Advancements in Applied Mathematics and Computational Physics

Advancements in Applied Mathematics and Computational Physics

Guest Editors

Branislav Randjelovic
Branislav Vlahovic

MDPI

Basel • Beijing • Wuhan • Barcelona • Belgrade • Novi Sad • Cluj • Manchester

Guest Editors
Branislav Randjelovic
Department of Mathematics
Faculty of Electronic Engineering
University of Nis
Nis
Serbia

Branislav Vlahovic
Department of Physics
North Carolina Central University
Durham, NC
USA

Editorial Office
MDPI AG
Grosspeteranlage 5
4052 Basel, Switzerland

This is a reprint of the Special Issue, published open access by the journal *Axioms* (ISSN 2075-1680), freely accessible at: https://www.mdpi.com/journal/axioms/special_issues/D5G2L7BO30.

For citation purposes, cite each article independently as indicated on the article page online and as indicated below:

Lastname, A.A.; Lastname, B.B. Article Title. *Journal Name* **Year**, *Volume Number*, Page Range.

ISBN 978-3-7258-5199-7 (Hbk)
ISBN 978-3-7258-5200-0 (PDF)
https://doi.org/10.3390/books978-3-7258-5200-0

Contents

About the Editors

Branislav Randjelovic

Branislav Randjelovic graduated with a degree in Electrical Engineering and Computer Science from the University of Nis in 1994; an MSc in Mathematical methods in Electrical Engineering in 2002; and a PhD in Technical Science and Applied Mathematics in 2015. He is an Associated Professor at the Department of Mathematics at the Faculty of Electrical Engineering, University of Nis, and is also an Associated Professor at the Department of Teaching Methods at the Faculty of Teachers Education, University of Kosovska Mitrovica. He has participated in 13 scientific projects, being the coordinator for one of these projects. He was engaged in pre-university education and adult education, as Head of the Institute for Educational Quality and Evaluation of Serbia and as Director of the Regional teacher training Center of Nis. During that work, he has been the coordinator of more than 100 domestic or international educational projects. Branislav has contributed to more than 200 scientific publications, 133 of which are in international conferences, books, and theses, and 41 are in international journals with referees.

Branislav Vlahovic

Branislav Vlahovic is a Professor of Physics in the Department of Mathematics and Physics at North Carolina Central University (NCCU) and is also the Director of the NSF Computational Center of Research Excellence in Science and Technology, the NASA University Research Center for Aerospace Devices, as well as at the DHS Center for Detectors. He earned his undergraduate and graduate degrees from the University of Zagreb, Croatia, and held positions at the Ruđer Bošković Institute (1980–1990), Duke University (1990–1995), and jointly at Jefferson National Laboratory and NCCU (1995–2000). Since 1995, he has been a faculty member at NCCU. Dr. Vlahovic has received numerous awards for his contributions to research and education, including the prestigious Oliver Max Gardner Award, which is the highest statewide honor presented by the University of North Carolina. He has served as principal investigator on multiple grants funded by NASA, NSF, DOE, DOD, and DHS, and has authored more than 400 peer-reviewed publications spanning theoretical and experimental nuclear and hypernuclear physics, materials science, nanotechnology, photonics, photovoltaics, chemistry, cosmology, genomics, and mathematics. He is also a member of the European Academy of Sciences and Arts.

Preface

The aim and purpose of this Special Issue Reprint are to present various methods and new solutions to explain the nature of matter, biophysical systems, and systems in technical sciences in the frame of overall reality, using the latest achievements in applied mathematics and computational physics.

The focus is on new results and solutions in contemporary applied mathematics and computational physics. It covers a broad range of topics to provide new insights into the exploration of the world of electronics, physical electronics, nuclear and hyper-nuclear physics, nanotechnology, material science, photonics and photovoltaics, cosmology, genomics, and nature.

Branislav Randjelovic and Branislav Vlahovic
Guest Editors

axioms

Article

Basic Computational Algorithms for Representing an Aircraft Flight (Calculation of 3D Displacement and Displaying)

Adan Ramirez-Lopez

Department of Industrial Engineering, Technological and Autonomous Institute of Mexico (ITAM), Rio Hondo #1 col. Progreso Tizapan, Mexico City ZP 01080, Mexico; adan.ramirez@itam.mx

Abstract: This manuscript describes the computational process to calculate an airplane path and display it in a 2D and 3D coordinate system on a computer screen. The airplane movement is calculated as a function of its dynamic's conditions according to physical and logical theory. Here, the flight is divided into maneuvers and the aircraft conditions are defined as boundary conditions. Then the aircraft position is calculated using nested loops, which execute the calculation procedure at every step time (Δt). The calculation of the aircraft displacement is obtained as a function of the aircraft speed and heading angles. The simulator was created using the C++ programming language, and each part of the algorithm was compiled independently to reduce the source code, allow easy modification, and improve the programming efficiency. Aerial navigation involves very complex phenomena to be considered for an appropriate representation; moreover, in this manuscript, the influence of the mathematical approach to properly represent the aircraft flight is described in detail. The flight simulator was successfully tested by simulating some basic theoretical flights with different maneuvers, which include stationary position, running along the way, take off, and some movements in the airspace. The maximum aircraft speed tested was 120 km/h, the maximum maneuver time was 12 min, and the space for simulation was assumed to be without obstacles. Here, the geometrical description of path and speed is analyzed according to the symmetric and asymmetric results. Finally, an analysis was conducted to evaluate the approach of the numerical methods used; after that, it was possible to confirm that precision increased as the step time was reduced. According to this analysis, no more than 500 steps are required for a good approach in the calculation of the aircraft displacement.

Keywords: flight simulator; programming algorithms; calculation of aircraft position; graphical display of aircraft path; 3D computer animation; numerical approaching

MSC: 00A71; 00A72

1. Introduction

The flight of an airplane is a very complex problem; there are many factors and variables involved. Some of these factors depend on human and external factors such as the route of the flight, the pilot's ability, the geography of the terrain, the weather, etc. Some of these factors depend on the aircraft's features, such as its speed and aerodynamic design [1–5]. Moreover, aeronautical has always been one of the pioneer industries in developing new technologies to increase performance and improve designs [5–7]. Consequently, authors in this area have worked on creating flight simulators, especially in order to reduce costs for training pilots, operational times, and risks [3–6,8–13]. Simulation is a huge area in aeronautics due to not only the flight can be simulated [7–11,14–20], there are some situations and conditions can vary or can be represented computationally such as flying operations, marketing, programming of routes, design of mechanical compounds etc. [3–7,12–16,21–27]. Other authors have worked on creating flight simulators, especially in order to reduce costs for training pilots, operational times, and risks [6–10,21–26]. The use of physical and computer simulations is desirable not only for training pilots; but, also to evaluate their performance and certification [13–16,23–30]. Thus, many authors have developed and programmed flight simulators in order to reproduce situations that happen during real flights and other complex problems in aeronautics, aerodynamics and aerial navigation [1–3,12–15,27–33].

Many of the aeronautical engineers developed physical flight simulators that reproduced some of the basic aircraft navigation instruments [5–7]. Their efforts were driven to create functional cabins where pilots could be trained, and they learned what to do in certain situations. As time went on, the aeronautical industry became interested in electronic and computer sciences; aeronautical engineers were pioneers in incorporating these technologies into airplanes [6–11,14–18]. Then, with the increase in computer capacities such as data speed management and storage, the improvement in programming methods and techniques has made it possible to develop more complex algorithms and computer simulators for flying [5,6].

Bruce Artwick [7–10,14–17] created the first consumer flight simulator software. His original work for Apple II software was purchased by Microsoft and eventually became Microsoft Flight Simulator. Artwick founded the company SubLogic after graduating from the University of Illinois at Urbana-Champaign in 1977, which released the first version of Flight Simulator the following year. Artwick worked for Hughes Aircraft in Culver City, California. It was here that he realized he could create his own 3D dynamic graphics on 6800-based machines. In his thesis of May 1975, called "A versatile computer generated dynamic light display" he showed a model of the flight of an aircraft on a computer screen [8–11,18–23]. With this, Artwick proved that it was possible to use the 6800 processor, which was the first available microcomputer, to handle the graphics and calculations of the specifications needed to create a real-time flight simulation [1–3,5–8].

The algorithms for representing an aircraft flight described in this work are based on the calculation as a single particle under certain speed and time of application conditions; these are so elementary, but they are a platform for including more complex integrations and calculations during an aircraft flight, such as the influence of the wind, the mechanical and aero-dynamical forces, the post-representation of the aircraft position in a virtual environment, etc.

2. Basic Assumptions and Reading Data

In this research, the aircraft flight is treated as an ideal set of planned operations in an ordered sequence. Then the flight is divided into maneuvers and the control variables are aircraft flying conditions such as the aircraft speed, heading angles, and defined times. Then a maneuver is assumed to be the defined group of airplane conditions to be executed during a period of time; thus, a change or remaining on any condition at any time defines the beginning and ending of a maneuver [10–15,18–20,24–30]. Nevertheless, there is a minimum of information required that defines the original aircraft status at the beginning of the simulation [24–26,34–41].

The general information about the aircraft is the divisions (steps) for analyzing the flight and the maximum takeoff weight (MTOW), which is defined as the aircraft weight at the beginning of the simulation. Thus, a volume for the fuel deposit must be declared according to the following restrictions:

(a) The fuel weight cannot be equal or minor to zero ($V_{tank} \leq 0$).
(b) The fuel weight cannot be equal or major to the MTOW ($V_{tank} \geq$ MTOW). This is a basic logical assumption. Here, fuel capacity of tank must be input in (l).

Then a specific fuel consumption rate is defined in (l/km) or (l/min). This consumption is assumed to be constant during the flight simulation; at least a consumption coefficient as a function of the cruise speed was defined. All restrictions were programmed using sentences (if) verifying and conditioning the reading data process [6–10,29–33,42].

All the corresponding warnings were programmed in order to avoid errors during reading data; if any of these restrictions occur, a window with an appropriate message is displayed with a brief explanation in order to correct them [1–3,6–9,27–32]. Then, the following assumptions were programmed and included to simulate the flights.

(1) Only one single flight is simulated.
(2) The simulation begins at the initial time ($t_{sim} = 0$).
(3) The simulated flight is divided into maneuvers (using an integer data type).
(4) The information about every maneuver is used as boundary conditions for the aircraft conditions.
(5) The maneuvers defined cannot be equal or minor to one ($n \leq 1$).
(6) The initial conditions for beginning the simulation are established in maneuver (0). For simulations in this work, the airplane was defined as being in stationary conditions.
(7) The times for maneuvers cannot be equals or minors to zero ($t_n \leq 0$).
(8) The values defined for every maneuver are modified at every step time ($t + \Delta t$) according to the previous values until they reach the latest; then, the change is not instantaneous; it is performed step by step during every maneuver.
(9) The aircraft speed is assumed to be in the same direction as the aircraft heading angle. Thus, the aircraft speed is a result of the total propulsion force.
(10) The aircraft with an initial speed equal to zero ($v_{An=0} = 0$) is considered to be in repose or stopped on the ground.
(11) The vertical aircraft speed is assumed to be absolute in the same direction as the pitching angle.
(12) The values for every maneuver, such as heading angles or aircraft vertical speed, can adopt positive or negative values without restrictions, with the exception of the aircraft speed.

A computational array is used to store and order the information about every maneuver. The array was defined as: Matdat [a][b]; this matrix stores floating data types for all the maneuvers. The location occupied by the variable [a] is used to store and identify the maneuver [a = n]. This location is also used to validate and take the appropriate values during simulation. The location occupied by the variable [b] is used to identify any variable as follows:

Matdat [a][[b = 1] Horizontal aircraft speed (v_{HAn}).
Matdat [a][[b = 2] Vertical aircraft speed (v_{VAn}).
Matdat [a][[b = 3] Heading angle (α_n).
Matdat [a][[b = 4] Rolling angle ($\alpha_{heading}$).
Matdat [a][[b = 5] Maneuver time (t_n).

In addition, the locations for the variables [b] are also predefined as a matrix with extra locations for storing all of the calculated variables after the execution of the calculation process. Here, the sub-indexes (n) refer to the corresponding maneuver.

The first step in developing a flight simulator is to create a virtual environment on the computer screen where the user can appreciate the aircraft path [1–4,7–10,34–41]. The aircraft movement must be represented appropriately, and physical and mathematical equations must be solved using the programming of numerical methods. Several authors have developed methods for solving geometrical and mathematical problems using repetitive operations and procedures [3–6,9–13,27–33,42]. This kind of problem can be easily programmed using any programming language. Here, code was generated using C++, and nesting numerical procedures were to be solved [29–34,39,41].

Time, aircraft speed, and angular positions during every maneuver are used as initial and final conditions to create a simulation of the aircraft's animation, and the resulted information is used as input to create an animation of the movement as would be in the aeronautical instruments [29–31,37–41]. Then, in this work, the main procedure is a calculation routine that contains the equations for calculating the aircraft displacement along the 3D position. These are solved at every step time (Δt) inside an executed nested loop using the boundary conditions defined by the user. Then, inside this procedure, are included independent subroutines with the code for calculating the graphical information to represent every aircraft instrument. The procedure is described as follows:

(a) Reading the data included general information about the aircraft conditions and the number of maneuvers during the flight. Then specific speed, time duration, and directional conditions of every maneuver are read.
(b) Options for new reading and modification are valuable tools; after this, different display animations were also programmed.
(c) An algorithm to make the simulation is executed, then a calculation of the aircraft displacement is performed, and the information is used to represent the instrument animation.
(d) Options for saving information are included.

In order to represent a landscape for the flight to be simulated, the following facts were assumed to represent computationally the surface and the flight directions:

The North Pole corresponds to 0° according to the angular position shown in Figure 1. And the clockwise direction is assumed to be positive to measure any heading angle. Then, 90° corresponds to the east, 180° corresponds to the south, and 270° corresponds to the west; nevertheless, this condition can be modified according to the sense of the turn; for example, −90° can also correspond to the west, −180 to the south, and −270° to the east. This fact is due to the aircraft's heading angle being taken as a function of its turning movement.

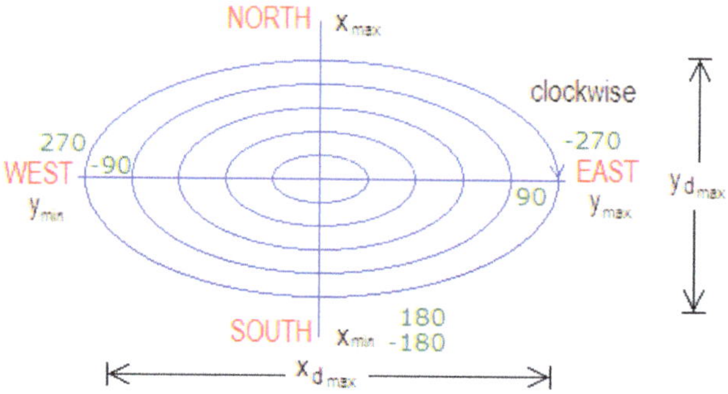

Figure 1. Assumptions for the graphical representation of the surface and the heading angle (direction of flight) according with earth position.

The flow chart shown in Figure 2 represents the general operations of the flight simulator developed. Here, the reading data process is the first action executed. Initially, the general information for the aircraft is read because it is absolutely required to start the calculation process; then the system executes the reading process for the maneuvers. This process appears in better detail in Figure 3, where the procedure to read the data and store it in the computational array is described [3–6,13–16,23–32]. This process is repeated from maneuver (0) until the latest maneuver (nt). In Figure 2, there is a shaded subroutine in the left part. This routine is included to be executed at the beginning to make a pre-calculus about the aircraft flight. The loops and parts of the routines inside are so similar to those in Figure 4a,b. These procedures are so similar, which is why all the procedures were compiled independently and included as separate libraries [27–33,42]. This fact provides easy identification and modification but also makes them more versatile. The execution time of this subroutine is very short, and its inclusion eliminates the necessity of using additional memory resources or saving unnecessary data. Here (ts) is the simulation time, and the step time (Δt) is calculated as a function of the steps defined to analyze the flight. Finally, the flowchart in Figure 3 shows an option to save the information or quit. The option for saving the information would create a new file named by the pilot (user) and save the data in a row and column format for easy identification.

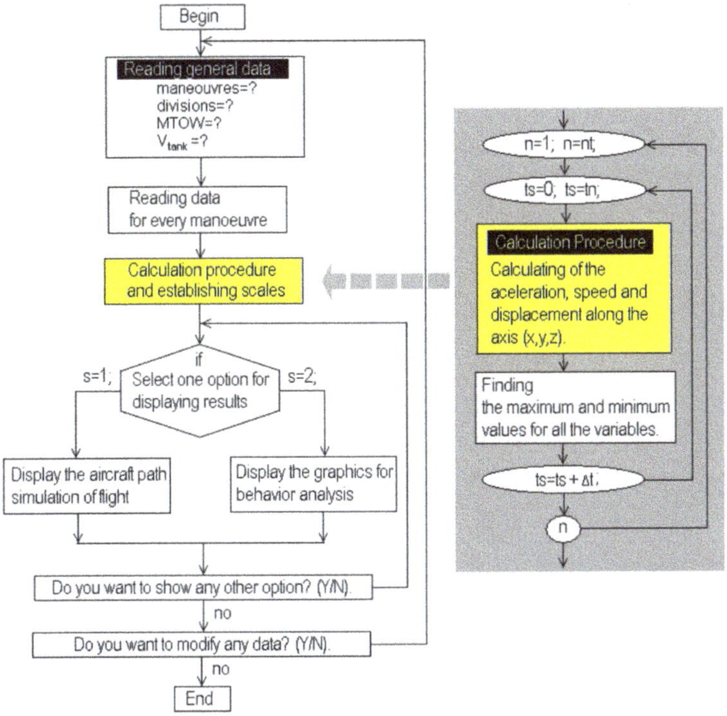

Figure 2. General flowchart for the flight simulator developed.

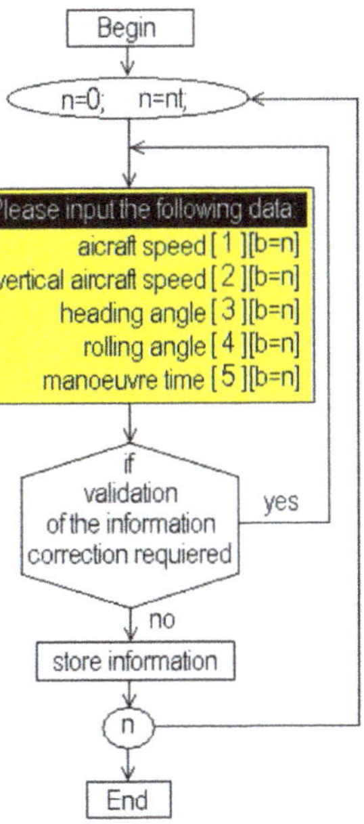

Figure 3. Flowchart for the reading data routine for each maneuver.

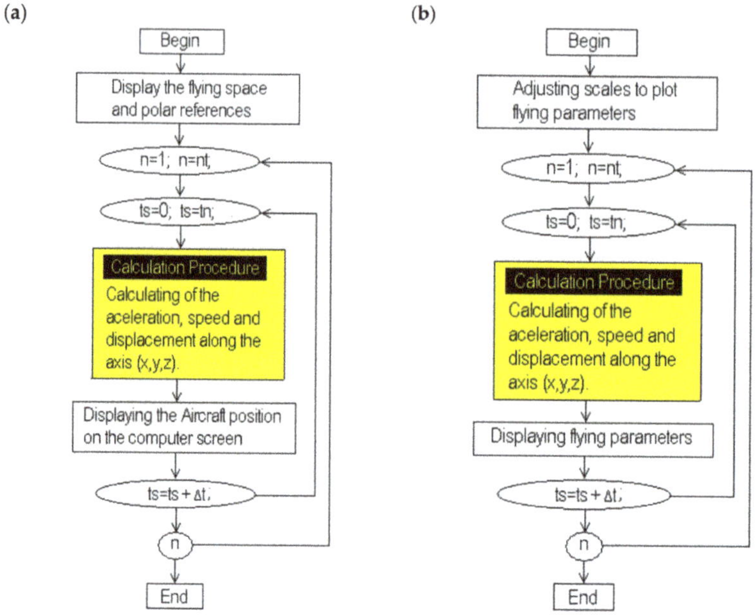

Figure 4. Flowchart for selecting any option to display the results. (**a**) Option for display the aircraft path and (**b**) option for display graphics and performance of the aircraft.

The processes for selecting and displaying the results are shown in the flowcharts in Figure 4a,b. Here, the calculation process is again included during the execution of the simulation loop because it is the same for both options. Each figure indicates the procedure to be executed according to the selection made. In Figure 4a, the virtual aerial space is traced, including the north–south and east–west directions. Then the calculation procedure is executed to display the aircraft path [4–7,15–19,22–31]. The flowchart in Figure 4b corresponds to the option developed to analyze the aircraft performance; here, a screen to display the aircraft speed and displacement is drawn according to the calculated scales [27–33,42]. The routines developed for this purpose were also compiled separately because they are executed many times to display different flight parameters. The flowchart shown in Figure 5 is used to obtain the maximum and minimum values for the displacement of the aircraft along axis (x); a pair of sentences (if) is used for these purposes; the algorithm uses two different comparison procedures that are included in the calculation loop just after the execution of the calculation procedure. This procedure can be repeated for the displacement along the axes (y) and (z); moreover, this procedure can also be nested and used again to compare, obtain, and store the maximum and minimum values of all the variables involved, eliminating unnecessary code.

The aircraft flight involves the calculation of the 3D aircraft displacement; the calculation is performed in the nested loops as a function of speed and the time conditions defined. Simultaneously, a comparison to obtain the minimum and maximum positions for a good fit with the computer screen pixels resolution is performed [9–14,22–32]. All procedures in Figures 2–5 were compiled separately in order to be executed independently, and then a quick calculation about the total distances traveled by the aircraft can be obtained. And the display of the displacement is shown only if it is required by the user.

Procedures in shaded areas are nested in the executed loops according to the user requirements; the routine in the flowchart in Figure 5 is also compiled separately and then included during the execution of the nested loops. It is absolutely required to obtain the minimum and maximum values of the aircraft displacement and then draw on the screen the flight; moreover, this procedure is repeated again for the (y) and (z) axes, which are also necessary for it.

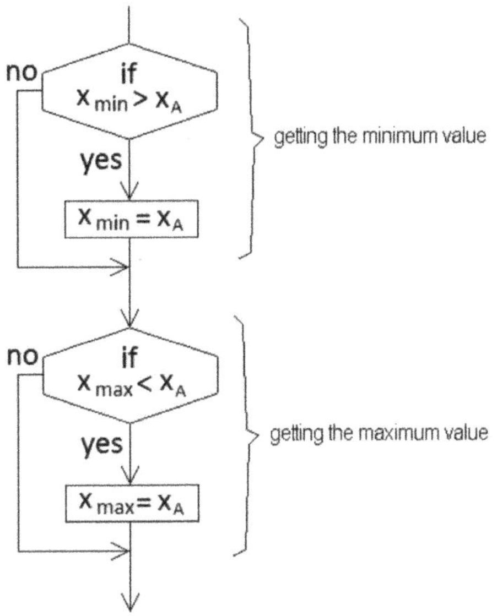

Figure 5. Flowchart sentence to find the maximum and minimum values for the aircraft displacement along the (x) axis.

3. Calculation Procedure

The calculation procedure involves the solution of the equations for calculating the aircraft path, as described next:

The time of a flight results from the sum of all the partial maneuver times, as shown in Equation (1). Here (n) is the maneuvers, (t_n) is the time of every maneuver, and (nt) is the number of maneuvers.

$$t_{flight} = \sum_{n=1}^{n=nt} t_n \tag{1}$$

According to Equations (2) and (3), the values of displacement and acceleration can be obtained as a function of the aircraft speed. Here, the super indexes (n) and (n − 1) correspond to the latest and previous maneuvers, respectively.

$$d = \Delta v \Delta t = (v^n - v^{n-1})(t^n - t^{n-1}) \tag{2}$$

$$a = \frac{\Delta v}{\Delta t} = \frac{(v^n - v^{n-1})}{(t^n - t^{n-1})} \tag{3}$$

These equations treat the problem using general assumptions; nevertheless, it is necessary to calculate the displacement and acceleration for every reference axis (x, y, z) using Equations (4) to (6) and (7) to (9), respectively. These equations can be nested inside a computational loop as a part of the calculation procedure; then, the equations for the aircraft movement (10) and (11) are solved, providing instantaneous values for acceleration and displacement.

$$x = (v_x^n - v_x^{n-1})(t^n - t^{n-1}) \tag{4}$$

$$y = (v_y^n - v_y^{n-1})(t^n - t^{n-1}) \tag{5}$$

$$z = (v_z^n - v_z^{n-1})(t^n - t^{n-1}) \tag{6}$$

$$a_x = \frac{(v_x^n - v_x^{n-1})}{(t^n - t^{n-1})} \tag{7}$$

$$a_y = \frac{(v_y^n - v_y^{n-1})}{(t^n - t^{n-1})} \tag{8}$$

$$a_z = \frac{(v_z^n - v_z^{n-1})}{(t^n - t^{n-1})} \tag{9}$$

$$\frac{dx}{dt} + \frac{dy}{dt} + \frac{dz}{dt} = \frac{d_{tot}}{dt} \tag{10}$$

$$\frac{dv_x}{dt} + \frac{dv_y}{dt} + \frac{dv_z}{dt} = \frac{dv_{tot}}{dt} \tag{11}$$

In order to solve these equations and calculate the aircraft position at every moment during the simulation, it is necessary to establish a step time (Δt) using Equation (12). This value is used as a criterion to determine the precision of the simulation. Here (nt) is the step number, which is an integer data type input by the pilot who runs the simulation. As this number is increased, the step time (Δt) becomes shorter, and the simulation precision improves.

$$\Delta t = \frac{t_n}{nt} \tag{12}$$

Then Equations (13) to (15) are used to calculate the distances for scaling the aircraft flight on the computer screen.

$$x_{d\max} = x_{\max} - x_{\min} \tag{13}$$

$$y_{d\max} = y_{\max} - y_{\min} \tag{14}$$

$$z_{d\max} = z_{\max} - z_{\min} \tag{15}$$

The distances for the aircraft flight can be obtained from Equations (16) to (18). Equation (16) is the general form of the equation between 2 points in a 3D system; but it must be modified in order to calculate the distance from the starting point to the aircraft at every moment, as is shown in Equation (17); then Equation (18) can be nested in a computer loop to calculate the aircraft displacement.

$$d_{total} = \sqrt{(x_{tot})^2 + (y_{tot})^2 + (z_{tot})^2} \tag{16}$$

$$d^n = \sqrt{(x^n - x^{n-1})^2 + (y^n - y^{n-1})^2 + (z^n - z^{n-1})^2} \tag{17}$$

$$d^{t+\Delta t} = \sqrt{(x^t - x^{t-\Delta t})^2 + (y^t - y^{t-\Delta t})^2 + (z^t - z^{t-\Delta t})^2} \tag{18}$$

4. Computer Simulation of Flights

During the flight simulation, the aircraft is placed in the original position (0,0,0) at the initial time (t = 0). Then every maneuver is calculated, and the aircraft position is computed and displayed. A virtual grid terrain is used as a reference for the aerial space where the simulation is executed.

The aircraft path is placed on the computer screen as a function of the transition from a 3D system to a 2D graphical representation. According to this, projected and real paths are displayed in order to provide a complimentary reference. The projected path is that the aircraft is describing over flat terrain, and the real path is that described by the aircraft considering the vertical displacement as a function of the step time (Δt).

Table 1 shows the information declared for the analyzed flights. The flights are 7 and 5 maneuvers; (v_{hor}) and (v_{vert}) are the horizontal and vertical speeds of the aircraft, and (α) is the heading angle.

Table 1. Information for the flights to be simulated (conditions for every maneuver).

Flight					1			
Maneuver	0	1	2	3	4	5	6	7
v_{hor} (km/h)	0	100	120	100	110.5	100	97.25	95.45
v_{vert} (km/h)	0	0	25	5	0	−2.2	15.55	12.25
$\alpha_{heading}$ (°)	45	45	45	180	180	450	450	270
t (min)	0	2.5	2.35	6	6	3.25	5.25	12.25
Flight					2			
Maneuver	0	1	2	3	4	5		
v_{hor} (km/h)	0	100	120	110	100	100		
v_{vert} (km/h)	0	0	15	10	10	−5		
$\alpha_{heading}$ (°)	0	0	0	90	360	450		
t (min)	0	2.5	3.5	6	6	4.55		
Flight					3			
Maneuver	0	1	2	3	4	5		
v_{hor} (km/h)	0	100	120	105	100	100		
v_{vert} (km/h)	0	0	5.55	15	10	−4.5		
$\alpha_{heading}$ (°)	0	0	0	90	90	0		
t (min)	0	2	2.55	3.2	4.25	10.05		

Figure 6a,b shows snapped screens from the simulator. These figures correspond to the flight (1) displayed using different angles over the terrain in order to test the graphical display using rotation and screen scaling tools. These views can be obtained by solving Equations (19) to (21). Here ($\alpha_{terrain}$) is a reference used to provide an inclined view over the terrain.

$$x_{dist} = \frac{\left(x^t - x^{t-\Delta t}\right)}{x_{dmax}} \cos(\alpha_{terrain}) \tag{19}$$

$$y_{dist} = \frac{\left(y^t - y^{t-\Delta t}\right)}{y_{dmax}} \sin(\alpha_{terrain}) \tag{20}$$

$$z_{dist} = \frac{\left(z^t - z^{t-\Delta t}\right)}{z_{dmax}} \tag{21}$$

Finally, Equations (22)–(24) are used for scaling the aircraft path over the terrain. Here (tot_{pix}) is the variable used to display the aircraft path using a congruent scale for the computer screen. Then (n_{pix}, n_{piy} and n_{piz}) are the aircraft displacement values expressed in pixels.

$$n_{pix\quad x} = tot_{pix}\left[\frac{d_x{}^{t+\Delta t}}{d_{xmax}}\right] \tag{22}$$

$$n_{pix\quad y} = tot_{pix}\left[\frac{d_y{}^{t+\Delta t}}{d_{y\max}}\right] \tag{23}$$

$$n_{pix\quad z} = tot_{pix}\left[\frac{d_z{}^{t+\Delta t}}{d_{z\max}}\right] \tag{24}$$

A brief description of the flight (1) simulated using the information in Table 1 is explained next; these explanations can be confirmed by watching the aircraft path on Figure 6a,b. Here can be observed the geometrical path in a simulated flat terrain; some maneuvers are symmetrical, but others are non-symmetrical according to speed conditions. The aircraft in this flight is initially placed on the ground at 45° (north–east direction) and then runs over the road and takes off in the same direction and turns to the right (clockwise); maintains a direction towards the south, then turns again to the right and maintains a new direction to the east; finally, turns left to the north and west against clockwise.

(a)

(b)

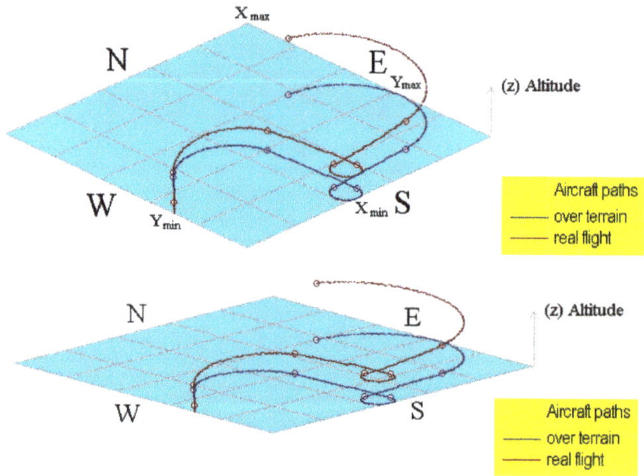

Figure 6. Computational representation of the aircraft path for flight (1) using different terrain angles. (**a**) Using 20° and (**b**) using 8°.

The computational tool developed to incline the terrain is very useful and versatile to provide a different point of view of the built aircraft paths. Here, the path over terrain can be easily identified because it is never out of the shaded area.

Maneuver 1. The aircraft is initially in stationary conditions; then it runs in order to prepare for take-off. The aircraft speed changes from ($v_x{}^{n=0}$ = 0) to ($v_x{}^{n=1}$ = 100 km/h) at the end of the first maneuver. There are no modifications to the lateral or vertical speed; the aircraft just runs over the reference plane. The heading direction is +45°, which corresponds to 45° measured from the North Pole direction. This run delays 2.50 min.

Maneuver 2. During this maneuver, the aircraft takes off, continues accelerating until it reaches $v_x{}^{n=2}$ = 120 km/h. Here, the aircraft increases its vertical speed until $v_z{}^{n=2}$ = 25 km/h. Then the projected and real aircraft paths are separated; the projected path is always traced as a function of the reference plane, and the real path is displayed considering the aircraft altitude over the terrain. This maneuver delays 2.35 min, and the heading angle remains +45°. So, the slope in the line for this segment indicates that the aircraft has taken off from the highway at the same heading angle, describing a line with a smoothed slope.

Maneuver 3. Here the aircraft decelerates slightly until ($v_x{}^{n=3}$ = 100 km/h); the vertical speed is decreased until ($v_z{}^{n=3}$ = 5 km/h); nevertheless, the aircraft continues ascending due to the vertical speed value continuing to be positive. Moreover, during this maneuver the aircraft's heading route is modified from +45° to 180°. So, the original aircraft direction north–east now is towards south. Then the aircraft turns to the right. This maneuver is executed for 6 min, so the advanced distance is longer than those in previous maneuvers.

Maneuver 4. Here the aircraft accelerates slightly again until ($v_x^{n=4}$ = 110 km/h); the vertical speed is nearly invariable ($v_z^{n=4}$ = 0 km/h). In addition, the heading angle remains in a south direction, so the segment of the path for this maneuver is a straight line.

Maneuver 5. Here the aircraft decelerates lightly until ($v_x^{n=5}$ = 100 km/h); the vertical speed becomes negative ($v_z^{n=5}$ = −2.20 km/h); and the aircraft suddenly turns from 180° to 450°, changing the heading route to the east. A turn is quickly performed in 3.25 min, during a light descent. Thus, the path described for this maneuver is a little elliptical arc.

Maneuver 6. The aircraft increases its propulsion and its vertical speed, but the same heading angle remains; so, the aircraft direction also remains towards the east with a slight increment in altitude.

Maneuver 7. Finally, the aircraft speed is slightly decreased, but although the vertical speed is also slightly decreased, the ascending rate remains considerable. Thus, a notorious increment in the aircraft's altitude can be observed during this maneuver. Moreover, the aircraft changes its heading angle towards the west during the longest period of time.

Speed curves are lines for the initial maneuvers when the aircraft runs along the way, and others are sinusoidal or second-grade curves. Some of these present conditions of symmetry or asymmetry as a function of the aircraft acceleration and the modification of the aircraft direction. In maneuvers 5 and 7, the speed curves are sinusoidal and are inverted for both axes (x, y). This can be considered a partially symmetric or inverted symmetry condition.

The aircraft performance and behavior during a flight can be analyzed along the axis (x, y, z). Figure 7a,b shows the evolution of the flight (1). Both figures use a dual time scale for the horizontal axis, indicating the maneuver duration just below. The maximum and minimum values are indicated on the vertical axis, which were obtained from the simulation. Figure 7a shows the aircraft speeds for each referred axis; here, the speed on the axis (x) shows the following features:

The aircraft is initially in a stop position ($v_z^{n=0}$ = 0 km/h). Then the speed is increased until ($v_z^{n=1}$ = 100 km/h) at the end of the first maneuver. Here, a straight line with a constant slope is displayed, evidencing the aircraft's acceleration. Another line with a minor but constant slope was obtained for the second maneuver due to the increased speed, but at a minor rate. For the third maneuver, the speed curve has a negative slope due to the aircraft having modified its heading route. Then this condition changes the plotting of the speed. During the fourth maneuver, the speed is slightly increased, but with a negative implication, so the slope is nearly horizontal, thus the line with a lightly negative slope can be appreciated. During the fifth maneuver the aircraft's speed decreased slightly, but it modified its heading direction from 180° to 450°, or from the south to the east, including a quick turn rotation, and the plotting conditions were modified again, resulting in a sinusoidal line segment. During the sixth maneuver the aircraft speed is slightly decreased, but the final plotting position of the fifth remains because the heading angle also remains constant. Finally, during the seventh maneuver, the aircraft changes the heading condition from east to west, becoming the line in this segment with a positive slope until it reaches a maximum value for the North Pole direction; then, the slope becomes negative, forming the end of the curve that corresponds to the final turn position.

The speed curves change geometrically with every maneuver as a function of the simulation conditions. The segments are influenced by the heading angle changes, which modify the direction of the slopes. During flight (1), the heading changes conducted by the aircraft on maneuvers three and five were performed turning towards the right; nevertheless, the final heading changes were performed turning towards the left. Moreover, the maneuver times (t_n) also influence the aircraft displacement. So, it is possible to mention the following facts after analyzing the speed curve for the (y) axis:

During the first and second maneuvers the speed behavior is represented by 2 lines with constant slopes in the same way as for the axis (x). Nevertheless, the curve for the third maneuver is very different due to the heading changing from 45° to 180°. Here a maximum is reached for a position east to 90°. Then the curve changes its slope to negative until the end of this maneuver. During the fourth maneuver, the heading remains invariable with a slight increment in the aircraft speed, resulting in a quasi-horizontal line. The aircraft modifies its heading during the fifth maneuver; here a sinusoidal curve is appreciated, but the starting and ending angles are different in comparison with the curve for the speed on the axis (x); the maximum and minimum positions on curves for the analysis over these axes are in mathematical correspondence with the inflection points for the (x) axis. After this, the aircraft remains with a constant heading angle, and for the sixth maneuver, a new sinusoidal curve is shown for the final maneuver due to the heading angle change.

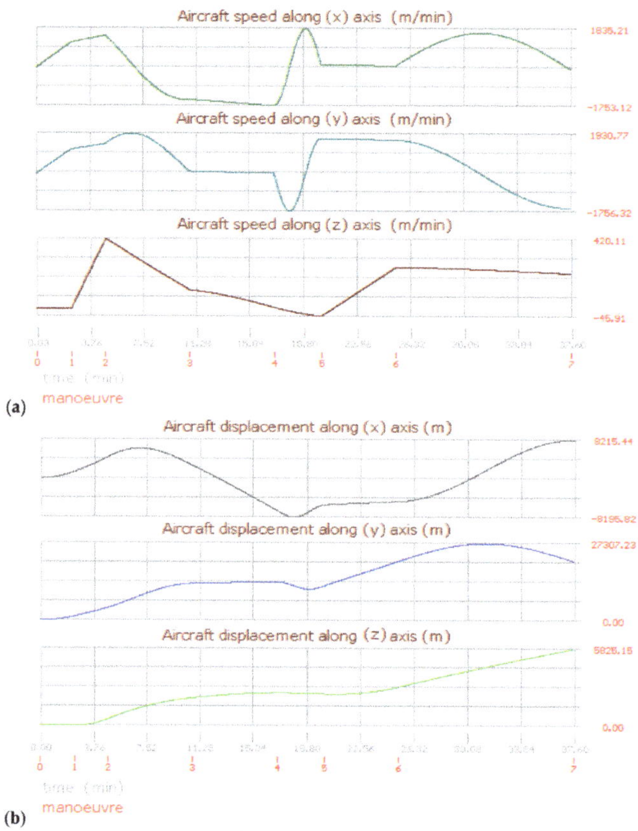

Figure 7. Aircraft performance graphics for flight (1) (**a**) Aircraft speed. (**b**) Aircraft displacement.

The vertical speed (v_z) is very easy to understand due to all the segments being lineal. Here, initially, the aircraft runs over the reference plane ($v_z = 0$); this first maneuver is represented by a horizontal line. During the second maneuver the aircraft takes off; then, the curve has a very vertical positive slope. For the third, fourth, and fifth maneuvers, the vertical speed decreases at different rates, although the aircraft remains always ascending. For the sixth and seventh maneuvers, the vertical speed is increased, but also at a different rate, so the slope changes from positive to negative.

The displacement curves for flight (1) are shown in Figure 7b. Thus, it is possible to mention the following facts about the curve on the axis (x):

The curve begins at an initial speed equal to zero; the displacement curves are different than speed curves due to the displacement rate not being constant ($v_{HA} = d_{HA}/dt$). During the third maneuver, the displacement reaches its maximum value, and then the slope becomes negative due to the route change. On the fourth maneuver, the heading angle remains unchanged, and the displacement is a line with a negative slope. During the fifth maneuver, the aircraft turns suddenly, changing its heading angle; here, a little inverse curved form with a quasi-flat ending is appreciated. During the sixth maneuver, the aircraft route remains the same; consequently, the curve is lineal. Finally, during the last maneuver, a sinusoidal form is the result of the route change.

Analyzing the curve for displacement on the axis (y), the displacement is similar to the curve for (d_x) for the first two maneuvers due to the aircraft speed and acceleration being at the same heading angles. On the third maneuver, the heading angle changes, and the displacement along (y) is lightly decreased. On the fourth maneuver, the effective displacement is increased, but the heading angle is nearly perpendicular to the axis (y), so the displacement about this axis is a horizontal line. During the fifth maneuver, the aircraft turns quickly 270°, turning in the east direction in a short period of time. On the sixth maneuver, the aircraft remains at the same heading angle, resulting in a line with a nearly invariable positive slope. Finally, during the last maneuver, the form of a circular semi-arc is displayed due to the turning again.

The displacement along the vertical axis (z) is shown below. Here, the aircraft begins remaining on the ground during the take-off run. Then the aircraft's altitude begins to increase during the second maneuver. The aircraft continues increasing its altitude for the next maneuvers, but at different rates, so the slopes are also different. With the exception of the fifth maneuver, which was defined with a negative value. Then it is important to mention that if a negative value is defined on any maneuver for the vertical speed, the aircraft remains ascending until the transition of values becomes negative ($v_z^{t+\Delta t} < 0$).

Figures 8–11 show the aircraft path, speed, and displacement curves corresponding to the flights (2) and (3), respectively. Here, differences and similarities in comparison with flight (1) can be appreciated. Moreover, the influence of aircraft speed, heading angles, and maneuver times can also be appreciated.

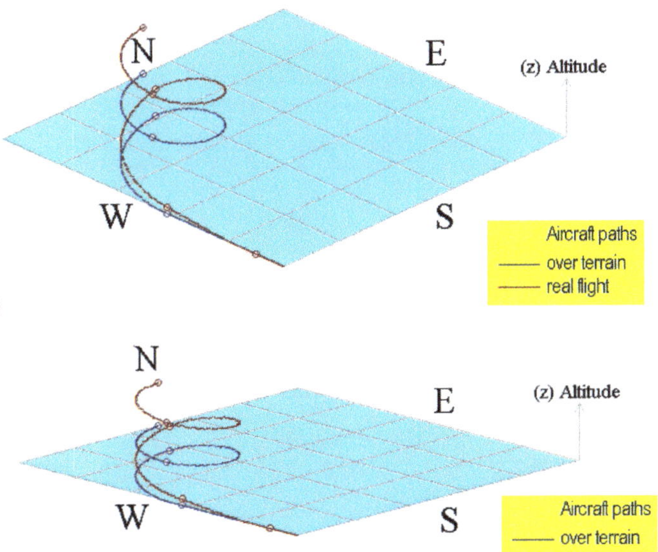

(a)

(b)

Figure 8. Computational representation of the aircraft path for flight (2) using different terrain angles. (**a**) Using 20° and (**b**) using 8°.

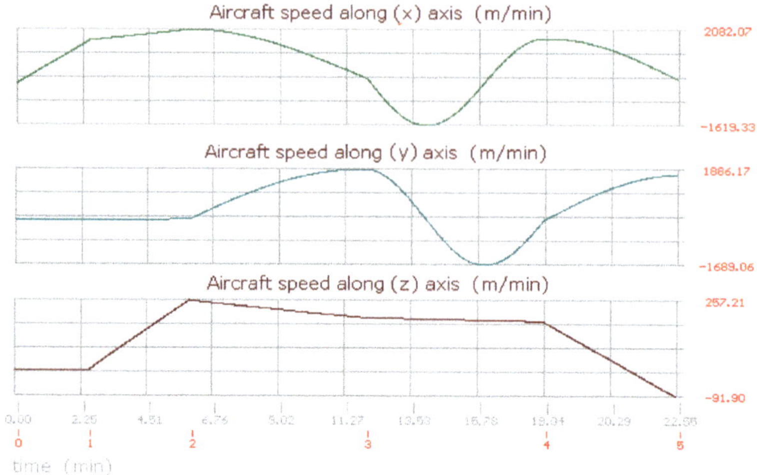

(a)

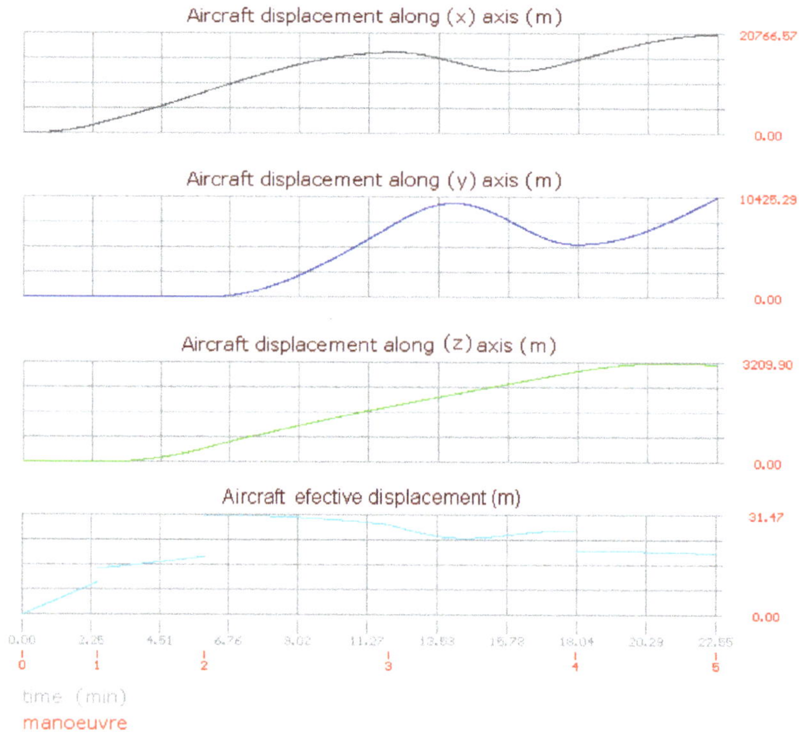

(b)

Figure 9. Aircraft performance graphics for flight (2). (**a**) Aircraft speed. (**b**) Aircraft displacement.

The aircraft on this flight is stationary with a direction to the north equal to 0°. Then it runs over the road and takes off in the same direction. On the next maneuver, the heading angles are always greater than the previous; thus, the aircraft always turns to the right in a clockwise direction. Moreover, the vertical speed is positive, the aircraft ascends until the fourth maneuver, and until the last maneuver, the aircraft lightly descends due to the final vertical speed being negative. Figure 8a,b shows the aircraft displacement over different terrain angles for view, evidencing the importance of displaying the flight path.

The flights were divided for analysis purposes into maneuvers with particular conditions of aircraft horizontal and vertical speed; a route angle and time endurance are defined; then the displacement is calculated. Then, all the equations in the manuscript are solved using an integration numerical Runge–Kutta method, which is very easy to program using nested loops with a minimal computational effort. Although increasing the steps for calculation is an easy way, there are some variables involved in the simulation that affect the final approach; therefore, it will be absolutely necessary to increase these in the following cases.

(a) If the aircraft's horizontal and vertical speeds are increased.
(b) If the endurance time of the maneuver is increased.

Other parameters influence the aircraft route, as follows:

If the heading angle is greater than in the previous maneuver, the aircraft will turn to the right.

(a) If the heading angle is less than in the previous maneuver, the aircraft will turn to the left.
(b) It is important to remember that a simulation is considered precise when a very accurate calculation of the aircraft's position in space is obtained. Additionally, mathematical and physical theory must be applicable to different conditions with the same certainty.

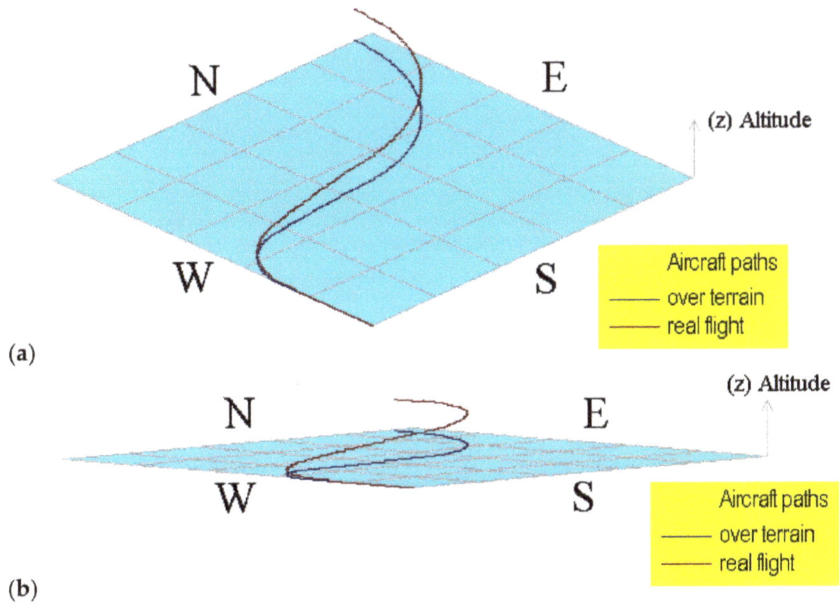

Figure 10. Computational representation of the aircraft path for flight (3) using different terrain angles. (**a**) Using 20° and (**b**) using 5°.

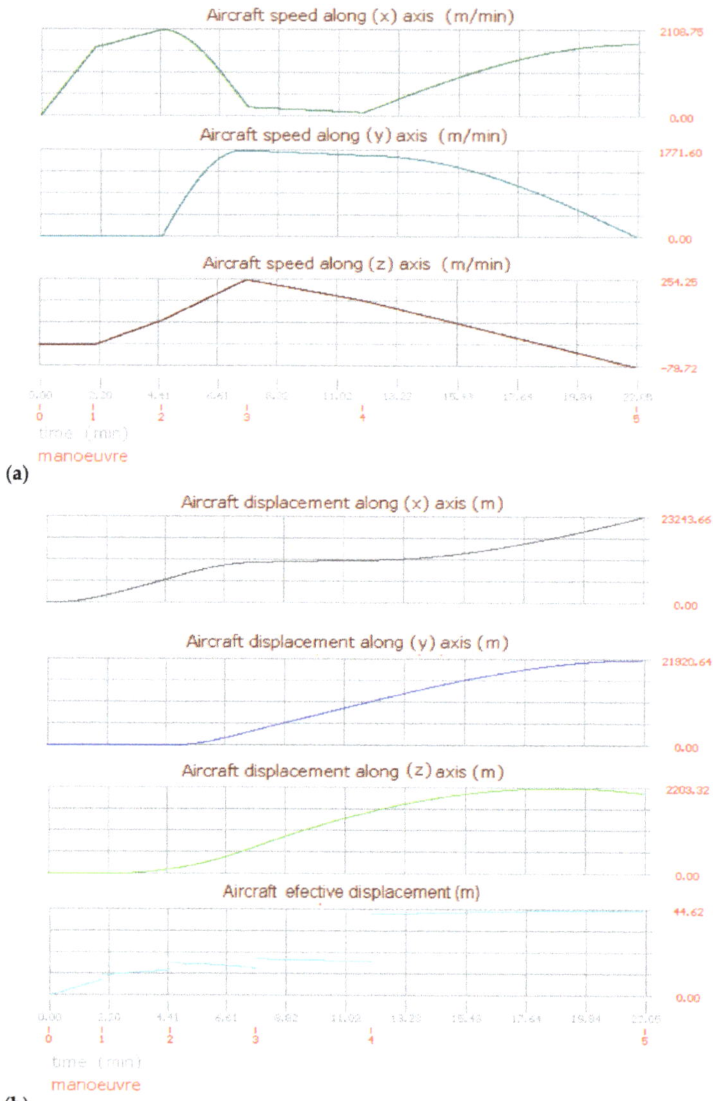

Figure 11. Aircraft performance graphics for flight (3). (**a**) Aircraft speed. (**b**) Aircraft displacement.

5. Evaluation of Approaching

In order to evaluate the numerical method programmed for the simulator, approaches and errors were analyzed by executing the nested routines in the simulator with different divisions (steps) reproducing the 3 flights defined in Table 1. Similar curves resulted for the three flights. The results for flight (2) have been chosen to evidence the error and approaching obtained and are shown in Figures 12–15. These curves show the evolution of the final distances calculated for the aircraft path. The distances (dx), (dy), and (dz) are the distances flown along every axis, and (d_{tot}) is the total distance from the origin of the aircraft flight. All of them were measured from the original starting point of the flight, assumed to be the position (0,0,0) towards the corresponding displacement axes. Their description of content is as follows:

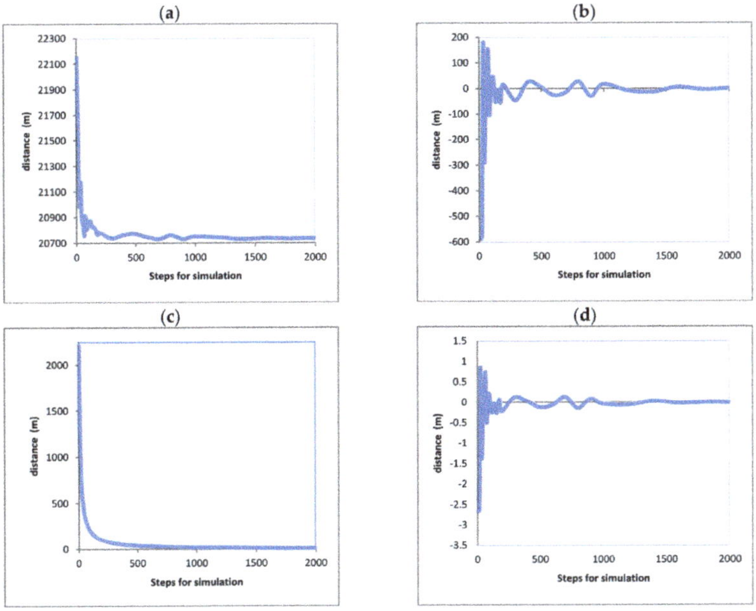

Figure 12. Calculated approaching for flight (1) curves for axis (x) direction Sud-North. (**a**) considering displacement values. (**b**) considering the previous calculated value. (**c**) considering the division of the displacement between the number of steps. (**d**) considering the approaching to the final value.

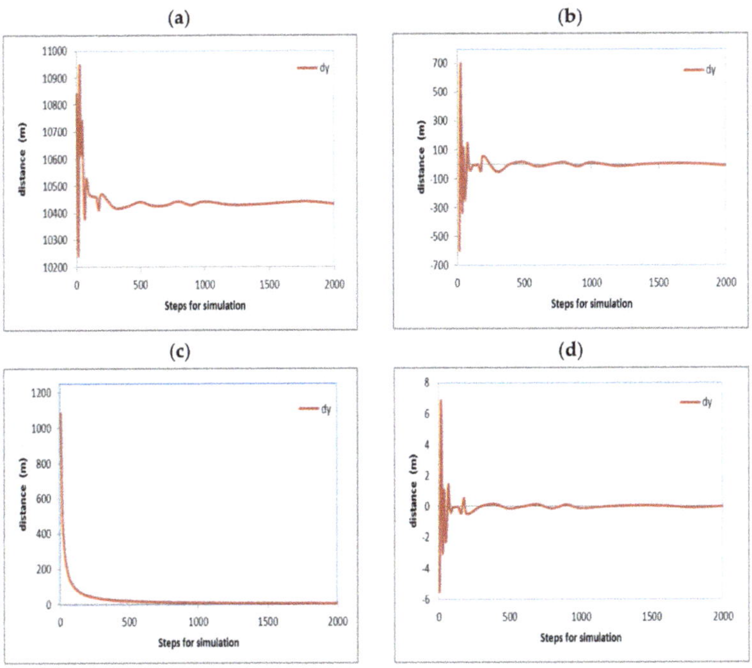

Figure 13. Calculated approaching for flight (1) curves for axis (y) direction Est-West. (**a**) considering displacement values. (**b**) considering the previous calculated value. (**c**) considering the division of the displacement between the number of steps. (**d**) considering the approaching to the final value.

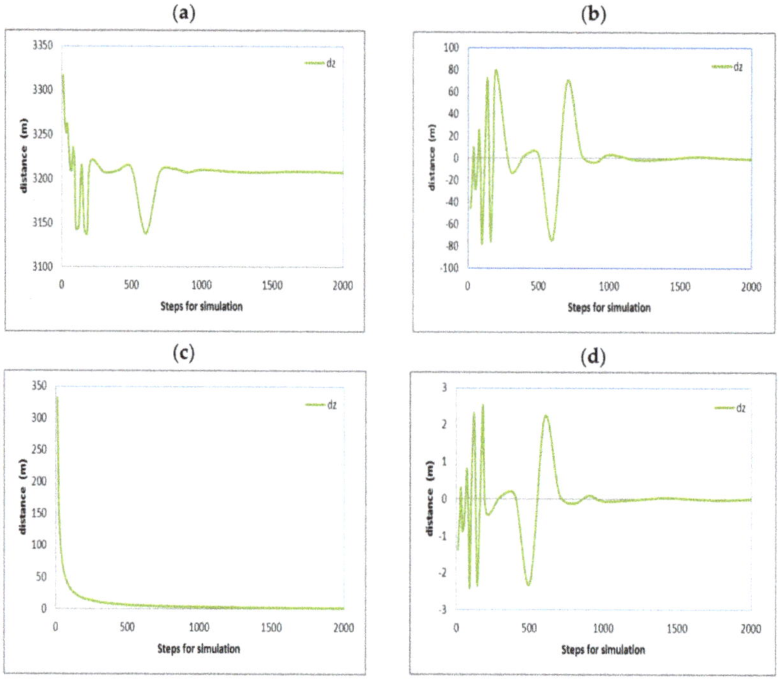

Figure 14. Calculated approaching for flight (1) curves for axis (z) this is for the altitude. (**a**) considering displacement values. (**b**) considering the previous calculated value. (**c**) considering the division of the displacement between the number of steps. (**d**) considering the approaching to the final value.

Approaching every displacement axis, the total displacement will be described. Figure 12a–d shows the displacement for the (x) axis with different criteria of approaching that are described next; similarly, Figure 13a–d shows the displacement for the (y) axis, Figure 14a–d shows the displacement for the (z) axis, and Figure 15a–d shows the total aircraft displacement, respectively. In all these figures, the values of displacement are plotted as a function of the steps for calculation. But different criteria for approaching are evaluated in order to achieve improvements.

Curves (12a, 13a, 14a, and 15a) show the fluctuation of the displacements along the directions (x), (y), (z), and the total aircraft displacement, respectively, evidencing that the final distances tend to adopt an invariable value. The reduction in this variation indicates that error is reduced and approaching is improved as the steps for analysis are increased.

The vertical axis in Figures 12a, 13a and 15a represents the displacement along the respective axis "x" for direction north–south and "y" for direction east–west and the total displacement. In contrast, the vertical values in Figures 12b, 13b and 15b are so minor because they were calculated using Equation (25). Additionally, the curves in Figures 12c, 13c and 15c were obtained using Equation (26), and the curves in Figures 12d, 13d and 15d were obtained using Equation (27).

Curves (12b, 13b, 14b, and 15b) show the fluctuation of the values calculated for the distances for the (x), (y), and (z) axes and the total aircraft displacement. Respectively. All these curves tend to zero because the values were obtained from the subtraction of the values with the previous calculation (with steps 1). This also means that the error is reduced as the steps for calculation are increased. The values in these curves were obtained using Equation (25). Here, (dx) is the distance on the axis (x); this equation is also solved again for the (y), (z) axes, and the total distance. The sub-index (ns) refers to the number of steps used for calculation. And the super index (t = total) means that the value corresponds to the latest calculated displacement in the latest step of the latest maneuver; this is at the end of the simulation.

$$dx^b = dx_{ns}^{t=total} - dx_{ns-1}^{t=total} \tag{25}$$

Curves (12c, 13c, 14c, and 15c) show the fluctuation of the values calculated for the distances for axis (x), (y), and (z) axes and the total aircraft displacement, respectively, divided by the steps used, also evidencing that the final values tend to be zero. This means that the error tends to be reduced again. Although these curves tend quickly to zero, they are not considered the best evidence of a good approach. The curves resulted after the application of Equation (26) to the final displacement values calculated; all these curves immediately tend to zero. Nevertheless, this approaching calculation is not the most reliable because (ns) is always increasing; thus, the next value will always be minor.

$$dx^c = \frac{dx_{ns}^{t=total}}{ns} \tag{26}$$

Curves (12d, 13d, 14d, and 15d) show the fluctuation of the values calculated for the distances for the (x), (y), and (z) axes and the total aircraft displacement, respectively, minus the previous value and divided by the previous value, also evidencing that the final values tend to be zero. This means that the error tends to be reduced again. These curves result from the application of Equation (27). All of these curves tend to zero, but there are positive and negative variations that diminish.

$$dx^d = \frac{dx_{ns}^{t=total} - dx_{ns-1}^{t=total}}{dx_{ns-1}^{t=total}} \tag{27}$$

Fluctuations on these curves can be positives or negatives due to the change in heading angles and the steps used for calculation; fluctuations for the axis (z) were major in contrast with the (x) and (y) axes, but they are not according to the scales on the vertical axes.

These curves evidence the following facts for flight (2):

The difference between the displacements calculated tends to a final value; then the error in the calculation is reduced as the number of steps is increased, as could be expected for any integration method; thus, the approaching is improved. The same behavior can be appreciated for every analyzed axis and for the total displacement.

According to the steps used for the calculation of the flights, it is possible to affirm the following facts for all the analyzed axes:

Using 10 to 100 steps, the approaching is bad.

Using 100 to 1000 steps, the approaching is notoriously improved. The fluctuations in the calculated values are damped.

Using 1000 to 2000 steps, the approaching was not significantly improved, which is why it can be considered not absolutely required.

It is important to mention that horizontal aircraft speeds are often higher than vertical speeds, but these can be so different depending on the aircraft type and capacity. For major speeds, it will be necessary to calculate the displacement using more steps.

The maneuver time has a strong influence on the approaching; the increment in steps is the best way to improve approaching for long times.

The aircraft speed also has a strong influence over calculation; increasing the steps for calculation reduces the errors and improves approaching if the aircraft speed is increased, as is appreciated in Figures 12–15. Moreover, fluctuations are so high in the vertical axis (z) due to altitude, with minor values in comparison with horizontal displacements. Additionally, it must be noted that a particular approaching can be calculated for every maneuver since everyone has particular data. Nevertheless, for this work, it was decided to do it for the completed flights.

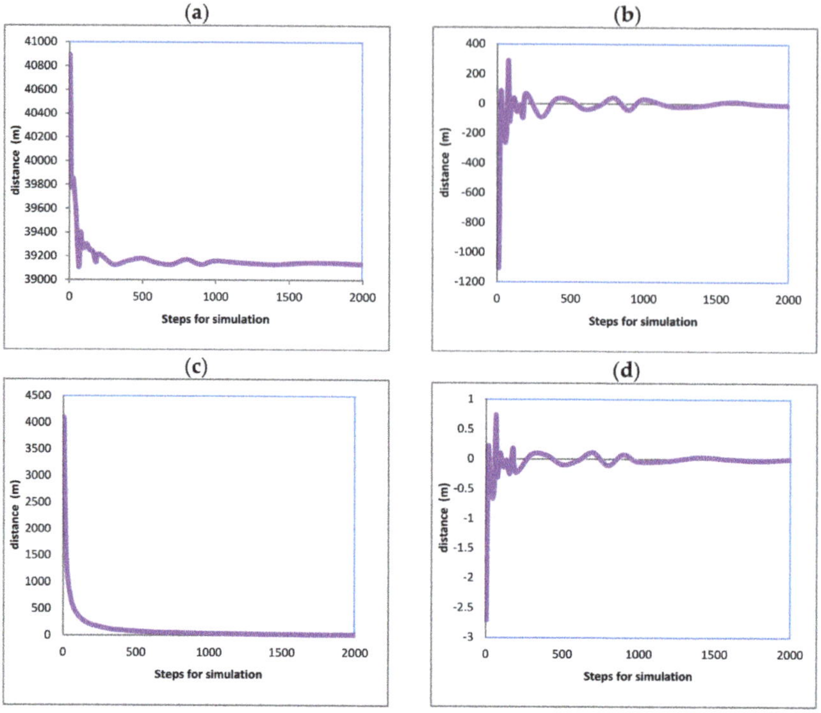

Figure 15. Calculated approaching for flight (1) curves for total distance measured for the original point assumed as the aircraft was in a stationary position at (0,0,0). (**a**) considering displacement values. (**b**) considering the previous calculated value. (**c**) considering the division of the displacement between the number of steps. (**d**) considering the approaching to the final value.

In addition, the displacement values for every flight along the 3 axes and the final displacement using 10,000 steps were calculated, which are considered enough for a very good approaching. The results shown are in Table 2, and additional curves resulted from the application of Equation (28) are shown in Figure 16a–d. The application of these equations shows the approaching as an error in percentage, referring to the value calculated using a large number of steps, and can also be used for comparison.

$$dx = 100\left[1 - \left(\frac{dx_{ns}^{t=total}}{dx_{ns=10{,}000}^{t=total}}\right)\right] \tag{28}$$

Table 2. Calculated distances along the axis (x, y, z) and total measured from the aircraft origin for every simulated flight.

Flight	dx	dy	dz	dtot
1	8214	20,976	5825	62,019
2	20,724	10,432	3136	39,123
3	23,250	21,871	2071	37,755

(a)
Analysis for distance along (x) axis

(b)
Analysis for distance along (y) axis

(c)
Analysis for distance along (z) axis

(d)
Analysis for the total displacemnt

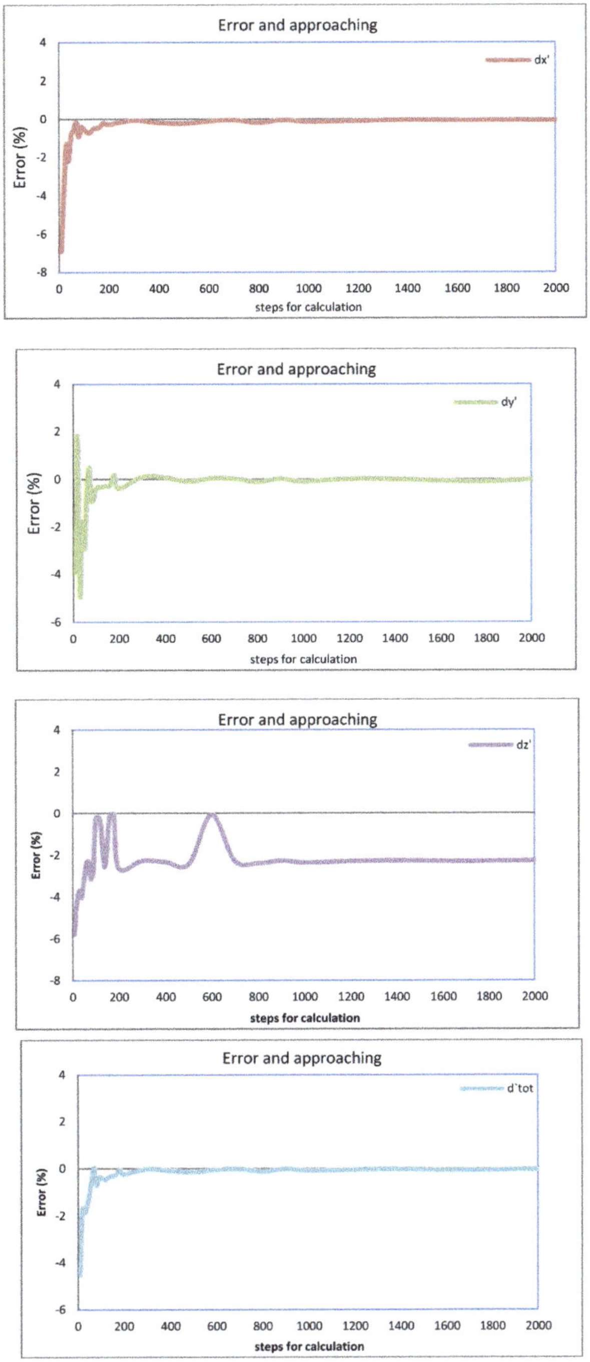

Figure 16. Reduction in the error calculated for flight (1) over every axis of displacement. Analysis for every displacement calculated (**a**) for Sud-North direction. (**b**) for Est-West direction. (**c**) for altitude. (**d**) for total displacement.

According to the graph shown in Figure 16a, a good approach is obtained using more than 400 steps for analysis because it tends to zero with such minimal variation. Maximum variations are from (−7.2%) when less than 100 steps are used. In the case of the direction east–west on axis (y), there is a similar damping behavior as the steps are increased, but at the beginning, variations are positive and negative. The maximum variations are between (−4%) and (2%). Although, in the same way as for axis (x), both curves tend to a final true value with a variation almost equal to zero. Thus, it can be considered that the variation over 400 steps is not so significant, and the solution is so close to the real, final true values. In the axis (z) for the altitude where the aircraft is flying, there is a variation until 800 steps; moreover, for 2000 steps, there is a variation of (2%). This variation is considerable, but it must be taken into account that the distance over this axis is so minor in comparison with the distances on the axes (x) and (y) and over the total distance. In Figure 16d, the same behavior is observed, and the curve is so similar to those in Figure 16a,b, evidencing the stronger influence of the much longer distances traveled on the horizontal axes as was shown in the flight path.

6. Discussion

According to the results obtained, it is possible to affirm that any aircraft flight condition can be properly calculated and represented computationally with the algorithm developed. Moreover, the approaching calculation can be easily improved by increasing the number of calculation steps. In addition, no more than 500 steps are needed for a good approach, although for different speeds and times of maneuvers, approaching analysis must be performed; this work can be quickly carried out with a minor computational effort. For immediate future studies, the information calculated can be employed to represent the aircraft instrument animation in a virtual environment to develop a more complex simulator. Some of the potential topics that can be developed from this work are the following:

(a) Computational representation of the aircraft instruments can be employed to train pilots or just to show students and enthusiasm their function described with theoretical support.
(b) Planning of aircraft flights and representation of flights in a basic virtual environment, including obstacles such as a defined geography for terrain. This option can provide tools for planning operations with safe air flying conditions.
(c) More complex calculations, including wind components or weather conditions, influence the aircraft path and the calculation of forces to correct.
(d) Simulation of many flights in one single environment is very important in order to avoid collisions and plan airport operations.
(e) Simulation of flights under pilot control using the computer keyboard with no defined data, considering manual control.
(f) Planning and correction of more sophisticated maneuvers and comparison between manual and automatic aircraft navigation.
(g) Calculation of application forces on stabilizers, flaps, slats, spoilers, rudders, elevators, etc.
(h) Inclusion of aero-dynamical behavior as a function of aircraft features.

In the algorithm developed, there are no limits on time or speed conditions that can be input for the aircraft flight simulated; appropriate warnings were programmed to avoid errors during input data; and the information about the aircraft displacement can be saved as is calculated in an independent file if required.

7. Conclusions

The algorithms developed to represent the aircraft path in 2D and 3D computational representation were successfully tested and represent the aircraft path appropriately during flights.

According to the conditions defined for the flights, simulated symmetrical and asymmetrical speeds and path segments can be observed on the maneuvers as a function of the aircraft direction and acceleration.

The reading data and modification options processes were also considered appropriate.

The options for analyzing the flights were also successfully tested and provided the information required.

The influence of the aircraft speed and maneuver time on the aircraft displacement is properly described with this algorithm.

The main and subroutines of the simulator were properly compiled; computational equipment with huge or specific features is not needed. No additional code is required on the algorithms, the computational effort is not significant; moreover, the execution time is short for a good approaching; thus, the simulator is efficient.

Increment of the steps used for calculation becomes short the step time (Δt) reducing errors and improving approaching.

Funding: This research received no external finance.

Institutional Review Board Statement: Not applicable.

Data Availability Statement: All information is in the manuscript.

Acknowledgments: The author wish to thanks to their institutions: Technological and Autonomous Institute of México (ITAM), Mexican Association of Culture and National Counsel of Humanities, Science and Technology (CONAHCyT).

Conflicts of Interest: The author declares no conflicts of interest.

References

1. Jukes, M. Aircraft Display Systems. In *Progress in Astronautics and Aeronautics*; Professional Engineering Publishing: London, UK, 2004.
2. Chorley, R.A. Seventy Years of Instruments and Displays 3RD Folland Lecture. *Aeronaut. Vol.* **1976**, *80*, 323–342. [CrossRef]
3. Coombs, L.F.E. *The Aircraft Cockpit*; Patrick Stephens Ltd.: Wellingborough, UK, 1990; pp. 12–25, 36–45 & 54–59.
4. Tanner, J. *The Official Air Publication for the Lancaster Mk I and III 1942–1945*; Arms and Armours: London, UK, 1977; pp. 32–47, 55–72.
5. Wise, J.A.; Hopkin, V.D.; Garland, D.J. *Handbook of Aviation Human Factors*, 2nd ed.; CRC Press, Taylor and Francis: Boca Raton, FL, USA, 2010; Chapters 1, 2, 13 & 19.
6. Carr, G.P.; Montemerlo, M.D. (Eds.) *Aerospace Crew Station Design: Proceedings of a Course Given at the International Center for Transportation Studies (ICTS) Amalfi, Italy—October 19–22, 1983*; Elsevier Science Publishers B.V.: Amsterdam, The Netherlands, 1984.
7. FAA. *Pilot's Handbook of Aeronautical Knowledge*; US Department of Transportation: Newcastle, WA, USA, 2008; Chapters 1, 4 & 28.
8. FAA; U.S. Department of Transportation. *Instrument Flying Handbook*; US Department of Transportation: Newcastle, WA, USA, 2012; Chapter 5.
9. Barspul, M. A Review of Flight Simulation Techniques. *Prog. Aerosp. Sci.* **1990**, *27*, 1–120. [CrossRef]
10. Baarspul, M.; Mulder, J.A.; Nieuwpoort, A.M.H.; Breeman, J.H. Mathematical Model Identification for Flight Simulation, Based on Flight and Taxi Tests. In *Flight Simulation—Recent Developments in Technology and Use, International Conference Proceedings*; The Royal Aeronautical Society: London, UK, 1988.
11. Nicholas, O.P.; Giles, J.A.; Williams, D.A. Development of in-flight Simulation Aircraft for Research and Training in U.K. In *AGARD Conference Proceedings No. 408 on "Flight Simulation"*; North Atlantic Treaty Organization: Cambridge, UK, 1985; pp. 24–35.
12. Faconti, V. Evolution of Flight Simulator Instructional Capabilities: The First Fifty Years. In *50 Years of Flight Simulation, Conference Proceedings*; The Royal Aeronautical Society: London, UK, 1979; Session 2; pp. 51–74.
13. Hellings, G.; Emms, E.T. A Visual System for Flight Simulators. *Br. Commun. Electron.* **1960**, *7*, 334–337.
14. Tomlinson, B.N. Motion Software for a Research Flight Simulator. In *Advances in Flight Simulation-Visual and Motion Systems, International Conference Proceedings*; The Royal Aeronautical Society: London, UK, 1986; pp. 64–80.
15. Hanke, C.R. Volume I: Mathematical model, NASA CR-1756. In *The Simulation of a Large Jet Transport Aircraft*; NASA: Washington, CA, USA, 1971.
16. Dunn, W.H.; Eldert, C.; Levonian, P.V. A Digital Computer for use in and Operational Flight Trainer. *IRE Trans. Electron. Comput.* **1955**, *4*, 55–63. [CrossRef]
17. Prathap, G. The Displacement-Type Finite Element Approach—From Art to Science. *Prog. Aerosp. Sci.* **1994**, *30*, 295–405. [CrossRef]
18. Adorian, P.; Staynes, W.N.; Bolton, M. The Evolution of the Flight Simulator. In *50 Years of Flight Simulation, Conference Proceedings*; The Royal Aeronautical Society: London, UK, 1979; Session 1; pp. 1–23.
19. Mulder, J.A.; Chu, Q.P.; Sridhar, J.K.; Breeman, J.H.; Laban, M. Non-linear aircraft flight path reconstruction review and new advances. *Prog. Aerosp. Sci.* **1999**, *35*, 673–726. [CrossRef]

20. Roudbari, A.; Saghafi, F. Intelligent Modeling and Identification of Aircraft Nonlinear Flight. *Chin. J. Aeronaut.* **2014**, *27*, 759–771. [CrossRef]
21. Cutler, A.E. Environmental Realism in Flight Simulators. *Radio Electron. Eng.* **1966**, *31*, 1–16. [CrossRef]
22. Liu, F.; Wang, L.; Tan, X. Digital Virtual Flight testing and Evaluation Method for Flight Characteristics Airworthiness Compliance of Civil Aircraft Based on HQRM. *Chin. J. Aeronaut.* **2015**, *28*, 112–120. [CrossRef]
23. Filippone, A. Comprehensive Analysis of Transport Aircraft Flight Performance. *Prog. Aerosp. Sci.* **2008**, *44*, 192–236. [CrossRef]
24. Gołębiewski, M.; Galant-Gołębiewska, M.; Jasiński, R. Flight Simulator's Energy Consumption Depending on the Conditions of the Air Operation. *Energies* **2022**, *15*, 580. [CrossRef]
25. Kozuba, J.; Bondaruk, A. Flight simulator as an essential device supporting the process of shaping pilot's situational awareness. In Proceedings of the International Conference of Scientific Paper AFASES 2014, Brasov, Romania, 22–24 May 2014.
26. Galant, M.; Nowak, M.; Kardach, M.; Maciejewska, M.; Łęgowik, A. Using the simulation technique to improve efficiency in general aviation Using the Simulation Technique To Improve Efficiency in General Aviation. *AIP Conf. Proc.* **2019**, *2078*, 20097. [CrossRef]
27. Epperson, J.F. *An Introduction to Numerical Methods and Analysis*; John Wiley & Sons, Inc.: Hoboken, NJ, USA, 2013.
28. Chapra, S.C. *Numerical Methods for Engineers*, 7th ed.; Mc Graw Hill: New York, NY, USA, 2015.
29. Venkateshan, S.P.; Swaminathan, P. *Computational Methods in Engineering*; Elsevier: Amsterdam, The Netherlands, 2013.
30. Ortega, J.M.; Grimshaw, A.S. *An Introduction to C++ and Numerical Methods*; Oxford University Press: Oxford, UK, 1998.
31. Flowers, B.H. *An Introduction to Numerical Methods in C++*; Oxford University Press: Oxford, UK, 2000.
32. Weiskamp, K.; Heiny, L. *Power Graphics Using Turbo C++*; John Wiley & Sons Inc.: Hoboken, NJ, USA, 1994.
33. Heiny, L. *Advanced Graphics Programming Using C/C++*; Wiley: Hoboken, NJ, USA, 1993.
34. Howe, R.M. Transfer Function and Characteristic Root Errors for Fixed-Step Integration Algorithms. *Trans. Soc. Comput. Simul.* **1985**, *2*, 293–320.
35. Howe, R.M. The Use of Real-time Predictor-corrector Integration for Flight Simulation. In Proceedings of the SCS Simulation Conference Simulators V, Orlando, FL, USA, 18–21 April 1988; pp. 38–42.
36. Hoogstraten, J.A.; Moesdijk, G.A.J. Modular programming structure applied to the simulation of non-linear aircraft models. In *IMACS Conference Proceedings 'Simulation in Engineering Sciences'*; Elsevier Science Publishers: Nantes, France, 1983.
37. Falcone, M. Numerical methods for differential game based on partial differential equations. *Int. Game Theory Rev.* **2006**, *8*, 231–272. [CrossRef]
38. Lin, Y.; Zhang, J.-W.; Liu, H. An algorithm for trajectory prediction of flight plan based on relative motion between positions. *Front. Inform. Technol. Electron. Eng.* **2018**, *19*, 905–916. [CrossRef]
39. Zhu, D. On the Applications of Numerical Methods to Aircraft Running Dynamics. In *Computational Mechanics '95*; Atluri, S.N., Yagawa, G., Cruse, T., Eds.; Springer: Berlin/Heidelberg, Germany, 1995. [CrossRef]
40. Scholz, D.; Thorbeck, J. Computer Based Training in Aircraft Design Education. In *ICAS: ICAS 2000 CD-ROM Proceedings (22nd International Congress of Aeronautical Sciences, Harrogate, UK, 27 August–1 September 2000)*; Paper: ICAS-2000-1.7.3; Optimage: Edinburgh, UK, 2000; ISBN 0953399125.
41. Jiang, S.-Y.; Luo, X.; He, L. Research on Method of Trajectory Prediction in Aircraft Flight Based on Aircraft Performance and Historical Track Data. *Math. Probl. Eng.* **2021**, *2021*, 6688213. [CrossRef]
42. Ascher, U.M.; Greif, C. *A First Course in Numerical Methods*; Siam: Philadelphia, PA, USA, 2011. [CrossRef]

axioms

MDPI

rticle

An Optimization Problem for Computing Predictive Potential of General Sum/Product-Connectivity Topological Indices of Physicochemical Properties of Benzenoid Hydrocarbons

akander Hayat [1,*,†], Azri Arfan [1], Asad Khan [2,*,†], Haziq Jamil [1] and Mohammed J. F. Alenazi [3]

1 Mathematical Sciences, Faculty of Science, Universiti Brunei Darussalam, Jln Tungku Link, Gadong BE1410, Brunei; 19b9052@ubd.edu.bn (A.A.); haziq.jamil1@ubd.edu.bn (H.J.)

2 Metaverse Research Institute, School of Computer Science and Cyber Engineering, Guangzhou University, Guangzhou 510006, China

3 Department of Computer Engineering, College of Computer and Information Sciences (CCIS), King Saud University, Riyadh 11451, Saudi Arabia; mjalenazi@ksu.edu.sa

* Correspondence: sakander.hayat@ubd.edu.bn (S.H.); asad@gzhu.edu.cn (A.K.)

† These authors contributed equally to this work.

Abstract: For a graph $G = (V_G, E_G)$, a degree-based graphical index GI_d takes the general form $GI_d = \sum_{xy \in E_G} \phi(d_x, d_y)$, where ϕ is a symmetric map and d_i is the degree of $i \in V_G$. For $\alpha \in \mathbb{R}$, if $\phi = (d_x d_y)^\alpha$ (resp. $\phi = (d_x + d_y)^\alpha$), the index is called the general product-connectivity R_α (resp. general sum-connectivity SCI_α) index. In this paper, by formulating an optimization problem, we determine the value(s) of α, for which the linear/multiple correlation coefficient of R_α and SCI_α with physicochemical properties of benzenoid hydrocarbons is the strongest. This, in turn, fills some research gaps left by similar studies in this area.

Keywords: chemical graph theory; graph; benzenoid hydrocarbon; boiling point; enthalpy of formation; general sum-connectivity index; general product-connectivity index; optimization

MSC: 05C92; 05C90; 05C09

1. Introduction

Structure–property modeling employs molecular descriptors [1] to generate regression models correlating the physicochemical, biological, or thermodynamic properties of chemical compounds. Degree-based graphical indices are a class of graph-theoretic molecular descriptors that gained popularity in efficiently correlating the physicochemical properties of benzenoid hydrocarbons (BHs). In 1975, Randić introduced the connectivity index, commonly referred to as the Randić index (cf. [2]). Over the years, this index has emerged as the predominant molecular descriptor in Quantitative Structure–Property Relationship (QSPR) and Quantitative Structure–Activity Relationship (QSAR) studies (cf. [2]). Its mathematical properties have been extensively examined, as succinctly outlined in two recent monographs [2,3]. Moreover, various modifications and alternative formulations of this index have been proposed in the scientific literature (cf. [4,5]). In the present discourse, we also explore a closely affiliated variant of the connectivity index, denoted as the sum-connectivity index [6]. For some recent progress on the structure–property modeling of the physicochemical properties of nanostructures and bio-molecular networks, we refer to [7–10].

In order to test the quality of a certain class of molecular graphical descriptors, it is customary to conduct comparative testing by selecting suitable test molecules and their particular chemical properties. Gutman and Tošović [11] tested the quality of degree-dependent graphical descriptors for correlating the physicochemical properties of ismeric octanes (representatives of alkanes). Malik et al. [12] extended this study of degree-based molecular indices from octane-isomers to benzenoid hydrocarbons (BHs). Hayat et al. [13] (resp. Hayat et al. [14]) further extended the work from physicochemical properties to the quantum-theoretical (resp. thermodynamic) properties of BHs.

In their study, Gutman and Tošović [11] selected isomeric octanes as test molecules, whereas, other studies [11,12,14] opted for the lower 20–30 BHs as test molecules for their investigation. Moreover, Gutman and Tošović [11] and Malik et al. [12] selected the normal boiling point (bp) and the standard enthalpy of formation ΔH_f^o to represent physicochemical characteristics. Van der Waals and intermolecular forms of interactions are represented by bp, whereas, ΔH_f^o advocates for the thermal characteristics of a compound. On the other hand, the total π-electronic energy (E_π) was selected to represent quantum-theoretical characteristics by Hayat et al. [13] and the entropy and heat capacity were selected to advocate for thermodynamic properties by Hayat et al. [14].

All of the aforementioned quality testing revealed the strong potential of both general product-connectivity R_α and sum-connectivity SCI_α indices to efficiently correlate the physicochemical, thermodynamical, and quantum-theoretical characteristics of benzenoid hydrocarbons. For instance, Malik et al. [12] showed that, among all degree-based descriptors, R_{-1} and SCI_{-2} are the top two indices in correlating physicochemical characteristics of BHs. Similarly, Hayat et al. [13] showcased that $SCI_{-\frac{1}{2}}$ and $R_{-0.2661}$ are the best descriptors in predicting the E_π of BHs, whereas Hayat et al. [14] showed that SCI_{-3} and R_{-1} are best two indices for correlating the thermodynamic properties of BHs. However, the disadvantage to these studies is that they consider both R_α and SCI_α in their comparative testing for only finite values of α, i.e., $\alpha \in \left\{\pm\frac{1}{2} \pm 1, \pm 2\right\}$. Since both R_α and SCI_α deliver strong potential in correlating various properties of BHs, it is natural to consider these indices by considering the general $\alpha \in \mathbb{R} \setminus \{0\}$. Note that there might be a possibility that some other nonlinear function $\phi(d_x, d_y)$, for instance considering other powers of α, could work even better. However, the current study is restricted to investigating the estimation potential of R_α and SCI_α only.

In summary, current comparative studies considered R_α and SCI_α for $\alpha \in \left\{\pm\frac{1}{2} \pm 1, \pm 2\right\}$ and showed that both R_α and SCI_α with some of these values of α correlate well with the physicochemical properties as well as the total π-electron energy (E_π) of benzenoid hydrocarbons (BHs). For instance, Malik et al. [12] showed that R_{-1} and SCI_{-2} are the top two best degree-based predictors for correlating the physicochemical properties of BHs. Moreover, Hayat et al. [13] showed that $SCI_{-\frac{1}{2}}$ correlates well with the E_π of BHs. The only limitation of these studies was that they considered R_α and SCI_α for $\alpha \in \left\{\pm\frac{1}{2} \pm 1, \pm 2\right\}$ only. So, if R_α and SCI_α deliver good predictors for these fixed integral values, both R_α and SCI_α might deliver even better predictors if we consider the general values of $\alpha \in \mathbb{R} \setminus \{0\}$.

In this paper, we determine the value(s) of α for which both SCI_α and R_α deliver strong predictive potential for the physicochemical properties of BHs. Multiple correlation and regression analyses were also conducted to find the best α for which the strongest multiple correlation is delivered both by SCI_α and R_α simultaneously. Following Gutman and Tošović [11], the physicochemical properties bp and ΔH_f^o were selected as the test properties of BHs. Moreover, 22 lower BHs were selected as the test molecules as the public availability of the experimental values of bp and ΔH_f^o is ensured for these test molecules. A computational method was used to calculate the SCI_α and R_α of these 22 BHs and then a detailed statistical analysis was conducted to find the suitable values of α for which both SCI_α and R_α deliver strong predictive potential.

2. Mathematical Preliminaries

For a chemical graph $G = (V_G, E_G)$, a degree-based graphical index GI_d takes the general form $GI_d = \sum_{xy \in E_G} \phi(d_x, d_y)$, where ϕ is a symmetric map and d_i is the degree of $i \in V_G$. The *product-connectivity index* of G, proposed by Randić in [15] back in 1975, is one of the earliest degree-based graphical indices. Later on, the index was renamed as the Randić index. Mathematically, it takes $\phi = (d_x d_y)^{-\frac{1}{2}}$ in GI_d. Thus, the product-connectivity descriptor $R(G)$ is defined as :

$$R(G) = GI_d, \text{ where } \phi(d_x, d_y) = \frac{1}{\sqrt{d_x d_y}} \tag{1}$$

The diversity of its applicability in cheminformatics makes the Randić index one of most-studied structure graphical descriptors. For instance, its mathematical and chemical properties were extensively examined in [2,16–19].

Introduced by Zhou and Trinajstić [6], the *sum-connectivity index* is another degree-related molecular graphical descriptor. For a graph G, it considers $\phi = (d_x + d_y)^{-\frac{1}{2}}$ in GI_d. Therefore, the sum-connectivity $SCI(G)$ of G has the defining structure:

$$SCI(G) = GI_d, \text{ where } \phi(d_x, d_y) = \frac{1}{\sqrt{d_x + d_y}} \tag{2}$$

The reader is suggested [12,13,20,21] for further studies on both applicative and mathematical perspectives of the sum-connectivity index.

The successful applicability of the product-connectivity and sum-connectivity indices motivated researchers to consider variants of these descriptors. Perhaps, the most well-studied variants are the generalized variants of the product- and sum-connectivity indices. For $\alpha \in \mathbb{R}$, if $\phi = (d_x d_y)^\alpha$ (resp. $\phi = (d_x + d_y)^\alpha$), the index is called the *general product-connectivity* R_α (resp. *general sum-connectivity* SCI_α) index. The general product-connectivity index was put forward by Bollobás and Erdös [4] in 1998 while generalizing the classical $R(G)$ index:

$$R_\alpha(G) = GI_d, \text{ where } \phi(d_x, d_y) = (d_x d_y)^\alpha, \tag{3}$$

where $\alpha \in \mathbb{R} \setminus \{0\}$. There have been numerous contributions in the chemical and mathematical literature published on the general product-connectivity index, see, for example, [2,22–25].

Similarly, Zhou and Trinajstić [26] in 2010 proposed the general sum-connectivity index with the following defining structure:

$$SCI_\alpha(G) = GI_d, \text{ where } \phi(d_x, d_y) = (d_x + d_y)^\alpha, \tag{4}$$

where $\alpha \in \mathbb{R} \setminus \{0\}$. A detailed mathematical treatment is reported in [27–30]. The application perspective of SCI_α is reported in Gutman and Tošović [11] and Hayat et al. [14]. Obviously,

$$R(G) = R_{-0.5}(G)$$
$$SCI(G) = SCI_{-0.5}(G)$$

In the field of statistics, the *correlation coefficient* between two finite-mean random variables X and Y is defined to be $\rho_{XY} = \text{cov}(X, Y)/\sigma_X\sigma_Y \in [-1, 1]$, where cov is the covariance function, and σ_X and σ_Y represent the standard deviations of the random variables X and Y, respectively. The correlation coefficient measures both the direction and strength of the linear relationship between a *predictor* Y and a response variable X. For a series of k measurements of these variables, denoted by x_n and y_n $(n = 1, 2, \ldots, k)$, the value ρ_{XY} is estimated by

$$r_{xy} = \frac{\sum_{n=1}^{k}(x_n - \bar{x})(y_n - \bar{y})}{\sqrt{\sum_{n=1}^{k}(x_n - \bar{x})^2}\sqrt{\sum_{n=1}^{k}(y_n - \bar{y})^2}}, \tag{5}$$

where $\bar{x} = \frac{1}{k}\sum_{n=1}^{k} x_n$ and $\bar{y} = \frac{1}{k}\sum_{n=1}^{k} y_n$. Values of $|\rho_{XY}|$ closer to 1 indicate a strong linear relationship between X and Y.

The correlation coefficient is strongly linked to the concept of the *linear regression* of Y against X by assuming a *regression line* $Y = aX + b + \epsilon$ where ϵ represents random errors, and $\{a, b \in \mathbb{R}\}$ are coefficients to be estimated. The *ordinary least squares* method is typically employed, with closed-form solutions of the estimators $\hat{a}$ and $\hat{b}$ for a and b, respectively, being readily available and widely known. In particular, for this *simple linear regression* model, $\hat{a} = r_{xy}s_y/s_x$, where s_x and s_y are the unbiased estimators of σ_x and σ_Y, respectively, while $\hat{b} = \bar{y} - \hat{a}\bar{x}$. Evidently, the correlation is related to the slope of the regression line.

The *standard error of fit* and correlation coefficient are both key goodness-of-fit measures in regression analysis. The standard error of fit is defined as

$$s(Y,X) = \sqrt{\frac{1}{k-2}\sum_{n=1}^{k}(y_n - y_n')^2} \tag{6}$$

where $y_n' = \hat{a}x_n + \hat{b}$ (the regression line's resulting predicted value). This quantifies how much the observed values deviate from the values predicted by the model. Using various types of mathematical or statistical software, they can be calculated.

The linear regression model can be extended to include multiple predictors, e.g., $X_1, \ldots, X_p$. Suppose we have two predictors X_1 and X_2, we may define the *multiple correlation* measure between these predictors and a single response variable Y as follows:

$$R = \sqrt{\begin{pmatrix} r_{x_1y} & r_{x_2y} \end{pmatrix} \begin{pmatrix} 1 & r_{x_1x_2} \\ r_{x_2x_1} & 1 \end{pmatrix}^{-1} \begin{pmatrix} r_{x_1y} \\ r_{x_2y} \end{pmatrix}} \in [0,1].$$

In the context of multiple linear regression, the quantity R^2 is usually referred to as the *coefficient of determination*. It is interpreted as the proportion of variability in the response variable Y that is accounted for by the predictor variables X_1 and X_2. The value R, thus, provides a measure of the correlation between the observed values of Y and the values predicted by the multiple linear regression model involving X_1 and X_2.

3. Materials and Methods

Every benzenoid hydrocarbon can be inherently depicted through a benzenoid system, defined as a finite, connected plane graph devoid of cut vertices, wherein each internal face is enclosed by a regular hexagon possessing sides of unit length.

The following definitions, as presented in [31], are applicable. Let B be a benzenoid system with v vertices and p hexagons. For any path $p_1 - p_2 - \cdots - p_{\ell+1}$ of length ℓ ($\ell \in \mathbb{N}, \ell \geq 1$) within B, the associated vertex degree sequence is defined as $(d_{p_1}, d_{p_2}, \ldots, d_{p_{\ell+1}})$. Subsequently, a *fjord, cove, bay,* and *fissure* refer to paths with degree sequences (2, 3, 3, 3, 3, 2), (2, 3, 3, 3, 2), (2, 3, 3, 2), and (2, 3, 2), respectively. These paths are traversed along the perimeter of B, as depicted in Figure 1. Fjords, coves, bays, and fissures are all considered different types of *inlets*. The number of inlets, k, is then defined as the total number of fjords, coves, bays, and fissures summed.

Suppose a benzenoid system B has p hexagons, k inlets, and v vertices. Let n_{ij} denote the number of B's edges that satisfies the conditions $d_a = i$ and $d_b = j$, where d_a and d_b, respectively, are the degrees of the ends a and b of an edge. By Lemma 1 in [31], we have

$$n_{22} = v - 2p - k + 2, \quad n_{23} = 2k, \quad n_{33} = 3p - k - 3. \tag{7}$$

By (3) and (7), the benzenoid system B has the general product-connectivity index as follows:

$$\begin{aligned} R_\alpha(B) &= n_{22}4^\alpha + n_{23}6^\alpha + n_{33}9^\alpha \\ &= (4^\alpha)v + (3\cdot 9^\alpha - 2\cdot 4^\alpha)p + (2\cdot 6^\alpha - 4^\alpha - 9^\alpha)k - 3\cdot 9^\alpha + 2\cdot 4^\alpha, \end{aligned} \tag{8}$$

By (4) and (7), the benzenoid system B has the general sum-connectivity index as follows:

$$\begin{aligned} SCI_\alpha(B) &= n_{22}4^\alpha + n_{23}5^\alpha + n_{33}6^\alpha \\ &= (4^\alpha)v + (3\cdot 6^\alpha - 2\cdot 4^\alpha)p + (2\cdot 5^\alpha - 4^\alpha - 6^\alpha)k - 3\cdot 6^\alpha + 2\cdot 4^\alpha, \end{aligned} \tag{9}$$

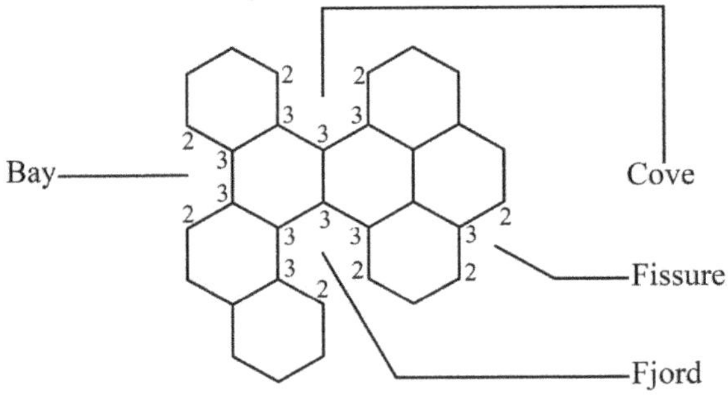

Figure 1. Fissure , cove, bay, and fjord in a benzenoid system.

We employ (8) and (9) to compute the R_α and SCI_α for the 22 lower BHs given in Table 1. Table 1 provides information on the molecular structure, normal boiling point (bp), and standard enthalpy of formation (ΔH_f^o) for various polycyclic aromatic hydrocarbons (PAHs). Additionally, Table 2 presents data on the general product-connectivity index R_α and the general sum-connectivity index SCI_α for the 22 lower BHs.

Table 1. The structural configuration of molecules, along with the experimental data pertaining to the standard enthalpy of formation (ΔH_f^o) and the normal boiling point (bp), is provided for a set of 22 lower benzenoid hydrocarbons.

Molecule	Structure	ΔH_f^o	bp
Benzene		75.2	80.1
Naphthalene		141	218
Phenanthrene	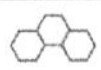	202.7	338
Anthracene	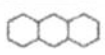	222.6	340
Chrysene	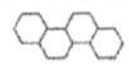	271.1	431
Benzo[a]anthracene	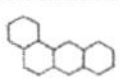	277.1	425
Triphenylene	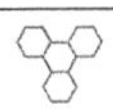	275.1	429
Tetracene	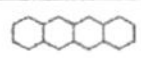	310.5	440
Benzo[a]pyrene	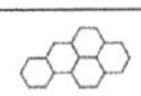	296	496
Benzo[e]pyrene	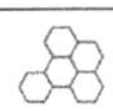	289.9	493
Perylene	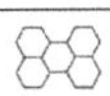	319.2	497
Anthanthrene	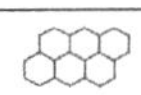	323	547
Benzo[ghi]perylene	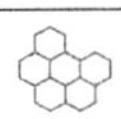	301.2	542

Table 1. *Cont.*

Molecule	Structure	ΔH_f^o	bp
Dibenzo[a,c]anthracene	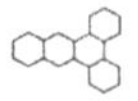	348	535
Dibenzo[a,h]anthracene	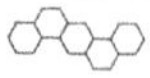	335	535
Dibenzo[a,j]anthracene	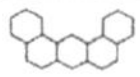	336.3	531
Picene	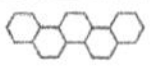	336.9	519
Coronene		296.7	590
Dibenzo(a,h)pyrene	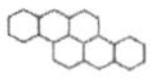	375.6	596
Dibenzo(a,i)pyrene	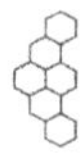	366	594
Dibenzo(a,l)pyrene	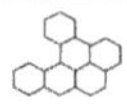	393.3	595
Pyrene		221.3	393

Table 2. The general product-connectivity index R_α and the general sum-connectivity index SCI_α of the 22 lower benzenoid hydrocarbons.

Molecule	R_α	SCI_α
Benzene	$6 \cdot 4^\alpha$	$6 \cdot 4^\alpha$
Naphthalene	$6 \cdot 4^\alpha + 4 \cdot 6^\alpha + 9^\alpha$	$6 \cdot 4^\alpha + 4 \cdot 5^\alpha + 6^\alpha$
Phenanthrene	$7 \cdot 4^\alpha + 6 \cdot 6^\alpha + 3 \cdot 9^\alpha$	$7 \cdot 4^\alpha + 6 \cdot 5^\alpha + 3 \cdot 6^\alpha$
Anthracene	$6 \cdot 4^\alpha + 8 \cdot 6^\alpha + 2 \cdot 9^\alpha$	$6 \cdot 4^\alpha + 8 \cdot 5^\alpha + 2 \cdot 6^\alpha$
Chrysene	$8 \cdot 4^\alpha + 8 \cdot 6^\alpha + 5 \cdot 9^\alpha$	$8 \cdot 4^\alpha + 8 \cdot 5^\alpha + 5 \cdot 6^\alpha$
Benzo[a]anthracene	$7 \cdot 4^\alpha + 10 \cdot 6^\alpha + 4 \cdot 9^\alpha$	$7 \cdot 4^\alpha + 10 \cdot 5^\alpha + 4 \cdot 6^\alpha$
Triphenylene	$9 \cdot 4^\alpha + 6 \cdot 6^\alpha + 6 \cdot 9^\alpha$	$9 \cdot 4^\alpha + 6 \cdot 5^\alpha + 6 \cdot 6^\alpha$
Tetracene	$6 \cdot 4^\alpha + 12 \cdot 6^\alpha + 3 \cdot 9^\alpha$	$6 \cdot 4^\alpha + 12 \cdot 5^\alpha + 3 \cdot 6^\alpha$
Benzo[a]pyrene	$7 \cdot 4^\alpha + 10 \cdot 6^\alpha + 7 \cdot 9^\alpha$	$7 \cdot 4^\alpha + 10 \cdot 5^\alpha + 7 \cdot 6^\alpha$
Benzo[e]pyrene	$8 \cdot 4^\alpha + 8 \cdot 6^\alpha + 8 \cdot 9^\alpha$	$8 \cdot 4^\alpha + 8 \cdot 5^\alpha + 8 \cdot 6^\alpha$
Perylene	$8 \cdot 4^\alpha + 8 \cdot 6^\alpha + 8 \cdot 9^\alpha$	$8 \cdot 4^\alpha + 8 \cdot 5^\alpha + 8 \cdot 6^\alpha$
Anthanthrene	$6 \cdot 4^\alpha + 12 \cdot 6^\alpha + 9 \cdot 9^\alpha$	$6 \cdot 4^\alpha + 12 \cdot 5^\alpha + 9 \cdot 6^\alpha$
Benzo[ghi]perylene	$7 \cdot 4^\alpha + 10 \cdot 6^\alpha + 10 \cdot 9^\alpha$	$7 \cdot 4^\alpha + 10 \cdot 5^\alpha + 10 \cdot 6^\alpha$
Dibenzo[a,c]anthracene	$9 \cdot 4^\alpha + 10 \cdot 6^\alpha + 7 \cdot 9^\alpha$	$9 \cdot 4^\alpha + 10 \cdot 5^\alpha + 7 \cdot 6^\alpha$
Dibenzo[a,h]anthracene	$8 \cdot 4^\alpha + 12 \cdot 6^\alpha + 6 \cdot 9^\alpha$	$8 \cdot 4^\alpha + 12 \cdot 5^\alpha + 6 \cdot 6^\alpha$
Dibenzo[a,j]anthracene	$8 \cdot 4^\alpha + 12 \cdot 6^\alpha + 6 \cdot 9^\alpha$	$8 \cdot 4^\alpha + 12 \cdot 5^\alpha + 6 \cdot 6^\alpha$
Picene	$9 \cdot 4^\alpha + 10 \cdot 6^\alpha + 7 \cdot 9^\alpha$	$9 \cdot 4^\alpha + 10 \cdot 5^\alpha + 7 \cdot 6^\alpha$
Coronene	$6 \cdot 4^\alpha + 12 \cdot 6^\alpha + 12 \cdot 9^\alpha$	$6 \cdot 4^\alpha + 12 \cdot 5^\alpha + 12 \cdot 6^\alpha$
Dibenzo(a,h)pyrene	$8 \cdot 4^\alpha + 12 \cdot 6^\alpha + 9 \cdot 9^\alpha$	$8 \cdot 4^\alpha + 12 \cdot 5^\alpha + 9 \cdot 6^\alpha$

Table 2. *Cont.*

Molecule	R_α	SCI_α
Dibenzo(a,i)pyrene	$8 \cdot 4^\alpha + 12 \cdot 6^\alpha + 9 \cdot 9^\alpha$	$8 \cdot 4^\alpha + 12 \cdot 5^\alpha + 9 \cdot 6^\alpha$
Dibenzo(a,l)pyrene	$9 \cdot 4^\alpha + 10 \cdot 6^\alpha + 10 \cdot 9^\alpha$	$9 \cdot 4^\alpha + 10 \cdot 5^\alpha + 10 \cdot 6^\alpha$
Pyrene	$6 \cdot 4^\alpha + 8 \cdot 6^\alpha + 5 \cdot 9^\alpha$	$6 \cdot 4^\alpha + 8 \cdot 5^\alpha + 5 \cdot 6^\alpha$

4. Results and Discussion

Recall that the general product-connectivity index R_α and the general sum-connectivity index SCI_α considering a range of values α exhibit a high degree of accuracy in predicting the boiling point and enthalpy of formation for the lower benzenoid hydrocarbons (BHs).

First, we employed the method described in Section 3 to evaluate the exact analytical expressions for R_α and SCI_α for the 22 lower BHs provided in Table 1. In particular, we utilized expressions for R_α and SCI_α in (8) and (9), respectively, to compute their exact values. Note that, we only needed the number of vertices v, the number of inlets k, and the number of hexagons p for a given hexagonal system to compute its R_α and SCI_α values. The next example explains the methodology in Section 3 to compute the general sum- and product-connectivity indices for a given BH graph.

Example 1. *Let us consider the graph of phenanthrene, e.g., P from Table 1. Then, P comprises two fissures, one bay (three inlets in total), three hexagons, and 14 vertices. Thus,* $v = 14$, $k = 3$, *and* $p = 3$. *Using these values in* (8) *and* (9), *we obtain:*

$$\begin{aligned} R_\alpha(P) &= 7 \cdot 4^\alpha + 6 \cdot 6^\alpha + 3 \cdot 9^\alpha \\ SCI_\alpha(P) &= 7 \cdot 4^\alpha + 6 \cdot 5^\alpha + 3 \cdot 6^\alpha. \end{aligned}$$

By using this method for all the graphs in Table 1, we generated the data in Table 2.

From the data shown in Table 2, we generated four curves, as illustrated in Figures 2–5. For these 22 lower BHs, the correlation coefficient curves for their physicochemical properties (bp in Figures 2 and 3; ΔH_f^0 in Figures 4 and 5) and the indices (R_α or SCI_α) are drawn in the respective figures in solid lines, distinguished by colors.

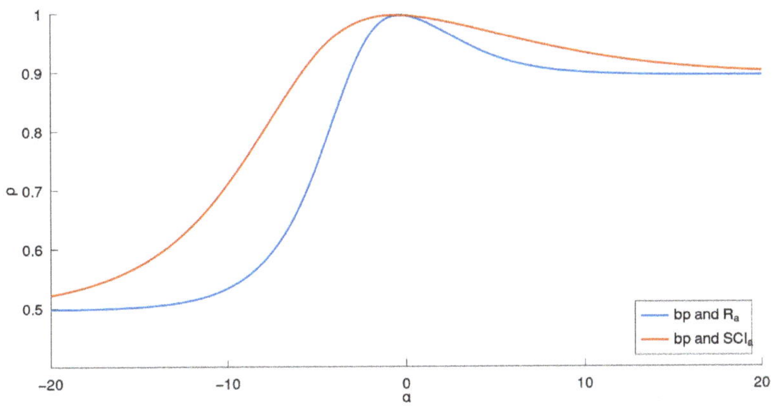

Figure 2. Correlation coefficient curves between general indices and bp of lower benzenoids (far view).

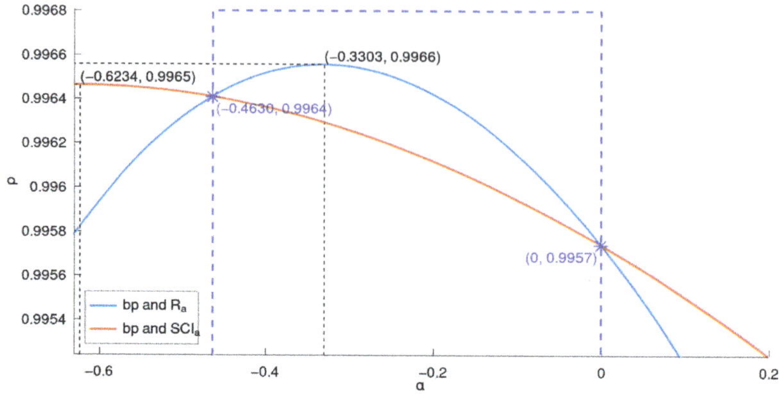

Figure 3. Correlation coefficient curves between general indices and bp of lower benzenoids.

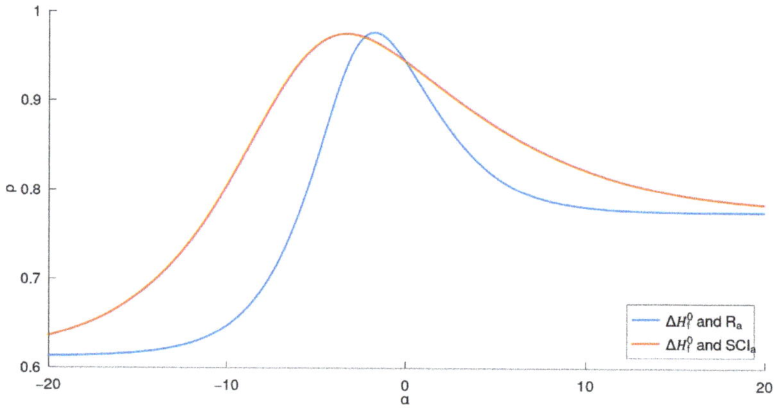

Figure 4. Correlation coefficient curves between general indices and ΔH_f^0 of lower benzenoids (far view).

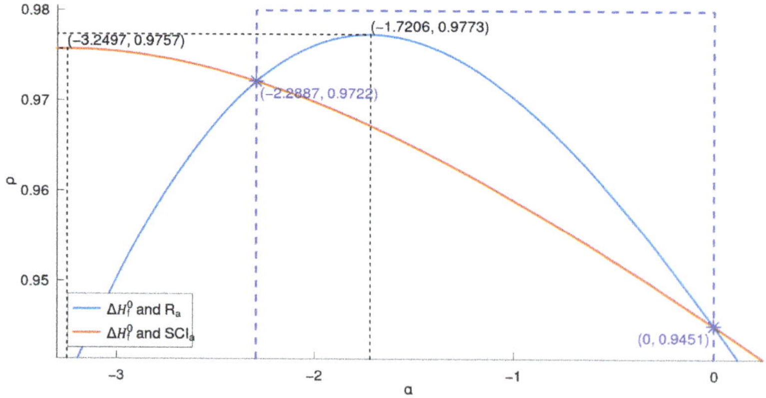

Figure 5. Correlation coefficient curves between general indices and ΔH_f^0 of lower benzenoids.

Comparing the two general indices, the general product-connectivity index R_α is the best measure of the boiling point bp for BHs for $\alpha \in (-0.4630, 0)$, as shown in Figure 3, while for any other α, the sum-connectivity index SCI_α is the best. On the other hand, as measures of the enthalpy of formation ΔH_f^0 of benzenoid hydrocarbons, the general product-connectivity index R_α is better for $\alpha \in (-2.2887, 0)$, as can be seen in Figure 5, while for any other α, the sum-connectivity index SCI_α is better.

There exists a good correlation between bp and R_α when α is in some interval. For example, for $\alpha \in [-1.154217, 0.681350]$, bp and R_α have a correlation coefficient greater than 0.996558. Similarly, there also exists—for α in different intervals—a good correlation between bp and SCI_α, between ΔH_f^0 and R_α, and between ΔH_f^0 and SCI_α, as shown in Figure 6.

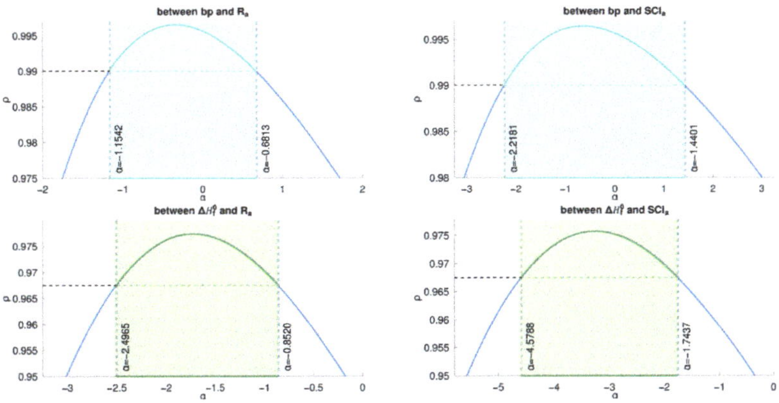

Figure 6. Intervals for good ρ for bp-R_α, bp-SCI_α, ΔH_f^0-R_α, ΔH_f^0-SCI_α for lower BHs.

By Figures 3 and 5, we have that, for the 22 lower BHs, $R_{-0.3303}$ and $R_{-1.7205}$ are the most linearly correlated with bp and ΔH_f^0, respectively, among all product-connectivity indices, and $SCI_{-0.6233}$ and $SCI_{-3.2496}$ are the most linearly correlated with bp and ΔH_f^0, respectively, among all sum-connectivity indices. The linear correlations (with 95% confidence intervals) between the physicochemical properties (bp and ΔH_f^0) and both of the aforementioned indices, respectively, are given below:

$$\begin{aligned} bp &= 39.693_{\pm 1.540} - 42.183_{\pm 20.161}\, R_{-0.33030}, \\ \rho(bp, R_{-0.33030}) &= 0.996558, s(bp, R_{-0.33030}) = 10.9571, \end{aligned} \tag{10}$$

$$\begin{aligned} bp &= 59.430_{\pm 2.334} - 40.884_{\pm 20.388}\, SCI_{-0.62336}, \\ \rho(bp, SCI_{-0.62336}) &= 0.996463, s(bp, SCI_{-0.62336}) = 11.1067, \end{aligned} \tag{11}$$

$$\begin{aligned} \Delta H_f^0 &= 300.943_{\pm 30.399} - 85.181_{\pm 38.305}\, R_{-1.72056}, \\ \rho(\Delta H_f^0, R_{-1.72056}) &= 0.977344, s(\Delta H_f^0, R_{-1.72056}) = 16.5206, \end{aligned} \tag{12}$$

$$\begin{aligned} \Delta H_f^0 &= 2486.468_{\pm 260.362} - 82.232_{\pm 39.402}\, SCI_{-3.24966}, \\ \rho(E, SCI_{-3.24966}) &= 0.975715, s(E, SCI_{-3.24966}) = 17.0968, \end{aligned} \tag{13}$$

Note that s and ρ are the standard error of fit and correlation coefficient, respectively. Figure 7 shows scatter plots between the boiling point bp and the indices $R_{-0.33030}$ and

$SCI_{-0.62336}$, and scatter plots between the enthalpy of formation ΔH_f^0 and the indices $R_{-1.72056}$ and $SCI_{-3.24966}$ for the 30 lower benzenoids.

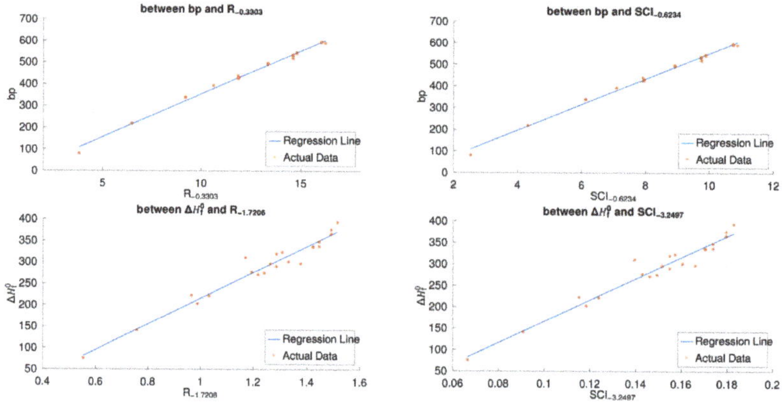

Figure 7. Scatter plots of bp-$R_{-0.33030}$, bp-$SCI_{-0.62336}$, ΔH_f^0-$R_{-1.72056}$, ΔH_f^0-$SCI_{-3.24966}$ for lower benzenoids.

It is obvious from (10)–(13) that the product-connectivity indices $R_{-0.33030}$ and $R_{-1.72056}$, respectively, are the best for measuring the boiling point and enthalpy of formation among all the examined indices. All the Octave codes have been made publicly accessible. See the Supplimentary Information at the end of the paper.

Recall that Gutman and Tošović [11] considered bp and ΔH_f^0 to be representatives of physicochemical properties. Moreover, they considered isomeric octanes as test molecules. We applied our study on the 18 isomeric octanes and the preliminary results showed that the value(s) of α for the 22 lower BHs yielding a good estimate of bp and ΔH_f^0 were not the same as they were for isomeric octanes. Thus, the current study and the corresponding intervals/values of α are limited to BHs only. However, we expect a similar behavior for other BHs (different from the 22 lower BHs considered in this study) as well.

5. Simultaneous Predictive Potential of R_α and SCI_α

In this section, we are interested in finding value(s) of α for which the correlation of either R_α or SCI_α with both properties bp and ΔH_f^0 simultaneously is the strongest. In order to achieve that, we need to consider the multiple correlation coefficient of either R_α or SCI_α with both bp and ΔH_f^0 by treating them as two independent variables. Let $Y = R_\alpha$ be the dependent variable and $X_1 = bp,\ X_2 = \Delta H_f^0$ be the two independent variables. Note that the multiple correlation determines the relationship with one dependent and more than one independent variable. Since there are two representatives of physicochemical properties, i.e., bp and ΔH_f^0, we employ multiple correlation between one graphical descriptor $GI_d \in \{R_\alpha, SCI_\alpha\}$ and the two chosen properties $X_1 = bp,\ X_2 = \Delta H_f^0$. This was able to deliver the predictive potential of a descriptor with the two properties simultaneously rather than determining .the correlation strength of the considered descriptor with both properties individually.

In the case where the response variable y depends on an unknown parameter $\alpha \in \mathbb{R}$, the value of multiple correlation ρ above also depends on α, i.e., $\rho := \rho(\alpha)$. A preliminary plot of $\rho(\alpha)$ in the region $-10 < \alpha < 10$ reveals a unimodal shape with a maxima in this region. A built-in optimizer in the R programming language was employed that yielded the value $\hat{\alpha} = -0.319$ that maximizes the multiple correlation value $\rho(\hat{\alpha}) = 0.997$. Figure 8 presents the corresponding plot elaborating this calculation.

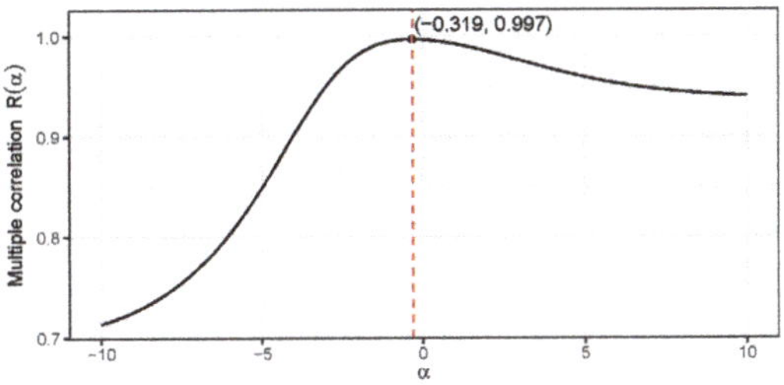

Figure 8. Plot delivering the value $\hat{\alpha} = -0.319$ for R_α, which maximizes the multiple correlation value $\rho(\hat{\alpha}) = 0.997$.

Figure 9 exhibits the matrix plot showing the distribution of the variables as well as the bivariate relationships between them (using the optimal value $\hat{\alpha}$).

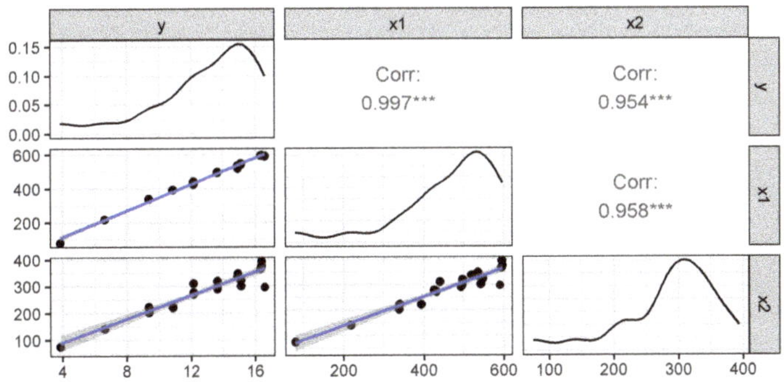

Figure 9. Distribution of variables $Y = R_\alpha$ and $X_1 = bp$, $X_2 = \Delta H_f^o$ and the bivariate relationships between them. Moreover, the main diagonal entries present the distribution of data points. The *** denotes the continuance of decimal expression.

Next, we study the multiple correlation $\rho := \rho(\alpha)$ between $Y = SCI_\alpha$ and the two chosen physicochemical properties $X_1 = bp$, $X_2 = \Delta H_f^o$. In the case where the response variables y depends on an unknown parameter $\alpha \in \mathbb{R}$, the value of R above also depends on α, i.e., $\rho := \rho(\alpha)$. A preliminary plot of $\rho(\alpha)$ in the region $-10 < \alpha < 10$ again reveals a unimodal shape with a maxima in this region. This time, the built in R optimizer yielded the value $\hat{\alpha} = -0.553$, so $\rho(\hat{\alpha}) = 0.996$. Figure 10 presents the corresponding plot elaborating these values.

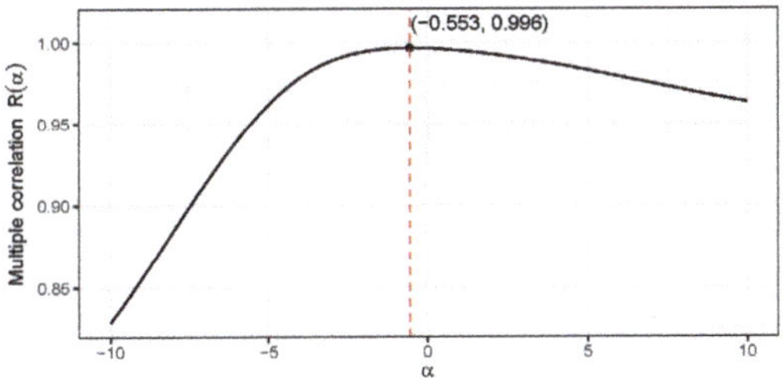

Figure 10. Plot delivering the value $\hat{\alpha} = -0.553$ for SCI_α, which maximizes the multiple correlation value $\rho(\hat{\alpha}) = 0.996$.

Figure 11 exhibits the matrix plot, showing the distribution of the variables as well as the bivariate relationships between them (using the optimal value $\hat{\alpha}$).

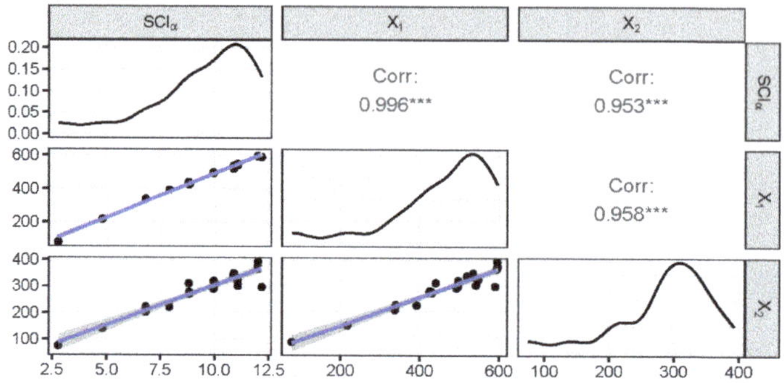

Figure 11. Distribution of variables $Y = SCI_\alpha$ and $X_1 = bp$, $X_2 = \Delta H_f^0$ and the bivariate relationships between them. Moreover, the main diagonal entries present the distribution of data points. The *** denotes the continuance of decimal expression.

6. Conclusions

We showed in this paper that there is good correlation between the boiling point (bp) and general product-connectivity index (R_α), between bp and the general sum-connectivity index (SCI_α), between the enthalpy of formation (ΔH_f^0) and R_α, and between ΔH_f^0 and SCI_α when α is in some intervals (as in Figure 6) for benzenoid hydrocarbons. Moreover, for $\alpha \in (-0.4630, 0)$ and $\alpha \in (-2.2887, 0)$ (marked with blue dashed lines in Figures 3 and 5), R_α rather than SCI_α is a better measure of the boiling point and enthalpy of formation, respectively, of G. For an α outside those intervals, SCI_α is a better measure of both the boiling point and enthalpy of formation of G.

7. Future Work

This paper examined the correlation power of the general product-connectivity index and general sum-connectivity index to determine the boiling point (bp) of benzenoid hydrocarbons, and their correlation power to determine the enthalpy of formation (ΔH_f^0) of benzenoid hydrocarbons. We propose further studies to similarly examine other generalized valency-based indices in determining the bp and ΔH_f^0 of benzenoid hydrocarbons. We also propose the following open problem:

Problem 2. *Can one use a learning technique to learn a nonlinear function $\phi(d_x, d_y)$ of minimal complexity that is a best predictor of GI_d?*

Supplementary Materials: Octave 7.2 scripts used to generate results and draw Figures 2–7 are provided on GitHub: https://github.com/AzriArfan/Correl_of_RandSCI_between_bpandH (accessed on 10 March 2024).

Author Contributions: Conceptualization, S.H. and H.J.; Methodology, A.A.; Software, A.K. and H.J.; Validation, S.H. and M.J.F.A.; Formal analysis, A.A. and A.K.; Investigation, A.A. and A.K.; Resources, H.J. and M.J.F.A.; Data curation, H.J. and M.J.F.A.; Writing—original draft, A.A.; Writing—review & editing, S.H., H.J. and M.J.F.A.; Supervision, A.K.; Project administration, S.H.; Funding acquisition, A.K. All authors have read and agreed to the published version of the manuscript.

Funding: S.H. is supported by UBD Faculty Research Grant with Grant Number UBD/RSC H/1.4/FICBF(b)/2022/053 and the National Natural Science Foundation of China (No. 622260-101). A.K. is supported by the Key Laboratory of Philosophy and Social Sciences in Guangdong Province of Maritime Silk Road of Guangzhou University (No. GD22TWCXGC15), the National Natural Sci-

69. Hassanabadi, H.; Hosseinpour, M. Thermodynamic properties of neutral particle in the presence of topological defects in magnetic cosmic string background. *Eur. Phys. J. C* **2016**, *76*, 553. [CrossRef]
70. Eshghi, M.; Mehraban, H. Study of a 2D charged particle confined by a magnetic and AB flux fields under the radial scalar power potential. *Eur. Phys. J. Plus* **2017**, *132*, 121. [CrossRef]
71. Ikot, A.N.; Lutfuoglu, B.C.; Ngwueke, M.I.; Udoh, M.E.; Zare, S.; Hassanabadi, H. Klein-Gordon equation particles in exponential-type molecule potentials and their thermodynamic properties in D dimensions. *Eur. Phys. J. Plus* **2016**, *131*, 419. [CrossRef]
72. Hassanabadi, H.; Sargolzaeipor, S.; Yazarloo, B.H. Thermodynamic properties of the three-dimensional Dirac oscillator with Aharonov–Bohm field and magnetic monopole potential. *Few-Body Syst.* **2015**, *56*, 115. [CrossRef]
73. Castellano, G. Thermodynamic potentials for simple magnetic systems. *J. Magn. Magn. Mater.* **2003**, *260*, 146. [CrossRef]
74. Vitória, R.L.L.; Moy, T.; Belich, H. Thermodynamics Properties of a Quantum Particle Confined into Two Elastic Concentric Spheres. *Few-Body Syst.* **2022**, *63*, 51. [CrossRef]
75. Nwabuzor, P.; Edet, C.; Ndem, Ikot, A.; Okorie, U.; Ramantswana, M.; Horchani, R.; Abdel-Aty, A.-H.; Rampho, G. Analyzing the Effects of Topological Defect (TD) on the Energy Spectra and Thermal Properties of LiH, TiC and I_2 Diatomic Molecules. *Entropy* **2021**, *23*, 1060. [CrossRef] [PubMed]
76. Hassanabadi, H.; Hosseini, S.S.; Boumali, A.; Zarrinkamar, S. The statistical properties of Klein-Gordon oscillator in noncommutative space. *J. Math. Phys.* **2014**, *55*, 033502. [CrossRef]
77. Hassanabadi, S.; K.říž; J.; Chung, W.S.; Lütfüoğlu, B.C.; Maghsoodi, E.; Hassanabadi, H. Thermodynamics of the Schwarzschild and Reissner-Nordström black holes under higher-order generalized uncertainty principle. *Eur. Phys. J. Plus* **2021**, *136*, 918. [CrossRef]
78. Zhang, M.-Y.; Chen, H.; Hassanabadi, H.; Long, Z.-W.; Yang, H. Thermodynamic topology of Kerr-Sen black holes via Rényi statistics. *Phys. Lett. B* **2024**, *856*, 138885. [CrossRef]
79. Martín-Martínez, E.; Smith, A.R.H.; Terno, D.R. Spacetime structure and vacuum entanglement. *Phys. Rev. D* **2016**, *93*, 044001. [CrossRef]

axioms

MDPI

Article

Eigenvalue Spectra of Rabi Models with Infinite Matrix Representations

Hongbin Liang [1], Shucan Xia [1], Yixiang Chen [1], Yuguo Su [2,*] and Jie Chen [3,*]

1 College of Media Engineering, Communication University of Zhejiang, Hangzhou 310018, China; lhb@cuz.edu.cn (H.L.); shucanxia@cuz.edu.cn (S.X.)
2 School of Science, Zhejiang University of Science and Technology, Hangzhou 310023, China
3 Institute for Quantum Technology and Engineering Computing, School of JiaYang, Zhejiang Shuren University, Hangzhou 310015, China
* Correspondence: suyuguo@zust.edu.cn (Y.S.); chenjie@zjsru.edu.cn (J.C.)

Abstract: We investigate the relationship between confluent Heun functions and the eigenvalue spectra of infinite matrices related to the semi-classical and quantum Rabi models, revealing distinct connections in each case. In the semi-classical model, the eigenvalues are explicitly expressed through confluent Heun functions, whereas in the quantum Rabi model, they are determined by zeros of a condition involving confluent Heun functions. Our findings establish a unified framework for solving the eigenvalue problem of infinite-dimensional unbounded matrices related to the Rabi models. We derive some new identities for confluent Heun functions, enabling simplifications and broader applications in mathematics and physics. The explicit eigenvalue expressions in the semi-classical case align with approximate results from earlier studies, while the derived conditions for the quantum model provide a concise and unified form, encompassing special cases that are typically treated as exceptions. We also discuss the energy spectrum of the quantum Rabi model, uncovering intriguing phenomena and patterns. Our results deepen the understanding of Rabi models and extend their potential applications in quantum optics and quantum information.

Keywords: Rabi model; confluent Heun function; infinite matrix; quantum optics; eigenvalue problem

MSC: 81Q05; 81Q80; 35Q40; 35Q41; 81Q93

1. Introduction

The Rabi model, initially proposed by Isidor I Rabi in 1936 [1,2], describes the interaction between a two-level atom and a classical oscillating magnetic field. It is one of the simplest and most fundamental models for studying matter–light interactions and has served as a basis for various areas in quantum physics [3–7], including quantum optics, quantum information, and condensed matter physics. A widely used approximation, the Jaynes–Cummings model applies when the coupling between the two-level system and the oscillator is weak, allowing certain terms in the Hamiltonian to be neglected, which is the rotating wave approximation (RWA) [8–14]. In recent years, advancements in experimental techniques have allowed the exploration of regimes beyond the applicability of the Jaynes–Cummings model, particularly the ultra-strong and deep-strong coupling regimes. In these regimes, the RWA fails, and the full regimes of the Rabi model must be used to accurately describe the system.

24. Wang, G.; Li, C.; Cappellaro, P. Observation of Symmetry-Protected Selection Rules in Periodically Driven Quantum Systems. *Phys. Rev. Lett.* **2021**, *127*, 140604. [CrossRef] [PubMed]
25. Schmidt, H.J. The Floquet Theory of the Two-Level System Revisited. *Z. für Naturforschung A* **2018**, *73*, 705–731. [CrossRef]
26. Lu, T.; Miao, X.; Metcalf, H. Bloch theorem on the Bloch sphere. *Phys. Rev. A* **2005**, *71*, 061405(R). [CrossRef]
27. Creffield, C. Location of crossings in the Floquet spectrum of a driven two-level system. *Phys. Rev. B* **2003**, *67*, 165301. [CrossRef]
28. Xie, Q. Floquet states and quasienergies of a periodically driven two-level system. *J. Phys. B* **2009**, *42*, 105501. [CrossRef]
29. Shirley, J.H. Solution of the Schrödinger Equation with a Hamiltonian Periodic in Time. *Phys. Rev.* **1965**, *138*, B979–B987. [CrossRef]
30. Ronveaux, A. *Heun's Differential Equations*; Oxford University: Oxford, UK, 1995.
31. Slavyanov, S.Y.; Lay, W. *Special Functions: A Unified Theory Based on Singularities*; Oxford University: Oxford, UK, 2000.
32. Ishkhanyan, A.M.; Grigoryan, A.E. Fifteen classes of solutions of the quantum two-state problem in terms of the confluent Heun function. *J. Phys. A* **2014**, *47*, 465205. [CrossRef]
33. Llorente, J.M.G.; Plata, J. Tunneling control in a two-level system. *Phys. Rev. A* **1992**, *45*, R6958–R6961. [CrossRef]
34. Barata, J.C.A.; Wreszinski, W.F. Strong-Coupling Theory of Two-Level Atoms in Periodic Fields. *Phys. Rev. Lett.* **2000**, *84*, 2112–2115. [CrossRef]
35. Angelo, R.M.; Wreszinski, W.F. Two-level quantum dynamics, integrability, and unitary NOT gates. *Phys. Rev. A* **2005**, *72*, 034105. [CrossRef]
36. Frasca, M. Third-order correction to localization in a two-level driven system. *Phys. Rev. B* **2005**, *71*, 073301. [CrossRef]
37. Wu, Y.; Yang, X. Strong-Coupling Theory of Periodically Driven Two-Level Systems. *Phys. Rev. Lett.* **2007**, *98*, 013601. [CrossRef]
38. Kayanuma, Y. Role of phase coherence in the transition dynamics of a periodically driven two-level system. *Phys. Rev. A* **1994**, *50*, 843–845. [CrossRef] [PubMed]
39. Grossmann, F.; Dittrich, T.; Jung, P.; Hänggi, P. Coherent transport in a periodically driven bistable system. *J. Statist. Phys.* **1993**, *70*, 229–245. [CrossRef]
40. Wu, Y.; Yang, X.; Xiao, Y. Analytical Method for Yrast Line States in Interacting Bose-Einstein Condensates. *Phys. Rev. Lett.* **2001**, *86*, 2200–2203. [CrossRef]
41. Wu, Y.; Yang, X. Analytical results for energy spectrum and eigenstates of a Bose-Einstein condensate in a Mott insulator state. *Phys. Rev. A* **2003**, *68*, 013608. [CrossRef]
42. Zhong, H.; Hai, W.; Lu, G.; Li, Z. Incoherent control in a non-Hermitian Bose-Hubbard dimer. *Phys. Rev. A* **2011**, *84*, 013410. [CrossRef]
43. Takagi, T.; Wakayama, M.; Tanaka, K.; Kunihiro, N.; Kimoto, K.; Duong, D. *Mathematical Modelling for Next-Generation Cryptography: CREST Crypto-Math Project*; Mathematics for Industry; Springer Nature: Singapore, 2017.
44. Li, Z.M.; Batchelor, M.T. Addendum to 'Algebraic equations for the exceptional eigenspectrum of the generalized Rabi model'. *J. Phys. A Math. Theor.* **2016**, *49*, 369401. [CrossRef]
45. Li, Z.M.; Batchelor, M.T. Algebraic equations for the exceptional eigenspectrum of the generalized Rabi model. *J. Phys. A Math. Theor.* **2015**, *48*, 454005. [CrossRef]
46. Judd, B.R. Exact solutions to a class of Jahn-Teller systems. *J. Phys. C Solid State Phys.* **1979**, *12*, 1685–1692. [CrossRef]
47. Kimoto, K.; Reyes-Bustos, C.; Wakayama, M. Determinant Expressions of Constraint Polynomials and the Spectrum of the Asymmetric Quantum Rabi Model. *Int. Math. Res. Not.* **2020**, *2021*, 9458–9544. [CrossRef]
48. Kuś, M. On the spectrum of a two-level system. *J. Math. Phys.* **1985**, *26*, 2792–2795. [CrossRef]
49. Motygin, O.V. On evaluation of the confluent Heun functions. In Proceedings of the 2018 Days on Diffraction (DD), St. Petersburg, Russia, 4–8 June 2018; IEEE: Piscataway, NJ, USA, 2018; pp. 223–229. [CrossRef]

axioms

MDPI

Article

Finite Volume Method and Its Applications in Computational Fluid Dynamics

Abdulkafi Mohammed Saeed *,† and Thekra Abdullah Fayez Alfawaz †

Department of Mathematics, College of Science, Qassim University, Buraydah 51452, Saudi Arabia; 441212381@qu.edu.sa
* Correspondence: abdulkafi.ahmed@qu.edu.sa
† These authors contributed equally to this work.

Abstract: Various numerical techniques have been developed to address multiple problems in computational fluid dynamics (CFD). The finite volume method (FVM) is a numerical technique used for solving partial differential equations that represent conservation laws by dividing the domain into control volumes and ensuring flux balance at their boundaries. Its conservative characteristics and capability to work with both structured and unstructured grids make it suitable for addressing issues related to fluid flow, heat transfer, and diffusion. This article introduces an FVM for the linear advection and nonlinear Burgers' equations through a fifth-order targeted essentially non-oscillatory (TENO5) scheme. Numerical experiments showcase the precision and effectiveness of TENO5, emphasizing its benefits for computational fluid dynamics (CFD) simulations.

Keywords: linear advection equation; nonlinear Burgers' equation; finite volume method; targeted essentially non-oscillatory scheme; error analysis

MSC: 35B45; 35D30; 35D35

1. Introduction

Computational fluid dynamics (CFD) refers to the numerical analysis of systems involving fluid motion, heat transfer, and related phenomena, such as chemical reactions, through computer simulations. This computational approach is widely applied across both industrial and non-industrial sectors.

CFD techniques play a crucial role in various industries, such as the design, research, development, and production of aircraft and jet engines. Furthermore, CFD has found extensive application across an array of other industries, demonstrating its wide-ranging impact and utility [1,2].

The finite volume method (FVM) is a numerical technique developed to solve partial differential equations (PDEs) that encapsulate various conservation laws, including those related to mass, momentum, and energy. By integrating these equations over well-defined control volumes, the FVM effectively transforms them into a system of algebraic equations. This transformation is crucial as it inherently preserves local conservation properties, ensuring that fundamental physical principles are maintained. Over the years, the finite volume method has undergone significant evolution, adapting to tackle increasingly complex challenges within the field of computational fluid dynamics (CFD). Its versatility and robustness render it a recommended choice for simulating fluid flow across a wide range of applications, from aerospace engineering to environmental modeling [1–4].

https://doi.org/10.3390/axioms14050359

ence Foundation of China (No. 622260-101) and by the Ministry of Science and Technology of China (No. WGXZ2023054L). M.J.F.A. extends his appreciation to Researcher Supporting Project number (RSPD2024R582), King Saud University, Riyadh, Saudi Arabia.

Data Availability Statement: No new data were created or analyzed in this study. Data sharing is not applicable to this article.

Conflicts of Interest: The authors declare no conflicts of interest.

References

1. Gutman, I.; Furtula, B. *Novel Molecular Structure Descriptors—Theory and Applications I*; University of Kragujevac: Kragujevac, Serbia, 2010.
2. Trinajstić, N.; Li, X.; Gutman, I. Mathematical aspects of Randić-type molecular structure descriptors. *Croat. Chem. Acta* **2006**, *79*, A31–A32.
3. Gutman, I.; Furtula B. (Eds.) *Recent Results in the Theory of Randić Index*; University of Kragujevac, Kragujevac, Serbia, 2008.
4. Bollobás, B.; Erdös, P. Graphs of extremal weights. *Ars Comb.* **1998**, *50*, 225. [CrossRef]
5. Devillers, J.; Balaban, A.T. *Topological Indices and Related Descriptors in QSAR and QSPR*; Gordon and Breach: Amsterdam, The Netherlands, 1999.
6. Zhou, B.; Trinajstić, N. On a novel connectivity index. *J. Math. Chem.* **2009**, *46*, 1252–1270. [CrossRef]
7. Ullah, A.; Aurangzeb; Zaman, S. A new perspective on the modeling and topological characterization of H-Naphtalenic nanosheets with applications. *J. Mol. Model.* **2022**, *28*, 211. [CrossRef]
8. Ullah, A.; Shamsudin; Zaman, S.; Hamraz, A. Zagreb Connection topological descriptors and structural property of the triangular chain structures. *Phys. Scr.* **2023**, *8*, 025009. [CrossRef]
9. Ullah, A.; Zaman, S.; Hamraz, A.; Muzammal, M. On the construction of some bioconjugate networks and their structural modeling via irregularity topological indices. *Eur. Phys. J. E* **2023**, *46*, 72. [CrossRef]
10. Ullah, A.; Zaman, S.; Hussain, A.; Jabeen, A.; Belay, M.B. Derivation of mathematical closed form expressions for certain irregular topological indices of 2D nanotubes. *Sci. Rep.* **2023**, *13*, 11187. [CrossRef]
11. Gutman, I.; Tošović, J. Testing the quality of molecular structure descriptors. Vertex-degree-based topological indices. *J. Serb. Chem. Soc.* **2013**, *78*, 805–810. [CrossRef]
12. Malik, M.Y.H.; Binyamin, M.A.; Hayat, S. Correlation ability of degree-based topological indices for physicochemical properties of polycyclic aromatic hydrocarbons with applications. *Polycycl. Aromat. Compd.* **2022**, *42*, 6267–6281. [CrossRef]
13. Hayat, S.; Khan, S.; Khan, A.; Liu, J.-B. Valency-based molecular descriptors for measuring the π-electronic energy of lower polycyclic aromatic hydrocarbons. *Polycycl. Aromat. Compd.* **2022**, *42*, 1113–1129. [CrossRef]
14. Hayat, S.; Suhaili, N.; Jamil, H. Statistical significance of valency-based topological descriptors for correlating thermodynamic properties of benzenoid hydrocarbons with applications. *Comput. Theor. Chem.* **2023**, *1227*, 114259. [CrossRef]
15. Randić, M. Characterization of molecular branching. *J. Am. Chem. Soc.* **1975**, *97*, 6609–6615. [CrossRef]
16. Cruz, R.; Gutman, I.; Rada, J. On benzenoid systems with minimal number of inlets. *J. Serb. Chem. Soc.* **2013**, *78*, 1351–1357. [CrossRef]
17. Furtula, B.; Gutman, I. Comparing energy and Randić energy. *Maced. J. Chem. Chem. Eng.* **2013**, *32*, 117–123. [CrossRef]
18. Randić, M. The connectivity index 25 years after. *J. Mol. Graph. Model.* **2001**, *20*, 19–35. [CrossRef] [PubMed]
19. Todeschini, R.; Consonni, V. *Handbook of Molecular Descriptors*; John Wiley & Sons: Hoboken, NJ, USA, 2008.
20. Wang, S.; Zhou, B.; Trinajstić, N. On the sum-connectivity index. *Filomat* **2011**, *25*, 29–42. [CrossRef]
21. Xing, R.; Zhou, B.; Trinajstić, N. Sum-connectivity index of molecular trees. *J. Math. Chem.* **2010**, *48*, 583–591. [CrossRef]
22. Balister, P.; Bollobás, B.; Gerke, S. The generalized Randić index of trees. *J. Graph Theory* **2007**, *56*, 270–286. [CrossRef]
23. Li, J.; Li, Y. The asymptotic value of the zeroth-order Randić index and sum-connectivity index for trees. *Appl. Math. Comput.* **2015**, *266*, 1027–1030. [CrossRef]
24. Li, F.; Ye, Q. Second order Randić index of fluoranthene-type benzenoid systems. *Appl. Math. Comput.* **2015**, *268*, 534–546. [CrossRef]
25. Li, X.; Zheng, J. Extremal chemical trees with minimum or maximum general Randić index. *MATCH Commun. Math. Comput. Chem.* **2006**, *55*, 381–390.
26. Zhou, B.; Trinajstić, N. On general sum-connectivity index. *J. Math. Chem.* **2010**, *47*, 210–218. [CrossRef]
27. Akhter, S.; Imran, M.; Raza, Z. Bounds for the general sum-connectivity index of composite graphs. *J. Ineq. Appl.* **2017**, *2017*, 76. [CrossRef] [PubMed]
28. Du, Z.; Zhou, B.; Trinajstić, N. On the general sum-connectivity index of trees. *Appl. Math. Lett.* **2011**, *24*, 402–405. [CrossRef]
29. Milovanović, I.Ž.; Milovanović, E.I.; Matejić, M. Some inequalities for general sum-connectivity index. *MATCH Commun. Math. Comput. Chem.* **2018**, *79*, 477–489.

30. Zaman, S. Cacti with maximal general sum-connectivity index. *J. Appl. Math. Comput.* **2021**, *65*, 147–160. [CrossRef]
31. Rada, J.; Araujo, O.; Gutman, I. Randić index of benzenoid systems and phenylenes. *Croat. Chem. Acta* **2001**, *74*, 225–235.

axioms

MDPI

Article

Biequivalent Planar Graphs

Bernard Piette

Department of Mathematical Sciences, Durham University, Durham DH1 3LE, UK; b.m.a.g.piette@durham.ac.uk

Abstract: We define biequivalent planar graphs, which are a generalisation of the uniform polyhedron graphs, as planar graphs made out of two families of equivalent nodes. Such graphs are required to identify polyhedral cages with geometries suitable for artificial protein cages. We use an algebraic method, which is followed by an algorithmic method, to determine all such graphs with up to 300 nodes each with valencies ranging between three and six. We also present a graphic representation of every graph found.

Keywords: planar graphs; Cayley graphs; uniform polyhedron; regular solids; polyhedral cages; protein cage

MSC: 00A69

1. Introduction

Recently, we showed that to construct a polyhedral cage (p-cages for short) one must use planar graphs to characterise how the different faces of a p-cage are linked together [1]. P-cages are assemblies of regular or nearly regular polygons but with holes. The nodes of the graph correspond to the faces of the p-cage, while the edges determine which of the faces are sharing an edge. P-cages correspond to the mathematical description of the geometry of artificial protein cages, which are being developed for targeted drug delivery [2]. To form spontaneously, such protein cages must be symmetric so that each face is equivalent, modulo a rotation, to all the other faces. The simplest p-cages candidates for artificial protein cages are hence p-cages made out of a single type of polygon, where all the faces are equivalent, thus having modulo rotation [3]. To be good candidates, p-cages must have small holes, and each face should have at least four neighbours each. Unfortunately, the number of such p-cages is relatively small. As an alternative, it is natural to consider protein cages made out of two types of polygons. In [4], we have constructed such p-cages but with the restriction that each face of a given type must be connected to face of the other type. Unfortunately, very few of these p-cages have small holes.

The next step is then to construct p-cages made out of two types of polygons but allowing each face to be adjacent to any type of face. To achieve this task, as explained in [1], one must characterise all the planar graphs made out of two families of nodes such that the nodes of a given family are equivalent to each other modulo to achieve automorphism of the graph. Planar graphs for which all the nodes are equivalent to each other correspond to the planar graphs of all the convex uniform polyhedra [5] (They are examples of Cayley graphs). The aim of this paper is to determine a list of all the planar graphs made out of two equivalent types of nodes with valencies ranging from three to six. This restriction comes from the fact that the faces of a p-cage must have at least three neighbours and cannot have more than six without being heavily irregular.

Artificial protein cages have been experimentally generated by a number of research groups. One of the first ones was the TRAP-cage made out of 24 hendecagonal faces, which are also called TRAP-rings [2,6]. More recently, a smaller protein cage was shown to be made out of 12 of the same TRAP-protein hendecagonal rings [7].

A number of other artificial protein cages have been made experimentally [8–11]. These cages are similar to virus capsids but require metal atoms to bind together [12]. The motivation to create these protein nanocages is to develop new method of drug delivery [13–17] by enclosing the drug inside such cages. By adding to the protein cages receptors that can bind to a target cell, such as cancer cells for example [13], the protein cages can be *swallowed* by the cell, where the drug is then released [18]. For expensive drugs, this method would greatly reduce the cost of medical treatment, and as only the targeted cells receives the drug, thus greatly reducing the side effects. Our ultimate aim it to identify geometries that can be used by nanobioengineers to create new protein cages.

The study of the structure of protein cages is quite new, and most investigations have so far been mostly experimental [19,20]. The formal mathematical description of polyhedral cages, as well as the connection between their structure and planar graphs, were identified in our previous work [1].

Graphs do occur in a number of areas of science such as the study of complex protein networks [21], quantum field theory [22], neurology [23], or mathematics [24]. The symmetry of graphs has been studied extensively [25], but here, we restrict ourselves to planar graphs. As we have stated above, planar graphs where all the nodes are equivalent, modulo of an automorphism of the graphs, and correspond to the planar graphs of convex uniform polyhedra. In this paper, we are constructing planar graphs made out of two families of equivalent nodes.

2. Characteristics of Potential Graphs

We define a biequivalent planar graph as a planar graph made out of nodes split in two families such that any node of a given family can be mapped to any other node of the same family via an automorphism of the graph. For the reasons mentioned in the introduction, in what follows, we restrict ourselves to graphs with a node valency ranging from three to six. Notice that loops are excluded from planar graphs.

Each planar graph is made of a number of nodes connected together by edges that then define faces. Each face is then characterised by the number of nodes from each family, as well as their cyclic order around the face. To be equivalent, the nodes of a given family must all be adjacent to the same type of faces and in the same order. To find biequivalent graphs, we start by using the Euler formula that states that for any planar graph consisting of F faces, E edges, and V nodes/vertices, the following condition is always satisfied: $V - E + F = 2$. This will allow us to find restrictions on the number of nodes, as well as the number and types of faces belonging to the graphs. We must emphasise that in the Euler formula, the outside of the graph is considered as a face. This is easy to understand when one visualises the graphs as a planar projection of a 3D polyhedron.

Considering planar graphs made out of V_1 nodes of type 1, with each having valency L_1 and V_2 nodes of type 2 of valency L_2, we denote $n(i_1, i_2)$ as the number of faces with i_1 nodes of type 1 and i_2 nodes of type 2. Then, we have that the total number of edges E and faces F are given by

$$E = \sum_{j=1,2} \frac{1}{2} L_j V_j \quad (1)$$

$$F = \sum_{i_1} \sum_{i_2} n(i_1, i_2). \quad (2)$$

Moreover,

$$V_1 = \sum_{i_1} \frac{i_1}{L_1} \sum_{i_2} n(i_1, i_2)$$

$$V_2 = \sum_{i_2} \frac{i_2}{L_2} \sum_{i_1} n(i_1, i_2). \quad (3)$$

Then, as a result,

$$V = V_1 + V_2 \quad = \quad \sum_{i_1}\sum_{i_2}\left(\frac{i_1}{L_1} + \frac{i_2}{L_2}\right)n(i_1, i_2). \tag{4}$$

Substituting these expressions for F, E, and V into the Euler formula, we have

$$\sum_{i_1}\sum_{i_2} n(i_1, i_2)\left(1 + \frac{i_1}{L_1} + \frac{i_2}{L_2}\right) - \frac{1}{2}\sum_{i_1}\sum_{i_2}(i_1 + i_2)n(i_1, i_2) = 2. \tag{5}$$

Now, by multiplying (5) by $2L_1L_2$, we obtain

$$\sum_{i_1}\sum_{i_2} n(i_1, i_2)(2\,L_1\,L_2 + i_1L_2(2 - L_1) + i_2L_1(2 - L_2)) = 4\,L_1\,L_2. \tag{6}$$

If each node of type j belongs to v_{j,i_1,i_2} faces with i_1 nodes of type 1 and i_2 nodes of type 2, we have

$$V_1 \quad = \quad \frac{i_1\,n(i_1, i_2)}{v_{1,i_1,i_2}}, \tag{7}$$

and similarly for any i_2:

$$V_2 = \frac{i_2\,n(i_1, i_2)}{v_{2,i_1,i_2}}. \tag{8}$$

Indeed, for every face with i_1 nodes of type 1 and i_2 nodes of type 2, $i_1 n(i_1, i_2)$ is the number of nodes of type 1, and V_1 is multiplied by the number of faces of that type adjacent to nodes of type 1 and similarly for nodes of type 2. This only works because all the nodes of a given type are equivalent.

Then, by definition, we also have

$$\sum_{i_2}\sum_{i_1} v_{1,i_1,i_2} = L_1, \qquad \sum_{i_1}\sum_{i_2} v_{2,i_1,i_2} = L_2\,. \tag{9}$$

To construct all biequivalent planar graphs, we must find the integers i_1, i_2, and $n(i_1, i_2)$ satisfying (6). We must then compute V_1 and V_2 using (3) and reject the cases where V_1 and V_2 are not integers. We must next compute v_{1,i_1,i_2} and v_{2,i_1,i_2} using (7) and (8), thus keeping only the cases for which they are integers that satisfy (9).

To do so, we have written a computer program (available from zenodo), which when given values for L_1 and L_2, scans all the possible combinations of $n(i_1, i_2)$ polygons made out of i_1 type 1 and i_2 type 2 nodes, thus considering polygonal faces such that $3 \leq i_1 + i_2 \leq 10$, with a maximum of 300 faces.

We have restricted ourselves to decagonal faces, because they are the largest polygons occurring in Archimedean solids and also because they already lead to p-cages with very large holes. We restricted ourselves to 300 faces to capture all the graphs, which are derivatives of the planar graphs corresponding to the Archimedean solids. We did so for $3 \leq L_1 \leq 6$ and $L_1 \leq L_2 \leq 6$. When $L_1 = L_2 = 3$, the program completes in a few minutes, but for $L_1 = 5, L_2 = 6$ it ran for 3 months on a powerful workstation. We did run the program for larger polygons and more faces (up to 1000) for some of the smaller values of L_1 and L_2 but did not obtain any more graphs other than the one derived from the prisms and antiprisms, of which there is an infinite number.

The program generates a list of potential graph characteristics (PGCs) of the type

[4 5;	5 4 0, 10 2 1;	2 0, 2 1;	5 1;	10 2]
valencies	faces 0 & 1	node 1	node 2	# nodes

The first two numbers correspond to the valencies of the graphs 4 and 5 for nodes of type 1 and 2, respectively. The value `5 4 0, 10 2 1` indicates that the graph is made out of five squares of valency, four nodes, and 10 triangles made out of two valency 4 and one valency 5 nodes. The value `2 0, 2 1` indicates that the type 1 nodes are adjacent to two faces of type 0 (the squares) and two faces of type 1 (the triangles). The value `5 1` indicates that the nodes of type 2 are adjacent to five faces of type 1. The value `10 2` specifies that there are 10 nodes of type 1 and 2 nodes of type 2. The total number of faces is hence 15 in this case.

Between the nine pairs of valencies considered and after filtering out double entries when $L_1 = L_2$ and in cases where there are no edges linking the two types of nodes, the program generated over 30,000 PGCs, but only just over 1% of these correspond to an actual planar graph. As an example of an impossible graph, the PGC `[3 3; 1 0 4, 2 2 1, 2 4 0; 1 1, 2 2; 1 1, 2 0; 4 2]` specifies that the type 2 nodes must be adjacent to two squares `0 4`, but as there is only one square, this is not possible.

As the next step, we must consider all the PGCs and try to convert them into actual graphs, thus discarding those for which this is not possible.

3. Construction of the Graphs

3.1. The Faces of the Graph

Each graph is made out of the faces and nodes as specified in the PGC described in the previous section. A face with i_1 nodes of type 1 and i_2 nodes of type 2 can assume different configurations referring to the order in which the nodes are distributed. For example, up to cyclic rotations, an hexagon $(2,4)$ can have the following configurations: $(1,2,2,1,2,2)$, $(1,2,1,2,2,2)$, or $(1,1,2,2,2,2)$. In the first case, all the nodes 1 are equivalent, and there are two types of nodes of type 2 (Some nodes 2 have the cyclic sequence $1,2,2,1,2$ on the right, while others have $2,1,2,2,1$). For the last two cases, there are two types of node 1 and four types of node 2. In what follows, we refer to these as the C-signature of the face, and we call $N_c(i_1,i_2)$ the number of different C-signatures for the face (i_1,i_2). We then label these configurations as $C_j(i_1,i_2)$, where $j \in [1, N_c(i_1,i_2)]$ indexes the different configurations. In the example above, $N_c(2,4) = 3$, $C_1(2,4) := (1,2,2,1,2,2)$, $C_2(2,4) := (1,2,1,2,2,2)$, and $C_3(2,4) := (1,1,2,2,2,2)$.

The cycle of the configuration, $Cy_{C_j(i_1,i_2)}$, is the smallest number of single cyclic rotations needed to recover the configuration. In the example above, we have $Cy_{C_1(2,4)} = 3$ and $Cy_{C_2(2,4)} = Cy_{C_3(2,4)} = 6$.

Each node on a face will have an index number, as well as a reduced index number corresponding to the lowest index amongst all the equivalent nodes of the same type. The reduced index of index i is simply $i \bmod Cy_{C_j(i_1,i_2)}$ (Notice that the index corresponds to an offset and hence starts at 0). For example, the reduced indices of $1,2,2,1,2,2$ are $(0,1,2,0,1,2)$, while the reduced indices of $(1,2,1,2,2,2)$ and $(1,1,2,2,2,2)$ are the actual indices: $(0,1,2,3,4,5)$.

We call the node multiplicity of a face configuration $C_J(i_1,i_2)$ as the number of nonequivalent nodes of type t that it contains, and we label it as $M_{tC_J(i_1,i_2)}$. The multiplicity of a type t node for a given configuration is simply given by $M_{tC_J(i_1,i_2)} = i_t / Cy_{C_j(i_1,i_2)}$.

In the example above, $M_{1C_1(2,4)} = 1$, and $M_{1C_2(2,4)} = M_{1C_3(2,4)} = 2$; as well, $M_{2C_1(2,4)} = 2$, and $M_{2C_2(2,4)} = M_{2C_3(2,4)} = 4$.

Having described the faces of the graph, we must now consider the nodes.

3.2. The Nodes of the Graph

The planar graphs we are considering are of two types and can be of different valencies. Each node of a given type will be surrounded by a sequence of faces of the different types, and to be equivalent, that sequence must be the same for every node, thus being modulo for a cyclic rotation.

As described above, each node of type t will be surrounded by v_{t,i_1,i_2} faces made out of i_1 nodes of type 1 and i_2 nodes of type 2, and for the type t nodes to be equivalent, it is not just the type of face that must be in the same sequence, but the C-signatures of these faces must be in the same sequence as well. Moreover, every nodes of type t must have the same reduced indices for each of the matching face signatures in the sequence. By convention, we label them in the anticlockwise order.

Figure 1 illustrates this as an example where the nodes of type 1 have valency 3, and the nodes of type 2, marked with a read dot, have valency 4. The graph is made out of two triangles, $(0,3)$, and nine squares, $(2,2)$. So, we have $N_c(0,3) = 2$ and $N_c(2,2) = 9$, and we define $C_1(0,3) = (2,2,2)$, $C_1(2,2) = (1,2,1,2)$, and $C_2(2,2) = (1,1,2,2)$. Notice that one of the 222 face sits *outside* the graph, but if we picture the graph as a polyhedron, it corresponds to the bottom of the polyhedron. In what follows, we call that face the outside face.

The nodes of type 1 have the face sequence $(C_1(2,2), C_2(2,2), C_2(2,2))$ with the corresponding reduce indices $(0,1,0)$. This also means that $v_{1,0,3} = 0$, and $v_{1,2,2} = 3$. The multiplicity of the face configurations are then $M_{1,C_1(0,3)} = 0$, $M_{1,C_1(2,2)} = 1$, and $M_{1,C_2(2,2)} = 2$.

The nodes of type 2 have the face sequence $(C_1(0,3), C_2(2,2), C_1(2,2), C_2(2,2))$ with the corresponding reduced indices $(0,2,1,3)$. This also means that $v_{2,0,3} = 1$, and $v_{2,2,2} = 3$. The multiplicity of the face configurations are then $M_{2,C_1(0,3)} = 1$, $M_{2,C_1(2,2)} = 1$, and $M_{2,C_2(2,2)} = 2$.

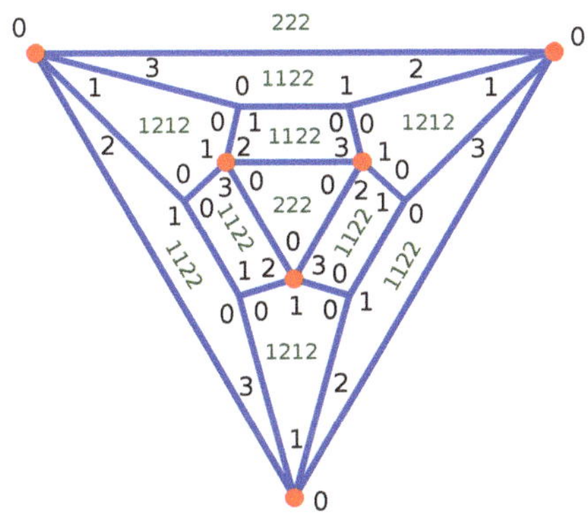

Figure 1. Graph made out of six valency 3 nodes (type 1), six valency 4 nodes (type 2) and the following faces: 2 $C_1(0,3) = (2,2,2)$, 3 $C_1(2,2) = (1,2,1,2)$, and 6 $C_2(2,2) = (1,1,2,2)$. $N_c(0,3) = 2$, and $N_c(2,2) = 9$. The reduced indices of each node are the black digits in the corner of each face.

Notice that the sum of the multiplicities of a type t node for the different configurations must be less than or equal to v_{t,i_1,i_2}:

$$\sum_j M_{tC_j(i_1,i_2)} \leq v_{t,i_1,i_2}. \tag{10}$$

In the example above, we have

$$\begin{aligned} M_{1C_1(0,3)} &= 0 \leq v_{1,0,3} = 0 \\ M_{2C_1(0,3)} &= 1 \leq v_{2,0,3} = 1 \\ M_{1C_1(2,2)} + M_{1C_2(2,2)} &= 1+2 \leq v_{1,2,2} = 3 \\ M_{2C_1(2,2)} + M_{2C_2(2,2)} &= 1+2 \leq v_{2,2,2} = 3. \end{aligned} \tag{11}$$

To determine the possible arrangements of faces around a node, we must consider all the permutations of the different face signatures for each of their possible configurations. For example, if a trivalent node of type 1 is surrounded by one $(1,2)$ face and two $(2,4)$ faces, the possible arrangements are as follows: (We order the faces in the anticlockwise order around the node, and the nodes are also ordered in the anticlockwise order around a face. The first node on the face signature is the node considered).

- (1,2,2), (1,1,2,2,2,2), (1,1,2,2,2,2)
- (1,2,2), (1,2,2,2,2,1), (1,1,2,2,2,2)
- (1,2,2), (1,2,2,2,2,1), (1,2,2,2,2,1)
- (1,2,2), (1,1,2,2,2,2), (1,2,2,2,2,1)

The first three configurations are illustrated in the same order in Figure 2, where we see that only the second configuration leads to compatible nodes. Indeed, not all configurations are compatible, and the neighbouring faces must have matching node types: on the first arrangement, the second face must have a second node of type 2 to match the $(1,2,2)$ face, and the two hexagons have a node mismatch above the green dot. One sees graphically that the only compatible configuration is the middle one: $(1,2),(1,2,2,2,2,1),(1,1,2,2,2,2)$.

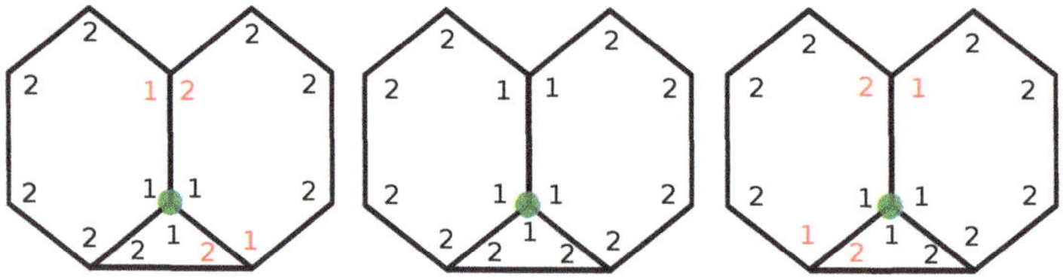

Figure 2. Fitting of a $(1,2,2)$ triangle and two $1,1,2,2,2,2$ hexagon around a trivalent node. The green dot corresponds to the node being fitted. Red labels indicate incompatible node types.

If we denote as $C_j(i_1,i_2)[k]$ the kth index of the configuration $C_j(i_1,i_2)$, the condition is that if A and B are two successive configurations in that order around a node with respective index a and b for the node, we must have

$$A[(a-1) \bmod P_A] = B[(b+1) \bmod P_B] \tag{12}$$

where P_A and P_B are the number of edges of, respectively, face A and B.

To construct a graph from a given PGC, we start by selecting a C-signature for each of the faces making the graph. For both types of node, we order the different faces around the node, as well as select a reduced index of the node for each face. We then pick a face as the outside face, as well as a node on that face. We then try to add the different faces around that node in the preselected order. Once a node is completed, we move to the adjacent node and keep working our way through all the nodes but stop when the addition of a face leads to a node type clash. We must then move one step backward and skip the addition of the previous face. One must also stop and move one step back when all the faces or all the nodes have been used. This is a recursive algorithm which, in some cases, can take a very long time. When the graph is completed, one can stop and move on to the next potential node and face configuration.

To find all the possible graphs for a given PGC, we must consider all the possible combinations of the face C-signatures, as well as all the possible orders of these faces around each type of node. This leads to a very large number of possibilities, but most of them can be easily ruled out using simple matching node incompatibility, as described above.

To understand how to construct a graph, we start by describing how to deconstruct one. If we start from a full graph and remove a given face, keeping the nodes and the edges belonging to the other faces, the graph acquires a hole (the graph still looks the same, as we have not removed any edges yet, but the removed face should be viewed as a hole in the graph). We then remove a second face by removing the edges common to the holes and that face. In the process, the hole becomes larger. We keep removing faces adjacent to the hole until we are left with the outside face with just a hole in it.

To build a graph, we proceed the other way round, thus starting from the outside face and adding faces inside the hole. We must consider every type of face that the graph is made of, as well as every rotation of the nodes. There is a very large number of ways to do this: many face additions can be ruled out by the constrains described above. When adding any face at a given location fails to satisfy all the constraints, we must remove the previous face and try again with another face instead. This is a recursive algorithm. We output a graph when it is completed.

We have written a computer program, available from Zenodo, (the link is given at the end of the paper), which builds a planar graph using the algorithm described above, thus using as input a PGC generated by the program described in the previous section.

It is usually best to take the largest face as the outside face, but sometimes, taking a different face generates or rejects a graph much faster. For some parameters, the program takes several weeks to complete, but in most cases, the graphs are rejected within a few minutes.

Some of the graphs have a chiral symmetry and hence correspond to two different graphs. Most of the time, the characteristics of a potential graph correspond to a single graph, modulo to the chiral symmetry, but in some instances, they actually correspond to two or even three totally different graphs.

Some graphs can be excluded easily though. For example, the graph corresponding to the PGC `[3 4; 1 6 0, 2 0 3, 2 3 0, 2 3 1; 1 0, 1 2, 1 3; 1 3, 3 1; 6 2]` has to contain one hexagon made out of valency 3 nodes, as well as a triangle made out of valency 3 nodes (see Figure 3a). The triangle `3 0` must share an edge with the hexagon `6 0` so that two of the valency 3 nodes are adjacent to a `3 0` and a `6 0` face. The remaining two edges of the triangle must then be shared with an edge from the `3 1`, but as a result, the third node of the triangle is adjacent to two `3 1`, which is not one as requested.

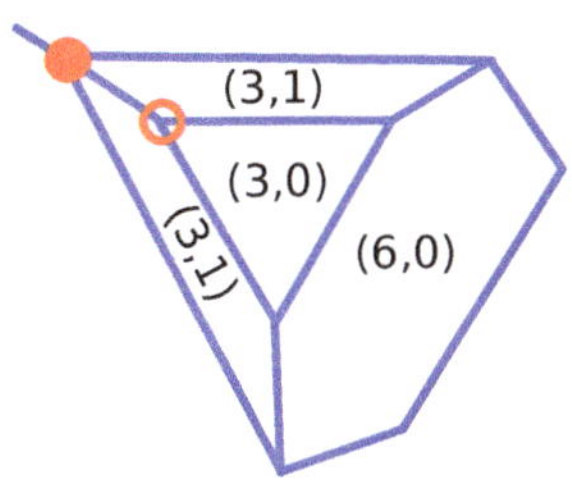

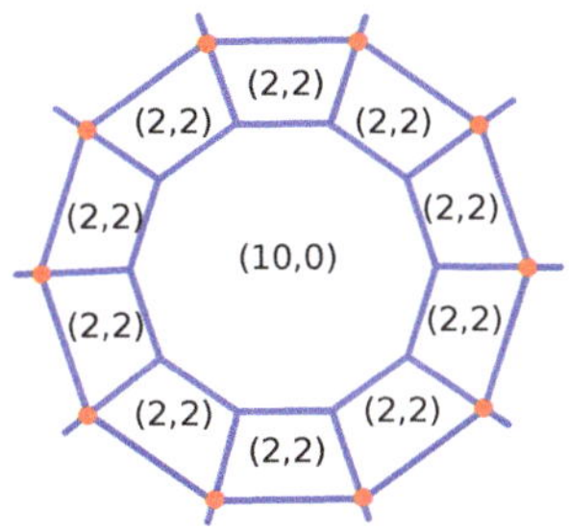

Figure 3. Examples of impossible PGCs: (**a**) `34_F9_1-6-0_2-0-3_2-3-0_2-3-1_V6_2`; (**b**) `34_F122_10-0-8_12-10-0_120-2-2_V120_80`.

As another example, the PGC `[3 4; 10 0 8, 12 10 0, 120 2 2; 1 2, 2 3; 1 1, 3 3; 120 80]` specifies that each face `10 0` must be surrounded by `10 2 2` forming a compound decagon (see Figure 3b). We must then find a way to form the planar graph of a uniform polyhedra made out of twelve decagons and ten octagons, but this is known to not exist, as there is no corresponding regular polyhedron.

We have run our computer program to construct all the biequivalent graphs with valencies ranging from three to six and made at most 300 faces ranging from triangle to decagons. In the next section, we describe each of these graphs.

4. Results

Most of the biequivalent graphs can be seen as modifications of the planar graph of a uniform polyhedron, where extra nodes and edges are added in symmetrically. So, we will present these graphs as different categories of such modifications, but we will start with the graphs derived from simple polygons. As shown in Appendix A, there are no planar graphs made exclusively out of valency 6 nodes. As a result, we can only consider the following pairs of valency values (L_1, L_2): `(3,3)`, `(3,4)`, `(3,5)`, `(3,6)`, `(4,4)`, `(4,5)`,

(4,6), (5,5) and (5,6). The data files describing the PGC, the graph connectivities, and the vector graphic representations of the graphs are available from Zenodo.

The drawing of a graph depends on the choice of the outside face, and most of the time, we have chosen the largest polygon for it. The connectivity between the different nodes, on the other hand, remains the same, regardless of the chosen outside face, and a description of each graph as a set of pair of nodes linked together can be found as plain text files available from Zenodo.

Most graphs can be seen as a member of a family of similarly obtained graphs, such as, for example, the addition of a pyramid on the bases of prisms. As we have identified over 400 different graphs, we only include one example of each family in the main text, but the supplementary file contains a graphic representation of every graph that we have found. On the figures, the nodes of type 2 are indicated with a red dot.

The names of the graphs are derived from their PGC and are of the type $d_1d_2\_Fn\_n_1 - i_{1,1} - i_{1,2}\_n_2 - i_{2,1} - i_{2,2}\_\cdots\_n_k - i_{k,1} - i_{k,2}\_Vv_1\_v_2$, where d_1 and d_2, with $d_1 \leq d_2$, are the valencies of the nodes, n is the total number of faces of the graph, n_j is the number of faces of type $i_{k,1}, i_{k,2}$, and v_k is the number of nodes of type k. For example, |45_F15_5-4-0_10-2-1_V10_2| is a graph made out of ten valency 4 nodes and two valency 5 nodes, with a total of fifteen faces: five squares $(4,0)$ and ten triangles $(2,1)$. When more than one graph correspond to a given PGC, we add the suffix _a, _b, or _c at the end of the name to differentiate them. We also add a * after the p-cage name when the graph is chiral.

To describe the families of graphs, we sometimes use some parameters, say P, and include an arithmetic expression inside curly brackets. For example, {2P+1} should be thought of as the value of $2P+1$.

We now proceed by describing each graph and how they can be described as modifications of known structures. As an abuse of language, we use the names of regular solids to refer to their planar graphs.

In what follows, we will be using some graph components to describe the biequivalent graphs. They are presented in Figure 4, where the blue dots represent the nodes that will be linked to the rest of the graph. We will also use the following abbreviations: P-gone for a polygon with P edges, P-star for a polygonal star with P branches, P-fan for polygonal fan with P blades, split P-fan for a split polygonal fan with P blades, inverted P-fan for inverted polygonal fans with P blades, and P-mosaic for mosaic with a P-gon at its centre. We also refer to pyramids, prisms, and antiprisms with a P-gonal base as, respectively, P-pyramids, P-prisms, and P-antiprisms.

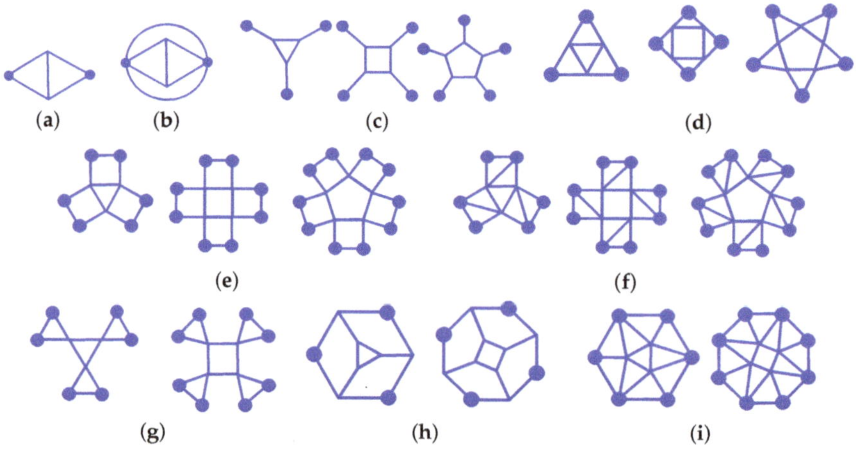

Figure 4. (**a**) 2D diamond, (**b**) 2D bubble diamond, (**c**) linked P-gon. (**d**) polygonal stars, (**e**) polygonal fans, (**f**) polygonal split fans, (**g**) polygonal inverted fans, (**h**) linked P-gon face, (**i**) mosaic polygon.

4.1. Special Graphs

Some graphs do not fall in any special category and should be considered as special:

- Two alternating diamonds: **34_F8_4-1-3_4-2-1_V4_4**, (see Figure 5a).
- One 2D diamond and one 2D bubble diamond: **36_F8_4-1-2_4-2-1_V4_2**, (see Figure 5b)
- Three 2D diamonds: **36_F9_3-2-2_6-2-1_V6_2**, (see Figure 5c)
- Multitriangles: **45_F12_4-2-1_8-1-2_V4_4** (see Figure 5d).

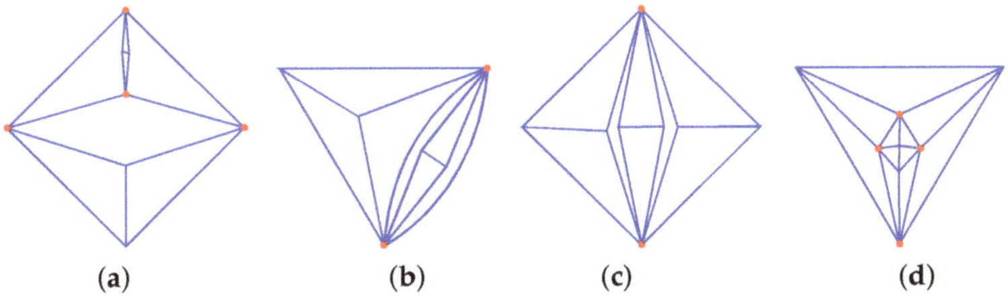

Figure 5. Special graphs: (**a**) **34_F8_4-1-3_4-2-1_V4_4**, (**b**) **36_F8_4-1-2_4-2-1_V4_2**, (**c**) **36_F9_3-2-2_6-2-1_V6_2**, (**d**) **45_F12_4-2-1_8-1-2_V4_4**.

4.2. Polygonal Dressing Graphs

- Replacing every second edge of a 2P-gone by a 2D diamond yields the following: **33_F2P+2_2-P-2P_2P-2-1_VP_P**, $P = 4, 6, 8$, (see Figure 6a,b)

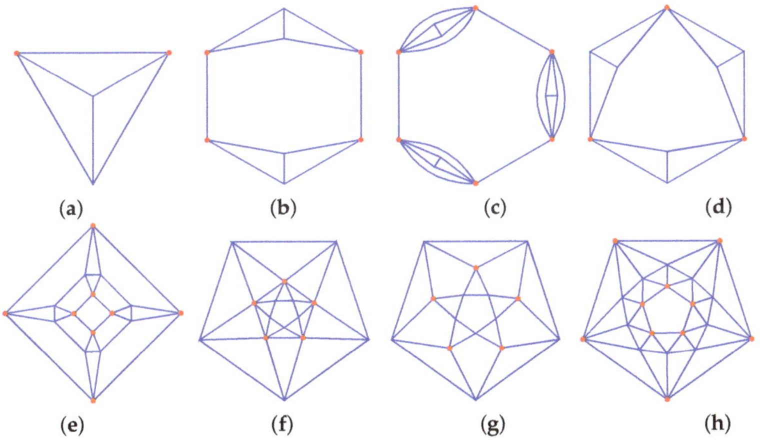

Figure 6. Dressed polygons: (**a**) **33_F4_2-1-2_2-2-1_V2_2**, (**b**) **33_F6_2-2-4_4-2-1_V4_4**, (**c**) **35_F14_2-0-6_6-1-2_6-2-1_V6_6**, (**d**) **34_F8_2-3-3_6-2-1_V6_3**, (**e**) **44_F18_2-0-4_8-2-1_8-2-2_V8_8**, (**f**) **46_F18_2-4-0_8-1-2_8-2-1_V8_4**. (**g**) **44_F17_2-5-0_5-2-2_10-2-1_V10_9**, (**h**) **55_F32_2-0-5_10-1-2_20-2-1_V10_10**.

- Replacing every second edge of a 2P-gon by a 2D bubble diamond yields the following: **35_F{4P+2}_2-0-{2P}_{2P}-1-2_{2P}-2-1_V{2P}_{2P}**, $P = 2, 3, 4, 5$ (see Figure 6c).
- P joined up 2D diamonds yield the following: **34_F{2P+2}_2-{P}-{P}_{2P}-2-1_V4_2**, $P = 2, 3, 4, 5$, (see Figure 6d)
- Inverted P-fans on both sides of a P-gon: **44_F{4P+2}_2-0-P_{2P}-2-1_{2P}-2-2_V{2P}_{2P}**, $P \geq 3$. (see Figure 6e).
- Two back-to-back P-stars on a polygon: **46_F{4P+2}_2-0-P_{2P}-1-2_{2P}-2-1_V{2P}_{P}**, $P \geq 3$. (see Figure 6f).
- Two back-to-back P-stars: **44_F{3P+2}_2-P-0_P-2-2_2P}-2-1_V{2P}_{P}**, $P \geq 3$. (see Figure 6g).
- Two P-mosaics back to back: **55_F{6P+2}_2-0-P_{2P}-1-2_{4P}-2-1_V{2P}_{2P}**, $P \geq 3$. When $P = 3$, this is an icosahedron. (see Figure 6h).

4.3. Pyramid Derived Graphs

- P-pyramids with graphs of the following type: **3P_F{P+1}_1-P-0_0-P-2-1_VP_1**, $P = 3 - 6$. (see Figure 7a).
- Two P-pyramids joined at the base: **4P_F{2P}_{2P}-1-2_V2_P**, $P = 3,4,5,6$. $P = 4$ is the octahedron. (see Figure 7b).
- P squares joined at a vertex, with two of them joined together: **3P_F{2P}_2P-1-3_V{2P}_2**. (see Figure 7c).
- Two truncated P-pyramids joined at the base: **34_F{2P+2}_2-P-0_{2P}-2-2_V{2P}_P**, $P \geq 3$, (see Figure 7d).

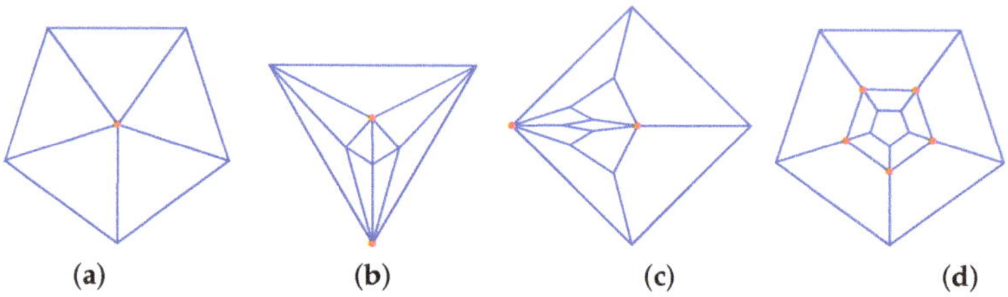

Figure 7. Dressed polygons: (**a**) **35_F6_1-5-0_5-2-1_V5_1**, (**b**) **45_F10_10-1-2_V5_2**, (**c**) **35_F10_10-3-1_V10_2**, (**d**) **34_F12_2-5-0_10-2-2_V10_5**.

4.4. Prism Derived Graphs

- The nodes of the prisms can be split in two symmetric subsets in two different ways: top base and bottom base nodes, **F{P+2}_1-0-P_1-P-0_P-2-2_VP_P** (see Figure 8a), or, for even P values, alternating nodes on top and bottom base **F{2P}_{2P}-2-{P/2}-{P/2}_P-2-2_V6_6_a** * (see Figure 8b), as well as **F{2P}_{2P}-2-{P/2}-{P/2}_P-2-2_V6_6_b** (see Figure 8c).
- P-prisms with a P-pyramid on each base: **3P_F{3P}_P-0-4_{2P}-1-2_V2_{2P}** $P \geq 3$ (see Figure 8d).
- P-risms with 4-pyramids on the square faces: **44_F{4P+2}_2-0-P_{4P}-1-2_V{P}_{2P}** $P \geq 3$, (see Figure 8e).
- P-prism with a truncated 4-pyramid on each side face: **35_F{5P+2}_2-0-P_P-4-0_{4P}_2-2_V{2P}_{2P}** *, $P \leq 3$ (see Figure 8f).
- P-prisms with a truncated P-pyramid on each base: **34_F{3P+2}_2-P-0_P-0-4_{2P}-2-2_V{2P}_{2P}**, $P \leq 3$ (see Figure 8g).
- P-prisms where the base is replaced by a linked P-gon: **33_F14_2-0-P_{2P}-3-2_V{2P}_{2P}**, $P \geq 3$ (see Figure 8h).
- A P-prism where every other side is split in two triangles: **34_F{3P+2}_2-P-P_P-2-2_{2P}-1-2_V{2P}_{2P}** *, $P = 2p, p \geq 1$ (see Figure 9a–c).
- P-prisms where every side edge becomes a 2D diamond: **34_F{3P+2}_2-0-P_P-2-4_{2P}-2-1_V{2P}_{2P}**, $P \geq 3$, (see Figure 9d)
- P-prisms where the links between the two bases become a 2D bubble diamond: **36_F{5P+2}_2-0-P_P-0-4_{2P}-1-2_{2P}-2-1_V{2P}_{2P}**, $P \geq 3$, (see Figure 9e)
- P-prisms where the edges joining the bases are split into a square, and the two new nodes are merged with the adjacent one, hence tiling the sides of the prism with squares: **34_F{3P+2}_2-0-P_{3P}-2-2_V{2P}_{2P}**, $P \geq 3$, (see Figure 9f).
- P-prims with P-star bases, where $P \geq 3$: **34_F{3P+2}_2-0-P_P-4-2_{2P}-1-2_V{2P}_{2P}** (see Figure 9g).
- A 2P-prism where the squares are split asymmetrically into two triangles: **35_F{4P+2}_2-P-P_{4P}-1-2_V{2P}_{2P}**, $P \geq 2$ (see Figure 9h).
- P-prisms where the squares are split into four triangles and one square: **36_F{5P+2}_2-0-P_P-2-2_{4P}-1-2_V{2P}_{2P}** *, $P \geq 3$, (see Figure 9i).
- P-prisms where every other vertex between the two bases becomes a 2D diamond: **35_F{4P+2}_2-0-P_{2P}-1-3_{2P}_2-1_V{2P}_{2P}** *, $P \geq 3$, (see Figure 9j).

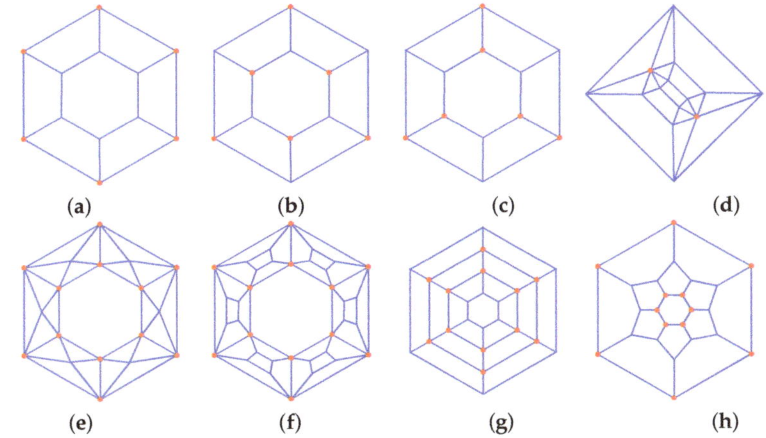

Figure 8. Prism-derived graphs: (a) **33_F8_1-0-6_1-6-0_6-2-2_V6_6**, (b) **33_F8_2-3-3_6-2-2_V6_6_a** *, (c) **33_F8_2-3-3_6-2-2_V6_6_b**, (d) **46_F18_6-4-0_12-2-1_V12_2**, (e) **45_F26_2-0-6_24-1-2_V6_12**, (f) **35_F32_2-0-6_6-4-0_24-2-2_V24_12**, (g) **34_F20_2-6-0_6-0-4_12-2-2_V12_12**, (h) **33_F14_2-0-6_12-3-2_V12_12**.

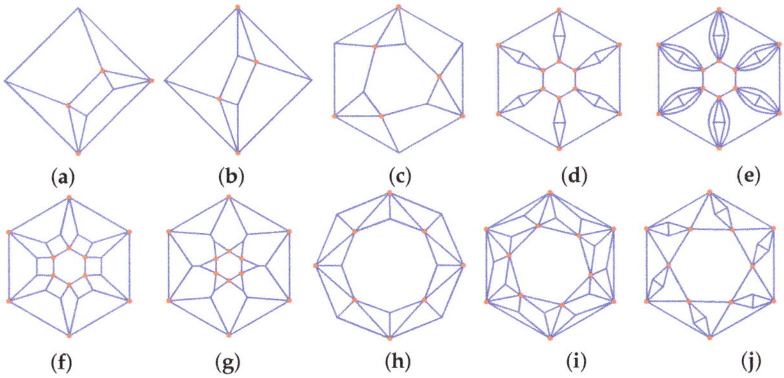

Figure 9. Prism-derived graphs: (a) **34_F8_4-1-2_4-2-2_V4_4_a** (parallel cut), (b) **34_F8_4-1-2_4-2-2_V4_4_b** *, (c) **34_F11_2-3-3_3-2-2_6-1-2_V6_6** *, (d) **34_F20_2-0-6_6-2-4_12-2-1_V12_12**, (e) **36_F32_2-0-6_6-0-4_12-1-2_12-2-1_V12_12**, (f) **34_F20_2-0-6_18-2-2_V12_12**, (g) **34_F20_2-0-6_6-4-2_12-1-2_V12_12** (h) **35_F18_2-4-4_16-1-2_V8_8**, (i) **36_F32_2-0-6_6-2-2_24-1-2_V12_12** *, (j) **35_F26_2-0-6_12-1-3_12-2-1_V12_12** *.

- P-prisms where the faces are split into two squares and two triangles: **35_F{4P+2}_2-0-P_{2P}-1-2_{2P}_2-2_V{2P}_{2P}**, $P \geq 3$. This can be done in three different ways (see Figure 10a–c).
- P-prism with a P-star on each base: **45_F{5P+2}_2-P-0_P-0-4_{2P}-1-2_{2P}-2-1_V{2P}_{2P}**, $P \geq 3$, (see Figure 10d).
- P-prisms where the squares are split into three triangles and a square: **45_F{5P+2}_2-0-P_P-2-2_{2P}-1-2_{2P}-2-1_V{2P}_{2P}** *, $P \geq 3$, (see Figure 10e).
- P-prisms where the squares are split into six triangles: **46_F{6P+2}_2-0-P_{2P}-2-1_{4P}-1-2_V{2P}_{2P}** *, $P \geq 3$, (see Figure 10f).

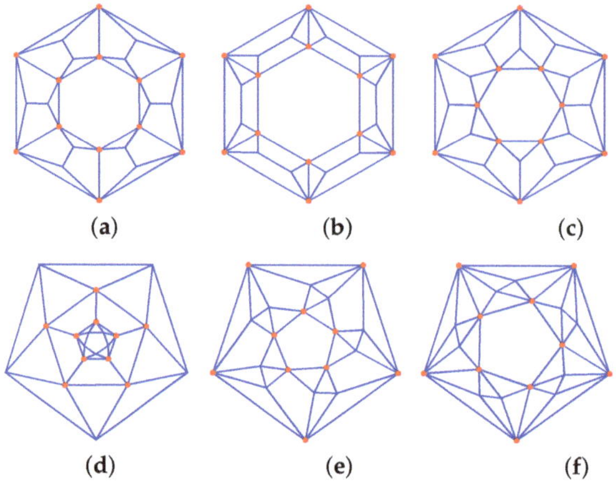

Figure 10. Prism-derived graphs: (a) **35_F26_2-0-6_12-1-2_12-2-2_V12_12_a**, (b) **35_F26_2-0-6_12-1-2_12-2-2_V12_12_b**, (c) **35_F26_2-0-6_12-1-2_12-2-2_V12_12_c**, (d) **45_F27_2-5-0_5-0-4_10-1-2_10-2-1_V10_10**, (e) **F27_2-0-5_5-2-2_10-1-2_10-2-1_V10_10** *, (f) **46_F32_2-0-5_10-2-1_20-1-2_V10_10** *.

4.5. Antiprism-Derived Graphs

- P-antiprisms where the two types of nodes are on each of the bases: **44_F{2P+2}_1-0-P_1-P-0_P-1-2_P-2-1_VP_P**, $P \geq 3$ (see Figure 11a).
- P-antiprisms where the two types of nodes alternate between the bases: **44_F{2P+2}_2-{P/2}-{P/2}_P-1-2_P-2-1_VP_P** *, $P \geq 4$ even, (see Figure 11b).
- P-antiprisms with a P-pyramid on each base: **P5_F{4P}_{2P}-0-3_{2P}-1-2_V{2P}_{2P}**, $P = 3, 4, 5, 6$, (see Figure 11c).
- P-antiprisms with two truncated P-gonal base pyramids: **35_F{4P+2}_2-P-0_{2P}-0-3_{2P}_2-2_V{2P}_{2P}**, $P \geq 3$, (see Figure 11d).
- P-antiprism with a P-star base: **44_F{4P+2}_2-P-0_{2P}-1-3_{2P}-2-1_V{2P}_{2P}**, $P \geq 3$, (see Figure 11e).
- P-antiprisms with P-fans added to the two bases: **46_F{6P+2}_2-P-0_{2P}-0-3_{2P}-1-2_{2P}-2-1_V{2P}_{2P}** *, $P \geq 3$, (see Figure 11f).

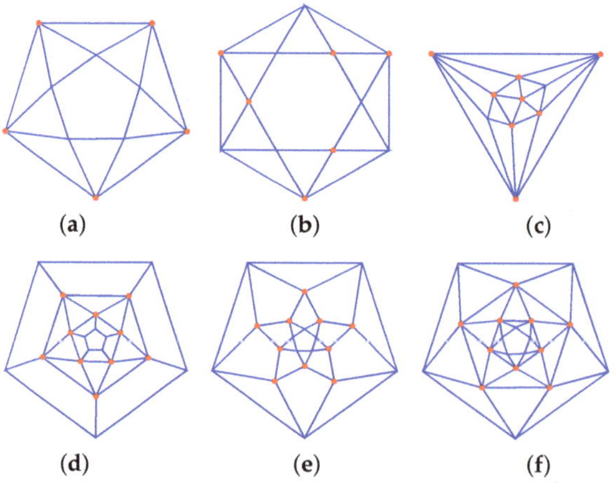

Figure 11. Antiprism-derived graphs: (a) **44_F12_1-0-5_1-5-0_5-1-2_5-2-1_V5_5**, (b) **44_F14_2-3-3_6-1-2_6-2-1_V6_6** *, (c) **45_F16_8-0-3_8-1-2_V2_8**, (d) **35_F22_2-5-0_10-0-3_10-2-2_V10_10**, (e) **44_F22_2-5-0_10-1-3_10-2-1_V10_10**, (f) **46_F32_2-5-0_10-0-3_10-1-2_10-2-1_V10_10**.

4.6. Platonic Solids-Derived Graphs

The nodes of the Platonic solids can be split into two symmetric families, but these graphs will also be characterised as part of other categories further done.

- Tetrahedron: **33_F4_2-1-2_2-2-1_V2_2.**
- Cube: **33_F6_6-3-1_V6_2.**
- Octahedron: **44_F8_8-2-1_V4_2.**
- Dodecahedron: **33_F12_2-5-0_10-2-3_V10_10.**
- Icosahedron: selecting two nodes on the poles of the solid **55_F20_10-2-1_10-3-0_V10_2.**
- Icosahedron: selecting six nodes on the equator: **55_F20_2-3-0_6-2-1_12-1-2_V6_6.**
- Platonic solids where the vertices become polygons, and the edges become two squares so that the faces of the solids end up with twice as many edges:
    - Tetrahedron: **34_F20_4-0-3_4-3-3_12-2-2_V12_12.**
    - Cube: **34_F38_6-4-4_8-0-3_24-2-2_V24_24.**
    - Octahedron: **34_F38_6-0-4_8-3-3_24-2-2_V24_24** (see Figure 12a).
    - Dodecahedron: **34_F92_12-5-5_20-0-3_60-2-2_V60_60.**
    - Icosahedron: **34_F92_12-0-5_20-3-3_60-2-2_V60_60.**
- Platonic solids where a pyramid is placed on four faces:
    - Octhedron: **36_F16_4-0-3_12-1-2_V4_6** (see Figure 12b).
    - Icosahedron: **36_F28_12-1-2_16-0-3_V4_12.**
- Platonic solids where some faces become truncated pyramids:
    - Tetrahedron: **36_F16_4-3-0_12-2-2_V12_4.**
    - Octahedron: **36_F20_4-0-3_4-3-0_12-2-2_V12_6** (see Figure 12c).
    - Icosahedron: **36_F32_4-3-0_12-2-2_16-0-3_V12_12.**
- Platonic solids where some P-gonal faces become P-stars. Doing this, the tetrahedron becomes an octahedron, the cube becomes an the octahedron, and both become a cuboctahedron, while the dodecahedron and icosahedron both become an icosidodecahedron.
- Platonic solid where a face becomes a linked P-gon:
    - Tetrahedron: **33_F10_4-3-0_6-4-2_V12_4.**
    - Cube: **33_F18_6-4-0_12-4-2_V24_8** (see Figure 12d).
    - Octahedron: **34_F20_8-3-0_12-4-2_V24_6.**
    - Dodecahedron: **33_F42_12-5-0_30-4-2_V60_20.**
    - Icosahedron: **35_F50_20-3-0_30-4-2_V60_12.**
- Platonic solids where every edge becomes a 2D diamond. The octahedron and icosahedron lead to graphs with valency exceeding 6:
    - Tetrahedron: **36_F16_4-3-3_12-2-1_V12_4,**
    - Cube: **36_F30_6-4-4_24-2-1_V24_8** (see Figure 12e),
    - Dodecahedron: **36_F72_12-5-5_60-2-1_V60_20.**
- Platonic solids where some edges become a 2D bubble diamond:
    - Tetrahedron: **36_F12_4-0-3_4-1-2_4-2-1_V4_4.**
    - Dodecahedron: **36_F52_12-0-5_20-1-2_20-2-1_V20_20** (see Figure 12f).
- Octahedrom where every other face is a P-star: **44_F20_4-3-0_4-3-3_12-2-1_V12_6** (see Figure 12g).
- Platonic solids with inverted P-fans replacing the faces. The octahedron and the icosahedron have, respectively, valency 4 and 5 nodes, and this leads to graphs with a valency exceeding six:
    - Tetrahedron: **46_F22_4-3-0_6-2-2_12-2-1_V12_4.**
    - Cube: **46_F42_6-4-0_12-2-2_24-2-1_V24_8.**
    - Dodecahedron: **46_F102_12-5-0_30-2-2_60-2-1_V60_20.**

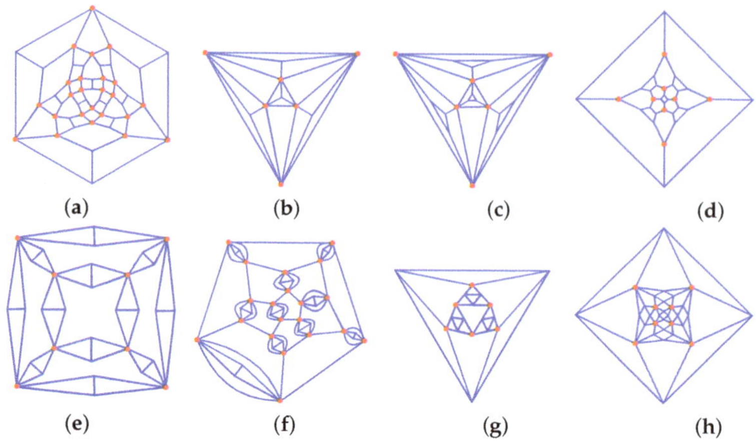

Figure 12. Platonic solids-derived graphs: (**a**) **34_F38_6-0-4_8-3-3_24-2-2_V24_24**, (**b**) **36_F16_4-0-3_12-1-2_V4_6**, (**c**) **36_F20_4-0-3_4-3-0_12-2-2_V12_6**, (**d**) **33_F18_6-4-0_12-4-2_V24_8**, (**e**) **36_F30_6-4-4_24-2-1_V24_8**, (**f**) **36_F52_12-0-5_20-1-2_20-2-1_V20_20**. (**g**) **44_F20_4-3-0_4-3-3_12-2-1_V12_6**, (**h**) **46_F42_6-4-0_12-2-2_24-2-1_V24_8**.

4.7. Archimedean Solids-Derived Graphs

- Truncated Platonic solids (the nodes of the other Archimedean solids cannot be split into two equivalent families):
  - Truncated octahedron: **33_F14_6-2-2_8-3-3_V12_12**.
  - Truncated cube: **33_F14_4-0-3_4-3-0_6-4-4_V12_12**.
  - Truncated cuboctahedron: **33_F26_6-4-4_8-3-3_12-2-2_V24_24** (see Figure 13a).
  - Truncated icosidodecahedron: **33_F62_12-5-5_20-3-3_30-2-2_V60_60**.
- Solids where a pyramid is placed on some of the faces of the truncated Platonic solids. Only the face that does not touch similar faces can be tiled like this, as otherwise, the equivalence is broken:
  - Truncated tetrahedron (triangles): **34_F16_4-0-6_12-1-2_V4_12** (see Figure 13b).
  - Truncated tetrahedron (hexagons): **56_F28_4-3-0_24-2-1_V12_4**.
  - Truncated cube (triangles): **34_F30_6-0-8_24-1-2_V8_24**.
  - Truncated octahedron (squares): **44_F32_8-6-0_24-2-1_V24_6**.
  - Truncated octahedron (hexagons): **56_F54_6-4-0_48-2-1_V24_8**.
  - Truncated dodecahedron (triangles): **34_F72_12-0-10_60-1-2_V20_60**.
  - Truncated icosahedron (pentagons): **45_F80_20-6-0_60-2-1_V60_12**.
  - Truncated icosahedron (hexagons): **56_F132_12-5-0_120-2-1_V60_20**.
- Solids where a pyramid is placed on some faces of the Archimedean solids:
  - Cuboctahedron (every other triangle): **35_F22_4-0-3_6-0-4_12-1-2_V4_12**.
  - Cuboctahedron (triangles): **36_F30_6-0-4_24-1-2_V8_12**.
  - Cuboctahedron (squares): **46_F32_8-0-3_24-1-2_V6_12**.
  - Rhombicuboctahedron (triangles): **35_F42_18-0-4_24-1-2_V8_24** (see Figure 13c).
  - Rhombicuboctahedron (6 squares): **45_F44_8-0-3_12-0-4_24-1-2_V6_24**.
  - Rhombicuboctahedron (8 squares): **46_F62_6-0-4_8-0-3_48-1-2_V12_24**.
  - Icosidodecahedron (triangles): **36_F72_12-0-5_60-1-2_V20_30**.
  - Icosidodecahedron (pentagons): **56_F80_20-0-3_60-1-2_V12_30**.
  - Snub dodecahedron (pentagons): **56_F140_60-1-2_80-0-3_V12_60 ***.
  - Snub dodecahedron (20 triangles): **36_F132_12-0-5_60-0-3_60-1-2_V20_60 ***.
  - Rhombicosididecahedron (triangles): **35_F102_12-0-5_30-0-4_60-1-2_V20_60**.
  - Rhombicosididecahedron (squares): **46_F152_12-0-5_20-0-3_120-1-2_V30_60**.
  - Rhombicosididecahedron (pentagons): **55_F110_20-3-0_30-4-0_60-2-1_V60_12**.

- Truncated pyramid on truncated Platonic solids:
  - Truncated tetrahedron (triangles): **34_F20_4-0-6_4-3-0_12-2-2_V12_12** (see Figure 13d).
  - Truncated tetrahedron (hexagons): **35_F32_4-0-3_4-6-0_24-2-2_V24_12**.
  - Truncated cube (triangles): **34_F38_6-0-8_8-3-0_24-2-2_V24_24**.
  - Truncated cube (octagons): **35_F62_6-8-0_8-0-3_48-2-2_V48_24**.
  - Truncated dodecahedron (decagons): **35_F152_12-10-0_20-0-3_120-2-2_V120_60**.
  - Truncated icosahedron (pentagon): **34_F92_12-5-0_20-0-6_60-2-2_V60_60**.
  - Truncated icosahedron (hexagon): **35_F152_12-0-5_20-6-0_120-2-2_V120_60**.
  - Truncated octahedron (squares): **34_F38_6-4-0_8-0-6_24-2-2_V24_24**.
  - Truncated octahedron (hexagons): **35_F62_6-0-4_8-6-0_48-2-2_V48_24**.
  - Truncated dodecahedron (triangles): **34_F82_12-0-10_20-3-0_60-2-2_V60_60**.
- Truncated pyramid on other Archimedean solids:
  - Snub cube (squares): **36_F62_6-4-0_24-2-2_32-0-3_V24_24** *.
  - Snub cube (8 triangles): **36_F62_6-0-4_8-3-0_24-0-3_24-2-2_V24_24** *.
  - Rhombicuboctahedron (triangles): **35_F50_8-3-0_18-0-4_24-2-2_V24_24**.
  - Snub dodecahedron (pentagons): **36_F152_12-5-0_60-2-2_80-0-3_V60_60** *.
  - Snub dodecahedron (triangles): **36_F152_12-0-5_20-3-0_60-0-3_60-2-2_V60_60** *.
  - Cuboctahedron (squares): **36_F38_6-4-0_8-0-3_24-2-2_V24_12**.
  - Cuboctahedron(triangles): **36_F38_6-0-4_8-3-0_24-2-2_V24_12**.
  - Cuboctahedron (every other triangles): **35_F26_4-0-3_4-3-0_6-0-4_12-2-2_V12_12**.
  - Rhombicuboctahedron (6 squares): **35_F50_6-4-0_8-0-3_12-0-4_24-2-2_V24_24**.
  - Rhombicuboctahedron (8 squares): **36_F74_6-0-4_8-0-3_12-4-0_48-2-2_V48_24**.
  - Icosidodecahedron (pentagons): **36_F92_12-5-0_20-0-3_60-2-2_V60_30**.
  - Icosidodecahedron (triangles): **36_F92_12-0-5_20-3-0_60-2-2_V60_30**.
  - Rhombicosidodecahedron (triangles): **35_F122_12-0-5_20-3-0_30-0-4_60-2-2_V60_60**.
  - Rhombicosidodecahedron (pentagons): **35_F122_12-5-0_20-0-3_30-0-4_60-2-2_V60_60**.
- Archimedean solids where some P-gonal faces become P-stars. This is only possible when there is a P-fold rotation symmetry around the center of the P-gonal face:
  - Truncated tetrahedron (triangles): **34_F20_4-0-3_4-6-3_12-1-2_V12_12**.
  - Truncated octahedron (squares): **34_F38_6-0-4_8-6-3_24-1-2_V24_24**.
  - Truncated icosahedron (pentagons): **34_F92_12-0-5_20-6-3_60-1-2_V60_60**.
  - Cuboctahedron (triangles): **44_F38_6-4-4_8-3-0_24-2-1_V24_12**.
  - Cuboctahedron (every other triangle): **44_F26_4-0-3_4-3-0_6-2-4_12-2-1_V12_12**.
  - Cuboctahedron (squares): **44_F38_6-4-0_8-3-3_24-2-1_V24_12**.
  - Rhombicuboctahedron (triangles): **44_F50_6-0-4_8-3-0_12-2-4_24-2-1_V24_24**.
  - Rhombicuboctahedron (squares): **44_F50_6-0-4_8-3-0_12-4-2_24-1-2_V24_24**.
  - Icosidodecahedron(triangles): **44_F92_12-5-5_20-3-0_60-2-1_V60_30**.
  - Icosidodecahedron (pentagons): **44_F92_12-0-5_20-3-3_60-2-1_V60_30**.
  - Snub cube (squares): **45_F62_6-4-0_8-0-3_24-1-3_24-2-1_V24_24** *.
  - Snub cube (eight triangles): **45_F62_6-0-4_8-3-0_24-1-3_24-2-1_V24_24** *.
  - Snub dodecahedron (pentagons): **45_F152_12-5-0_20-0-3_60-1-3_60-2-1_V60_60** *.
  - Snub dodecahedron (20 triangles): **45_F152_12-0-5_20-3-0_60-1-3_60-2-1_V60_60** *.
  - Rhombicosidodecahedron (triangles): **44_F122_12-0-5_20-3-0_30-2-4_60-2-1_V60_60**.
  - Rhombicosidodecahedron (pentagons): **44_F122_12-0-5_20-3-0_30-4-2_60-1-2_V60_60**.
- Archimedean solids with some P-faces filled with a P-stars.
  A P-star-filled cuboactahedron and icosidodecahedron have valency 8 nodes. The following solids have nodes with valencies that are too large: truncated cubes (octagons), truncated octagons (hexagons), snub cubes, snub dodecahedrons, truncated dodecahedrons (decagons), and truncated icosahedron (hexagons).

- Truncated tetrahedron (triangles): **45_F32_4-0-6_4-3-0_12-1-2_12-2-1_V12_12** (see Figure 13f).
- Truncated tetrahedron (hexagons): **45_F32_4-0-3_4-3-0_12-1-3_12-2-1_V12_12 ***.
- Truncated cube (triangles): **45_F62_6-0-8_8-3-0_24-1-2_24-2-1_V24_24.**
- Truncated octahedron (squares): **45_F62_6-4-0_8-0-6_24-1-2_24-2-1_V24_24.**
- Truncated dodecahedron (triangles): **45_F152_12-0-10_20-3-0_60-1-2_60-2-1_V60_60.**
- Truncated icosahedron (pentagons): **45_F152_12-5-0_20-0-6_60-1-2_60-2-1_V60_60.**
- Cuboctahedron (four triangles): **34_F20_4-0-3_4-6-3_12-1-2_V12_12.**
- Rhomicuboctahedron (six squares): **46_F74_6-4-0_8-0-3_12-0-4_24-1-2_24-2-1_V24_24.**
- Rhomicuboctahedron (triangles): **46_F74_8-3-0_18-0-4_24-1-2_24-2-1_V24_24.**
- Rhomicosidodecahedron (pentagon): **46_F182_12-5-0_20-0-3_30-0-4_60-1-2_60-2-1.**
- Rhomicosidodecahedron (triangles): **46_F182_12-0-5_20-3-0_30-0-4_60-1-2_60-2-1.**

• Linked P-gon-filled truncated Platonic solids:

- Truncated tetrahedron: **34_F20_4-0-3_4-3-0_12-2-3_V12_12 ***.
- Truncated cube: **34_F38_6-4-0_8-0-3_24-2-3_V24_24 *** (see Figure 13g).
- Truncated octahedron: **34_F38_6-0-4_8-3-0_24-2-3_V24_24 ***.
- Truncated dodecahedron: **34_F92_12-5-0_20-0-3_60-2-3_V60_60 ***.
- Truncated icosahedron: **34_F92_12-0-5_20-3-0_60-2-3_V60_60 ***.

• Archimedean solids where a face becomes a linked P-gon. When applying this to the cuboctahedron, one obtains the truncated cube and the truncated octahedron. When applying this to the icosidodecahedron, one obtains the truncated dodecahedron and the truncated icosahedron. This cannot be applied to the truncated Platonic solids, as this gives the same solid (truncation face) of an nonequivalent graph (adjacent faces):

- The snub cube (eight triangles) gives **34_F38_6-0-4_8-3-0_24-2-3_V24_24** (a linked P-gon-filled truncated octahedron).
- The snub cube (squares) gives **34_F38_6-4-0_8-0-3_24-2-3_V24_24** (a linked P-gon-filled truncated cube).
- The snub dodecahedron (20 triangles) gives **34_F92_12-0-5_20-3-0_60-2-3_V60_60** (a linked P-gon-filled truncated icosahedron).
- The snub dodecahedron (pentagons) gives **34_F92_12-5-0_20-0-3_60-2-3_V60_60** (a linked P-gon-filled truncated dodecahedron).
- Rhombicuboctahedron: **35_F26_6-0-4_8-3-0_12-4-4_V24_24** (see Figure 13h),.
- Rhombicosidodecahedron: **33_F62_12-0-5_20-3-0_30-4-4_V60_60.**

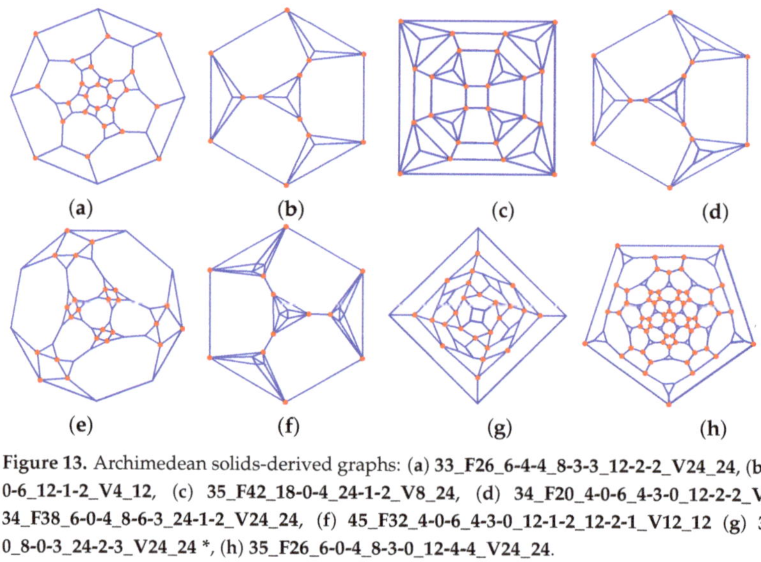

Figure 13. Archimedean solids-derived graphs: (**a**) **33_F26_6-4-4_8-3-3_12-2-2_V24_24**, (**b**) **34_F16_4-0-6_12-1-2_V4_12**, (**c**) **35_F42_18-0-4_24-1-2_V8_24**, (**d**) **34_F20_4-0-6_4-3-0_12-2-2_V12_12**, (**e**) **34_F38_6-0-4_8-6-3_24-1-2_V24_24**, (**f**) **45_F32_4-0-6_4-3-0_12-1-2_12-2-1_V12_12** (**g**) **34_F38_6-4-0_8-0-3_24-2-3_V24_24 ***, (**h**) **35_F26_6-0-4_8-3-0_12-4-4_V24_24**.

- Truncated Platonic solids where some the 2P faces are filled with P-fans ($P > 2$). This can be done in two different ways:
  - Truncated tetrahedron: **45_F32_4-0-3_4-3-0_12-1-2_12-2-2_V12_12_a**.
  - Truncated tetrahedron: **45_F32_4-0-3_4-3-0_12-1-2_12-2-2_V12_12_b**.
  - Truncated cube 1: **45_F62_6-4-0_8-0-3_24-1-2_24-2-2_V24_24_a** (see Figure 14a).
  - Truncated cube 2: **45_F62_6-4-0_8-0-3_24-1-2_24-2-2_V24_24_b** (see Figure 14b).
  - Truncated cctahedron 1: **45_F62_6-0-4_8-3-0_24-1-2_24-2-2_V24_24_a**.
  - Truncated octahedron 2: **45_F62_6-0-4_8-3-0_24-1-2_24-2-2_V24_24_b**.
  - Truncated dodecahedron 1: **45_F152_12-5-0_20-0-3_60-1-2_60-2-2_V60_60_a**.
  - Truncated dodecahedron 2: **45_F152_12-5-0_20-0-3_60-1-2_60-2-2_V60_60_b**.
  - Truncated icosahedron 1: **45_F152_12-0-5_20-3-0_60-1-2_60-2-2_V60_60_a**.
  - Truncated icosahedron 2: **45_F152_12-0-5_20-3-0_60-1-2_60-2-2_V60_60_b**.
- Archimedean solids where squares are split into two squares and two triangles. This can be done in two different ways:
  - Rhombicubotcahedron: **36_F62_6-0-4_8-0-3_24-1-2_24-2-2_V24_24_a** (see Figure 14c).
  - Rhombicubotcahedron: **36_F62_6-0-4_8-0-3_24-1-2_24-2-2_V24_24_b** (see Figure 14d).
  - Rhombicosidodecahedron: **36_F152_12-0-5_20-0-3_60-1-2_60-2-2_V60_60_a**.
  - Rhombicosidodecahedron: **36_F152_12-0-5_20-0-3_60-1-2_60-2-2_V60_60_b**.
- Truncated Platonic solids with 2P-gon faces split into P squares:
  - Truncated tetrahedron: **34_F16_4-0-3_12-1-3_V4_12** *.
  - Truncated cube: **44_F32_8-3-0_24-3-1_V24_6** *.
  - Truncated octahedron: **34_F30_6-0-4_24-1-3_V8_24** * (see Figure 14e).
  - Truncated icosahedron: **34_F72_12-0-5_60-1-3_V20_60** *.
  - Truncated dodecahedron: **45_F80_20-3-0_60-3-1_V60_12** *.
- As truncated Platonic solids have a 2-fold symmetry around the centre of the edges shared by two identical faces, one can replace the edge with a 2D diamond. For the truncated cube and truncated dodecahedron, this leads to faces with more than 10 edges:
  - Truncated tetrahedron: **34_F20_4-0-3_4-3-6_12-2-1_V12_12**.
  - Truncated octahedron: **34_F38_6-0-4_8-3-6_24-2-1_V24_24** (see Figure 14f).
  - Truncated icosahedron: **34_F92_12-0-5_20-3-6_60-2-1_V48_60**.
- Archimedean solids with squares linking triangles are split into two triangles and a square. This requires a 2-fold rotation symmetry of the solid around the split square:
  - Split cuboctahedron: **35_F26_4-0-3_4-3-3_6-2-2_12-1-2_V12_12** * (see Figure 14g).
  - Rhombicuboctahedron: **35_F50_6-4-4_8-0-3_12-2-2_24-1-2_V24_24** *.
  - Rhombicuboctahedron: **35_F50_6-0-4_8-3-3_12-2-2_24-1-2_V24_24** *.
  - Rhombicosidodecahedron: **35_F122_12-0-5_20-3-3_30-2-2_60-1-2_V60_60** *.
  - Rhombicosidodecahedron: **35_F122_12-5-5_20-0-3_30-2-2_60-1-2_V60_60** *.
- Archimedean solids where some edges become a 2D bubble diamonds:
  - Truncated tetrahedron: **36_F32_4-0-3_4-0-6_12-1-2_12-2-1_V12_12** (see Figure 14h).
  - Truncated cube: **36_F62_6-0-8_8-0-3_24-1-2_24-2-1_V24_24**.
  - Truncated octahedron: **36_F62_6-0-4_8-0-6_24-1-2_24-2-1_V24_24**.
  - Truncated dodecahedron: **36_F152_12-0-10_20-0-3_60-1-2_60-2-1_V60_60**.
  - Truncated icosahedron: **36_F152_12-0-5_20-0-6_60-1-2_60-2-1**.

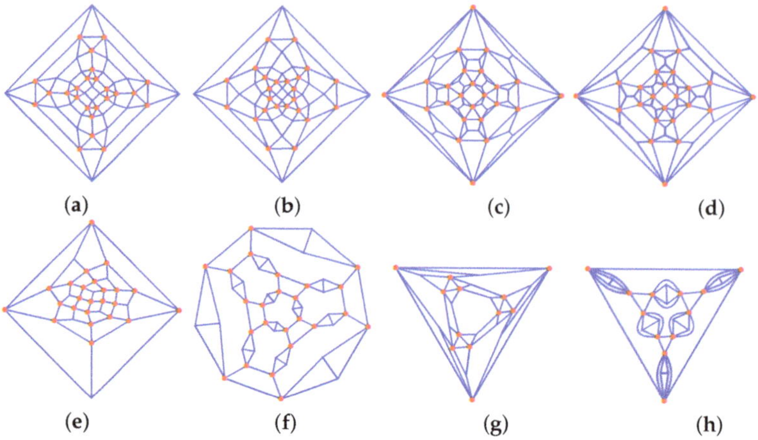

Figure 14. Archimedean solids-derived graphs: (a) **45_F62_6-4-0_8-0-3_24-1-2_24-2-2_V24_24_a**, (b) **45_F62_6-4-0_8-0-3_24-1-2_24-2-2_V24_24_b**, (c) **36_F62_6-0-4_8-0-3_24-1-2_24-2-2_V24_24_a**, (d) **36_F62_6-0-4_8-0-3_24-1-2_24-2-2_V24_24_b**, (e) **34_F30_6-0-4_24-1-3_V8_24** *, (f) **34_F38_6-0-4_8-3-6_24-2-1_V24_24**, (g) **35_F26_4-0-3_4-3-3_6-2-2_12-1-2_V12_12** *, (h) **36_F32_4-0-3_4-0-6_12-1-2_12-2-1_V12_12**.

- Archimedean solids where some squares are split intro four triangles:
  - Cuboctahedron: **36_F32_4-0-3_4-3-3_24-1-2_V12_12** * (see Figure 15a).
  - Rhombicuboctahedron: **36_F32_4-0-3_4-3-3_24-1-2_V12_12** *.
  - Rhombicuboctahedron: **36_F62_6-4-4_8-0-3_48-1-2_V24_24** *.
  - Rhombicosidodecahedron: **36_F152_12-0-5_20-3-3_120-1-2_V60_60** *.
  - Rhombicosidodecahedron: **36_F152_12-5-5_20-0-3_120-1-2_V60_60** *.
- Truncated Platonic solids where the faces are replaced by P-fans. This can only be done with valency 3 graphs without exceeding the maximum valency, which we consider as follows:
  - Truncated tetrahedron: **44_F26_4-0-3_4-3-0_18-2-2_V12_12**.
  - Truncated cube and truncated octahedron: **44_F26_4-0-3_4-3-0_6-2-4_12-2-1_V12_12** (see Figure 14b).
  - Truncated dodecahedron and truncated icosahedron: **44_F122_12-0-5_20-3-0_90-2-2_V60_60**.
- Archimedean solids where the squares are split into four triangles to form braided links:
  - Cuboctahedron: **45_F32_4-0-3_4-3-3_12-1-2_12-2-1_V12_12** *.
  - Rhombicuboctahedron that is parallel braided: **45_F62_6-0-4_8-3-3_24-1-2_24-2-1_V24_24** *.
  - Rhombicuboctahedron that is perpendicular braided: **45_F62_6-4-4_8-0-3_24-1-2_24-2-1_V24_24** * (see Figure 14c).
  - Rhombicosidodecahedron that is parallel braided: **45_F152_12-5-0_20-0-3_60-1-3_60-2-1_V60_6** *.
  - Rhombicosidodecahedron that is perpendicular braided: **45_F152_12-5-5_20-0-3_60-1-2_60-2-1_V60_60** *.
- Truncated Platonic solids with 2P-gonal faces replaced by split P-fans. For the truncated cube and truncated icosahedron, this leads to nodes with valencies exceeding six:
  - Truncated tetrahedron: **55_F38_4-0-3_4-3-0_6-2-2_12-1-2_12-2-1_V12_12** *.
  - Truncated octahedron: **55_F74_6-0-4_8-3-0_12-2-2_24-1-2_24-2-1_V24_24** * (see Figure 14d).

  - Truncated dodecahedron: **55_F182_12-0-5_20-3-0_30-2-2_60-1-2_60-2-1_V60_60** *.
- Truncated Platonic solids where the faces are P-mosaics:
  - Truncated tetrahedron: **56_F44_4-0-3_4-3-0_12-2-1_24-1-2_V12_12** *.
  - Truncated cube: **56_F86_6-4-0_8-0-3_24-2-1_48-1-2_V24_24** *.
  - Truncated octahedron: **56_F86_6-0-4_8-3-0_24-2-1_48-1-2_V24_24** *.
  - Truncated icosahedron: **56_F212_12-0-5_20-3-0_60-2-1_120-1-2_V60_60** *.
  - Truncated dodecahedron: **56_F212_12-5-0_20-0-3_60-2-1_120-1-2_V60_60** *.

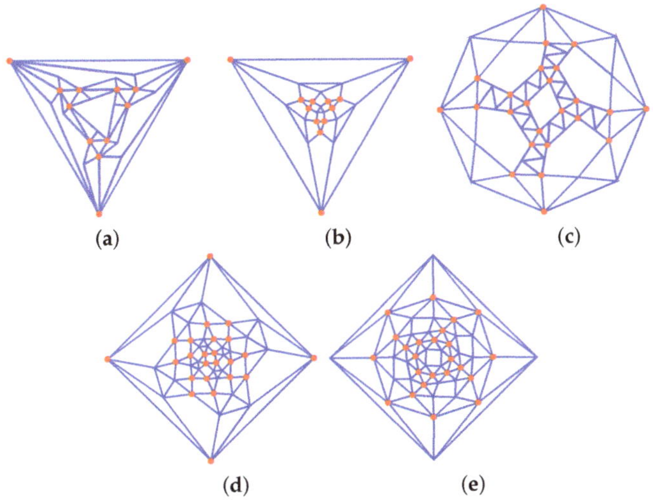

Figure 15. Archimedean solids-derived graphs: (a) **36_F32_4-0-3_4-3-3_24-1-2_V12_12** *, (b) **44_F26_4-0-3_4-3-0_18-2-2_V12_12**, (c) **45_F62_6-4-4_8-0-3_24-1-2_24-2-1_V24_24** *, (d) **55_F74_6-0-4_8-3-0_12-2-2_24-1-2_24-2-1_V24_24** *, (e) **56_F86_6-4-0_8-0-3_24-2-1_48-1-2_V24_24** *.

4.8. Other Solids-Derived Graphs

- For solids with valency 4 nodes and a 2-fold rotational symmetry around each node, one can replace the node with a 2D diamond:
  - Octahedron: **34_F20_8-3-3_12-1-2_V12_12** * (see Figure 16a).
  - Cuboctahedron: **34_F38_6-4-4_8-3-3_24-1-2_V24_24** * (see Figure 16b).
  - Icosidodecahedron: **34_F92_12-5-5_20-3-3_60-1-2_V60_60** * (see Figure 16c).

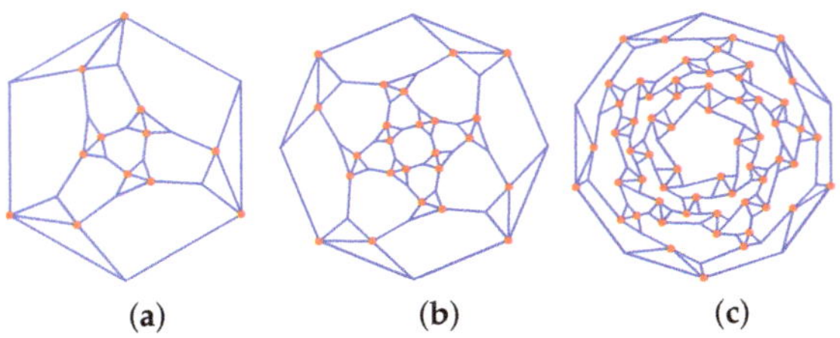

Figure 16. Other solids-derived graphs: (a) **34_F20_8-3-3_12-1-2_V12_12** *, (b) **34_F38_6-4-4_8-3-3_24-1-2_V24_24** *, (c) **34_F92_12-5-5_20-3-3_60-1-2_V60_60** *.

4.9. Dual of Archimedean Solids Graphs

The planar graphs of the dual of Archimedean solids with two inequivalent type of faces have nodes that can be split into two families. These are the following:

- Triakis tetrahedron: **36_F12_12-1-2_V4_4** (see Figure 17a).
- Triakis hexahedron: **46_F24_24-1-2_V6_8** (see Figure 17b).

- Pentakis dodecahedron: **56_F60_60-1-2_V12_20** (see Figure 17c).
- Rhomic dodecahedron: **34_F12_12-2-2_V8_6** (see Figure 17d).
- Rhomic tricontahedron: **35_F30_30-2-2_V20_12** (see Figure 17e).

The planar graphs of the dual of the truncated cube and the truncated dodecahedron have valencies exceeding six and are hence not presented here.

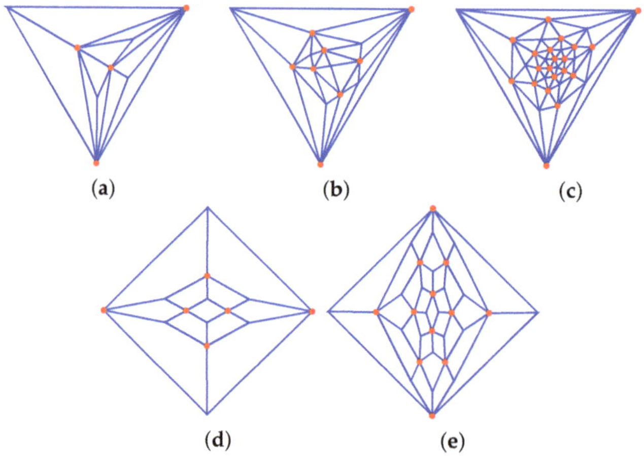

Figure 17. Archimedean solids-derived graphs: (**a**) Triakis tetrahedron: **36_F12_12-1-2_V4_4**. (**b**) Triakis hexahedron: **46_F24_24-1-2_V6_8**. (**c**) Pentakis dodecahedron: **56_F60_60-1-2_V12_20**. (**d**) Rhomic dodecahedron: **34_F12_12-2-2_V8_6**. (**e**) Rhomic tricontahedron: **35_F30_30-2-2_V20_12**.

5. Conclusions

In this paper, we have defined biequivalent graphs as graphs made out of two families of nodes equivalent in modulo to an automorphism of the graph. We have found 430 graphs made out of up to 300 faces ranging from triangles to decagons and with valencies ranging between three and six.

Supplementary Materials: The following supporting information can be downloaded at https://www.mdpi.com/article/10.3390/axioms13070437/s1. **graphs_full_list.pdf**: a graphic representation of all the graphs that we have identified.

Funding: This research was funded by the Leverhulme Trust Research Project Grants RPG-2020-306.

Data Availability Statement: The software to determine all the biequivalent planar graphs is available from Zenodo: https://doi.org/10.5281/zenodo.11059064. The PGC node links and vector graphics for all the graphs are available from Zenodo: https://doi.org/10.5281/zenodo.11059440.

Acknowledgments: I would like to thank Árpad Lukács for our useful discussions. Some of the graphics where created or edited using Inkscape: https://inkscape.org/ (accessed on 20 June 2024).

Conflicts of Interest: The author declares no conflicts of interest.

Abbreviations

The following abbreviations are used in this manuscript:

p-cage	Polyhedral cages
PGC	Potential graph characteristics
TRAP	trp RNA-binding attenuation protein

Appendix A

A maximal planar graph is a graph for which adding one edge would render the graph nonplanar. Every maximal planar graph is made out of triangles. This means that using F, E, and V for, respectively, the number of faces, edges, and nodes, we have

$$E = 3V - 6. \tag{A1}$$

As the sum of the valencies of each node of the graph is $2E$, the average valency of the graph is

$$\frac{2E}{V} = 6 - \frac{12}{V}. \tag{A2}$$

which is then strictly smaller than six. This means that maximal planar graphs must have at least one node of a valency less than six, and as nonmaximal graphs, they can be obtained by removing edges from some maximal graphs; this implies that it is impossible to have planar graphs where all the nodes have a valency of six.

References

1. Piette, B.M.A.G.; Kowalczyk, A.; Heddle, J.G. Characterization of near-miss connectivity-invariant homogeneous convex polyhedral cages. *Proc. R. Soc. A* **2022**, *478*, 20210679. [CrossRef] [PubMed]
2. Malay, A.D.; Heddle, J.G.; Tomita, S.; Iwasaki, K.; Miyazaki, N.; Sumitomo, K.; Yanagi, H.; Yamashita, I.; Uraoka, Y. Gold nanoparticle-induced formation of artificial protein capsids. *Nano Lett.* **2012**, *12*, 2056–2059. [CrossRef] [PubMed]
3. Piette, B.M.A.G.; Lukács, A. Near-Miss Symmetric Polyhedral Cages. *Symmetry* **2023**, *15*, 717. [CrossRef]
4. Piette, B.M.A.G.; Lukács, A. Near-Miss Bi-Homogenous Symmetric Polyhedral Cages. *Symmetry* **2023**, *15*, 1804. [CrossRef]
5. Coxeter, H.S.M. *Regular Polytopes*; Dover Publications: Mineola, NY, USA, 1973.
6. Malay, A.D.; Miyazaki, N.; Biela, A.; Chakraborti, S.; Majsterkiewicz, K.; Stupka, I.; Kaplan, C.S.; Kowalczyk, A.; Piette, B.M.; Hochberg, G.K.; et al. An ultra-stable gold-coordinated protein cage displaying reversible assembly. *Nature* **2019**, *569*, 438–442. [CrossRef] [PubMed]
7. Stupka, I.; Biela, A.P.; Piette, B.; Kowalczyk, A.; Majsterkiewicz, K.; Borzęcka-Solarz, K.; Naskalska, A.; Heddle, J.G. An artificial protein cage made from a 12-membered ring. *J. Mater. Chem. B* **2024**, *12*, 436–447. [CrossRef] [PubMed]
8. Chakraborti, S.; Lin, T.Y.; Glatt, S.; Heddle, J.G. Enzyme encapsulation by protein cages. *RSC Adv.* **2020**, *10*, 13293–13301. [CrossRef] [PubMed] [PubMed Central]
9. Gao, R.; Tan, H.; Li, S.; Ma, S.; Tang, Y.; Zhang, K.; Zhang, Z.; Fan, Q.; Yang, J.; Zhang, X.E.; et al. A prototype protein nanocage minimized from carboxysomes with gated oxygen permeability. *Proc. Natl. Acad. Sci. USA* **2022**, *119*, e2104964119. [CrossRef] [PubMed]
10. Zhu, J.; Avakyan, N.; Kakkis, A.; Hoffnagle, A.M.; Han, K.; Li, Y.; Zhang, Z.; Choi, T.S.; Na, Y.; Yu, C.J.; et al. Protein Assembly by Design. *Chem. Rev.* **2021**, *121*, 13701–13796. [CrossRef]
11. Percastegui, E.G.; Ronson, T.K.; Nitschke, J.R. Design and Applications of Water-Soluble Coordination Cages. *Chem. Rev.* **2020**, *120*, 13480–13544. [CrossRef]
12. Cristie-David, A.S.; Marsh, E.N.G. Metal-dependent assembly of a protein nano-cage. *Protein Sci.* **2019**, *28*, 1620–1629. [CrossRef] [PubMed]
13. Liang, Y.; Furukawa, H.; Sakamoto, K.; Inaba, H.; Matsuura, K. Anticancer Activity of Reconstituted Ribonuclease S-Decorated Artificial Viral Capsid. *ChemBioChem* **2022**, *23*, e202200220. [CrossRef] [PubMed]
14. Olshefsky, A.; Richardson, C.; Pun, S.H.; King, N.P. Engineering Self-Assembling Protein Nanoparticles for Therapeutic Delivery. *Bioconjug Chem.* **2022**, *33*, 2018–2034. [CrossRef] [PubMed]
15. Luo, X.; Liu, J. Ultrasmall Luminescent Metal Nanoparticles: Surface Engineering Strategies for Biological Targeting and Imaging. *Adv. Sci.* **2022**, *9*, e2103971. [CrossRef] [PubMed]
16. Naskalska, A.; Borzęcka-Solarz, K.; Różycki, J.; Stupka, I.; Bochenek, M.; Pyza, E.; Heddle, J.G. Artificial Protein Cage Delivers Active Protein Cargos to the Cell Interior. *Biomacromolecules* **2021**, *22*, 4146–4154. [CrossRef] [PubMed]
17. Edwardson, T.G.W.; Tetter, S.; Hilvert, D. Two-tier supramolecular encapsulation of small molecules in a protein cage. *Nat. Commun.* **2020**, *11*, 5410. [CrossRef] [PubMed]
18. Stupka, I.; Azuma, Y.; Biela, A.P.; Imamura, M.; Scheuring, S.; Pyza, E.; Woźnicka, O.; Maskell, D.P.; Heddle, J.G. Chemically induced protein cage assembly with programmable opening and cargo release. *Sci. Adv.* **2022**, *8*, eabj9424. [CrossRef] [PubMed]
19. Miller, J.E.; Castells-Graells, R.; Arbing, M.A.; Munoz, A.; Jiang, Y.X.; Espinoza, C.T.; Nguyen, B.; Moroz, P.; Yeates, T.O. Design of Beta-2 Microglobulin Adsorbent Protein Nanoparticles Biomolecules. *Biomolecules* **2023**, *13*, 1122. [CrossRef] [PubMed]
20. Sasaki, E.; Böhringer, D.; Van De Waterbeemd, M.; Leibundgut, M.; Zschoche, R.; Heck, A.J.; Ban, N.; Hilvert, D. Structure and assembly of scalable porous protein cages. *Nat. Commun.* **2017**, *8*, 14663. [CrossRef]

21. Mashaghi, A.R.; Ramezanpour, A.; Karimipour, V. Investigation of a protein complex network. *Eur. Phys. J. B* **2004**, *41*, 113–121 [CrossRef]
22. Bjorken, J.D.; Drell, S.D. *Relativistic Quantum Fields*; McGraw-Hill: New York, NY, USA, 1965.
23. Vecchio, F. Brain network connectivity assessed using graph theory in frontotemporal dementia. *Neurology* **2013**, *81*, 134–143 [CrossRef]
24. Biggs, N.; Lloyd, E.; Wilson, R. *Graph Theory*; Oxford University Press: Oxford, UK, 1986.
25. Biggs, N. *Algebraic Graph Theory*, 2nd ed.; Cambridge University Press: Cambridge, UK, 1993; pp. 118–140, ISBN 0-521-45897-8.

axioms

MDPI

Article

Special Geometric Objects in Generalized Riemannian Spaces

Marko Stefanović [1,†], Nenad Vesić [2,†], Dušan Simjanović [3,†] and Branislav Randjelović [4,5,*,†]

1 Faculty of Sciences and Mathematics, University of Niš, 18000 Niš, Serbia; marko.stefanovic@pmf.edu.rs
2 Mathematical Institute of Serbian Academy of Sciences and Arts, University of Belgrade, 11000 Belgrade, Serbia; n.o.vesic@turing.mi.sanu.ac.rs
3 Faculty of Information Technology, Metropolitan University, 11158 Belgrade, Serbia; dusan.simjanovic@metropolitan.ac.rs
4 Faculty of Electronic Engineering, University of Niš, 18000 Niš, Serbia
5 Faculty of Teachers Education, University of Priština in K. Mitrovica, Leposavić, 38218 Leposavic, Serbia
* Correspondence: bane@elfak.ni.ac.rs
† These authors contributed equally to this work.

Abstract: In this paper, we obtained the geometrical objects that are common in different definitions of the generalized Riemannian spaces. These objects are analogies to the Thomas projective parameter and the Weyl projective tensor. After that, we obtained some geometrical objects important for applications in physics.

Keywords: Riemannian space; invariant of Thomas type; invariant of Weyl type; invariant; pressure; energy density; spin tensor

MSC: 53B05; 53B21; 53B50

1. Introduction

In many research articles, books, and monographs, Riemannian and pseudo-Riemannian spaces have been studied. Some of the most significant authors who have developed the theory of these spaces are L. P. Eisenhart [1], N. S. Sinyukov [2], J. Mikeš and his research group [3–6], I. Hinterleitner [7,8], S. E. Stepanov [9], and many others.

An N-dimensional manifold $\mathcal{M}_N$ equipped with the regular symmetric metric tensor $g_{\underline{ij}}$, $g_{\underline{ij}} = g_{\underline{ji}}$ is [2–6,10,11] the (pseudo-)Riemannian space $\overset{g}{\mathbb{R}}_N$, where $\underline{ij}$ denote the symmetrization with respect to indices i and j. The affine connection (Levi–Civita connection) coefficients of the space $\overset{g}{\mathbb{R}}_N$ are the Christoffel symbols $\Gamma^i_{\underline{jk}}$, $\Gamma^i_{\underline{jk}} = \Gamma^i_{\underline{kj}}$, where $\Gamma^i_{\underline{jk}} = g^{\underline{i\alpha}}\Gamma_{\alpha.\underline{jk}}$, $\Gamma_{i.\underline{jk}} = \frac{1}{2}\big(g_{\underline{ji},k} - g_{\underline{jk},i} + g_{\underline{ik},j}\big)$.

One kind of covariant derivative with respect to the symmetric metric tensor $g_{\underline{ij}}$ is

$$a^i_{j|_g k} = a^i_{j,k} + \Gamma^i_{\underline{\alpha k}} a^\alpha_j - \Gamma^\alpha_{\underline{jk}} a^i_\alpha, \tag{1}$$

for a tensor a^i_j of the type $(1,1)$, the Christoffel symbols $\Gamma^i_{\underline{jk}}$ and the partial derivative $\partial/\partial x^k$ are denoted by commas.

One Ricci identity [2–6] is founded with respect to the covariant derivative (1), $a^i_{j|_g m|_g n} - a_{j|_g n|_g m} = a^\alpha_j \overset{g}{R}{}^i_{\alpha mn} - a^i_\alpha \overset{g}{R}{}^\alpha_{jmn}$. With respect to this identity, the curvature tensor, the Ricci tensor, and the scalar curvature of the associated space $\overset{g}{\mathbb{R}}_N$ are obtained

$$\overset{g}{R}{}^i_{jmn} = \Gamma^i_{\underline{jm},n} - \Gamma^i_{\underline{jn},m} + \Gamma^\alpha_{\underline{jm}}\Gamma^i_{\underline{\alpha n}} - \Gamma^\alpha_{\underline{jn}}\Gamma^i_{\underline{\alpha m}}, \tag{2}$$

$$\overset{g}{R}_{ij} = \overset{g}{R}{}^\alpha_{ij\alpha} = \Gamma^\alpha_{\underline{ij},\alpha} - \Gamma^\alpha_{\underline{i\alpha},j} + \Gamma^\alpha_{\underline{ij}}\Gamma^\beta_{\underline{\alpha\beta}} - \Gamma^\alpha_{\underline{i\beta}}\Gamma^\beta_{\underline{j\alpha}}, \tag{3}$$

$$\overset{g}{R} = g^{\underline{\alpha\beta}}\overset{g}{R}_{\alpha\beta} = g^{\underline{\alpha\beta}}(\Gamma^\gamma_{\underline{\alpha\beta},\gamma} - \Gamma^\gamma_{\underline{\alpha\gamma},\beta} + \Gamma^\gamma_{\underline{\alpha\beta}}\Gamma^\delta_{\underline{\gamma\delta}} - \Gamma^\gamma_{\underline{\alpha\delta}}\Gamma^\delta_{\underline{\beta\gamma}}). \tag{4}$$

Based on research articles (L. P. Eisenhart, [10,11]), many researchers have studied and developed the theories of generalized Riemannian spaces and special kinds of them. The physical meaning of curvature tensors in the sense of Eisenhart's definition is presented in [12].

The studies about the affine connection spaces with torsion are started by the research of L. P. Eisenhart [13]. An N-dimensional manifold $\mathcal{M}_N$ equipped with the affine connection with torsion ∇, whose coefficients are L^i_{jk}, $L^i_{jk} \not\equiv L^i_{kj}$, for at least one pair of indices (j,k), is the (general) affine connection space $\mathbb{GA}_N$.

The symmetric and antisymmetric parts of the coefficients L^i_{jk} are

$$L^i_{\underline{jk}} = \frac{1}{2}(L^i_{jk} + L^i_{kj}) \quad \text{and} \quad L^i_{\underset{\vee}{jk}} = \frac{1}{2}(L^i_{jk} - L^i_{kj}).$$

The tensor $T^i_{jk} = 2L^i_{\underset{\vee}{jk}}$ is the torsion tensor for the space $\mathbb{GA}_N$.

The manifold $\mathcal{M}_N$ equipped with the torsion-free affine connection $\overset{0}{\nabla}$, whose coefficients are $L^i_{\underline{jk}}$, is the associated space $\mathbb{A}_N$ of the space $\mathbb{GA}_N$.

One kind of covariant derivative with respect to the affine connection $\overset{0}{\nabla}$ is [2–6]:

$$a^i_{j|k} = a^i_{j,k} + L^i_{\underline{\alpha k}}a^\alpha_j - L^\alpha_{\underline{jk}}a^i_\alpha.$$

The corresponding Ricci-type identity is $a^i_{j|mn} - a^i_{j|nm} = a^\alpha_j R^i_{\alpha mn} - a^i_\alpha R^\alpha_{jmn}$, where

$$R^i_{jmn} = L^i_{\underline{jm},n} - L^i_{\underline{jn},m} + L^\alpha_{\underline{jm}}L^i_{\underline{\alpha n}} - L^\alpha_{\underline{jn}}L^i_{\underline{\alpha m}}, \tag{5}$$

is the curvature tensor of the space $\mathbb{A}_N$.

The Ricci tensor of the associated space $\mathbb{A}_N$ is

$$R_{ij} = R^\alpha_{ij\alpha} = L^\alpha_{\underline{ij},\alpha} - L^\alpha_{\underline{i\alpha},j} + L^\alpha_{\underline{ij}}L^\beta_{\underline{\alpha\beta}} - L^\alpha_{\underline{i\beta}}L^\beta_{\underline{j\alpha}}. \tag{6}$$

1.1. Generalized Riemannian Spaces

An N-dimensional manifold $\mathcal{M}_N$ equipped with the nonsymmetric metric tensor g_{ij} is [1] the generalized Riemannian space $\mathbb{G}\overset{g}{\mathbb{R}}_N$ (in the Eisenhart's sense).

The symmetric and antisymmetric parts of the metric tensor g_{ij} are

$$g_{\underline{ij}} = \frac{1}{2}(g_{ij} + g_{ji}) \quad \text{and} \quad g_{\underset{\vee}{ij}} = \frac{1}{2}(g_{ij} - g_{ji}).$$

We assume that the matrix $[g_{\underline{ij}}]$ is regular. In this case, g_{ij} is a metric tensor of some Riemannian space, which we denote as $\overset{g}{\mathbb{R}}_N$. Hence, the components $g^{\underline{ij}}$ of the contravariant metric tensor are $[g^{\underline{ij}}] = [g_{\underline{ij}}]^{-1}$. For this reason, the equality $g^{\underline{i\alpha}}g_{\underline{j\alpha}} = \delta^i_j$ holds for the

Kronecker δ-symbol δ^i_j. For this reason, the tensors $g_{\underline{ij}}$ and $g^{\underline{ij}}$ are used for lowering and raising the indices in the $\mathbb{G}\overset{g}{\mathbb{R}}_N$ space.

The affine connection coefficients of the $\mathbb{G}\overset{g}{\mathbb{R}}_N$ space are the generalized Christoffell symbols [1]:

$$\Gamma^i_{jk} = \frac{1}{2} g^{\underline{i\alpha}} \left(g_{j\alpha,k} - g_{jk,\alpha} + g_{\alpha k,j} \right).$$

One obtains that the symmetric and antisymmetric parts $\Gamma^i_{\underline{jk}} = \frac{1}{2}\left(\Gamma^i_{jk} + \Gamma^i_{kj}\right)$ and $\Gamma^i_{\underset{\vee}{jk}} = \frac{1}{2}\left(\Gamma^i_{jk} - \Gamma^i_{kj}\right)$ are

$$\Gamma^i_{\underline{jk}} = \frac{1}{2} g^{\underline{i\alpha}} \left(g_{\underline{j\alpha},k} - g_{\underline{jk},\alpha} + g_{\underline{\alpha k},j} \right),$$

$$\Gamma^i_{\underset{\vee}{jk}} = -\frac{1}{2} g^{\underline{i\alpha}} \left(g_{\underset{\vee}{\alpha j},k} + g_{\underset{\vee}{jk},\alpha} - g_{\underset{\vee}{\alpha k},j} \right).$$

The tensor $2\Gamma^i_{\underset{\vee}{jk}}$ is the torsion tensor for the space $\mathbb{G}\overset{g}{\mathbb{R}}_N$.

Motivated by the Einstein Metricity Condition

$$g_{ij\wr k} = g_{ij,k} - \Gamma^\alpha_{ik} g_{\alpha j} - \Gamma^\alpha_{kj} g_{i\alpha} = 0,$$

S. Ivanov and M. Lj. Zlatanović (see [14,15]) obtained the generalized Riemannian space $\mathbb{GR}_N$, whose metric tensor is g_{ij}, but the affine connection coefficients are

$$L^i_{jk} = \Gamma^i_{\underline{jk}} - \frac{1}{2} g^{\underline{i\alpha}} \left(T_{j\alpha k} + T_{k\alpha j} + g_{\underline{k\alpha}\underset{1}{|}j} + g_{\underline{\alpha j}\underset{1}{|}k} - g_{\underline{jk}\underset{1}{|}\alpha} \right) + T^i_{jk}, \tag{7}$$

for $g_{\underline{ij}\underset{1}{|}k} = g_{\underline{ij},k} - L^\alpha_{ik} g_{\underline{\alpha j}} - L^\alpha_{jk} g_{\underline{i\alpha}}$ and the torsion tensor T^i_{jk}, $T^i_{jk} = -T^i_{kj}$.

The curvature tensor and the Ricci tensor of the associated space $\mathbb{R}_N$ are given by ((5) and (6)). The scalar curvature of the associated space $\mathbb{R}_N$ is

$$R = g^{\underline{\alpha\beta}} \left(L^\gamma_{\underline{\alpha\beta},\gamma} - L^\gamma_{\underline{\alpha\gamma},\beta} + L^\gamma_{\underline{\alpha\beta}} L^\delta_{\underline{\gamma\delta}} - L^\gamma_{\underline{\alpha\delta}} L^\delta_{\underline{\beta\gamma}} \right), \tag{8}$$

for the corresponding affine connection coefficients $L^i_{\underline{jk}}$.

The $\mathbb{GR}_N$ space obtained and used in [14,15] is a special kind of affine connection space $\mathbb{GA}_N$ in Eisenhart's sense [13].

1.2. Mappings of Space $\mathbb{A}_N$

Invariants of different mappings are significant objects in mathematical research. Unlike in the theory of fixed points, where the existence of an object whose value does not change under the action of a function is noted [16,17], in differential geometry, specific geometric objects are determined that do not change under the action of different mappings [2–6,18,19].

The generalized Riemannian space $\mathbb{G}\overset{g}{\mathbb{R}}_N$ in the Eisenhart's sense [1] is the special case of the affine connection space $\mathbb{GA}_N$ (see [13]).

A diffeomorphism $f : \mathbb{A}_N \to \overline{\mathbb{A}}_N$, in which the affine connection $\overset{0}{\nabla}$ of the space $\mathbb{A}_N$ transforms to the affine connection $\overset{0}{\overline{\nabla}}$ of the space $\overline{\mathbb{A}}_N$ is *the mapping* of the space $\mathbb{A}_N$.

If the mapping f transforms the affine connection coefficients $\underline{L}^i_{jk}$ which correspond to the affine connection $\overset{0}{\nabla}$ of the space $\mathbb{A}_N$ to the affine connection coefficients $\overline{\underline{L}}^i_{jk}$ of the affine connection $\overset{0}{\overline{\nabla}}$ of the space $\overline{\mathbb{A}}_N$, the tensor

$$\underline{P}^i_{jk} = \overline{\underline{L}}^i_{jk} - \underline{L}^i_{jk}, \tag{9}$$

is the deformation tensor for the mapping f.

After adding a symmetric tensor $\underline{\pi}^i_{jk}$, $\underline{\pi}^i_{jk} = \underline{\pi}^i_{kj}$ of the type $(1,2)$ to the affine connection coefficient $\underline{L}^i_{jk}$, i.e., $\underline{L}^i_{jk} \to \underline{L}^i_{jk} + \underline{\pi}^i_{jk}$, one obtains the geometrical objects $\tilde{\underline{L}}^i_{jk}$ which are the coefficients of the corresponding (unique) affine connection $\overset{0}{\tilde{\nabla}}$. For this reason, any deformation tensor $\underline{P}^i_{jk}$ generates unique mapping $f : \mathbb{A}_N \to \overline{\mathbb{A}}_N$.

Geodesic Mappings of Space $\mathbb{A}_N$

A curve $\ell = (\ell^i(t))$ in the space $\mathbb{A}_N$ is a curve that satisfies the following system of partial differential equations [2–6]

$$\frac{\partial^2 \ell^i}{\partial t^2} + \underline{L}^i_{\alpha\beta}\frac{d\ell^\alpha}{dt}\frac{d\ell^\beta}{dt} = \rho\frac{d\ell^i}{dt},$$

for a scalar function ρ.

A mapping $f : \mathbb{A}_N \to \bar{\mathbb{A}}_N$, which any geodesic line of space $\mathbb{A}_N$ transmits to a geodesic line of the space $\bar{\mathbb{A}}_N$, is the geodesic mapping [2–6].

The basic equation of geodesic mapping f is

$$\bar{\underline{L}}^i_{jk} = \underline{L}^i_{jk} + \psi_j\delta^i_k + \psi_k\delta^i_j, \tag{10}$$

for a 1-form ψ_j.

N. S. Sinyukov [2] and J. Mikeš with his research group [3–6] contracted the equality (10) by i and k, expressed the 1-form ψ_j as $\psi_j = \dfrac{1}{N+1}\big(\bar{\underline{L}}^\alpha_{j\alpha} - \underline{L}^\alpha_{j\alpha}\big)$, substituted this expression into the basic Equation (12), and obtained that it is $\bar{T}^{g}{}^i_{jk} = T^{g}{}^i_{jk}$ for

$$T^i_{jk} = \underline{L}^i_{jk} - \frac{1}{N+1}\big(\underline{L}^\alpha_{j\alpha}\delta^i_k + \underline{L}^\alpha_{k\alpha}\delta^i_j\big), \tag{11}$$

and the corresponding $\bar{T}^i_{jk}$. The geometric object T^i_{jk} is the Thomas Projective parameter initially obtained by T. Thomas [20].

After that, N. S. Sinyukov [2] and J. Mikeš with his collaborators [3–6] applied H. Weyl's methodology [21] to obtain invariant from the transformation of curvature tensor R^i_{jmn} caused by the basic Equation (10):

$$\bar{R}^i_{jmn} = R^i_{jmn} + (\psi_{j|n} - \psi_j\psi_n)\delta^i_m - (\psi_{j|m} - \psi_j\psi_m)\delta^i_n + (\psi_{m|n} - \psi_{n|m})\delta^i_j. \tag{12}$$

They contracted the relation (12) by i and j, and obtained that it is $\psi_{m|n} - \psi_{n|m} = R_{mn} - \bar{R}_{mn}$. The contraction of relation (12) by i and n gave

$$\psi_{j|m} - \psi_j\psi_m = \left(\frac{N}{N^2-1}R_{jm} + \frac{1}{N^2-1}R_{mj}\right) - \left(\frac{N}{N^2-1}\bar{R}_{jm} + \frac{1}{N^2-1}\bar{R}_{mj}\right). \tag{13}$$

When substituting the expression (13) into the Equation (12), they obtained the equality $\bar{W}^i_{jmn} = W^i_{jmn}$ for

$$W^i_{jmn} = R^i_{jmn} + \frac{1}{N+1}\delta^i_j(R_{mn} - R_{nm}) + \frac{1}{N^2-1}\Big((NR_{jn} + R_{nj})\delta^i_n - (NR_{jm} + R_{mj})\delta^i_n\Big), \tag{14}$$

and the corresponding $\bar{W}^i_{jmn}$.

All of the traces $W^\alpha_{jm\alpha}, W^\alpha_{j\alpha n}, W^\alpha_{\alpha mn}$ vanish. For this reason, it is not possible to use the Weyl projective tensor to obtain an invariant for the geodesic mapping that is a linear monic polynomial of Ricci tensor R_{ij}.

The last presented methodology was used for obtaining invariants of mappings defined on a nonsymmetric affine connection space $\mathbb{GA}_N$. Many authors have obtained significant results in these generalizations. Some of them are M. S. Stanković [22–24], M. Lj. Zlatanović [22–26], S. M. Minčić [23], M. S. Najdanović [27], and many others.

Preferred Methodology for Obtaining Invariants of Mappings

Motivated by the basic Equation (10) for geodesic mapping $f : \mathbb{A}_N \to \bar{\mathbb{A}}_N$, with substituted $\psi_j = \frac{1}{N+1}(\bar{L}^\alpha_{\underline{j\alpha}} - L^\alpha_{\underline{j\alpha}})$,

$$\bar{L}^i_{\underline{jk}} = L^i_{\underline{jk}} + \frac{1}{N+1}(\bar{L}^\alpha_{\underline{j\alpha}}\delta^i_k + \bar{L}^\alpha_{\underline{k\alpha}}\delta^i_j) - \frac{1}{N+1}(L^\alpha_{\underline{j\alpha}}\delta^i_k + L^\alpha_{\underline{k\alpha}}\delta^i_j), \tag{10a}$$

the methodology for obtaining invariants of a mapping $F : \mathbb{A}_N \to \bar{\mathbb{A}}_N$ is developed in the following way [19]:

- The deformation tensor $\bar{L}^i_{\underline{jk}} - L^i_{\underline{jk}}$ is expressed as

$$\bar{L}^i_{jk} - L^i_{jk} = \bar{\omega}^i_{\underline{jk}} - \omega^i_{\underline{jk}}, \tag{15}$$

  for geometrical objects $\omega^i_{\underline{jk}} = \omega_{kj} \in \mathbb{R}_N$, $\bar{\omega}^i_{\underline{jk}} = \bar{\omega}^i_{\underline{kj}} \in \bar{\mathbb{R}}_N$.
- In the next step, it was concluded that $\bar{L}^i_{\underline{jk}} - \bar{\omega}^i_{\underline{jk}} = L^i_{\underline{jk}} - \omega^i_{\underline{jk}}$. In this way, it was proved that the geometrical object $\mathcal{T}^i_{\underline{jk}} = L^i_{\underline{jk}} - \omega^i_{\underline{jk}}$ is an invariant for the mapping F. The geometrical object $\mathcal{T}^i_{\underline{jk}}$ is the associated basic invariant of Thomas type for the mapping F.
- In the next, based on the equality

$$\bar{\mathcal{T}}^i_{\underline{jm},n} - \bar{\mathcal{T}}^i_{\underline{jn},m} + \bar{\mathcal{T}}^\alpha_{\underline{jm}}\bar{\mathcal{T}}^i_{\underline{\alpha n}} - \bar{\mathcal{T}}^\alpha_{\underline{jn}}\bar{\mathcal{T}}^i_{\underline{\alpha m}} = \mathcal{T}^i_{\underline{jm},n} - \mathcal{T}^i_{\underline{jn},m} + \mathcal{T}^\alpha_{\underline{jm}}\mathcal{T}^i_{\underline{\alpha n}} - \mathcal{T}^\alpha_{\underline{jn}}\mathcal{T}^i_{\underline{\alpha m}},$$

  the next invariant for mapping F is obtained:

$$\mathcal{W}^i_{jmn} = R^i_{jmn} - \omega^i_{\underline{jm}|n} + \omega^i_{\underline{jn}|m} + \omega^\alpha_{\underline{jm}}\omega^i_{\underline{\alpha n}} - \omega^\alpha_{\underline{jn}}\omega^i_{\underline{\alpha m}}. \tag{16}$$

  The invariant $\mathcal{W}^i_{jmn}$ is the associated basic invariant of the Weyl type for the mapping F.
- After contracting the difference $\bar{\mathcal{W}}^i_{jmn} - \mathcal{W}^i_{jmn} = 0$, another invariant W^i_{jmn} for the mapping F was obtained.
- The trace $\mathcal{W}^\alpha_{ij\alpha}$ is a linear monic function of the Ricci tensor, unlike the trace $W^\alpha_{ij\alpha}$.

By using this methodology, we proved that two invariants with respect to the transformation of curvature tensor R^i_{jmn} may be obtained [28]. The trace $\mathcal{W}^\alpha_{ij\alpha}$ of the first of these two invariants is a monic linear polynomial of Ricci tensor R_{ij}.

In this paper, we focused on the associated invariants of Thomas and Weyl type of the third class for a special mapping. These invariants are (see the Equations (2.6, 2.9) in [19]):

$$\mathcal{T}^{i}_{(3).jk} = L^{i}_{\underline{jk}} + \frac{1}{2}P^{i}_{\underline{jk}}, \tag{17}$$

$$\mathcal{W}^{i}_{(3).jmn} = R^{i}_{jmn} + \frac{1}{2}P^{i}_{\underline{jm}|n} - \frac{1}{2}P^{i}_{\underline{jn}|m}, \tag{18}$$

where R^{i}_{jmn} is the curvature tensor of the associated space $\mathbb{A}_N$ and $P^{i}_{\underline{jk}} = \frac{1}{2}(P^{i}_{jk} + P^{i}_{kj})$.

1.3. Variations and Variational Derivatives

Let $f(x)$ be a continuously differentiable function defined on the interval $[a,b]$, $a \ll x \ll b$, and let $F[x,y,z]$ be a function of three variables. The expression

$$J[f] = \int_a^b F[x, f(x), f'(x)]dx,$$

where $f(x)$ ranges over the set of all continuously differentiable functions defined on the interval $[a,b]$, is a functional [29].

The variational (or functional) derivative $\delta J/\delta f$ of the operator $J[f]$ is [29,30]

$$\int \frac{\delta J}{\delta f}\phi(x)dx = \lim_{\varepsilon\to 0}\frac{J[f+\varepsilon\phi] - J[f]}{\varepsilon} = \left[\frac{d}{d\varepsilon}J[f+\varepsilon\varphi]\right]_{\varepsilon=0},$$

where ϕ is an arbitrary function.

For a scalar $\mathcal{L} = \mathcal{L}[f]$ in four-dimensional space and the corresponding operator $S = \int d^4x\mathcal{L}$, it satisfies the equalities

$$\frac{\delta S}{\delta f} = \int d^4x \frac{\delta \mathcal{L}}{\delta f}\delta f \quad \text{and} \quad \frac{\delta S_1 S_2}{\delta f} = \frac{\delta S_1}{\delta f}S_2 + S_1\frac{\delta S_2}{\delta f}.$$

In particular, it holds the equality $\dfrac{\delta \overset{g}{R}}{\delta g^{\underline{ij}}} = \overset{g}{R}_{ij}$.

1.4. Motivation

The Einstein–Hilbert action that corresponds to the symmetric metric tensor $g_{\underline{ij}}$ is [31]

$$\overset{g}{S} = \int d^4x\sqrt{|g|}(\overset{g}{R} - 2\Lambda + \mathcal{L}_M),$$

for a term $\mathcal{L}_M$ describing any matter fields appearing in the theory, the metric determinant $g = \det[g_{\underline{ij}}]$ and the cosmological constant $\Lambda = 1.1056 \times 10^{-52}m^{-2}$.

The Einstein's equations of motion are

$$\overset{g}{R}_{ij} - \frac{1}{2}\overset{g}{R}g_{\underline{ij}} + \frac{1}{2}\Lambda g_{\underline{ij}} = \overset{g}{T}_{ij}, \tag{19}$$

where $\overset{g}{T}_{ij}$ is the energy–momentum tensor.

In [32], the energy–momentum tensor $\overset{g}{T}_{ij}$ is expressed as

$$\overset{g}{T}_{ij} = \overset{g}{\rho}u_iu_j + q_iu_j + q_ju_i - (\overset{g}{p}h_{ij} + \pi_{ij}),$$

for the energy density $\overset{g}{\rho}$, the pressure $\overset{g}{p}$, the 4-velocity u_i, $u_\alpha u^\alpha = 1$, the 1-form q_i such that $u_\alpha q^\alpha = 0$, the trace-free tensor π_{ij} of type $(0,2)$ which, together with the 4-velocity u_i, satisfies the equality $\pi_{i\alpha}u^\alpha = 0$ and the tensor $h_{ij} = g_{\underline{ij}} - u_i u_j$.

The next equalities are satisfied [32]:

$$\overset{g}{\rho} = \overset{g}{T}_{\alpha\beta}u^\alpha u^\beta, \quad \text{and} \quad \overset{g}{p} = -\frac{1}{3}\overset{g}{T}{}^\alpha_\alpha + \frac{1}{3}\overset{g}{T}_{\alpha\beta}u^\alpha u^\beta.$$

The following equalities are satisfied [12,33]

$$\overset{g}{p} = \frac{1}{3}\overset{g}{R}_{\alpha\beta}u^\alpha u^\beta + \frac{1}{6}\overset{g}{R} - \Lambda \quad \text{and} \quad \overset{g}{\rho} = \overset{g}{R}_{\alpha\beta}u^\alpha u^\beta - \frac{1}{2}\overset{g}{R} + \Lambda, \tag{20}$$

in the reference system $u^i = g^{\underline{i\alpha}}u_\alpha$, such as

$$\overset{g}{p}_1 = \frac{1}{3}\overset{g}{R}_{11} + \frac{1}{6}\overset{g}{R} - \Lambda \quad \text{and} \quad \overset{g}{\rho}_1 = \overset{g}{R}_{11} - \frac{1}{2}\overset{g}{R} + \Lambda, \tag{21}$$

in the comoving reference system $u^i = g^{\underline{i\alpha}}u_\alpha = \delta^i_1$.

2. Main Results

With respect to Equation (7), we conclude the existence of the unique mapping $f : \mathbb{GR}_N \to \overset{g}{\mathbb{GR}}_N$ whose deformation tensor is

$$P^i_{jk} = \frac{1}{2}g^{\underline{i\alpha}}\big(T_{j\alpha k} + T_{k\alpha j} + g_{\underline{k\alpha}\underset{1}{|}j} + g_{\underline{j\alpha}\underset{1}{|}k} - g_{\underline{jk}\underset{1}{|}\alpha}\big) - T^i_{jk}.$$

In this section, we realize the next purposes of this paper: (1) To obtain the associated invariants of Thomas and Weyl type of the third class for the mapping $f : \mathbb{GR}_N \to \overset{g}{\mathbb{GR}}_N$, whose deformation tensor is given by (9); (2) To study the transformation rules of the pressure p and the energy density ρ with respect to the mapping $f : \mathbb{GR}_4 \to \overset{g}{\mathbb{GR}}_4$.

2.1. Invariants

After symmetrizing the Equation (7) by j and k, one obtains

$$\Gamma^i_{\underline{jk}} = L^i_{\underline{jk}} + \frac{1}{2}g^{\underline{i\alpha}}\Big(T_{j\alpha k} + T_{k\alpha j} + g_{\underline{k\alpha}\underset{1}{|}j} + g_{\underline{\alpha j}\underset{1}{|}k} - g_{\underline{jk}\underset{1}{|}\alpha}\Big). \tag{22}$$

From the last equation, after using the equalities

$$\Gamma^i_{\underline{jk}} - L^i_{\underline{jk}} = -\frac{1}{2}\overline{P}^i_{\underline{jk}} - \big(-\frac{1}{2}P^i_{\underline{jk}}\big) = \overline{\omega}^i_{(3).jk} - \omega^i_{(3).jk},$$

one obtains

$$\omega^i_{(3).jk} = -\frac{1}{4}g^{\underline{i\alpha}}\big(T_{j\alpha k} + T_{k\alpha j} + g_{\underline{k\alpha}\underset{1}{|}j} + g_{\underline{\alpha j}\underset{1}{|}k} - g_{\underline{jk}\underset{1}{|}\alpha}\big). \tag{23}$$

Based on $L^i_{jk} = L^i_{\underline{jk}} + \frac{1}{2}T^i_{jk}$, we conclude that $g_{\underline{ij}\underset{1}{|}k} = g_{\underline{ij}|k} - \frac{1}{2}T^\alpha_{ik}g_{\underline{\alpha j}} - \frac{1}{2}T^\alpha_{jk}g_{\underline{i\alpha}}$ such as

$$g^{\underline{i\alpha}}\big(g_{\underline{k\alpha}\underset{1}{|}j} + g_{\underline{j\alpha}\underset{1}{|}k} - g_{\underline{jk}\underset{1}{|}\alpha}\big) = g^{\underline{i\alpha}}\big(g_{\underline{k\alpha}|j} + g_{\underline{j\alpha}|k} - g_{\underline{jk}|\alpha}\big) - g^{\underline{i\alpha}}\big(T_{k\alpha j} + T_{j\alpha k}\big).$$

Hence, the geometrical object $\omega^i_{(3).jk}$ given by (23) reduces to

$$\omega^i_{(3).jk} = -\frac{1}{4}g^{\underline{i\alpha}}\big(g_{\underline{k\alpha}|j} + g_{\underline{j\alpha}|k} - g_{\underline{jk}|\alpha}\big). \tag{23a}$$

After substituting the expression (23a) into the Equations (17) and (18) multiplied by $\frac{4}{3}$, one obtains

$$\widetilde{\mathcal{T}}^i_{(3).jk} = L^i_{\underline{jk}} + \frac{1}{4} g^{\underline{i\alpha}} \big(g_{\underline{k\alpha}|j} + g_{\underline{j\alpha}|k} - g_{\underline{jk}|\alpha} \big), \tag{24}$$

$$\begin{aligned} \widetilde{W}^i_{(3).jmn} &= R^i_{jmn} - \frac{1}{3} g^{\underline{i\alpha}} \big(R_{j\alpha mn} - g_{[\underline{m\alpha}|jn]} + g_{\underline{j[m}|\alpha n]} \big) \\ &\quad - \frac{1}{3} \big(g^{\underline{i\alpha}}_{|[m} g_{\underline{n]\alpha}|j} + g^{\underline{i\alpha}}_{|[m} g_{\underline{\alpha j}|n]} - g^{\underline{i\alpha}}_{|[m} g_{\underline{jn]}|\alpha} \big). \end{aligned} \tag{25}$$

The next theorem holds.

Theorem 1. *Let $f : \mathbb{GR}_N \to \overset{g}{\mathbb{GR}}_N$ be the mapping which transforms the generalized Riemannian space $\mathbb{GR}_N$ in the sense of Ivanov and Zlatanović's definition [14] of the generalized Riemannian space $\overset{g}{\mathbb{GR}}_N$ in the sense of Eisenhart's definition [1]. The geometrical objects $\widetilde{\mathcal{T}}^i_{(3).jk}$ and $\widetilde{W}^i_{(3).jmn}$, given by (24), (25), are the associated basic invariants of the Thomas and Weyl type of the third class for the mapping f.*

2.2. Physical Examples

In this part of the paper, we compare the pressures, energy densities, and state parameters generated by the spaces $\overset{g}{\mathbb{GR}}_4$ and $\mathbb{GR}_4$. We also assume that the equality $\frac{\delta R}{\delta g^{\underline{ij}}} = R_{ij}$ holds for the contravariant metric tensor $g^{\underline{ij}}$ obtained from the metric tensor $g_{\underline{ij}}$.

Let us consider the Einstein–Hilbert action

$$S = \int d^4x \sqrt{|g|} \big(R - 2\Lambda + \mathcal{L}_M \big), \tag{26}$$

for the scalar curvature of the associated Riemannian space $\mathbb{R}_4$ in the sense of the definition from [14,15].

As in [12], after varying the Einstein–Hilbert action (26) by $g^{\underline{ij}}$ we obtain

$$R_{ij} - \frac{1}{2} R g_{\underline{ij}} + \frac{1}{2} \Lambda g_{\underline{ij}} = T_{ij}.$$

In a reference system $u^i = g^{\underline{i\alpha}} u_\alpha$, the pressure and the energy density are

$$p = \frac{1}{3} R_{\alpha\beta} u^\alpha u^\beta + \frac{1}{6} R - \Lambda, \tag{27}$$

$$\rho = R_{\alpha\beta} u^\alpha u^\beta - \frac{1}{2} R + \Lambda, \tag{28}$$

for the 4-velocity (u^1, u^2, u^3, u^4).

In the comoving reference system $u^i = g^{\underline{i\alpha}} u_\alpha = \delta^i_1$, the pressure and the energy densitygiven by (27), (28) reduce to

$$p_1 = \frac{1}{3} R_{11} + \frac{1}{6} R - \Lambda, \tag{29}$$

$$\rho_1 = R_{11} - \frac{1}{2} R + \Lambda. \tag{30}$$

With respect to Equations (22) and (23a), we get

$$\Gamma^i_{\underline{jk}} = L^i_{\underline{jk}} + \frac{1}{2} g^{\underline{i\alpha}} \big(g_{\underline{k\alpha}|j} + g_{\underline{j\alpha}|k} - g_{\underline{jk}|\alpha} \big) \equiv L^i_{\underline{jk}} - 2\omega^i_{(3).jk}, \tag{22a}$$

for the tensor $\omega^i_{(3).jk}$ given by (23a).

After substituting the expression (22a) in Equations (3), (4), (6), and (8), one obtains

$$\overset{g}{R}_{ij} = R_{ij} - 2\big(\omega^{\alpha}_{(3).ij|\alpha} - \omega^{\alpha}_{(3).i\alpha|j}\big) + 4\big(\omega^{\alpha}_{(3).ij}\omega^{\beta}_{(3).\alpha\beta} - \omega^{\alpha}_{(3).i\beta}\omega^{\beta}_{(3).j\alpha}\big), \quad (31)$$

$$\overset{g}{R} = R - 2g^{\underline{\alpha\beta}}\big(\omega^{\gamma}_{(3).\alpha\beta|\gamma} - \omega^{\gamma}_{(3).\alpha\gamma|\beta}\big) + 4g^{\underline{\alpha\beta}}\big(\omega^{\gamma}_{(3).\alpha\beta}\omega^{\delta}_{(3).\gamma\delta} - \omega^{\gamma}_{(3).\alpha\delta}\omega^{\delta}_{(3).\beta\gamma}\big). \quad (32)$$

As we concluded above, the symmetric part of the deformation tensor for the mapping $f : \mathbb{GR}_4 \to \overset{g}{\mathbb{GR}}_4$ is $P^{i}_{\underline{jk}} = -2\omega^{i}_{(3).jk}$. Hence, the geometrical object $\omega^{i}_{(3).jk}\omega^{p}_{(3).qr}$ is an invariant for the mapping f. The contravariant symmetric metric tensor $g^{\underline{ij}}$ is also an invariant for the mapping f.

If one substitutes Equations (31) and (32) in the expressions (19)–(21), (27)–(30), one will complete the proof for the next theorem.

Theorem 2. *The mapping $f : \mathbb{GR}_4 \to \overset{g}{\mathbb{GR}}_4$ transforms the energy–momentum tensor T_{ij} to the energy–momentum tensor $\overset{g}{T}_{ij}$ by the rule*

$$\overset{g}{T}_{ij} = T_{ij} - 2\omega^{\alpha}_{(3).ij|\alpha} + 2\omega^{\alpha}_{(3).i\alpha|j} + g^{\underline{\alpha\beta}}\big(\omega^{\gamma}_{(3).\alpha\beta|\gamma} - \omega^{\gamma}_{(3).\alpha\gamma|\beta}\big)g_{\underline{ij}}.$$

The following equalities $\mathbf{E}_1 - \mathbf{E}_4$ are equivalent

$$\mathbf{E}_1 : \ T_{ij} = \overset{g}{T}_{ij}, \qquad \mathbf{E}_2 : \ \omega^{\alpha}_{(3).ij|\alpha} - \omega^{\alpha}_{(3).i\alpha|j} = \frac{1}{2}g^{\underline{\alpha\beta}}\big(\omega^{\gamma}_{(3).\alpha\beta|\gamma} - \omega^{\gamma}_{(3).\alpha\gamma|\beta}\big)g_{\underline{ij}},$$

$$\mathbf{E}_3 : \ \omega^{\alpha}_{(3).ij|\alpha} = \omega^{\alpha}_{(3).i\alpha|j}, \quad \mathbf{E}_4 : \ g^{\underline{\alpha\beta}}\big(\omega^{\gamma}_{(3).\alpha\beta|\gamma} - \omega^{\gamma}_{(3).\alpha\gamma|\beta}\big) = 0.$$

The pressures p and $\overset{g}{p}$ obtained with respect to the spaces $\mathbb{GR}_4$ and $\overset{g}{\mathbb{GR}}_4$ satisfy the equation

$$\overset{g}{p} = p - \frac{1}{3}\big(\omega^{\gamma}_{(3).\alpha\beta|\gamma} - \omega^{\gamma}_{(3).\alpha\gamma|\beta}\big)\cdot\big(2u^{\alpha}u^{\beta} + g^{\underline{\alpha\beta}}\big). \quad (33)$$

In the comoving reference system $u^i = g^{\underline{i\alpha}}u_\alpha = \delta^i_1$, the Equation (33) reduces to

$$\overset{g}{p}_1 = p_1 - \frac{2}{3}\big(\omega^{\alpha}_{(3).11|\alpha} - \omega^{\alpha}_{(3).1\alpha|1}\big) - \frac{1}{3}g^{\underline{\alpha\beta}}\big(\omega^{\gamma}_{(3).\alpha\beta|\gamma} - \omega^{\gamma}_{(3).\alpha\gamma|\beta}\big).$$

The pressure p is an invariant for the mapping $f : \mathbb{GR}_4 \to \overset{g}{\mathbb{GR}}_4$ if and only if

$$0 = \big(\omega^{\gamma}_{(3).\alpha\beta|\gamma} - \omega^{\gamma}_{(3).\alpha\gamma|\beta}\big)\cdot\big(2u^{\alpha}u^{\beta} + g^{\underline{\alpha\beta}}\big). \quad (34)$$

In the comoving reference system $u^i = g^{\underline{i\alpha}}u_\alpha = \delta^i_1$, the condition (34) reduces to

$$\omega^{\alpha}_{(3).11|\alpha} - \omega^{\alpha}_{(3).1\alpha|1} = -\frac{1}{2}g^{\underline{\alpha\beta}}\big(\omega^{\gamma}_{(3).\alpha\beta|\gamma} - \omega^{\gamma}_{(3).\alpha\gamma|\beta}\big).$$

The energy densities ρ and $\overset{g}{\rho}$ obtained with respect to the spaces $\mathbb{GR}_4$ and $\overset{g}{\mathbb{GR}}_4$ satisfy the equation

$$\overset{g}{\rho} = \rho - \big(\omega^{\gamma}_{(3).\alpha\beta|\gamma} - \omega^{\gamma}_{(3).\alpha\gamma|\beta}\big)\cdot\big(2u^{\alpha}u^{\beta} - g^{\underline{\alpha\beta}}\big).$$

In the comoving reference system $u^i = g^{\underline{i\alpha}}u_\alpha = \delta^i_1$, the Equation (33) reduces to

$$\overset{g}{\rho}_1 = \rho_1 - 2\big(\omega^{\alpha}_{(3).11|\alpha} - \omega^{\alpha}_{(3).1\alpha|1}\big) + g^{\underline{\alpha\beta}}\big(\omega^{\gamma}_{(3).\alpha\beta|\gamma} - \omega^{\gamma}_{(3).\alpha\gamma|\beta}\big).$$

The energy density ρ is an invariant for the mapping $f : \mathbb{GR}_4 \to \overset{g}{\mathbb{GR}}_4$ if and only if

$$0 = \left(\omega^{\gamma}_{(3).\alpha\beta|\gamma} - \omega^{\gamma}_{(3).\alpha\gamma|\beta}\right) \cdot \left(2u^{\alpha}u^{\beta} - g^{\underline{\alpha\beta}}\right). \tag{35}$$

In the comoving reference system $u^i = g^{\underline{i\alpha}} u_\alpha = \delta^i_1$, the condition (35) reduces to

$$\omega^{\alpha}_{(3).11|\alpha} - \omega^{\alpha}_{(3).1\alpha|1} = \frac{1}{2} g^{\underline{\alpha\beta}} \left(\omega^{\gamma}_{(3).\alpha\beta|\gamma} - \omega^{\gamma}_{(3).\alpha\gamma|\beta}\right).$$

The geometrical object $\omega^i_{(3).jk}$ used in this theorem is given by (23a).

2.3. Contorsion and Spin Tensors

The covariant contorsion tensor of space $\mathbb{GR}_N$ is

$$K_{ijk} = \frac{1}{2} g^{\underline{i\alpha}} \left(\underset{\vee}{L_{\alpha.jk}} - \underset{\vee}{L_{j.\alpha k}} + \underset{\vee}{L_{k.\alpha j}}\right).$$

The corresponding spin tensor is [34]

$$\sigma^i_{jk} = \frac{1}{\kappa} g^{\underline{i\alpha}} \left(\underset{\vee}{L_{i.j\alpha}} + \delta^i_j \underset{\vee}{L^{\alpha}_{k\alpha}} - \delta^i_k \underset{\vee}{L^{\alpha}_{j\alpha}}\right). \tag{36}$$

After lowering the index i in (36), we obtain the covariant spin tensor

$$\sigma_{ijk} = \frac{1}{\kappa} g^{\underline{\alpha\beta}} \left(g_{\underline{k\alpha}} \underset{\vee}{L_{i.j\beta}} + g_{\underline{ik}} \underset{\vee}{L_{j.\alpha\beta}} - g_{\underline{jk}} \underset{\vee}{L_{k.\alpha\beta}}\right) = \frac{1}{\kappa} \underset{\vee}{L_{i.jk}}.$$

3. Conclusions

In this paper, we connected different definitions of generalized Riemannian spaces through their corresponding mapping.

In Section 2.1, we obtained the associated invariants of Thomas and Weyl type for this mapping. The Purpose 1 of this paper is realized in this section.

In Section 2.2, we analyzed some physical terms and their changes with respect to transformation from one to another definition of the generalized Riemannian space. We obtained the necessary and sufficient conditions for these terms to be invariant under this transformation.

Author Contributions: All authors have equal contributions. Conceptualization, M.S., N.V., D.S. and B.R.; Methodology, M.S., N.V., D.S. and B.R.; Software, M.S., N.V., D.S. and B.R.; Validation, M.S., N.V., D.S. and B.R.; Formal analysis, M.S., N.V., D.S. and B.R.; Investigation, M.S., N.V., D.S. and B.R.; Resources, M.S., N.V., D.S. and B.R.; Data curation, M.S., N.V., D.S. and B.R.; Writing—original draft, M.S., N.V., D.S. and B.R.; Writing—review & editing, M.S., N.V., D.S. and B.R.; Visualization, M.S., N.V., D.S. and B.R.; Supervision, M.S., N.V., D.S. and B.R.; Project administration, M.S., N.V., D.S. and B.R.; Funding acquisition, M.S., N.V., D.S. and B.R. All authors have read and agreed to the published version of the manuscript.

Funding: This paper is partially supported by the Ministry of Science and Technological Development through grants 451-03-65/2024-03/200102 and 451-03-65/2024-03/200251.

Data Availability Statement: No new data were created or analyzed in this study. Data sharing is not applicable to this article.

Acknowledgments: Nenad Vesić wishes to thank the Serbian Ministry of Science, Technological Developments, and Patents, which financially supported this research through the Mathematical Institute of Serbian Academy of Sciences and Arts.

Conflicts of Interest: The authors declare no conflicts of interest.

References

1. Eisenhart, L.P. *Riemannian Geometry*; Princeton University Press: London, UK; Humphrey Milfold, Oxford University Press: Oxford, UK, 1926.
2. Sinyukov, N.S. *Geodesic Mappings of Riemannian Spaces*; Nauka: Moscow, Russia, 1979. (In Russian)
3. Mikeš, J.; Stepanova, E.; Vanžurová, A.; Bácsó, S.; Berezovski, V.E.; Chepurna, O.; Chodorová, M.; Chudá, H.; Gavrilchenko, M.L.; Haddad, M.L. *Differential Geometry of Special Mappings*; Palacký University: Olomouc, Czech Republic, 2019.
4. Mikeš, J.; Berezovski, V.E.; Stepanova, E.; Chudá, H. Geodesic Mappings and Their Generalizations. *J. Math. Sci.* **2016**, *217*, 607–623. [CrossRef]
5. Mikeš, J.; Stepanova, E.; Vanžurová, A.; Bácsó, S.; Berezovski, V.E.; Chepurna, O.; Chodorová, M.; Chudá, H.; Gavrilchenko, M.L.; Haddad, M.L. *Differential Geometry of Special Mappings*; Palacký University: Olomouc, Czech Republic, 2015.
6. Mikeš, J.; Vanžurová, A.; Hinterleitner, I. *Geodesic Mappings and Some Generalizations*; Palacký University: Olomouc, Czech Republic, 2009.
7. Hinterleitner, I. 4-planar Mappings of Quaternionic Kähler Manifolds. In *Geometric Methods in Physics, XXXI Workshop 2012 Trends in Mathematics*; Birkhäuser: Basel, Switzerland, 2013; pp. 187–193.
8. Hinterleitner, I.; Mikeš, J. Geodesic mappings of (pseudo-) Riemannian manifolds preserve class of differentiability. *Miskolc Math. Notes* **2013**, *14*, 575–582. [CrossRef]
9. Stepanov, S.E.; Mikeš, J. Betti and Tachibana numbers of compact Riemannian manifolds. *Diff. Geom. Appl.* **2013**, *31*, 486–495. [CrossRef]
10. Eisenhart, L.P. Generalized Riemannian Spaces. *Proc. Natl. Acad. Sci. USA* **1951**, *37*, 311–315. [CrossRef] [PubMed]
11. Eisenhart, L.P. Generalized Riemannian Spaces, II. *Proc. Natl. Acad. Sci. USA* **1952**, *38*, 505–508. [CrossRef] [PubMed]
12. Vesić, N.O. Cosmological Meaning of Geometric Curvatures. *Filomat* **2020**, *34*, 4107–4121. [CrossRef]
13. Eisenhart, L.P. *Non-Riemannian Geometry*; Courier Corporation: New York, NY, USA, 1927.
14. Ivanov, S.; Zlatanović, M. Connections on a non-symmetric (generalized) Riemannian manifold and gravity. *Class. Quantum Gravity* **2016**, *33*, 075016. [CrossRef]
15. Ivanov, S.; Zlatanović, M. Non-symmetric Riemannian gravity and Sasaki-Einstein 5-manifolds. *Class. Quantum Gravity* **2020**, *37*, 025002. [CrossRef]
16. Ješic, S.N.; Cirovic, N.A.; Nikolic, R.M.; Rand-elovic, B.M. A fixed point theorem in strictly convex *b*-fuzzy metric spaces. *AIMS Math.* **2023**, *8*, 20989–21000. [CrossRef]
17. Ranđelović, B.M.; Ćirović, N.A.; Ješic, S.N. A Characterisation of Completeness of *B*-Fuzzy Metric Spaces and Nonlinear Contractions. *Appl. Anal. Discret. Math.* **2021**, *15*, 233–242. [CrossRef]
18. Simjanović, D.J.; Vesić, N.O. Novel Invariants for Almost Geodesic Mappings of the Third Type. *Miskolc Math. Notes* **2021**, *22*, 961–975. [CrossRef]
19. Vesić, N.O. Basic Invariants of Geometric Mappings. *Miskolc Math. Notes* **2020**, *21*, 473–487. [CrossRef]
20. Thomas, T.Y. On the projective and equi-projective geometries of paths. *Proc. Nat. Acad. Sci. USA* **1925**, *11*, 199–203. [CrossRef] [PubMed]
21. Weyl, H. Zur infinitesimal geometrie: Einordnung der projectiven und der konformen auffssung. *Gott. Nachrichten* **1921**, *11* , 99–112.
22. Stanković, M.S.; Ćirić, M.S.; Zlatanović, M.L. Geodesic mappings of equiaffine and anti-equiaffine general affine connection spaces preserving torsion. *Filomat* **2012**, *26*, 439–451. [CrossRef]
23. Stanković, M.S.; Minčić, S.M.; Velimirović, L.S.; Zlatanović, M.L. On Equitorsion Geodesic Mappings of General Affine Connection Space. *Rend. Semin. Mat. 'Universita' Padova/Math. J. Univ. Padova* **2010**, *124*, 77–90. [CrossRef]
24. Stanković, M.S.; Zlatanović, M.L.; Velimirović, L.S. Equitorsion Holomorphically Projective Mappings of Generalized Kählerian Space of the Second Kind. *Int. Electron. J. Geom.* **2010**, *3*, 26–39.
25. Zlatanović, M.L. New projective tensors for equitorsion geodesic mappings. *Appl. Math. Lett.* **2012**, *25*, 890–897. [CrossRef]
26. Zlatanović, M.L.; Stanković, V.M. Some invariants of holomorphically projective mappings of generalized Kählerian spaces. *J. Math. Anal. Appl.* **2018**, *458*, 601–610. [CrossRef]
27. Najdanović, M.S.; Zlatanović, M.L.; Hinterleitner, I. Conformal and Geodesic Mappings of Generalized Equidistant Spaces. *Publ. Inst. Math.* **2015**, *98*, 71–84. [CrossRef]
28. Vesić, N.O.; Milenković, V.M.; Stanković, M.S. Two Invariants for Geometric Mappings. *Axioms* **2022**, *11*, 239. [CrossRef]
29. Gelfand, I.M.; Fomin, S.V. *Calculus of Variations*; Silverman, R.A., Translator; Revised English Edition; Prentice-Hall, Inc.: Hoboken, NJ, USA, 1963.
30. Blau, M. *Lecture Notes on General Relativity*; Albert Einstein Center for Fundamental Physics, Universität Bern: Bern, Switzerland, 2015.
31. Sean, C.M. *Spacetime and Geometry: An Introduction to General Relativity*; Addison-Wesley: San Franciso, CA, USA, 2004.
32. Madsen, M.S. Scalar Fields Curved Spacetimes. *Class. Quantum Gravity* **1988**, *5*, 627–639. [CrossRef]

33. Vesić, N.O.; Dimitrijević, D.D.; Simjanović, D.J. Generalized Riemannian Spaces With Respect to 4-Velocity Vectors and Functions of State Parameters. *Filomat* **2020**, *35*, 1519–1541. [CrossRef]
34. Hehl, F.W.; von der Heyde, P.; Kerlick, G.D.; Nester, J.M. General relativity with spin and torison: Foundations and prospects. *Rev. Mod. Phys.* **1976**, *48*, 393–416. [CrossRef]

axioms

MDPI

Article

Well-Posedness of the Schrödinger–Korteweg–de Vries System with Robin Boundary Conditions on the Half-Line

Po-Chun Huang [1,*] and Bo-Yu Pan [2]

1 Department of Mathematics, National Tsing Hua University, Hsinchu 300044, Taiwan
2 Department of Applied Mathematics, National Chung Hsing University, Taichung 402, Taiwan; pan740102@gmail.com
* Correspondence: d917205@oz.nthu.edu.tw

Abstract: The Schrödinger–Korteweg–de Vries (SKdV) system can describe the nonlinear dynamics of phenomena such as Langmuir and ion acoustic waves, which are highly valuable for studying wave behavior and interactions. The SKdV system has wide-ranging applications in physics and applied mathematics. In this article, we investigate the local well-posedness of the SKdV system with Robin boundary conditions and polynomial terms in the Sobolev space. We want to enhance the applicability of this type of SKdV system. Our verification process is as follows: We estimate Fokas solutions for the Robin problem with external forces. Next, we define an iteration map in suitable solution space and prove the iteration map is a contraction mapping and onto some closed ball $B(0,r)$. Finally, by the contraction mapping theorem, we obtain the uniqueness solution. Moreover, we show that the data-to-solution map is locally Lipschitz continuous and conclude with the well-posedness of the SKdV system.

Keywords: Schrödinger–Korteweg–de Vries system; the local well-posedness of the Schrödinger–Korteweg–de Vries system; unified transform method; Robin boundary condition

MSC: 35A01; 35A02

1. Introduction and Main Results

1.1. Introduction

In this article, we study the local well-posedness of the following Schrödinger–Korteweg–de Vries (SKdV) system:

$$\begin{cases} i\partial_t u + \partial_x^2 u = P(u)v, & x \in (0,\infty),\ t \in (0,T), \\ \partial_t v + \partial_x^3 v = Q(v)v_x, & x \in (0,\infty),\ t \in (0,T), \\ u(x,0) = u_0(x) \in H_x^s(0,\infty),\ v(x,0) = v_0(x) \in H_x^s(0,\infty), & x \in [0,\infty), \\ u_x(0,t) - \gamma_1 u(0,t) = g_1(t) \in H_t^{(2s-1)/4}(0,T), & t \in (0,T),\ \gamma_1 \geq 1, \\ v_x(0,t) - \gamma_2 v(0,t) = g_2(t) \in H_t^{s/3}(0,T), & t \in (0,T),\ \gamma_2 > 0, \end{cases}$$

where $0 < T < 1, 3/4 < s < 1$, $u(x,t)$ is a complex-valued function, $v(x,t)$ is a real-valued function, and

$$P(u) = \sum_{i=0}^{m} a_i u^i \text{ and } Q(v) = \sum_{j=0}^{n} b_j v^j$$

are polynomials, where a_i and b_j are constants. Well-posedness guarantees the reliability and predictive accuracy of equation models in various fields, making it essential for scientific research, engineering applications, and decision-making. According to our current understanding from studies on the SKdV system, we investigate the local well-posedness of the SKdV system with Robin boundary conditions. We consider the local well-posedness of the SKdV system with Robin boundary conditions from a mathematical point of view.

The right side of the equals sign of this system is composed of polynomials mainly because we hope to use polynomials to approximate any arbitrary continuous function, allowing it to be applied to different SKdV systems.

Next, we introduce the SKdV system. The SKdV system is a coupled nonlinear partial differential system consisting of the Schrödinger equation, which describes complex-valued functions, and the Korteweg–de Vries (KdV) equation, which describes real-valued functions. The Schrödinger equation characterizes the temporal evolution of the wave function, while the KdV equation describes the propagation and interaction of nonlinear waves. This system integrates the properties of two types of waves: short waves (described by the Schrödinger equation) and long waves (described by the KdV equation), making it highly applicable to the study of wave phenomena and dynamic behavior.

The SKdV system has wide applications in physics and applied mathematics. In the study of nonlinear waves, the SKdV system can describe the nonlinear dynamics of phenomena such as Langmuir waves and ion acoustic waves, which is very useful for studying wave behavior and interactions [1,2]. In plasma physics, the SKdV system is used to describe wave phenomena in plasmas, such as the interactions between Langmuir waves and ion acoustic waves. This is crucial to understanding the properties and behavior of plasmas [3–7]. In fluid dynamics, the SKdV system is used to study wave phenomena in fluids, such as the nonlinear interactions between short and long waves, and to describe the behavior of water waves under nonlinear and dispersive effects [8,9]. In the field of optics, the SKdV system can be used to describe nonlinear wave and dispersion effects in optical fibers. This helps to understand the propagation characteristics of light in optical fibers and the impact of nonlinear effects on wave behavior [10]. In wave dynamics, the SKdV system is used to describe the propagation and interaction of water waves, which has important applications in oceanography and marine engineering. For example, this system can be used to study the resonant interactions between short and long waves on the water surface [11]. In the control theory of dynamical systems, the SKdV system is used to study the dynamic behavior and control methods of systems [12]. In fractal dynamics, the SKdV system is used to describe dynamical systems with fractal characteristics, and the behavior and properties of such systems are further studied [13,14]. In the study of chaotic synchronization, the SKdV system is used to investigate synchronization phenomena and control methods in chaotic systems [15]. These applications demonstrate the versatile use of the SKdV system in various fields and provide a deep understanding of the dynamic behavior of such systems and control methods.

We present some relatively new research on the SKdV system. Shang, Li, and Li [16] investigate traveling wave solutions of a coupled Schrödinger–Korteweg–de Vries equation using the generalized coupled trial equation method. The researchers have utilized this method to discover a series of exact traveling wave solutions, which hold significant importance in understanding various processes in dusty plasma. This study provides an effective solution for nonlinear evolution equation systems and highlights the practical applications of these equations in physics. Khan, Khan, and Ahmad [17] investigated the fractal fractional nonlinear Korteweg–de-Vries–Schrödinger system with a power law kernel. The study utilizes the Yang transform and Caputo fractional fractal operator, applying the Yang transform homotopy perturbation method to solve this system. The research aims to analyze the existence and uniqueness of the solution and provides graphical representations of the results. The article also involves fixed point theory and nonlinear functional analysis to delve into this challenging mathematical problem. Noor, Alotaibi, Shah, Ismaeel, and El-Tantawy [18] analyze solitary waves and nonlinear oscillations of the fractional Schrödinger–KdV equation using the Caputo Operator framework. They employ the Laplace residual power series method (LRPSM) to study this model and compare the resulting approximations with exact solutions in the integer case. Their research shows that the approximations are highly accurate and more stable over large space-time domains.

Now, we present recent articles that discuss the existence, uniqueness, and well-posedness of solutions associated with the SKdV system. Guo and Miao [6] studied the well-posedness of the Cauchy problem for the SKdV system. By establishing global well-posedness in specific function spaces, this research explored the nonlinear dynamics equations describing one-dimensional Langmuir and ion acoustic waves. The work focused on the mathematical properties of the system, the existence and uniqueness of solutions, and the relationship between the electric field of Langmuir oscillations and low-frequency density perturbations. Corcho and Linares [12] studied the well-posedness of the Cauchy problem for the SKdV system. The authors studied the local well-posedness for weak initial data and obtained well-posedness results for data in Sobolev space $L^2(\mathbb{R}) \times H^{-\frac{3}{4}+}$. These results also led to global well-posedness in energy space $H^1(\mathbb{R}) \times H^1(\mathbb{R})$. The authors improved upon previous research on the well-posedness of the SKdV system. Matheus [19] showed that the Cauchy problem for the SKdV system with periodic functions is globally well-posed in the energy space $H^1 \times H^1$. The study used the I-method introduced by Colliander et al. and improved the results of Arbieto et al. on the global well-posedness of the SKdV system. The author conducted a thorough investigation and proof of the global well-posedness of the SKdV system for periodic functions. Guo and Wang [7] studied the well-posedness of the SKdV system, in particular, for initial data in the Sobolev spaces $L^2(\mathbb{R}) \times H^{-3/4}(\mathbb{R})$ and $H^s(\mathbb{R}) \times H^{-3/4}(\mathbb{R})$ $(s > -1/16)$. The article introduced F^s-type spaces to handle the KdV component and coupling terms of the system, overcoming difficulties arising from the lack of scale invariance through unified estimates of multipliers. The authors demonstrated the local well-posedness of the SKdV system for certain initial data under resonance conditions.

Wang and Cui [20] established the local well-posedness of the Cauchy problem for the SKdV system in different function spaces. Using bilinear estimates and other techniques, the authors presented results on the local well-posedness of the system under certain conditions. Guo, Ma, and Zhang [21] investigated the global existence and uniqueness of solutions for the fractional SKdV system. Using the contraction method, the authors addressed local existence and uniqueness and proved the global existence of solutions over time using a priori estimates. Cavalcante and Corcho [10] studied the local progress theory of the SKdV system on the half-line. Cavalcante and Corcho [22] studied the well-posedness and lower bounds of the growth of weighted norms for the SKdV system on the half-line. The authors studied the initial boundary value problem for the SKdV system, analyzing the growth of the weighted norms of the solutions over time. By studying the dynamical properties and norm growth of the SKdV system, they determined the well-posedness and lower bounds, thus gaining a deeper understanding of the behavior and characteristics of this nonlinear evolution system. Chen [23] studied the periodic solutions of the SKdV system, in particular, the influence of boundary and external forces on the solutions. The author discussed the existence of theorems for periodic, quasi-periodic, and nearly periodic solutions, investigating their properties and characteristics under various conditions. The focus was on the stability and periodicity of the solutions, as well as on the influence of external forces on the dynamical behavior of the system. Compaan, Shin, and Tzirakis [24] studied the well-posedness of the SKdV system on the half-line. By applying multilinear harmonic analysis techniques, the authors improved the well-posedness theory based on L^2 solutions. They studied the local well-posedness and global existence of the system and proposed theorems describing the behavior of the solutions. In addition, they discussed the smoothing effects and the growth of the solutions under different parameter conditions. Himonas and Yan [11] investigated the well-posedness of the initial boundary value problem for the SKdV system on the half-line. Using the Fokas unified transform method, they analyzed the well-posedness of the problem, discussing linear space-time estimates and quadratic/cubic estimates in Bourgain space.

After introducing the SKdV system, the main research of this paper will be presented next.

1.2. Main Results

In this paper, we demonstrate the local well-posedness of the SKdV system presented below.

$$\begin{cases} i\partial_t u + \partial_x^2 u = P(u)v, & x \in (0,\infty),\ t \in (0,T), \\ \partial_t v + \partial_x^3 v = Q(v)v_x, & x \in (0,\infty),\ t \in (0,T), \\ u(x,0) = u_0(x),\ v(x,0) = v_0(x), & x \in [0,\infty), \\ u_x(0,t) - \gamma_1 u(0,t) = g_1(t), & t \in (0,T),\ \gamma_1 \geq 1, \\ v_x(0,t) - \gamma_2 v(0,t) = g_2(t), & t \in (0,T),\ \gamma_2 > 0, \end{cases} \tag{1}$$

where $0 < T < 1$, $u(x,t)$ is a complex-valued function, $v(x,t)$ is a real-valued function,

$$P(u) = \sum_{i=0}^{m} a_i u^i \text{ and } Q(v) = \sum_{j=0}^{n} b_j v^j$$

are polynomials, a_i and b_j are constants, and $u_0(x) \in H_x^s(0,\infty)$ and $v_0(x) \in H_x^s(0,\infty)$ are initial data with $3/4 < s < 1$. The boundary data $g_1(t) \in H_t^{(2s-1)/4}(0,T)$ and $g_2(t) \in H_t^{s/3}(0,T)$ are suggested by the time regularity of the boundary value problems (BVPs) for the corresponding linear equations.

In this article, we demonstrate the local well-posedness of the initial boundary value problem (IBVP) (1). The proof consists of four steps. In the first step, we replace the nonlinear terms $P(u)v$ and $Q(v)v_x$ with external forces and apply the unified transform method (UTM) to solve the corresponding linear IBVPs. In the second step, we derive linear estimates using the UTM formula, considering data and forcing in suitable spaces. (The UTM and its applications were introduced by Fokas [25–28].) In the third step, we define an iteration map in a suitable solution space by the UTM formula with the forcing terms replaced by the nonlinearities and prove that the iteration map is a contraction map and onto some closed ball $B(0,r)$, and by the contraction mapping theorem, the IBVP (1) has a unique solution. Finally, in the fourth step, we prove the local Lipschitz continuity of the data-to-solution map, thereby confirming the local well-posedness of the IBVP (1).

In [29], the authors mentioned the advantages of UTM over other standard methods and gave some examples for discussion. The UTM complements the standard method for the following reasons: In situations where the standard method can produce an explicit solution, the UTM can also do so, and the solution formula obtained is equivalent; it is more efficient than the standard method. It is versatile and can generate solution formulas for many problems that cannot be solved by classical methods, especially problems with higher than second-order derivatives; the standard method is a collection of methods for specific equations and boundary conditions, while the UTM uses the same idea. The UTM can generate explicit solution formulas and determine in a straightforward way how many and which boundary conditions lead to a well-formulated problem, especially for problems with higher than second-order derivatives. The solution can be efficiently evaluated by various means, such as parameterization of the integration path, to make the integral easy to evaluate by numerical methods, asymptotic methods like the steep descent method, the residue theorem, etc. Background knowledge is limited to knowledge of Fourier transform and inverse Fourier transform pairs, the residue theorem, and Jordan's lemma.

Now, we provide an overview of Sobolev spaces. For $s \in \mathbb{R}$, the Sobolev space $H^s(\mathbb{R})$ consists of all tempered distributions F with the finite norm:

$$\| F \|_{H^s(\mathbb{R})} \doteq \left(\int_{\mathbb{R}} (1+\xi^2)^s |\widehat{F}(\xi)|^2 d\xi \right)^{\frac{1}{2}},$$

where the Fourier transform $\widehat{F}(\xi)$ is defined by

$$\widehat{F}(\xi) \doteq \int_{\mathbb{R}} e^{-ix\xi} F(x)dx.$$

Additionally, for an interval $(a,b) \subset \mathbb{R}$ which may extend to infinity on either side, the Sobolev space $H^s(a,b)$ is defined as

$$H^s(a,b) = \left\{ \begin{array}{l} f : f = F|_{(a,b)}, \text{ where } F \in H^s(\mathbb{R}) \\ \text{and } \| f \|_{H^s(a,b)} \doteq \inf_{F \in H^s(\mathbb{R})} \| F \|_{H^s(\mathbb{R})} < \infty \end{array} \right\}.$$

Solving the forced linear Robin IBVP using the UTM leads us to the following Fourier transform.

Definition 1 (Fourier transform on the half-line). *For a test function $\psi(x)$ which is defined on $(0,\infty)$, its half-line Fourier transform is expressed as*

$$\widehat{\psi}(k) \doteq \int_0^\infty e^{-ikx} \psi(x)dx, \tag{2}$$

where $k \in \mathbb{C}$ and $\Im(k) \leq 0$. Here, $\Im(k)$ and $\Re(k)$ denote the imaginary and real parts of k, respectively.

Remark 1. *For Equation (2), it is evident that if ψ is an integrable function on $(0,\infty)$, then $\widehat{\psi}(k)$ is well-defined for $\Im(k) \leq 0$. In fact, within the more suitable space $L^2(0,\infty)$, the half-line Fourier transform can be defined. Specifically, ψ in $L^2(0,\infty)$ can be extended to the entire real line by defining $\psi(x) = 0$ for $x < 0$, resulting in a function in $L^2(\mathbb{R})$. Consequently, the half-line Fourier transform of ψ can be expressed using the same formula as the Fourier transform for its extension to the real line. Thus, the inverse of this transform can also be derived, which corresponds to the inverse Fourier transform on the real line.*

Let's start by outlining the first step of our approach to solving the Robin problem related to the forced linear Schrödinger equation and the forced linear KdV equation:

$$\begin{cases} iu_t + u_{xx} = f_1(x,t), & x \in (0,\infty),\ 0 < t < T < 1, \\ u(x,0) = u_0(x) \in H_x^s(0,\infty), & x \in [0,\infty), \\ u_x(0,t) - \gamma_1 u(0,t) = g_1(t) \in H_t^{\frac{2s-1}{4}}(0,T), & 0 < t < T < 1,\ \gamma_1 \geq 1 \end{cases} \tag{3}$$

and

$$\begin{cases} v_t + v_{xxx} = f_2(x,t), & x \in (0,\infty),\ 0 < t < T < 1, \\ v(x,0) = v_0(x) \in H_x^s(0,\infty), & x \in [0,\infty), \\ v_x(0,t) - \gamma_2 v(0,t) = g_2(t) \in H_t^{\frac{s}{3}}(0,T), & 0 < t < T < 1,\ \gamma_2 > 0, \end{cases} \tag{4}$$

respectively. By the UTM formulation, the solution to (3) is denoted by

$$\begin{aligned} u(x,t) &\doteq S_{LS}[u_0, g_1; f_1](x,t) \\ &= \frac{1}{2\pi} \int_{\mathbb{R}} e^{ikx - ik^2 t} \left(\widehat{u_0}(k) - i \int_0^t e^{ik^2 y} \widehat{f}_1(k,y)dy \right) dk \\ &+ \frac{1}{2\pi} \int_{\partial D_1^+} e^{ikx - ik^2 t} \frac{k - i\gamma_1}{k + i\gamma_1} \left(\widehat{u_0}(-k) - i \int_0^t e^{ik^2 y} \widehat{f}_1(k,y)dy \right) dk \\ &- \frac{i}{\pi} \int_{\partial D_1^+} e^{ikx - ik^2 t} \frac{k}{k + i\gamma_1} \left(\int_0^t e^{ik^2 y} g_1(y)dy \right) dk, \end{aligned} \tag{5}$$

where

$$\widehat{u_0}(k) = \int_0^\infty e^{-ikx} u_0(x)dx,\ \Im(k) \leq 0,$$

and the solution of (4) is denoted by

$$\begin{aligned} v(x,t) &\doteq S_{LK}[v_0, g_2; f_2](x,t) \\ &= \frac{1}{2\pi}\int_{\mathbb{R}} e^{ikx+ik^3t}(\widehat{v_0}(k) + F(k,t))dk \\ &+ \frac{1}{2\pi}\int_{\partial D_2^+} e^{ikx+ik^3t}\frac{(k-i(\alpha+1)\gamma_2)(F(\alpha k,T)+\widehat{v_0}(\alpha k))}{\alpha(k+i\gamma_2)}dk \\ &- \frac{1}{2\pi}\int_{\partial D_2^+} e^{ikx+ik^3t}\frac{(k(\alpha+1)-i\gamma_2)(F(\alpha^2 k,T)+\widehat{v_0}(\alpha^2 k))}{\alpha(k+i\gamma_2)}dk \\ &+ \frac{3i}{2\pi}\int_{\partial D_2^+} e^{ikx+ik^3t}\frac{k^2}{k+i\gamma_2}\widetilde{g_2}(k^3,T)dk, \end{aligned} \tag{6}$$

where $\alpha = e^{i2\pi/3}$,

$$\begin{aligned} \widehat{v_0}(k) &= \int_0^\infty e^{-ikx} v_0(x)dx,\ \Im(k) \leq 0, \\ \widetilde{g_2}(k^3,\tau) &\doteq \int_0^\tau e^{-ik^3t} g_2(t)dt,\ k \in \mathbb{C}, \\ F(k,\tau) &\doteq \int_0^\tau e^{-ik^3t}\widehat{f_2}(k,t)dt = \int_0^\tau e^{-ik^3t}\Big(\int_0^\infty e^{-ikx} f_2(x,t)dx\Big)dt,\ \Im(k) \leq 0, \end{aligned}$$

and D_1^+ and D_2^+ are represented in Figure 1.

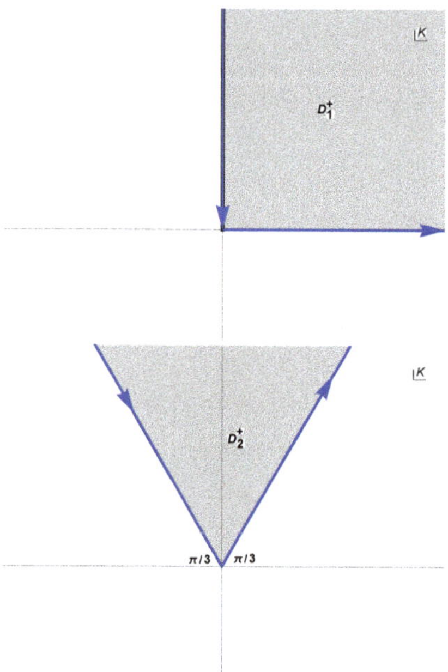

Figure 1. The positively oriented boundaries and regions for D_1^+ and D_2^+.

Next, we outline the second step, which involves estimating the Hadamard norm of the UTM solution formulas $S_{LS}[u_0, g_1; f_1]$ (5) and $S_{LK}[v_0, g_2; f_2]$ (6) based on the Sobolev norms of the data and a suitable norm of the forcing. In particular, we have the following linear estimates. The linear estimate for the Schrödinger equation IBVP is as follows:

Theorem 1 (The linear estimate for the Schrödinger equation IBVP [30]). *Suppose* $1/2 < s < 3/2$, $u_0(x) \in H_x^s(0,\infty)$, *and* $g_1(t) \in H_t^{(2s-1)/4}(0,T)$. *Then, the solution* $u = S_{LS}[u_0, g_1; f_1] \in C([0,T]; H_x^s(0,\infty))$ *of the forced linear Schrödinger equation IBVP (3) given by (5) satisfies the estimate:*

$$\begin{aligned} &\sup_{t\in[0,T]} \| u(t) \|_{H_x^s(0,\infty)} + \sup_{x\in[0,\infty)} \| u(x) \|_{H_t^{\frac{2s+1}{4}}(0,T)} \\ &\le C_s \left(\| u_0 \|_{H_x^s(0,\infty)} + \| g_1 \|_{H_t^{\frac{2s-1}{4}}(0,T)} + \sqrt{T} \sup_{t\in[0,T]} \| f_1(t) \|_{H_x^s(0,\infty)} \right), \end{aligned} \tag{7}$$

where $C_s = C(s) > 0$ *is a constant depending on* s.

We can use a similar proof process for Theorem 1.2 in [30] to obtain the above theorem. The linear estimate for the KdV equation IBVP is as follows:

Theorem 2 (The linear estimate for the KdV equation IBVP [31]). *Suppose* $1/2 < s < 3/2$, $v_0(x) \in H_x^s(0,\infty)$, *and* $g_2(t) \in H_t^{s/3}(0,T)$. *Then, the solution* $v = S_{LK}[v_0, g_2; f_2] \in C([0,T]; H_x^s(0,\infty))$ *of the forced linear KdV equation IBVP (4) given by (6) satisfies the estimate:*

$$\begin{aligned} &\sup_{t\in[0,T]} \| v(t) \|_{H_x^s(0,\infty)} \\ &\le d_s \left(\| v_0 \|_{H_x^s(0,\infty)} + \| g_2 \|_{H_t^{\frac{s}{3}}(0,T)} + T^{\frac{3-2s}{6}} \left(\int_0^T \| f_2(t) \|^2_{H_x^s(0,\infty)} dt \right)^{\frac{1}{2}} \right), \end{aligned} \tag{8}$$

where $d_s = d(s) > 0$ *is a constant depending on* s.

We can find the above theorem in [31].

In the third and fourth steps, our objective is to prove the uniqueness of the solution for (1) and to demonstrate that the data-to-solution map is locally Lipschitz continuous. To achieve this, for $s > 1/2$ and $0 < T < 1$, we define two Banach spaces X_T and Y_T:

$$X_T \doteq C([0,T]; H_x^s(0,\infty)) \cap C\left([0,\infty); H_t^{\frac{2s+1}{4}}(0,T) \right)$$

with the norm

$$\| u \|_{X_T} = \sup_{t\in[0,T]} \| u(t) \|_{H_x^s(0,\infty)} + \sup_{x\in[0,\infty)} \| u(x) \|_{H_t^{\frac{2s+1}{4}}(0,T)} \tag{9}$$

and

$$Y_T \doteq \left\{ \begin{array}{l} v \in C([0,T]; H_x^s(0,\infty)) : \\ \| v \|_{Y_T} \doteq \Lambda^T(v) = \max\left\{ \Lambda_{1,s}^T(v), \Lambda_{2,s}^T(v), \Lambda_3^T(v), \Lambda_4^T(v) \right\} < \infty \end{array} \right\}, \tag{10}$$

where the norms $\Lambda_{1,s}^T(v), \Lambda_{2,s}^T(v), \Lambda_3^T(v), \Lambda_4^T(v)$ are defined as

$$\Lambda_{1,s}^T(v) = \sup_{t\in[0,T]} \| v(t) \|_{H_x^s(0,\infty)}, \ \Lambda_{2,s}^T(v) = \left(\sup_{x\in[0,\infty)} \int_0^T |D_x^s \partial_x v(x,t)|^2 dt \right)^{\frac{1}{2}}, \tag{11}$$

$$\Lambda_3^T(v) = \left(\int_0^\infty \sup_{t\in[0,T]} |v(x,t)|^2 dx\right)^{\frac{1}{2}}, \ \Lambda_4^T(v) = \left(\int_0^T \sup_{x\in[0,\infty)} |\partial_x v(x,t)|^4 dt\right)^{\frac{1}{4}}, \tag{12}$$

where D_x^s is defined by

$$|D_x^s v(x,t)|^2 \doteq \begin{cases} |\partial_x^s v(x,t)|^2, \ s \in \mathbb{N}, \\ \int_0^\infty \frac{\left|\partial_x^{\lfloor s \rfloor} v(x+\zeta,t) - \partial_x^{\lfloor s \rfloor} v(x,t)\right|^2}{\zeta^{1+2\beta}} d\zeta, \end{cases}$$

where $\lfloor s \rfloor \in \mathbb{Z}^+ \cup \{0\}$, $s = \lfloor s \rfloor + \beta$, and $0 < \beta < 1$.

Then, we define the complete metric space $\mathbb{X}_T$ and the data space D as

$$\mathbb{X}_T \doteq X_T \times Y_T = \{(u,v) : u \in X_T, \ v \in Y_T\}$$

with the norm

$$\| (u,v) \|_{\mathbb{X}_T} = \| u \|_{X_T} + \| v \|_{Y_T} . \tag{13}$$

The data space

$$D = H_x^s(0,\infty) \times H_t^{\frac{2s-1}{4}}(0,T) \times H_x^s(0,\infty) \times H_t^{\frac{s}{3}}(0,T)$$

with the norm

$$\| (u_0, g_1, v_0, g_2) \|_D = \| u_0 \|_{H_x^s(0,\infty)} + \| g_1 \|_{H_t^{\frac{2s-1}{4}}(0,T)} + \| v_0 \|_{H_x^s(0,\infty)} + \| g_2 \|_{H_t^{\frac{s}{3}}(0,T)}, \tag{14}$$

for $(u_0, g_1, v_0, g_2) \in D$.

We then present the main result of this work using the definitions provided above.

Theorem 3 (The local well-posedness of the SKdV system). *Consider the SKdV system (1). Suppose $3/4 < s < 1$ and $0 < T < 1$. For the data $u_0, v_0 \in H_x^s(0,\infty)$, $g_1(t) \in H_t^{(2s-1)/4}(0,T)$, and $g_2(t) \in H_t^{s/3}(0,T)$.*

Then, there exist $\mathfrak{K}_s = \mathfrak{K}(s) > 0$ and $\widetilde{C}_s = \widetilde{C}(s) > 0$ which are constants depending on s, and $T^* = \min\{T, T_1, T_2\} > 0$, where

$$r = \max\left\{1, \sqrt{\frac{3}{2}} \widetilde{C_s}^{-1}, 2\mathfrak{K}_s^* \| (u_0, g_1, v_0, g_2) \|_D \right\},$$

$$n_0 = \max\{m,n\}, \ A = \max\{|a_0|, |a_1|, \cdots, |a_m|\}, \ B = \max\{|b_0|, |b_1| \cdots, |b_n|\},$$

$$T_1 = \frac{1}{64(A(m+1) + \sqrt{10}B)^6 (\mathfrak{K}_s^*)^{6n_0+6} r^{6n_0+6}},$$

and

$$T_2 = \frac{1}{64(A(m^2+m+1) + \sqrt{5}B(2^{n+1}(n+1) + 2^n n^3)^{\frac{1}{2}})^6 (\mathfrak{K}_s^*)^{6n_0+6} r^{6n_0}},$$

such that the SKdV system (1) has a unique solution $(u,v) \in \mathbb{X}_{T^*}$ and the solution satisfies the size estimate

$$\| (u,v) \|_{\mathbb{X}_{T^*}} \leq r.$$

Furthermore, the data-to-solution map $(u_0, g_1, v_0, g_2) \longmapsto (u, v)$ *is locally Lipschitz continuous.*

According to the above theorem, we have proven that under certain conditions there will be a unique solution to the SKdV system (1). Regarding the difficulty in studying the local well-posedness of the SKdV system: The SKdV system will involve the algebraic property of the nonlinear estimation term. In two-dimensional space, $H_x^s(\mathbb{R}^2)$ must be in $s > 1$, even in $n \geq 2$ dimensional space, and $H_x^s(\mathbb{R}^n)$ must be in $s > n/2$ to satisfy the algebraic property. This is a major challenge for existing estimation techniques for the KdV equation.

To facilitate calculations and presentation, we use the following notations.

Remark 2. *For two quantities* $\mathcal{A}$ *and* $\mathcal{B}$ *that depend on one or several variables, we write* $\mathcal{A} \lesssim \mathcal{B}$ *if there exists a positive constant c such that* $\mathcal{A} \leq c\mathcal{B}$*. If* $\mathcal{A} \lesssim \mathcal{B}$ *and* $\mathcal{B} \lesssim \mathcal{A}$*, then we denote this relationship by* $\mathcal{A} \simeq \mathcal{B}$*.*

In Section 2, we provide some tools that will be used in later sections. Section 3 outlines the proof of Theorem 2 in preparation for the proof in Section 5. In Sections 4 and 5, we define a new space, give the Λ-norm estimates for the UTM solution of the forced linear KdV IBVP (4), and finish the proof of Proposition 2. In Section 6, we define the iteration map and demonstrate that it is a contraction mapping onto a closed ball. We then use the contraction mapping theorem to establish the uniqueness of the solution. Additionally, in Lemma 12, we show that the data-to-solution map is locally Lipschitz continuous. Finally, we complete the proof of Theorem 3.

Regarding Section 6, since we consider the SKdV system with polynomial nonlinear terms, the proof of existence and uniqueness of solutions is more complex than in [30–33]. In proving that the iteration map is both onto and a contraction, more considerations about the lifetime of the solution are required. For example, the coefficients and degrees of the polynomials affect the length of the existence time, and the size of the unique solution also requires additional considerations based on the data norm and the corresponding range of s. Furthermore, in proving the data-to-solution aspect of local well-posedness, the determination of the lifetime requires more complicated estimates due to the polynomial nonlinear terms in the SKdV system. For example, the existence range of the solution is also affected by the coefficients and degrees of the polynomials. Therefore, the estimates in Section 6 extend and apply the results of [30–33].

In this paper, we consider the SKdV system with polynomial nonlinear terms and Robin boundary conditions and discuss linear space-time estimates and the polynomial nonlinear terms in Sobolev space. This differs from the work of Himonas and Yan [11], who considered the SKdV system under Dirichlet boundary conditions and discussed linear space-time estimates and quadratic/cubic estimates in Bourgain space.

2. Preliminary Results and Some Useful Tools

This section provides some tools that will be used in later sections.

Lemma 1 ([33])**.** *If* $r = r_R + ir_I$ *with* $r_I > 0$*, then*

$$\left|e^{irkx} - e^{irk\zeta}\right| \leq \sqrt{2}\left(1 + \frac{|r_R|}{r_I}\right)\left|e^{-r_Ikx} - e^{-r_Ik\zeta}\right|, \; \forall k, x, \zeta \geq 0.$$

Lemma 2 ([33])**.** *Suppose* $\phi(k) \in L_k^2(0, \infty)$*. Then, the map*

$$\phi(k) \longmapsto \int_0^\infty e^{-ky}\phi(k)dk$$

is bounded from $L^2_k(0,\infty)$ *into* $L^2_y(0,\infty)$ *with*

$$\| \int_0^\infty e^{-ky}\phi(k)dk \|_{L^2_y(0,\infty)} \leq \sqrt{\pi} \| \phi(k) \|_{L^2_k(0,\infty)} .$$

Lemma 3 ([32]). *For* $m_1 < m < m_2$*, we have*

$$\| f \|_{H^m} \leq \| f \|_{H^{m_1}}^{\frac{m_2-m}{m_2-m_1}} \| f \|_{H^{m_2}}^{\frac{m-m_1}{m_2-m_1}} .$$

Lemma 4 ([34]). *If* $s > n/2$*, then* $H^s_x(\mathbb{R}^n)$ *is an algebra with respect to the product of functions. That is, if* f *and* g *in* $H^s_x(\mathbb{R}^n)$*, then* $fg \in H^s_x(\mathbb{R}^n)$ *with*

$$\| fg \|_{H^s_x(\mathbb{R}^n)} \leq (C_1)_s \| f \|_{H^s_x(\mathbb{R}^n)} \| g \|_{H^s_x(\mathbb{R}^n)},$$

for some constant $(C_1)_s > 0$ *depending on s.*

For the following lemma, we define the following operator

$$D^r U^2(t)R(x) \doteq \int_{\mathbb{R}} e^{ikx+ik^3t}(ik)^r \widehat{R}(k)dk \simeq \int_{\mathbb{R}} e^{ikx+ik^3t}|k|^r \widehat{R}(k)dk, \tag{15}$$

where $\widehat{R}(k)$ is the Fourier transform of $R(x)$.

Lemma 5 ([31,35–37]). *For* $R \in L^2_x(\mathbb{R})$*, the operator* $D^{\frac{1}{4}}U^2(t)R(x)$ *defined by (15) is bounded from* L^2_x *into* $L^4[\mathbb{R}_t; L^\infty_x(0,\infty)]$*; that is, it satisfies the estimate*

$$\| D^{\frac{1}{4}}U^2(t)R(x) \|_{L^4[\mathbb{R}_t;L^\infty_x(\mathbb{R})]} \leq C_T \| R \|_{L^2_x(\mathbb{R})},$$

for some constant $C_T > 0$.

For the following lemma, we define the operator

$$\Delta^r R(x,t) \doteq \int_0^\infty e^{ia\tau^{\frac{1}{3}}x+i\tau t}\tau^r \widehat{R}(\tau)d\tau, \tag{16}$$

where $\widehat{R}(\tau)$ is the Fourier transform of $R(t)$.

Lemma 6 ([35,38]). *For* $R \in L^2_t(\mathbb{R})$*, the operator* $\Delta^{\frac{-1}{4}}R$ *defined by* (16) *is bounded from* L^2_t *into* $L^4[\mathbb{R}_t; L^\infty_x(0,\infty)]$*; that is, it satisfies the estimate*

$$\| \Delta^{\frac{-1}{4}}R(x,-t) \|_{L^4[\mathbb{R}_t;L^\infty_x(0,\infty)]} = \| \Delta^{\frac{-1}{4}}R(x,t) \|_{L^4[\mathbb{R}_t;L^\infty_x(0,\infty)]} \leq C_T \| R \|_{L^2_t(\mathbb{R})},$$

for some constant $C_T > 0$.

Lemma 7 ([32]). *If* $\mu \in [0,\infty)$, $\beta \in (0,1)\backslash\left\{\frac{1}{2}\right\}$*, and*

$$\Delta(\mu,\frac{1}{\mu},\beta) \doteq \int_0^\infty \int_0^\infty \frac{(e^{-\mu x} - e^{-\mu y})\left(e^{\frac{-x}{\mu}} - e^{\frac{-y}{\mu}}\right)}{|x-y|^{1+2\beta}}dxdy,$$

then

$$\Delta(\mu,\frac{1}{\mu},\beta) = C_\beta\left(\mu + \frac{1}{\mu}\right)^{-1}\left(\mu^{2\beta} + \left(\frac{1}{\mu}\right)^{2\beta} - \left(\mu + \frac{1}{\mu}\right)^{2\beta}\right),$$

where

$$C_\beta = \begin{cases} \frac{\Gamma(1-2\beta)}{\beta}, & \beta \in (0, \frac{1}{2}), \\ \frac{\pi}{\beta \sin(2\pi\beta)\Gamma(2\beta)}, & \beta \in (\frac{1}{2}, 1), \end{cases}$$

and we obtain the estimate

$$\Delta(\mu, \frac{1}{\mu}, \beta) \lesssim C_\beta\left(\mu + \frac{1}{\mu}\right)^{-1}, \; C_\beta > 0, \; \beta \in (0,1)\backslash\left\{\frac{1}{2}\right\}.$$

3. Sketch the Proof of the Theorem 2

This section details the proof of Theorem 2 by breaking down the Robin problem for the forced linear KdV equation into four simpler problems. In Section 3.2, we use Theorems 4 and 5 from Section 3.1 to derive estimates for the IBVPs.

3.1. The Discussion of the Reduced Pure IBVP for the Linear KdV Equation

In this subsection, Theorems 4 and 5 analyze a fundamental Robin problem related to the linear KdV equation and are key tools for estimating the linear IBVPs (III) and (IV) discussed in Section 3.2.

3.1.1. Reduced Pure IBVP

We begin with the most basic linear KdV equation IBVP on the half-line. That is, the homogeneous IBVP with zero initial data and nonzero boundary data.

Furthermore, we assume that the boundary data $g \in H_t^{s/3}(\mathbb{R})$ extends $g_2 \in H_t^{s/3}(0,T)$, which is compactly supported in the interval $[0,2]$, and

$$\| g \|_{H_t^{s/3}(\mathbb{R})} \leq 2 \| g_2 \|_{H_t^{s/3}(0,T)} . \tag{17}$$

This specific problem, referred to as the reduced pure IBVP, can be formulated as follows:

$$\begin{cases} \omega_t + \omega_{xxx} = 0 & x \in (0,\infty), \; 0 < t < 2, \\ \omega(x,0) = 0, & x \in [0,\infty), \\ \omega_x(0,t) - \gamma_2\omega(0,t) = g(t) \in H_t^{\frac{s}{3}}(\mathbb{R}), & t \in [0,2], \; \gamma_2 > 0. \end{cases} \tag{18}$$

According to the UTM formula, the solution to (18) is

$$\begin{aligned} \omega(x,t) = S_{LK}[0,g;0](x,t) &= \frac{3i}{2\pi}\int_{\partial D_2^+} e^{ikx+ik^3t}\frac{k^2}{k+i\gamma_2}\tilde{g}(k^3,T)dk \\ &= \omega_1(x,t) + \omega_2(x,t). \end{aligned} \tag{19}$$

We use the parameterization $k \longmapsto ak$ or a^2k, with $a = e^{i\pi/3}$, where

$$\omega_1(x,t) = \frac{-3i}{2\pi}\int_0^\infty e^{iakx-ik^3t}\frac{k^2}{ak+i\gamma_2}\tilde{g}(-k^3,T)dk, \tag{20}$$

$$\omega_2(x,t) = \frac{-3i}{2\pi}\int_0^\infty e^{ia^2kx+ik^3t}\frac{k^2}{a^2k+i\gamma_2}\tilde{g}(k^3,T)dk. \tag{21}$$

Our objective is to estimate the Hadamard norm of the solution to the IBVP (18). The following theorem, which we found in [31], addresses this estimation.

Theorem 4 (Reduced linear KdV IBVP with Sobolev data [31]). *Let $s \geq 0$. For a test function g which is compactly supported in the interval $[0,2]$, the solution (19) to the Robin problem (18) satisfies the estimate*

$$\sup_{t\in\mathbb{R}} \| \omega(t) \|_{H_x^s(0,\infty)} \leq \widetilde{(C_3)}_s \| g \|_{H_t^{\frac{s}{3}}(\mathbb{R})}, \tag{22}$$

where $\widetilde{(C_3)}_s$ is a constant depending on s.

3.1.2. Homogeneous IBVP with Zero Initial Data

In this subsection, we consider the pure IBVP:

$$\begin{cases} \widetilde{\omega}_t + \widetilde{\omega}_{xxx} = 0 & x \in (0,\infty),\ t \in [0,T], \\ \widetilde{\omega}(x,0) = 0, & x \in [0,\infty), \\ \widetilde{\omega}_x(0,t) - \gamma_2 \widetilde{\omega}(0,t) = g_2(t) \in H_t^{\frac{s}{3}}(0,T), & t \in [0,T],\ \gamma_2 > 0. \end{cases} \tag{23}$$

We will extend the boundary data $g_2(t)$ from the interval $[0,T]$ to the entire real line $\mathbb{R}$. Our goal is to define a function $g(t) \in H_t^{\frac{s}{3}}(\mathbb{R})$ with g compactly supported in the interval $[0,2]$ as an extension of $g_2(t) \in H_t^{\frac{s}{3}}(0,T)$. For $1/2 < s < 3/2$, g is defined by

$$g(t) = \begin{cases} E_\theta(t), & t \in (0,2), \\ 0, & t \in (0,2)^c, \end{cases}$$

where $\theta \in C_0^\infty(\mathbb{R})$ with $|\theta(t)| \leq 1$ for all $t \in \mathbb{R}$, $\theta(t) = 1$ for all $|t| \leq 1$, $\theta(t) = 0$ for all $|t| \geq 2$, and $E_\theta = \theta(t)E(t)$. Here, $E \in H_t^{\frac{s}{3}}(\mathbb{R})$ is an extension of $g_2 \in H_t^{\frac{s}{3}}(0,T)$ such that

$$\| E \|_{H_t^{\frac{s}{3}}(\mathbb{R})} \leq 2 \| g_2 \|_{H_t^{\frac{s}{3}}(0,T)}.$$

Consequently, we have that g is compactly supported in the interval $[0,2]$ and (17):

$$\| g \|_{H_t^{\frac{s}{3}}(\mathbb{R})} \leq 2 \| g_2 \|_{H_t^{\frac{s}{3}}(0,T)}, \text{ for } \frac{1}{2} < s < \frac{3}{2}.$$

Thus, for IBVP (23), we can derive the following two inequalities: one for space estimates and one for time estimates.

$$\begin{aligned} \sup_{t\in[0,T]} \| \widetilde{\omega}(t) \|_{H_x^s(0,\infty)} &\leq \widetilde{(C_3)}_s \| g \|_{H_t^{\frac{s}{3}}(\mathbb{R})}, \text{ (by Theorem 4)} \\ &\leq 2\widetilde{(C_3)}_s \| g_2 \|_{H_t^{\frac{s}{3}}(0,T)}, \text{ for } \frac{1}{2} < s < \frac{3}{2}, \text{ (by (17))}, \end{aligned}$$

where $\widetilde{(C_3)}_s$ is a constant depending on s.

Therefore, we obtain the following result:

Theorem 5. *For $1/2 < s < 3/2$ and the boundary data test function $g_2 \in H_t^{\frac{s}{3}}(0,T)$. The solution for the IBVP (23) which satisfies the following Hadamard space estimate:*

$$\sup_{t\in[0,T]} \| S[0,g_2;0](t) \|_{H_x^s(0,\infty)} \leq 2\widetilde{(C_3)}_s \| g_2 \|_{H_t^{\frac{s}{3}}(0,T)},$$

where $\widetilde{(C_3)}_s$ is a constant depending on s.

3.2. The Norm Estimates of the Forced Linear KdV Equation IBVP (4) (Theorem 2)

In this subsection, we will prove Theorem 2 by breaking down the forced linear KdV equation into four simpler problems.

3.2.1. Decomposition into Simple Problems

To prove Theorem 2, we start by decomposing the forced linear IBVP (4) into a combination of the following problems:

(I) The homogeneous linear initial value problem (IVP):

$$\begin{cases} V_t + V_{xxx} = 0, & x \in \mathbb{R},\ t \in (0,T), \\ V(x,0) = V_0(x) \in H_x^s(\mathbb{R}), & x \in \mathbb{R}, \end{cases} \tag{24}$$

where $V_0 \in H_x^s(\mathbb{R})$ is an extension of the initial datum $v_0 \in H_x^s(0,\infty)$ such that

$$\| V_0 \|_{H_x^s(\mathbb{R})} \leq 2 \| v_0 \|_{H_x^s(0,\infty)} \tag{25}$$

with the solution to IVP (24) expressed using the Duhamel formula

$$V(x,t) = S[V_0;0](x,t) = \frac{1}{2\pi}\int_{\mathbb{R}} e^{ikx+ik^3t}\widehat{V_0}(k)dk, \tag{26}$$

where the Fourier transform with respect to the spatial variable $\widehat{V_0}(\zeta)$ is defined by

$$\widehat{V_0}(\zeta) = \int_{\mathbb{R}} e^{-i\zeta k} V_0(k)dk,\ \zeta \in \mathbb{R}.$$

(II) The forced linear IVP with zero initial condition:

$$\begin{cases} W_t^* + W_{xxx}^* = F_2(x,t), & x \in \mathbb{R},\ t \in (0,T), \\ W^*(x,0) = 0, & x \in \mathbb{R}, \end{cases} \tag{27}$$

where $F_2(x,t) \in C([0,T]; H_x^s(\mathbb{R}))$ is an extension of $f_2(x,t) \in C([0,T]; H_x^s(0,\infty))$, which satisfies

$$\| F_2 \|_{L^2([0,T];H_x^s(\mathbb{R}))} \leq 2 \| f_2 \|_{L^2([0,T];H_x^s(0,\infty))} . \tag{28}$$

The solution to IVP (27) is expressed using the Duhamel formula

$$\begin{aligned} W^*(x,t) = S[0;F_2](x,t) &= \frac{1}{2\pi}\int_{\mathbb{R}}\left(\int_0^t e^{ikx+ik^3(t-t')}\widehat{F_2}(k,t')dt'\right)dk \\ &= \int_0^t S[F_2(\cdot,t');0](x,t-t')dt'. \end{aligned} \tag{29}$$

(III) The linear IBVP on the half-line:

$$\begin{cases} v_t^\# + v_{xxx}^\# = 0 & x \in (0,\infty),\ t \in (0,T), \\ v^\#(x,0) = 0, & x \in [0,\infty), \\ v_x^\#(0,t) - \gamma_2 v^\#(0,t) = G_1(t), & t \in [0,T],\ \gamma_2 > 0, \end{cases} \tag{30}$$

where $G_1(t) \doteq g_2(t) - V_x(0,t) - W_x^*(0,t)$ and $v^\# = S[0,G_0;0]$ is the solution of (30).

(IV) Homogeneous linear IBVP with zero initial condition:

$$\begin{cases} v_t^* + v_{xxx}^* = 0 & x \in (0,\infty),\ t \in (0,T), \\ v^*(x,0) = 0, & x \in [0,\infty), \\ v_x^*(0,t) - \gamma_2 v^*(0,t) = H_1(t), & t \in [0,T],\ \gamma_2 > 0, \end{cases} \tag{31}$$

where $H_1(t) \doteq \gamma_2(V(0,t) + W^*(0,t))$ and $v^* = S[0, H_1; 0]$ is the solution of (31).

By applying the superposition principle, the UTM solution (6) of the linear IBVP (4) is expressed as follows: for $x > 0$ and $0 < t < T$,

$$S_{LK}[v_0, g_2; f_2] = S[V_0; 0]|_{x>0} + S[0; F_2]|_{x>0} + S[0, G_1; 0] + S[0, H_1; 0], \tag{32}$$

where the four terms on the right-hand side correspond to the solutions of problems (24), (27), (30), and (31), respectively.

3.2.2. The Estimates for the Linear IVPs

We begin by analyzing the components of (32). First, we will estimate the solutions of the homogeneous linear IVP (24) and the forced linear IVP with zero initial condition (27) in Sobolev spaces. The following two theorems from [31] provide the necessary estimates for these IVPs.

Theorem 6 ([31])**.** *The function V defined by formula (26) solves the linear KdV IVP (24) and satisfies the following estimates:*

1. *Space estimate:*

$$\sup_{t\in[0,T]} \| V(t) \|_{H_x^s(\mathbb{R})} = \| V_0 \|_{H_x^s(\mathbb{R})}, \ s \in \mathbb{R}. \tag{33}$$

2. *Time estimates:*

$$\sup_{x\in\mathbb{R}} \| V(x) \|_{H_t^{\frac{s+1}{3}}(0,T)} \leq (C_6)_s \| V_0 \|_{H_x^s(\mathbb{R})}, \ s \in \mathbb{R}, \tag{34}$$

$$\sup_{x\in\mathbb{R}} \| V_x(x) \|_{H_t^{\frac{s}{3}}(\mathbb{R})} \leq (C_7)_s \| V_0 \|_{H_x^s(\mathbb{R})}, \ s \in \mathbb{R}, \tag{35}$$

where $(C_6)_s$ and $(C_7)_s$ are constants depending on s.

Having analyzed the homogeneous linear IVP (24), we now turn to the estimation of the forced linear IVP with zero initial condition (27).

Theorem 7 ([31])**.** *The solution $W^* = S[0; F_2]$ of the forced linear IVP (27) given by (29) admits the following senses:*

1. *Space estimate:*

$$\sup_{t\in[0,T]} \| W^*(t) \|_{H_x^s(\mathbb{R})} \leq (C_8)_s T^{\frac{1}{2}} \left(\int_0^T \| F_2(\cdot, t') \|^2_{H_x^s(\mathbb{R})} \, dt' \right)^{\frac{1}{2}}, \ s \in \mathbb{R}. \tag{36}$$

2. *Time estimates:*

$$\sup_{x\in\mathbb{R}} \| W^*(x) \|_{H_t^{\frac{s+1}{3}}(0,T)} \leq (C_9)_s T^{\frac{2-s}{3}} \| F_2 \|_{L^2([0,T];\, H_x^s(\mathbb{R}))}, \ \frac{1}{2} < s < 2, \tag{37}$$

$$\sup_{x\in\mathbb{R}} \| W_x^*(x) \|_{H_t^{\frac{s}{3}}(0,T)} \leq (C_{10})_s T^{\frac{3-2s}{6}} \| F_2 \|_{L^2([0,T];\, H_x^s(\mathbb{R}))}, \ 0 \leq s < \frac{3}{2}, \tag{38}$$

where $(C_8)_s$, $(C_9)_s$, and $(C_{10})_s$ are constants depending on s.

3.2.3. Proof of Theorem 2

In this subsection, we establish Theorem 2 by utilizing Theorems 4–7.

According to Theorem 5, we obtain the following inequality:

$$\sup_{t\in[0,T]} \| S[0,G_1;0](t) \|_{H_x^{\frac{s}{3}}(0,\infty)} \leq 2\widetilde{(C_3)_s} \| G_1 \|_{H_t^{\frac{s}{3}}(0,T)}, \tag{39}$$

$$\sup_{t\in[0,T]} \| S[0,H_1;0](t) \|_{H_x^{\frac{s}{3}}(0,\infty)} \leq 2\widetilde{(C_3)_s} \| H_1 \|_{H_t^{\frac{s}{3}}(0,T)}. \tag{40}$$

According to (32), we have the following inequality:

$$\begin{aligned}
&\sup_{t\in[0,T]} \| S_{LK}[v_0, g_2; f_2] \|_{H_x^{\frac{s}{3}}(0,\infty)} \\
&\leq 2 \| v_0 \|_{H_x^{\frac{s}{3}}(0,\infty)} + 2(C_8)_s T^{\frac{1}{2}} \left(\int_0^T \| f_2(t) \|^2_{H_x^{\frac{s}{3}}(0,\infty)} dt \right)^{\frac{1}{2}} + 2\widetilde{(C_3)_s} \| G_1 \|_{H_t^{\frac{s}{3}}(0,T)} \\
&\quad + 2\widetilde{(C_3)_s} \| H_1 \|_{H_t^{\frac{s}{3}}(0,T)}, \text{ (by (25), (28), (33), (36), (39), (40)).}
\end{aligned}$$

We must estimate $\| G_1 \|_{H_t^{\frac{s}{3}}(0,T)}$ and $\| H_1 \|_{H_t^{\frac{s}{3}}(0,T)}$. Then, we obtain the following inequalities:

$$\begin{aligned}
\| G_1 \|_{H_t^{\frac{s}{3}}(0,T)} &= \| g_2(t) - V_x(0,t) - W_x^*(0,t) \|_{H_t^{\frac{s}{3}}(0,T)} \\
&\leq \| g_2 \|_{H_t^{\frac{s}{3}}(0,T)} + \| V_x(0,t) \|_{H_t^{\frac{s}{3}}(0,T)} + \| W_x^*(0,t) \|_{H_t^{\frac{s}{3}}(0,T)} \\
&\lesssim \| g_2 \|_{H_t^{\frac{s}{3}}(0,T)} + \| V_0 \|_{H_x^{\frac{s}{3}}(\mathbb{R})} + T^{\frac{3-2s}{6}} \| F_2 \|_{L^2([0,T];\, H_x^{\frac{s}{3}}(\mathbb{R}))}, \\
&\text{(by (35) and (38))} \\
&\lesssim \| g_2 \|_{H_t^{\frac{s}{3}}(0,T)} + \| v_0 \|_{H_x^{\frac{s}{3}}(0,\infty)} + T^{\frac{3-2s}{6}} \| f_2 \|_{L^2([0,T];H_x^{\frac{s}{3}}(0,\infty))}, \\
&\text{(by (25) and (28)),}
\end{aligned} \tag{41}$$

and

$$\begin{aligned}
\| H_1 \|_{H_t^{\frac{s}{3}}(0,T)} &= \| \gamma_2 V(0,t) + \gamma_2 W^*(0,t) \|_{H_t^{\frac{s}{3}}(0,T)} \\
&\leq \gamma_2 \| V(0,t) \|_{H_t^{\frac{s}{3}}(0,T)} + \gamma_2 \| W^*(0,t) \|_{H_t^{\frac{s}{3}}(0,T)} \\
&\leq \gamma_2 \| V(0,t) \|_{H_t^{\frac{s+1}{3}}(0,T)} + \gamma_2 \| W^*(0,t) \|_{H_t^{\frac{s+1}{3}}(0,T)} \\
&\leq (C_6)_s \gamma_2 \| V_0 \|_{H_x^{\frac{s}{3}}(\mathbb{R})} + (C_9)_s \gamma_2 T^{\frac{2-s}{3}} \| F_2 \|_{L^2([0,T];\, H_x^{\frac{s}{3}}(\mathbb{R}))}, \\
&\text{(by (34) and (37))} \\
&\leq 2(C_6)_s \gamma_2 \| v_0 \|_{H_x^{\frac{s}{3}}(0,\infty)} + 2(C_9)_s \gamma_2 T^{\frac{2-s}{3}} \| f_2 \|_{L^2([0,T];H_x^{\frac{s}{3}}(0,\infty))}, \\
&\text{(by (25) and (28)).}
\end{aligned} \tag{42}$$

Hence, by (41) and (42), we can yield (8):

$$\begin{aligned}
&\sup_{t\in[0,T]} \| S_{LK}[v_0, g_2; f_2] \|_{H_x^{\frac{s}{3}}(0,\infty)} \\
&\leq d_s \left(\| v_0 \|_{H_x^{\frac{s}{3}}(0,\infty)} + \| g_2 \|_{H_t^{\frac{s}{3}}(0,T)} + T^{\frac{3-2s}{6}} \left(\int_0^T \| f_2(t) \|^2_{H_x^{\frac{s}{3}}(0,\infty)} dt \right)^{\frac{1}{2}} \right),
\end{aligned}$$

which concludes this proof of Theorem 2.

4. About the New Solution Space and Some Estimates

One strategy to prove the existence of solutions to our Robin problem for the KdV equation on $(0,\infty)$ is to use (8) with f_2 replaced by $Q(v)v_x$. However, the Hadamard space $C([0,T];H_x^s(0,\infty))$ is not a suitable candidate due to the presence of the term

$$\int_0^T \| vv_x \|^2_{H_x^s(0,\infty)} dt.$$

This is precisely the necessary "algebraic property" (refer to Lemma 4).

Hence,

$$\| vv_x \|_{H_x^s(0,\infty)} \leq (C_1)_s \| v \|_{H_x^s(0,\infty)} \| v_x \|_{H_x^s(0,\infty)}$$

for closing the loop is not true. Therefore, we introduce a new solution space, a subspace of the Hadamard space, defined by specific Λ-norms.

The following lemma was proven in [33]; therefore, we omit its proof here. Below, we provide the bilinear estimate for the problem term.

Lemma 8 (Bilinear estimate on the half-line). *For $0 \leq s < 1$ and any u and v in Y_T, where the space Y_T is defined in (10), we have the bilinear estimate*

$$\begin{aligned} \| uv_x \|^2_{L^2([0,T];H_x^s(0,\infty))} &\doteq \int_0^T \| uv_x(t) \|^2_{H_x^s(0,\infty)} dt \\ &\leq T^{\frac{1}{2}}\left(\Lambda_3^T(u)\Lambda_4^T(v)\right)^2 + 2\left(\Lambda_3^T(u)\Lambda_{2,s}^T(v)\right)^2 + 2T^{\frac{1}{2}}\left(\Lambda_{1,s}^T(u)\Lambda_4^T(v)\right)^2. \end{aligned} \tag{43}$$

We now turn to the following useful lemma for our estimation.

Lemma 9. *For $1/2 < s < 1$ and $0 < T < 1$, we have the following results:*

$$\Lambda_3^T(uv) \leq \Lambda_{1,s}^T(u)\Lambda_3^T(v), \tag{44}$$

and

$$\Lambda_{1,s}^T(uv) \leq (C_1)_s\Lambda_{1,s}^T(u)\Lambda_{1,s}^T(v), \tag{45}$$

for $u, v \in C([0,T];H_x^s(0,\infty))$, where $(C_1)_s$ is a constant depending on s.

Proof. By definition of $\Lambda_3^T(uv)$,

$$\begin{aligned} \Lambda_3^T(uv) &= \left(\int_0^\infty \sup_{t\in[0,T]} |u(x,t)v(x,t)|^2 dx\right)^{\frac{1}{2}} \\ &\leq \left(\int_0^\infty \sup_{t\in[0,T]}\left(\sup_{x\in[0,\infty)} |u(x,t)|^2\right) \sup_{t\in[0,T]} |v(x,t)|^2 dx\right)^{\frac{1}{2}} \\ &\leq \left(\int_0^\infty \sup_{t\in[0,T]} \| u(t) \|^2_{H_x^s(0,\infty)} \sup_{t\in[0,T]} |v(x,t)|^2 dx\right)^{\frac{1}{2}}, \\ &\text{(by the Sobolev Imbedding Theorem for } s > 1/2) \\ &\leq \sup_{t\in[0,T]} \| u(t) \|_{H_x^s(0,\infty)} \left(\int_0^\infty \sup_{t\in[0,T]} |v(x,t)|^2 dx\right)^{\frac{1}{2}}, \\ &= \Lambda_{1,s}^T(u)\Lambda_3^T(v), \end{aligned}$$

we obtain Equation (44).

To estimate $\Lambda_{1,s}^T(uv)$:

$$\begin{aligned}\Lambda_{1.s}^T(uv) &= \sup_{t\in[0,T]} \| uv(t) \|_{H_x^s(0,\infty)} \\ &\leq \sup_{t\in[0,T]} \Big((C_1)_s \| u(t) \|_{H_x^s(0,\infty)} \| v(t) \|_{H_x^s(0,\infty)}\Big), \text{(by Lemma 4)} \\ &\leq (C_1)_s \left(\sup_{t\in[0,T]} \| u(t) \|_{H_x^s(0,\infty)}\right)\left(\sup_{t\in[0,T]} \| v(t) \|_{H_x^s(0,\infty)}\right) \\ &= (C_1)_s \Lambda_{1,s}^T(u)\Lambda_{1,s}^T(v),\end{aligned}$$

we obtain Equation (45). □

Finally, we obtain the following proposition.

Proposition 1. *For $1/2 < s < 1$ and $0 < T < 1$, we have the following results:*

$$\begin{aligned}&\int_0^T \| u_1u_2\cdots u_nv_x(t) \|_{H_x^s(0,\infty)}^2 dt \\ &\leq T^{\frac{1}{2}}\Big(\Lambda_{1,s}^T(u_1)\Lambda_{1,s}^T(u_2)\cdots\Lambda_{1,s}^T(u_{n-1})\Lambda_3^T(u_n)\Lambda_4^T(v)\Big)^2 \\ &\quad + 2\Big(\Lambda_{1,s}^T(u_1)\Lambda_{1,s}^T(u_2)\cdots\Lambda_{1,s}^T(u_{n-1})\Lambda_3^T(u_n)\Lambda_{2,s}^T(v)\Big)^2 \\ &\quad + 2((C_1)_s)^{2(n-1)}T^{\frac{1}{2}}\Big(\Lambda_{1,s}^T(u_1)\Lambda_{1,s}^T(u_2)\cdots\Lambda_{1,s}^T(u_n)\Lambda_4^T(v)\Big)^2 \\ &\leq 5\widetilde{C}_s^{2(n-1)} \| u_1 \|_{Y_T}^2 \| u_2 \|_{Y_T}^2 \cdots \| u_n \|_{Y_T}^2 \| v \|_{Y_T}^2,\end{aligned} \tag{46}$$

where $n \geq 2$, $n \in \mathbb{N}$, and $\widetilde{C}_s = \max\{1, (C_1)_s\}$.

Proof. We use mathematical induction to prove this lemma.

In the first part, we assume $n = 2$. We have

$$\begin{aligned}&\int_0^T \| u_1u_2v_x(t) \|_{H_x^s(0,\infty)}^2 dt \\ &\leq T^{\frac{1}{2}}\Big(\Lambda_3^T(u_1u_2)\Lambda_4^T(v)\Big)^2 + 2\Big(\Lambda_3^T(u_1u_2)\Lambda_{2,s}^T(v)\Big)^2 + 2T^{\frac{1}{2}}\Big(\Lambda_{1,s}^T(u_1u_2)\Lambda_4^T(v)\Big)^2, \\ &\quad \text{(by Lemma 8)} \\ &\leq T^{\frac{1}{2}}\Big(\Lambda_{1,s}^T(u_1)\Lambda_3^T(u_2)\Lambda_4^T(v)\Big)^2 + 2\Big(\Lambda_{1,s}^T(u_1)\Lambda_3^T(u_2)\Lambda_{2,s}^T(v)\Big)^2 \\ &\quad + 2T^{\frac{1}{2}}\Big((C_1)_s\Lambda_{1,s}^T(u_1)\Lambda_{1,s}^T(u_2)\Lambda_4^T(v)\Big)^2, \text{ (by Lemmas 4 and 9)} \\ &\leq 5\widetilde{C}_s^{2(n-1)} \| u_1 \|_{Y_T}^2 \| u_2 \|_{Y_T}^2 \| v \|_{Y_T}^2 .\end{aligned}$$

Therefore, when $n = 2$, the inequality (46) holds.

In the second part, we assume $n = k > 2$ and the following inequality

$$\begin{aligned}&\int_0^T \| u_1u_2\cdots u_kv_x(t) \|_{H_x^s(0,\infty)}^2 dt \\ &\leq T^{\frac{1}{2}}\Big(\Lambda_{1,s}^T(u_1)\Lambda_{1,s}^T(u_2)\cdots\Lambda_{1,s}^T(u_{k-1})\Lambda_3^T(u_k)\Lambda_4^T(v)\Big)^2 \\ &\quad + 2\Big(\Lambda_{1,s}^T(u_1)\Lambda_{1,s}^T(u_2)\cdots\Lambda_{1,s}^T(u_{k-1})\Lambda_3^T(u_k)\Lambda_{2,s}^T(v)\Big)^2 \\ &\quad + 2((C_1)_s)^{2(k-1)}T^{\frac{1}{2}}\Big(\Lambda_{1,s}^T(u_1)\Lambda_{1,s}^T(u_2)\cdots\Lambda_{1,s}^T(u_k)\Lambda_4^T(v)\Big)^2 \\ &\leq 5\widetilde{C}_s^{2(k-1)} \| u_1 \|_{Y_T}^2 \| u_2 \|_{Y_T}^2 \cdots \| u_k \|_{Y_T}^2 \| v \|_{Y_T}^2\end{aligned} \tag{47}$$

holds.

Then, when $n = k+1$, we obtain

$$\begin{aligned}
&\int_0^T \| u_1u_2\cdots u_{k+1}v_x(t) \|^2_{H_x^{\frac{s}{3}}(0,\infty)} \, dt \\
&\le T^{\frac{1}{2}}\Big(\Lambda^T_{1,s}(u_1)\Lambda^T_{1,s}(u_2)\cdots\Lambda^T_{1,s}(u_{k-1})\Lambda^T_3(u_ku_{k+1})\Lambda^T_4(v)\Big)^2 \\
&\quad + 2\Big(\Lambda^T_{1,s}(u_1)\Lambda^T_{1,s}(u_2)\cdots\Lambda^T_{1,s}(u_{k-1})\Lambda^T_3(u_ku_{k+1})\Lambda^T_{2,s}(v)\Big)^2 \\
&\quad + 2((C_1)_s)^{2(k-1)}T^{\frac{1}{2}}\Big(\Lambda^T_{1,s}(u_1)\Lambda^T_{1,s}(u_2)\cdots\Lambda^T_{1,s}(u_{k-1})\Lambda^T_{1,s}(u_ku_{k+1})\Lambda^T_4(v)\Big)^2, \\
&\quad \text{(by Formula (47))} \\
&\le T^{\frac{1}{2}}\Big(\Lambda^T_{1,s}(u_1)\Lambda^T_{1,s}(u_2)\cdots\Lambda^T_{1,s}(u_k)\Lambda^T_3(u_{k+1})\Lambda^T_4(v)\Big)^2 \\
&\quad + 2\Big(\Lambda^T_{1,s}(u_1)\Lambda^T_{1,s}(u_2)\cdots\Lambda^T_{1,s}(u_k)\Lambda^T_3(u_{k+1})\Lambda^T_{2,s}(v)\Big)^2 \\
&\quad + 2((C_1)_s)^{2(k-1)}T^{\frac{1}{2}}\Big(\Lambda^T_{1,s}(u_1)\Lambda^T_{1,s}(u_2)\cdots\Lambda^T_{1,s}(u_{k-1})(C_1)_s\Lambda^T_{1,s}(u_k)\Lambda^T_{1,s}(u_{k+1})\Lambda^T_4(v)\Big)^2, \\
&\quad \text{(by Lemma 9)} \\
&\le T^{\frac{1}{2}}\Big(\Lambda^T_{1,s}(u_1)\Lambda^T_{1,s}(u_2)\cdots\Lambda^T_{1,s}(u_k)\Lambda^T_3(u_{k+1})\Lambda^T_4(v)\Big)^2 \\
&\quad + 2\Big(\Lambda^T_{1,s}(u_1)\Lambda^T_{1,s}(u_2)\cdots\Lambda^T_{1,s}(u_k)\Lambda^T_3(u_{k+1})\Lambda^T_{2,s}(v)\Big)^2 \\
&\quad + 2((C_1)_s)^{2k}T^{\frac{1}{2}}\Big(\Lambda^T_{1,s}(u_1)\Lambda^T_{1,s}(u_2)\cdots\Lambda^T_{1,s}(u_{k-1})\Lambda^T_{1,s}(u_k)\Lambda^T_{1,s}(u_{k+1})\Lambda^T_4(v)\Big)^2 \\
&\le 5\widetilde{C}_s^{2k} \| u_1 \|^2_{Y_T} \| u_2 \|^2_{Y_T} \cdots \| u_{k+1} \|^2_{Y_T} \| v \|^2_{Y_T}.
\end{aligned}$$

Therefore, when $n = k+1$, the inequality (46) holds.

By mathematical induction, we finish the proof of inequality (46). □

Refining our solution space from $C([0,T]; H_x^s(0,\infty)$ to Y_T requires additional estimates for the UTM solution $S_{LK}[v_0, g_2; f_2]$ of (4). Therefore, $S_{LK}[v_0, g_2; f_2]$ must be estimated using the Λ-norms (11) and (12), which define the norm (10) of Y_T.

These new linear estimates are presented in the following proposition and are proven in Section 5.

Proposition 2 (Λ-norms estimates for the forced linear IBVP). *For $3/4 < s < 1$, the solution $S_{LK}[v_0, g_2; f_2]$ of the forced linear KdV IBVP (4) defined by the UTM formula (6) admits the estimate:*

$$\begin{aligned}
&\Lambda^T(S_{LK}[v_0, g_2; f_2]) &(48)\\
&\le (d_2)_s\left(\| v_0 \|_{H_x^s(0,\infty)} + \| g_2 \|_{H_t^{\frac{s}{3}}(0,T)} + T^{\frac{3-2s}{6}}\left(\int_0^T \| f_2(t) \|^2_{H_x^s(0,\infty)} \, dt\right)^{\frac{1}{2}}\right),
\end{aligned}$$

where $(d_2)_s > 0$ is a constant depending on s.

5. The Proof of Proposition 2 (About the Norms Estimates of the Forced Linear KdV IBVP)

In this section, we will prove Proposition 2. Recall that $S_{LK}[v_0, g_2; f_2]$ (32) is the solution of the forced linear KdV IBVP (4),

$$S_{LK}[v_0, g_2; f_2] = S[V_0; 0]|_{x>0} + S[0; F_2]|_{x>0} + S[0, G_1; 0] + S[0, H_1; 0],$$

where $S[V_0; 0]$ is the solution of the linear IVP (24).

$S[0;F_2]$ is the solution of the forced linear IVP (27), and $S[0,G_1;0]$ and $S[0,H_1;0]$ are the solution of the linear IVP (30) and (31), respectively. Now, we must estimate the Λ-norms for $S_{LK}[v_0,g_2;f_2]$. We decompose the estimate into four cases:

(A) We estimate the $\Lambda^T_{1,s}$-norm for $S_{LK}[v_0,g_2;f_2]$ to obtain

$$\Lambda^T_{1,s}(S_{LK}[v_0,g_2;f_2]) \lesssim \| v_0 \|_{H^s_x(0,\infty)} + \| g_2 \|_{H_t^{\frac{s}{3}}(0,T)} + T^{\frac{3-2s}{6}}\left(\int_0^T \| f_2(t) \|^2_{H^s_x(0,\infty)} dt\right)^{\frac{1}{2}}; \tag{49}$$

(B) We estimate the $\Lambda^T_{2,s}$-norm for $S_{LK}[v_0,g_2;f_2]$ to obtain

$$\Lambda^T_{2,s}(S_{LK}[v_0,g_2;f_2]) \lesssim \| v_0 \|_{H^s_x(0,\infty)} + \| g_2 \|_{H_t^{\frac{s}{3}}(0,T)} + T^{\frac{3-2s}{6}}\left(\int_0^T \| f_2(t) \|^2_{H^s_x(0,\infty)} dt\right)^{\frac{1}{2}}; \tag{50}$$

(C) When $s > 3/4$, we estimate the Λ^T_3-norm for $S_{LK}[v_0,g_2;f_2]$ to obtain

$$\Lambda^T_3(S_{LK}[v_0,g_2;f_2]) \lesssim \| v_0 \|_{H^s_x(0,\infty)} + \| g_2 \|_{H_t^{\frac{s}{3}}(0,T)} + T^{\frac{3-2s}{6}}\left(\int_0^T \| f_2(t) \|^2_{H^s_x(0,\infty)} dt\right)^{\frac{1}{2}}; \tag{51}$$

(D) We estimate the Λ^T_4-norm for $S_{LK}[v_0,g_2;f_2]$ to obtain

$$\Lambda^T_4(S_{LK}[v_0,g_2;f_2]) \lesssim \| v_0 \|_{H^s_x(0,\infty)} + \| g_2 \|_{H_t^{\frac{s}{3}}(0,T)} + T^{\frac{3-2s}{6}}\left(\int_0^T \| f_2(t) \|^2_{H^s_x(0,\infty)} dt\right)^{\frac{1}{2}}. \tag{52}$$

Since

$$\begin{aligned}&\Lambda^T(S_{LK}[v_0,g_2;f_2])\\ &= \max\Big\{\Lambda^T_{1,s}(S_{LK}[v_0,g_2;f_2]), \Lambda^T_{2,s}(S_{LK}[v_0,g_2;f_2]), \Lambda^T_3(S_{LK}[v_0,g_2;f_2]), \Lambda^T_4(S_{LK}[v_0,g_2;f_2])\Big\},\end{aligned}$$

and by (49), (50), (51), and (52), we can yield that (48)

$$\begin{aligned}&\Lambda(S[v_0,g_2;f_2])\\ &\lesssim \| v_0 \|_{H^s_x(0,\infty)} + \| g_2 \|_{H_t^{\frac{s}{3}}(0,T)} + T^{\frac{3-2s}{6}}\left(\int_0^T \| f_2(t) \|^2_{H^s_x(0,\infty)} dt\right)^{\frac{1}{2}}, \text{ for } \frac{3}{4} < s < 1.\end{aligned}$$

Therefore, the proof of Proposition 2 is complete.

We will now proceed to prove statements (A), (B), (C), and (D).

(A) The estimate of $\Lambda^T_{1,s}$-norm for $S_{LK}[v_0,g_2;f_2]$ is as follows: For $3/4 < s < 1$,

$$\begin{aligned}&\Lambda^T_{1,s}(S_{LK}[v_0,g_2;f_2])\\ &= \Lambda^T_{1,s}\big(S[V_0;0]|_{x>0} + S[0;F_2]|_{x>0} + S[0,G_1;0] + S[0,H_1;0]\big)\\ &\le \sup_{t\in[0,T]} \| S[V_0;0]|_{x>0} \|_{H^s_x(0,\infty)} + \sup_{t\in[0,T]} \| S[0;F_2]|_{x>0} \|_{H^s_x(0,\infty)}\\ &\quad + \sup_{t\in[0,T]} \| S[0,G_1;0] \|_{H^s_x(0,\infty)} + \sup_{t\in[0,T]} \| S[0,H_1;0] \|_{H^s_x(0,\infty)}\\ &\lesssim \| v_0 \|_{H^s_x(0,\infty)} + \| g_2 \|_{H_t^{\frac{s}{3}}(0,T)} + T^{\frac{3-2s}{6}}\left(\int_0^T \| f_2(t) \|^2_{H^s_x(0,\infty)} dt\right)^{\frac{1}{2}},\end{aligned}$$

(by (25), (28), (33), (36), (39), (40), (41), and (42).

In fact, by (8), we can attain (49).

(B) The estimate of $\Lambda^T_{2,s}$-norm for $S_{LK}[v_0,g_2;f_2]$ is as follows: For $3/4<s<1$,

$$
\begin{aligned}
&\Lambda^T_{2,s}(S_{LK}[v_0,g_2;f_2])\\
&=\Lambda^T_{2,s}\big(S[V_0;0]|_{x>0}+S[0;F_2]|_{x>0}+S[0,G_1;0]+S[0,H_1;0]\big)\\
&=\left(\sup_{x\in[0,\infty)}\int_0^T\left|D^s_x\partial_x\big(S[V_0;0]|_{x>0}+S[0;F_2]|_{x>0}+S[0,G_1;0]+S[0,H_1;0]\big)\right|^2dt\right)^{\frac12}\\
&\lesssim\underbrace{\left(\sup_{x\in[0,\infty)}\int_0^T|D^s_x\partial_xS[V_0;0]|^2dt\right)^{\frac12}}_{(a)}+\underbrace{\left(\sup_{x\in[0,\infty)}\int_0^T|D^s_x\partial_xS[0;F_2]|^2dt\right)^{\frac12}}_{(b)}\\
&\quad+\underbrace{\left(\sup_{x\in[0,\infty)}\int_0^T|D^s_x\partial_xS[0,G_1;0]|^2dt\right)^{\frac12}}_{(c)}+\underbrace{\left(\sup_{x\in[0,\infty)}\int_0^T|D^s_x\partial_xS[0,H_1;0]|^2dt\right)^{\frac12}}_{(d)}.
\end{aligned}
$$

We must estimate (a), (b), (c), and (d); then, we attain the following results:

We estimate (a) as follows:

$$
\begin{aligned}
(a)&=\left(\sup_{x\in[0,\infty)}\int_0^T\left|\int_0^\infty\frac{|V_x(x+\zeta,t)-V_x(x,t)|^2}{\zeta^{1+2\beta}}d\zeta\right|dt\right)^{\frac12}\\
&=\left(\sup_{x\in[0,\infty)}\int_0^T\left(\int_0^\infty\frac{\left|\int_{\mathbb{R}}ke^{ikx+ik^3t}\left(e^{ik\zeta}-1\right)\widehat{V_0}(k)dk\right|^2}{2\pi\zeta^{1+2\beta}}d\zeta\right)dt\right)^{\frac12},
\end{aligned}
$$

(let $\eta=k^3$ and by the Parseval's Theorem)

$$
\begin{aligned}
&\le\left(\sup_{x\in[0,\infty)}\int_0^\infty\left(\frac{\int_{\mathbb{R}}\left|e^{i\eta^{\frac13}x}\left(e^{i\eta^{\frac13}\zeta}-1\right)\frac{\widehat{V_0}(\eta^{\frac13})}{3\eta^{\frac13}}\right|^2d\eta}{\zeta^{1+2\beta}}\right)d\zeta\right)^{\frac12}\\
&=\frac13\left(\sup_{x\in[0,\infty)}\int_{\mathbb{R}}\left|\frac{\widehat{V_0}(\eta^{\frac13})}{3\eta^{\frac13}}\right|^2\left(\int_0^\infty\frac{\left|e^{i\eta^{\frac13}\zeta}-1\right|^2}{\zeta^{1+2\beta}}d\zeta\right)d\eta\right)^{\frac12}\\
&=\frac13\left(\sup_{x\in[0,\infty)}\int_{\mathbb{R}}\left|\frac{\widehat{V_0}(\eta^{\frac13})}{3\eta^{\frac13}}\right|^2\left(\int_0^\infty\frac{4\sin^2\left(\frac{\eta^{\frac13}\zeta}{2}\right)}{\zeta^{1+2\beta}}d\zeta\right)d\eta\right)^{\frac12},\ (\text{let } y=\frac{\eta^{\frac13}\zeta}{2})\\
&\simeq\frac13\left(\sup_{x\in[0,\infty)}\int_{\mathbb{R}}\left|\frac{\widehat{V_0}(\eta^{\frac13})}{\eta^{\frac13}}\right|^2\eta^{\frac{2\beta}{3}}\left(\int_0^1\frac{\sin^2y}{y^{1+2\beta}}dy+\lim_{\tau\to\infty}\int_1^\tau\frac{\sin^2y}{y^{1+2\beta}}dy\right)d\eta\right)^{\frac12}\\
&\lesssim\left(\sup_{x\in[0,\infty)}\int_{\mathbb{R}}\left|\frac{\widehat{V_0}(\eta^{\frac13})}{\eta^{\frac13}}\right|^2\eta^{\frac{2\beta}{3}}d\eta\right)^{\frac12},\ (\text{let } \eta=k^3)\\
&=\left(\int_{\mathbb{R}}3\left|\widehat{V_0}(k)\right|^2k^{2\beta}dk\right)^{\frac12}\le\left(\int_{\mathbb{R}}3\left|\widehat{V_0}(k)\right|^2(1+k^2)^\beta dk\right)^{\frac12}\lesssim\|V_0\|_{H^s_x(\mathbb{R})}.
\end{aligned}
$$

Therefore, we derive the following inequality:

$$(a) \lesssim \| V_0 \|_{H^s_x(\mathbb{R})} \leq 2 \| v_0 \|_{H^s_x(0,\infty)}, \text{ (by (25))}. \quad (53)$$

We estimate (b) as follows:

$$\begin{aligned}
(b) &= \left(\sup_{x\in[0,\infty)} \int_0^T |D^s_x \partial_x S[0;F_2]|^2 dt \right)^{\frac{1}{2}} \\
&= \left(\sup_{x\in[0,\infty)} \int_0^T \left| D^s_x \partial_x \left(\int_0^t S[F_2(\cdot,t');0](x,t-t')dt' \right) \right|^2 dt \right)^{\frac{1}{2}} \\
&\leq \left(\sup_{x\in[0,\infty)} \int_0^T \left(\int_0^t \left| D^s_x \partial_x S[F_2(\cdot,t');0](x,t-t') \right| dt' \right)^2 dt \right)^{\frac{1}{2}} \\
&\leq \sup_{x\in[0,\infty)} \int_0^T \left(\int_{t'}^T \left| D^s_x \partial_x S[F_2(\cdot,t');0](x,t-t') \right|^2 dt \right)^{\frac{1}{2}} dt' \\
&\leq \sup_{x\in[0,\infty)} \int_0^T \left(\int_0^T \left| D^s_x \partial_x S[F_2(\cdot,t');0](x,\tau) \right|^2 d\tau \right)^{\frac{1}{2}} dt', \text{ (let } \tau = t-t') \\
&\leq \int_0^T \left(\sup_{x\in[0,\infty)} \int_0^T \left| D^s_x \partial_x S[F_2(\cdot,t');0](x,\tau) \right|^2 d\tau \right)^{\frac{1}{2}} dt' = \int_0^T \Lambda^T_{2,s}\left(S[F_2(\cdot,t');0]\right) dt' \\
&\lesssim \int_0^T \| F_2(t') \|_{H^s_x(\mathbb{R})} dt', \text{ (by (53))} \\
&\leq T^{\frac{1}{2}} \left(\int_0^T \| F_2(t') \|^2_{H^s_x(\mathbb{R})} dt' \right)^{\frac{1}{2}} \leq 2T^{\frac{1}{2}} \left(\int_0^T \| f_2(t') \|^2_{H^s_x(0,\infty)} dt' \right)^{\frac{1}{2}}, \text{ (by (28))}.
\end{aligned}$$

Hence, we derive the following inequality:

$$(b) \lesssim T^{\frac{1}{2}} \left(\int_0^T \| f_2(t') \|^2_{H^s_x(0,\infty)} dt' \right)^{\frac{1}{2}}. \quad (54)$$

To estimate (c) and (d), we consider the UTM solution formula

$$S_{LK}[0,g;0] = \omega_1 + \omega_2, \quad (55)$$

where

$$\begin{aligned}
\omega_1(x,t) &= \frac{-3i}{2\pi} \int_0^\infty e^{iakx - ik^3 t} \frac{k^2}{ak + i\gamma_2} \widetilde{g}(-k^3,T) dk, \\
\omega_2(x,t) &= \frac{-3i}{2\pi} \int_0^\infty e^{ia^2 kx + ik^3 t} \frac{k^2}{a^2 k + i\gamma_2} \widetilde{g}(k^3,T) dk.
\end{aligned}$$

We assume

$$\chi_{[0,T]} = \begin{cases} 1, & \text{if } x \in [0,T], \\ 0, & \text{if } x \in \mathbb{R} \backslash [0,T]. \end{cases}$$

Now, we estimate $\Lambda^T_{2,s}(\omega_1)$, and the estimate of $\Lambda^T_{2,s}(\omega_2)$ is similar to the estimate of $\Lambda^T_{2,s}(\omega_1)$.

$$
\begin{aligned}
\left(\Lambda_{2,s}^{T}(\omega_1)\right)^2 &= \sup_{x\in[0,\infty)} \int_0^T |D_x^s \partial_x \omega_1(x,t)|^2 dt \\
&= \sup_{x\in[0,\infty)} \int_0^T \left(\int_0^\infty \frac{|\partial_x\omega_1(x+\zeta,t) - \partial_x\omega_1(x,t)|^2}{\zeta^{1+2\beta}} d\zeta \right) dt \\
&\simeq \sup_{x\in[0,\infty)} \int_0^T \left(\int_0^\infty \frac{\left| \int_0^\infty e^{iakx-ik^3t}\left(e^{iak\zeta}-1\right)\frac{k^3}{ak+i\gamma_2}\widehat{\mathcal{X}_{[0,T]}g}(-k^3)dk \right|^2}{2\pi\zeta^{1+2\beta}} d\zeta \right) dt \\
&\leq \sup_{x\in[0,\infty)} \int_0^\infty \left(\int_0^T \frac{\left| \int_{-\infty}^0 e^{-ia\tau^{\frac{1}{3}}x+i\tau t}\left(e^{-ia\tau^{\frac{1}{3}}\zeta}-1\right)\frac{-\tau}{-a\tau^{\frac{1}{3}}+i\gamma_2}\widehat{\mathcal{X}_{[0,T]}g}(\tau)d\tau \right|^2}{2\pi\zeta^{1+2\beta}|\tau|^{\frac{2}{3}}} dt \right) d\zeta,
\end{aligned}
$$

(by Fubini's Theorem and let $\tau = -k^3$)

$$
\leq \sup_{x\in[0,\infty)} \int_0^\infty \left(\frac{\int_{-\infty}^0 \left| e^{-ia\tau^{\frac{1}{3}}x}\left(e^{-ia\tau^{\frac{1}{3}}\zeta}-1\right)\widehat{\mathcal{X}_{[0,T]}g}(\tau) \right|^2 d\tau}{\zeta^{1+2\beta}} \right) d\zeta,
$$

(by Parseval's Theorem)

$$
\begin{aligned}
&\leq \sup_{x\in[0,\infty)} \int_0^\infty \left(\frac{\int_{-\infty}^0 e^{\sqrt{3}\tau^{\frac{1}{3}}x}\left| e^{\frac{\sqrt{3}}{2}\tau^{\frac{1}{3}}\zeta}-1\right|^2 \left|\widehat{\mathcal{X}_{[0,T]}g}(\tau)\right|^2 d\tau}{\zeta^{1+2\beta}}, \right) d\zeta, \text{ (by Lemma 1)} \\
&\leq \int_0^\infty \left(\frac{\int_{-\infty}^0 \left| e^{\frac{\sqrt{3}}{2}\tau^{\frac{1}{3}}\zeta}-1\right|^2 \left|\widehat{\mathcal{X}_{[0,T]}g}(\tau)\right|^2 d\tau}{\zeta^{1+2\beta}} \right) d\zeta \\
&= \int_{-\infty}^0 \left|\widehat{\mathcal{X}_{[0,T]}g}(\tau)\right|^2 \left(\int_0^\infty \frac{\left| e^{\frac{\sqrt{3}}{2}\tau^{\frac{1}{3}}\zeta}-1\right|^2}{\zeta^{1+2\beta}} d\zeta \right) d\tau \lesssim \int_{-\infty}^0 \left|\widehat{\mathcal{X}_{[0,T]}g}(\tau)\right|^2 \left(\frac{\sqrt{3}}{2}\tau^{\frac{1}{3}}\right)^{2\beta} d\tau,
\end{aligned}
$$

(let $r = -\frac{\sqrt{3}}{2}\tau^{\frac{1}{3}}\zeta$, and by $\int_0^\infty \frac{(1-e^{-r})^2}{r^{1+2\beta}}dr < \infty$)

$$
\leq \int_{\mathbb{R}} \left(1+\tau^2\right)^{\frac{\beta}{3}} \left|\widehat{\mathcal{X}_{[0,T]}g}(\tau)\right|^2 d\tau = \| \mathcal{X}_{[0,T]}g \|^2_{H_t^{\frac{\beta}{3}}(\mathbb{R})} \leq \| g \|^2_{H_t^{\frac{s}{3}}(\mathbb{R})}.
$$

We can estimate $\Lambda_{2,s}^T(\omega_2)$ in a similar way. Hence, we obtain the following inequalities:

$$
\Lambda_{2,s}^T(\omega_1) \lesssim \| g \|_{H_t^{\frac{s}{3}}(\mathbb{R})}, \quad \Lambda_{2,s}^T(\omega_2) \lesssim \| g \|_{H_t^{\frac{s}{3}}(\mathbb{R})}. \tag{56}
$$

According to (17) and (56), we obtain

$$
\Lambda_{2,s}^T(S[0,g;0]) \lesssim \Lambda_{2,s}^T(\omega_1) + \Lambda_{2,s}^T(\omega_2) \lesssim \| g \|_{H_t^{\frac{s}{3}}(\mathbb{R})} \leq 2 \| g_2 \|_{H_t^{\frac{s}{3}}(0,T)}. \tag{57}
$$

Therefore, we can have the following results:

$$
\begin{aligned}
(c) \lesssim & \| G_1 \|_{H_t^{\frac{s}{3}}(0,T)} = \| g_2(t) - V_x(0,t) - W_x^*(0,t) \|_{H_t^{\frac{s}{3}}(0,T)}, \\
& \text{(by (17), (30), and (57))} \\
& \leq \| g_2 \|_{H_t^{\frac{s}{3}}(0,T)} + \| V_x(0,t) \|_{H_t^{\frac{s}{3}}(0,T)} + \| W_x^*(0,t) \|_{H_t^{\frac{s}{3}}(0,T)} \\
& \leq \| g_2 \|_{H_t^{\frac{s}{3}}(0,T)} + (C_7)_s \| V_0 \|_{H_x^s(\mathbb{R})} + (C_{10})_s T^{\frac{3-2s}{6}} \| F_2 \|_{L^2([0,T];\, H_x^s(\mathbb{R}))}, \\
& \text{(by (35) and (38))} \\
& \leq \| g_2 \|_{H_t^{\frac{s}{3}}(0,T)} + 2(C_7)_s \| v_0 \|_{H_x^s(0,\infty)} + 2(C_{10})_s T^{\frac{3-2s}{6}} \| f_2 \|_{L^2([0,T];H_x^s(0,\infty))}, \\
& \text{(by (25) and (28))} \\
& \lesssim \| v_0 \|_{H_x^s(0,\infty)} + \| g_2 \|_{H_t^{\frac{s}{3}}(0,T)} + T^{\frac{3-2s}{6}} \left(\int_0^T \| f_2(t) \|^2_{H_x^s(0,\infty)} \, dt \right)^{\frac{1}{2}},
\end{aligned} \tag{58}
$$

and

$$
\begin{aligned}
(d) \lesssim & \| H_1 \|_{H_t^{\frac{s}{3}}(0,T)} = \| \gamma_2 V(0,t) + \gamma_2 W^*(0,t) \|_{H_t^{\frac{s}{3}}(0,T)}, \\
& \text{(by (17), (31), and (57))} \\
& \leq |\gamma_2| \, \| V(0,t) \|_{H_t^{\frac{s}{3}}(0,T)} + |\gamma_2| \, \| W(0,t) \|_{H_t^{\frac{s}{3}}(0,T)} \\
& \leq |\gamma_2| \, \| V(0,t) \|_{H_t^{\frac{s+1}{3}}(0,T)} + |\gamma_2| \, \| W(0,t) \|_{H_t^{\frac{s+1}{3}}(0,T)} \\
& \leq (C_6)_s |\gamma_2| \, \| V_0 \|_{H_x^s(\mathbb{R})} + (C_9)_s |\gamma_2| T^{\frac{2-s}{3}} \| F_2 \|_{L^2([0,T];\, H_x^s(\mathbb{R}))}, \\
& \text{(by (34) and (37))} \\
& \leq 2(C_6)_s |\gamma_2| \, \| v_0 \|_{H_x^s(0,\infty)} + 2(C_9)_s |\gamma_2| T^{\frac{2-s}{3}} \| f_2 \|_{L^2([0,T];H_x^s(0,\infty))}, \\
& \text{(by (25) and (28))} \\
& \lesssim \| v_0 \|_{H_x^s(0,\infty)} + T^{\frac{2-s}{3}} \left(\int_0^T \| f_2(t) \|^2_{H_x^s(0,\infty)} \, dt \right)^{\frac{1}{2}}.
\end{aligned} \tag{59}
$$

According to (53), (54), (58), and (59), we obtain (50):

$$
\begin{aligned}
& \Lambda_{2,s}^T(S_{LK}[v_0, g_2; f_2]) \\
& \lesssim \| v_0 \|_{H_x^s(0,\infty)} + \| g_2 \|_{H_t^{\frac{s}{3}}(0,T)} + T^{\frac{3-2s}{6}} \left(\int_0^T \| f_2(t) \|^2_{H_x^s(0,\infty)} \, dt \right)^{\frac{1}{2}}.
\end{aligned}
$$

(C) The estimate of Λ_3^T-norm for $S_{LK}[v_0, g_2; f_2]$ is as follows: For $3/4 < s < 1$,

$$
\begin{aligned}
& \Lambda_3^T(S_{LK}[v_0, g_2; f_2]) \\
& = \left(\int_0^\infty \sup_{t \in [0,T]} |S_{LK}[v_0, g_2; f_2](x,t)|^2 dx \right)^{\frac{1}{2}} \\
& = \left(\int_0^\infty \sup_{t \in [0,T]} \left| S[V_0; 0]|_{x>0} + S[0; F_2]|_{x>0} + S[0, G_1; 0] + S[0, H_1; 0] \right|^2 dx \right)^{\frac{1}{2}} \\
& \lesssim \Lambda_3^T(S[V_0; 0]) + \Lambda_3^T(S[0; F_2]) + \Lambda_3^T(S[0, G_1; 0]) + \Lambda_3^T(S[0, H_1; 0]).
\end{aligned}
$$

We must estimate $\Lambda_3^T(S[V_0; 0])$, $\Lambda_3^T(S[0; F_2])$, $\Lambda_3^T(S[0, G_1; 0])$, and $\Lambda_3^T(S[0, H_1; 0])$.

The estimate of $\Lambda_3^T(S[V_0;0])$ according to (25) in [37] is

$$\Lambda_3^T(S[V_0;0]) \leq (C_{14})_s(1+T)^\rho \parallel v_0 \parallel_{H_x^s(0,\infty)}, \text{ for } s,\rho > \frac{3}{4}. \quad (60)$$

The estimate of $\Lambda_3^T(S_{LK}[0;F_2])$ is as follows:

$$\begin{aligned}
&\Lambda_3^T(S_{LK}[0;F_2]) \quad (61)\\
&= \left(\int_0^\infty \sup_{t\in[0,T]} \left|\int_0^t S_{LK}[F_2(\cdot,t');0](x,t-t')dt'\right|^2 dx\right)^{\frac{1}{2}},
\end{aligned}$$

(since $\left|S_{LK}[F_2(\cdot,t');0](x,t-t')\right| \leq \sup_{\tau\in[0,T]} \left|S_{LK}[F_2(\cdot,t');0](x,\tau)\right|, 0 \leq t' \leq t \leq T, x \in [0,\infty)$,

and let $\tau = t - t'$),

$$\begin{aligned}
&\leq \left(\int_0^\infty \left|\int_0^T \sup_{\tau\in[0,T]} \left|S_{LK}[F_2(\cdot,t');0](x,\tau)\right|dt'\right|^2 dx\right)^{\frac{1}{2}}\\
&\leq \int_0^T \left(\int_0^\infty \sup_{\tau\in[0,T]} \left|S_{LK}[F_2(\cdot,t');0](x,\tau)\right|^2 dx\right)^{\frac{1}{2}} dt'\\
&= \int_0^T \Lambda_3^T\left(S_{LK}[F_2(\cdot,t');0]\right)dt'\\
&\lesssim \int_0^T (1+T)^\rho \parallel f_2(t') \parallel_{H_x^s(0,\infty)} dt', \text{ (by (60))}\\
&\lesssim (1+T)^\rho T^{\frac{1}{2}} \left(\int_0^T \parallel f_2(t) \parallel^2_{H_x^s(0,\infty)} dt\right)^{\frac{1}{2}}, \text{ for } s,\rho > \frac{3}{4}.
\end{aligned}$$

The estimates of $\Lambda_3^T(S_{LK}[0,G_1;0])$ and $\Lambda_3^T(S_{LK}[0,H_1;0])$ are as follows: We consider the UTM solution formula (55) and

$$\begin{aligned}
\Lambda_3^T(S_{LK}[0,g;0]) &= \Lambda_3^T(\omega_1+\omega_2)\\
&\leq \sqrt{2}\left(\int_0^\infty \sup_{t\in[0,T]} |\omega_1(x,t)|^2 dx\right)^{\frac{1}{2}} + \sqrt{2}\left(\int_0^\infty \sup_{t\in[0,T]} |\omega_2(x,t)|^2 dx\right)^{\frac{1}{2}}\\
&= \sqrt{2}\Lambda_3^T(\omega_1) + \sqrt{2}\Lambda_3^T(\omega_2).
\end{aligned}$$

We will estimate $\Lambda_3^T(\omega_1)$, noting that the estimate for $\Lambda_3^T(\omega_2)$ follows similarly to that of $\Lambda_3^T(\omega_1)$.

$$\begin{aligned}
\Lambda_3^T(\omega_1) &= \left(\int_0^\infty \sup_{t\in[0,T]} |\omega_1(x,t)|^2 dx\right)^{\frac{1}{2}}\\
&\leq \left(\int_0^\infty \sup_{t\in[0,T]} \left(\int_0^\infty e^{-\frac{\sqrt{3}}{2}kx} k\left|\widehat{\chi_{[0,T]}g}(-k^3)\right|dk\right)^2 dx\right)^{\frac{1}{2}}\\
&= \left(\int_0^\infty \sup_{t\in[0,T]} \left(\int_0^\infty e^{-ky} k\left|\widehat{\chi_{[0,T]}g}(-k^3)\right|dk\right)^2 \frac{2}{\sqrt{3}}dy\right)^{\frac{1}{2}}, \text{ (let } y = \frac{\sqrt{3}}{2}x)\\
&\lesssim \left(\int_0^\infty k^2\left|\widehat{\chi_{[0,T]}g}(-k^3)\right|^2 dk\right)^{\frac{1}{2}}, \text{ (by Lemma 2)}\\
&\leq \left(\int_{\mathbb{R}}\left|\widehat{\chi_{[0,T]}g}(\eta)\right|^2 d\eta\right)^{\frac{1}{2}}, \text{ (let } \eta = -k^3)\\
&= \parallel \chi_{[0,T]}g \parallel_{L^2(\mathbb{R})} \leq \parallel g \parallel_{H_t^{\frac{s}{3}}(\mathbb{R})}.
\end{aligned}$$

We can estimate $\Lambda_3^T(\omega_2)$ in the same way. Hence, we obtain the following inequalities:

$$\Lambda_3^T(\omega_1) \lesssim \| g \|_{H_t^{\frac{s}{3}}(\mathbb{R})}, \ \Lambda_3^T(\omega_2) \lesssim \| g \|_{H_t^{\frac{s}{3}}(\mathbb{R})}.$$

Hence, we can yield that

$$\Lambda_3^T(S_{LK}[0, g; 0]) \lesssim \| g \|_{H_t^{\frac{s}{3}}(\mathbb{R})} \le 2 \| g_2 \|_{H_t^{\frac{s}{3}}(0,T)}, \text{ (by (17))}. \tag{62}$$

Therefore, we can have the following results:

$$\begin{aligned}
&\Lambda_3^T(S[0, G_1; 0]) \\
&\lesssim \| G_1 \|_{H_t^{\frac{s}{3}}(0,T)} = \| g_2(t) - V_x(0,t) - W_x^*(0,t) \|_{H_t^{\frac{s}{3}}(0,T)}, \\
&\quad \text{(by (17), (18), (30), and (62))} \\
&\le \| g_2 \|_{H_t^{\frac{s}{3}}(0,T)} + \| V_x(0,t) \|_{H_t^{\frac{s}{3}}(0,T)} + \| W_x^*(0,t) \|_{H_t^{\frac{s}{3}}(0,T)} \\
&\le \| g_2 \|_{H_t^{\frac{s}{3}}(0,T)} + (C_7)_s \| V_0 \|_{H_x^s(\mathbb{R})} + (C_{10})_s T^{\frac{3-2s}{6}} \| F_2 \|_{L^2([0,T];\, H_x^s(\mathbb{R}))}, \\
&\quad \text{(by (35) and (38))} \\
&\le \| g_2 \|_{H_t^{\frac{s}{3}}(0,T)} + 2(C_7)_s \| v_0 \|_{H_x^s(0,\infty)} + 2(C_{10})_s T^{\frac{3-2s}{6}} \| f_2 \|_{L^2([0,T];H_x^s(0,\infty))}, \\
&\quad \text{(by (25) and (28))} \\
&\lesssim \| v_0 \|_{H_x^s(0,\infty)} + \| g_2 \|_{H_t^{\frac{s}{3}}(0,T)} + T^{\frac{3-2s}{6}} \left(\int_0^T \| f_2(t) \|_{H_x^s(0,\infty)}^2 \, dt \right)^{\frac{1}{2}},
\end{aligned} \tag{63}$$

and

$$\begin{aligned}
\Lambda_3^T(S[0, H_1; 0]) &\lesssim \| H_1 \|_{H_t^{\frac{s}{3}}(0,T)} = \| \gamma_2 V(0,t) + \gamma_2 W^*(0,t) \|_{H_t^{\frac{s}{3}}(0,T)}, \\
&\quad \text{(by (17), (18), (30), and (62))} \\
&\le |\gamma_2| \| V(0,t) \|_{H_t^{\frac{s}{3}}(0,T)} + |\gamma_2| \| W^*(0,t) \|_{H_t^{\frac{s}{3}}(0,T)} \\
&\le |\gamma_2| \| V(0,t) \|_{H_t^{\frac{s+1}{3}}(0,T)} + |\gamma_2| \| W^*(0,t) \|_{H_t^{\frac{s+1}{3}}(0,T)} \\
&\le (C_6)_s |\gamma_2| \| V_0 \|_{H_x^s(\mathbb{R})} + (C_9)_s |\gamma_2| T^{\frac{2-s}{3}} \| F_2 \|_{L^2([0,T];\, H_x^s(\mathbb{R}))}, \\
&\quad \text{(by (34) and (37))} \\
&\le 2(C_6)_s |\gamma_2| \| v_0 \|_{H_x^s(0,\infty)} + 2(C_9)_s |\gamma_2| T^{\frac{2-s}{3}} \| f_2 \|_{L^2([0,T];H_x^s(0,\infty))}, \\
&\quad \text{(by (25) and (28))} \\
&\lesssim \| v_0 \|_{H_x^s(0,\infty)} + T^{\frac{2-s}{3}} \left(\int_0^T \| f_2(t) \|_{H_x^s(0,\infty)}^2 \, dt \right)^{\frac{1}{2}}.
\end{aligned} \tag{64}$$

According to (60), (61), (63), and (64), we obtain (51):

$$\begin{aligned}
&\Lambda_3^T(S_{LK}[v_0, g_2; f_2]) \\
&\lesssim \| v_0 \|_{H_x^s(0,\infty)} + \| g_2 \|_{H_t^{\frac{s}{3}}(0,T)} + T^{\frac{3-2s}{6}} \left(\int_0^T \| f_2(t) \|_{H_x^s(0,\infty)}^2 \, dt \right)^{\frac{1}{2}}, \text{ for } s > \frac{3}{4}.
\end{aligned}$$

(D) The estimate of Λ_4^T-norm for $S_{LK}[v_0, g_2; f_2]$ is as follows: For $3/4 < s < 1$,

$$\begin{aligned}
&\Lambda_4^T(S_{LK}[v_0, g_2; f_2]) \\
&= \left(\int_0^T \sup_{x\in[0,\infty)} |\partial_x S_{LK}[v_0, g_2; f_2](x,t)|^4 dt\right)^{\frac{1}{4}} \\
&= \left(\int_0^T \sup_{x\in[0,\infty)} |\partial_x S[V_0;0]|_{x>0} + \partial_x S[0;F_2]|_{x>0} + \partial_x S[0,G_1;0] + \partial_x S[0,H_1;0]|^4 dt\right)^{\frac{1}{4}} \\
&\lesssim \left(\int_0^T \sup_{x\in[0,\infty)} \left(|\partial_x S[V_0;0]|^2 + |\partial_x S[0;F_2]|^2 + |\partial_x S[0,G_1;0]|^2 + |\partial_x S[0,H_1;0]|^2\right)^2 dt\right)^{\frac{1}{4}} \\
&\lesssim \Lambda_4^T(S[V_0;0]) + \Lambda_4^T(S[0;F_2]) + \Lambda_4^T(S[0,G_1;0]) + \Lambda_4^T(S[0,H_1;0]).
\end{aligned}$$

We must estimate $\Lambda_4^T(S[V_0;0])$, $\Lambda_4^T(S[0;F_2])$, $\Lambda_4^T(S[0,G_1;0])$, and $\Lambda_4^T(S[0,H_1;0])$.

The estimate of $\Lambda_4^T(S_{LK}[V_0;0])$ is as follows: we define the operator

$$D^r U^2(t)R(x) \doteq \int_{\mathbb{R}} e^{ikx+ik^3t}(ik)^r \widehat{R}(k)dk \simeq \int_{\mathbb{R}} e^{ikx+ik^3t}|k|^r \widehat{R}(k)dk,$$

where $\widehat{R}(k)$ denotes the Fourier transform of $R(x)$.

Now, we apply Lemma 5 to estimate $\Lambda_4^T(S_{LK}[V_0;0])$:

$$\begin{aligned}
\Lambda_4^T(S_{LK}[V_0;0]) &= \left(\int_0^T \sup_{x\in[0,\infty)} |\partial_x V(x,t)|^4 dt\right)^{\frac{1}{4}} \qquad (65)\\
&= \left(\int_0^T \sup_{x\in[0,\infty)} \left|\frac{1}{2\pi}\int_{\mathbb{R}} ike^{ikx+ik^3t}\widehat{V_0}(k)dk\right|^4 dt\right)^{\frac{1}{4}}, \\
&\left(\text{let } R(x) = \frac{1}{2\pi}\int_{\mathbb{R}} e^{ikx}\widehat{R}(k)dk \text{ and } \widehat{R}(k) = k^{\frac{3}{4}}\widehat{V_0}(k)\right) \\
&= \left(\int_0^T \sup_{x\in[0,\infty)} \left|\frac{1}{2\pi}D^{\frac{1}{4}}U^2(t)R(x)\right|^4 dt\right)^{\frac{1}{4}} \\
&\leq \left(\int_0^T \| D^{\frac{1}{4}}U^2(t)R(x) \|^4_{L_x^\infty(\mathbb{R})} dt\right)^{\frac{1}{4}} \\
&\leq \| D^{\frac{1}{4}}U^2(t)R(x) \|_{L^4[\mathbb{R}_t;L_x^\infty(\mathbb{R})]} \lesssim \| R \|_{L_x^2(\mathbb{R})}, \text{ (by Lemma 5)} \\
&= \left(\int_{\mathbb{R}} |R(x)|^2 dx\right)^{\frac{1}{2}} = \left(\int_{\mathbb{R}} |\widehat{R}(k)|^2 dk\right)^{\frac{1}{2}} \\
&\leq \left(\int_{\mathbb{R}} \left(1+k^2\right)^{\frac{3}{4}} \left|\widehat{V_0}(k)\right|^2 dk\right)^{\frac{1}{2}} = \| V_0 \|_{H_x^{\frac{3}{4}}(\mathbb{R})} \leq 2 \| v_0 \|_{H_x^s(0,\infty)}, \text{ for } s \geq \frac{3}{4}.
\end{aligned}$$

Hence, we can yield that

$$\Lambda_4^T(S_{LK}[V_0;0]) \lesssim 2 \| v_0 \|_{H_x^s(0,\infty)}, \text{ for } s \geq \frac{3}{4}. \qquad (66)$$

The estimate of $\Lambda_4^T(S_{LK}[0;F_2])$ is as follows:

$$
\begin{aligned}
&\Lambda_4^T(S_{LK}[0;F_2]) \\
&= \left(\int_0^T \sup_{x\in[0,\infty)} |\partial_x S_{LK}[0;F_2](x,t)|^4 dt\right)^{\frac{1}{4}} \\
&\leq \left(\int_0^T \left(\int_0^t \sup_{x\in[0,\infty)} \left|\partial_x S_{LK}[F_2(\cdot,t^{'});0](x,t-t^{'})\right| dt^{'}\right)^4 dt\right)^{\frac{1}{4}}, \\
&\leq \int_0^T \left(\int_{t^{'}}^T \sup_{x\in[0,\infty)} \left|\partial_x S_{LK}[F_2(\cdot,t^{'});0](x,t-t^{'})\right|^4 dt\right)^{\frac{1}{4}} dt^{'},
\end{aligned}
$$

(by Minkowski's integral inequality)

$$
\leq \int_0^T \left(\int_0^T \sup_{x\in[0,\infty)} \left|\partial_x S_{LK}[F_2(\cdot,t^{'});0](x,\tau)\right|^4 d\tau\right)^{\frac{1}{4}} dt^{'}
$$

(let $\tau = t - t^{'}$)

$$
\begin{aligned}
&= \int_0^T \Lambda_4^T\left(S_{LK}[F_2(\cdot,t^{'});0]\right) dt^{'} \lesssim \int_0^T \| f_2(t^{'}) \|_{H_x^s(0,\infty)} dt^{'}, \text{ (by (65))} \\
&\leq T^{\frac{1}{2}} \left(\int_0^T \| f_2(t^{'}) \|^2_{H_x^s(0,\infty)} dt^{'}\right)^2, \text{ (by the Cauchy–Schwartz inequality).}
\end{aligned}
$$

Hence, we can yield that

$$
\Lambda_4^T(S_{LK}[0;F_2]) \lesssim T^{\frac{1}{2}} \left(\int_0^T \| f_2(t^{'}) \|^2_{H_x^s(0,\infty)} dt^{'}\right)^2.
$$

The estimate of $\Lambda_4^T(S_{LK}[0,G_1;0])$ and $\Lambda_4^T(S_{LK}[0,H_1;0])$ are as follows: According to the UTM solution formula (55) and

$$
\begin{aligned}
\Lambda_4^T(S[0,g;0]) &= \Lambda_4^T(\omega_1 + \omega_2) \\
&\lesssim \left(\int_0^T \sup_{t\in[0,T]} |\partial_x \omega_1(x,t)|^4 dx\right)^{\frac{1}{4}} + \left(\int_0^T \sup_{t\in[0,T]} |\partial_x \omega_2(x,t)|^4 dx\right)^{\frac{1}{4}} \\
&= \Lambda_4^T(\omega_1) + \Lambda_4^T(\omega_2).
\end{aligned}
$$

We will estimate $\Lambda_4^T(\omega_1)$, noting that the estimate for $\Lambda_4^T(\omega_2)$ follows similarly to that of $\Lambda_4^T(\omega_1)$.

$$
\begin{aligned}
\Lambda_4^T(\omega_1) &= \left(\int_0^T \sup_{x\in[0,\infty)} \left|\frac{-3i}{2\pi}\int_0^\infty iake^{iakx-ik^3t}\frac{k^2}{ak+i\gamma_2}\widetilde{g}(-k^3,T)dk\right|^4 dt\right)^{\frac{1}{4}}, \text{ (let } \tau = k^3) \\
&\simeq \left(\int_0^T \sup_{x\in[0,\infty)} \left|ia\int_0^\infty e^{ia\tau^{\frac{1}{3}}x-i\tau t}\tau^{\frac{-1}{4}}\frac{\tau^{\frac{7}{12}}}{a\tau^{\frac{1}{3}}+ir_2}\widehat{\mathcal{X}_{[0,T]}g}(-\tau)d\tau\right|^4 dt\right)^{\frac{1}{4}},
\end{aligned}
$$

(let $R(t) = \frac{1}{2\pi}\int_{\mathbb{R}} e^{i\tau t}\widehat{R}(\tau)d\tau$, $\widehat{R}(\tau) = \frac{\tau^{\frac{7}{12}}}{a\tau^{\frac{1}{3}}+i\gamma_2}\widehat{\mathcal{X}_{[0,T]}g}(-\tau)$ for $\tau \geq 0$ and $\widehat{R}(\tau) = 0$ for $\tau < 0$)

$$
\begin{aligned}
&= \left(\int_0^T \sup_{x\in[0,\infty)} \left|\int_0^\infty e^{ia\tau^{\frac{1}{3}}x-i\tau t}\tau^{\frac{-1}{4}}\widehat{R}(\tau)d\tau\right|^4 dt\right)^{\frac{1}{4}} = \left(\int_0^T \sup_{x\in[0,\infty)} \left|\Delta^{\frac{-1}{4}} R(x,-t)\right|^4 dt\right)^{\frac{1}{4}} \\
&\lesssim \| R \|_{L_t^2(\mathbb{R})}, \text{ (by Lemma 6)} \\
&= \| \widehat{R} \|_{L_\tau^2(\mathbb{R})} = \left(\int_{\mathbb{R}} \left|\frac{\tau^{\frac{7}{12}}}{a\tau^{\frac{1}{3}}+i\gamma_2}\widehat{\mathcal{X}_{[0,T]}g}(-\tau)\right|^2 d\tau\right)^{\frac{1}{2}} \leq \left(\int_{\mathbb{R}} |\tau|^{\frac{1}{2}} \left|\widehat{\mathcal{X}_{[0,T]}g}(-\tau)\right|^2 d\tau\right)^{\frac{1}{2}} \\
&\lesssim \| g \|_{H_t^{\frac{s}{3}}(\mathbb{R})} \lesssim \| g_2 \|_{H_t^{\frac{s}{3}}(0,T)}, \text{ for } s \geq \frac{3}{4}.
\end{aligned}
$$

We can estimate $\Lambda_4^T(\omega_2)$ in the same way. Hence, we obtain the following inequalities:

$$\Lambda_4^T(\omega_1) \lesssim \| g_2 \|_{H_t^{\frac{s}{3}}(0,T)}, \ \Lambda_4^T(\omega_2) \lesssim \| g_2 \|_{H_t^{\frac{s}{3}}(0,T)}, \text{ for } s \geq \frac{3}{4},$$

then

$$\Lambda_4^T(S_{LK}[0,g;0]) \lesssim \| g_2 \|_{H_t^{\frac{s}{3}}(0,T)}. \tag{67}$$

Therefore, we can have the following results:

$$\begin{aligned}
&\Lambda_4^T(S[0,G_1;0]) \\
&\lesssim \| G_0 \|_{H_t^{\frac{s}{3}}(0,T)} = \| g_2(t) - V_x(0,t) - W_x^*(0,t) \|_{H_t^{\frac{s}{3}}(0,T)}, \\
&\quad \text{(by (17), (18), (30), and (67))} \\
&\leq \| g_2 \|_{H_t^{\frac{s}{3}}(0,T)} + \| V_x(0,t) \|_{H_t^{\frac{s}{3}}(0,T)} + \| W_x^*(0,t) \|_{H_t^{\frac{s}{3}}(0,T)} \\
&\leq \| g_2 \|_{H_t^{\frac{s}{3}}(0,T)} + (C_7)_s \| V_0 \|_{H_x^s(\mathbb{R})} + (C_{10})_s T^{\frac{3-2s}{6}} \| F_2 \|_{L^2([0,T];\, H_x^s(\mathbb{R}))}, \\
&\quad \text{(by (35) and (38))} \\
&\leq \| g_2 \|_{H_t^{\frac{s}{3}}(0,T)} + 2(C_7)_s \| v_0 \|_{H_x^s(0,\infty)} + 2(C_{10})_s T^{\frac{3-2s}{6}} \| f_2 \|_{L^2([0,T];H_x^s(0,\infty))}, \\
&\quad \text{(by (25) and (28))} \\
&\lesssim \| v_0 \|_{H_x^s(0,\infty)} + \| g_2 \|_{H_t^{\frac{s}{3}}(0,T)} + T^{\frac{3-2s}{6}} \left(\int_0^T \| f_2(t) \|_{H_x^s(0,\infty)}^2 \, dt \right)^{\frac{1}{2}} dt,
\end{aligned}$$

and

$$\begin{aligned}
\Lambda_4^T(S[0,H_1;0]) \lesssim \| H_1 \|_{H_t^{\frac{s}{3}}(0,T)} &= \| \gamma_2 V(0,t) + \gamma_2 W^*(0,t) \|_{H_t^{\frac{s}{3}}(0,T)}, \\
&\text{(by (17), (18), (31), and (67))} \\
&\leq |\gamma_2| \, \| V(0,t) \|_{H_t^{\frac{s}{3}}(0,T)} + |\gamma_2| \, \| W^*(0,t) \|_{H_t^{\frac{s}{3}}(0,T)} \\
&\leq |\gamma_2| \, \| V(0,t) \|_{H_t^{\frac{s+1}{3}}(0,T)} + |\gamma_2| \, \| W^*(0,t) \|_{H_t^{\frac{s+1}{3}}(0,T)} \\
&\leq (C_6)_s |\gamma_2| \, \| V_0 \|_{H_x^s(\mathbb{R})} + (C_9)_s |\gamma_2| T^{\frac{2-s}{3}} \| F_2 \|_{L^2([0,T];\, H_x^s(\mathbb{R}))}, \\
&\text{(by (34) and (37))} \\
&\leq 2(C_6)_s |\gamma_2| \, \| v_0 \|_{H_x^s(0,\infty)} + 2(C_9)_s |\gamma_2| T^{\frac{2-s}{3}} \| f_2 \|_{L^2([0,T];H_x^s(0,\infty))}, \\
&\text{(by (25) and (28))} \\
&\lesssim \| v_0 \|_{H_x^s(0,\infty)} + T^{\frac{2-s}{3}} \left(\int_0^T \| f_2(t) \|_{H_x^s(0,\infty)}^2 \, dt \right)^{\frac{1}{2}}.
\end{aligned} \tag{68}$$

Now, by combining the estimates (66)–(68), we obtain (52):

$$\Lambda_4^T(S_{LK}[v_0,g_2;f_2]) \lesssim \| v_0 \|_{H_x^s(0,\infty)} + \| g_2 \|_{H_t^{\frac{s}{3}}(0,T)} + T^{\frac{3-2s}{6}} \left(\int_0^T \| f_2(t) \|_{H_x^s(0,\infty)}^2 \, dt \right)^{\frac{1}{2}}, \text{ for } s \geq \frac{3}{4}.$$

Since

$$\begin{aligned}
&\Lambda^T(S_{LK}[v_0,g_2;f_2]) \\
&= \max\left\{ \Lambda_{1,s}^T(S_{LK}[v_0,g_2;f_2]), \Lambda_{2,s}^T(S_{LK}[v_0,g_2;f_2]), \Lambda_3^T(S_{LK}[v_0,g_2;f_2]), \Lambda_4^T(S_{LK}[v_0,g_2;f_2]) \right\},
\end{aligned}$$

and by (50)∼(52), we obtain (48):

$$\Lambda^T(S_{LK}[v_0, g_2; f_2])$$
$$\leq (d_2)_s \left(\| v_0 \|_{H_x^s(0,\infty)} + \| g_2 \|_{H_t^{\frac{s}{3}}(0,T)} + T^{\frac{3-2s}{6}} \left(\int_0^T \| f_2(t) \|^2_{H_x^s(0,\infty)} dt \right)^{\frac{1}{2}} \right),$$

for $3/4 < s < 1$, where $(d_2)_s > 0$ is a constant depending on s. Therefore, the proof of Proposition 2 is complete.

6. The Proof of Theorem 3 (About Solving the SKdV System in Sobolev Spaces)

In this section, we first define the iteration map. Next, Lemmas 10 and 11 demonstrate that the iteration map is a contraction and maps onto a closed ball. By the contraction mapping theorem, the solution is unique. Finally, Lemma 12 shows that the data-to-solution map is locally Lipschitz continuous. With these results, we complete the proof of Theorem 3.

Now, we define the iteration map:

$$(u, v) \longmapsto \Phi_{T^*} \times \Psi_{T^*}(u, v) \doteq (\Phi_{T^*}(u, v), \Psi_{T^*}(u, v)),$$

which is derived from the UTM formulas (5) and (6) for the forced linear SKdV IBVP, with the forcing terms replaced by the nonlinearities, and localized appropriately. Let $0 < T^* \leq T < 1$. More precisely we have

$$\Phi_{T^*}(u, v) \doteq S_{LS}[u_0, g_1; P(u)v],$$
$$\Psi_{T^*}(u, v) \doteq S_{Lk}[v_0, g_2; Q(v)v_x].$$

The iteration map E is defined by

$$E(u, v) = (\Phi_{T^*}(u, v), \Phi_{T^*}(u, v)) = (S_{LS}[u_0, g_1; P(u)v], S_{Lk}[v_0, g_2; Q(v)v_x]). \quad (69)$$

We will prove the iteration map (69) is a contraction map in the complete metric space $\mathbb{X}_{T^*} = X_{T^*} \times Y_{T^*}$, where

$$\mathbb{X}_{T^*} = \{(u, v) : u \in X_{T^*}, v \in Y_{T^*}\},$$

and where

$$X_{T^*} = C([0, T^*]; H_x^s(0, \infty)) \cap C\left([0, \infty); H_t^{\frac{2s+1}{4}}(0, T^*)\right),$$
$$Y_{T^*} = C([0, T^*]; H_x^s(0, \infty)),$$

with

$$\| u \|_{X_{T^*}} = \sup_{t \in [0, T^*]} \| u \|_{H_x^s(0,\infty)} + \sup_{x \in [0,\infty)} \| u \|_{H_t^{\frac{2s+1}{4}}(0,T^*)},$$
$$\| v \|_{Y_{T^*}} = \Lambda^{T^*}(v) = \max\left\{\Lambda_{1,s}^{T^*}(v), \Lambda_{2,s}^{T^*}(v), \Lambda_3^{T^*}(v), \Lambda_4^{T^*}(v)\right\},$$

and

$$\| (u, v) \|_{\mathbb{X}_{T^*}} = \| u \|_{X_{T^*}} + \| v \|_{Y_{T^*}} . \quad (70)$$

Next, when $3/4 < s < 1$, we define a closed ball $B(0,r) = \{(u,v) \in \mathbb{X}_{T^*} :\| (u,v) \|_{\mathbb{X}_{T^*}} \leq r\}$, where

$$\widetilde{C}_s = \max\{1, (C_1)_s\}, \tag{71}$$

$$\mathfrak{K}_s^* = \max\Big\{C_s, (C_1)_s, (C_2)_s, \cdots, (C_{11})_s, d_s, (d_2)_s, \widetilde{C}_s\Big\}, \tag{72}$$

$$r = \max\left\{2\mathfrak{K}_s^* \| (u_0, g_1, v_0, g_2) \|_D, 1, \sqrt{\frac{3}{2}}\widetilde{C}_s^{-1}\right\}. \tag{73}$$

In the following lemma, we identify the constraint on T^* to ensure that $E(u,v)$ maps onto $B(0,r)$.

Lemma 10. *The iteration map $E(u,v)$ onto $B(0,r)$, when the following condition on T^* holds:*

$$0 < T^* \leq \min\{T, T_1\}, \tag{74}$$

where

$$n_0 = \max\{m, n\},$$
$$A = \max\{|a_0|, |a_1|, |a_2|, \cdots, |a_m|\},$$
$$B = \max\{|b_0|, |b_1|, |b_2|, \cdots, |b_n|\},$$
$$T_1 = \frac{1}{64(A(m+1) + \sqrt{10}B)^6(\mathfrak{K}_s^*)^{6n_0+6} r^{6n_0+6}}.$$

Proof. For $(u,v) \in B(0,r)$,

$$\begin{aligned} \| E(u,v) \|_{\mathbb{X}_{T^*}} &= \| (S_{LS}[u_0, g_1; P(u)v], S_{LK}[v_0, g_2; Q(v)v_x]) \|_{\mathbb{X}_{T^*}} \\ &= \| S_{LS}[u_0, g_1; P(u)v] \|_{X_{T^*}} + \| S_{LK}[v_0, g_2; Q(v)v_x] \|_{Y_{T^*}}, \end{aligned}$$

we must estimate the $\| S_{LS}[u_0, g_1; P(u)v] \|_{X_{T^*}}$ and $\| S_{LK}[v_0, g_2; Q(v)v_x] \|_{Y_{T^*}}$.

First, the estimate for $\| S_{LK}[v_0, g_2; Q(v)v_x] \|_{Y_{T^*}}$:

$$\begin{aligned} &\| S_{LK}[v_0, g_2; Q(v)v_x] \|_{Y_{T^*}} = \Lambda^{T^*}(S_{LK}[v_0, g_2; Q(v)v_x]) \\ &\leq (d_2)_s \left(\| v_0 \|_{H_x^s(0,\infty)} + \| g_2 \|_{H_t^{\frac{s}{3}}(0,T)} + (T^*)^{\frac{3-2s}{6}} \left(\int_0^{T^*} \| Q(v)v_x \|^2_{H_x^s(0,\infty)} dt \right)^{\frac{1}{2}} \right), \\ &\text{(by Proposition 2)}, \end{aligned} \tag{75}$$

where the term:

$$\begin{aligned} &\int_0^{T^*} \| Q(v)v_x \|^2_{H_x^s(0,\infty)} dt = \int_0^{T^*} \left\| \left(\sum_{j=0}^n b_j v^j \right) v_x \right\|^2_{H_x^s(0,\infty)} dt \\ &\leq \sum_{j=0}^n |b_j|^2 \int_0^{T^*} \| v^j v_x \|^2_{H_x^s(0,\infty)} dt = \sum_{j=0}^n |b_j|^2 \left(5\widetilde{C}_s^{2(j-1)} \| v \|^{2j}_{Y_{T^*}} \| v \|^2_{Y_{T^*}} \right), \quad \text{(by (46))} \\ &\leq 5B^2 \sum_{j=0}^n \widetilde{C}_s^{2(j-1)} r^{2j+2} = 5B^2 \frac{\widetilde{C}_s^{-2} r^2 \left(\widetilde{C}_s^{2(n+1)} r^{2(n+1)} - 1 \right)}{\widetilde{C}_s^2 r^2 - 1}. \end{aligned} \tag{76}$$

We combine the estimates (75) and (76) such that we obtain the following result:

$$\| S_{LK}[v_0, g_2; Q(v)v_x] \|_{Y_{T^*}} \le (d_2)_s \left(\| v_0 \|_{H_x^s(0,\infty)} + \| g_2 \|_{H_t^{\frac{s}{3}}(0,T)} + (T^*)^{\frac{3-2s}{6}} \left(5B^2 \frac{\widetilde{C}_s^{-2} r^2 \left(\widetilde{C}_s^{2(n+1)} r^{2(n+1)} - 1 \right)}{\widetilde{C}_s^2 r^2 - 1} \right)^{\frac{1}{2}} \right). \tag{77}$$

Next, we estimate $\| S_{LS}[u_0, g_1; P(u)v] \|_{X_{T^*}}$ for $0 < T^* < T$:

$$\begin{aligned} &\| S_{LS}[u_0, g_1; P(u)v] \|_{X_{T^*}} \\ &= \sup_{t\in[0,T^*]} \| S_{LS}[u_0, g_1; P(u)v] \|_{H_x^s(0,\infty)} + \sup_{x\in[0,\infty)} \| S_{LS}[u_0, g_1; P(u)v] \|_{H_t^{\frac{2s+1}{4}}(0,T^*)} \\ &\le C_s \left(\| u_0 \|_{H_x^s(0,\infty)} + \| g_1 \|_{H_t^{\frac{2s-1}{4}}(0,T)} + \sqrt{T^*} \sup_{t\in[0,T^*]} \| P(u)v \|_{H_x^s(0,\infty)} \right), \text{(by Theorem 1)}, \end{aligned} \tag{78}$$

and the term:

$$\begin{aligned} \sup_{t\in[0,T^*]} \| P(u)v \|_{H_x^s(0,\infty)} &= \sup_{t\in[0,T^*]} \left\| \left(\sum_{i=0}^m a_i u^i \right) v \right\|_{H_x^s(0,\infty)} \\ &\le \sup_{t\in[0,T^*]} \sum_{i=0}^m A (C_1)_s^i \| u \|_{H_x^s(0,\infty)}^i \| v \|_{H_x^s(0,\infty)}, \text{ (by Lemma 4)} \\ &\le \sum_{i=0}^m A (C_1)_s^i r^{(i+1)}. \end{aligned} \tag{79}$$

By (78) and (79), we obtain the following result:

$$\| S_{LS}[u_0, g_1; P(u)v] \|_{X_{T^*}} \le C_s \left(\| u_0 \|_{H_x^s(0,\infty)} + \| g_1 \|_{H_t^{\frac{2s-1}{4}}(0,T^*)} + (m+1)\sqrt{T^*} A (\mathfrak{K}_s^*)^m r^{(m+1)} \right). \tag{80}$$

By (77) and (80), we attain

$$\begin{aligned} &\| E(u,v) \|_{\mathbb{X}_{T^*}} \\ &\le (d_2)_s \left(\| v_0 \|_{H_x^s(0,\infty)} + \| g_2 \|_{H_t^{\frac{s}{3}}(0,T^*)} + (T^*)^{\frac{3-2s}{6}} \left(5B^2 \frac{\widetilde{C}_s^{-2} r^2 \left(\widetilde{C}_s^{2(n+1)} r^{2(n+1)} - 1 \right)}{\widetilde{C}_s^2 r^2 - 1} \right)^{\frac{1}{2}} \right) \\ &+ C_s \left(\| u_0 \|_{H_x^s(0,\infty)} + \| g_1 \|_{H_t^{\frac{2s-1}{4}}(0,T^*)} + (m+1)\sqrt{T^*} A (\mathfrak{K}_s^*)^m r^{(m+1)} \right) \\ &\le \mathfrak{K}_s^* \left(\| (u_0, g_1, v_0, g_2) \|_D + (m+1)(T^*)^{\frac{1}{6}} A (\mathfrak{K}_s^*)^m r^{m+1} + \sqrt{10} (T^*)^{\frac{1}{6}} B \widetilde{C}_s^n r^{(n+2)} \right), \\ &\text{(by (73) and (72))} \\ &\le \frac{r}{2} + \left((m+1)A + \sqrt{10}B \right) (T^*)^{\frac{1}{6}} (\mathfrak{K}_s^*)^{(n_0+1)} r^{(n_0+2)}. \end{aligned}$$

Now, we want to choose T^* such that

$$\frac{r}{2} + \left((m+1)A + \sqrt{10}B \right) (T^*)^{\frac{1}{6}} (\mathfrak{K}_s^*)^{(n_0+1)} r^{(n_0+2)} \le r$$

holds. Therefore,

$$0 < T^* \le \min\{T, T_1\}$$

is satisfied. Hence, when T^* satisfies (74), the iteration map E is onto $B(0,r)$. □

Next, we identify the constraint on T^* under which E is a contraction on $B(0,r)$, as described in the following lemma.

Lemma 11. *The iteration map $E(u,v)$ is a contraction on $B(0,r)$, when the following condition on T^* holds:*

$$0 < T^* \leq \min\{T, T_2\}, \tag{81}$$

where

$$T_2 = \frac{1}{64\left(A(m^2+m+1)+\sqrt{5}B\left(2^{(n+1)}(n+1)+2^n n^3\right)^{\frac{1}{2}}\right)^6 (\mathfrak{K}_s^*)^{6n_0+6} r^{6n_0}}.$$

Proof. For $(u_1,v_1),(u_2,v_2) \in B(0,r)$, we have the following inequality:

$$\begin{aligned}
&\| E(u_1,v_1) - E(u_2,v_2) \|_{\mathbb{X}_{T^*}} \\
&= \| (S_{LS}[0,0;P(u_1)v_1 - P(u_2)v_2], S_{LK}[0,0;Q(v_1)(v_1)_x - Q(v_2)(v_2)_x]) \|_{\mathbb{X}_{T^*}} \\
&= \| S_{LS}[0,0;P(u_1)v_1 - P(u_2)v_2] \|_{X_{T^*}} + \| S_{LK}[0,0;Q(v_1)(v_1)_x - Q(v_2)(v_2)_x] \|_{Y_{T^*}} \\
&= C_s\sqrt{T^*} \underbrace{\sup_{t\in[0,T^*]} \| P(u_1)v_1 - P(u_2)v_2 \|_{H_x^s(0,\infty)}}_{(A)} \\
&\quad + d_s(T^*)^{\frac{3-2s}{6}} \Bigg(\underbrace{\int_0^{T^*} \| Q(v_1)(v_1)_x - Q(v_2)(v_2)_x \|^2_{H_x^s(0,\infty)}\, dt}_{(B)} \Bigg)^{\frac{1}{2}},
\end{aligned}$$

(by Theorems 1 and 2).

Now, we estimate (A). There exists $\delta \in [0,1]$; we derive the following estimation of (A):

$$\begin{aligned}
&\sup_{t\in[0,T^*]} \| P(u_1)v_1 - P(u_2)v_2 \|_{H_x^s(0,\infty)} \\
&= \sup_{t\in[0,T^*]} \| P(u_1)(v_1-v_2) + P'(\delta u_1 + (1-\delta)u_2)(u_1-u_2)v_2 \|_{H_x^s(0,\infty)} \\
&\leq \sup_{t\in[0,T^*]} \left(\| P(u_1)(v_1-v_2) \|_{H_x^s(0,\infty)} + \| P'(\delta u_1 + (1-\delta)u_2)(u_1-u_2)v_2 \|_{H_x^s(0,\infty)} \right) \\
&= \sup_{t\in[0,T^*]} \left(\| \left(\sum_{i=0}^m a_i(u_1)^i\right)(v_1-v_2) \|_{H_x^s(0,\infty)} + \| \left(\sum_{i=1}^m ia_i(\delta u_1 + (1-\delta)u_2)^{i-1}\right)(u_1-u_2)v_2 \|_{H_x^s(0,\infty)} \right) \\
&\leq \sum_{i=0}^m |a_i| \sup_{t\in[0,T^*]} \| (u_1)^i(v_1-v_2) \|_{H_x^s(0,\infty)} + \sum_{i=1}^m |ia_i| \sup_{t\in[0,T^*]} \| (\delta u_1 + (1-\delta)u_2)^{i-1}(u_1-u_2)v_2 \|_{H_x^s(0,\infty)} \\
&\leq (\mathfrak{K}_s^*)^m \sum_{i=0}^m |a_i| \sup_{t\in[0,T^*]} \| (u_1) \|^i_{H_x^s(0,\infty)} \| (v_1-v_2) \|_{H_x^s(0,\infty)} \\
&\quad + (\mathfrak{K}_s^*)^m \sum_{i=1}^m |ia_i| \sup_{t\in[0,T^*]} \| \delta u_1 + (1-\delta)u_2 \|^{i-1}_{H_x^s(0,\infty)} \| (u_1-u_2) \|_{H_x^s(0,\infty)} \| v_2 \|_{H_x^s(0,\infty)},
\end{aligned}$$

(by Lemma 4 and $\mathfrak{K}_s^* \geq \max\{1,(C_1)_s\}$)

$$\leq (\mathfrak{K}_s^*)^m A \| (u_1,v_1) - (u_2,v_2) \|_{\mathbb{X}_{T^*}} \left(\sum_{i=0}^m r^i + m\sum_{i=1}^m r^i \right), \tag{82}$$

(by (9)~(12) and by (13) with $T = T^*$).

By $r \geq 1$, we derive the inequality

$$\sup_{t\in[0,T^*]} \| P(u_1)v_1 - P(u_2)v_2 \|_{H^s_x(0,\infty)} \leq (m^2+m+1)A(\mathfrak{K}^*_s)^m r^m \| (u_1,v_1)-(u_2,v_2) \|_{\mathbb{X}_{T^*}} . \tag{83}$$

Now, we estimate (B). There exists $\delta_1 \in [0,1]$; we obtain the following estimation of (B):

$$\begin{aligned}
&\int_0^{T^*} \| Q(v_1)(v_1)_x - Q(v_2)(v_2)_x \|^2_{H^s_x(0,\infty)} dt \\
&\leq 2\int_0^{T^*} \Big(\| Q(v_1)(v_1-v_2)_x \|^2_{H^s_x(0,\infty)} + \| Q'(\delta_1 v_1 + (1-\delta_1)v_2)(v_1-v_2)(v_2)_x \|^2_{H^s_x(0,\infty)} \Big) dt \\
&\leq 2^{n+1}\sum_{j=0}^{n} |b_j|^2 \int_0^{T^*} \| (v_1)^j (v_1-v_2)_x \|^2_{H^s_x(0,\infty)} dt \\
&\quad + 2^n \sum_{j=1}^{n} |jb_j|^2 \int_0^{T^*} \| (\delta_1 v_1 + (1-\delta_1)v_2)^{j-1}(v_1-v_2)(v_2)_x \|^2_{H^s_x(0,\infty)} dt \\
&\leq 2^{n+1}5(\mathfrak{K}^*_s)^{2(n-1)} \sum_{j=0}^{n} |b_j|^2 \| v_1 \|^{2j}_{Y_{T^*}} \| v_1 - v_2 \|^2_{Y_{T^*}} \\
&\quad + 2^n 5(\mathfrak{K}^*_s)^{2(n-1)} \sum_{j=1}^{n} |jb_j|^2 \| \delta_1 v_1 + (1-\delta_1)v_2 \|^{2(j-1)}_{Y_{T^*}} \| v_1 - v_2 \|^2_{Y_{T^*}} \| v_2 \|^2_{Y_{T^*}},
\end{aligned}$$

(by Proposition 1 and $\mathfrak{K}^*_s \geq \max\Big\{1, \widetilde{C}_s\Big\}$)

$$\leq 2^n 5(\mathfrak{K}^*_s)^{2(n-1)} B^2 \| (u_1,v_1)-(u_2,v_2) \|^2_{\mathbb{X}_{T^*}} \left(2\sum_{j=0}^{n} r^{2j} + n^2 \sum_{j=1}^{n} r^{2j} \right) \tag{84}$$

By $r \geq 1$, we obtain the following inequality

$$\begin{aligned}
&\int_0^{T^*} \| Q(v_1)(v_1)_x - Q(v_2)(v_2)_x \|^2_{H^s_x(0,\infty)} dt \\
&\leq (2^{n+1}(n+1) + 2^n n^3)5B^2(\mathfrak{K}^*_s)^{2(n-1)} r^{2n} \| (u_1,v_1)-(u_2,v_2) \|^2_{\mathbb{X}_{T^*}} .
\end{aligned} \tag{85}$$

By (83) and (85), we attain

$$\begin{aligned}
&\| E(u_1,v_1) - E(u_2,v_2) \|_{\mathbb{X}_{T^*}} \\
&\leq C_s(\mathfrak{K}^*_s)^m (T^*)^{\frac{1}{2}} (m^2+m+1)Ar^m \| (u_1,v_1)-(u_2,v_2) \|_{\mathbb{X}_{T^*}} \\
&\quad + d_s(T^*)^{\frac{3-2s}{6}} \Big((2^{n+1}(n+1) + 2^n n^3)5B^2(\mathfrak{K}^*_s)^{2(n-1)} r^{2n} \| (u_1,v_1)-(u_2,v_2) \|^2_{\mathbb{X}_{T^*}} \Big)^{\frac{1}{2}} \\
&\leq \mathfrak{K}^*_s(T^*)^{\frac{1}{6}} \Big((m^2+m+1)A(\mathfrak{K}^*_s)^m r^m + \Big((2^{n+1}(n+1) + 2^n n^3)5B^2 r^{2n} (\mathfrak{K}^*_s)^{2n-1} \Big)^{\frac{1}{2}} \Big) \\
&\quad \| (u_1,v_1)-(u_2,v_2) \|_{\mathbb{X}_{T^*}} \\
&\leq \Big((m^2+m+1)A + \sqrt{5}B\Big((2^{n+1}(n+1) + 2^n n^3) \Big)^{\frac{1}{2}} \Big) (\mathfrak{K}^*_s)^{n_0+1} (T^*)^{\frac{1}{6}} r^{n_0} \| (u_1,v_1)-(u_2,v_2) \|_{\mathbb{X}_{T^*}} .
\end{aligned}$$

Therefore, we need the following condition to help us prove that E is a contraction on $B(0,r)$:

$$\Big((m^2+m+1)A + \sqrt{5}B\Big((2^{n+1}(n+1) + 2^n n^3) \Big)^{\frac{1}{2}} \Big) (\mathfrak{K}^*_s)^{n_0+1} (T^*)^{\frac{1}{6}} r^{n_0} \leq \frac{1}{2}.$$

Therefore,

$$0 < T^* \leq \min\{T, T_2\}$$

is satisfied. Hence, when T^* satisfies (81), the iteration map E is a contraction on $B(0,r)$. □

Now, by choosing the lifespan

$$T^* = \min\{T, T_1, T_2\}, \tag{86}$$

we ensure that T^* satisfies both (74) and (81). Consequently, the iteration map is a contraction and maps onto $B(0,r)$. Thus, the equation $(u,v) = E(u,v)$ has a unique solution $(u,v) \in B(0,r) \subset \mathbb{X}_{T^*}$.

Next, we will demonstrate that the data-to-solution map $(u_0, g_1, v_0, g_2) \longmapsto (u,v)$ is locally Lipschitz continuous.

We consider the two different data (u_0, g_1, v_0, g_2) and $(\mathcal{U}_0, \mathcal{G}_1, \mathcal{V}_0, \mathcal{G}_2)$ that lie within a ball $B_\rho \subset D$ of radius $\rho > 0$ centered at a distance $\mathcal{R}$ from the origin, where

$$D = H_x^s(0,\infty) \times H_t^{\frac{2s-1}{4}}(0,T) \times H_x^s(0,\infty) \times H_t^{\frac{s}{3}}(0,T)$$

with the norm (14). We set $(u,v) = E(u,v)$ and $(\mathcal{U},\mathcal{V}) = E(\mathcal{U},\mathcal{V})$, and $T_{(u,v)}$ and $T_{(\mathcal{U},\mathcal{V})}$ are the lifespans of those solutions given according to (86). Since

$$\max\{\| (u_0,, g_1 v_0, g_2) \|_D, \| (\mathcal{U}_0, \mathcal{G}_1, \mathcal{V}_0, \mathcal{G}_2) \|_D\} \leq \rho + \mathcal{R},$$

we have

$$T_{(u,v)} = \min\left\{T, T_{1,(u,v)}, T_{2,(u,v)}\right\} \geq T_c, \quad T_{(\mathcal{U},\mathcal{V})} = \min\left\{T, T_{1,(\mathcal{U},\mathcal{V})}, T_{2,(\mathcal{U},\mathcal{V})}\right\} \geq T_c,$$

where

$$\begin{aligned}
r^* &= \max\left\{2\mathfrak{K}_s^*(\rho + \mathcal{R}), 1, \sqrt{\frac{3}{2}\widetilde{C}_s^{-1}}\right\}, \\
T_{1,c} &= \frac{1}{64(A(m+1) + \sqrt{10}B)^6 (\mathfrak{K}_s^*)^{6n_0+6} (r^*)^{6n_0+6}}, \\
T_{2,c} &= \frac{1}{64\left(A(m^2+m+1) + \sqrt{5}B(2^{(n+1)}(n+1) + 2^n n^3)^{\frac{1}{2}}\right)^6 (\mathfrak{K}_s^*)^{6n_0+6} (r^*)^{6n_0}}, \\
T_c &= \min\{T, T_{1,c}, T_{2,c}\}.
\end{aligned} \tag{87}$$

Since $T_{(u,v)}, T_{(\mathcal{U},\mathcal{V})} \geq T_c$, both solutions (u,v) and $(\mathcal{U},\mathcal{V})$ are valid for any $0 < t \leq T_c$. We denote $\mathbb{X}_{T_c}$ as the solution space $\mathbb{X}_{T^*}$ with $T^* = T_c$. Clearly, $\mathbb{X}_{T_c} \subset \mathbb{X}_{T_{(u,v)}}$ and $\mathbb{X}_{T_c} \subset \mathbb{X}_{T_{(\mathcal{U},\mathcal{V})}}$, where $\mathbb{X}_{T_{(u,v)}}$ and $\mathbb{X}_{T_{(\mathcal{U},\mathcal{V})}}$ represent the solution spaces $\mathbb{X}_{T^*}$ with $T^* = T_{(u,v)}$ and $T^* = T_{(\mathcal{U},\mathcal{V})}$, respectively.

The following lemma demonstrates that the data-to-solution map $(u_0, v_0, g_0, h_0) \longmapsto (u,v)$ is locally Lipschitz continuous.

Lemma 12. *Given*

$$\widetilde{r}_1 = \left(\frac{1}{2\left(A(n_0^2+n_0+1) + \sqrt{5}B\left(2^{(n_0+1)}(n_0+1)+2^{n_0}n_0^3\right)^{\frac{1}{2}} \right)(\mathfrak{K}_s^*)^{n_0+1}(T_c)^{\frac{1}{6}}} - 1 \right)^{\frac{1}{n_0}},$$

$$\widetilde{r}_2 = \left(\frac{1}{\left(A(n_0^2+n_0+1) + \sqrt{5}B\left(2^{(n_0+1)}(n_0+1)+2^{n_0}n_0^3\right)^{\frac{1}{2}} \right)(\mathfrak{K}_s^*)^{n_0+1}(T_c)^{\frac{1}{6}}} - 1 \right)^{\frac{1}{n_0}},$$

$$r_c = \min\left\{1, \widetilde{r}_1, \frac{\widetilde{r}_2}{2}\right\}.$$

For any $(u,v), (\mathcal{U},\mathcal{V}) \in B(0,r_c) \subset \mathbb{X}_{T_c}$ with data in the ball B_ρ, we obtain the following inequality:

$$\| (u,v) - (\mathcal{U},\mathcal{V}) \|_{\mathbb{X}_{T_c}} \leq 2\mathfrak{K}_s^* \| (u_0, g_1, v_0, g_2) - (\mathcal{U}_0, \mathcal{G}_1, \mathcal{V}_0, \mathcal{G}_2) \|_D . \tag{88}$$

Hence, the data-to-solution map $(u_0, g_1, v_0, g_2) \longmapsto (u,v)$ is locally Lipschitz continuous.

Proof. For any $(u,v), (\mathcal{U},\mathcal{V}) \in B(0,r_c) \subset \mathbb{X}_{T_c}$ with data in the ball B_ρ, we have the following inequality:

$$\begin{aligned}
&\| (u,v) - (\mathcal{U},\mathcal{V}) \|_{\mathbb{X}_{T_c}} = \| E(u,v) - E(\mathcal{U},\mathcal{V}) \|_{\mathbb{X}_{T_c}} \\
&= \| (S_{LS}[u_0, g_1; P(u)v], S_{LK}[v_0, g_2; Q(v)v_x]) - (S_{LS}[\mathcal{U}_0, \mathcal{G}_1; P(\mathcal{U})\mathcal{V}], S_{LK}[\mathcal{V}_0, \mathcal{G}_2; Q(\mathcal{V})\mathcal{V}_x]) \|_{\mathbb{X}_{T_c}} \\
&\leq \underbrace{\| (S_{LS}[u_0 - \mathcal{U}_0, g_1 - \mathcal{G}_1; 0], S_{LK}[v_0 - \mathcal{V}_0, g_2 - \mathcal{G}_2; 0]) \|_{\mathbb{X}_{T_c}}}_{(C)} \\
&\quad + \underbrace{\| (S_{LS}[0,0; P(u)v - P(\mathcal{U})\mathcal{V}], S_{LK}[0,0; Q(v)v_x - Q(\mathcal{V})\mathcal{V}_x]) \|_{\mathbb{X}_{T_c}}}_{(D)}
\end{aligned}$$

Now, we estimate (C):

$$\begin{aligned}
&\| (S_{LS}[u_0 - \mathcal{U}_0, g_1 - \mathcal{G}_1; 0], S_{LK}[v_0 - \mathcal{V}_0, g_2 - \mathcal{G}_2; 0]) \|_{\mathbb{X}_{T_c}} \\
&= \| S_{LS}[u_0 - \mathcal{U}_0, g_1 - \mathcal{G}_1; 0] \|_{X_{T_c}} + \| S_{LK}[v_0 - \mathcal{V}_0, g_2 - \mathcal{G}_2; 0] \|_{Y_{T_c}}, \quad \text{(by (70) with } T^* = T_c) \\
&\leq C_s \left(\| u_0 - \mathcal{U}_0 \|_{H_x^s(0,\infty)} + \| g_1 - \mathcal{G}_1 \|_{H_t^{\frac{2s-1}{4}}(0,T)} \right) + (d_2)_s \left(\| v_0 - \mathcal{V}_0 \|_{H_x^s(0,\infty)} + \| g_2 - \mathcal{G}_2 \|_{H_t^{\frac{s}{3}}(0,T)} \right), \\
&\quad \text{(by (7) and (48) with } T = T_c) \\
&\leq \mathfrak{K}_s^* \| (u_0, , g_1, v_0, g_2) - (\mathcal{U}_0, \mathcal{G}_1, \mathcal{V}_0, \mathcal{G}_2) \|_D .
\end{aligned} \tag{89}$$

Next, we estimate (D):

$$
\begin{aligned}
&\| (S_{LS}[0,0;P(u)v-P(\mathcal{U})\mathcal{V}],S_{LK}[0,0;Q(v)v_x-Q(\mathcal{V})\mathcal{V}_x]) \|_{\mathbb{X}_{T_c}} \\
&=\| S_{LS}[0,0;P(u)v-P(\mathcal{U})\mathcal{V}] \|_{X_{T_c}} + \| S_{LK}[0,0;Q(v)v_x-Q(\mathcal{V})\mathcal{V}_x] \|_{Y_{T_c}}, \quad \text{(by (70) with } T^*=T_c) \\
&\le \mathfrak{K}_s^* T_c^{\frac{1}{6}} \left(\underbrace{\sup_{t\in[0,T_c]} \| P(u)v-P(\mathcal{U})\mathcal{V} \|_{H_x^s(0,\infty)}}_{(E)} + \left(\underbrace{\int_0^{T_c} \| Q(v)v_x-Q(\mathcal{V})\mathcal{V}_x \|^2_{H_x^s(0,\infty)}\, dt}_{(F)} \right)^{\frac{1}{2}} \right), \\
&\quad \text{(by (7) and (48) with } T^*=T_c, \text{ and } \mathfrak{K}_s^* \ge \max\{C_s,(d_2)_s\}) \\
&\le \mathfrak{K}_s^* T_c^{\frac{1}{6}} \| (u,v)-(\mathcal{U},\mathcal{V}) \|_{\mathbb{X}_{T_c}} \left((\mathfrak{K}_s^*)^m A \left(\sum_{i=0}^m r_c^i + m \sum_{i=1}^m r_c^i \right) \right. \\
&\qquad \left. + \left(2^n 5 (\mathfrak{K}_s^*)^{2(n-1)} B^2 \left(2 \sum_{j=0}^n r_c^{2j} + n^2 \sum_{j=1}^n r_c^{2j} \right) \right)^{\frac{1}{2}} \right), \\
&\quad \text{(by (82) and (84) with } T^*=T_c, r=r_c, u_1=u, v_1=v, u_2=\mathcal{U}, \text{ and } v_2=\mathcal{V}, \\
&\quad \text{we obtain the estimates of } (E) \text{ and } (F)) \\
&\le \mathfrak{K}_s^* T_c^{\frac{1}{6}} \| (u,v)-(\mathcal{U},\mathcal{V}) \|_{\mathbb{X}_{T_c}} \Big((m^2+m+1) A (\mathfrak{K}_s^*)^m (1+r_c^m) \\
&\qquad + \left((2^{n+1}(n+1) + 2^n n^3) 5 B^2 (\mathfrak{K}_s^*)^{2(n-1)} (1+r_c^{2n}) \right)^{\frac{1}{2}} \Big) \\
&\le \left((n_0^2+n_0+1)A + \sqrt{5}B \left(2^{n_0+1}(n_0+1) + 2^{n_0} n_0^3 \right)^{\frac{1}{2}} \right) (\mathfrak{K}_s^*)^{n_0+1} T_c^{\frac{1}{6}} (1+r_c^{n_0}) \| (u,v)-(\mathcal{U},\mathcal{V}) \|_{\mathbb{X}_{T_c}}.
\end{aligned} \tag{90}
$$

By (89) and (90), we derive the following inequality:

$$
\begin{aligned}
&\| (u,v)-(\mathcal{U},\mathcal{V}) \|_{\mathbb{X}_{T_c}} \\
&\le \mathfrak{K}_s^* \| (u_0,g_1,v_0,g_2) - (\mathcal{U}_0,\mathcal{G}_1,\mathcal{V}_0,\mathcal{G}_2) \|_D \\
&+ \left((n_0^2+n_0+1)A + \sqrt{5}B \left((2^{n_0+1}(n_0+1) + 2^{n_0} n_0^3) \right)^{\frac{1}{2}} \right) (\mathfrak{K}_s^*)^{n_0+1} T_c^{\frac{1}{6}} (1+r_c^{n_0}) \| (u,v)-(\mathcal{U},\mathcal{V}) \|_{\mathbb{X}_{T_c}}.
\end{aligned}
$$

Therefore, we derive the following inequality:

$$
\begin{aligned}
&\| (u,v)-(\mathcal{U},\mathcal{V}) \|_{\mathbb{X}_{T_c}} \\
&\le \frac{\mathfrak{K}_s^* \| (u_0,g_1,v_0,g_2) - (\mathcal{U}_0,\mathcal{G}_1,\mathcal{V}_0,\mathcal{G}_2) \|_D}{1 - \left((n_0^2+n_0+1)A + \sqrt{5}B(2^{n_0+1}(n_0+1) + 2^{n_0} n_0^3)^{\frac{1}{2}} \right) (\mathfrak{K}_s^*)^{n_0+1} T_c^{\frac{1}{6}} (1+r_c^{n_0}))}.
\end{aligned}
$$

Hence, when we set

$$
r_c = \min\left\{ 1, \widetilde{r}_1, \frac{\widetilde{r}_2}{2} \right\},
$$

where

$$\widetilde{r}_1 = \left(\frac{1}{2\left(A(n_0^2+n_0+1) + \sqrt{5}B(2^{(n_0+1)}(n_0+1) + 2^{n_0}n_0^3)^{\frac{1}{2}} \right)(\mathfrak{K}_s^*)^{n_0+1}(T_c)^{\frac{1}{6}}} - 1 \right)^{\frac{1}{n_0}},$$

$$\widetilde{r}_2 = \left(\frac{1}{\left(A(n_0^2+n_0+1) + \sqrt{5}B(2^{(n_0+1)}(n_0+1) + 2^{n_0}n_0^3)^{\frac{1}{2}} \right)(\mathfrak{K}_s^*)^{n_0+1}(T_c)^{\frac{1}{6}}} - 1 \right)^{\frac{1}{n_0}},$$

then the two inequalities

$$\frac{1}{1 - \left((n_0^2+n_0+1)A + \sqrt{5}B(2^{n_0+1}(n_0+1) + 2^{n_0}n_0^3)^{\frac{1}{2}} \right)(\mathfrak{K}_s^*)^{n_0+1}T_c^{\frac{1}{6}}(1+r_c^{n_0}))} \leq 2$$

and

$$\left((n_0^2+n_0+1)A + \sqrt{5}B\left(2^{n_0+1}(n_0+1) + 2^{n_0}n_0^3\right)^{\frac{1}{2}} \right)(\mathfrak{K}_s^*)^{n_0+1}T_c^{\frac{1}{6}}(1+r_c^{n_0})) < 1$$

hold with the definition of T_c (87). Therefore, we have established (88), which confirms that the data-to-solution map is locally Lipschitz continuous. The proof of Lemma 12 is complete. □

We are now in a position to prove Theorem 3. We set the lifespan

$$T^* = \min\{T, T_1, T_2\},$$

where

$$r = \max\left\{ 2\mathfrak{K}_s^* \parallel (u_0, g_1, v_0, g_2) \parallel_D, 1, \sqrt{\frac{3}{2}}\widetilde{C}_s^{-1} \right\},$$

$$T_1 = \frac{1}{64(A(m+1) + \sqrt{10}B)^6(\mathfrak{K}_s^*)^{6n_0+6}r^{6n_0+6}},$$

$$T_2 = \frac{1}{64\left(A(m^2+m+1) + \sqrt{5}B(2^{(n+1)}(n+1) + 2^n n^3)^{\frac{1}{2}} \right)^6 (\mathfrak{K}_s^*)^{6n_0+6}r^{6n_0}},$$

and then, by Lemma 10 to Lemma 12, the proof of Theorem 3 is complete.

Author Contributions: B.-Y.P. is the first author and P.-C.H. is the corresponding author. P.-C.H. and B.-Y.P. wrote the main manuscript text. All authors reviewed the manuscript. All authors have read and agreed to the published version of the manuscript.

Funding: This research received no external funding.

Data Availability Statement: The original contributions presented in the study are included in the article, further inquiries can be directed to the corresponding author/s.

Acknowledgments: We sincerely appreciate Hsin-Yuan Huang at National Yang Ming Chiao Tung University in Taiwan for his invaluable guidance, unwavering encouragement, and support in this field. Additionally, B.-Y.P. would like to extend gratitude to Ya-Lun Tsai for his generous support provided through the grant from the National Science Council in Taiwan.

Conflicts of Interest: The authors declare no conflicts of interest.

References

1. Makhankov, V.G. On stationary solutions of the Schrödinger equation with a self-consistent potential satisfying Boussinesq's equation. *Phys. Lett. A* **1974**, *50*, 42–44. [CrossRef]
2. Nishikawa, K.; Hojo, H.; Mima, K.; Ikezi, H. Coupled nonlinear electron plasma and ion-acoustic waves. *Phys. Rev. Lett.* **1974**, *33*, 148–151. [CrossRef]
3. Arbieto, A.; Corcho, A.J.; Matheus, C. Rough solutions for the periodic Schrödinger–Korteweg–de Vries system. *J. Differ. Equ.* **2006**, *230* 295–336. [CrossRef]
4. Benilov, E.S.; Burtsev, S.P. To the integrability of the equations describing the Langmuir-wave-ion-acoustic-wave interaction. *Phys. Let.* **1983**, *98A*, 256–258. [CrossRef]
5. Bourgain, J. Fourier transform restriction phenomena for certain lattice subsets and applications to nonlinear evolution equations II. The KdV-equation. *Geom. Funct. Anal.* **1993**, *3*, 209–262. [CrossRef]
6. Guo, B.; Miao, C. Well-posedness of the Cauchy problem for the coupled system of the Schrödinger-KdV equations. *Acta Math. Sin. (Engl. Ser.)* **1999**, *15*, 215–224. [CrossRef]
7. Guo, Z.; Wang, Y. On the well-posedness of the Schrödinger-Korteweg-de Vries system. *J. Differ. Equ.* **2010**, *249*, 2500–2520. [CrossRef]
8. Guo, B.; Feng-Xin, C. Finite-dimensional behavior of global attractors for weakly damped and forced KdV equations coupling with nonlinear Schrödinger equations. *Nonlinear Anal. Theory Methods Appl.* **1997**, *29*, 569–584.
9. Kawahara, T.; Sugimoto, N.; Ponce, G.; Kakutani, T. Nonlinear interaction between short and long capillary-gravity waves. *J. Phys. Soc. Jpn.* **1975**, *39*, 1379–1386. [CrossRef]
10. Cavalcante, M.; Corcho, A.J. The initial-boundary value problem for the Schrödinger–Korteweg–de Vries system on the half-line. *Commun. Contemp. Math.* **2019**, *21*, 1850066. [CrossRef]
11. Himonas, A.A.; Yan, F. The Schrödinger-Korteweg-de Vries system on the half-line. *Appl. Numer. Math.* **2024**, *199*, 32–58. [CrossRef]
12. Corcho, A.J.; Linares, F. Well-posedness for the Schrödinger-Korteweg-de Vries system. *Trans. Am. Math. Soc.* **2007**, *359*, 4089–4106. [CrossRef]
13. Guo, X.; Xu, M. Some physical applications of fractional Schrödinger equation. *J. Math. Phys.* **2006**, *47*, 082104. [CrossRef]
14. Hilfer, R. *Applications of Fractional Calculus in Physics*; World Scientific: Singapore, 2000.
15. Deng, W. Generalized synchronization in fractional order systems. *Phys. Rev. E* **2007**, *75*, 056201. [CrossRef] [PubMed]
16. Shang, J.; Wenhe, L.; Da, L. Traveling wave solutions of a coupled Schrödinger-Korteweg-de Vries equation by the generalized coupled trial equation method. *Heliyon* **2023**, *9*, e15695. [CrossRef] [PubMed]
17. Khan, A.; Khan, A.U.; Ahmad, S. Investigation of fractal fractional nonlinear Korteweg-de-Vries-Schrödinger system with Power Law Kernel. *Phys. Scr.* **2023**, *98*, 085202. [CrossRef]
18. Noor, S.; Alotaibi, B.M.; Shah, R.; Ismaeel, S.M.E.; El-Tantawy, S.A. On the solitary waves and nonlinear oscillations to the fractional Schrödinger-KdV equation in the framework of the Caputo operator. *Symmetry* **2023**, *15*, 1616. [CrossRef]
19. Matheus, C. Global well-posedness of NLS-KdV systems for periodic functions. *Electron. J. Differ. Equ.* **2007**, *2006*, 20.
20. Wang, H.; Cui, S. The Cauchy problem for the Schrödinger–KdV system. *J. Differ. Equ.* **2011**, *250*, 3559–3583. [CrossRef]
21. Guo, B.; Ma, B.; Zhang, J. Global existence and uniqueness of the solution for the generalized Schrödinger–KdV system. In *Frontiers in Differential Geometry, Partial Differential Equations and Mathematical Physics*; World Scientific: Singapore, 2014; pp. 69–86.
22. Cavalcante, M.; Corcho, A.J. Well-posedness and lower bounds of the growth of weighted norms for the Schrödinger–Korteweg–de Vries interactions on the half-line. *J. Evol. Equ.* **2020**, *20*, 1563–1596. [CrossRef]
23. Chen, M. Recurrent solutions of the Schrödinger-KdV system with boundary forces. *Discret. Contin. Dyn.-Syst.-B* **2021**, *26*, 5149–5170. [CrossRef]
24. Compaan, E.; Shin, W.; Tzirakis, N. Well-posedness for the Schrödinger-KdV system on the half-line. *J. Math. Anal. Appl.* **2024**, *537*, 128313. [CrossRef]
25. Fokas, A.S. A unified transform method for solving linear and certain nonlinear PDEs. *Proc. R. Soc. Lond. Ser. A* **1997**, *453*, 1411–1443. [CrossRef]
26. Fokas, A.S. On the integrability of linear and nonlinear partial differential equations. *J. Math. Phys.* **2000**, *41*, 4188–4237. [CrossRef]
27. Fokas, A.S. Integrable nonlinear evolution equations on the half-line. *Commun. Math. Phys.* **2002**, *230*, 1–39. [CrossRef]
28. Fokas, A.S. *A Unified Approach to Boundary Value Problems CBMS-NSF Regional Conference Series in Applied Mathematics*; SIAM: Philadelphia, PA, USA, 2008.
29. Deconinck, B.; Trogdon, T.; Vasan, V. The method of Fokas for solving linear partial differential equations. *SIAM Rev.* **2014**, *56*, 159–186. [CrossRef]
30. Himonas, A.A.; Mantzavinos, D. The nonlinear Schrödinger equation on the half-line with a Robin boundary condition. *Anal. Math. Phys.* **2021**, *11*, 157. [CrossRef]
31. Himonas, A.A.; Madrid, C.; Yan, F. The Neumann and Robin problems for the Korteweg-de Vries equation on the half-line. *J. Math. Phys.* **2021**, *62*, 111503. [CrossRef]
32. Fokas, A.S.; Himonas, A.A.; Mantzavinos, D. The nonlinear Schrödinger equation on the half-line. *Trans. Am. Math. Soc.* **2017**, *369*, 681–709. [CrossRef]
33. Fokas, A.S.; Himonas, A.; Mantzavinos, D. The Korteweg-de Vries equation on the half-line. *Nonlinearity* **2016**, *29*, 489–527. [CrossRef]

34. Linares, F.; Ponce, G. *Introduction to Nonlinear Dispersive Equations*; Universitext; Springer: New York, NY, USA, 2009.
35. Himonas, A.A.; Mantzavinos, D.; Yan, F. The Korteweg-de Vries equation on an interval. *J. Math. Phys.* **2019**, *60*, 051507. [CrossRef]
36. Kenig, C.E.; Ponce, G.; Vega, L. On the (generalized) Korteweg–de Vries equation. *Duke Math. J.* **1989**, *59*, 585–610. [CrossRef]
37. Kenig, C.E.; Ponce, G.; Vega, L. Well-posedness of the initial value problem for the Korteweg–de Vries equation. *J. Am. Math. Soc.* **1991**, *4*, 323–347. [CrossRef]
38. Yan, F. Well-posedness of a higher dispersion KdV equation on the half-line. *J. Math. Phys.* **2020**, *61*, 081506. [CrossRef]

axioms

MDPI

Article

Combined Compact Symplectic Schemes for the Solution of Good Boussinesq Equations

Zhenyu Lang [1], Xiuling Yin [2,*], Yanqin Liu [2], Zhiguo Chen [2] and Shuxia Kong [2]

1 School of Mathematics and Statistics, Shandong University of Technology, Zibo 255049, China; 23411011065@sdut.edu.cn
2 School of Mathematics and Big Data, Dezhou University, Dezhou 253023, China; chenzhiguo@dzu.edu.cn (Z.C.); kongshuxia@dzu.edu.cn (S.K.)
* Correspondence: yinllmm@163.com; Tel.: +86-1831-591-6282

Abstract: Good Boussinesq equations are considered in this work. First, we apply three combined compact schemes to approximate spatial derivatives of good Boussinesq equations. Then, three fully discrete schemes are developed based on a symplectic scheme in the time direction, which preserves the symplectic structure. Meanwhile, the convergence and conservation of the fully discrete schemes are analyzed. Finally, we present numerical experiments to confirm our theoretical analysis. Both our analysis and numerical tests indicate that the fully discrete schemes are efficient in solving the spatial derivative mixed equation.

Keywords: Hamiltonian system; good Boussinesq equation; symplectic scheme; combined compact scheme; conservation

MSC: 65M06; 65M12; 65Z05; 70H15

1. Introduction

Boussinesq equations are important mathematical–physical models for characterizing ocean mixing, atmospheric convection, and intra-Earth convection. They play a key role in fields such as Earth sciences, meteorology, and oceanography. The study of Boussinesq equations is of great value because it helps us to better understand hydrodynamic behavior, especially in terms of thermal convection, ocean currents, and atmospheric phenomena. In addition, the study of Boussinesq equations is essential for the development of numerical models for weather forecasting, climate research, and oceanography. Such studies have also helped to uncover the fundamental principles that govern fluid motion and heat transfer, contributing to advances in fields such as engineering, environmental science, and geophysics. The good Boussinesq (GB) equation and its various extensions have been broadly analyzed in the existing literature, such as a closed-form solution for the two-soliton interaction in [1], a highly complicated mechanism for the solitary wave interaction in [2], and the nonlinear stability and convergence of some simple finite difference schemes in [3]. Among recent works concerning the numerical solution of PDEs, a significant number address the Schrödinger equation; see [4–11]. In [5,6], the authors use the Cubic B-Spline Galerkin Method. This method has also been studied for the MRLW equation in [12]. In [11], the authors use a combined compact difference method to solve the Schrödinger equation, and this scheme preserves the structure. This method originated from [13], and it can also be found in [14–17]. In addition, many works related to GB equations can be found in [18–24]. Boussinesq equations have also been investigated in [25,26].

In solving PDEs numerically, high-order compact (HOC) schemes are often used to discretize spatial derivatives. For example, HOC schemes have been applied to solve steady convection–diffusion equations [15], nonlinear Schrödinger equations [11], Klein–Gordon–Schrödinger equations [27], and GB equations [20]. Compared with general finite difference schemes, HOC schemes have the advantages of smaller error rates and higher accuracy under the same calculation amount. However, for PDEs with multiple-order spatial derivatives, such as the good Boussinesq equation $u_{tt} = -u_{xxxx} + u_{xx} + \left(u^2\right)_{xx}$, the advantages of classical HOC schemes are often offset. If multiple HOC schemes are used to discretize multiple spatial derivatives simultaneously, it is necessary to perform multiple matrix inverse operations, which will reduce the computational efficiency and affect the accuracy. In [11], the combined high-order compact (CHOC) scheme is used to approximate PDEs with multiple-order spatial derivatives and achieve some discrete conservation laws, and the proposed CHOC scheme overcomes the above shortcomings of the compact scheme and is worth popularizing. In this work, we study the CHOC schemes of GB equations with two spatial derivatives.

In this work, three CHOC schemes for good Boussinesq equations are derived. Applying a Taylor analysis to an equality combining the solution u and its first derivative and second derivative yields the first three-point CHOC scheme. This scheme has sixth-order precision and extensive applications. Then, similarly, we propose the second three-point eight-order scheme by using a combination of the first, second, and third derivatives of the solution. Since the two schemes have a large number of matrix operations and complex formulations, the third scheme is designed finally by combining the solution and its second derivative and fourth derivative, which greatly simplifies the matrix operations and ensures certain accuracy. In this scheme, through simpler computation, the relationship between the solution and its fourth-order derivative, as well as the relationship between the solution and its second-order derivative, can be directly obtained, which cannot be achieved with the first two schemes described in this work. Finally, we use the three schemes to simulate a motion invariant and a conservation law and summarize the structure-preserving property of these schemes. At the same time, compared with a three-point compact scheme with sixth-order accuracy derived by Chu and Fan in 1998 [13], our schemes are more accurate for GB equations.

In this work, we consider fully discrete schemes for the linear good Boussinesq equation

$$\partial_t^2 u = \partial_x^2 u - \partial_x^4 u, \tag{1}$$

where $0 \le x \le L, t > 0$, L is a constant. The following nonlinear good Boussinesq equation is also numerically solved, as follows:

$$\partial_t^2 u = \partial_x^2 u - \partial_x^4 u + \partial_x^2 (u^2). \tag{2}$$

We consider the initial conditions and periodic boundary conditions as follows:

$$u(t,0) = u(t,L),\ u(0,x) = f_1(x), u_t(0,x) = f_2(x), 0 \le x \le L. \tag{3}$$

2. Establishment of the CHOC Scheme

In this work, we introduce three schemes for the discretization of spatial derivatives. To detail the CHOC scheme, we introduce a uniform grid $x_0 < x_1 \cdots < x_N$ with $x_j = x_0 + jh$ and $h = \frac{x_L - x_0}{N}, j = 1, 2, \cdots, N$. First, we introduce the first scheme (4) and (5)

$$\alpha_1\left(u'_{j+1} + u'_{j-1}\right) + u'_j + \beta_1 h\left(u''_{j+1} - u''_{j-1}\right) + \gamma_1 \frac{u_{j+1} - u_{j-1}}{h} = 0, \tag{4}$$

$$\alpha_2\left(\frac{u'_{j+1} - u'_{j-1}}{h}\right) + u''_j + \beta_2\left(u''_{j+1} + u''_{j-1}\right) + \gamma_2 \frac{u_{j+1} - 2u_j + u_{j-1}}{h^2} = 0, \tag{5}$$

where $\alpha_1, \beta_1, \gamma_1$ and $\alpha_2, \beta_2, \gamma_2$ are coefficients to be determined according to the accuracy of the approximation. The three-point CHOC scheme for the combination of the first and second derivatives aims to relate u_j, u'_j, u''_j to their neighbors $u_{j-1}, u'_{j-1}, u''_{j-1}$ and $u_{j+1}, u'_{j+1}, u''_{j+1}$.

This scheme approximates the first-order derivative and second-order derivative of u separately using the above combinations to numerically solve the Schrödinger equation in [11].

By applying Taylor expansion to Equations (4) and (5), we can obtain the following Tables 1 and 2. Here, the last row denotes the summation of each corresponding column. The tables related to Taylor expansion and discussed subsequently are similarly constructed.

Table 1. Taylor series of scheme (4).

Term	$u_j h^{-1}$	u_j'	$u_j'' h$	$u_j''' h^2$	$u_j^{(4)} h^3$	$u_j^{(5)} h^4$	$u_j^{(6)} h^5$	$u_j^{(7)} h^6$	$u_j^{(8)} h^7$
$\alpha_1 u_{j+1}'$	0	α_1	α_1	$\frac{\alpha_1}{2!}$	$\frac{\alpha_1}{3!}$	$\frac{\alpha_1}{4!}$	$\frac{\alpha_1}{5!}$	$\frac{\alpha_1}{6!}$	$\frac{\alpha_1}{7!}$
$\alpha_1 u_{j-1}'$	0	α_1	$-\alpha_1$	$\frac{\alpha_1}{2!}$	$-\frac{\alpha_1}{3!}$	$\frac{\alpha_1}{4!}$	$-\frac{\alpha_1}{5!}$	$\frac{\alpha_1}{6!}$	$-\frac{\alpha_1}{7!}$
u_j'	0	1	0	0	0	0	0	0	0
$\beta_1 u_{j+1}'' h$	0	0	β_1	β_1	$\frac{\beta_1}{2!}$	$\frac{\beta_1}{3!}$	$\frac{\beta_1}{4!}$	$\frac{\beta_1}{5!}$	$\frac{\beta_1}{6!}$
$-\beta_1 u_{j-1}'' h$	0	0	$-\beta_1$	β_1	$-\frac{\beta_1}{2!}$	$\frac{\beta_1}{3!}$	$-\frac{\beta_1}{4!}$	$\frac{\beta_1}{5!}$	$-\frac{\beta_1}{6!}$
$\frac{\gamma_1}{h} u_{j+1}$	γ_1	γ_1	$\frac{\gamma_1}{2!}$	$\frac{\gamma_1}{3!}$	$\frac{\gamma_1}{4!}$	$\frac{\gamma_1}{5!}$	$\frac{\gamma_1}{6!}$	$\frac{\gamma_1}{7!}$	$\frac{\gamma_1}{8!}$
$-\frac{\gamma_1}{h} u_{j-1}$	$-\gamma_1$	γ_1	$-\frac{\gamma_1}{2!}$	$\frac{\gamma_1}{3!}$	$-\frac{\gamma_1}{4!}$	$\frac{\gamma_1}{5!}$	$-\frac{\gamma_1}{6!}$	$\frac{\gamma_1}{7!}$	$-\frac{\gamma_1}{8!}$
Σ	0	y_{11}	0	y_{12}	0	y_{13}	0	y_{14}	0

Table 2. Taylor series of scheme (5).

Term	$u_j h^{-2}$	$u_j' h^{-1}$	u_j''	$u_j''' h$	$u_j^{(4)} h^2$	$u_j^{(5)} h^3$	$u_j^{(6)} h^4$	$u_j^{(7)} h^5$	$u_j^{(8)} h^6$
$\frac{\alpha_2}{h} u_{j+1}'$	0	α_2	α_2	$\frac{\alpha_2}{2!}$	$\frac{\alpha_2}{3!}$	$\frac{\alpha_2}{4!}$	$\frac{\alpha_2}{5!}$	$\frac{\alpha_2}{6!}$	$\frac{\alpha_2}{7!}$
$-\frac{\alpha_2}{h} u_{j-1}'$	0	$-\alpha_2$	α_2	$-\frac{\alpha_2}{2!}$	$\frac{\alpha_2}{3!}$	$-\frac{\alpha_2}{4!}$	$\frac{\alpha_2}{5!}$	$-\frac{\alpha_2}{6!}$	$\frac{\alpha_1}{7!}$
u_j''	0	0	1	0	0	0	0	0	0
$\beta_2 u_{j+1}''$	0	0	β_2	β_2	$\frac{\beta_2}{2!}$	$\frac{\beta_2}{3!}$	$\frac{\beta_2}{4!}$	$\frac{\beta_2}{5!}$	$\frac{\beta_2}{6!}$
$\beta_2 u_{j-1}''$	0	0	β_2	$-\beta_2$	$\frac{\beta_2}{2!}$	$-\frac{\beta_2}{3!}$	$\frac{\beta_2}{4!}$	$-\frac{\beta_2}{5!}$	$\frac{\beta_2}{6!}$
$\frac{\gamma_2}{h^2} u_{j+1}$	γ_2	γ_2	$\frac{\gamma_2}{2!}$	$\frac{\gamma_2}{3!}$	$\frac{\gamma_2}{4!}$	$\frac{\gamma_2}{5!}$	$\frac{\gamma_2}{6!}$	$\frac{\gamma_2}{7!}$	$\frac{\gamma_2}{8!}$
$-2\frac{\gamma_2}{h^2} u_j$	$-2\gamma_2$	0	0	0	0	0	0	0	0
$\frac{\gamma_2}{h^2} u_{j-1}$	γ_2	$-\gamma_2$	$\frac{\gamma_2}{2!}$	$-\frac{\gamma_2}{3!}$	$\frac{\gamma_2}{4!}$	$-\frac{\gamma_2}{5!}$	$\frac{\gamma_2}{6!}$	$-\frac{\gamma_2}{7!}$	$\frac{\gamma_2}{8!}$
Σ	0	0	y_{21}	0	y_{22}	0	y_{23}	0	y_{24}

To obtain this scheme with sixth-order convergence, the above coefficients must satisfy the following algebraic equations:

$$\begin{cases} y_{11} = 2(\alpha_1 + \gamma_1) + 1 = 0, \\ y_{12} = \alpha_1 + 2\left(\beta_1 + \frac{\gamma_1}{3!}\right) = 0, \\ y_{13} = 2\left(\frac{\alpha_1}{4!} + \frac{\beta_1}{3!} + \frac{\gamma_1}{5!}\right) = 0, \end{cases} \tag{6}$$

and

$$\begin{cases} y_{21} = 2(\alpha_2 + \beta_2) + \gamma_2 + 1 = 0, \\ y_{22} = \frac{\alpha_2}{3} + \beta_2 + \frac{\gamma_2}{12} = 0, \\ y_{23} = \frac{\alpha_2}{5!} + \frac{\beta_2}{4!} + \frac{\gamma_2}{6!} = 0. \end{cases} \tag{7}$$

The solutions of the above equations are

$$\alpha_1 = \frac{7}{16}, \beta_1 = -\frac{1}{16}, \gamma_1 = -\frac{15}{16},$$

and

$$\alpha_2 = \frac{9}{8}, \beta_2 = -\frac{1}{8}, \gamma_2 = -3.$$

Therefore, schemes (4) and (5) possess the specific forms

$$\frac{1}{16}\left(7u'_{j+1} + 16u'_j + 7u'_{j-1}\right) - \frac{h}{16}\left(u''_{j+1} - u''_{j-1}\right) = \frac{15}{16h}(u_{j+1} - u_{j-1}), \tag{8}$$

$$\frac{9}{8h}\left(u'_{j+1} - u'_{j-1}\right) - \frac{1}{8}\left(u''_{j+1} - 8u''_j + u''_{j-1}\right) = \frac{3}{h^2}(u_{j+1} - 2u_j + u_{j-1}). \tag{9}$$

After conducting a thorough analysis, it is determined that this scheme has relatively limited applicability. Its usage often necessitates complex matrix operations, and it is insufficient for differential equations involving certain high-order derivatives. In the good Boussinesq equation under study in this work, a fourth-order spatial derivative is involved. To obtain the numerical solutions of good Boussinesq equations, we require the discretization of $\partial_x^4 u$ and $\partial_x^2 u$. Here, we adopt the combination of the function values of u and its first-order derivative and second-order derivative to represent the fourth-order spatial derivative

$$u_j^{(4)} = -\frac{36}{h^4}(u_{j+1} - 2u_j + u_{j-1}) + \frac{21}{h^3}\left(u'_{j+1} + u'_{j-1}\right) - \frac{3}{h^2}\left(u''_{j+1} + u''_{j-1}\right). \tag{10}$$

Under periodic boundary conditions, by combining (8) and (9), we have

$$\begin{cases} A_{11}U_x + A_{12}U_{xx} = A_{13}U, \\ A_{21}U_x + A_{22}U_{xx} = A_{23}U. \end{cases} \tag{11}$$

where

$$A_{11} = \frac{1}{16}\begin{bmatrix} 16 & 7 & & & 7 \\ 7 & 16 & 7 & & \\ & \ddots & \ddots & \ddots & \\ & & 7 & 16 & 7 \\ 7 & & & 7 & 16 \end{bmatrix}, A_{12} = -\frac{h}{16}\begin{bmatrix} 0 & 1 & & & -1 \\ -1 & 0 & 1 & & \\ & \ddots & \ddots & \ddots & \\ & & -1 & 0 & 1 \\ 1 & & & -1 & 0 \end{bmatrix}, A_{13} = \frac{15}{16h}\begin{bmatrix} 0 & 1 & & & -1 \\ -1 & 0 & 1 & & \\ & \ddots & \ddots & \ddots & \\ & & -1 & 0 & 1 \\ 1 & & & -1 & 0 \end{bmatrix},$$

$$A_{21} = \frac{9}{8h}\begin{bmatrix} 0 & 1 & & & -1 \\ -1 & 0 & 1 & & \\ & \ddots & \ddots & \ddots & \\ & & -1 & 0 & 1 \\ 1 & & & -1 & 0 \end{bmatrix}, A_{22} = -\frac{1}{8}\begin{bmatrix} -8 & 1 & & & 1 \\ 1 & -8 & 1 & & \\ & \ddots & \ddots & \ddots & \\ & & 1 & -8 & 1 \\ 1 & & & 1 & -8 \end{bmatrix}, A_{23} = \frac{3}{h^2}\begin{bmatrix} -2 & 1 & & & 1 \\ 1 & -2 & 1 & & \\ & \ddots & \ddots & \ddots & \\ & & 1 & -2 & 1 \\ 1 & & & 1 & -2 \end{bmatrix}.$$

By solving (11), we can obtain $U_x = G \cdot U, U_{xx} = H \cdot U, G = A^{-1}B, H = A^{-1}C$, where $A = A_{11}A_{22} - A_{12}A_{21}, B = A_{22}A_{13} - A_{12}A_{23}, C = A_{11}A_{23} - A_{21}A_{13}$. For (10), we have

$$\begin{bmatrix} u_1^{(4)} \\ u_2^{(4)} \\ \vdots \\ u_{N-1}^{(4)} \\ u_N^{(4)} \end{bmatrix} = -\frac{36}{h^4}\begin{bmatrix} -2 & 1 & & & 1 \\ 1 & -2 & 1 & & \\ & \ddots & \ddots & \ddots & \\ & & 1 & -2 & 1 \\ 1 & & & 1 & -2 \end{bmatrix}\begin{bmatrix} u_1 \\ u_2 \\ \vdots \\ u_{N-1} \\ u_N \end{bmatrix} + \frac{21}{h^3}\begin{bmatrix} 0 & 1 & & & -1 \\ -1 & 0 & 1 & & \\ & \ddots & \ddots & \ddots & \\ & & -1 & 0 & 1 \\ 1 & & & -1 & 0 \end{bmatrix}\begin{bmatrix} u'_1 \\ u'_2 \\ \vdots \\ u'_{N-1} \\ u'_N \end{bmatrix} - \frac{3}{h^2}\begin{bmatrix} 0 & 1 & & & 1 \\ 1 & 0 & 1 & & \\ & \ddots & \ddots & \ddots & \\ & & 1 & 0 & 1 \\ 1 & & & 1 & 0 \end{bmatrix}\begin{bmatrix} u''_1 \\ u''_2 \\ \vdots \\ u''_{N-1} \\ u''_N \end{bmatrix},$$

where

$$B_1 = -\frac{3}{h^2}\begin{bmatrix} 0 & 1 & & & 1 \\ 1 & 0 & 1 & & \\ & \ddots & \ddots & \ddots & \\ & & 1 & 0 & 1 \\ 1 & & & 1 & 0 \end{bmatrix}.$$

By substituting $U_x = G \cdot U, U_{xx} = H \cdot U$ into this, the above expression can be represented as follows:

$$\partial_x^4 U = -\frac{12}{h^2}A_{23} \cdot U + \frac{56}{3h^2}A_{21}G \cdot U + B_1 H \cdot U. \tag{12}$$

Let $\mathrm{M} = \mathrm{B}_1 \cdot \mathrm{H} + \frac{56}{3\mathrm{h}^2}\mathrm{A}_{21} \cdot \mathrm{G} - \frac{12}{\mathrm{h}^2}\mathrm{A}_{23}$. We will use the following schemes for the spatial derivatives:

$$\begin{cases} \partial_x^4 U = \mathrm{M} \cdot U, \\ \partial_x^2 U = \mathrm{H} \cdot U. \end{cases} \tag{13}$$

Next, we will obtain the second CHOC scheme with eighth-order accuracy with the combination of the first, second, and third derivatives relating u_j, u_j', u_j'', u_j''' to their neighbors $u_{j-1}, u_{j-1}', u_{j-1}'', u_{j-1}'''$ and $u_{j+1}, u_{j+1}', u_{j+1}'', u_{j+1}'''$. The generalization of (4) and (5) to the case of three derivatives similarly yields the following CHOC scheme:

$$\alpha_1\left(u_{j+1}' + u_{j-1}'\right) + u_j' + \beta_1 h\left(u_{j+1}'' - u_{j-1}''\right) + \omega_1 h^2\left(u_{j+1}''' + u_{j-1}'''\right) + \gamma_1 \frac{u_{j+1} - u_{j-1}}{h} = 0, \tag{14}$$

$$\alpha_2\left(\frac{u_{j+1}' - u_{j-1}'}{h}\right) + u_j'' + \beta_2\left(u_{j+1}'' + u_{j-1}''\right) + \omega_2 h\left(u_{j+1}''' - u_{j-1}'''\right) + \gamma_2 \frac{u_{j+1} - 2u_j + u_{j-1}}{h^2} = 0, \tag{15}$$

$$\alpha_3\left(\frac{u_{j+1}' + u_{j-1}'}{h}\right) + u_j''' + \beta_3\left(\frac{u_{j+1}'' - u_{j-1}''}{h}\right) + \omega_3\left(u_{j+1}''' + u_{j-1}'''\right) + \gamma_3 \frac{u_{j+1} - u_{j-1}}{h^3} = 0, \tag{16}$$

where $\alpha_1, \beta_1, \omega_1, \gamma_1$ and $\alpha_2, \beta_2, \omega_2, \gamma_2$ and $\alpha_3, \beta_3, \omega_3, \gamma_3$ are coefficients to be determined according to the accuracy of the approximation. Through the Taylor expansion of Equations (14)–(16), we can obtain Tables 3–5.

Table 3. Taylor series of scheme (14).

Term	$u_j h^{-1}$	u_j'	$u_j'' h$	$u_j''' h^2$	$u_j^{(4)} h^3$	$u_j^{(5)} h^4$	$u_j^{(6)} h^5$	$u_j^{(7)} h^6$	$u_j^{(8)} h^7$
$\alpha_1 u_{j+1}'$	0	α_1	α_1	$\frac{\alpha_1}{2!}$	$\frac{\alpha_1}{3!}$	$\frac{\alpha_1}{4!}$	$\frac{\alpha_1}{5!}$	$\frac{\alpha_1}{6!}$	$\frac{\alpha_1}{7!}$
$\alpha_1 u_{j-1}'$	0	α_1	$-\alpha_1$	$\frac{\alpha_1}{2!}$	$-\frac{\alpha_1}{3!}$	$\frac{\alpha_1}{4!}$	$-\frac{\alpha_1}{5!}$	$\frac{\alpha_1}{6!}$	$-\frac{\alpha_1}{7!}$
u_j'	0	1	0	0	0	0	0	0	0
$\beta_1 u_{j+1}'' h$	0	0	β_1	β_1	$\frac{\beta_1}{2!}$	$\frac{\beta_1}{3!}$	$\frac{\beta_1}{4!}$	$\frac{\beta_1}{5!}$	$\frac{\beta_1}{6!}$
$-\beta_1 u_{j-1}'' h$	0	0	$-\beta_1$	β_1	$-\frac{\beta_1}{2!}$	$\frac{\beta_1}{3!}$	$-\frac{\beta_1}{4!}$	$\frac{\beta_1}{5!}$	$-\frac{\beta_1}{6!}$
$\omega_1 u_{j+1}''' h^2$	0	0	0	ω_1	ω_1	$\frac{\omega_1}{2!}$	$\frac{\omega_1}{3!}$	$\frac{\omega_1}{4!}$	$\frac{\omega_1}{5!}$
$\omega_1 u_{j-1}''' h^2$	0	0	0	ω_1	$-\omega_1$	$\frac{\omega_1}{2!}$	$-\frac{\omega_1}{3!}$	$\frac{\omega_1}{4!}$	$-\frac{\omega_1}{5!}$
$\frac{\gamma_1}{h} u_{j+1}$	γ_1	γ_1	$\frac{\gamma_1}{2!}$	$\frac{\gamma_1}{3!}$	$\frac{\gamma_1}{4!}$	$\frac{\gamma_1}{5!}$	$\frac{\gamma_1}{6!}$	$\frac{\gamma_1}{7!}$	$\frac{\gamma_1}{8!}$
$-\frac{\gamma_1}{h} u_{j-1}$	$-\gamma_1$	γ_1	$-\frac{\gamma_1}{2!}$	$\frac{\gamma_1}{3!}$	$-\frac{\gamma_1}{4!}$	$\frac{\gamma_1}{5!}$	$-\frac{\gamma_1}{6!}$	$\frac{\gamma_1}{7!}$	$-\frac{\gamma_1}{8!}$
Σ	0	y_{11}	0	y_{12}	0	y_{13}	0	y_{14}	0

To obtain these schemes with the eighth order, they must satisfy the algebraic equations

$$\begin{cases} y_{11} = 2(\alpha_1 + \gamma_1) + 1 = 0, \\ y_{12} = \alpha_1 + 2\left(\beta_1 + \omega_1 + \frac{\gamma_1}{3!}\right) - 0, \\ y_{13} = 2\left(\frac{\alpha_1}{4!} + \frac{\beta_1}{3!} + \frac{\omega_1}{2!} + \frac{\gamma_1}{5!}\right) = 0, \\ y_{14} = 2\left(\frac{\alpha_1}{6!} + \frac{\beta_1}{5!} + \frac{\omega_1}{4!} + \frac{\gamma_1}{7!}\right) = 0, \end{cases} \tag{17}$$

and

$$\begin{cases} y_{21} = 2\left(\alpha_2 + \beta_2 + \frac{\gamma_2}{2!}\right) + 1 = 0, \\ y_{22} = 2\left(\frac{\alpha_2}{3!} + \frac{\beta_2}{2!} + \omega_2 + \frac{\gamma_2}{4!}\right) = 0, \\ y_{23} = 2\left(\frac{\alpha_2}{5!} + \frac{\beta_2}{4!} + \frac{\omega_2}{3!} + \frac{\gamma_2}{6!}\right) = 0, \\ y_{24} = 2\left(\frac{\alpha_2}{7!} + \frac{\beta_2}{6!} + \frac{\omega_2}{5!} + \frac{\gamma_2}{8!}\right) = 0, \end{cases} \tag{18}$$

and

$$\begin{cases} y_{31} = 2(\alpha_3 + \gamma_3) = 0, \\ y_{32} = 2\left(\frac{\alpha_3}{2!} + \beta_3 + \omega_3 + \frac{\gamma_3}{3!}\right) + 1 = 0, \\ y_{33} = 2\left(\frac{\alpha_3}{4!} + \frac{\beta_3}{3!} + \frac{\omega_3}{2!} + \frac{\gamma_3}{5!}\right) = 0, \\ y_{34} = 2\left(\frac{\alpha_3}{6!} + \frac{\beta_3}{5!} + \frac{\omega_3}{4!} + \frac{\gamma_3}{7!}\right) = 0. \end{cases} \tag{19}$$

Table 4. Taylor series of scheme (15).

Term	$u_j h^{-2}$	$u_j' h$	u_j''	$u_j''' h$	$u_j^{(4)} h^2$	$u_j^{(5)} h^3$	$u_j^{(6)} h^4$	$u_j^{(7)} h^5$	$u_j^{(8)} h^6$
$\frac{\alpha_2}{h} u_{j+1}'$	0	α_2	α_2	$\frac{\alpha_2}{2!}$	$\frac{\alpha_2}{3!}$	$\frac{\alpha_2}{4!}$	$\frac{\alpha_2}{5!}$	$\frac{\alpha_2}{6!}$	$\frac{\alpha_2}{7!}$
$-\frac{\alpha_2}{h} u_{j-1}'$	0	$-\alpha_2$	α_2	$-\frac{\alpha_2}{2!}$	$\frac{\alpha_2}{3!}$	$-\frac{\alpha_2}{4!}$	$\frac{\alpha_2}{5!}$	$-\frac{\alpha_2}{6!}$	$\frac{\alpha_2}{7!}$
u_j''	0	0	1	0	0	0	0	0	0
$\beta_2 u_{j+1}''$	0	0	β_2	β_2	$\frac{\beta_2}{2!}$	$\frac{\beta_2}{3!}$	$\frac{\beta_2}{4!}$	$\frac{\beta_2}{5!}$	$\frac{\beta_2}{6!}$
$\beta_2 u_{j-1}''$	0	0	β_2	$-\beta_2$	$\frac{\beta_2}{2!}$	$-\frac{\beta_2}{3!}$	$\frac{\beta_2}{4!}$	$-\frac{\beta_2}{5!}$	$\frac{\beta_2}{6!}$
$\omega_2 u_{j+1}''' h$	0	0	0	ω_2	ω_2	$\frac{\omega_2}{2!}$	$\frac{\omega_2}{3!}$	$\frac{\omega_2}{4!}$	$\frac{\omega_2}{5!}$
$-\omega_2 u_{j-1}''' h$	0	0	0	$-\omega_2$	ω_2	$-\frac{\omega_2}{2!}$	$\frac{\omega_2}{3!}$	$-\frac{\omega_2}{4!}$	$\frac{\omega_2}{5!}$
$\frac{\gamma_2}{h^2} u_{j+1}$	γ_2	γ_2	$\frac{\gamma_2}{2!}$	$\frac{\gamma_2}{3!}$	$\frac{\gamma_2}{4!}$	$\frac{\gamma_2}{5!}$	$\frac{\gamma_2}{6!}$	$\frac{\gamma_2}{7!}$	$\frac{\gamma_2}{8!}$
$-\frac{2\gamma_2}{h^2} u_j$	$-2\gamma_2$	0	0	0	0	0	0	0	0
$\frac{\gamma_2}{h^2} u_{j-1}$	γ_2	$-\gamma_2$	$\frac{\gamma_2}{2!}$	$-\frac{\gamma_2}{3!}$	$\frac{\gamma_2}{4!}$	$-\frac{\gamma_2}{5!}$	$\frac{\gamma_2}{6!}$	$-\frac{\gamma_2}{7!}$	$\frac{\gamma_2}{8!}$
Σ	0	0	y_{21}	0	y_{22}	0	y_{23}	0	y_{24}

Table 5. Taylor series of scheme (16).

Term	$u_j h^{-3}$	$u_j' h^{-2}$	$u_j'' h^{-1}$	u_j'''	$u_j^{(4)} h$	$u_j^{(5)} h^2$	$u_j^{(6)} h^3$	$u_j^{(7)} h^4$	$u_j^{(8)} h^5$
$\frac{\alpha_3}{h^2} u_{j+1}'$	0	α_3	α_3	$\frac{\alpha_3}{2!}$	$\frac{\alpha_3}{3!}$	$\frac{\alpha_3}{4!}$	$\frac{\alpha_3}{5!}$	$\frac{\alpha_3}{6!}$	$\frac{\alpha_3}{7!}$
$\frac{\alpha_3}{h^2} u_{j-1}'$	0	α_3	$-\alpha_3$	$\frac{\alpha_3}{2!}$	$-\frac{\alpha_3}{3!}$	$\frac{\alpha_3}{4!}$	$-\frac{\alpha_3}{5!}$	$\frac{\alpha_3}{6!}$	$-\frac{\alpha_3}{7!}$
u_j'''	0	0	0	1	0	0	0	0	0
$\frac{\beta_3}{h} u_{j+1}''$	0	0	β_3	β_3	$\frac{\beta_3}{2!}$	$\frac{\beta_3}{3!}$	$\frac{\beta_3}{4!}$	$\frac{\beta_3}{5!}$	$\frac{\beta_3}{6!}$
$-\frac{\beta_3}{h} u_{j-1}''$	0	0	$-\beta_3$	β_3	$-\frac{\beta_3}{2!}$	$\frac{\beta_3}{3!}$	$-\frac{\beta_3}{4!}$	$\frac{\beta_3}{5!}$	$-\frac{\beta_3}{6!}$
$\omega_3 u_{j+1}'''$	0	0	0	ω_3	ω_3	$\frac{\omega_3}{2!}$	$\frac{\omega_3}{3!}$	$\frac{\omega_3}{4!}$	$\frac{\omega_3}{5!}$
$\omega_3 u_{j-1}'''$	0	0	0	ω_3	$-\omega_3$	$\frac{\omega_3}{2!}$	$-\frac{\omega_3}{3!}$	$\frac{\omega_3}{4!}$	$-\frac{\omega_3}{5!}$
$\frac{\gamma_3}{h^3} u_{j+1}$	γ_3	γ_3	$\frac{\gamma_3}{2!}$	$\frac{\gamma_3}{3!}$	$\frac{\gamma_3}{4!}$	$\frac{\gamma_3}{5!}$	$\frac{\gamma_3}{6!}$	$\frac{\gamma_3}{7!}$	$\frac{\gamma_3}{8!}$
$-\frac{\gamma_3}{h^3} u_{j-1}$	$-\gamma_3$	γ_3	$-\frac{\gamma_3}{2!}$	$\frac{\gamma_3}{3!}$	$-\frac{\gamma_3}{4!}$	$\frac{\gamma_3}{5!}$	$-\frac{\gamma_3}{6!}$	$\frac{\gamma_3}{7!}$	$-\frac{\gamma_3}{8!}$
Σ	0	y_{31}	0	y_{32}	0	y_{33}	0	y_{34}	0

Their unique solutions are

$$\alpha_1 = \frac{19}{32}, \beta_1 = -\frac{1}{8}, \omega_1 = \frac{1}{96}, \gamma_1 = -\frac{35}{32}$$

and

$$\alpha_2 = \frac{29}{16}, \beta_2 = -\frac{5}{16}, \omega_2 = \frac{1}{48}, \gamma_2 = -4$$

and

$$\alpha_3 = -\frac{105}{16}, \beta_3 = \frac{15}{8}, \omega_3 = -\frac{3}{16}, \gamma_3 = \frac{105}{16}$$

respectively. Therefore, schemes (14)–(16) have the following specific forms:

$$\frac{1}{32}\left(19u'_{j+1} + 32u'_j + 19u'_{j-1}\right) - \frac{h}{8}\left(u''_{j+1} - u''_{j-1}\right) + \frac{h^2}{96}\left(u'''_{j+1} + u'''_{j-1}\right) = \frac{35}{32h}(u_{j+1} - u_{j-1}), \tag{20}$$

$$\frac{\left(29u'_{j+1} - 29u'_{j-1}\right)}{16h} - \frac{\left(5u''_{j+1} - 16u''_j + 5u''_{j-1}\right)}{16} + \frac{h\left(u'''_{j+1} - u'''_{j-1}\right)}{48} = \frac{4(u_{j+1} - 2u_j + u_{j-1})}{h^2}, \tag{21}$$

$$\frac{\left(105u'_{j+1} + 105u'_{j-1}\right)}{-16h^2} + \frac{\left(15u''_{j+1} - 15u''_{j-1}\right)}{8h} - \frac{\left(3u'''_{j+1} - 16u'''_j + 3u'''_{j-1}\right)}{16} = \frac{105(u_{j+1} - u_{j-1})}{-16h^3}. \tag{22}$$

This three-point scheme possesses eighth-order accuracy and involves three derivatives, so it is more applicable and allows for greater accuracy in comparison to (4) and (5). Under periodic boundary conditions, by combining (20)–(22), we have

$$\begin{cases} B_{11}U_x + B_{12}U_{xx} + B_{13}U_{xxx} = B_{14}U, \\ B_{21}U_x + B_{22}U_{xx} + B_{23}U_{xxx} = B_{24}U, \\ B_{31}U_x + B_{32}U_{xx} + B_{33}U_{xxx} = B_{34}U. \end{cases} \tag{23}$$

where

$$B_{11} = \frac{19}{32}\begin{bmatrix} \frac{32}{19} & 1 & & & 1 \\ 1 & \frac{32}{19} & 1 & & \\ & \ddots & \ddots & \ddots & \\ & & 1 & \frac{32}{19} & 1 \\ 1 & & & 1 & \frac{32}{19} \end{bmatrix}, B_{12} = -\frac{h}{8}\begin{bmatrix} 0 & 1 & & & -1 \\ -1 & 0 & 1 & & \\ & \ddots & \ddots & \ddots & \\ & & -1 & 0 & 1 \\ 1 & & & -1 & 0 \end{bmatrix}, B_{13} = \frac{h^2}{96}\begin{bmatrix} 0 & 1 & & & 1 \\ 1 & 0 & 1 & & \\ & \ddots & \ddots & \ddots & \\ & & 1 & 0 & 1 \\ 1 & & & 1 & 0 \end{bmatrix},$$

$$B_{14} = \frac{35}{32h}\begin{bmatrix} 0 & 1 & & & -1 \\ -1 & 0 & 1 & & \\ & \ddots & \ddots & \ddots & \\ & & -1 & 0 & 1 \\ 1 & & & -1 & 0 \end{bmatrix}, B_{21} = \frac{29}{16h}\begin{bmatrix} 0 & 1 & & & -1 \\ -1 & 0 & 1 & & \\ & \ddots & \ddots & \ddots & \\ & & -1 & 0 & 1 \\ 1 & & & -1 & 0 \end{bmatrix}, B_{22} = -\frac{5}{16}\begin{bmatrix} -\frac{16}{5} & 1 & & & 1 \\ 1 & -\frac{16}{5} & 1 & & \\ & \ddots & \ddots & \ddots & \\ & & 1 & -\frac{16}{5} & 1 \\ 1 & & & 1 & -\frac{16}{5} \end{bmatrix},$$

$$B_{23} = \frac{h}{48}\begin{bmatrix} 0 & 1 & & & -1 \\ -1 & 0 & 1 & & \\ & \ddots & \ddots & \ddots & \\ & & -1 & 0 & 1 \\ 1 & & & -1 & 0 \end{bmatrix}, B_{24} = \frac{4}{h^2}\begin{bmatrix} -2 & 1 & & & 1 \\ 1 & -2 & 1 & & \\ & \ddots & \ddots & \ddots & \\ & & 1 & -2 & 1 \\ 1 & & & 1 & -2 \end{bmatrix}, B_{31} = -\frac{105}{16h^2}\begin{bmatrix} 0 & 1 & & & -1 \\ -1 & 0 & 1 & & \\ & \ddots & \ddots & \ddots & \\ & & -1 & 0 & 1 \\ 1 & & & -1 & 0 \end{bmatrix},$$

$$B_{32} = \frac{15}{8h}\begin{bmatrix} 0 & 1 & & & -1 \\ -1 & 0 & 1 & & \\ & \ddots & \ddots & \ddots & \\ & & -1 & 0 & 1 \\ 1 & & & -1 & 0 \end{bmatrix}, B_{33} = -\frac{3}{16}\begin{bmatrix} -\frac{16}{3} & 1 & & & 1 \\ 1 & -\frac{16}{3} & 1 & & \\ & \ddots & \ddots & \ddots & \\ & & 1 & -\frac{16}{3} & 1 \\ 1 & & & 1 & -\frac{16}{3} \end{bmatrix}, B_{34} = -\frac{105}{16h^3}\begin{bmatrix} 0 & 1 & & & -1 \\ -1 & 0 & 1 & & \\ & \ddots & \ddots & \ddots & \\ & & -1 & 0 & 1 \\ 1 & & & -1 & 0 \end{bmatrix}.$$

Next, we adopt the combination of the function values of u and its first, second, and third derivatives to represent the fourth-order spatial derivative

$$u_j^{(4)} = -\frac{72}{h^4}(u_{j+1} - 2u_j + u_{j-1}) + \frac{183}{4h^3}\left(u'_{j+1} - u'_{j-1}\right) - \frac{39}{4h^2}\left(u''_{j+1} + u''_{j-1}\right) + \frac{3}{4h}\left(u'''_{j+1} - u'''_{j-1}\right). \tag{24}$$

In light of solving (23), we can obtain

$$\begin{cases} \partial_x U = \mathrm{G}^* \cdot U, \\ \partial_x^2 U = \mathrm{H}^* \cdot U, \\ \partial_x^3 U = \mathrm{I} \cdot U, \end{cases} \tag{25}$$

where $\mathrm{G}^* = \mathrm{D}^{-1}\mathrm{D}_1, \mathrm{H}^* = \mathrm{D}^{-1}\mathrm{D}_2, \mathrm{I} = \mathrm{D}^{-1}\mathrm{D}_3$. For $\mathrm{D}, \mathrm{D}_1, \mathrm{D}_2$ and D_3, we have

$$\begin{cases} \mathrm{D} = \mathrm{B}_{11}\mathrm{B}_{22}\mathrm{B}_{33} + \mathrm{B}_{12}\mathrm{B}_{23}\mathrm{B}_{31} + \mathrm{B}_{13}\mathrm{B}_{21}\mathrm{B}_{32} - \mathrm{B}_{11}\mathrm{B}_{23}\mathrm{B}_{32} - \mathrm{B}_{12}\mathrm{B}_{21}\mathrm{B}_{33} - \mathrm{B}_{13}\mathrm{B}_{22}\mathrm{B}_{31}, \\ \mathrm{D}_1 = \mathrm{B}_{14}\mathrm{B}_{22}\mathrm{B}_{33} + \mathrm{B}_{14}\mathrm{B}_{23}\mathrm{B}_{31} + \mathrm{B}_{13}\mathrm{B}_{21}\mathrm{B}_{34} - \mathrm{B}_{11}\mathrm{B}_{23}\mathrm{B}_{34} - \mathrm{B}_{14}\mathrm{B}_{21}\mathrm{B}_{33} - \mathrm{B}_{13}\mathrm{B}_{24}\mathrm{B}_{31}, \\ \mathrm{D}_2 = \mathrm{B}_{11}\mathrm{B}_{22}\mathrm{B}_{34} + \mathrm{B}_{12}\mathrm{B}_{24}\mathrm{B}_{31} + \mathrm{B}_{14}\mathrm{B}_{21}\mathrm{B}_{32} - \mathrm{B}_{13}\mathrm{B}_{24}\mathrm{B}_{31} - \mathrm{B}_{14}\mathrm{B}_{21}\mathrm{B}_{33} - \mathrm{B}_{11}\mathrm{B}_{23}\mathrm{B}_{34}, \\ \mathrm{D}_3 = \mathrm{B}_{11}\mathrm{B}_{22}\mathrm{B}_{34} + \mathrm{B}_{12}\mathrm{B}_{24}\mathrm{B}_{31} + \mathrm{B}_{14}\mathrm{B}_{21}\mathrm{B}_{32} - \mathrm{B}_{11}\mathrm{B}_{24}\mathrm{B}_{32} - \mathrm{B}_{12}\mathrm{B}_{21}\mathrm{B}_{34} - \mathrm{B}_{14}\mathrm{B}_{22}\mathrm{B}_{31}. \end{cases} \tag{26}$$

Substituting $U_x = \mathrm{G}^* \cdot U, U_{xx} = \mathrm{H}^* \cdot U, U_{xxx} = \mathrm{I} \cdot U$ into (24) gives

$$\partial_x^4 U = -\frac{18}{\mathrm{h}^2}\mathrm{B}_{24} \cdot U - \frac{366}{h^4}\mathrm{B}_{12}\mathrm{G}^* \cdot U + \frac{936}{h^4}\mathrm{B}_{13}\mathrm{H}^* \cdot U - \frac{6}{h^2}\mathrm{B}_{12}\mathrm{I} \cdot U. \tag{27}$$

Let $\mathrm{M}^* = \frac{936}{h^4}\mathrm{B}_{13}\mathrm{H}^* - \frac{366}{h^4}\mathrm{B}_{12}\mathrm{G}^* - \frac{18}{h^2}\mathrm{B}_{24} - \frac{6}{h^2}\mathrm{B}_{12}\mathrm{I}$. We will obtain the following discrete schemes of the spatial derivative, as follows:

$$\begin{cases} \partial_x^4 U = \mathrm{M}^* \cdot U, \\ \partial_x^2 U = \mathrm{H}^* \cdot U. \end{cases} \tag{28}$$

For the above scheme, we find that the matrix operation becomes complicated. To obtain the discrete form of $\partial_x^2 u$ and $\partial_x^4 u$ according to (14)–(16), we require many matrix operations, and the subsequent simulation of the numerical solution will be more difficult. Thus, we consider constructing a direct combination of $\partial_x^2 u, \partial_x^4 u$ and u to devise the third CHOC scheme. This scheme will maintain sixth-order precision and can be used to easily obtain the discrete forms of $\partial_x^2 u$ and $\partial_x^4 u$, which will be more pertinent and accurate. This scheme has the following formulation:

$$\alpha_1\left(\frac{u''_{j+1} + u''_{j-1}}{2}\right) + u''_j + \beta_1 h^2\left(\frac{u^{(4)}_{j+1} + u^{(4)}_{j-1}}{2}\right) = \gamma_1\frac{u_{j+1} - 2u_j + u_{j-1}}{h^2}, \tag{29}$$

$$\alpha_2\left(\frac{u''_{j+1} - 2u''_j + u''_{j-1}}{h^2}\right) + u^{(4)}_j + \beta_2\left(\frac{u^{(4)}_{j+1} + u^{(4)}_{j-1}}{2}\right) = \gamma_2\frac{u_{j+2} - 4u_{j+1} + 6u_j - 4u_{j-1} + u_{j-2}}{h^4}. \tag{30}$$

We apply Taylor expansion to (29) to obtain

$$
\begin{aligned}
LHS &= u_j'' + \alpha_1\left(\frac{u_{j+1}'' + u_{j-1}''}{2}\right) + \beta_1 h^2\left(\frac{u_{j+1}^{(4)} + u_{j-1}^{(4)}}{2}\right) \\
&= u_j'' + \alpha_1\left(u_j'' + \frac{h^2}{2!}u_j^{(4)} + \frac{h^4}{4!}u_j^{(6)} + o\left(h^6\right)\right) + \beta_1 h^2\left(u_j^{(4)} + \frac{h^2}{2!}u_j^{(6)} + \frac{h^4}{4!}u_j^{(8)} + o\left(h^6\right)\right) \\
&= (1+\alpha_1)u_j'' + \left(\frac{\alpha_1}{2!} + \beta_1\right)h^2 u_j^{(4)} + \left(\frac{\alpha_1}{4!} + \frac{\beta_1}{2!}\right)h^4 u_j^{(6)} + o\left(h^6\right), \\
RHS &= \gamma_1\left(\frac{u_{j+1} - 2u_j + u_{j-1}}{h^2}\right) \\
&= \gamma_1\left(u_j'' + \frac{u_j^{(4)}}{12}h^2 + \frac{u_j^{(6)}}{360}h^4\right) + o\left(h^6\right).
\end{aligned}
$$

To obtain the scheme with sixth-order accuracy, the coefficients must satisfy the algebraic equations

$$
\begin{cases}
1 + \alpha_1 = \frac{\gamma_1}{2!}, \\
\frac{\alpha_1}{2!} + \beta_1 = \frac{\gamma_1}{4!}, \\
\frac{\alpha_1}{4!} + \frac{\beta_1}{2!} = \frac{\gamma_1}{6!},
\end{cases}
\Rightarrow
\begin{cases}
\alpha_1 = \frac{14}{61}, \\
\beta_1 = -\frac{3}{244}, \\
\gamma_1 = \frac{75}{61}.
\end{cases}
$$

Similarly, for (30), we have

$$
\begin{aligned}
LHS &= u_j^{(4)} + \alpha_2\left(u_j^{(4)} + \frac{u_j^{(6)}}{12}h^2 + \frac{u_j^{(8)}}{360}h^4\right) + \beta_2\left(u_j^{(4)} + \frac{u_j^{(6)}h^2}{2!} + \frac{u_j^{(8)}h^4}{4!}\right) + o\left(h^6\right) \\
&= (1+\alpha_2+\beta_2)u_j^{(4)} + \left(\frac{\alpha_2}{12} + \frac{\beta_2}{2!}\right)h^2 u_j^{(6)} + \left(\frac{\alpha_2}{360} + \frac{\beta_2}{4!}\right)h^4 u_j^{(8)} + o\left(h^6\right), \\
RHS &= \gamma_2\frac{u_{j+2} - 4u_{j+1} + 6u_j - 4u_{j-1} + u_{j-2}}{h^4} + o\left(h^6\right) \\
&= \gamma_2\left(\frac{2^5 - 2^3}{4!}u_j^{(4)} + \frac{2^7 - 2^3}{6!}h^2 u_j^{(6)} + \frac{2^9 - 2^3}{8!}h^4 u_j^{(8)}\right) + o\left(h^6\right).
\end{aligned}
$$

To obtain the scheme with sixth-order accuracy, the coefficients must satisfy the algebraic equations

$$
\begin{cases}
1 + \alpha_2 + \beta_2 = \frac{2^5-2^3}{4!}\gamma_2, \\
\frac{\alpha_2}{12} + \frac{\beta_2}{2!} = \frac{2^7-2^3}{6!}\gamma_2, \\
\frac{\alpha_2}{360} + \frac{\beta_2}{4!} = \frac{2^9-2^3}{8!}\gamma_2,
\end{cases}
\Longrightarrow
\begin{cases}
\alpha_2 = \frac{6}{7}, \\
\beta_2 = \frac{5}{7}, \\
\gamma_2 = \frac{18}{7}.
\end{cases}
$$

Under periodic boundary conditions, for (29) and (30), we obtain

$$
\begin{cases}
A_{11}^* U_{xx} + A_{12}^* U_{xxxx} = A_{13}^* U, \\
A_{21}^* U_{xx} + A_{22}^* U_{xxxx} = A_{23}^* U.
\end{cases}
\tag{31}
$$

where

$$
A_{11}^{*}=\frac{7}{61}\begin{bmatrix}\frac{61}{7} & 1 & & & 1\\ 1 & \frac{61}{7} & 1 & & \\ & \ddots & \ddots & \ddots & \\ & & 1 & \frac{61}{7} & 1\\ 1 & & & 1 & \frac{61}{7}\end{bmatrix},A_{12}^{*}=-\frac{3h^2}{488}\begin{bmatrix}0 & 1 & & & 1\\ 1 & 0 & 1 & & \\ & \ddots & \ddots & \ddots & \\ & & 1 & 0 & 1\\ 1 & & & 1 & 0\end{bmatrix},A_{13}^{*}=\frac{75}{61h^2}\begin{bmatrix}-2 & 1 & & & 1\\ 1 & -2 & 1 & & \\ & \ddots & \ddots & \ddots & \\ & & 1 & -2 & 1\\ 1 & & & 1 & -2\end{bmatrix},
$$

$$
A_{21}^{*}=\frac{6}{7h^2}\begin{bmatrix}-2 & 1 & & & 1\\ 1 & -2 & 1 & & \\ & \ddots & \ddots & \ddots & \\ & & 1 & -2 & 1\\ 1 & & & 1 & -2\end{bmatrix},A_{22}^{*}=\frac{5}{14}\begin{bmatrix}\frac{14}{5} & 1 & & & 1\\ 1 & \frac{14}{5} & 1 & & \\ & \ddots & \ddots & \ddots & \\ & & 1 & \frac{14}{5} & 1\\ 1 & & & 1 & \frac{14}{5}\end{bmatrix},A_{23}^{*}=\frac{18}{7h^4}\begin{bmatrix}6 & -4 & 1 & & & & 1 & -4\\ -4 & 6 & -4 & 1 & & & & 1\\ 1 & -4 & 6 & -4 & 1 & & & \\ & \ddots & \ddots & \ddots & \ddots & \ddots & & \\ & & \ddots & \ddots & \ddots & \ddots & \ddots & \\ & & & \ddots & \ddots & \ddots & \ddots & 1\\ 1 & & & & 1 & -4 & 6 & -4\\ -4 & 1 & & & & 1 & -4 & 6\end{bmatrix}.
$$

With (31), we can readily derive U_{xx} and U_{xxxx} via the expressions of U. This significantly streamlines the matrix operations. By solving (31), we can obtain

$$
\begin{cases}\partial_x^2 U = G_1\cdot U,\\ \partial_x^4 U = H_1\cdot U.\end{cases} \tag{32}
$$

where $G_1 = A_1^{-1}B_1, H_1 = A_1^{-1}C_1$. For A_1, B_1, C_1, we have

$$
\begin{cases}A_1 = A_{11}^{*}A_{22}^{*} - A_{12}^{*}A_{21}^{*},\\ B_1 = A_{22}^{*}A_{13}^{*} - A_{12}^{*}A_{23}^{*},\\ C_1 = A_{11}^{*}A_{23}^{*} - A_{21}^{*}A_{13}^{*}.\end{cases} \tag{33}
$$

Additionally, the following high-order compact (HOC) scheme is presented in the existing literature [28]. For good Boussinesq equations, the above scheme has higher spatial accuracy compared to the scheme given in [28].

$$
\alpha_1 u''_{j-1} + u''_j + \alpha_1 u''_{j+1} = b_1\frac{u_{j+2}-2u_j+u_{j-2}}{4h^2} + a_1\frac{u_{j+1}-2u_j+u_{j-1}}{h^2}, \tag{34}
$$

$$
\begin{aligned}\alpha_2 u^{(4)}_{j-1} + u^{(4)}_j + \alpha_2 u^{(4)}_{j+1} &= b_2\frac{u_{j+3}-9u_{j+1}+16u_j-9u_{j-1}+u_{j-3}}{6h^4}\\ &+a_2\frac{u_{j+2}-4u_{j+1}+6u_j-4u_{j-1}+u_{j-2}}{h^4},\end{aligned} \tag{35}
$$

for (34) and (35), according to [28], we have $\alpha_1 = \frac{2}{11}$, $\alpha_2 = \frac{7}{26}$, $a_1 = \frac{12}{11}$, $a_2 = \frac{19}{13}$, $b_1 = \frac{3}{11}$, $b_2 = \frac{1}{13}$. Therefore, we can also express this HOC scheme in the same way as in the three aforementioned schemes, where we denote

$$
\begin{cases}\partial_x^4 U = S_2\cdot U,\\ \partial_x^2 U = S_1\cdot U.\end{cases} \tag{36}
$$

3. Establishment of the Fully Discrete Scheme

Let τ be a temporal step size and $t_n = n\tau, n = 0, 1, 2, \cdots, M$, where $M = T/\tau$. Denote the approximation of $u(x, t_n)$ by u^n. Define the following operators:

$$\delta_t u^{n+\frac{1}{2}} = \frac{u^{n+1} - u^n}{\tau}, \quad u^{n+\frac{1}{2}} = \frac{u^n + u^{n+1}}{2}.$$

Let $v = u_t$, and the considered good Boussinesq equation can be written as

$$\partial_t v = \partial_x^2 u - \partial_x^4 u + \partial_x^2 (u^2).$$

Applying the CHOC scheme (13) to the spatial derivatives of the above equation gives

$$v_t = -M \cdot u + H \cdot u + H \cdot u^2 = N \cdot u + H \cdot u^2,$$

where $N = H - M$. By applying a symplectic midpoint scheme with second-order accuracy to the above equation, we obtain the following fully discrete scheme:

$$u^{n+1} = u^n + \frac{\tau}{2}\left(v^n + v^{n+1}\right), \tag{37}$$

$$-\frac{\tau}{2} N \cdot u^{n+1} + v^{n+1} = \frac{\tau}{2} N \cdot u^n + v^n + \frac{\tau}{2} H \cdot \left\{ \left(u^2\right)^n + \left(u^2\right)^{n+1} \right\}. \tag{38}$$

Similarly, using CHOC scheme (28) for the spatial derivatives yields

$$v_t = -M^* \cdot u + H^* \cdot u + H^* \cdot u^2 = N^* \cdot u + H^* \cdot u^2,$$

where $N^* = H^* - M^*$. We obtain the corresponding fully discrete scheme

$$-\frac{\tau}{2} N^* \cdot u^{n+1} + v^{n+1} = \frac{\tau}{2} N^* \cdot u^n + v^n + \frac{\tau}{2} H^* \cdot \left\{ \left(u^2\right)^n + \left(u^2\right)^{n+1} \right\}. \tag{39}$$

Applying the CHOC scheme (31) for the spatial derivatives gives

$$v_t = -H_1 \cdot u + G_1 \cdot u + G_1 \cdot u^2 = N_1 \cdot u + G_1 \cdot u^2,$$

where $N_1 = G_1 - H_1$. We similarly obtain the following fully discrete scheme:

$$-\frac{\tau}{2} N_1 \cdot u^{n+1} + v^{n+1} = \frac{\tau}{2} N_1 \cdot u^n + v^n + \frac{\tau}{2} G_1 \cdot \left\{ \left(u^2\right)^n + \left(u^2\right)^{n+1} \right\}. \tag{40}$$

Applying the HOC scheme (34) and (35) for the spatial derivatives gives

$$v_t = -S_2 \cdot u + S_1 \cdot u + S_1 \cdot u^2 = S_3 \cdot u + S_1 \cdot u^2,$$

where $S_3 = S_1 - S_2$. We also similarly obtain the following fully discrete scheme:

$$-\frac{\tau}{2} S_3 \cdot u^{n+1} + v^{n+1} = \frac{\tau}{2} S_3 \cdot u^n + v^n + \frac{\tau}{2} S_1 \cdot \left\{ \left(u^2\right)^n + \left(u^2\right)^{n+1} \right\}. \tag{41}$$

By combining (38)–(41) with (37), respectively, we always obtain the algebraic equation as follows:

$$A \cdot T^{n+1} = B \cdot T^n + F\left(T^{n+1}, T^n\right),$$

where A and B are some invertible tridiagonal matrices depending on the corresponding scheme, $T^n = [u^n, v^n]^\top$, and F is the corresponding nonlinear term.

For simplicity, we will denote the schemes corresponding to (38)–(41) by CHOC-A, CHOC-B, CHOC-C, and HOC, respectively.

4. Conservation Laws of CHOC Schemes

Under periodic boundary condition (3) with $L = 1$, some good Boussinesq equations have certain conservation laws. Below, we consider periodic domain $[0, 1]$.

Theorem 1. *Let $\|\cdot\|$ denote the standard L^2-norm for 1-periodic functions. Then, along with $\partial_t^2 u = -\partial_x^4 u$, the quadratic functional*

$$\|u_t\|^2 + \|u_{xx}\|^2 \tag{42}$$

is invariant. Thus, it is an integral of motion.

Proof. According to (3), after multiplying both sides of $\partial_t^2 u = -\partial_x^4 u$ by u_t and integrating it by parts, we have

$$\int_0^1 u_t \cdot u_{tt} dx = -\int_0^1 u_{xx} \cdot u_{txx} dx. \tag{43}$$

For (43), we take integration with respect to t to obtain

$$\int_0^t \int_0^1 u_t \cdot u_{tt}\, dx\, dt = -\int_0^t \int_0^1 u_{xx} u_{txx}\, dx\, dt.$$

$$\Rightarrow \int_0^1 u_t^2(x,t)\, dx + \int_0^1 u_{xx}^2(x,t)\, dx = \int_0^1 u_t^2(x,0)\, dx + \int_0^1 u_{xx}^2(x,0)\, dx.$$

Therefore, we have (42). □

Theorem 2. *For nonlinear Boussinesq Equation (2), the following conservation law is satisfied:*

$$\int_0^1 u_t(x,t)\, dx = \int_0^1 v^0(x)\, dx. \tag{44}$$

If $\int_0^1 v^0(x)\, dx = 0$, then we obtain the conservation law as follows:

$$\int_0^1 u(x,t)\, dx = \int_0^1 u^0(x)\, dx. \tag{45}$$

Proof. For $t \in [0, T]$, integrating with respect to x on both sides of (2), we obtain

$$\int_0^1 u_{tt} dx = \int_0^1 (u_{xx} - \partial_x^4 u + (u^2)_{xx}) dx.$$

According to (3), the integration on the right side of the above equation is 0, i.e.,

$$\int_0^1 u_{tt} dx = 0.$$

Taking integration with respect to t yields $\int_0^1 u_t(x,t)dx = \int_0^1 v^0(x)dx$, which is (44). If $\int_0^1 v^0(x)\, dx = 0$, then $\int_0^1 u_t(x,t)dx = 0$, which gives (45) by integration with respect to t.

First, we are interested in the discrete versions of Theorems 1 and 2 under numerical analysis for CHOC schemes. To this end, we list some important properties of circulant matrices [11]. A matrix written in the form

$$Circ(c_0, c_1, c_2 \cdots c_{N-1}) = \begin{bmatrix} c_0 & c_1 & c_2 & \cdots & c_{N-1} \\ c_{N-1} & c_0 & c_1 & \cdots & c_{N-2} \\ \cdots & \ddots & \ddots & \ddots & \cdots \\ c_2 & c_3 & \ddots & \ddots & c_1 \\ c_1 & c_2 & \cdots & c_{N-1} & c_0 \end{bmatrix}$$

is said to be a circulant matrix.

All of the matrices $A_{ij}(i,j = 1,2.)$, $B_{ij}(i,j = 1,2,3.)$, $A^*_{ij}(i,j = 1,2.)$ are circulant. There are a number of favorable characteristics of this type of matrix.

We list some of them in the following; these are useful in analyzing our schemes. □

Proposition 1 ([11,27]). *If A, B are circulant matrices with the same number of rows and columns, then we have the following.*

(i) $A + B, A - B, AB$ *are circulant matrices.*
(ii) *If* A^{-1} *is well defined, then* A^{-1} *is also a circulant matrix.*
(iii) *A, B are commutators,* $AB = BA$.
(iv) *If A, B are symmetric and positive definite matrices, then* $AB = BA$ *is a symmetric and positive definite matrix.*
(v) *The eigenvalue of the circulant matrix above is* $\lambda_j = \sum_{k=0}^{N-1} c_k e^{-ik\theta_j}$ *with the corresponding eigenvector* $w_j = \frac{1}{N}\left[1, e^{-i\theta_j}, \cdots, e^{-i(N-1)\theta_j}\right]^{\top}$.

With Proposition 1, we can obtain the following proposition.

Proposition 2. *For the matrices in the CHOC solvers (13), (28), (31), and the HOC solver (36), we have the following:*

(i) $A_{11}, A_{22}, -A_{23}, B_{22}, B_{33}, A^*_{11}, A^*_{22}, A^*_{23}$ *are symmetric and positive definite.*
(ii) $A_{12}, A_{13}, A_{21}, B_{12}, B_{14}, B_{21}, B_{23}, B_{34}$ *are skew-symmetric.*
(iii) $B_{11}, B_{13}, B_{24}, B_{31}, B_{32}, A^*_{12}, A^*_{13}, A^*_{21}, S_1$ *are symmetric.*
(iv) A, A^{-1}, D, A_1, C_1 *are symmetric and positive definite;* D_1, D_3 *are skew-symmetric; and* D_2, B_1 *are symmetric.*
(v) M^*, H_1, S_2 *are symmetric and positive definite;* G, G^*, I, *are skew-symmetric; and* H, M, H^*, G_1, N, N^*, N_1, S_1 *are symmetric.*
(vi) *All of these are circulant.*

Proof. The conclusions (i)–(iv) and (vi) can be observed or be verified from Proposition 1. The result (v) can be derived from the last conclusion in Proposition 1 by finding their eigenvalues. □

Theorem 3. *Define*

$$w^n = (v^n, v^n) + (u^n, R \cdot u^n),$$

where (u,v) *is the standard unitary inner product at the discrete level for finite-dimensional sequence vectors,* $v^n = \left[v_1^n, v_2^n, \cdots, v_{NX}^n\right]^{\top}, u^n = \left[u_1^n, u_2^n, \cdots, u_{NX}^n\right]^{\top}$. *R is the matrix coefficient when approximating the fourth-order spatial derivative expressed by M (13),* M^* *(28),* H_1 *(31),* S_2 *(36). Then, for CHOC solvers (13), (28), (31), and HOC solver (36) to solve* $\partial_t^2 u = -\partial_x^4 u$, *the numerical solutions satisfy that*

$$\omega^{n+1} = w^n. \tag{46}$$

Moreover, for M^* *(28),* H_1 *(31) and* S_2 *(36), there exists C such that* $C^{\top} \cdot C = R$; *therefore,*

$$w^n = (v^n, v^n) + (C \cdot u^n, C \cdot u^n).$$

Proof. Since $v = u_t$, we have $v_t = -u_{xxxx}$, and its discrete scheme is

$$\frac{v^{n+1} - v^n}{\tau} = -\frac{Ru^{n+1} + Ru^n}{2}.$$

By multiplying $\frac{u^{n+1}-u^n}{\tau}=\frac{v^{n+1}+v^n}{2}$ on both sides of the above formula, we have

$$\frac{(v^{n+1}+v^n)^{\top}(v^{n+1}-v^n)}{2\tau}=-\frac{(v^{n+1}+v^n)^{\top}}{2}\cdot\frac{Ru^{n+1}+Ru^n}{2}.$$

Therefore, we obtain that

$$\left(v^{n+1}\right)^{\top}\left(v^{n+1}\right)-(v^n)^{\top}(v^n)=-\left(u^{n+1}\right)^{\top}R\cdot\left(u^{n+1}\right)-(u^n)^{\top}R\cdot(u^n),$$
$$\left(v^{n+1}\right)^{\top}\left(v^{n+1}\right)+\left(u^{n+1}\right)^{\top}\left(R\cdot u^{n+1}\right)=(v^n)^{\top}(v^n)+(u^n)^{\top}(R\cdot u^n),$$

which is $\omega^{n+1}=\omega^n$. Taking into account the symmetric positivity of M^* (28), H_1 (31), and $S_2(36)$, there exists C such that $C^{\top}\cdot C=R$, which yields

$$(u^n,R\cdot u^n)=(C\cdot u^n)^{\top}(C\cdot u^n).$$

Therefore, we obtain

$$w^n=(v^n,v^n)+(C\cdot u^n,C\cdot u^n).$$

□

Theorem 4. *For the nonlinear good Boussinesq Equation (2) with periodic boundary conditions, the schemes CHOC-A, CHOC-B, CHOC-C, and HOC satisfy the following discrete conservation law:*

$$\overline{u^n}=h\sum_{j=1}^{NX}u_j^n\equiv\overline{u^0} \tag{47}$$

provided that $\overline{v^0}=0$.

Proof. Firstly, we consider scheme CHOC-A to solve nonlinear system (2) and have the following formula:

$$u^{n+1}=u^n+\tau\left(\frac{v^n+v^{n+1}}{2}\right),v^{n+1}=v^n+\frac{\tau}{2}N\left(u^{n+1}+u^n\right)+\frac{\tau}{2}H\left[(u^n)^2+\left(u^{n+1}\right)^2\right]. \tag{48}$$

By calculation, we obtain that

$$v^{n+1}=v^n+\frac{\tau}{2}\left(E-\frac{\tau^2}{4}N\right)^{-1}\left\{\tau Nv^n+2Nu^n+H\left[(u^n)^2+\left(u^{n+1}\right)^2\right]\right\}. \tag{49}$$

We construct the following iterative algorithm:

$$\begin{aligned}v^{n+1}_{(k+1)}&=v^n+\frac{\tau}{2}\left(E-\frac{\tau^2}{4}N\right)^{-1}\left\{\tau Nv^n+2Nu^n+H\left[(u^n)^2+\left(u^{n+1}_{(k)}\right)^2\right]\right\},\\ u^{n+1}_{(k+1)}&=u^n+\tau\left(\frac{v^n+v^{n+1}_{(k+1)}}{2}\right),\end{aligned} \tag{50}$$

where $k=0,1,\ldots$ and $u^{n+1}_{(0)}=u^n$. Then, we find that

$$\lim_{k\to\infty}u^{n+1}_{(k)}=u^{n+1},\ \lim_{k\to\infty}v^{n+1}_{(k)}=v^{n+1}. \tag{51}$$

Considering $\overline{v^0}=0$ and the symmetry of N,H, we can obtain $\overline{v^{n+1}_{(k+1)}}=\overline{v^n}=0,\overline{u^{n+1}_{(k+1)}}=\overline{u^n}$. The limit (51) yields $\overline{v^{n+1}}=0,\overline{u^{n+1}}=\overline{u^n}$. The conservation identity (47) for schemes CHOC-B, CHOC-C, and HOC can be derived similarly.

For the linear good Boussinesq Equation (1), we have the following equivalent Hamiltonian system:

$$\begin{cases} u_t = v, \\ v_t = u_{xx} - u_{xxxx}, \end{cases} \tag{52}$$

with the Hamiltonian function $H = -\frac{1}{2}\int (v^2 + u_x^2 + u_{xx}^2 + V^2(u))dx$. Thus, we obtain the symplectic conservation law as follows:

$$w(t) = \int du \wedge dv dx = w(0). \tag{53}$$

Symplectic schemes for Hamiltonian systems are proven to be more efficient than non-symplectic schemes for long-time numerical computations and are widely applied to practical problems arising in many fields of science and engineering. These include celestial mechanics, quantum physics, statistics, and so on (see [16,29–31]). Next, we will demonstrate that the considered schemes are symplectic. □

Theorem 5. *For linear GB Equation (1), the schemes CHOC-A, CHOC-B, CHOC-C, and HOC are symplectic with the following conservation law:*

$$w^n = h\sum_{j=1}^{NX} du_j^n \wedge dv_j^n = w^0. \tag{54}$$

Proof. For (38), scheme $CHOC - A$ has the formula as follows:

$$\begin{bmatrix} -\frac{\tau}{2}N & E \\ E & -\frac{\tau}{2}E \end{bmatrix}\begin{bmatrix} U^{n+1} \\ V^{n+1} \end{bmatrix} = \begin{bmatrix} \frac{\tau}{2}N & E \\ E & \frac{\tau}{2}E \end{bmatrix}\begin{bmatrix} U^n \\ V^n \end{bmatrix}.$$

Therefore, through extensive calculation, scheme CHOC-A is shown to be symplectic. Similarly, the schemes CHOC-B, CHOC-C, and HOC are also symplectic. □

5. Numerical Experiments

In this section, we present some numerical results to illustrate the above theoretical analysis of the CHOC and HOC schemes, mainly focusing on the convergence and discrete conservation laws for numerical solutions of the GB equation. Our numerical results were obtained via MATLAB 2022a.

First, for the linear GB equation, we take the initial value $f(x) = sin(x)$ and exact solution $u(x,t) = \sin(x)\cos\left(\sqrt{2}t\right)$. Here, we focus on issues within a limited space–time domain $[0, 2\pi] \times [0, T]$. The L_2 and L_∞ norms of the errors between the numerical solution and exact solution are defined, respectively, as

$$\|e^n(h,\tau)\|_2 = \sqrt{h\Sigma_j\left(U_j^n - u_j^n\right)^2}, \quad \|e^n(h,\tau)\|_\infty = \max_j\left|U_j^n - u_j^n\right|,$$

where $U_j^n = u(x_j, t_n)$ is the exact solution and u_j^n is the numerical solution. The convergence order in the space and time directions is defined as $order1$ and $order2$, respectively,

$$order1 = \frac{\ln(\|e(h_1,\tau)\|/\|e(h_2,\tau)\|)}{\ln(h_1/h_2)}, \quad order2 = \frac{\ln(\|e(h,\tau_1)\|/\|e(h,\tau_2)\|)}{\ln(\tau_1/\tau_2)}.$$

First, we test the convergence order of $CHOC - A$, $CHOC - B$, $CHOC - C$, HOC and take different step sizes in the direction to be considered, while taking a very small step size in the other direction.

Table 6 lists the errors of the numerical solution and exact solution under the L_2 and L_∞ norms, as well as the spatial convergence order calculated with $order1$ for the four schemes while taking different spatial step sizes. In order to render the error in the time direction relatively negligible, we take the time step size $\tau = 10^{-4}$.

Next, Table 7 shows the ratio of the numerical errors in Table 6, calculated with

$$\frac{\text{Numerical error by } CHOC-B \text{ } or \text{ } CHOC-C}{\text{Numerical error by } CHOA \text{ scheme}}.$$

Table 8 shows the ratio of the numerical errors in Table 6 calculated with

$$\frac{\text{Numerical error by } CHOC-B \text{ } or \text{ } CHOC-C}{\text{Numerical error by } HOC \text{ scheme}}.$$

Table 9 lists the errors of the numerical solution and exact solution under the L_2 and L_∞ norms, as well as the time convergence order calculated with *order*2 when the four schemes take different time step sizes. In order to render the error in the spatial direction relatively negligible, we take the spatial step size $h = \frac{2\pi}{80}$.

This indicates that the two additional CHOC schemes derived from CHOC-A are more accurate than the CHOC-A and HOC schemes.

Secondly, for the linear principal part of the GB equation, we simulate the discrete conservation law (46) in time interval $[0,15]$, which is measured with the following approximate motion-invariant error: $\omega^n - \omega^0$.

Thirdly, we consider the nonlinear GB equation (2) with an exact solitary wave solution as follows:

$$u(x,t) = -A\,\text{sech}^2\left[\left(\frac{P}{2}\right)(\xi - \xi_0)\right], \quad \xi = x - ct, \quad (x,t) \in [-50,50] \times [0,1],$$

where $0 < P < 1$, $A = \frac{3P^2}{2}$, $\xi_0 = (1-P^2)^{1/2}$. Below, we take a moderate amplitude $A = 0.5\,, \xi_0 = 0$ and take step sizes $h = 0.5\,, \tau = 0.01$. We simulate the discrete conservation law (47) in time interval $[0,15]$, which is measured with the following approximate motion-invariant error: $\overline{u^n} - \overline{u^0}$. We also test three CHOC schemes for the interaction of two solitary waves governed by the nonlinear GB equation. In this work, we set different amplitudes A of 1 and 0.25, with corresponding initial phases ξ of -60 and -80, respectively. We also take step sizes $h = 0.5\,, \tau = 0.01$. The experimental results indicate that all three *CHOC* schemes effectively simulate the interaction of the two solitary waves, and the results are similar. Therefore, we only present the simulation results for the CHOC-C scheme at different time instances.

Table 6. Numerical errors of u_j^n with $\tau = 10^{-4}$.

h	*Scheme*	$\|e^n\|_2$	**Order**	$\|e^n\|_\infty$	**Order**
$\frac{2\pi}{5}$	$CHOC-A$	7.629×10^{-3}	–	4.1841×10^{-3}	–
	$CHOC-B$	7.4229×10^{-4}	–	3.9829×10^{-4}	–
	$CHOC-C$	9.4958×10^{-4}	–	5.0952×10^{-4}	–
	HOC	8.7936×10^{-4}	–	6.1928×10^{-4}	–
$\frac{2\pi}{10}$	$CHOC-A$	4.203×10^{-4}	4.1816	2.3058×10^{-4}	4.1816
	$CHOC-B$	9.4353×10^{-6}	6.2978	5.0628×10^{-6}	6.2977
	$CHOC-C$	1.348×10^{-5}	6.1384	7.2331×10^{-6}	6.1384
	HOC	2.4481×10^{-5}	5.1667	1.3136×10^{-5}	5.5590
$\frac{2\pi}{15}$	$CHOC-A$	8.0998×10^{-5}	4.0609	4.5682×10^{-5}	3.9927
	$CHOC-B$	7.9367×10^{-7}	6.1054	4.4533×10^{-7}	5.9952
	$CHOC-C$	1.1673×10^{-6}	6.0338	6.5498×10^{-7}	5.9236
	HOC	2.1169×10^{-6}	6.0374	1.1878×10^{-6}	5.9272

Table 6. *Cont.*

h	*Scheme*	$\|e^n\|_2$	Order	$\|e^n\|_\infty$	Order
$\frac{2\pi}{20}$	$CHOC-A$	2.5403×10^{-5}	4.0307	1.4288×10^{-5}	4.0402
	$CHOC-B$	1.3599×10^{-7}	6.1321	7.6726×10^{-8}	6.1129
	$CHOC-C$	2.0994×10^{-7}	5.9636	1.1844×10^{-7}	5.9448
	HOC	3.7792×10^{-7}	5.9893	2.1322×10^{-7}	5.9702
$\frac{2\pi}{25}$	$CHOC-A$	1.0361×10^{-5}	4.0190	5.8447×10^{-6}	4.0059
	$CHOC-B$	3.2376×10^{-8}	6.4316	1.823×10^{-8}	6.4406
	$CHOC-C$	5.7932×10^{-8}	5.7701	3.262×10^{-8}	5.7784
	HOC	1.0185×10^{-7}	5.8760	5.7347×10^{-8}	5.8850

Table 7. The ratio of the numerical errors among different CHOC schemes of u_j^n with $\tau=10^{-4}$.

h	$CHOC-B$		$CHOC-C$	
	Rate e_2^u	*Rate* e_∞^u	*Rate* e_2^u	*Rate* e_∞^u
$\frac{2\pi}{5}$	0.097	0.095	0.124	0.122
$\frac{2\pi}{10}$	0.022	0.022	0.032	0.031
$\frac{2\pi}{15}$	0.0098	0.0097	0.0144	0.0143
$\frac{2\pi}{20}$	0.0053	0.0054	0.0083	0.0083
$\frac{2\pi}{25}$	0.0031	0.0031	0.0056	0.0056

Table 8. The ratio of the numerical errors among different schemes of u_j^n with $\tau=10^{-4}$.

h	$CHOC-B$		$CHOC-C$	
	Rate e_2^u	*Rate* e_∞^u	*Rate* e_2^u	*Rate* e_∞^u
$\frac{2\pi}{5}$	0.8441	0.6432	1.8	0.8228
$\frac{2\pi}{10}$	0.3854	0.3854	0.5506	0.5506
$\frac{2\pi}{15}$	0.3749	0.3749	0.5514	0.5514
$\frac{2\pi}{20}$	0.3598	0.3598	0.5555	0.5555
$\frac{2\pi}{25}$	0.3179	0.3179	0.5688	0.5688

Table 9. Verification of temporal convergence rate with $h=\frac{2\pi}{80}$.

τ	*Scheme*	$\|e^n\|_2$	Order	$\|e^n\|_\infty$	Order
$\frac{1}{40}$	$CHOC-A$	5.5718×10^{-6}	–	1.1056×10^{-5}	–
	$CHOC-B$	5.574×10^{-6}	–	1.106×10^{-5}	–
	$CHOC-C$	5.574×10^{-6}	–	1.106×10^{-5}	–
	HOC	5.574×10^{-6}	–	1.106×10^{-5}	–
$\frac{1}{80}$	$CHOC-A$	1.4094×10^{-6}	1.9831	2.8058×10^{-6}	1.9783
	$CHOC-B$	1.4116×10^{-6}	1.9814	2.8101×10^{-6}	1.9764
	$CHOC-C$	1.4116×10^{-6}	1.9814	2.8101×10^{-6}	1.9764
	HOC	1.4116×10^{-6}	1.9814	2.8101×10^{-6}	1.9764
$\frac{1}{160}$	$CHOC-A$	3.5297×10^{-7}	1.9975	7.0373×10^{-7}	1.9953
	$CHOC-B$	3.5515×10^{-7}	1.9908	7.0808×10^{-7}	1.9886
	$CHOC-C$	3.5514×10^{-7}	1.9909	7.0806×10^{-7}	1.9887
	HOC	3.5514×10^{-7}	1.9909	7.0807×10^{-7}	1.9887

Table 9. *Cont.*

τ	Scheme	$\|\|e^n\|\|_2$	Order	$\|\|e^n\|\|_\infty$	Order
$\frac{1}{320}$	$CHOC-A$	8.689×10^{-8}	2.0223	1.7336×10^{-7}	2.0213
	$CHOC-B$	8.907×10^{-8}	1.9954	1.7772×10^{-7}	1.9943
	$CHOC-C$	8.9065×10^{-8}	1.9955	1.777×10^{-7}	1.9944
	HOC	8.9069×10^{-8}	1.9954	1.7771×10^{-7}	1.9944
$\frac{1}{640}$	$CHOC-A$	2.0124×10^{-8}	2.1103	4.0162×10^{-8}	2.1099
	$CHOC-B$	2.2307×10^{-8}	1.9974	4.4534×10^{-8}	1.9966
	$CHOC-C$	2.2301×10^{-8}	1.9978	4.4511×10^{-8}	1.9972
	HOC	2.2305×10^{-8}	1.9976	4.452×10^{-8}	1.9970

Finally, we give three-dimensional waveform diagrams of the exact solution and numerical solution of the three schemes. We also give a comparison between the numerical solution and the exact solution.

6. Conclusions

In this work, for a GB equation, we construct three combined high-order compact symplectic schemes, which are $CHOC-A$, $CHOC-B$, and $CHOC-C$. The schemes satisfy the discrete conservation laws corresponding to the structure-preserving property of the GB equation. Equations (46), (47) and (54) indicate the types of stability of the schemes. $CHOC$ schemes improve the efficiency of the traditional HOC method in simulating such differential equations with multiple-order spatial derivatives, such as GB equations. $CHOC$ schemes make full use of the information of all of the involved derivative values, which leads to fewer nodes and higher-accuracy schemes. Therefore, it mitigates the difficulties of boundary treatment. Finally, the $CHOC$ scheme is more accurate than the HOC scheme with the same order.

In the numerical experiments, we first test the convergence order of $CHOC-A, CHOC-B$, $CHOC-C$, and HOC by taking different step sizes in the direction to be considered and taking very small step sizes in the other direction. In Table 6, we list the spatial convergence order of $CHOC-A, CHOC-B, CHOC-C$, and HOC. We can observe that scheme $CHOC-A$ is of fourth-order accuracy in space. Schemes $CHOC-B$, $CHOC-C$, and HOC are of sixth-order accuracy in space. In line with Tables 7 and 8, we can conclude that $CHOC-B$ and $CHOC-C$ are more accurate for the GB equation than $CHOC-A$ and HOC, and $CHOC-B$ is also superior to $CHOC-C$. In Table 9, we list the time convergence order of $CHOC-A$, $CHOC-B$, $CHOC-C$, and HOC. We can observe that the schemes are of two orders in time. Also, from Figure 1, we can observe that the $CHOC-C$ scheme effectively simulate the interaction of the two solitary waves with the nonlinear GB Equation (2).

Second, from the approximate motion-invariant error simulation depicted in Figures 2–5, we can see that the three $CHOC$ schemes and the HOC scheme satisfy the discrete conservation law (46) for linear GB equations.

Next, we observe Figures 6–9. We find that the errors are small enough; in other words, the three $CHOC$ schemes and the HOC scheme satisfy the conservation law (47) for nonlinear GB Equation (2).

Finally, we use the three $CHOC$ schemes to numerically simulate the solitary wave solutions with the nonlinear good Boussinesq Equation (2). From Figures 10–13, we can observe that the numerical solutions fit the waveforms of the exact solutions well.

When the equation contains multiple spatial derivatives or there are higher-order derivatives, it may be difficult to accurately solve the discrete formulas for these spatial derivatives. In this case, we can use some software, such as Maple, or perform a simulation through numerical methods. In the future, we will also construct combined compact difference schemes to solve more general Boussinesq equations and other PDEs.

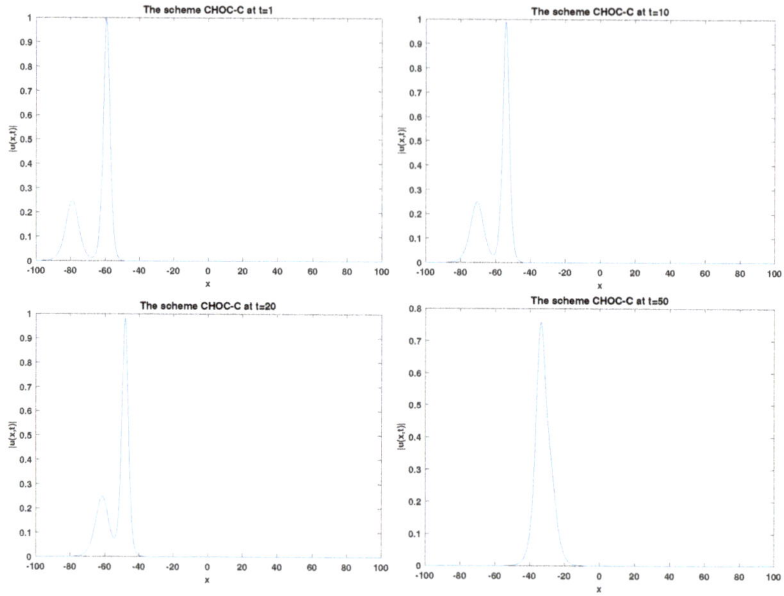

Figure 1. The interaction of two solitary waves in $CHOC-C$, when $h = 0.5$, $\tau = 0.01$.

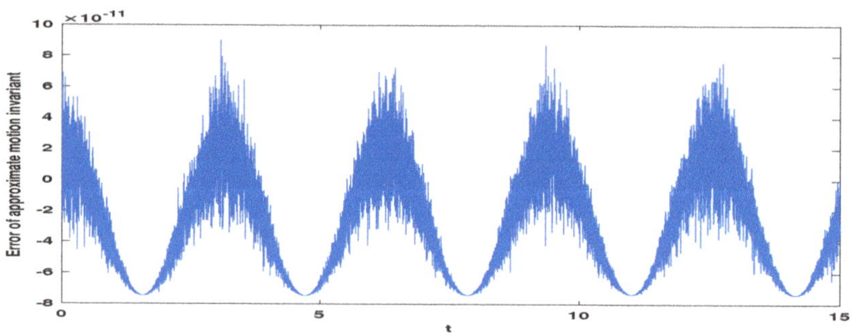

Figure 2. Approximate motion−invariant error diagram for $CHOC-A$ when $h = \frac{2\pi}{80}$, $\tau = 0.001$.

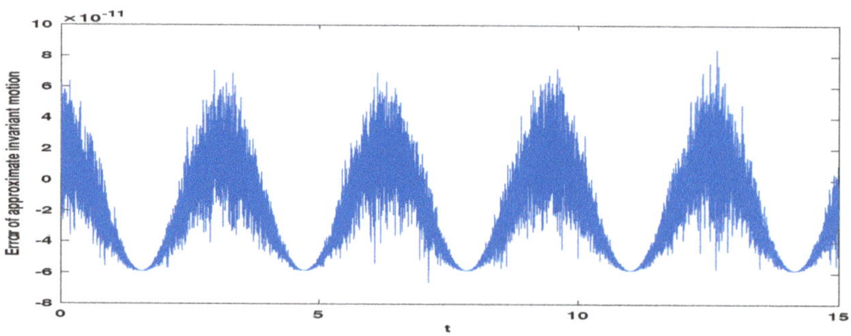

Figure 3. Approximate motion−invariant error diagram for $CHOC-B$ when $h = \frac{2\pi}{80}$, $\tau = 0.001$.

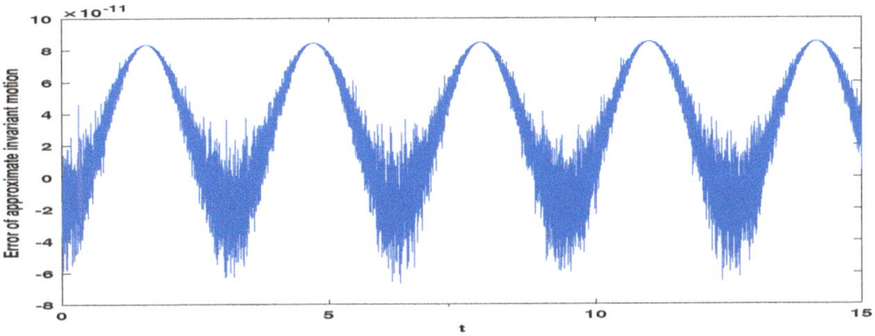

Figure 4. Approximate motion−invariant error diagram for $CHOC-C$ when $h=\frac{2\pi}{80}, \tau=0.001$.

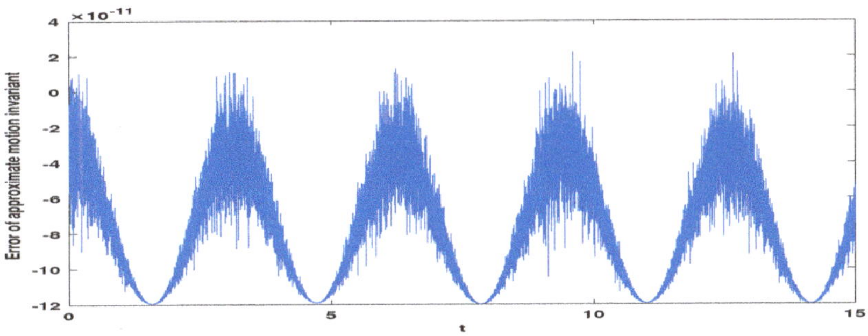

Figure 5. Approximate motion−invariant error diagram for HOC when $h=\frac{2\pi}{80}, \tau=0.001$.

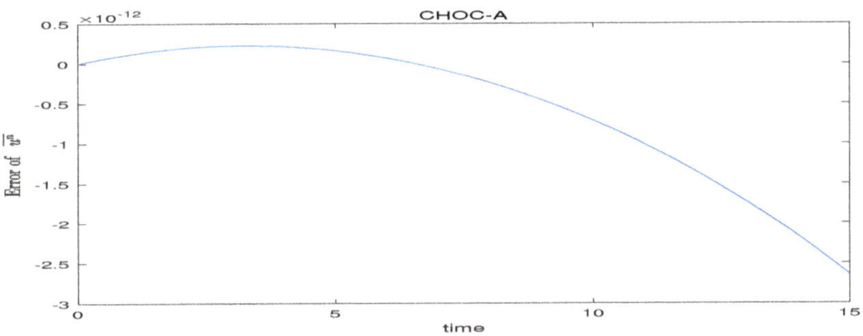

Figure 6. $\overline{u^n}$ error diagram for $CHOC-A$ when $h=0.5, \tau=0.01$.

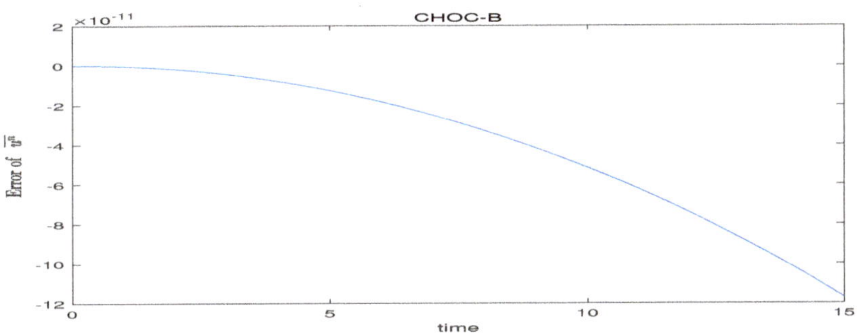

Figure 7. $\overline{u^n}$ error diagram for $CHOC-B$ when $h=0.5, \tau=0.01$.

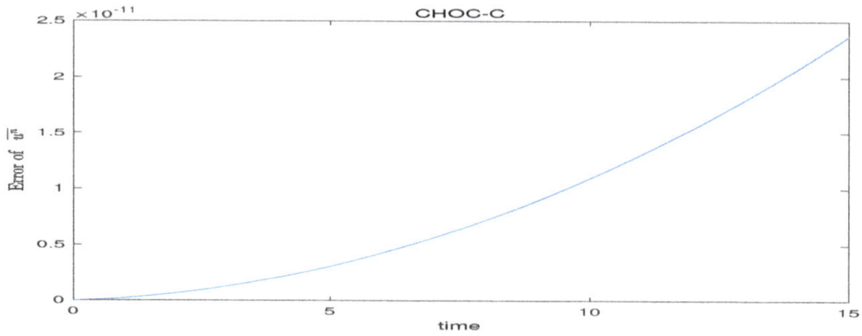

Figure 8. $\overline{u^n}$ error diagram for $CHOC - C$ when $h = 0.5, \tau = 0.01$.

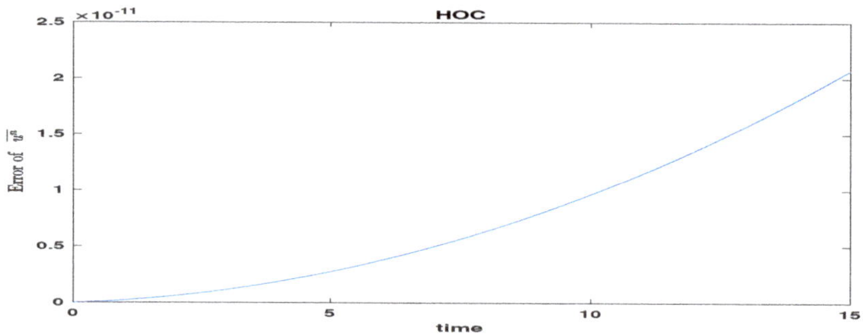

Figure 9. $\overline{u^n}$ error diagram for HOC when $h = 0.5, \tau = 0.01$.

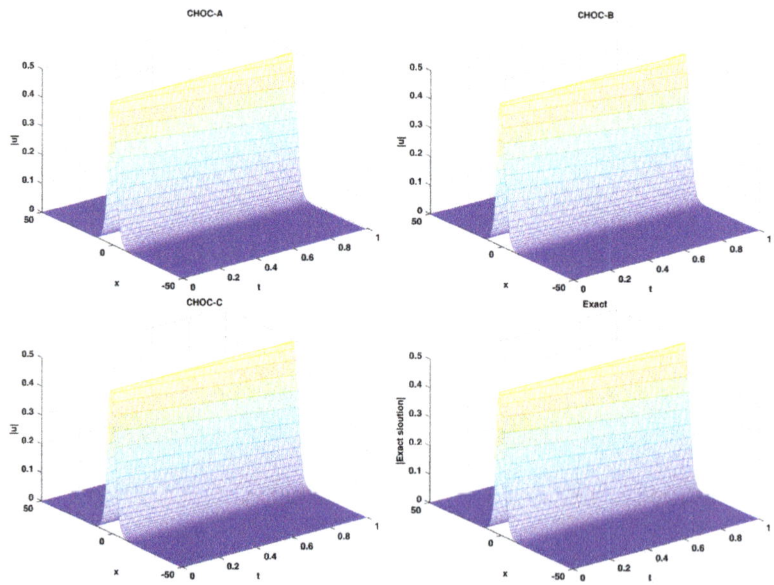

Figure 10. For $h = 0.5\,, \tau = 0.01$, the three-dimensional waveform diagrams of the $CHOC - A$, $CHOC - B$, and $CHOC - C$ schemes and the three-dimensional waveform diagram of the exact solution are shown.

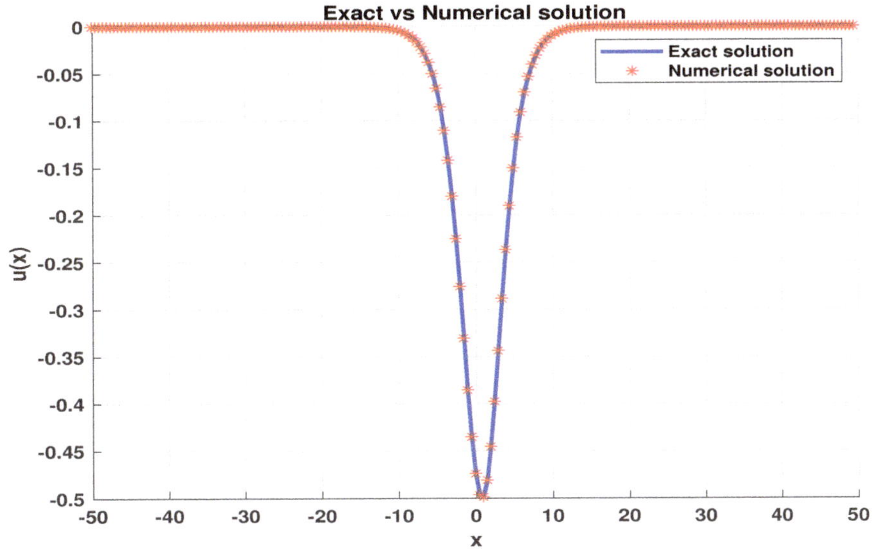

Figure 11. The case of $h = 0.5$, at time $T = 1$. The exact solution vs. the numerical solution of $CHOC - A$.

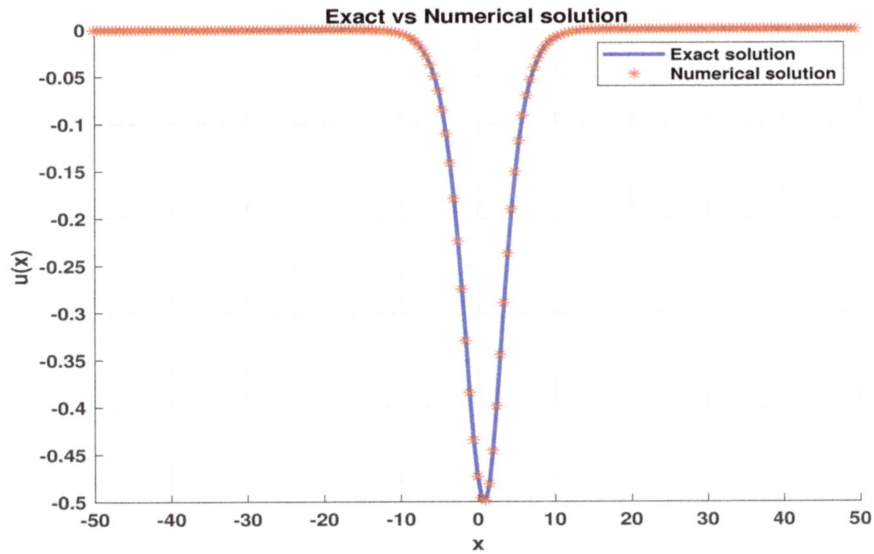

Figure 12. The case of $h = 0.5$, at time $T = 1$. The exact solution vs. the numerical solution of $CHOC - B$.

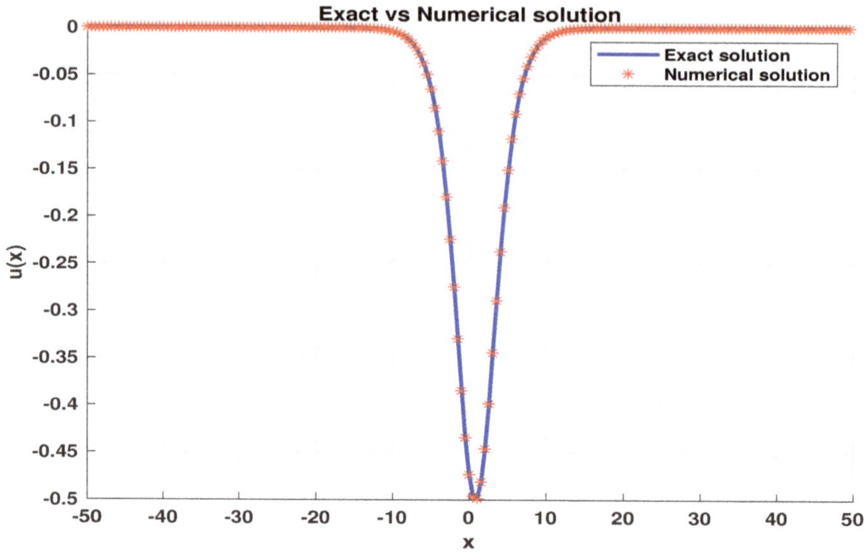

Figure 13. The case of $h = 0.5$, at time $T = 1$. The exact solution vs. the numerical solution of $CHOC - C$.

Author Contributions: Conceptualization, Z.L. and X.Y.; methodology, Z.L. and X.Y.; software, Z.L. and X.Y.; validation, Z.L., X.Y., Y.L., Z.C., and S.K.; formal analysis, Z.L. and X.Y.; investigation, Z.L., X.Y., Y.L., Z.C., and S.K.; resources, X.Y.; data curation, Z.L. and X.Y.; writing—original draft preparation, Z.L. and X.Y.; writing—review and editing, Z.L. and X.Y.; visualization, Z.L. and X.Y.; supervision, X.Y.; project administration, X.Y.; funding acquisition, X.Y. All authors have read and agreed to the published version of the manuscript.

Funding: This work is supported by the Natural Science Foundations of Shandong (No. ZR2023MA062, ZR202204010001), the Science and Technology Plan Project of Dezhou (No. 2021dzkj1638) and the Research Platform Project of Dezhou University (No. 2023XKZX024).

Institutional Review Board Statement: Not applicable.

Informed Consent Statement: Not applicable.

Data Availability Statement: The original contributions presented in the study are included in the article, further inquiries can be directed to the corresponding author. (Matlab 2022a codes can be provided if required).

Conflicts of Interest: The authors declare no conflicts of interest

References

1. Manotanjan, V.S.; Mitchell, A.R.; Morris, J.L. Numerical solutions of the good Boussinesq equation. *Siam. J. Sci. Stat. Comput.* **1984**, *5*, 946–957. [CrossRef]
2. Manotanjan, V.S.; Ortega, T.; Sanz-Serna, J.M. Soliton and antisoliton interactions in the "good" Boussinesq equation. *J. Math. Phys.* **1988**, *29*, 1964–1968. [CrossRef]
3. Ortega, T.; Sanz-Serna, J.M. Nonlinear stability and convergence of finite-difference methods for the "good" Boussinesq equation *Numer. Math.* **1990**, *58*, 215–229. [CrossRef]
4. Guo, Z.W.; Jiang, T.S.; Vasil'ev, V.I.; Wang, G. Complex structure-preserving method for Schrodinger equations in quaternionic quantum mechanics. *Numer. Algorithms* **2023**, *150*, 1–17. [CrossRef]
5. Iqbal, A.; Abd Hamid, N.N.; Ismail, A.I.M. Soliton Solution of Schrödinger Equation Using Cubic B-Spline Galerkin Method *Fluids* **2019**, *4*, 108. [CrossRef]
6. Iqbal, A.; Abd Hamid, N.N.; Ismail, A.I.M. Cubic B-spline Galerkin method for numerical solution of the coupled nonlinear Schrödinger equation. *Math. Comput. Sim.* **2020**, *174*, 32–44. [CrossRef]

7. Jiang, T.S.; Wang, G.; Guo, Z.W.; Zhang, D. Algebraic algorithms for a class of Schrodinger equations in split quaternionic mechanics. *Math. Math. Methods. Appl. Sci.* **2024**, *47*, 5349–5354. [CrossRef]
8. Hu, H.Z.; Chen, Y.P.; Zhou, J.W. Two-grid finite element method for time-fractional nonlinear schrodinger equation. *J. Comput. Math.* **2024**, *42*, 1124–1144. [CrossRef]
9. Jiang, T.S.; Guo, Z.W.; Zhang, D.; Vasil'ev, V.I. A fast algorithm for the Schrödinger equation in quaternionic quantum mechanics. *Appl. Math. Lett.* **2024**, *150*, 108975. [CrossRef]
10. Jiang, T.S.; Zhang, Z.Z.; Jiang, Z.W. Algebraic techniques for Schrodinger equations in split quaternionic mechanics. *Comput. Math. Appl.* **2018**, *75*, 2217–2222. [CrossRef]
11. Wang, L.; Kong, L.H.; Chen, M.; Zhu, P.; Guo, H. Structure-Preserving Combined High-Order Compact Schemes for Multiple Order Spatial Derivatives Differential Equations. *J. Sci. Comput.* **2023**, *96*, 8. [CrossRef]
12. Haq, F.; Islam, I.; Tirmizi, I.A. A numerical technique for solution of the MRLW equation using quartic B-splines. *Appl. Math. Model* **2010**, *34*, 4151–4160. [CrossRef]
13. Chu, P.C.; Fan, C. A three-point combined compact difference scheme. *J. Comput. Phys.* **1998**, *140*, 370–399. [CrossRef]
14. Kaur, Deepti.; R.K. Mohanty. Highly accurate compact difference scheme for fourth order parabolic equation with Dirichlet and Neumann boundary conditions. *Appl. Numer. Math.* **2020**, *378*, 125202.
15. Wang, R.F.; Wang, W.H.; Yang, J.H. Containing High Order Compact Scheme Source of Steady Convection-Diffusion Equation. *Sci. Discov.* **2016**, *4*, 156–160. [CrossRef]
16. Chen, B.; He, D.; Pan, K. A linearized high-order combined compact difference scheme for multidimensional coupled Burgers equations. *Numer. Math. Theor. Methods. Appl.* **2018**, *11*, 299–320. [CrossRef]
17. Yu, C.H.; Wang, D.; He, Z.; Pähtz, T. An optimized dispersion–relation-preserving combined compact difference scheme to solve advection equations. *J. Comput. Phys.* **2015**, *300*, 92–115. [CrossRef]
18. Zhang, C.; Wang, H.; Huang, J.F.; Wang, C.; Yue, X.Y. A second order operator splitting numerical scheme for the "good" Boussinesq equation. *Appl. Numer. Math.* **2017**, *119*, 179–193. [CrossRef]
19. Chen, M.; Kong, L.H.; Hong, Y. Efficient structure-preserving schemes for good Boussinesq equation. *Math. Meth. Appl. Sci.* **2018**, *41*, 1743–1752. [CrossRef]
20. Hu, W.P.; Deng, Z.C. Multi-symplectic method for generalized Boussinesq equation. *Appl. Math. Mech.* **2008**, *29*, 927–932. [CrossRef]
21. Cienfuegos, R.; Barthélemy, E.; Bonneton, P. A fourth-order compact finite volume scheme for fully nonlinear and weakly dispersive Boussinesq-type equations. Part II: Boundary conditions and validation. *Int. J. Numer. Methods Fluids.* **2007**, *53*, 1423–1455. [CrossRef]
22. Frutos, J.D.; Ortega, T.; Sanz-Serna, J.M. Pseudospectral method for the "good" Boussinesq equation. *Math. Comput.* **1991**, *57*, 109–122.
23. Oh, S.; Stefanov, A. Improved local well-posedness for the periodic "good" Boussinesq equation. *J. Differ. Equ.* **2013**, *254*, 4047–4065. [CrossRef]
24. Farah, L.; Scialom, M. On the periodic "good" Boussinesq equation. *Proc. Am. Math. Soc.* **2010**, *138*, 953–964. [CrossRef]
25. Zou, Z.L. Higher order Boussinesq equations. *Ocean Eng.* **1999**, *26*, 767–792. [CrossRef]
26. Ucar, Y.; Esen, A.; Karaagac, B. Numerical solutions of Boussinesq equation using Galerkin finite element method. *Wiley* **2020**, *37*, 1612–1630. [CrossRef]
27. Kong, L.H.; Chen, M.; Yin, X. A novel kind of efficient symplectic scheme for Klein-Gordon-Schrödinger equation. *Appl. Numer. Math.* **2019**, *135*, 481–496. [CrossRef]
28. Lele, S.K. Compact finite difference schemes with spectral-like solution. *J. Comput. Phys.* **1992**, *103*, 16–42. [CrossRef]
29. Bridges, T.J.; Reich, S. Multi-symplectic integrators: Numerical schemes for Hamiltonian PDEs that conserve symplecticity. *Phys. Lett. A* **2001**, *284*, 184–193. [CrossRef]
30. Shen, J.; Xu, J.; Yang, J. A new class of efficient and robust energy stable schemes for gradient flows. *SIAM Rev.* **2019**, *61*, 474–506. [CrossRef]
31. Jiménez, S.; Vázquez. L. *Some Remarks on Conservative and Symplectic Schemes*; World Scientific: Singapore, 1991; pp. 151–162.

axioms

MDPI

Article

The Robin Problems in the Coupled System of Wave Equations on a Half-Line

Po-Chun Huang [1] and Bo-Yu Pan [2,*]

[1] Department of Mathematics, National Tsing Hua University, Hsinchu 300044, Taiwan; d917205@oz.nthu.edu.tw
[2] Department of Applied Mathematics, National Chung Hsing University, Taichung 402, Taiwan
* Correspondence: pan740102@gmail.com or panboyu@dragon.nchu.edu.tw

Abstract: This article investigates the local well-posedness of a coupled system of wave equations on a half-line, with a particular emphasis on Robin boundary conditions within Sobolev spaces. We provide estimates for the solutions to linear initial-boundary-value problems related to the coupled system of wave equations, utilizing the Unified Transform Method in conjunction with the Hadamard norm while considering the influence of external forces. Furthermore, we demonstrate that replacing the external force with a nonlinear term alters the iteration map defined by the unified transform solutions, making it a contraction map in a suitable solution space. By employing the contraction mapping theorem, we establish the existence of a unique solution. Finally, we show that the data-to-solution map is locally Lipschitz continuous, thus confirming the local well-posedness of the coupled system of wave equations under consideration.

Keywords: coupled wave system; local well-posedness of the coupled system of wave equations; Robin boundary condition; unified transform method

MSC: 35-XX; 35A01; 35A02

1. Introduction and Main Results

1.1. Introduction

In this article, we consider the following system of coupled wave equations with Robin boundary conditions:

$$\begin{cases} u_{tt} = u_{xx} + u^2 v, & x \in (0,\infty),\ t \in (0,T), \\ v_{tt} = v_{xx} + uv^2, & x \in (0,\infty),\ t \in (0,T), \\ (u,v)(x,0) = (u_0,v_0)(x), & x \in [0,\infty), \\ (u_t,v_t)(x,0) = (u_*,v_*)(x), & x \in [0,\infty), \\ u_x(0,t) - \varpi_1 u(0,t) = \gamma_1(t), & t \in [0,T], \\ v_x(0,t) - \varpi_2 v(0,t) = \gamma_2(t), & t \in [0,T], \end{cases} \tag{1}$$

where $0 < T < 1$ and $\varpi_i \geq 1$ for $i = 1,2$; $u(x,t)$ and $v(x,t)$ are real-valued functions; $u_0(x)$, $v_0(x)$, $u_*(x)$, $v_*(x)$ are initial data in $H_x^s(0,\infty)$; and $\gamma_1(t), \gamma_2(t)$ are boundary data in $H_t^{s-1}(0,T)$. The Robin boundary conditions model the dynamic balance of partial energy reflection and absorption at a system's boundary. It is widely applied in simulating interactions in fields such as acoustics, electromagnetics, elastic waves, and heat conduction.

The primary objective of this article is to employ the Unified Transform Method (UTM) to derive UTM formulas for the linear initial-boundary-value problems (IBVPs) associated with the system (1). We then provide estimates for these UTM formulas and utilize them to construct an iteration map in a suitable function space, which allows us to prove the local well-posedness of (1). For readers interested in UTM and its application to proving the local well-posedness of various equations, please refer to the articles [1–6].

Typically, the solution of IBVPs for linear partial differential equations with constant coefficients involves methods such as the separation of variables and specific integral transforms. These classical methods apply only to problems with particular boundary conditions. Fokas' UTM not only handles the problems solvable by these classical methods but also extends to address issues that classical methods cannot resolve. Moreover, the UTM can clearly determine which boundary value problems are well-posed. Additionally, the paper [7] highlights several key benefits of the UTM compared to standard methods:

- Efficiency: The UTM offers a more efficient means of providing explicit solutions compared to standard methods, and it is capable of addressing problems involving higher-order derivatives that classical approaches may not handle effectively.
- Unified Approach: The UTM provides a consistent framework applicable to a wide range of problems, facilitating the determination of necessary boundary conditions for well-posedness, even in complex scenarios.
- Flexible Evaluation: Solutions obtained through the UTM can be efficiently evaluated using various techniques, including integration path parameterization, asymptotic methods, or the residue theorem.
- Minimal Knowledge Required: The UTM necessitates only a basic understanding of Fourier transforms, the residue theorem, and Jordan's lemma, making it accessible to those with fundamental knowledge in these areas.

Based on the advantages of the UTM outlined above, this article applies the UTM to derive the UTM formulas for the linear wave equations on the half-line. We then investigate whether these formulas remain valid for data in broader, appropriate Sobolev spaces and conduct a deeper analysis of the linear wave equations on the half-line. This approach ultimately helps us prove the local well-posedness of (1).

Next, we explain the motivation behind considering the system (1). From a mathematical perspective, we are curious whether the UTM can help us establish the local well-posedness of the following system:

$$\begin{cases} u_{tt} = u_{xx} + f(u,v), \\ v_{tt} = v_{xx} + g(u,v), \end{cases} \tag{2}$$

where f and g are polynomial functions of u and v. Furthermore, we can also consider f and g as continuous functions of u and v.

Given that many results already exist on the local well-posedness of the coupled Klein–Gordon equations, we chose to study the distinct system (1). Our subsequent research will investigate the system (2).

The coupled system of Klein–Gordon equations is

$$\begin{cases} u_{tt} = u_{xx} + h_u(u,v), \\ v_{tt} = d^2 v_{xx} + h_v(u,v), \end{cases}$$

where $h(u,v)$ is a nonlinear coupling potential function, and d is the ratio of the sound speeds in the u- and v-components. The system describes the long-wave dynamics of a pair of coupled one-dimensional periodic particle chains [8]. The elements of each chain are connected through linear coupling, while the chains interact via nonlinear coupling.

When $h(u,v) = \frac{a^2u^2}{2} + \frac{b^2v^2}{2} + \frac{c^2u^2v^2}{2}$, where u and v are scalar fields of masses a and b, respectively, and c is the interaction constant, the system models the motion of charged mesons in an electromagnetic field. For readers interested in the coupled system of Klein–Gordon equations, please refer to [9–14].

We now present recent studies that explore the existence, uniqueness, and well-posedness of solutions for coupled systems of wave equations. In [15], the authors establish the well-posedness and exponential stability of a strongly coupled Klein–Gordon system in a bounded domain with smooth boundaries, considering the effect of locally distributed viscoelastic damping. In their research, the authors employ microlocal analysis tools and a unique continuation principle to address the challenges posed by integral terms. They also formulate a perturbation problem to obtain the exponential decay rate. The conclusions show that under suitable initial conditions, the system achieves exponential energy decay, thereby proving the stability of the system.

In [16], the authors investigated the local well-posedness of the one-dimensional nonlinear wave equation on a half-line. They used the UTM to help analyze the problem's local well-posedness.

In [17], the authors study a coupled system of two biharmonic equations with damping and source terms of variable-exponent nonlinearities under mixed boundary value conditions. They investigate the existence and uniqueness of weak solutions. By applying Green's formula, the authors derive an integral equation for the weak solution and then prove the existence and uniqueness of the solution using the fixed-point theorem. Additionally, they establish a blow-up result for negative-initial energy solutions within a finite time.

In [18], the authors investigate the global existence, uniqueness, and uniform stability of the solution energy for the Klein–Gordon system. They employ the Faedo–Galerkin method with compactness arguments and the energy method to prove the existence and uniqueness of the global solution. Additionally, they demonstrate that under specific boundary conditions, the solutions of the system exhibit stable asymptotic behavior over time.

In [19], the authors study the global existence theory for a system of wave equations with variable-exponent nonlinearities. They use the Galerkin method and compactness properties to prove the existence of solutions and further demonstrate that these solutions stabilize towards a stationary state under sufficient regularity conditions.

In [20], the authors investigate the existence of periodic solutions for a Klein–Gordon system with linear coupling and prove that as the coupling constant approaches zero, these solutions converge to those of the uncoupled wave equation. The results highlight the high regularity and stability of the solutions.

In [21], the authors investigate a coupled system of wave equations with coupled Robin boundary conditions, employing group methods to study the issues of approximate boundary controllability and approximate boundary synchronization. The authors provide an algebraic lemma, which generalizes Kalman's criterion or the Hautus test. They also establish the well-posedness of the coupled system of wave equations with coupled Robin boundary conditions. Additionally, the authors demonstrate the equivalence between the approximate controllability of the system and the D-observability of its adjoint system under certain conditions.

In [22], the authors study a coupled system of two nonlinear hyperbolic equations, where the exponents in the damping and source terms are variables. They establish the existence and uniqueness of solutions by using the Faedo–Galerkin approximation and the Banach fixed-point theorem to prove the existence and uniqueness of weak solutions. Additionally, they apply the energy method to demonstrate that certain solutions with positive-initial energy blow-up in a finite time.

In [23], the authors analyze the solutions of the nonlinear Klein–Gordon equation, presenting necessary and sufficient conditions for finite-time blow-up based on new mass properties of ordinary differential equations. They refine Levine's concavity method and also prove the global existence of solutions and their asymptotic behavior under specific initial energy conditions.

After introducing the coupled systems of wave equations under consideration, the next subsection will present the main results of this article.

1.2. Main Results

Now, we briefly outline the process through which we establish the local well-posedness of the system (1). The proof is carried out in four steps. First, we replace the nonlinear terms u^2v and v^2u with external forces, allowing us to derive UTM formulas for the corresponding linear IBVPs. Second, using these UTM formulas, we derive linear estimates that account for the data and forcing terms in appropriate functional spaces. Third, we define an iterative mapping in the chosen solution space, substituting the nonlinear terms for the external forces. We then prove that this mapping is a contraction onto a closed ball $B(0,r)$, ensuring the existence of a unique solution by applying the contraction mapping theorem. Finally, we show that the data-to-solution map is locally Lipschitz continuous, thus confirming the local well-posedness of the IBVP (1).

Before introducing the main theorem of this article, we will briefly define some terms. For $s \in \mathbb{R}$, the Sobolev space $H^s(\mathbb{R})$ consists of all tempered distributions F that have a finite norm given by

$$\| F \|_{H^s(\mathbb{R})} \doteq \left(\int_{\xi \in \mathbb{R}} (1+\xi^2)^s |\widehat{F}(\xi)|^2 d\xi \right)^{\frac{1}{2}}, \tag{3}$$

where $\widehat{F}(\xi)$ denotes the Fourier transform of F, defined by

$$\widehat{F}(\xi) \doteq \int_{\mathbb{R}} e^{-ix\xi} F(x) dx.$$

Additionally, for any open interval (a,b) in $\mathbb{R}$, the Sobolev space $H^s(a,b)$ is defined as

$$H^s(a,b) = \left\{ \begin{array}{l} f : f = F|_{(a,b)}, \text{ where } F \in H^s(\mathbb{R}) \\ \text{and } \| f \|_{H^s(a,b)} \doteq \inf_{F \in H^s(\mathbb{R})} \| F \|_{H^s(\mathbb{R})} < \infty \end{array} \right\}.$$

When we apply the UTM to solve the forced linear Robin IBVP, it yields the following Fourier transform.

Definition 1 (Half-Line Fourier Transform). *Let $\Phi(x)$ be a test function defined on the interval $(0,\infty)$. The Fourier transform of $\Phi(x)$, restricted to the half-line, is expressed as*

$$\widehat{\Phi}(k) \doteq \int_0^\infty \Phi(x) e^{-ikx}\, dx, \tag{4}$$

where $k \in \mathbb{C}$ and $\Im(k) \leq 0$. Here, $\Re(k)$ and $\Im(k)$ denote the real and imaginary components of k, respectively.

Remark 1. *In the case of Equation (4), it is straightforward to observe that if Φ is integrable over the interval $(0,\infty)$, the Fourier transform $\widehat{\Phi}(k)$ is well-defined for values of k where $\Im(k) \leq 0$. Furthermore, the half-line Fourier transform extends naturally within the space $L^2(0,\infty)$. A function $\Phi \in L^2(0,\infty)$ can be extended to the entire real line by defining it as zero for all $x < 0$, thereby embedding Φ into $L^2(\mathbb{R})$. This allows the half-line Fourier transform to be written similarly to the standard Fourier transform for functions defined on $\mathbb{R}$. Consequently, the inverse transform can also be defined analogously to the inverse Fourier transform on the full real line.*

First, we will outline the first step in our strategy for tackling the Robin boundary problem associated with the forced linear wave equations. For the nonlinear IBVP (1), the corresponding linear problem is the forced linear IBVP:

$$\begin{cases} u_{tt} = u_{xx} + f(x,t), & x \in (0,\infty),\ t \in (0,T), \\ v_{tt} = v_{xx} + g(x,t), & x \in (0,\infty),\ t \in (0,T), \\ (u,v)(x,0) = (u_0,v_0)(x), & x \in [0,\infty), \\ (u_t,v_t)(x,0) = (u_*,v_*)(x), & x \in [0,\infty), \\ u_x(0,t) - \varpi_1 u(0,t) = \gamma_1(t), & t \in [0,T], \\ v_x(0,t) - \varpi_2 v(0,t) = \gamma_2(t), & t \in [0,T], \end{cases} \tag{5}$$

where $\varpi_i \geq 1$, for $i = 1,2$, and $0 < T < 1$.

The IBVP (5) can be separated into two parts, (6) and (7):

$$\begin{cases} u_t = u_1, \\ (u_1)_t = u_{xx} + f(x,t), \\ u(x,0) = u_0(x),\ u_1(x,0) = u_*(x), \\ u_x(0,t) - \varpi_1 u(0,t) = \gamma_1(t), \end{cases} \tag{6}$$

and

$$\begin{cases} v_t = v_1, \\ (v_1)_t = v_{xx} + g(x,t), \\ v(x,0) = v_0(x),\ v_1(x,0) = v_*(x), \\ v_x(0,t) - \varpi_2 v(0,t) = \gamma_2(t). \end{cases} \tag{7}$$

Next, we briefly explain how to use the UTM to derive the corresponding formulas for (6). A similar process can be applied to (7) to obtain its UTM formulas. For Equation (6), we can express it as

$$\partial_t Q + \Lambda(-i\partial_x)Q = F, \text{ where } Q = \begin{bmatrix} u \\ u_1 \end{bmatrix},\ \Lambda(k) = \begin{bmatrix} 0 & -1 \\ k^2 & 0 \end{bmatrix}, \text{ and } F = \begin{bmatrix} 0 \\ f(x,t) \end{bmatrix}.$$

The first step in applying UTM to (6) is to rewrite the above system of equations in a divergence form as

$$(e^{-ikxI+\Lambda(k)t}Q)_t - (e^{-ikxI+\Lambda(k)t}M(x,t,k)Q)_x = e^{-ikxI+\Lambda(k)t}F, \tag{8}$$

where I is a 2-dimensional identity matrix and the vector $M(x,t,k)$ is a differential matrix operator which is defined by

$$M(x,t,k) = i\left.\frac{\Lambda(k) - \Lambda(l)}{k-l}\right|_{l=-i\partial_x}.$$

We refer to this form (8) as the local relation.

In the next step, we integrate the local relation over an infinite strip in the (x,t)-plane. Applying Green's Theorem allows us to convert the area integrals into boundary integrals along the domain's boundary. Through this process, we obtain the following global relation:

$$\widehat{Q_0}(k) - e^{\Lambda(k)t}\hat{Q}(k,t) - G(k,t) = \int_0^t e^{\Lambda(k)t'}\hat{F}(k,t')dt',$$

where

$$Q_0 = \begin{bmatrix} u_0(x) \\ u_*(x) \end{bmatrix},\ \widehat{Q_0}(k) = \int_0^\infty e^{-ikx}Q_0(x)dx,\ \hat{Q}(k,t) = \int_0^\infty e^{-ikx}Q(x,t)dx,$$

$$G(k,t) = \int_0^t e^{\Lambda(k)x}M(0,x,k)Q_0(x)dx,\ \hat{F}(k,t) = \int_0^\infty e^{-ikx}F(x,t)dx.$$

Then, we apply the inverse Fourier transform to the global relation, and we have a solution formula with unknown boundary conditions. We can use the symmetry relation of $\Lambda(k)$ replacing k by $-k$ to solve the unknown boundary condition; then, we obtain the UTM formulas (9) and (10) for (6). A similar process can be applied to (7) to obtain its UTM formulas (11) and (12).

Due to the complexity and length of the detailed calculations in this section, interested readers are encouraged to refer to references [16,24] for further details.

The UTM formulas for (6) and (7):

$$
\begin{aligned}
u(x,t) &\doteq S_1[u_0,u_*,\gamma_1;f](x,t) \\
&= \frac{1}{2\pi}\int_{-\infty}^{\infty}\frac{ie^{ikx}}{2i\sqrt{k^2}}\left(\sqrt{k^2}e^{-i\sqrt{k^2}t}+\sqrt{k^2}e^{i\sqrt{k^2}t}\right)\left(\widehat{u_0}(k)+\left(\frac{\varpi_1+ik}{-\varpi_1+ik}\right)\widehat{u_0}(-k)\right)dk \\
&+\frac{1}{2\pi}\int_{-\infty}^{\infty}\frac{e^{ikx}}{2i\sqrt{k^2}}\left(e^{i\sqrt{k^2}t}-e^{-i\sqrt{k^2}t}\right)\left(\widehat{u_*}(k)+\left(\frac{\varpi_1+ik}{-\varpi_1+ik}\right)\widehat{u_*}(-k)\right)dk \\
&+\frac{1}{2\pi}\int_{-\infty}^{\infty}\frac{e^{ikx}}{\sqrt{k^2}}\left(\frac{k}{-\varpi_1+ik}\right)\left(e^{-i\sqrt{k^2}t}\widetilde{\gamma_{11}}(k,t)-e^{i\sqrt{k^2}t}\widetilde{\gamma_{12}}(k,t)\right)dk \\
&+\frac{1}{2\pi}\int_{-\infty}^{\infty}\frac{e^{ikx}}{2i\sqrt{k^2}}\left[e^{i\sqrt{k^2}t}\left(\widehat{f_2}^*(k,t)+\left(\frac{\varpi_1+ik}{-\varpi_1+ik}\right)\widehat{f_2}^*(-k,t)\right)\right. \\
&\left.-e^{-i\sqrt{k^2}t}\left(\widehat{f_1}^*(k,t)+\left(\frac{\varpi_1+ik}{-\varpi_1+ik}\right)\widehat{f_1}^*(-k,t)\right)\right]dk
\end{aligned} \tag{9}
$$

and

$$
\begin{aligned}
u_1(x,t) &\doteq S_2[u_0,u_*,\gamma_1;f](x,t) \\
&= \frac{1}{2\pi}\int_{-\infty}^{\infty}\frac{e^{ikx}}{2i\sqrt{k^2}}\left(k^2e^{-i\sqrt{k^2}t}-k^2e^{i\sqrt{k^2}t}\right)\left(\widehat{u_0}(k)+\left(\frac{\varpi_1+ik}{-\varpi_1+ik}\right)\widehat{u_0}(-k)\right)dk \\
&+\frac{1}{2\pi}\int_{-\infty}^{\infty}\frac{e^{ikx}}{2}\left(e^{-i\sqrt{k^2}t}+e^{i\sqrt{k^2}t}\right)\left(\widehat{u_*}(k)+\left(\frac{\varpi_1+ik}{-\varpi_1+ik}\right)\widehat{u_*}(-k)\right)dk \\
&+\frac{1}{2\pi}\int_{-\infty}^{\infty}-ie^{ikx}\left(\frac{k}{-\varpi_1+ik}\right)\left(e^{i\sqrt{k^2}t}\widetilde{\gamma_{12}}(k,t)+e^{-i\sqrt{k^2}t}\widetilde{\gamma_{11}}(k,t)\right)dk \\
&+\frac{1}{2\pi}\int_{-\infty}^{\infty}\frac{e^{ikx}}{2}\left[e^{-i\sqrt{k^2}t}\left(\widehat{f_1}^*(k,t)+\left(\frac{\varpi_1+ik}{-\varpi_1+ik}\right)\widehat{f_1}^*(-k,t)\right)\right. \\
&\left.+e^{i\sqrt{k^2}t}\left(\widehat{f_2}^*(k,t)+\left(\frac{\varpi_1+ik}{-\varpi_1+ik}\right)\widehat{f_2}^*(-k,t)\right)\right]dk,
\end{aligned} \tag{10}
$$

where

$$
\widehat{f_1}^*(k,t)=\int_0^t\int_0^{\infty}e^{-ikx+i\sqrt{k^2}s}f(x,s)dxds,\quad \widehat{f_2}^*(k,t)=\int_0^t\int_0^{\infty}e^{-ikx-i\sqrt{k^2}s}f(x,s)dxds,
$$

$$
\widetilde{\gamma_{11}}(k,t)=\int_0^t e^{i\sqrt{k^2}s}\gamma_1(s)ds,\quad \widetilde{\gamma_{12}}(k,t)=\int_0^t e^{-i\sqrt{k^2}s}\gamma_1(s)ds
$$

and

$$
\begin{aligned}
v(x,t) &\doteq S_1[v_0,v_*,\gamma_2;g](x,t) \\
&= \frac{1}{2\pi}\int_{-\infty}^{\infty}\frac{ie^{ikx}}{2i\sqrt{k^2}}\left(\sqrt{k^2}e^{-i\sqrt{k^2}t}+\sqrt{k^2}e^{i\sqrt{k^2}t}\right)\left(\widehat{v_0}(k)+\left(\frac{\varpi_2+ik}{-\varpi_2+ik}\right)\widehat{v_0}(-k)\right)dk \\
&+\frac{1}{2\pi}\int_{-\infty}^{\infty}\frac{e^{ikx}}{2i\sqrt{k^2}}\left(e^{i\sqrt{k^2}t}-e^{-i\sqrt{k^2}t}\right)\left(\widehat{v_*}(k)+\left(\frac{\varpi_2+ik}{-\varpi_2+ik}\right)\widehat{v_*}(-k)\right)dk \\
&+\frac{1}{2\pi}\int_{-\infty}^{\infty}\frac{e^{ikx}}{\sqrt{k^2}}\left(\frac{k}{-\varpi_2+ik}\right)\left(e^{-i\sqrt{k^2}t}\widetilde{\gamma_{21}}(k,t)-e^{i\sqrt{k^2}t}\widetilde{\gamma_{22}}(k,t)\right)dk \\
&+\frac{1}{2\pi}\int_{-\infty}^{\infty}\frac{e^{ikx}}{2i\sqrt{k^2}}\left[e^{i\sqrt{k^2}t}\left(\widehat{g_2}^*(k,t)+\left(\frac{\varpi_2+ik}{-\varpi_2+ik}\right)\widehat{g_2}^*(-k,t)\right)\right. \\
&\left.-e^{-i\sqrt{k^2}t}\left(\widehat{g_1}^*(k,t)+\left(\frac{\varpi_2+ik}{-\varpi_2+ik}\right)\widehat{g_1}^*(-k,t)\right)\right]dk
\end{aligned} \tag{11}
$$

and

$$\begin{aligned}
v_1(x,t) &\doteq S_2[v_0, v_*, \gamma_2; g](x,t) \\
&= \frac{1}{2\pi}\int_{-\infty}^{\infty} \frac{e^{ikx}}{2i\sqrt{k^2}}\left(k^2 e^{-i\sqrt{k^2}t} - k^2 e^{i\sqrt{k^2}t}\right)\left(\widehat{v_0}(k) + \left(\frac{\omega_2 + ik}{-\omega_2 + ik}\right)\widehat{v_0}(-k)\right)dk \\
&+ \frac{1}{2\pi}\int_{-\infty}^{\infty} \frac{e^{ikx}}{2}\left(e^{-i\sqrt{k^2}t} + e^{i\sqrt{k^2}t}\right)\left(\widehat{v_*}(k) + \left(\frac{\omega_2 + ik}{-\omega_2 + ik}\right)\widehat{v_*}(-k)\right)dk \\
&+ \frac{1}{2\pi}\int_{-\infty}^{\infty} \frac{e^{ikx}}{2i\sqrt{k^2}}\left(\frac{2k}{-\omega_2 + ik}\right)\left(\sqrt{k^2}e^{i\sqrt{k^2}t}\widetilde{\gamma_{22}}(k,t) + \sqrt{k^2}e^{-i\sqrt{k^2}t}\widetilde{\gamma_{21}}(k,t)\right)dk \\
&+ \frac{1}{2\pi}\int_{-\infty}^{\infty} \frac{e^{ikx}}{2}\left[e^{-i\sqrt{k^2}t}\left(\widehat{g_1}^*(k,t) + \left(\frac{\omega_2 + ik}{-\omega_2 + ik}\right)\widehat{g_1}^*(-k,t)\right)\right. \\
&\left. + e^{i\sqrt{k^2}t}\left(\widehat{g_2}^*(k,t) + \left(\frac{\omega_2 + ik}{-\omega_2 + ik}\right)\widehat{g_2}^*(-k,t)\right)\right]dk
\end{aligned} \tag{12}$$

where

$$\widehat{g_1}^*(k,t) = \int_0^t \int_0^\infty e^{-ikx + i\sqrt{k^2}s} g(x,s)dxds, \quad \widehat{g_2}^*(k,t) = \int_0^t \int_0^\infty e^{-ikx - i\sqrt{k^2}s} g(x,s)dxds,$$

$$\widetilde{\gamma_{21}}(k,t) = \int_0^t e^{i\sqrt{k^2}s}\gamma_2(s)ds, \quad \widetilde{\gamma_{22}}(k,t) = \int_0^t e^{-i\sqrt{k^2}s}\gamma_2(s)ds.$$

Next, we present the second step, which involves estimating the Hadamard norm of the UTM Formulas (9)–(12) in connection with the Sobolev norms of the data as well as a suitable norm for the forcing terms. Specifically, we derive the following linear estimates.

Theorem 1 (Linear estimates for the wave equations with Robin boundary condition). *Consider the wave Equations (6) and (7). Suppose* $\frac{1}{2} < s < 1$, $0 < T < 1$, $u_0 \in H_x^s(0,\infty)$, $u_* \in H_x^s(0,\infty)$, $v_0 \in H_x^s(0,\infty)$, $v_* \in H_x^s(0,\infty)$, $\gamma_1 \in H_t^{s-1}(0,T)$, *and* $\gamma_2 \in H_t^{s-1}(0,T)$. *Then, the UTM Formulas (9)–(12) define the solutions* (u, u_1) *and* (v, v_1) *to the forced-linear wave-Equation IBVPs (6) and (7), and they satisfy the following estimates:*

$$\begin{aligned}
&\sup_{t\in[0,T]} \| u(t) \|_{H_x^s(0,\infty)} + \sup_{x\in[0,\infty)} \| u(x) \|_{H_t^s(0,T)} \\
&\le C_s\left(\| u_0 \|_{H_x^s(0,\infty)} + \| u_* \|_{H_x^s(0,\infty)} + \| \gamma_1 \|_{H_t^{s-1}(0,T)} + \sqrt{T}\sup_{t\in[0,T]} \| f(t) \|_{H_x^s(0,\infty)}\right),
\end{aligned} \tag{13}$$

and

$$\begin{aligned}
&\sup_{t\in[0,T]} \| v(t) \|_{H_x^s(0,\infty)} + \sup_{x\in[0,\infty)} \| v(x) \|_{H_t^s(0,T)} \\
&\le d_s\left(\| v_0 \|_{H_x^s(0,\infty)} + \| v_* \|_{H_x^s(0,\infty)} + \| \gamma_2 \|_{H_t^{s-1}(0,T)} + \sqrt{T}\sup_{t\in[0,T]} \| g(t) \|_{H_x^s(0,\infty)}\right),
\end{aligned} \tag{14}$$

where $C_s > 0$ *and* $d_s > 0$ *are constants depending on s.*

In the subsequent third and fourth steps, our objective is to prove the uniqueness of the solution for (1) and to establish the local Lipschitz continuity of the data-to-solution mapping. To facilitate this, we define two Banach spaces, referred to as X and D, under the conditions $s > 1/2$ and $0 < T^* \le T < 1$, as detailed below:

$$X = (C([0,T^*]; H_x^s(0,\infty)) \cap C([0,\infty); H_t^s(0,T^*)))^2$$

with the following norm:

$$\| (u,v) \|_X = \sup_{t\in[0,T^*]} \| u(t) \|_{H_x^s(0,\infty)} + \sup_{x\in[0,\infty)} \| u(x) \|_{H_t^s(0,T^*)} + \sup_{t\in[0,T^*]} \| v(t) \|_{H_x^s(0,\infty)} + \sup_{x\in[0,\infty)} \| v(x) \|_{H_t^s(0,T^*)} .$$

The data space

$$D = H_x^s(0,\infty) \times H_x^s(0,\infty) \times H_x^s(0,\infty) \times H_x^s(0,\infty) \times H_t^{s-1}(0,T) \times H_t^{s-1}(0,T)$$

with the data norm

$$\| (u_0,u_*,v_0,v_*,\gamma_1,\gamma_2) \|_D = \| u_0 \|_{H_x^s(0,\infty)} + \| u_* \|_{H_x^s(0,\infty)} + \| v_0 \|_{H_x^s(0,\infty)} + \| v_* \|_{H_x^s(0,\infty)} + \| \gamma_1 \|_{H_t^{s-1}(0,T)} + \| \gamma_2 \|_{H_t^{s-1}(0,T)} .$$

Having established the above definitions, we now present the main result of this study.

Theorem 2 (Local well-posedness of the coupled wave system on the half-line). *Consider the coupled wave system (1). Suppose* $1/2 < s < 1$, $u_0 \in H_x^s(0,\infty)$, $v_0 \in H_x^s(0,\infty)$, $u_* \in H_x^s(0,\infty)$, $v_* \in H_x^s(0,\infty)$, $\gamma_1(t) \in H_t^{s-1}(0,T)$, *and* $\gamma_2(t) \in H_t^{s-1}(0,T)$. *Then, there exists* T^*, $0 < T^* \le T < 1$, *with*

$$T^* = min\left\{ T, \frac{1}{2304(C_s^*)^{10} \| (u_0,u_*,v_0,v_*,\gamma_1,\gamma_2) \|_D^{\frac{4}{5}}} \right\},$$

such that the coupled wave system (1) has a unique solution $(u,v) \in X$ *which satisfies the size estimate*

$$\| (u,v) \|_X \le 2C_s^* \| (u_0,u_*,v_0,v_*,\gamma_1,\gamma_2) \|_D,$$

where $C_s^* > 0$ *is a constant depending on* s.

Furthermore, the data-to-solution map $\{u_0,u_*,v_0,v_*,\gamma_1,\gamma_2\} \longmapsto (u,v)$ *is locally Lipschitz continuous.*

Based on the aforementioned theorem, we have demonstrated the local well-posedness of the coupled wave system (1).

In this article, we conclude that the UTM can be employed to derive UTM formulas for the linear IBVPs associated with system (1). We then provide estimates for these UTM formulas and use them to construct an iteration map in a suitable function space, ultimately proving Theorem 2 to establish the local well-posedness of the system (1).

This article is organized as follows: In Section 2, we introduce a variety of tools that will be used in the subsequent sections. Section 3 focuses on transforming the IBVP (6) into one with zero initial data and simplified boundary conditions, which facilitates estimating the corresponding solution for the linear wave equation IBVP. These estimates are essential for the proof provided in Section 4, where we conclude the proof of Theorem 1. In Section 5, we define the iteration map and demonstrate that it functions as a contraction mapping onto a closed ball, employing the contraction mapping theorem to establish the uniqueness of the solution. Furthermore, in Lemma 7, we show that the data-to-solution map is locally Lipschitz continuous. Finally, we conclude with the proof of Theorem 2.

2. Preliminary Results

In this section, we present several tools that will be utilized in the following sections.

Remark 2. *The norm of Sobolev–Slodobeckii spaces on time is*

$$\| u(x) \|^2_{H^s_t(0,T)} = \begin{cases} \sum_{j=0}^{\lfloor s \rfloor} \| \partial_t^j u(x) \|^2_{L^2_t(0,T)} + \| \partial_t^{\lfloor s \rfloor} u(x) \|^2_\beta, & \text{for } s \in \mathbb{R}^+ \backslash \mathbb{Z}^+, \\ \sum_{j=0}^{\lfloor s \rfloor} \| \partial_t^j u(x) \|^2_{L^2_t(0,T)}, & \text{for } s \in \mathbb{Z}^+, \end{cases}$$

where $0 < \beta < 1$ *and* $\lfloor s \rfloor = s - \beta \in \mathbb{Z}^+ \cup \{0\}$. *The fractional norm* $\| \cdot \|_\beta$ *is defined by*

$$\| u(x) \|^2_\beta \doteq \int_0^T \int_0^{T-t} \frac{|u(x,t+\zeta) - u(x,t)|^2}{\zeta^{1+2\beta}} d\zeta dt, \ \forall \beta \in (0,1).$$

Lemma 1 ([25] Ch.3). *For* $m_1 < m < m_2$, *we have*

$$\| f \|_{H^m} \leq (\| f \|_{H^{m_1}})^{\frac{m_2-m}{m_2-m_1}} (\| f \|_{H^{m_2}})^{\frac{m-m_1}{m_2-m_1}}.$$

Lemma 2 ([25] Ch.3). *If* $s > \frac{n}{2}$, *then* $H^s(\mathbb{R}^n)$ *is an algebra with respect to the product of functions. That is, if* f *and* $g \in H^s(\mathbb{R}^n)$, *then* $fg \in H^s(\mathbb{R}^n)$ *with*

$$\| fg \|_{H^s(\mathbb{R}^n)} \leq C_s \| f \|_{H^s(\mathbb{R}^n)} \| g \|_{H^s(\mathbb{R}^n)},$$

for some constant $C_s > 0$, *which is a constant depending on* s.

Lemma 3 ([26] CH.8). *Suppose that* (X, μ_1) *and* (Y, μ_2) *are two* σ*—finite measure spaces and* $F : X \times Y \to \mathbb{R}$ *is measurable. Then, Minkowski's integral inequality is*

$$\left(\int_Y \left| \int_X F(x,y) d\mu_1(x) \right|^p d\mu_2(y) \right)^{\frac{1}{p}} \leq \int_X \left(\int_Y |F(x,y)|^p d\mu_2(y) \right)^{\frac{1}{p}} d\mu_1(x),$$

for $1 \leq p < \infty$.

Theorem 3 ([26] CH.13). *If* $f \in L^1(\mathbb{R}^n)$, *then at every point* x *of the Lebesque set of* f,

$$f(x) = \lim_{t \to 0} \frac{1}{(2\pi)^n} \int_{\mathbb{R}^n} \widehat{f}(y) e^{ix \cdot y} e^{-t|y|^2} dy. \tag{15}$$

In addition, if $\widehat{f} \in L^1(\mathbb{R}^n)$, *then at every Lebesque point* x *of* f,

$$f(x) = \frac{1}{(2\pi)^n} \int_{\mathbb{R}^n} \widehat{f}(y) e^{ix \cdot y} dy. \tag{16}$$

In particular, (15) and (16) hold a.e. in $\mathbb{R}^n$ *and at every point of continuity of* f.

Theorem 4 ([27]). *For each* $f \in L^2$, *a function* $\hat{f} \in L^2$, *so that the following properties hold:*

(*i*) *If* $f \in L^1 \cap L^2$;
(*ii*) *For every* $f \in L^2$, $\| \hat{f} \|_2 = \| f \|_2$;
(*iii*) *The mapping* $f \longmapsto \hat{f}$ *is a Hilbert space isomorphism of* L^2 *onto* L^2;
(*iv*) *The following symmetric relation exists between* f *and* $\hat{f}$: *If*

$$\phi_A(t) = \int_{-A}^{A} f(x) e^{-ixt} dm(t) \text{ and } \psi_A(x) = \int_{-A}^{A} \hat{f}(t) e^{ixt} dm(t),$$

then

$$\parallel \phi_A - \hat{f} \parallel_2 \rightarrow 0 \text{ and } \parallel \psi_A - f \parallel_2 \rightarrow 0 \text{ as } A \rightarrow 0. \tag{17}$$

Theorem 5 ([28]). *If Ω satisfies a uniform interior cone condition (that is, there exists a fixed cone k_Ω such that each $x \in \Omega$ is the vertex of a cone $k_\Omega(x) \subset \bar{\Omega}$ and congruent to k_Ω), then there is an embedding*

$$W^{k,p}(\Omega) \begin{array}{l} \nearrow L^{\frac{np}{(n-kp)}}, \text{ for } kp < n, \\ \searrow C_B^m(\Omega), \text{ for } 0 \leq m < k - \frac{n}{p}, \end{array}$$

where

$$C_B^m(\Omega) = \{u \in C^m(\Omega) | D^\alpha u \in L^\infty(\Omega) \text{ for } |\alpha| \leq m\}.$$

To facilitate our calculations and enhance the clarity of our presentation, we introduce the following notations.

Remark 3. *Given two quantities $\mathbb{A}$ and $\mathbb{B}$ that may depend on one or more variables, we denote $\mathbb{A} \lesssim \mathbb{B}$ when there exists a positive constant c such that $\mathbb{A} \leq c\mathbb{B}$. If both inequalities $\mathbb{A} \lesssim \mathbb{B}$ and $\mathbb{B} \lesssim \mathbb{A}$ hold, we express this relationship as $\mathbb{A} \simeq \mathbb{B}$.*

3. The Reduced Pure Linear Robin Problem and Sobolev Space Estimates

In this section, we will demonstrate Theorem 6, which provides estimates of the solution to the linear wave equation IBVP, and will help us to prove Theorem 1 in Section 4.

We begin our analysis with the fundamental IBVP for the linear wave equation defined on the half-line. This involves considering the homogeneous IBVP with zero initial data and non-zero boundary conditions.

Moreover, we assume that the boundary data γ_ℓ is a test function of time, where $\gamma_\ell \in H_t^{s-1}(\mathbb{R})$ is an extension of $\gamma_1 \in H_t^{s-1}(0,T)$ such that

$$\parallel \gamma_\ell \parallel_{H_t^{s-1}(\mathbb{R})} \leq 2 \parallel \gamma_1 \parallel_{H_t^{s-1}(0,T)}, \text{ for } \frac{1}{2} < s < 1, \tag{18}$$

and γ_ℓ is compactly supported within the interval $[0, 2]$.

This particular problem, referred to as the reduced pure IBVP, can be expressed as follows:

$$\begin{cases} w_t = w_1, & x \in (0,\infty),\ t \geq 0, \\ (w_1)_t = w_{xx}, & x \in (0,\infty),\ t \geq 0, \\ w(x,0) = 0,\ w_t(x,0) = 0, & x \in [0,\infty), \\ w_x(0,t) - \varpi_1 w(0,t) = \gamma_\ell(t), & t \geq 0. \end{cases} \tag{19}$$

By employing the UTM Formulas (9) and (10), we can derive the corresponding UTM formulas for the reduced pure initial-boundary-value problem (IBVP) (19):

$$\begin{aligned} w(x,t) &= S_1[0,0,\gamma_\ell;0](x,t) \\ &= \frac{1}{2\pi}\int_{-\infty}^{\infty} e^{ikx}\Big(\frac{k}{|k|(-\varpi_1 + ik)}\Big)\big(e^{-i|k|t}\widetilde{\gamma_{\ell_1}}(k,t) - e^{i|k|t}\widetilde{\gamma_{\ell_2}}(k,t)\big)dk, \end{aligned} \tag{20}$$

and

$$\begin{aligned} w_1(x,t) &= S_2[0,0,\gamma_\ell;0](x,t) \\ &= -\frac{1}{2\pi}\int_{-\infty}^{\infty} e^{ikx}\Big(\frac{ik}{-\varpi_1 + ik}\Big)\big(e^{-i|k|t}\widetilde{\gamma_{\ell_2}}(k,t) + e^{i|k|t}\widetilde{\gamma_{\ell_1}}(k,t)\big)dk, \end{aligned} \tag{21}$$

where

$$\widetilde{\gamma_{\ell_1}}(k,t) = \int_0^t e^{i\sqrt{k^2}s}\gamma_\ell(s)ds, \quad \widetilde{\gamma_{\ell_2}}(k,t) = \int_0^t e^{-i\sqrt{k^2}s}\gamma_\ell(s)ds.$$

In the subsequent result, we evaluate the solutions (20) and (21) within the Hadamard space.

Theorem 6. *(Estimates for the Pure IBVP on the Half-Line) Let $1/2 < s < 3/2$ and consider the boundary data test function $\gamma_\ell \in H_t^{s-1}(\mathbb{R})$, which is compactly supported within the interval $[0,2]$. The solution to the reduced pure initial-boundary-value problem (IBVP) (19) satisfies the following Hadamard space estimates:*

$$\sup_{t\in[0,2]} \| S_1[0,0,\gamma_\ell;0](t) \|_{H_x^s(0,\infty)} \leq (C_1)_s \| \gamma_\ell \|_{H_t^{s-1}(\mathbb{R})}, \tag{22}$$

$$\sup_{t\in[0,2]} \| S_2[0,0,\gamma_\ell;0](t) \|_{H_x^{s-1}(0,\infty)} \leq (C_1)_s \| \gamma_\ell \|_{H_t^{s-1}(\mathbb{R})}, \tag{23}$$

and time estimates:

$$\sup_{x\in[0,\infty)} \| S_1[0,0,\gamma_\ell;0](x) \|_{H_t^s(0,2)} \leq (C_1)_s \| \gamma_\ell \|_{H_t^{s-1}(\mathbb{R})}, \tag{24}$$

$$\sup_{x\in[0,\infty)} \| S_2[0,0,\gamma_\ell;0](x) \|_{H_t^{s-1}(0,2)} \leq (C_1)_s \| \gamma_\ell \|_{H_t^{s-1}(\mathbb{R})}, \tag{25}$$

where $s \in \mathbb{R}$ and $(C_1)_s > 0$ is a constant that depends on s.

Proof. We will first present the proof for the space estimate given in (22). To perform this, we will analyze Equation (20):

$$\begin{aligned} w(x,t) &= S_1[0,0,\gamma_\ell;0](x,t) \\ &= \frac{1}{2\pi}\int_{-\infty}^{\infty} e^{ikx}\Big(\frac{k}{|k|(-\omega_1+ik)}\Big)\Big(e^{-i|k|t}\widetilde{\gamma_{\ell_1}}(k,t) - e^{i|k|t}\widetilde{\gamma_{\ell_2}}(k,t)\Big)dk \\ &= \underbrace{\frac{1}{2\pi}\int_{-\infty}^{0} e^{ikx}\Big(\frac{-1}{-\omega_1+ik}\Big)\Big(e^{ikt}\widetilde{\gamma_{\ell_1}}(k,t) - e^{-ikt}\widetilde{\gamma_{\ell_2}}(k,t)\Big)dk}_{(A)} \\ &\quad \underbrace{+\frac{1}{2\pi}\int_{0}^{\infty} e^{ikx}\Big(\frac{1}{-\omega_1+ik}\Big)\Big(e^{-ikt}\widetilde{\gamma_{\ell_1}}(k,t) - e^{ikt}\widetilde{\gamma_{\ell_2}}(k,t)\Big)dk}_{(B)}. \end{aligned}$$

Regarding equations (A) and (B), we deduce that the space Fourier transform of W is given by

$$\widehat{w}^x(k,t) = \begin{cases} \frac{(-1)(e^{ikt}\widetilde{\gamma_{\ell_1}}(k,t) - e^{-ikt}\widetilde{\gamma_{\ell_2}}(k,t))}{-\omega_1+ik}, & k\in(-\infty,0], \\ \frac{(e^{-ikt}\widetilde{\gamma_{\ell_1}}(k,t) - e^{ikt}\widetilde{\gamma_{\ell_2}}(k,t))}{-\omega_1+ik}, & k\in[0,\infty). \end{cases}$$

Applying (3), we derive the following inequality:

$$
\begin{aligned}
&\| S_1[0,0,\gamma_\ell;0](x,t) \|^2_{H^s_x(0,\infty)} = \int_{\mathbb{R}} (1+k^2)^s |\widehat{w}^x(k,t)|^2 dk \\
&= \int_{-\infty}^{0} (1+k^2)^s |\widehat{w}^x(k,t)|^2 dk + \int_{0}^{\infty} (1+k^2)^s |\widehat{w}^x(k,t)|^2 dk \\
&\lesssim \int_{-\infty}^{0} (1+k^2)^{s-1} \Big(\Big|\widetilde{\gamma_{\ell_1}}(k,t)|^2 + |\widetilde{\gamma_{\ell_2}}(k,t)\Big|^2 \Big) dk \quad + \int_{0}^{\infty} (1+k^2)^{s-1} \Big(\Big|\widetilde{\gamma_{\ell_1}}(k,t)|^2 + |\widetilde{\gamma_{\ell_2}}(k,t)\Big|^2 \Big) dk \\
&= \int_{-\infty}^{0} (1+k^2)^{s-1} \Big(\Big| \int_0^t e^{-iks}\gamma_\ell(s)ds \Big|^2 + \Big| \int_0^t e^{iks}\gamma_\ell(s)ds \Big|^2 \Big) dk \\
&\quad + \int_{0}^{\infty} (1+k^2)^{s-1} \Big(\Big| \int_0^t e^{iks}\gamma_\ell(s)ds| \Big|^2 + \Big| \int_0^t e^{-iks}\gamma_\ell(s)ds \Big|^2 \Big) dk \\
&= \int_{-\infty}^{0} (1+k^2)^{s-1} \Big(\Big| \int_{\mathbb{R}} e^{-iks}\chi_{[0,t]}(s)\gamma_\ell(s)ds \Big|^2 + \Big| \int_{\mathbb{R}} e^{iks}\chi_{[0,t]}(s)\gamma_\ell(s)ds \Big|^2 \Big) dk \\
&\quad + \int_{0}^{\infty} (1+k^2)^{s-1} \Big(\Big| \int_{\mathbb{R}} e^{iks}\chi_{[0,t]}(s)\gamma_\ell(s)ds \Big|^2 + \Big| \int_{\mathbb{R}} e^{-iks}\chi_{[0,t]}(s)\gamma_\ell(s)ds \Big|^2 \Big) dk \\
&= \int_{-\infty}^{0} (1+k^2)^{s-1} \Big(\Big| \widehat{\chi_{[0,t]}\gamma_\ell}(k) \Big|^2 + \Big| \widehat{\chi_{[0,t]}\gamma_\ell}(-k) \Big|^2 \Big) dk \\
&\quad + \int_{0}^{\infty} (1+k^2)^{s-1} \Big(\Big| \widehat{\chi_{[0,t]}\gamma_\ell}(-k)|^2 + |\widehat{\chi_{[0,t]}\gamma_\ell}(k) \Big|^2 \Big) dk \\
&= \int_{\mathbb{R}} (1+k^2)^{s-1} |\widehat{\chi_{[0,t]}\gamma_\ell}(k)|^2 dk + \int_{\mathbb{R}} (1+k^2)^{s-1} |\widehat{\chi_{[0,t]}\gamma_\ell}(-k)|^2 dk \\
&= \| \chi_{[0,t]}\gamma_\ell \|^2_{H_t^{s-1}(\mathbb{R})} + \| \chi_{[0,t]}\gamma_\ell \|^2_{H_t^{s-1}(\mathbb{R})} \lesssim \| \gamma_\ell \|^2_{H_t^{s-1}(\mathbb{R})} .
\end{aligned}
$$

Hence, we have Equation (22):

$$
\sup_{t\in[0,2]} \| S_1[0,0,\gamma_\ell;0](t) \|_{H^s_x(0,\infty)} \leq (C_1)_s \| \gamma_\ell \|_{H_t^{s-1}(\mathbb{R})} .
$$

Next, we begin proving the space estimate (23). We examine Equation (21):

$$
\begin{aligned}
w_1(x,t) &= S_2[0,0,\gamma_\ell;0](x,t) \\
&= -\frac{1}{2\pi} \int_{-\infty}^{\infty} e^{ikx} \Big(\frac{ik}{-\varpi_1 + ik} \Big) \big(e^{-i|k|t}\widetilde{\gamma_{\ell_2}}(k,t) + e^{i|k|t}\widetilde{\gamma_{\ell_1}}(k,t) \big) dk \\
&= \underbrace{-\frac{1}{2\pi} \int_{-\infty}^{0} e^{ikx} \Big(\frac{ik}{-\varpi_1 + ik} \Big) \big(e^{ikt}\widetilde{\gamma_{\ell_2}}(k,t) + e^{-ikt}\widetilde{\gamma_{\ell_1}}(k,t) \big) dk}_{(C)} \\
&\quad \underbrace{-\frac{1}{2\pi} \int_{0}^{\infty} e^{ikx} \Big(\frac{ik}{-\varpi_1 + ik} \Big) \big(e^{-ikt}\widetilde{\gamma_{\ell_2}}(k,t) + e^{ikt}\widetilde{\gamma_{\ell_1}}(k,t) \big)}_{(D)} .
\end{aligned}
$$

Regarding Equations (C) and (D), we deduce that the space Fourier transform of W_1 is given by

$$
\widehat{w_1}^x(k,t) = \begin{cases} \frac{-ik}{-\varpi_1+ik} \big(e^{ikt}\widetilde{\gamma_{\ell_2}}(k,t) + e^{-ikt}\widetilde{\gamma_{\ell_1}}(k,t) \big), \ k \in (-\infty,0], \\ \frac{-ik}{-\varpi_1+ik} \big(e^{-ikt}\widetilde{\gamma_{\ell_2}}(k,t) + e^{ikt}\widetilde{\gamma_{\ell_1}}(k,t) \big), \ k \in (0,\infty). \end{cases}
$$

Applying (3), we derive the following inequality:

$$
\begin{aligned}
&\| S_2[0,0,\gamma_\ell;0](x,t) \|^2_{H_x^{s-1}(0,\infty)} = \int_{\mathbb{R}} (1+k^2)^{s-1} |\widehat{w_1}^x(k,t)|^2 dk \\
&= \int_{-\infty}^0 (1+k^2)^{s-1} |\widehat{w_1}^x(k,t)|^2 dk + \int_0^\infty (1+k^2)^{s-1} |\widehat{w_1}^x(k,t)|^2 dk \\
&= \int_{-\infty}^0 (1+k^2)^{s-1} \Big| \frac{-ik}{-\varpi_1 + ik} (e^{ikt}\widetilde{\gamma_{\ell_2}}(k,t) + e^{-ikt}\widetilde{\gamma_{\ell_1}}(k,t)) \Big|^2 dk \\
&\quad + \int_0^\infty (1+k^2)^{s-1} \Big| \frac{-ik}{-\varpi_1 + ik} (e^{-ikt}\widetilde{\gamma_{\ell_2}}(k,t) + e^{ikt}\widetilde{\gamma_{\ell_1}}(k,t)) \Big|^2 dk \\
&\lesssim \int_{-\infty}^0 (1+k^2)^{s-1} \Big(\Big| \widetilde{\gamma_{\ell_2}}(k,t) \Big|^2 + |\widetilde{\gamma_{\ell_1}}(k,t)\Big)^2 \Big) dk + \int_0^\infty (1+k^2)^{s-1} \Big(\Big| \widetilde{\gamma_{\ell_2}}(k,t)\Big|^2 + |\widetilde{\gamma_{\ell_1}}(k,t) \Big)^2 \Big) dk \\
&= \int_{-\infty}^0 (1+k^2)^{s-1} \Big(\Big| \int_0^t e^{-i\sqrt{k^2}s} \gamma_\ell(s) ds \Big|^2 + \Big| \int_0^t e^{i\sqrt{k^2}s} \gamma_\ell(s) ds \Big|^2 \Big) dk \\
&\quad + \int_0^\infty (1+k^2)^{s-1} \Big(\Big| \int_0^t e^{-i\sqrt{k^2}s} \gamma_\ell(s) ds \Big|^2 + \Big| \int_0^t e^{i\sqrt{k^2}s} \gamma_\ell(s) ds \Big|^2 \Big) dk \\
&= \int_{-\infty}^0 (1+k^2)^{s-1} \Big(\Big| \int_{\mathbb{R}} e^{iks} \chi_{[0,t]}(s) \gamma_\ell(s) ds \Big|^2 + \Big| \int_{\mathbb{R}} e^{-iks} \chi_{[0,t]}(s) \gamma_\ell(s) ds \Big|^2 \Big) dk \\
&\quad + \int_0^\infty (1+k^2)^{s-1} \Big(\Big| \int_{\mathbb{R}} e^{-iks} \chi_{[0,t]}(s) \gamma_\ell(s) ds \Big|^2 + \Big| \int_{\mathbb{R}} e^{iks} \chi_{[0,t]}(s) \gamma_\ell(s) ds \Big|^2 \Big) dk \\
&= \int_{-\infty}^\infty (1+k^2)^{s-1} |\widehat{\chi_{[0,t]}\gamma_\ell}(k)|^2 dk + \int_{-\infty}^\infty (1+k^2)^{s-1} |\widehat{\chi_{[0,t]}\gamma_\ell}(-k)|^2 dk \\
&= \| \chi_{[0,t]}\gamma_\ell \|^2_{H_t^{s-1}(\mathbb{R})} + \| \chi_{[0,t]}\gamma_\ell \|^2_{H_t^{s-1}(\mathbb{R})} \lesssim \| \gamma_\ell \|^2_{H_t^{s-1}(\mathbb{R})} .
\end{aligned}
$$

Hence, we have Equation (23):

$$
\sup_{[0,2]} \| S_2[0,0,\gamma_\ell;0](x,t) \|_{H_x^{s-1}(0,\infty)} \leq (C_1)_s \| \gamma_\ell \|_{H_t^{s-1}(\mathbb{R})} .
$$

Next, we proceed to prove the time estimates (24) and (25). First, we consider the estimate of $\| S_1[0,0,\gamma_\ell;0](x,t) \|_{H_t^s(0,2)}$ as follows:

$$
\begin{aligned}
&\| S_1[0,0,\gamma_\ell;0](x,t) \|_{H_t^s(0,2)} \\
&= \Big\| \frac{1}{2\pi} \int_{-\infty}^0 e^{ikx} \Big(\frac{-1}{-\varpi_1 + ik} \Big) (e^{ikt}\widetilde{\gamma_{\ell_1}}(k,t) - e^{-ikt}\widetilde{\gamma_{\ell_2}}(k,t)) dk \\
&\quad + \frac{1}{2\pi} \int_0^\infty e^{ikx} \Big(\frac{1}{-\varpi_1 + ik} \Big) (e^{-ikt}\widetilde{\gamma_{\ell_1}}(k,t) - e^{ikt}\widetilde{\gamma_{\ell_2}}(k,t)) dk \Big\|_{H_t^s(0,2)}, \\
&\leq \underbrace{\Big\| \frac{1}{2\pi} \int_{-\infty}^0 e^{ikt} e^{ikx} \Big(\frac{-1}{-\varpi_1 + ik} \Big) \widetilde{\gamma_{\ell_1}}(k,t) dk \Big\|_{H_t^s(0,2)}}_{(E)} + \underbrace{\Big\| \frac{1}{2\pi} \int_{-\infty}^0 e^{-ikt} e^{ikx} \Big(\frac{-1}{-\varpi_1 + ik} \Big) \widetilde{\gamma_{\ell_2}}(k,t) dk \Big\|_{H_t^s(0,2)}}_{(F)} \\
&\quad + \underbrace{\Big\| \frac{1}{2\pi} \int_0^\infty e^{-ikt} e^{ikx} \Big(\frac{1}{-\varpi_1 + ik} \Big) \widetilde{\gamma_{\ell_1}}(k,t) dk \Big\|_{H_t^s(0,2)}}_{(G)} + \underbrace{\Big\| \frac{1}{2\pi} \int_0^\infty e^{ikt} e^{ikx} \Big(\frac{1}{-\varpi_1 + ik} \Big) \widetilde{\gamma_{\ell_2}}(k,t) dk \Big\|_{H_t^s(0,2)}}_{(H)} .
\end{aligned}
$$

Applying Theorem 3, we derive the following inequality:

$$(E)^2 \leq \| \frac{1}{2\pi}\int_{-\infty}^{0} e^{ikt}e^{ikx}(\frac{-1}{-\omega_1+ik})\widetilde{\gamma_{\ell_1}}(k,t)dk \|^2_{H_t^s(\mathbb{R})}$$
$$\lesssim \int_{\mathbb{R}}(1+k^2)^{s-1}|\widehat{\chi_{[0,t]}\gamma_\ell}(k)|^2dk \leq \| \gamma_\ell \|^2_{H_t^{s-1}(\mathbb{R})},$$
$$(F)^2 \leq \| \frac{1}{2\pi}\int_{-\infty}^{0} e^{-ikt}e^{ikx}(\frac{-1}{-\omega_1+ik})\widetilde{\gamma_{\ell_2}}(k,t)dk \|^2_{H_t^s(\mathbb{R})}$$
$$= \| \frac{1}{2\pi}\int_{0}^{\infty} e^{ikt}e^{-ikx}(\frac{-1}{-\omega_1-ik})\widetilde{\gamma_{\ell_2}}(k,t)dk \|^2_{H_t^s(\mathbb{R})}$$
$$\lesssim \int_{\mathbb{R}}(1+k^2)^{s-1}|\widehat{\chi_{[0,t]}\gamma_\ell}(k)|^2dk \leq \| \gamma_\ell \|^2_{H_t^{s-1}(\mathbb{R})}.$$

Following a similar proof process as used for the estimates of $(E)^2$ and $(F)^2$ above, we also derive the following results:

$$(G)^2 \leq \| \gamma_\ell \|^2_{H_t^{s-1}(\mathbb{R})}, \quad (H)^2 \leq \| \gamma_\ell \|^2_{H_t^{s-1}(\mathbb{R})}.$$

Thus, we can conclude that

$$\| S_1[0,0,\gamma_\ell;0](x,t) \|_{H_t^s(0,2)} \lesssim \| \gamma_\ell \|_{H_t^{s-1}(\mathbb{R})},$$

and then, we have Equation (24):

$$\sup_{x\in[0,\infty)} \| S_1[0,0,\gamma_\ell;0](x) \|_{H_t^s(0,2)} \leq (C_1)_s \| \gamma_\ell \|_{H_t^{s-1}(\mathbb{R})}.$$

Following a similar proof process as in (24), we can derive Equation (25):

$$\sup_{x\in[0,\infty)} \| S_2[0,0,\gamma_\ell;0](x) \|_{H_t^{s-1}(0,2)} \leq (C_1)_s \| \gamma_\ell \|_{H_t^{s-1}(\mathbb{R})}.$$

We finish the proof of Theorem 6. □

4. The Proof of Theorem 1 (about the Forced Linear IBVP Estimates)

In this section, we utilize Theorem 6 to perform the space and time estimates for (36) and (38). We establish the fundamental linear estimates (13) and (14), thereby completing the proof of Theorem 1. We begin by breaking down the forced linear IBVP (6) into a combination of simple IVPs and IBVPs.

4.1. Decomposition into a Superposition of IVPs and IBVPs

In this subsection, we focus on proving Theorem 1. Our approach begins with decomposing the forced linear IBVP (6) into a superposition of the following problems.

Let $U_0 \in H_x^s(\mathbb{R})$ and $U_* \in H_x^s(\mathbb{R})$ represent extensions of the initial data $u_0 \in H_x^s(0,\infty)$ and $u_* \in H_x^s(0,\infty)$, respectively, such that

$$\| U_0 \|_{H_x^s(\mathbb{R})} \leq 2 \| u_0 \|_{H_x^s(0,\infty)}, \ s \geq 0, \tag{26}$$
$$\| U_* \|_{H_x^s(\mathbb{R})} \leq 2 \| u_* \|_{H_x^s(0,\infty)}, \ s \geq 0, \tag{27}$$

and F be an extension of the forcing term f such that

$$\sup_{t\in[0,T]} \| F(t) \|_{H_x^s(\mathbb{R})} \leq 2 \sup_{t\in[0,T]} \| f(t) \|_{H_x^s(0,\infty)}, \ s > 0. \tag{28}$$

Based on the definitions of U_0, U_*, and F established, we initiate our approach by breaking down the IBVP (6) into a combination of the following component problems:

(I) The homogeneous linear IVP:

$$\begin{cases} U_t = U_1, & x \in \mathbb{R},\ t \in (0,T), \\ (U_1)_t = U_{xx}, & x \in \mathbb{R},\ t \in (0,T), \\ U(x,0) = U_0(x), U_t(x,0) = U_*(x), & x \in \mathbb{R}. \end{cases} \tag{29}$$

Using the Fourier transform, we derive the following solutions:

$$\begin{aligned} U(x,t) &= \widetilde{S_1}[U_0, U_*; 0](x,t) \\ &= \frac{1}{2\pi} \int_{-\infty}^{\infty} \frac{e^{ikx}}{2i|k|} \left[\left(e^{-i|k|t} + e^{i|k|t} \right) \left(i|k|\widehat{U_0} \right) + \left(e^{i|k|t} - e^{-i|k|t} \right) \widehat{U_*} \right] dk, \end{aligned} \tag{30}$$

$$\begin{aligned} U_1(x,t) &= \widetilde{S_2}[U_0, U_*; 0](x,t) \\ &= \frac{1}{4\pi} \int_{-\infty}^{\infty} e^{ikx} \left[\left(e^{i|k|t} - e^{-i|k|t} \right) \left(i|k|\widehat{U_0} \right) + \left(e^{i|k|t} + e^{-i|k|t} \right) \widehat{U_*} \right] dk, \end{aligned} \tag{31}$$

where

$$\widehat{U_0}(\xi) = \int_{x \in \mathbb{R}} e^{-i\xi x} U_0(x) dx, \ \ \widehat{U_*}(\xi) = \int_{x \in \mathbb{R}} e^{-i\xi x} U_*(x) dx.$$

(II) The forced linear IVP with zero initial condition:

$$\begin{cases} W_t = W_1, & x \in \mathbb{R},\ t \in (0,T), \\ (W_1)_t = W_{xx} + F(x,t), & x \in \mathbb{R},\ t \in (0,T), \\ W(x,0) = W_t(x,0) = 0, & x \in \mathbb{R}. \end{cases} \tag{32}$$

Using the Fourier transform, we derive the following solutions:

$$W(x,t) = \widetilde{S_1}[0,0;F](x,t) = \frac{1}{2\pi} \int_0^t \int_{-\infty}^{\infty} \frac{e^{ikx}}{2i|k|} \widehat{F}(k,s) \left(e^{i|k|(t-s)} - e^{-i|k|(t-s)} \right) dkds, \tag{33}$$

$$W_1(x,t) = \widetilde{S_2}[0,0;F](x,t) = \frac{1}{4\pi} \int_0^t \int_{-\infty}^{\infty} e^{ikx} \widehat{F}(k,s) \left(e^{i|k|(t-s)} + e^{-i|k|(t-s)} \right) dkds, \tag{34}$$

where

$$\widehat{W}(\xi,t) = \int_{x \in \mathbb{R}} e^{-ix\xi} W(x,t) dx.$$

(III) The linear IBVP on the half-line:

$$\begin{cases} (\widetilde{u})_t &= \widetilde{u_1}, & x \in (0,\infty),\ t \in (0,T), \\ (\widetilde{u_1})_t &= \widetilde{u}_{xx}, & x \in (0,\infty),\ t \in (0,T), \\ \widetilde{u}(x,0) = \widetilde{u}_t(x,0) &= 0, & x \in [0,\infty), \\ \widetilde{u}_x(0,t) - \varpi_1 \widetilde{u}(0,t) &= \gamma_1(t) \quad U_x(0,t) - W_x(0,t) & \\ &\doteq G_0(t), & t \in [0,T], \end{cases} \tag{35}$$

where $\varpi_1 \geq 1$, and with the solution

$$\widetilde{u}(x,t) = S_1[0,0,G_0;0](x,t) \tag{36}$$

(IV) The homogeneous linear IBVP with zero initial condition:

$$\begin{cases} (u^*)_t &= u_1^*, & x \in (0,\infty), t \in (0,T), \\ (u_1^*)_t &= u_{xx}^*, & x \in (0,\infty), t \in (0,T), \\ u^*(x,0) = u_t^*(x,0) &= 0, & x \in [0,\infty), t \in (0,T), \\ u_x^*(0,t) - \varpi_1 u^*(0,t) &= \varpi_1 U(0,t) + \varpi_1 W(0,t) & \\ &\doteq H_0(t), & t \in [0,T], \end{cases} \tag{37}$$

where $\varpi_1 \geq 1$, and with the solution

$$u^*(x,t) = S_1[0,0,H_0;0](x,t). \tag{38}$$

By utilizing the superposition principle, the UTM solutions (9) and (10) for the linear IBVPs (6) have been represented as

$$\begin{aligned} S_1[u_0,u_*,\gamma_1;f](x,t) = &\widetilde{S_1}[U_0,U_*;0]|_{x>0} + \widetilde{S_1}[0,0;F]|_{x>0} \\ &+ S_1[0,0,G_0;0](x,t) + S_1[0,0,H_0;0](x,t), \end{aligned} \tag{39}$$

where the four terms on the right-hand side of (39) correspond to the solutions of the respective problems (29), (32), (35) and (37), respectively.

4.2. The Estimations for the Linear IVPs in Sobolev Spaces

In this subsection, we will derive the space and time estimates for the components of (39), namely $\widetilde{S_1}[U_0,U_*;0]|_{x>0}$, $\widetilde{S_1}[0,0;F]|_{x>0}$, $S_1[0,0,G_0;0](x,t)$, and $S_1[0,0,H_0;0](x,t)$.

Theorem 7 (Estimates for Homogeneous IVP (29)). *The solutions $U = \widetilde{S_1}[U_0,U_*;0]$ and $U_1 = \widetilde{S_2}[U_0,U_*;0]$ of the linear IVP (29) given by Formulas (30) and (31) admit the estimates*

$$\sup_{t\in[0,T]} \| U(t) \|_{H_x^s(\mathbb{R})} \leq (C_2)_s(\| U_0 \|_{H_x^s(\mathbb{R})} + \| U_* \|_{H_x^s(\mathbb{R})}),\ s \in \mathbb{R}, \tag{40}$$

$$\sup_{t\in[0,T]} \| U_1(t) \|_{H_x^{s-1}(\mathbb{R})} \leq (C_2)_s(\| U_0 \|_{H_x^s(\mathbb{R})} + \| U_* \|_{H_x^s(\mathbb{R})}),\ s \in \mathbb{R}, \tag{41}$$

$$\sup_{x\in[0,\infty)} \| U(x) \|_{H_t^s(0,T)} \leq (C_2)_s(\| U_0 \|_{H_x^s(\mathbb{R})} + \| U_* \|_{H_x^s(\mathbb{R})}),\ s > 0, \tag{42}$$

$$\sup_{x\in[0,\infty)} \| U_1(x) \|_{H_t^{s-1}(0,T)} \leq (C_2)_s(\| U_0 \|_{H_x^s(\mathbb{R})} + \| U_* \|_{H_x^s(\mathbb{R})}),\ s > 1, \tag{43}$$

where $(C_2)_s > 0$ is a constant depending on s.

Proof. First, we will prove (40). We will analyze the solution formula given in (30):

$$\begin{aligned} U(x,t) &= \widetilde{S_1}[U_0,U_*;0](x,t) \\ &= \frac{1}{2\pi}\int_{-\infty}^{\infty} \frac{e^{ikx}}{2i|k|}\Big[\Big(e^{-i|k|t}+e^{i|k|t}\Big)\Big(i|k|\widehat{U_0}(k)\Big) + \Big(e^{i|k|t}-e^{-i|k|t}\Big)\widehat{U_*}(k)\Big]dk \\ &= \frac{1}{2\pi}\int_{-\infty}^{0} \frac{e^{ikx}}{-2ik}\Big[\Big(e^{ikt}+e^{-ikt}\Big)\Big(-ik\widehat{U_0}(k)\Big) + \Big(e^{-ikt}-e^{ikt}\Big)\widehat{U_*}(k)\Big]dk \\ &+ \frac{1}{2\pi}\int_{0}^{\infty} \frac{e^{ikx}}{2ik}\Big[\Big(e^{-ikt}+e^{ikt}\Big)\Big(ik\widehat{U_0}(k)\Big) + \Big(e^{ikt}-e^{-ikt}\Big)\widehat{U_*}(k)\Big]dk. \end{aligned}$$

Now, we will calculate the estimate for $\|U(t)\|^2_{H_x^s(\mathbb{R})}$:

$$
\begin{aligned}
&\| U(t) \|^2_{H^s_x(\mathbb{R})} \\
&\lesssim \| \frac{1}{2\pi}\int_{-\infty}^{0} e^{ikx}\left(\frac{1}{-2ik}\left(\left(e^{ikt}+e^{-ikt}\right)\left(-ik\widehat{U_0}(k)\right)+\left(e^{-ikt}-e^{ikt}\right)\widehat{U_*}(k)\right)\right)dk \|^2_{H^s_x(\mathbb{R})} \\
&\quad + \| \frac{1}{2\pi}\int_{0}^{\infty} e^{ikx}\left(\frac{1}{2ik}\left(\left(e^{-ikt}+e^{ikt}\right)\left(ik\widehat{U_0}(k)\right)+\left(e^{ikt}-e^{-ikt}\right)\widehat{U_*}(k)\right)\right)dk \|^2_{H^s_x(\mathbb{R})} \\
&\leq \int_{\mathbb{R}}\left(1+k^2\right)^s\left|\frac{1}{-2ik}\left(\left(e^{ikt}+e^{-ikt}\right)\left(-ik\widehat{U_0}(k)\right)+\left(e^{-ikt}-e^{ikt}\right)\widehat{U_*}(k)\right)\right|^2 dk \\
&\quad + \int_{\mathbb{R}}\left(1+k^2\right)^s\left|\frac{1}{2ik}\left(\left(e^{-ikt}+e^{ikt}\right)\left(ik\widehat{U_0}(k)\right)+\left(e^{ikt}-e^{-ikt}\right)\widehat{U_*}(k)\right)\right|^2 dk \\
&\text{(by Theorem 3)} \\
&\lesssim \underbrace{\int_{\mathbb{R}}\left(1+k^2\right)^s\left|\left(e^{ikt}+e^{-ikt}\right)\widehat{U_0}(k)\right|^2 dk}_{(A)} + \underbrace{\int_{\mathbb{R}}\left(1+k^2\right)^s\left|\frac{\left(e^{-ikt}-e^{ikt}\right)}{-2ik}\widehat{U_*}(k)\right|^2 dk}_{(B)},
\end{aligned}
$$

where

$$
\begin{aligned}
(A) &= \int_{\mathbb{R}}\left(1+k^2\right)^s\left|\left(e^{ikt}+e^{-ikt}\right)\widehat{U_0}(k)\right|^2 dk \lesssim \int_{\mathbb{R}}\left(1+k^2\right)^s\left|\widehat{U_0}(k)\right|^2 dk = \| U_0 \|^2_{H^s_x(\mathbb{R})}, \\
(B) &= \int_{\mathbb{R}}\left(1+k^2\right)^s\left|\frac{\left(e^{-ikt}-e^{ikt}\right)}{-2ik}\widehat{U_*}(k)\right|^2 dk = \int_{\mathbb{R}}\left(1+k^2\right)^s\left|\frac{-2i\sin(kt)}{-2ik}\widehat{U_*}(k)\right|^2 dk \\
&\lesssim \int_{\mathbb{R}}\left(1+k^2\right)^s\left|\frac{kt}{k}\right|\left|\widehat{U_*}(k)\right|^2 dk \lesssim \| U_* \|^2_{H^s_x(\mathbb{R})}, \ (\text{as } t\in[0,T],\ T<1).
\end{aligned}
$$

Thus, we can conclude that

$$
\| U(t) \|^2_{H^s_x(\mathbb{R})} \lesssim \| U_0 \|^2_{H^s_x(\mathbb{R})} + \| U_* \|^2_{H^s_x(\mathbb{R})},\ \forall t\in[0,T],\ T<1,
$$

and then, we have the inequality (40):

$$
\sup_{t\in[0,T]} \| U(t) \|_{H^s_x(\mathbb{R})} \leq (C_2)_s(\| U_0 \|_{H^s_x(\mathbb{R})} + \| U_* \|_{H^s_x(\mathbb{R})}),\ s\in\mathbb{R}.
$$

Second, we proceed with the proof of (41). We examine the solution Formula (31):

$$
\begin{aligned}
U_1(x,t) &= \widetilde{S_2}[U_0,U_*;0](x,t) \\
&= \frac{1}{4\pi}\int_{-\infty}^{\infty} e^{ikx}\left(\left(e^{i|k|t}-e^{-i|k|t}\right)\left(i|k|\widehat{U_0}(k)\right)+\left(e^{i|k|t}+e^{-i|k|t}\right)\widehat{U_*}(k)\right)dk \\
&= \underbrace{\frac{1}{4\pi}\int_{-\infty}^{0} e^{ikx}\left(\left(e^{-ikt}-e^{ikt}\right)\left(-ik\widehat{U_0}(k)\right)+\left(e^{-ikt}+e^{ikt}\right)\widehat{U_*}(k)\right)dk}_{(C)} \\
&\quad + \underbrace{\frac{1}{4\pi}\int_{0}^{\infty} e^{ikx}\left(\left(e^{ikt}-e^{-ikt}\right)\left(ik\widehat{U_0}(k)\right)+\left(e^{ikt}+e^{-ikt}\right)\widehat{U_*}(k)\right)dk}_{(D)},
\end{aligned}
$$

then

$$
\| U_1(t) \|^2_{H^{s-1}_x(\mathbb{R})} \lesssim \| (C) \|^2_{H^{s-1}_x(\mathbb{R})} + \| (D) \|^2_{H^{s-1}_x(\mathbb{R})}.
$$

At this point, we calculate Equation (C) to derive the following inequality:

$$\begin{aligned}
&\| (C) \|^2_{H^{s-1}_x(\mathbb{R})} \\
=&\| \frac{1}{4\pi}\int_{-\infty}^{0} e^{ikx}\Big(\Big(e^{-ikt}-e^{ikt}\Big)\Big(-ik\widehat{U_0}(k)\Big)+\Big(e^{-ikt}+e^{ikt}\Big)\widehat{U_*}(k)\Big)dk \|^2_{H^{s-1}_x(\mathbb{R})} \\
\leq& \int_{\mathbb{R}}\Big(1+k^2\Big)^{s-1}\Big|\Big(e^{-ikt}-e^{ikt}\Big)\Big(-ik\widehat{U_0}(k)\Big)+\Big(e^{-ikt}+e^{ikt}\Big)\widehat{U_*}(k)\Big|^2 dk, \text{ (by Theroem 3)} \\
\lesssim& \int_{\mathbb{R}}\Big(1+k^2\Big)^{s-1}\Big(1+k^2\Big)\Big|\widehat{U_0}(k)\Big|^2 dk+\int_{\mathbb{R}}\Big(1+k^2\Big)^{s-1}\Big|\widehat{U_*}(k)\Big|^2 dk \\
\leq& \int_{\mathbb{R}}\Big(1+k^2\Big)^{s}\Big|\widehat{U_0}(k)\Big|^2 dk+\int_{\mathbb{R}}\Big(1+k^2\Big)^{s}\Big|\widehat{U_*}(k)\Big|^2 dk = \| U_0 \|^2_{H^s_x(\mathbb{R})}+\| U_* \|^2_{H^s_x(\mathbb{R})}\,.
\end{aligned} \tag{44}$$

Following a similar proof process as used for the estimates of (C) in (44), we also derive the results:

$$\| (D) \|^2_{H^{s-1}_x(\mathbb{R})} \lesssim \| U_0 \|^2_{H^s_x(\mathbb{R})}+\| U_* \|^2_{H^s_x(\mathbb{R})}\,. \tag{45}$$

By combining Formulas (44) and (45), we arrive at the inequality (41):

$$\sup_{t\in[0,T]} \| U_1(t) \|_{H^{s-1}_x(\mathbb{R})} \leq (C_2)_s\Big(\| U_0 \|_{H^s_x(\mathbb{R})}+\| U_* \|_{H^s_x(\mathbb{R})}\Big),\ s\in\mathbb{R}.$$

Third, we start with the proof of (42). We examine the solution Formula (30):

$$\begin{aligned}
U(x,t) &= \widetilde{S_1}[U_0,U_*;0](x,t) \\
&= \frac{1}{2\pi}\int_{-\infty}^{\infty}\frac{e^{ikx}}{2i|k|}\Big(\Big(e^{-i|k|t}+e^{i|k|t}\Big)\Big(i|k|\widehat{U_0}(k)\Big)+\Big(e^{i|k|t}-e^{-i|k|t}\Big)\widehat{U_*}(k)\Big)dk \\
&= \frac{1}{2\pi}\int_{-\infty}^{\infty}\frac{e^{ikx}}{2i|k|}\Big(2\cos(|k|t)\Big(i|k|\widehat{U_0}(k)\Big)+(2i\sin(|k|t))\widehat{U_*}(k)\Big)dk \\
&= \frac{1}{2\pi}\int_{-\infty}^{\infty}e^{ikx}\Big(\cos(|k|t)\widehat{U_0}(k)+\frac{\sin(|k|t)}{|k|}\widehat{U_*}(k)\Big)dk.
\end{aligned}$$

For the time estimate, we express $U(x,t)$ as

$$U(x,t) = I_1(x,t)+I_2(x,t), \tag{46}$$

where

$$\begin{aligned}
I_1(x,t) &= \frac{1}{2\pi}\int_{-\infty}^{\infty}e^{ikx}Q(k)\Big(\cos(|k|t)\widehat{U_0}(k)+\frac{\sin(|k|t)}{|k|}\widehat{U_*}(k)\Big)dk, \\
I_2(x,t) &= \frac{1}{4\pi}\int_{-\infty}^{\infty}e^{ikx}(1-Q(k))\left(\Big(e^{-i|k|t}+e^{i|k|t}\Big)\widehat{U_0}(k)+\frac{\Big(e^{i|k|t}-e^{-i|k|t}\Big)\widehat{U_*}(k)}{ik}\right)dk,
\end{aligned}$$

and $Q(k)\in C_0^\infty(\mathbb{R})$ is a smooth cut-off function, which is defined by

$$Q(k) = \begin{cases} 1, & \text{if } |k|\leq 1, \\ 0, & \text{if } |k|\geq 2, \end{cases} \quad \text{and } 0\leq Q(k)\leq 1.$$

Now, we will calculate the equations $I_1(x,t)$ and $I_2(x,t)$ in the following parts $(\mathcal{A})$ and $(\mathcal{B})$, respectively.

($\mathcal{A}$) The estimation of I_1:
For $\mu \in \mathbb{N}_0$, by Remark 2, the definition for $\| I_1(x) \|_{H_t^{\mu}(0,T)}$ is

$$\| I_1(x) \|^2_{H_t^{\mu}(0,T)} = \sum_{j=0}^{\mu} \| \partial_t^j I_1(x) \|^2_{L_t^2(0,T)},$$

where $\mathbb{N}_0 = \mathbb{N} \cup \{0\}$, and $\mathbb{N}$ is the set of natural numbers. For $j \in \mathbb{N}$, by the definition of $Q(k)$,

$$\begin{aligned}|\partial_t^j I_1(x,t)| &\leq \frac{1}{2\pi}\int_{-2}^{2} |k|^j Q(k)\left|\widehat{\mathcal{U}_0}(k)\right| dk + \frac{1}{2\pi}\int_{-2}^{2} |k|^{j-1} Q(k)\left|\widehat{\mathcal{U}_*}(k)\right| dk \\ &\leq \frac{2^{j-1}}{\pi}\int_{-2}^{2}\left|\widehat{\mathcal{U}_0}(k)\right| dk + \frac{2^{j-2}}{\pi}\int_{-2}^{2}\left|\widehat{\mathcal{U}_*}(k)\right| dk \\ &\leq 2^{j-1}\left(\int_{-2}^{2}\left(1+k^2\right)^{-s} dk\right)^{\frac{1}{2}}\left(\int_{\mathbb{R}}\left(1+k^2\right)^{s}\left|\widehat{\mathcal{U}_0}(k)\right|^2 dk\right)^{\frac{1}{2}} \\ &\quad + 2^{j-2}\left(\int_{-2}^{2}\left(1+k^2\right)^{-s} dk\right)^{\frac{1}{2}}\left(\int_{\mathbb{R}}\left(1+k^2\right)^{s}\left|\widehat{\mathcal{U}_*}(k)\right|^2 dk\right)^{\frac{1}{2}} \\ &\lesssim 2^{j-1} \| \mathcal{U}_0 \|_{H_x^s(\mathbb{R})} + 2^{j-2} \| \mathcal{U}_* \|_{H_x^s(\mathbb{R})}.\end{aligned} \tag{47}$$

Hence, for any $j \in \mathbb{N}$, by (47), we derive the following two inequalities:

$$\begin{aligned}\| \partial_t^j I_1(x,t) \|_{L_t^2(0,T)} &= \left(\int_0^T |\partial_t^j I_1(x,t)|^2 dt\right)^{\frac{1}{2}} \\ &\lesssim \left(\int_0^T \left(2^{j-1} \| \mathcal{U}_0 \|_{H_x^s(\mathbb{R})} + 2^{j-2} \| \mathcal{U}_* \|_{H_x^s(\mathbb{R})}\right)^2 dt\right)^{\frac{1}{2}} \\ &\lesssim \left(\int_0^T 2^{2j-2} \| \mathcal{U}_0 \|^2_{H_x^s(\mathbb{R})} dt + \int_0^T 2^{2j-4} \| \mathcal{U}_* \|^2_{H_x^s(\mathbb{R})} dt\right)^{\frac{1}{2}} \\ &\leq 2^{j-1}\left(\int_0^T \| \mathcal{U}_0 \|^2_{H_x^s(\mathbb{R})} dt\right)^{\frac{1}{2}} + 2^{j-2}\left(\int_0^T \| \mathcal{U}_* \|^2_{H_x^s(\mathbb{R})} dt\right)^{\frac{1}{2}} \\ &\leq 2^{j-1}\sqrt{T}\left(\| \mathcal{U}_0 \|_{H_x^s(\mathbb{R})} + \| \mathcal{U}_* \|_{H_x^s(\mathbb{R})}\right),\end{aligned}$$

and

$$\begin{aligned}\| I_1(x,t) \|^2_{L_t^2(0,T)} &= \int_0^T |I_1(x,t)|^2 dt \\ &= \int_0^T \left|\frac{1}{2\pi}\int_{-\infty}^{\infty} e^{ikx} Q(k)\left(\cos(|k|t)\widehat{\mathcal{U}_0}(k) + \frac{\sin(|k|t)}{|k|}\widehat{\mathcal{U}_*}(k)\right) dk\right|^2 dt \\ &\leq \int_0^T \left(\int_{-2}^{2}\left(\left|\widehat{\mathcal{U}_0}(k)\right| + \left|\widehat{\mathcal{U}_*}(k)\right|\right) dk\right)^2 dt \\ &\lesssim \int_0^T \left(\int_{-2}^{2}\left|\widehat{\mathcal{U}_0}(k)\right| dk\right)^2 dt + \int_0^T \left(\int_{-2}^{2}\left|\widehat{\mathcal{U}_*}(k)\right| dk\right)^2 dt \\ &\leq \int_0^T \left(\int_{-2}^{2}\left(1+k^2\right)^{-s} dk\right)\left(\int_{\mathbb{R}}\left(1+k^2\right)^{s}\left|\widehat{\mathcal{U}_0}(k)\right|^2 dk\right) dt \\ &\quad + \int_0^T \left(\int_{-2}^{2}\left(1+k^2\right)^{-s} dk\right)\left(\int_{\mathbb{R}}\left(1+k^2\right)^{s}\left|\widehat{\mathcal{U}_*}(k)\right|^2 dk\right) dt \\ &\lesssim \left(\| \mathcal{U}_0 \|^2_{H_x^s(\mathbb{R})} + \| \mathcal{U}_* \|^2_{H_x^s(\mathbb{R})}\right), \ \left(\text{since } \int_{-2}^{2}\left(1+k^2\right)^{-s} dk \text{ is finite and } s > 0\right).\end{aligned}$$

Thus, we have the following two inequalities:

$$\| \partial_t^j I_1(x,t) \|_{L_t^2(0,T)} \lesssim 2^{j-1}\sqrt{T}\Big(\| U_0 \|_{H_x^s(\mathbb{R})} + \| U_* \|_{H_x^s(\mathbb{R})}\Big), \tag{48}$$

$$\| I_1(x,t) \|_{L_t^2(0,T)} \lesssim \| U_0 \|_{H_x^s(\mathbb{R})} + \| U_* \|_{H_x^s(\mathbb{R})} \,. \tag{49}$$

For $\mu \in \mathbb{N}$, by Formulas (48) and (49), we derive the following inequality:

$$\begin{aligned}
\| I_1(x) \|_{H_t^\mu(0,T)} &= \| I_1(x) \|_{L_t^2(0,T)} + \sum_{j=1}^{\mu} \| \partial_t^j I_1(x) \|_{L_t^2(0,T)} \\
&\lesssim \| U_0 \|_{H_x^s(\mathbb{R})} + \| U_* \|_{H_x^s(\mathbb{R})} + \sum_{j=1}^{\mu} 2^{j-1}\sqrt{T}(\| U_0 \|_{H_x^s(\mathbb{R})} + \| U_* \|_{H_x^s(\mathbb{R})}) \\
&\lesssim \| U_0 \|_{H_x^s(\mathbb{R})} + \| U_* \|_{H_x^s(\mathbb{R})} \,.
\end{aligned}$$

Thus, for $\mu \in \mathbb{N}$, we have the following inequality:

$$\| I_1(x) \|_{H_t^\mu(0,T)} \lesssim \| U_0 \|_{H_x^s(\mathbb{R})} + \| U_* \|_{H_x^s(\mathbb{R})} \,. \tag{50}$$

According to Lemma 1, for any $s > 0$ and $s \notin \mathbb{N}$, let $m_1 = \lfloor s \rfloor$ and $m_2 = \lfloor s \rfloor + 1$; then, we derive the following inequality:

$$\begin{aligned}
\| I_1 \|_{H^s(0,T)} &\leq \| I_1 \|_{H^{\lfloor s \rfloor}(0,T)}^{\lfloor s \rfloor + 1 - s} \| I_1 \|_{H^{\lfloor s \rfloor + 1}(0,T)}^{s - \lfloor s \rfloor} \\
&\lesssim \| U_0 \|_{H_x^s(\mathbb{R})} + \| U_* \|_{H_x^s(\mathbb{R})}, \text{ (by (49) and (50))}.
\end{aligned}$$

Thus, we derive the following inequality:

$$\| I_1 \|_{H^s(0,T)} \lesssim \| U_0 \|_{H_x^s(\mathbb{R})} + \| U_* \|_{H_x^s(\mathbb{R})}, \text{ for } s > 0. \tag{51}$$

($\mathcal{B}$) The estimation of I_2:
Now, we consider $I_2(x,t)$:

$$\begin{aligned}
I_2(x,t) &= \frac{1}{4\pi} \int_{-\infty}^{\infty} e^{ikx}(1 - Q(k)) \left(\left(e^{-i|k|t} + e^{i|k|t} \right) \left(\widehat{U_0}(k) \right) + \frac{\left(e^{i|k|t} - e^{-i|k|t} \right) \widehat{U_*}(k)}{ik} \right) dk \\
&= I_{21}(x,t) + I_{22}(x,t),
\end{aligned} \tag{52}$$

where

$$\begin{aligned}
I_{21}(x,t) &= \frac{1}{4\pi} \int_{|k| \geq 1} e^{ikx + i|k|t} \left(\widehat{U_0}(k) + \frac{\widehat{U_*}(k)}{ik} \right) dk, \\
I_{22}(x,t) &= \frac{1}{2\pi} \int_{|k| \geq 1} e^{ikx - i|k|t} \left(\widehat{U_0}(k) - \frac{\widehat{U_*}(k)}{ik} \right) dk.
\end{aligned}$$

Next, we will calculate $I_{21}(x,t)$ in the following:

$$\begin{aligned}
I_{21}(x,t) &= \frac{1}{4\pi} \int_{-\infty}^{-1} e^{ikx - ikt} \left(\widehat{U_0}(k) + \frac{\widehat{U_*}(k)}{ik} \right) dk + \frac{1}{4\pi} \int_{1}^{\infty} e^{ikx + ikt} \left(\widehat{U_0}(k) + \frac{\widehat{U_*}(k)}{ik} \right) dk \\
&= \frac{1}{4\pi} \int_{1}^{\infty} e^{-ikx + ikt} \left(\widehat{U_0}(-k) - \frac{\widehat{U_*}(-k)}{ik} \right) dk + \frac{1}{4\pi} \int_{1}^{\infty} e^{ikx + ikt} \left(\widehat{U_0}(k) + \frac{\widehat{U_*}(k)}{ik} \right) dk \\
&= \frac{1}{4\pi} \int_{1}^{\infty} e^{ikt} \left(e^{-ikx} \left(\widehat{U_0}(-k) - \frac{\widehat{U_*}(-k)}{ik} \right) + e^{ikx} \left(\widehat{U_0}(k) + \frac{\widehat{U_*}(k)}{ik} \right) \right) dk,
\end{aligned}$$

and

$$
\begin{aligned}
\| I_{21}(x,t) \|^2_{H^s_t(0,T)} &\leq \int_1^\infty \left(1+k^2\right)^s \left| e^{-ikx}\left(\widehat{U_0}(-k) - \frac{\widehat{U_*}(-k)}{ik}\right) + e^{ikx}\left(\widehat{U_0}(k) + \frac{\widehat{U_*}(k)}{ik}\right)\right|^2 dk \\
&\lesssim \int_1^\infty \left(1+k^2\right)^s \left|\widehat{U_0}(-k)\right|^2 dk + \int_1^\infty \left(1+k^2\right)^s \left|\frac{\widehat{U_*}(-k)}{ik}\right|^2 dk \\
&\quad + \int_1^\infty \left(1+k^2\right)^s \left|\widehat{U_0}(k)\right|^2 dk + \int_1^\infty \left(1+k^2\right)^s \left|\frac{\widehat{U_*}(k)}{ik}\right|^2 dk \\
&\lesssim \int_{\mathbb{R}} \left(1+k^2\right)^s \left|\widehat{U_0}(k)\right|^2 dk + \int_{\mathbb{R}} \left(1+k^2\right)^s \left|\widehat{U_*}(k)\right|^2 dk \\
&= \| U_0 \|^2_{H^s_x(\mathbb{R})} + \| U_* \|^2_{H^s_x(\mathbb{R})},
\end{aligned}
$$

and hence, we have the following inequality:

$$
\| I_{21}(x,t) \|_{H^s_t(0,T)} \lesssim \| U_0 \|_{H^s_x(\mathbb{R})} + \| U_* \|_{H^s_x(\mathbb{R})} \,. \tag{53}
$$

By employing a similar proof strategy as in (53), we obtain the following inequality:

$$
\| I_{22}(x,t) \|_{H^s_t(0,T)} \lesssim \| U_0 \|_{H^s_x(\mathbb{R})} + \| U_* \|_{H^s_x(\mathbb{R})} \,. \tag{54}
$$

Consequently, we obtain the following inequality:

$$
\begin{aligned}
\| U(x) \|_{H^s_t(0,T)} &\leq \| I_1(x,t) \|_{H^s_t(0,T)} + \| I_2(x,t) \|_{H^s_t(0,T)}, \ \text{(by (46))} \\
&\leq \| I_1(x,t) \|_{H^s_t(0,T)} + \| I_{21}(x,t) \|_{H^s_t(0,T)} + \| I_{22}(x,t) \|_{H^s_t(0,T)}, \ \text{(by (52))} \\
&\leq (C_2)_s(\| U_0 \|_{H^s_x(\mathbb{R})} + \| U_* \|_{H^s_x(\mathbb{R})}), \ \text{(by (51), (53) and (54))}.
\end{aligned}
$$

As a result, we establish the inequality (42):

$$
\sup_{x\in[0,\infty)} \| U(x) \|_{H^s_t(0,T)} \leq (C_2)_s(\| U_0 \|_{H^s_x(\mathbb{R})} + \| U_* \|_{H^s_x(\mathbb{R})}), \ s > 0.
$$

Ultimately, by employing a similar proof strategy as in (42), we establish (43):

$$
\sup_{x\in[0,\infty)} \| U_1(x) \|_{H^{s-1}_t(0,T)} \leq (C_2)_s(\| U_0 \|_{H^s_x(\mathbb{R})} + \| U_* \|_{H^s_x(\mathbb{R})}), \ s > 1.
$$

We finish this proof of Theorem 7. □

Now, we will show the estimates of W and W_1 in the following Theorem.

Theorem 8 (Sobolev-type estimates for the homogeneous linear IVP (32)). *The solutions $W = \widetilde{S_1}[0,0;F]$ and $W_1 = \widetilde{S_2}[0,0;F]$ of the linear IVP (32) given by Formulas (33) and (34) admit the following estimates:*

Space estimates:

$$
\sup_{t\in[0,T]} \| W(t) \|_{H^s_x(\mathbb{R})} \lesssim T \sup_{t\in[0,T]} \| F(t) \|_{H^s_x(\mathbb{R})}, \ s \in \mathbb{R}, \tag{55}
$$

$$
\sup_{t\in[0,T]} \| W_1(t) \|_{H^{s-1}_x(\mathbb{R})} \lesssim T \sup_{t\in[0,T]} \| F(t) \|_{H^s_x(\mathbb{R})}, \ s \in \mathbb{R}. \tag{56}
$$

Time estimates:

$$\sup_{x\in[0,\infty)} \| W(x) \|_{H_t^s(0,T)} \lesssim \sqrt{T} \sup_{t\in[0,T]} \| F(t) \|_{H_x^s(\mathbb{R})}, \ for\ \frac{1}{2} < s < 1, \quad (57)$$

$$\sup_{x\in[0,\infty)} \| W_1(x) \|_{H_t^{s-1}(0,T)} \lesssim \sqrt{T} \sup_{t\in[0,T]} \| F(t) \|_{H_x^s(\mathbb{R})}, \ for\ \frac{3}{2} < s < 2. \quad (58)$$

Proof. Using the Fourier transform, we have the solution formulas:

$$W(x,t) = \widetilde{S_1}[0,0;F](x,t) = \frac{1}{2\pi}\int_0^t \int_{-\infty}^{\infty} \frac{e^{ikx}}{2i|k|}\widehat{F}(k,t')(e^{i|k|(t-t')} - e^{-i|k|(t-t')})dkdt', \quad (59)$$
$$W_1(x,t) = \widetilde{S_2}[0,0;F](x,t) = \frac{1}{4\pi}\int_0^t \int_{-\infty}^{\infty} e^{ikx}\widehat{F}(k,t')(e^{i|k|(t-t')} + e^{-i|k|(t-t')})dkdt'.$$

First, we begin with the proof of (55). We will focus on estimating $\| W(t) \|_{H_x^s(\mathbb{R})}$:

$$\begin{aligned}
\| W(t) \|^2_{H_x^s(\mathbb{R})} &= \| \int_0^t \left(\frac{1}{2\pi}\int_{-\infty}^{\infty} \frac{e^{ikx}}{2i|k|}\widehat{F}(k,t')\left(e^{i|k|(t-t')} - e^{-i|k|(t-t')}\right)dk\right)dt' \|^2_{H_x^s(\mathbb{R})} \\
&= \| \int_0^t \widetilde{S_1}[0,F;0](x,t-t')dt' \|^2_{H_x^s(\mathbb{R})} \quad \text{(by (30))} \\
&\leq \left(\int_0^t \| \widetilde{S_1}[0,F;0](x,t-t') \|_{H_x^s(\mathbb{R})} dt'\right)^2 \\
&\leq \left(\int_0^T \sup_{t\in[0,T]} \| \widetilde{S_1}[0,F;0](x,t) \|_{H_x^s(\mathbb{R})} dt'\right)^2 \\
&= T^2\left(\sup_{t\in[0,T]} \| \widetilde{S_1}[0,F;0](t) \|_{H_x^s(\mathbb{R})}\right)^2.
\end{aligned}$$

Consequently, we obtain the following inequality:

$$\| W(t) \|_{H_x^s(\mathbb{R})} \leq T \sup_{t\in[0,T]} \| \widetilde{S_1}[0,F;0](t) \|_{H_x^s(\mathbb{R})}, \ \forall t \in [0,T].$$

As a result, we establish the inequality (55):

$$\begin{aligned}
\sup_{t\in[0,T]} \| W(t) \|_{H_x^s(\mathbb{R})} &\leq T \sup_{t\in[0,T]} \| \widetilde{S_1}[0,F;0](t) \|_{H_x^s(\mathbb{R})} \\
&\lesssim T \sup_{t\in[0,T]} \| F(t) \|_{H_x^s(\mathbb{R})}, \ s \in \mathbb{R}. \text{ (by (40))}.
\end{aligned}$$

Second, by employing a similar proof strategy as in (55), we can have the result (56):

$$\sup_{t\in[0,T]} \| W_1(t) \|_{H_x^{s-1}(\mathbb{R})} \lesssim T \sup_{t\in[0,T]} \| F(t) \|_{H_x^s(\mathbb{R})}, \ s \in \mathbb{R}.$$

Third, we start with the proof of (57). By Remark 2, the definition for $\| W(x) \|_{H_t^s(0,T)}$ is

$$\| W(x) \|^2_{H_t^s(0,T)} = \| W(x) \|^2_{L_t^2(0,T)} + \| W(x) \|^2_s, \ 0 \leq s < 1,$$

where

$$\| W(x) \|^2_s = \int_0^T \int_0^{T-t} \frac{|W(x,t+\xi) - W(x,t)|^2}{\xi^{1+2s}} d\xi dt.$$

Now, we will focus on estimating $\| W(x) \|_{L_t^2(0,T)}$:

$$\begin{aligned}
\| W(x) \|_{L_t^2(0,T)}^2 &= \int_0^T \left| \frac{1}{2\pi} \int_0^t \int_{-\infty}^{\infty} \frac{e^{ikx}}{2i|k|} \widehat{F}(k,t') \left(e^{i|k|(t-t')} - e^{-i|k|(t-t')} \right) dk dt' \right|^2 dt \\
&= \int_0^T \left| \int_0^t \widetilde{S_1}[0,F;0](x,t-t') dt' \right|^2 dt \\
&\leq \left(\int_0^T \left(\int_{t'}^T \left| \widetilde{S_1}[0,F;0](x,t-t') \right|^2 dt \right)^{\frac{1}{2}} dt' \right)^2, \text{ (by Lemma 3)} \\
&\leq \left(\int_0^T \left(\int_0^T \left| \widetilde{S_1}[0,F;0](x,\tau) \right|^2 d\tau \right)^{\frac{1}{2}} dt' \right)^2, \text{ (let } \tau = t - t') \\
&\leq \left(\int_0^T \| \widetilde{S_1}[0,F;0](x) \|_{H_\tau^s(0,T)} dt' \right)^2 \\
&\leq \left(\int_0^T \sup_{x \in [0,\infty)} \| \widetilde{S_1}[0,F;0](x) \|_{H_\tau^s(0,T)} dt' \right)^2 \\
&\lesssim \left(\int_0^T \| F(t) \|_{H_x^s(\mathbb{R})} dt' \right)^2, \text{ (by (42))} \\
&\leq T^2 \left(\sup_{t \in [0,T]} \| F(t) \|_{H_x^s(\mathbb{R})} \right)^2.
\end{aligned}$$

Consequently, we obtain the following inequality:

$$\| W(x) \|_{L_t^2(0,T)} \lesssim T \sup_{t \in [0,T]} \| F(t) \|_{H_x^s(\mathbb{R})} . \tag{60}$$

Next, we will focus on estimating $\| W(x) \|_s$. From Equation (59),

$$\begin{aligned}
W(x,t) = \widetilde{S_1}[0,0;F](x,t) &= \frac{1}{2\pi} \int_0^t \int_{-\infty}^{\infty} \frac{e^{ikx}}{2i|k|} \widehat{F}(k,t') \left(e^{i|k|(t-t')} - e^{-i|k|(t-t')} \right) dk dt' \\
&= \int_0^t \left(\frac{1}{2\pi} \int_{-\infty}^{\infty} \frac{e^{ikx}}{2i|k|} \widehat{F}(k,t') \left(e^{i|k|(t-t')} - e^{-i|k|(t-t')} \right) dk \right) dt' \\
&= \int_0^t \widetilde{S_1}[0,F;0](x,t-t') dt',
\end{aligned}$$

and then we obtain

$$\begin{aligned}
&W(x,t+\zeta) - W(x,t) \\
&= \int_0^{t+\zeta} \widetilde{S_1}[0,F;0](x,t+\zeta-t') dt' - \int_0^t \widetilde{S_1}[0,F;0](x,t-t') dt' \\
&= \int_0^t \left(\widetilde{S_1}[0,F;0](x,t+\zeta-t') - \widetilde{S_1}[0,F;0](x,t-t') \right) dt' \\
&\quad + \int_t^{t+\zeta} \widetilde{S_1}[0,F;0](x,t+\zeta-t') dt'.
\end{aligned} \tag{61}$$

From Equation (61), we derive the estimation of $\| W(x) \|_s^2$:

$$
\begin{aligned}
\| W(x) \|_s^2 &= \int_0^T \int_0^{T-t} \frac{|W(x,t+\zeta) - W(x,t)|^2}{\zeta^{1+2s}} d\zeta dt \\
&= \int_0^T \int_0^{T-t} \frac{1}{\zeta^{1+2s}} \bigg| \int_0^t \Big(\widetilde{S_1}[0,F;0](x,t+\zeta-t') - \widetilde{S_1}[0,F;0](x,t-t') \Big) dt' \\
&\quad + \int_t^{t+\zeta} \widetilde{S_1}[0,F;0](x,t+\zeta-t') dt' \bigg|^2 d\zeta dt \\
&\lesssim \underbrace{\int_0^T \int_0^{T-t} \frac{1}{\zeta^{1+2s}} \bigg| \int_0^t \Big(\widetilde{S_1}[0,F;0](x,t+\zeta-t') - \widetilde{S_1}[0,F;0](x,t-t') \Big) dt' \bigg|^2 d\zeta dt}_{(E)} \\
&\quad + \underbrace{\int_0^T \int_0^{T-t} \frac{1}{\zeta^{1+2s}} \bigg| \int_t^{t+\zeta} \widetilde{S_1}[0,F;0](x,t+\zeta-t') dt' \bigg|^2 d\zeta dt}_{(F)}.
\end{aligned}
$$

Now, we calculate the equations (E) and (F) to derive the following two inequalities:

$$
\begin{aligned}
(E) &= \int_0^T \int_0^{T-t} \frac{1}{\zeta^{1+2s}} \bigg| \int_0^t \Big(\widetilde{S_1}[0,F;0](x,t+\zeta-t') - \widetilde{S_1}[0,F;0](x,t-t') \Big) dt' \bigg|^2 d\zeta dt \\
&\leq \left(\int_0^T \left(\int_0^T \int_0^{T-t} \frac{1}{\zeta^{1+2s}} \Big| \widetilde{S_1}[0,F;0](x,t+\zeta-t') - \widetilde{S_1}[0,F;0](x,t-t') \Big|^2 d\zeta dt \right)^{\frac{1}{2}} dt' \right)^2, \\
&\quad \text{(by Lemma 3)} \\
&= \left(\int_0^T \| \widetilde{S_1}[0,F;0](x,t-t') \|_s \, dt' \right)^2 \leq \left(\int_0^T \| F(t) \|_{H_x^s(\mathbb{R})} dt' \right)^2, \text{ (by (42))} \\
&\leq \left(\int_0^T \sup_{t\in[0,T]} \| F(t) \|_{H_x^s(\mathbb{R})} dt' \right)^2 = \left(T \sup_{t\in[0,T]} \| F(t) \|_{H_x^s(\mathbb{R})} \right)^2,
\end{aligned} \tag{62}
$$

and

$$
\begin{aligned}
(F) &= \int_0^T \int_0^{T-t} \frac{1}{\zeta^{1+2s}} \bigg| \int_t^{t+\zeta} \widetilde{S_1}[0,F;0](x,t+\zeta-t') dt' \bigg|^2 d\zeta dt \\
&= \int_0^T \int_0^{T-t} \frac{1}{\zeta^{1+2s}} \bigg| \int_t^{t+\zeta} \left(\frac{1}{2\pi} \int_{-\infty}^{\infty} \frac{e^{ikx}}{2i|k|} \widehat{F}(k,t') \Big(e^{i|k|(t+\zeta-t')} - e^{-i|k|(t+\zeta-t')} \Big) dk \right) dt' \bigg|^2 d\zeta dt \\
&\leq \int_0^T \int_0^{T-t} \frac{1}{\zeta^{1+2s}} \left\| \frac{1}{2\pi} \int_t^{t+\zeta} \int_{-\infty}^{\infty} \frac{e^{ikx} \widehat{F}(k,t') \Big(e^{i|k|(t+\zeta-t')} - e^{-i|k|(t+\zeta-t')} \Big)}{2i|k|} dk dt' \right\|_{L_x^\infty(\mathbb{R})}^2 d\zeta dt \\
&\quad \left(\text{since } s > \frac{1}{2}, \text{ by Theorem 5 (the Sobolev Embedding Theorem)}\right) \\
&\leq \int_0^T \int_0^{T-t} \frac{1}{\zeta^{1+2s}} \left\| \frac{1}{2\pi} \int_t^{t+\zeta} \int_{-\infty}^{\infty} \frac{e^{ikx} \widehat{F}(k,t') \Big(e^{i|k|(t+\zeta-t')} - e^{-i|k|(t+\zeta-t')} \Big)}{2i|k|} dk dt' \right\|_{H_x^s(\mathbb{R})}^2 d\zeta dt \\
&= \int_0^T \int_0^{T-t} \frac{1}{\zeta^{1+2s}} \left\| \frac{1}{2\pi} \int_{-\infty}^{\infty} e^{ikx} \frac{\int_t^{t+\zeta} \widehat{F}(k,t') \Big(e^{i|k|(t+\zeta-t')} - e^{-i|k|(t+\zeta-t')} \Big) dt'}{2i|k|} dk \right\|_{H_x^s(\mathbb{R})}^2 d\zeta dt \\
&= \int_0^T \int_0^{T-t} \frac{1}{\zeta^{1+2s}} \left(\int_{\mathbb{R}} \Big(1+k^2\Big)^s \left| \frac{\int_t^{t+\zeta} \widehat{F}(k,t') \Big(e^{i|k|(t+\zeta-t')} - e^{-i|k|(t+\zeta-t')} \Big) dt'}{2i|k|} \right|^2 dk \right) d\zeta dt \\
&\quad \text{(by Theorem 3 and Theorem 4)}
\end{aligned}
$$

$$
\begin{aligned}
&= \int_0^T \int_0^{T-t} \frac{1}{\zeta^{1+2s}} \left(\int_{\mathbb{R}} \left(1+k^2\right)^s \left| \frac{1}{2i|k|} \int_t^{t+\zeta} \widehat{F}(k,t')\left(2i\sin\left(|k|(t+\zeta-t')\right)\right)dt' \right|^2 dk \right) d\zeta dt \\
&\le \int_0^T \int_0^{T-t} \frac{1}{\zeta^{1+2s}} \left(\int_{\mathbb{R}} \left(1+k^2\right)^s \left(\frac{1}{2|k|} \int_t^{t+\zeta} \left|\widehat{F}(k,t')\right| \cdot 2|k|(t+\zeta-t')dt' \right)^2 dk \right) d\zeta dt \\
&= \int_0^T \int_0^{T-t} \frac{1}{\zeta^{1+2s}} \left(\int_{\mathbb{R}} \left(1+k^2\right)^s \left(\int_t^{t+\zeta} \left|\widehat{F}(k,t')\right| (t+\zeta-t')dt' \right)^2 dk \right) d\zeta dt \\
&\le \int_0^T \int_0^{T-t} \frac{1}{\zeta^{1+2s}} \left(\int_t^{t+\zeta} \left(\int_{\mathbb{R}} \left(1+k^2\right)^s \left|\widehat{F}(k,t')\right|^2 (t+\zeta-t')^2 dk \right)^{\frac{1}{2}} dt' \right)^2 d\zeta dt
\end{aligned}
$$

(by Lemma 3 (Minkowski integral inequality))

$$
\begin{aligned}
&\le \int_0^T \int_0^{T-t} \frac{1}{\zeta^{1+2s}} \left(\int_t^{t+\zeta} (t+\zeta-t') \left(\int_{\mathbb{R}} \left(1+k^2\right)^s \left|\widehat{F}(k,t')\right|^2 dk \right)^{\frac{1}{2}} dt' \right)^2 d\zeta dt \\
&= \int_0^T \int_0^{T-t} \frac{1}{\zeta^{1+2s}} \left(\int_t^{t+\zeta} (t+\zeta-t') \parallel F(t') \parallel_{H_x^s(\mathbb{R})} dt' \right)^2 d\zeta dt \\
&= \sup_{t' \in [t,t+\zeta]} \parallel F(t') \parallel^2_{H_x^s(\mathbb{R})} \left(\int_0^T \int_0^{T-t} \zeta^{3-2s} d\zeta dt \right) \\
&\lesssim \sup_{t' \in [t,t+\zeta]} \parallel F(t') \parallel^2_{H_x^s(\mathbb{R})} T^{5-2s} \le \sup_{t' \in [0,T]} \parallel F(t') \parallel^2_{H_x^s(\mathbb{R})} T, \text{ (for } T<1).
\end{aligned}
$$

Consequently, we obtain the following inequality:

$$
(F) \lesssim T \sup_{t \in [0,T]} \parallel F(t) \parallel^2_{H_x^s(\mathbb{R})} . \tag{63}
$$

By (60), (62) and (63), we derive (57):

$$
\begin{aligned}
&\parallel W(x) \parallel^2_{H_t^s(0,T)} \lesssim \left(T \sup_{t \in [0,T]} \parallel F(t) \parallel^2_{H_x^s(\mathbb{R})} \right) \\
&\Longrightarrow \sup_{x \in [0,\infty)} \parallel W(x) \parallel_{H_t^s(0,T)} \lesssim \sqrt{T} \sup_{t \in [0,T]} \parallel F(t) \parallel_{H_x^s(\mathbb{R})}, \text{ for } \frac{1}{2} < s < 1 \text{ and } 0 < T < 1.
\end{aligned}
$$

Ultimately, by employing a similar proof strategy as in (57), we establish (58):

$$
\sup_{x \in [0,\infty)} \parallel W_1(x) \parallel_{H_t^{s-1}(0,T)} \lesssim \sqrt{T} \sup_{t \in [0,T]} \parallel F(t) \parallel_{H_x^s(0,T)}, \text{ for } \frac{3}{2} < s < 2 \text{ and } T < 1.
$$

We finish this proof of Theorem 8. □

4.3. *About the Proof of Therorem 1*

By applying the superposition principle, we can synthesize Theorem 6, Theorem 7, and Theorem 8 to derive Theorem 1 for the forced linear IVPs (6) and (7). Additionally, we incorporate the following time estimates:

$$\begin{aligned}\| G_0 \|_{H_t^{s-1}(0,T)} &= \| \gamma_1(t) - U_x(0,t) - W_x(0,t) \|_{H_t^{s-1}(0,T)} \\ &\leq \| \gamma_1(t) \|_{H_t^{s-1}(0,T)} + \| U_x(0,t) \|_{H_t^{s-1}(0,T)} \\ &\quad + \| W_x(0,t) \|_{H_t^{s-1}(0,T)}\end{aligned} \tag{64}$$

and

$$\begin{aligned}\| H_0 \|_{H_t^{s-1}(0,T)} &= \| \varpi_1 U(0,t) + \varpi_1 W(0,t) \|_{H_t^{s-1}(0,T)} \\ &\leq \varpi_1 \| U(0,t) \|_{H_t^{s-1}(0,T)} + \varpi_1 \| W(0,t) \|_{H_t^{s-1}(0,T)} .\end{aligned} \tag{65}$$

Thus, we need to estimate $\| U_x(0,t) \|_{H_t^{s-1}(0,T)}$ and $\| W_x(0,t) \|_{H_t^{s-1}(0,T)}$.

Lemma 4. *(Sobolev-type estimates) For $\frac{1}{2} < s < 1$, we obtain the following estimates:*

$$\sup_{x \in [0,\infty)} \| U_x(x) \|_{H_t^{s-1}(0,T)} \lesssim \| U_0 \|_{H_x^s(\mathbb{R})} + \| U_* \|_{H_x^s(\mathbb{R})} \tag{66}$$

and

$$\sup_{x \in [0,\infty)} \| W_x(x) \|_{H_t^{s-1}(0,T)} \lesssim \sqrt{T} \sup_{t \in [0,T]} \| F(t) \|_{H_x^s(\mathbb{R})} . \tag{67}$$

Proof. First, we begin the proof of (66). From Equation (30), we have

$$\begin{aligned}U(x,t) &= \frac{1}{2\pi} \int_{-\infty}^{0} \frac{e^{ikx}}{-2ik} \Big(\Big(e^{ikt} + e^{-ikt} \Big) \Big(-ik\widehat{U}_0(k) \Big) + \Big(e^{-ikt} - e^{ikt} \Big) \widehat{U}_*(k) \Big) dk \\ &\quad + \frac{1}{2\pi} \int_{0}^{\infty} \frac{e^{ikx}}{2ik} \Big(\Big(e^{-ikt} + e^{ikt} \Big) \Big(ik\widehat{U}_0(k) \Big) + \Big(e^{ikt} - e^{-ikt} \Big) \widehat{U}_*(k) \Big) dk.\end{aligned}$$

Thus, we obtain that

$$\begin{aligned}U_x(x,t) &= \frac{1}{2\pi} \int_{-\infty}^{0} e^{ikt} \Big(\frac{1}{2}(ik) e^{ikx} \widehat{U}_0(k) + \frac{1}{2} e^{ikx} \widehat{U}_*(k) \Big) dk \\ &\quad + \frac{1}{2\pi} \int_{-\infty}^{0} e^{-ikt} \Big(\frac{1}{2}(ik) e^{ikx} \widehat{U}_0(k) - \frac{1}{2} e^{ikx} \widehat{U}_*(k) \Big) dk \\ &\quad + \frac{1}{2\pi} \int_{0}^{\infty} e^{ikt} \Big(\frac{1}{2}(ik) e^{ikx} \widehat{U}_0(k) + \frac{1}{2} e^{ikx} \widehat{U}_*(k) \Big) dk \\ &\quad + \frac{1}{2\pi} \int_{0}^{\infty} e^{-ikt} \Big(\frac{1}{2}(ik) e^{ikx} \widehat{U}_0(k) - \frac{1}{2} e^{ikx} \widehat{U}_*(k) \Big) dk.\end{aligned}$$

According to Theorem 3, the estimation of $\| U_x(x) \|^2_{H_t^{s-1}(0,T)}$ is

$$
\begin{aligned}
\| U_x(x) \|^2_{H_t^{s-1}(0,T)} &\leq \| U_x(x) \|^2_{H_t^{s-1}(\mathbb{R})} \\
&\lesssim \| \frac{1}{2\pi} \int_{-\infty}^{0} e^{ikt} \left(\frac{1}{2}(ik) e^{ikx} \widehat{U}_0(k) + \frac{1}{2} e^{ikx} \widehat{U}_*(k) \right) dk \|^2_{H_t^{s-1}(\mathbb{R})} \\
&\quad + \| \frac{1}{2\pi} \int_{-\infty}^{0} e^{-ikt} \left(\frac{1}{2}(ik) e^{ikx} \widehat{U}_0(k) - \frac{1}{2} e^{ikx} \widehat{U}_*(k) \right) dk \|^2_{H_t^{s-1}(\mathbb{R})} \\
&\quad + \| \frac{1}{2\pi} \int_{0}^{\infty} e^{ikt} \left(\frac{1}{2} ik e^{ikx} \widehat{U}_0(k) + \frac{1}{2} e^{ikx} \widehat{U}_*(k) \right) dk \|^2_{H_t^{s-1}(\mathbb{R})} \\
&\quad + \| \frac{1}{2\pi} \int_{0}^{\infty} e^{-ikt} \left(\frac{1}{2} ik e^{ikx} \widehat{U}_0(k) - \frac{1}{2} e^{ikx} \widehat{U}_*(k) \right) dk \|^2_{H_t^{s-1}(\mathbb{R})} \\
&\leq \int_{\mathbb{R}} \left(1+k^2\right)^{s-1} \left| \frac{1}{2}(ik) e^{ikx} \widehat{U}_0(k) + \frac{1}{2} e^{ikx} \widehat{U}_*(k) \right|^2 dk \\
&\quad + \int_{\mathbb{R}} \left(1+k^2\right)^{s-1} \left| -\frac{1}{2} ik e^{-ikx} \widehat{U}_0(-k) - \frac{1}{2} e^{-ikx} \widehat{U}_*(-k) \right|^2 dk \\
&\quad + \int_{\mathbb{R}} \left(1+k^2\right)^{s-1} \left| \frac{1}{2} ik e^{ikx} \widehat{U}_0(k) + \frac{1}{2} e^{ikx} \widehat{U}_*(k) \right|^2 dk \\
&\quad + \int_{\mathbb{R}} \left(1+k^2\right)^{s-1} \left| -\frac{1}{2} ik e^{-ikx} \widehat{U}_0(-k) - \frac{1}{2} e^{-ikx} \widehat{U}_*(-k) \right|^2 dk \\
&\leq \int_{\mathbb{R}} \left(1+k^2\right)^{s-1} k^2 \left| \widehat{U}_0(k) \right|^2 dk + \int_{\mathbb{R}} \left(1+k^2\right)^{s-1} \left| \widehat{U}_*(k) \right|^2 dk \\
&\quad + \int_{\mathbb{R}} \left(1+k^2\right)^{s-1} k^2 \left| \widehat{U}_0(-k) \right|^2 dk + \int_{\mathbb{R}} \left(1+k^2\right)^{s-1} \left| \widehat{U}_*(-k) \right|^2 dk \\
&\quad + \int_{\mathbb{R}} \left(1+k^2\right)^{s-1} k^2 \left| \widehat{U}_0(k) \right|^2 dk + \int_{\mathbb{R}} \left(1+k^2\right)^{s-1} \left| \widehat{U}_*(k) \right|^2 dk \\
&\quad + \int_{\mathbb{R}} \left(1+k^2\right)^{s-1} k^2 \left| \widehat{U}_0(-k) \right|^2 dk + \int_{\mathbb{R}} \left(1+k^2\right)^{s-1} \left| \widehat{U}_*(-k) \right|^2 dk \\
&\lesssim \int_{\mathbb{R}} \left(1+k^2\right)^{s} \left| \widehat{U}_0(k) \right|^2 dk + \int_{\mathbb{R}} \left(1+k^2\right)^{s} \left| \widehat{U}_*(k) \right|^2 dk \\
&= \| U_0 \|^2_{H_x^s(\mathbb{R})} + \| U_* \|^2_{H_x^s(\mathbb{R})} .
\end{aligned}
$$

Consequently, we obtain the following inequality:

$$
\| U_x(x) \|^2_{H_t^{s-1}(0,T)} \lesssim \| U_0 \|^2_{H_x^s(\mathbb{R})} + \| U_* \|^2_{H_x^s(\mathbb{R})},
$$

and then we derive the following inequality (66):

$$
\sup_{x \in [0,\infty)} \| U_x(x) \|_{H_t^{s-1}(0,T)} \lesssim \left(\| U_0 \|_{H_x^s(\mathbb{R})} + \| U_* \|_{H_x^s(\mathbb{R})} \right).
$$

Next, we begin the proof of (67). We will consider Equation (59):

$$
W(x,t) = \widetilde{S_1}[0,0;F](x,t) = \frac{1}{2\pi} \int_0^t \int_{-\infty}^{\infty} \frac{e^{ikx}}{2i|k|} \widehat{F}(k,t') \left(e^{i|k|(t-t')} - e^{-i|k|(t-t')} \right) dk dt',
$$

and then, we derive that

$$
W_x(x,t) = \frac{1}{2\pi} \int_0^t \int_{-\infty}^{\infty} \frac{ik}{2i|k|} e^{ikx} \widehat{F}(k,t') \left(e^{i|k|(t-t')} - e^{-i|k|(t-t')} \right) dk dt'.
$$

The estimation of $\| W_x(x,t) \|_{H_t^s(\mathbb{R})}$ is

$$
\begin{aligned}
\| W_x(x,t) \|_{H_t^s(\mathbb{R})} &\leq \int_0^T \| \frac{1}{2\pi} \int_{-\infty}^{\infty} \frac{ik}{2i|k|} e^{ikx} \widehat{F}(k,t') \left(e^{i|k|(t-t')} - e^{-i|k|(t-t')} \right) dk \|_{H_t^s(\mathbb{R})} dt' \\
&= \int_0^T \| \frac{1}{2\pi} \int_{-\infty}^{0} \frac{-1}{2} e^{ikx} \widehat{F}(k,t') \left(e^{i|k|(t-t')} - e^{-i|k|(t-t')} \right) dk \\
&\quad + \frac{1}{2\pi} \int_0^{\infty} \frac{1}{2} e^{ikx} \widehat{F}(k,t') \left(e^{i|k|(t-t')} - e^{-i|k|(t-t')} \right) dk \|_{H_t^s(\mathbb{R})} dt' \\
&\leq \int_0^T \| \frac{1}{2\pi} \int_{-\infty}^{0} e^{-ikt} e^{ikx} e^{ikt'} \widehat{F}(k,t') dk \|_{H_t^s(\mathbb{R})} dt' \\
&\quad + \int_0^T \| \frac{1}{2\pi} \int_{-\infty}^{0} e^{ikt} e^{ikx} e^{-ikt'} \widehat{F}(k,t') dk \|_{H_t^s(\mathbb{R})} dt' \\
&\quad + \int_0^T \| \frac{1}{2\pi} \int_0^{\infty} e^{ikt} e^{ikx} e^{-ikt'} \widehat{F}(k,t') dk \|_{H_t^s(\mathbb{R})} dt' \\
&\quad + \int_0^T \| \frac{1}{2\pi} \int_0^{\infty} e^{-ikt} e^{ikx} e^{ikt'} \widehat{F}(k,t') dk \|_{H_t^s(\mathbb{R})} dt' \\
&= \int_0^T \| \frac{1}{2\pi} \int_0^{\infty} e^{ikt} e^{-ikx} e^{-ikt'} \widehat{F}(-k,t') dk \|_{H_t^s(\mathbb{R})} dt' \\
&\quad + \int_0^T \| \frac{1}{2\pi} \int_{-\infty}^{0} e^{ikt} e^{ikx} e^{-ikt'} \widehat{F}(k,t') dk \|_{H_t^s(\mathbb{R})} dt' \\
&\quad + \int_0^T \| \frac{1}{2\pi} \int_0^{\infty} e^{ikt} e^{ikx} e^{-ikt'} \widehat{F}(k,t') dk \|_{H_t^s(\mathbb{R})} dt' \\
&\quad + \int_0^T \| \frac{1}{2\pi} \int_{-\infty}^{0} e^{ikt} e^{-ikx} e^{-ikt'} \widehat{F}(-k,t') dk \|_{H_t^s(\mathbb{R})} dt' \\
&\leq \int_0^T \left(\int_{-\infty}^{\infty} \left(1+k^2\right)^s \left| e^{-ikx} e^{-ikt'} \widehat{F}(-k,t') \right|^2 dk \right)^{\frac{1}{2}} dt' \\
&\quad + \int_0^T \left(\int_{-\infty}^{\infty} \left(1+k^2\right)^s \left| e^{ikx} e^{-ikt'} \widehat{F}(k,t') \right|^2 dk \right)^{\frac{1}{2}} dt' \\
&\quad + \int_0^T \left(\int_{-\infty}^{\infty} \left(1+k^2\right)^s \left| e^{ikx} e^{-ikt'} \widehat{F}(k,t') \right|^2 dk \right)^{\frac{1}{2}} dt' \\
&\quad + \int_0^T \left(\int_{-\infty}^{\infty} \left(1+k^2\right)^s \left| e^{-ikx} e^{-ikt'} \widehat{F}(-k,t') \right|^2 dk \right)^{\frac{1}{2}} dt', \\
&\quad \text{(by Theorem 3 and Theorem 4)} \\
&= 4 \int_0^T \| F(t') \|_{H_x^s(\mathbb{R})} dt' \lesssim T \sup_{t \in [0,T]} \| F(t) \|_{H_x^s(\mathbb{R})} \leq \sqrt{T} \sup_{t \in [0,T]} \| F(t) \|_{H_x^s(\mathbb{R})} .
\end{aligned}
$$

Consequently, we obtain the following inequality:

$$\| W_x(x,t) \|_{H_t^s(\mathbb{R})} \lesssim \sqrt{T} \sup_{t \in [0,T]} \| F(t) \|_{H_x^s(\mathbb{R})} .$$

Since the inequality

$$\| W_x(x,t) \|_{H_t^{s-1}(\mathbb{R})} \leq \| W_x(x,t) \|_{H_t^s(\mathbb{R})},$$

we obtain the inequality

$$\| W_x(x,t) \|_{H_t^{s-1}(\mathbb{R})} \lesssim \sqrt{T} \sup_{t \in [0,T]} \| F(t) \|_{H_x^s(\mathbb{R})} .$$

As a result, we establish the inequality (67) as follows:

$$\sup_{x\in[0,\infty)} \| W_x(x,t) \|_{H_t^{s-1}(0,T)} \lesssim \sqrt{T} \sup_{t\in[0,T]} \| F(t) \|_{H_x^s(\mathbb{R})} .$$

We finish this proof of Lemma 4. □

Now, by applying Lemma 4 to Formulas (64) and (65), we derive the following inequalities:

$$\begin{aligned}
\| G_0 \|_{H_t^{s-1}(0,T)} &\leq \| \gamma_1(t) \|_{H_t^{s-1}(0,T)} + \| U_x(0,t) \|_{H_t^{s-1}(0,T)} + \| W_x(0,t) \|_{H_t^{s-1}(0,T)} \\
&\lesssim \| \gamma_1(t) \|_{H_t^{s-1}(0,T)} + \left(\| U_0 \|_{H_x^s(\mathbb{R})} + \| U_* \|_{H_x^s(\mathbb{R})} \right) + \sqrt{T} \sup_{t\in[0,T]} \| F(t) \|_{H_x^s(\mathbb{R})} \\
&\quad \text{(by (66) and (67))} \\
&\lesssim \| u_0 \|_{H_x^s(0,\infty)} + \| u_* \|_{H_x^s(0,\infty)} + \| \gamma_1 \|_{H_t^{s-1}(0,T)} + \sqrt{T} \sup_{t\in[0,T]} \| f(t) \|_{H_x^s(0,\infty)} \\
&\quad \text{(by (26)–(28))},
\end{aligned}$$

and

$$\begin{aligned}
\| H_0 \|_{H_t^{s-1}(0,T)} &\leq \varpi_1 \| U(0,t) \|_{H_t^{s-1}(0,T)} + \varpi_1 \| W(0,t) \|_{H_t^{s-1}(0,T)} \\
&\leq \varpi_1 \| U(0,t) \|_{H_t^{s}(0,T)} + \varpi_1 \| W(0,t) \|_{H_t^{s}(0,T)} \\
&\leq \varpi_1 \left(\| U_0 \|_{H_x^s(\mathbb{R})} + \| U_* \|_{H_x^s(\mathbb{R})} \right) + \varpi_1 \left(\sqrt{T} \sup_{t\in[0,T]} \| F(t) \|_{H_x^s(\mathbb{R})} \right) \\
&\quad \text{(by (42) and (57))} \\
&\lesssim \| u_0 \|_{H_x^s(0,\infty)} + \| u_* \|_{H_x^s(0,\infty)} + \sqrt{T} \sup_{t\in[0,T]} \| f(t) \|_{H_x^s(0,\infty)} \\
&\quad \text{(by (26)–(28))}.
\end{aligned}$$

According to Equation (39),

$$S_1[u_0,u_*,\gamma_1;f](x,t) = \widetilde{S_1}[U_0,U_*;0]|_{x>0} + \widetilde{S_1}[0,0;F]|_{x>0} + S_1[0,0,G_0;0](x,t) + S_1[0,0,H_0;0](x,t),$$

we obtain the following inequality:

$$\begin{aligned}
&\sup_{t\in[0,T]} \| S_1[u_0,u_*,\gamma_1;f](x,t) \|_{H_x^s(0,\infty)} \\
&\leq \sup_{t\in[0,T]} \| \widetilde{S_1}[U_0,U_*;0](t) \|_{H_x^s(0,\infty)} + \sup_{t\in[0,T]} \| \widetilde{S_1}[0,0;F](t) \|_{H_x^s(0,\infty)} \\
&\quad + \sup_{t\in[0,T]} \| S_1[0,0,G_0;0](t) \|_{H_x^s(0,\infty)} + \sup_{t\in[0,T]} \| S_1[0,0,H_0;0](t) \|_{H_x^s(0,\infty)} \\
&\lesssim \| U_0 \|_{H_x^s(\mathbb{R})} + \| U_* \|_{H_x^s(\mathbb{R})} + T \sup_{t\in[0,T]} \| F(t) \|_{H_x^s(\mathbb{R})} + \| G_0(t) \|_{H_t^{s-1}(0,T)} + \| H_0(t) \|_{H_t^{s-1}(0,T)} \\
&\quad \text{(by (18), (22), (40) and (55))} \\
&\lesssim \| u_0 \|_{H_x^s(0,\infty)} + \| u_* \|_{H_x^s(0,\infty)} + T \sup_{t\in[0,T]} \| f(t) \|_{H_x^s(0,\infty)} + \| \gamma_1 \|_{H_t^{s-1}(0,T)} \\
&\quad + \sqrt{T} \sup_{t\in[0,T]} \| f(t) \|_{H_x^s(0,\infty)} \quad \text{(by (26)–(28) and (64)–(67))} \\
&\lesssim \| u_0 \|_{H_x^s(0,\infty)} + \| u_* \|_{H_x^s(0,\infty)} + \| \gamma_1 \|_{H_t^{s-1}(0,T)} + \sqrt{T} \sup_{t\in[0,T]} \| f(t) \|_{H_x^s(0,\infty)} .
\end{aligned}$$

Consequently, we obtain the following inequality:

$$\sup_{t\in[0,T]} \| u(t) \|_{H_x^s(0,\infty)} \lesssim \| u_0 \|_{H_x^s(0,\infty)} + \| u_* \|_{H_x^s(0,\infty)} + \| \gamma_1 \|_{H_t^{s-1}(0,T)} + \sqrt{T} \sup_{t\in[0,T]} \| f(t) \|_{H_x^s(0,\infty)}, \tag{68}$$

and

$$\begin{aligned}
&\sup_{x\in[0,\infty)} \| S_1[u_0,u_*,\gamma_1;f](x,t) \|_{H_t^s(0,T)} \\
&\leq \sup_{x\in[0,\infty)} \| \widetilde{S}_1[U_0,U_*;0](x) \|_{H_t^s(0,T)} + \sup_{x\in[0,\infty)} \| \widetilde{S}_1[0,0;F](x) \|_{H_t^s(0,T)} \\
&\quad + \sup_{x\in[0,\infty)} \| S_1[0,0,G_0;0](x) \|_{H_t^s(0,T)} + \sup_{x\in[0,\infty)} \| S_1[0,0,H_0;0](x) \|_{H_t^s(0,T)} \\
&\lesssim \| U_0 \|_{H_x^s(\mathbb{R})} + \| U_* \|_{H_x^s(\mathbb{R})} + \sqrt{T} \sup_{t\in[0,T]} \| F(t) \|_{H_x^s(\mathbb{R})} + \| G_0(t) \|_{H_t^{s-1}(0,T)} \\
&\quad + \| H_0(t) \|_{H_t^{s-1}(0,T)} \ \text{(by (18), (24), (42) and (57))} \\
&\lesssim \| u_0 \|_{H_x^s(0,\infty)} + \| u_* \|_{H_x^s(0,\infty)} + \| \gamma_1 \|_{H_t^{s-1}(0,T)} + \sqrt{T} \sup_{t\in[0,T]} \| f(t) \|_{H_x^s(0,\infty)}
\end{aligned}$$

(by (26)–(28), (42), (57), (66) and (67)).

Therefore, we derive the following inequality:

$$\sup_{x\in[0,\infty)} \| u(x) \|_{H_t^s(0,T)} \lesssim \| u_0 \|_{H_x^s(0,\infty)} + \| u_* \|_{H_x^s(0,\infty)} + \| \gamma_1 \|_{H_t^{s-1}(0,T)} + \sqrt{T} \sup_{t\in[0,T]} \| f(t) \|_{H_x^s(0,\infty)} . \tag{69}$$

We combine Equations (68) and (69) and establish the following inequality (13):

$$\begin{aligned}
&\sup_{t\in[0,T]} \| u(t) \|_{H_x^s(0,\infty)} + \sup_{x\in[0,\infty)} \| u(x) \|_{H_t^s(0,T)} \\
&\leq C_s \left(\| u_0 \|_{H_x^s(0,\infty)} + \| u_* \|_{H_x^s(0,\infty)} + \| \gamma_1 \|_{H_t^{s-1}(0,T)} + \sqrt{T} \sup_{t\in[0,T]} \| f(t) \|_{H_x^s(0,\infty)} \right),
\end{aligned}$$

where $C_s > 0$ is a constant depending on s.

By employing a similar proof strategy as in (13), we can derive the inequality (14) below:

$$\begin{aligned}
&\sup_{t\in[0,T]} \| v(t) \|_{H_x^s(0,\infty)} + \sup_{x\in[0,\infty)} \| v(x) \|_{H_t^s(0,T)} \\
&\leq d_s \left(\| v_0 \|_{H_x^s(0,\infty)} + \| v_* \|_{H_x^s(0,\infty)} + \| \gamma_2 \|_{H_t^{s-1}(0,T)} + \sqrt{T} \sup_{t\in[0,T]} \| g(t) \|_{H_x^s(0,\infty)} \right),
\end{aligned}$$

where $d_s > 0$ is a constant depending on s. We finish this proof of Theorem 1.

Now, by applying Theorem 1 and combining the results from Equations (13) and (14), we obtain that

$$\begin{aligned}
&\sup_{t\in[0,T]} \| u(t) \|_{H_x^s(0,\infty)} + \sup_{x\in[0,\infty)} \| u(x) \|_{H_t^s(0,T)} + \sup_{t\in[0,T]} \| v(t) \|_{H_x^s(0,\infty)} + \sup_{x\in[0,\infty)} \| v(x) \|_{H_t^s(0,T)} \\
&\leq C_s^* \Big(\| u_0 \|_{H_x^s(0,\infty)} + \| u_* \|_{H_x^s(0,\infty)} + \| v_0 \|_{H_x^s(0,\infty)} + \| v_* \|_{H_x^s(0,\infty)} + \| \gamma_1 \|_{H_t^{s-1}(0,T)} \\
&\quad + \| \gamma_2 \|_{H_t^{s-1}(0,T)} + \sqrt{T} \sup_{t\in[0,T]} \| f(t) \|_{H_x^s(0,\infty)} + \sqrt{T} \sup_{t\in[0,T]} \| g(t) \|_{H_x^s(0,\infty)} \Big),
\end{aligned} \tag{70}$$

where $C_s^* = \max\{C_s, d_s\}$.

5. The Proof of Therorem 2 (about the Local Well-Posedness of the Coupled System of Wave Equations in Sobolev Spaces)

In this section, we begin by introducing the iteration map. Following this, Lemma 5 and Lemma 6 are presented to demonstrate that the iteration map is both a contraction and a self-map on a closed ball. By applying the contraction mapping theorem, we prove the uniqueness of the solution. Additionally, Lemma 7 establishes that the data-to-solution map is locally Lipschitz continuous. By leveraging these results, we conclude the proof of Theorem 2.

5.1. *Existence and Uniqueness*

In this subsection, we prove the existence and uniqueness of the solution for (1).

First, for $0 < T < 1$ and some $T^* \in (0,T)$, we set $f = u^2v$ and $g = uv^2$ in (9) and (11), respectively. And then, for data $D_1 = (u_0, u_*, v_0, v_*, \gamma_1, \gamma_2)$, we define the iteration map $(u,v) \longmapsto \mathcal{F}_{D_1}(u,v) \doteq (\Phi_{T^*}(u,v), \Psi_{T^*}(u,v))$, which is derived from Formulas (9) and (11) for the forced-linear wave-equation IBVPs (6) and (7). More precisely, we have

$$\Phi_{T^*}(u,v) \doteq S_1[u_0, u_*, \gamma_1; u^2v], \quad \Psi_{T^*}(u,v) \doteq S_1[v_0, v_*, \gamma_2; uv^2].$$

We will demonstrate that the iteration map

$$\mathcal{F}_{D_1}(u,v) \doteq (\Phi_{T^*}(u,v), \Psi_{T^*}(u,v)) = \Big(S_1[u_0, u_*, \gamma_1; u^2v], S_1[v_0, v_*, \gamma_2; uv^2]\Big)$$

is a contraction in the Banach space

$$X = (C([0,T^*]; H_x^s(0,\infty)) \cap C([0,\infty); H_t^s(0,T^*)))^2, \tag{71}$$

with the norm

$$\begin{aligned} \| (u,v) \|_X = & \sup_{t\in[0,T^*]} \| u(t) \|_{H_x^s(0,\infty)} + \sup_{x\in[0,\infty)} \| u(x) \|_{H_t^s(0,T^*)} \\ & + \sup_{t\in[0,T^*]} \| v(t) \|_{H_x^s(0,\infty)} + \sup_{x\in[0,\infty)} \| v(x) \|_{H_t^s(0,T^*)} . \end{aligned}$$

Next, we begin to prove that the map $(u,v) \longmapsto \mathcal{F}_{D_1}(u,v)$ is onto X. We consider a closed ball $B(0,r) = \{(u,v) \in X : \| (u,v) \|_X \le r\}$, where

$$C_s^* = \max\{C_s, d_s\}, \; r \doteq 2C_s^* \| (u_0, u_*, v_0, v_*, \gamma_1, \gamma_2) \|_D$$

and

$$\begin{aligned} \| (u_0, u_*, v_0, v_*, \gamma_1, \gamma_2) \|_D = & \| u_0 \|_{H_x^s(0,\infty)} + \| u_* \|_{H_x^s(0,\infty)} + \| v_0 \|_{H_x^s(0,\infty)} \\ & + \| v_* \|_{H_x^s(0,\infty)} + \| \gamma_1 \|_{H_t^{s-1}(0,T)} + \| \gamma_2 \|_{H_t^{s-1}(0,T)} . \end{aligned} \tag{72}$$

In the next lemma, we determine the condition on T^* under which $\mathcal{F}_{D_1}$ maps onto $B(0,r)$.

Lemma 5. *Let $C_s^* = \max\{C_s, d_s\}$ and $r = 2C_s^* \| (u_0, u_*, v_0, v_*, \gamma_1, \gamma_2) \|_D$. If the following condition for T^* given by*

$$0 < T^* \le \min\left\{T, \frac{1}{256(C_s^*)^{10} \| (u_0, u_*, v_0, v_*, \gamma_1, \gamma_2) \|_D^4}\right\} \tag{73}$$

is satisfied, then the iteration map $\mathcal{F}_{D_1}$ is onto $B(0,r)$.

Proof. For $(u,v) \in B(0,r)$, the following inequality holds:

$$
\begin{aligned}
&\| \mathcal{F}_{D_1}(u,v) \|_X = \| \left(S_1[u_0,u_*,\gamma_1;u^2v], S_1[v_0,v_*,\gamma_2;uv^2] \right) \|_X \\
&= \sup_{t\in[0,T^*]} \| S_1[u_0,u_*,\gamma_1;u^2v](t) \|_{H^s_x(0,\infty)} + \sup_{x\in[0,\infty)} \| S_1[u_0,u_*,\gamma_1;u^2v](x) \|_{H^s_t(0,T^*)} \\
&\quad + \sup_{t\in[0,T^*]} \| S_1[v_0,v_*,\gamma_2;uv^2](t) \|_{H^s_x(0,\infty)} + \sup_{x\in[0,\infty)} \| S_1[v_0,v_*,\gamma_2;uv^2](x) \|_{H^s_t(0,T^*)} \\
&\le C_s^* \Big(\| u_0 \|_{H^s_x(0,\infty)} + \| u_* \|_{H^s_x(0,\infty)} + \| v_0 \|_{H^s_x(0,\infty)} + \| v_* \|_{H^s_x(0,\infty)} + \| \gamma_1 \|_{H^{s-1}_t(0,T)} \\
&\quad + \| \gamma_2 \|_{H^{s-1}_t(0,T)} + \sqrt{T^*} \sup_{t\in[0,T^*]} \| u^2v \|_{H^s_x(0,\infty)} + \sqrt{T^*} \sup_{t\in[0,T^*]} \| uv^2 \|_{H^s_x(0,\infty)} \Big), \text{ (by (70))} \\
&= \frac{r}{2} + C_s^* \sqrt{T^*} \left(\sup_{t\in[0,T^*]} \| u^2v \|_{H^s_x(0,\infty)} + \sup_{t\in[0,T^*]} \| uv^2 \|_{H^s_x(0,\infty)} \right) \\
&\le \frac{r}{2} + C_s^* \sqrt{T^*} \left(C_s^2 r^3 + C_s^2 r^3 \right), \text{ (by Lemma 2)} \\
&\le \frac{r}{2} + 2(C_s^*)^3 \sqrt{T^*} r^3.
\end{aligned}
$$

Hence, we obtain the inequality

$$
\| \mathcal{F}_{D_1}(u,v) \|_X \le \frac{r}{2} + 2(C_s^*)^3 \sqrt{T^*} r^3.
$$

For $0 < T^* \le T$, in order to prove that $\mathcal{F}_{D_1}$ is onto on $B(0,r)$, we aim for the following inequality to hold:

$$
\frac{r}{2} + 2(C_s^*)^3 \sqrt{T^*} r^3 \le r,
$$

which is equivalent to

$$
0 < T^* \le \frac{1}{256(C_s^*)^{10} \| (u_0,u_*,v_0,v_*,\gamma_1,\gamma_2) \|_D^4}.
$$

Thus, when T^* satisfies the following condition (73):

$$
0 < T^* \le \min\left\{ T, \frac{1}{256(C_s^*)^{10} \| (u_0,u_*,v_0,v_*,\gamma_1,\gamma_2) \|_D^4} \right\},
$$

it follows that $\mathcal{F}_{D_1}$ is onto $B(0,r)$. □

Now, we begin to prove that the map $(u,v) \longmapsto \mathcal{F}_{D_1}(u,v)$ is a contraction in X. We establish the constraint on T^* such that $\mathcal{F}_{D_1}$ is a contraction on $B(0,r)$, for $C_s^* = \max\{C_s, d_s\}$ and $r = 2C_s^* \| (u_0,u_*,v_0,v_*,\gamma_1,\gamma_2) \|_D$. This is detailed in the following lemma.

Lemma 6. *Let $C_s^* = \max\{C_s, d_s\}$ and $r = 2C_s^* \| (u_0,u_*,v_0,v_*,\gamma_1,\gamma_2) \|_D$. If the following condition for T^* given by*

$$
0 < T^* \le \min\left\{ T, \frac{1}{2304(C_s^*)^{10} \| (u_0,u_*,v_0,v_*,\gamma_1,\gamma_2) \|_D^4} \right\} \tag{74}
$$

is satisfied, then the iteration map $\mathcal{F}_{D_1}$ is a contraction on $B(0,r)$.

Proof. For $(\bar{u}_1, \bar{v}_1), (\bar{u}_2, \bar{v}_2) \in B(0,r)$, the following inequality holds:

$$
\begin{aligned}
&\| \mathcal{F}_{D_1}(\bar{u}_1, \bar{v}_1) - \mathcal{F}_{D_1}(\bar{u}_2, \bar{v}_2) \|_X \\
&= \| \left(S_1[u_0, u_*, \gamma_1; \bar{u}_1^2 \bar{v}_1], S_1[v_0, v_*, \gamma_2; \bar{u}_1 \bar{v}_1^2] \right) - \left(S_1[u_0, u_*, \gamma_1; \bar{u}_2^2 \bar{v}_2], S_1[v_0, v_*, \gamma_2; \bar{u}_2 \bar{v}_2^2] \right) \|_X \\
&= \| \left(S_1[0,0,0; \bar{u}_1^2 \bar{v}_1 - \bar{u}_2^2 \bar{v}_2], S_1[0,0,0; \bar{u}_1 \bar{v}_1^2 - \bar{u}_2 \bar{v}_2^2] \right) \|_X \\
&= \sup_{t \in [0,T^*]} \| S_1[0,0,0; \bar{u}_1^2 \bar{v}_1 - \bar{u}_2^2 \bar{v}_2](t) \|_{H_x^s(0,\infty)} \\
&\quad + \sup_{x \in [0,\infty)} \| S_1[0,0,0; \bar{u}_1^2 \bar{v}_1 - \bar{u}_2^2 \bar{v}_2](x) \|_{H_t^s(0,T^*)} \\
&\quad + \sup_{t \in [0,T^*]} \| S_1[0,0,0; \bar{u}_1 \bar{v}_1^2 - \bar{u}_2 \bar{v}_2^2](t) \|_{H_x^s(0,\infty)} \\
&\quad + \sup_{x \in [0,\infty)} \| S_1[0,0,0; \bar{u}_1 \bar{v}_1^2 - \bar{u}_2 \bar{v}_2^2](x) \|_{H_t^s(0,T^*)} \\
&\le C_s^* \left(\sqrt{T^*} \sup_{t \in [0,T^*]} \| \bar{u}_1^2 \bar{v}_1 - \bar{u}_2^2 \bar{v}_2 \|_{H_x^s(0,\infty)} + \sqrt{T^*} \sup_{t \in [0,T^*]} \| \bar{u}_1 \bar{v}_1^2 - \bar{u}_2 \bar{v}_2^2 \|_{H_x^s(0,\infty)} \right), \\
&\quad \text{(by (70))} \\
&\le C_s^* \sqrt{T^*} \left(\sup_{t \in [0,T^*]} \| \bar{u}_1^2 (\bar{v}_1 - \bar{v}_2) \|_{H_x^s(0,\infty)} + \sup_{t \in [0,T^*]} \| (\bar{u}_1 + \bar{u}_2)(\bar{u}_1 - \bar{u}_2) \bar{v}_2 \|_{H_x^s(0,\infty)} \right. \\
&\qquad \left. + \sup_{t \in [0,T^*]} \| \bar{v}_1^2 (\bar{u}_1 - \bar{u}_2) \|_{H_x^s(0,\infty)} + \sup_{t \in [0,T^*]} \| (\bar{v}_1 - \bar{v}_2)(\bar{v}_1 + \bar{v}_2) \bar{u}_2 \|_{H_x^s(0,\infty)} \right) \\
&\le 6 (C_s^*)^3 r^2 \sqrt{T^*} \| (\bar{u}_1, \bar{v}_1) - (\bar{u}_2, \bar{v}_2) \|_X
\end{aligned}
$$

For $0 < T^* \le T$, in order to prove that $\mathcal{F}_{D_1}$ is a contraction, we aim for the following inequality to hold:

$$6 (C_s^*)^3 r^2 \sqrt{T^*} \le \frac{1}{2}$$

which is equivalent to

$$0 < T^* \le \min \frac{1}{2304 (C_s^*)^{10} \| (u_0, u_*, v_0, v_*, \gamma_1, \gamma_2) \|_D^4}.$$

Thus, when T^* satisfies the following condition (74):

$$0 < T^* \le \min \left\{ T, \frac{1}{2304 (C_s^*)^{10} \| (u_0, u_*, v_0, v_*, \gamma_1, \gamma_2) \|_D^4} \right\}$$

it follows that $\mathcal{F}_{D_1}$ is a contraction. □

We will now set the lifespan as follows:

$$T^* = \min \left\{ T, \frac{1}{2304 (C_s^*)^{10} \| (u_0, u_*, v_0, v_*, \gamma_1, \gamma_2) \|_D^4} \right\}. \quad (75)$$

This choice ensures that T^* satisfies both conditions (73) and (74). As a result, the iteration map $\mathcal{F}_{D_1}$ acts as a contraction and maps onto $B(0,r)$. Consequently, by applying the contraction mapping theorem, we conclude that Equation $(u,v) = \mathcal{F}_{D_1}(u,v)$ has a unique solution $(u,v) \in B(0,r) \subset X$.

5.2. Continuity of the Data-to-Solution Map

In this subsection, we will establish that the data-to-solution map $(u_0, u_*, v_0, v_*, r_1, r_2) \longmapsto (u,v)$ is locally Lipschitz continuous. This step is crucial for completing the proof of local well-posedness for the IBVP (1) on the half-line.

We consider two distinct sets of data $D_1 = (u_0, u_*, v_0, v_*, r_1, r_2)$ and $D_2 = (\mathcal{U}_0, \mathcal{U}_*, \mathcal{V}_0, \mathcal{V}_*, \mathcal{R}_1, \mathcal{R}_2)$. These datasets reside within a ball $B_\rho \subset D$ of radius $\rho > 0$ centered at a distance $\mathcal{R}$ from the origin, where

$$D = H_x^s(0,\infty) \times H_x^s(0,\infty) \times H_x^s(0,\infty) \times H_x^s(0,\infty) \times H_t^{s-1}(0,T) \times H_t^{s-1}(0,T)$$

with the norm (72).

Let $(u,v) = \mathcal{F}_{D_1}(u,v)$ and $(\mathcal{U},\mathcal{V}) = \mathcal{F}_{D_2}(\mathcal{U},\mathcal{V})$ represent the solutions corresponding to the IBVP (1). The lifespans of (u,v) and $(\mathcal{U},\mathcal{V})$ are denoted by $T_{(u,v)}$ and $T_{(\mathcal{U},\mathcal{V})}$, respectively, where

$$\begin{aligned} T_{(u,v)} &= \min\left\{T, \frac{1}{2304(C_s^*)^{10} \parallel (u_0, u_*, v_0, v_*, \gamma_1, \gamma_2) \parallel_D^4}\right\}, \\ T_{(\mathcal{U},\mathcal{V})} &= \min\left\{T, \frac{1}{2304(C_s^*)^{10} \parallel (\mathcal{U}_0, \mathcal{U}_*, \mathcal{V}_0, \mathcal{V}_*, \mathcal{R}_1, \mathcal{R}_2) \parallel_D^4}\right\}. \end{aligned}$$

Given that

$$\max\{\parallel (u_0, u_*, v_0, v_*, \gamma_1, \gamma_2) \parallel_D, \parallel (\mathcal{U}_0, \mathcal{U}_*, \mathcal{V}_0, \mathcal{V}_*, \mathcal{R}_1, \mathcal{R}_2) \parallel_D\} \leq \rho + \mathcal{R},$$

we can deduce that

$$\min\left\{T_{(u,v)}, T_{(\mathcal{U},\mathcal{V})}\right\} \geq \min\left\{T, \frac{1}{2304(C_s^*)^{10}(\mathcal{R}+\rho)^4}\right\} \doteq T_\eta.$$

Thus, both solutions (u,v) and $(\mathcal{U},\mathcal{V})$ are guaranteed to exist for any $0 < t \leq T_\eta$. For the lifespan T_η, we define the solution space X_η as the solution space X outlined in (71) with $T^* = T_\eta$.

In the upcoming lemma, we will demonstrate that the data-to-solution map $(u_0, u_*, v_0, v_*, r_1, r_2) \longmapsto (u,v)$ is locally Lipschitz continuous.

Lemma 7. *Let* $C_s^* = \max\{C_s, d_s\}$ *and* $r_\eta = \left(12(C_s^*)^3 T_\eta^{\frac{1}{2}}\right)^{-\frac{1}{2}}$. *For any* $(u,v), (\mathcal{U},\mathcal{V}) \in B(0,r_\eta) \subset X_\eta$ *with data in the ball* B_ρ, *we can establish the following inequality:*

$$\parallel (u,v) - (\mathcal{U},\mathcal{V}) \parallel_{X_\eta} \leq 2C_s^* \parallel (u_0, u_*, v_0, v_*, r_1, r_2) - (\mathcal{U}_0, \mathcal{U}_*, \mathcal{V}_0, \mathcal{V}_*, \mathcal{R}_1, \mathcal{R}_2) \parallel_D. \quad (76)$$

Hence, the data-to-solution map $(u_0, u_*, v_0, v_*, r_1, r_2) \longmapsto (u,v)$ *is locally Lipschitz continuous.*

Proof. For any $(u,v), (\mathcal{U},\mathcal{V}) \in B(0,r_\eta) \subset X_\eta$ with data in the ball B_ρ, we derive the following inequality:

$$
\begin{aligned}
&\| (u,v)-(\mathcal{U},\mathcal{V}) \|_{X_\eta} = \| \mathcal{F}_{D_1}(u,v)-\mathcal{F}_{D_2}(\mathcal{U},\mathcal{V}) \|_{X_\eta} \\
&= \| (S_1[u_0-\mathcal{U}_0, u_*-\mathcal{U}_*, r_1-\mathcal{R}_1; u^2v-\mathcal{U}^2\mathcal{V}], S_1[v_0-\mathcal{V}_0, v_*-\mathcal{V}_*, r_2-\mathcal{R}_2; uv^2-\mathcal{U}\mathcal{V}^2]) \|_{X_\eta} \\
&= \sup_{t\in[0,T_\eta]} \| S_1[u_0-\mathcal{U}_0, u_*-\mathcal{U}_*, r_1-\mathcal{R}_1; u^2v-\mathcal{U}^2\mathcal{V}](t) \|_{H_x^s(0,\infty)} \\
&\quad + \sup_{x\in[0,\infty)} \| S_1[u_0-\mathcal{U}_0, u_*-\mathcal{U}_*, r_1-\mathcal{R}_1; u^2v-\mathcal{U}^2\mathcal{V}](x) \|_{H_t^s(0,T_\eta)} \\
&\quad + \sup_{t\in[0,T_\eta]} \| S_1[v_0-\mathcal{V}_0, v_*-\mathcal{V}_*, r_2-\mathcal{R}_2; uv^2-\mathcal{U}\mathcal{V}^2](t) \|_{H_x^s(0,\infty)} \\
&\quad + \sup_{x\in[0,\infty)} \| S_1[v_0-\mathcal{V}_0, v_*-\mathcal{V}_*, r_2-\mathcal{R}_2; uv^2-\mathcal{U}\mathcal{V}^2](x) \|_{H_t^s(0,T_\eta)} \\
&\le C_s^*(\| u_0-\mathcal{U}_0 \|_{H_x^s(0,\infty)} + \| u_*-\mathcal{U}_* \|_{H_x^s(0,\infty)} + \| v_0-\mathcal{V}_0 \|_{H_x^s(0,\infty)} + \| v_*-\mathcal{V}_* \|_{H_x^s(0,\infty)} \\
&\qquad \| r_1-\mathcal{R}_1 \|_{H_t^{s-1}(0,\infty)} + \| r_2-\mathcal{R}_2 \|_{H_t^{s-1}(0,\infty)} + \sqrt{T_\eta} \sup_{t\in[0,T_\eta]} \| u^2v-\mathcal{U}^2\mathcal{V} \|_{H_x^s(0,\infty)} \\
&\qquad + \sqrt{T_\eta} \sup_{t\in[0,T_\eta]} \| uv^2-\mathcal{U}\mathcal{V}^2 \|_{H_x^s(0,\infty)}) \text{ (by (70))} \\
&\le C_s^* \| (u_0,u_*,v_0,v_*,r_1,r_2)-(\mathcal{U}_0,\mathcal{U}_*,\mathcal{V}_0,\mathcal{V}_*,\mathcal{R}_1,\mathcal{R}_2) \|_D \\
&\quad + C_s^*\sqrt{T_\eta}\Bigg(\sup_{t\in[0,T_\eta]} \| v(u-\mathcal{U})(u+\mathcal{U}) \|_{H_x^s(0,\infty)} + \sup_{t\in[0,T_\eta]} \| (u-\mathcal{U})v^2 \|_{H_x^s(0,\infty)} \\
&\qquad + \sup_{t\in[0,T_\eta]} \| \mathcal{U}(v-\mathcal{V})(v+\mathcal{V}) \|_{H_x^s(0,\infty)} + \sup_{t\in[0,T_\eta]} \| \mathcal{U}^2(v-\mathcal{V}) \|_{H_x^s(0,\infty)} \Bigg) \\
&\le C_s^* \| (u_0,u_*,v_0,v_*,r_1,r_2)-(\mathcal{U}_0,\mathcal{U}_*,\mathcal{V}_0,\mathcal{V}_*,\mathcal{R}_1,\mathcal{R}_2) \|_D + 6C_s^*C_s^2 r_\eta^2\sqrt{T_\eta} \| (u,v)-(\mathcal{U},\mathcal{V}) \|_{X_\eta} \\
&\le C_s^* \| (u_0,u_*,v_0,v_*,r_1,r_2)-(\mathcal{U}_0,\mathcal{U}_*,\mathcal{V}_0,\mathcal{V}_*,\mathcal{R}_1,\mathcal{R}_2) \|_D + 6(C_s^*)^3 r_\eta^2\sqrt{T_\eta} \| (u,v)-(\mathcal{U},\mathcal{V}) \|_{X_\eta}.
\end{aligned}
$$

Therefore, we derive the following inequality:

$$
\| (u,v)-(\mathcal{U},\mathcal{V}) \|_{X_\eta} \le \frac{C_s^*}{1-6(C_s^*)^3\sqrt{T_\eta}r_\eta^2} \| (u_0,u_*,v_0,v_*,r_1,r_2)-(\mathcal{U}_0,\mathcal{U}_*,\mathcal{V}_0,\mathcal{V}_*,\mathcal{R}_1,\mathcal{R}_2) \|_D .
$$

Hence, when we set

$$
r_\eta = \left(12(C_s^*)^3 T_\eta^{\frac{1}{2}}\right)^{-\frac{1}{2}},
$$

the following two inequalities hold:

$$
\frac{1}{1-6(C_s^*)^3\sqrt{T_\eta}r_\eta^2} \le 2 \text{ and } 1-6(C_s^*)^3\sqrt{T_\eta}r_\eta^2 > 0.
$$

Consequently, we can derive (76), demonstrating that the data-to-solution map is locally Lipschitz continuous. This concludes the proof of Lemma 7. □

Now, we can proceed to prove Theorem 2. We define the lifespan as

$$
T^* = min\left\{ T, \frac{1}{2304(C_s^*)^{10} \| (u_0,u_*,v_0,v_*,\gamma_1,\gamma_2) \|_D^4} \right\}.
$$

By utilizing Lemmas 5–7, we can finalize the proof of Theorem 2.

In conclusion, based on our previous experience, using classical methods to prove the local well-posedness of a system tends to be more cumbersome and restrictive compared to the UTM. The UTM facilitates the selection of appropriate Sobolev spaces for the boundary conditions of system (1), which simplifies subsequent estimates and the process of proving the local well-posedness of system (1). This article thus enhances our understanding of the utility of the UTM in establishing the local well-posedness of coupled wave equations, laying the foundation for future research on system (2).

Author Contributions: P.-C.H. is the first author and B.-Y.P. is the corresponding author. P.-C.H. and B.-Y.P. wrote the main manuscript text. All authors reviewed the manuscript. All authors have read and agreed to the published version of the manuscript.

Funding: This research received no external funding.

Data Availability Statement: The original contributions presented in the study are included in the article, further inquiries can be directed to the corresponding authors.

Acknowledgments: We wish to extend our sincere appreciation to Hsin-Yuan Huang from the National Yang Ming Chiao Tung University in Taiwan for his invaluable guidance, steadfast encouragement, and support in this field. Additionally, B.-Y.P. would like to thank Ya-Lun Tsai for his generous assistance provided through the grant from the National Science Council in Taiwan.

Conflicts of Interest: The authors declare no conflicts of interest.

References

1. Fokas, A.S. A unified transform method for solving linear and certain nonlinear PDEs. *Proc. R. Soc. Lond. Ser. A* **1997**, *453*, 1411–1443. [CrossRef]
2. Fokas, A.S. On the integrability of linear and nonlinear partial differential equations. *J. Math. Phys.* **2000**, *41*, 4188–4237. [CrossRef]
3. Fokas, A.S. Integrable nonlinear evolution equations on the half-line. *Comm. Math. Phys.* **2002**, *230*, 1–39. [CrossRef]
4. Fokas, A.S. *A Unified Approach to Boundary Value Problems*; CBMS-NSF Regional Conference Series in Applied Mathematics; SIAM: Philadelphia, PA, USA, 2008.
5. Huang, P.C.; Pan, B.Y. The Robin problems for the coupled system of reaction–diffusion equations. *Bound. Value Probl.* **2024**, *2024*, 29. [CrossRef]
6. Huang, P.C.; Pan, B.Y. Well-Posedness of the Schrödinger–Korteweg–de Vries System with Robin Boundary Conditions on the Half-Line. *Axioms* **2024**, *13*, 508. [CrossRef]
7. Deconinck, B.; Trogdon, T.; Vasan, V. The method of Fokas for solving linear partial differential equations. *SIAM Rev.* **2014**, *56*, 159–186. [CrossRef]
8. Akhatov, I.S.; Baikov, V.; Khusnutdinova, K. Non-linear dynamics of coupled chains of particles. *J. Appl. Math. Mech.* **1995**, *59*, 353–361. [CrossRef]
9. Zhang, J. On the standing wave in coupled non-linear Klein–Gordon equations. *Math. Methods Appl. Sci.* **2003**, *26*, 11–25. [CrossRef]
10. Khusnutdinova, K.R.; Silberschmidt, V.V. Lattice modelling of nonlinear waves in a bi-layer with delamination. *Proc. Estonian Acad. Sci. Phys. Math.* **2003**, *52*, 63–75. [CrossRef]
11. Khusnutdinova, K.R.; Pelinovsky, D. On the exchange of energy in coupled Klein–Gordon equations. *Wave Motion* **2003**, *38*, 1–10. [CrossRef]
12. Wang, Y.J. Non-existence of global solutions of a class of coupled non-linear Klein–Gordon equations with non-negative potentials and arbitrary initial energy. *IMA J. Appl. Math.* **2009**, *74*, 392–415. [CrossRef]
13. Liu, W.J. Global existence, asymptotic behavior and blow-up of solutions for coupled Klein–Gordon equations with damping terms. *Nonlinear Anal.* **2010**, *73*, 244–255. [CrossRef]
14. Nikan, O.; Avazzadeh, Z. A locally stabilized radial basis function partition of unity technique for the sine–Gordon system in nonlinear optics. *Math. Comput. Simul.* **2022**, *199*, 394–413. [CrossRef]
15. Faria, J.C.O.; Souza Franc, A.Y. Well-posedness and exponential stability for a Klein-Gordon system with locally distributed viscoelastic dampings in a past-history framework. *J. Differ. Equ.* **2023**, *346*, 108–144. [CrossRef]
16. Huang, H.Y.; Hsu, C.W. Well-Posedness of the One-Dimension Nonlinear Wave Equation on Half Line. Master's Thesis, National Yang Ming Chiao Tung University, Hsinchu, Taiwan, 2023. Available online: https://hdl.handle.net/11296/c9n627 (accessed on 13 May 2023).
17. Bouhoufani, O.; Messaoudi, S.A.; Alahyane, M. Existence, Blow up and Numerical approximations of Solutions for a Biharmonic Coupled System with Variable exponents. *Authorea* **2022**. [CrossRef]
18. Da Silva, C.O.P.; Louredo, A.T.; Miranda, M.M. Existence and asymptotic behavior of solutions for a Klein-Gordon system. *Methods Appl. Sci.* **2022**, *45*, 3865–3895. [CrossRef]

19. Messaoudi, S.A.; Talahmeh, A.A.; Al-Gharabli, M.M.; Alahyane, M. On the existence and stability of a nonlinear wave system with variable exponents. *Asymptot. Anal.* **2022**, *128*, 211–238. [CrossRef]
20. Chen, J.; Zhang, Z.; Chang, G.; Zhao, J. Periodic solutions to Klein–Gordon systems with linear couplings. *Adv. Nonlinear Stud.* **2021**, *21*, 633–660. [CrossRef]
21. Li, T.T.; Rao, B. Approximate boundary synchronization by groups for a coupled system of wave equations with coupled Robin boundary conditions. *ESAIM Control Optim. Calc. Var.* **2021**, *27*, 10. [CrossRef]
22. Messaoudi, S.A.; Bouhoufani, O.; Hamchi, I.; Alahyane, M. Existence and blow up in a system of wave equations with nonstandard nonlinearities. *Electron. J. Differ. Equ.* **2021**, *2021*, 1–33. [CrossRef]
23. Dimova, M.; Kolkovska, N.; Kutev, N. Global behavior of the solutions to nonlinear Klein–Gordon equation with critical initial energy. *Electron. Res. Arch.* **2020**, *28*, 671–689. [CrossRef]
24. Deconinck, B.; Guo, Q.; Shlizerman, E.; Vasan, V. Fokas's unified transform method for linear systems. *Q. Appl. Math.* **2018**, *76*, 463–488. [CrossRef]
25. Linares, F.; Ponce, G. *Introduction to Nonlinear Dispersive Equations*; Universitext; Springer: New York, NY, USA, 2009.
26. Wheeden, R.; Zygmund, A. *Measure and Integral: An Introduction to Real Analysis*; Marcel Dekker: New York, NY, USA, 1977.
27. Rudin, A. *Real and Complex Analysis, McGraw-Hill International Editions: Mathematics Series*; McGraw-Hill Publishing Co.: New York, NY, USA, 1987.
28. Gilbarg, D.; Trudinger, N.S. *Elliptic Partial Differential Equations of Second Order*; Springer: Berlin/Heidelberg, Germany, 2015.

axioms

MDPI

Article

The Characteristic Relation in Two-Dimensional Type I Intermittency[†]

Juan Colman [‡] and Sergio Elaskar [*,‡]

Departamento de Ingeniería Aeroespacial, FCEFyN, Universidad Nacional de Córdoba e Instituto de Estudios Avanzados en Ingeniería y Tecnología, CONICET, Córdoba 5000, Argentina; juan.colman@mi.unc.edu.ar

* Correspondence: selaskar@unc.edu.ar

[†] This article is a revised and expanded version of a paper entitled "Intermitencia en un mapa bidimensional", which was presented at XXXIX Congreso Argentino de Mecánica Computacional, Concordia, Argentina, 6–11 November 2023.

[‡] These authors contributed equally to this work.

Abstract: To explore intermittency in discrete systems with two or more degrees of freedom, we analyze the general characteristics of type I intermittency within a two-dimensional map. This investigation is carried out numerically, concentrating on the system's attractors, bifurcation diagrams, and the characteristic relation associated with type I intermittency. We present two methods for determining the laminar interval and the channel structure. Our computations yield numerical results for the average laminar length as a function of the control parameter, which we then compare with findings from intermittency in one-dimensional maps. We observe a strong agreement between the numerical data and the theoretical predictions.

Keywords: two-dimensional; map; intermittency; characteristic relation; laminar interval

MSC: 37D45; 37E05

1. Introduction

Chaotic intermittency is an interesting phenomenon observed in dynamical systems, characterized by a distinctive alternation between chaotic and laminar or regular behaviors. During the laminar phases, which may also be referred to as pseudo-equilibrium regions or pseudo-periodic solutions, the solution of the system moves close to the previous stable solution. In contrast, the bursts that occur during the chaotic phases signify a transition to irregular patterns. This duality highlights the complex nature of dynamical systems and the intricate balance between regular and chaotic behavior within their evolution. Understanding these dynamics is crucial for analyzing a wide range of complex systems, whether they are of natural or human origin [1]. Intermittency is a route that leads to chaos and has been found in physics, engineering, astronomy, chemistry, medicine, neurosciences, economics, biology, and genetics [2–23]. A more detailed description of chaotic intermittency could lead to a better understanding of these phenomena. Consequently, this area of research has the potential to provide significant benefits across various fields. Additionally, accurately describing chaotic intermittency is crucial for systems that have incomplete or unknown equations.

About 45 years ago, chaotic intermittency was classified into three distinct types, referred to as I, II, and III [9,24]. This classification depends on the bifurcation that gives rise to the intermittency. This bifurcation occurs when the eigenvalues of the system's Jacobian matrix—evaluated in the local solution—depart from the unit circle. Type I intermittency is characterized by an eigenvalue exiting the unit circle through +1, while type II involves two complex conjugated eigenvalues leaving the unit circle. Finally, type III is defined by an eigenvalue leaving the unit circle through -1 [25–27]. Subsequent research introduced additional types of chaotic intermittency, including on-off, eyelet, ring, in-out, type X, and type V (see [27,28] and references there).

One-dimensional maps, commonly referred to as Poincaré maps, offer an alternative for investigating chaotic intermittency. Two essential elements characterize these maps: a specific local map, which establishes the intermittency type, and a reinjection mechanism returning the trajectories from the chaotic dynamics to the regular phase. The core of this process is encapsulated in the reinjection probability density function (RPD). The RPD quantifies the probability of trajectories re-entering the laminar zone around an unstable or disappearing fixed point. When paired with the local map, the RPD function provides profound insights into the dynamical characteristics of the system. Determining the RPD function correctly is paramount for a comprehensive understanding of chaotic intermittency. However, extracting the RPD from experimental or numerical data can be quite challenging due to the vast amounts of data and the inherent statistical fluctuations. Various strategies have emerged for calculating the RPD function. Traditionally, the classical framework for chaotic intermittency has relied on the assumption of uniform reinjection within the laminar interval. Recently, two innovative methodologies have been developed to more accurately derive the RPD function. The first, the M function methodology, introduces a generalized power law for the RPD and has demonstrated remarkable accuracy for a wide range of one-dimensional maps exhibiting type I, II, III, and V intermittencies. This approach not only integrates the classical approximation but also accommodates uniform reinjection as a specific instance. The second methodology, known as the continuity technique, employs the Perron–Frobenius operator to effectively compute the reinjection probability density function. Like the M function methodology, the continuity technique has been validated across various maps displaying different types of intermittency. To gain deeper insights into the phenomenon of intermittency, it is also essential to consider other statistical functions, such as the probability density of laminar lengths, $\psi(l)$, the average laminar length, $\bar{l}$, and the characteristic relation $\bar{l} = \bar{l}(\varepsilon)$. These functions, however, are contingent on the RPD. Furthermore, the RPD and the related statistical functions that characterize chaotic intermittency are influenced by external noise and the lower boundary of reinjection (LBR). Remarkably, the M function methodology has been further refined to encompass both of these crucial aspects [27,28].

However, these previous studies only consider one-dimensional maps. In this paper, we are interested in analyzing chaotic intermittency in two-dimensional maps, more specifically, we analyze the characteristic relation, the dependence of the average laminar length, $\bar{l}$, with the control parameter ε for type I intermittency. To carry out this task, we study a 2D map introduced in [29], which exhibits type I intermittency. The researchers provided a comprehensive description of the structure of the reinjection channel and the trajectory within it, resulting in the establishment of scaling relations based on the trajectory.

The main objective of this paper is to investigate the phenomenon of chaotic intermittency. In addition, it includes a partial analysis of specific attractors within the system. However, this study does not aim to provide a comprehensive description of the system's attractors, and the methodology employed is not particularly well-suited for uncovering hidden chaotic attractors [30].

This study focuses on the dynamics of the system, examining the basins of attraction for different attractors, analyzing various trajectories within the channel, and calculating the exponents of the characteristic relation. The findings presented in this research serve as a preliminary exploration of the potential for extending the new theory of chaotic intermittency [27,28] to high-dimensional maps. This article is a revised and expanded version of a paper entitled "Intermitencia en un mapa bidimensional", which was presented at XXXIX Congreso Argentino de Mecánica Computacional, Concordia, Argentina in November 2023 [31].

This paper is organized as follows: In Section 2, we introduce the two-dimensional map and analyze the dynamics of the system. We describe the fixed points and assess their stability, followed by the presentation of bifurcation diagrams along with an explanation of the attraction basins. Section 3 explores the type I intermittency observed in the two-dimensional map. We illustrate this intermittency for various values of the control parameters, which correspond to different trajectories related to 14 cycles and 10 cycles. Finally, Section 4 summarizes the main conclusions and discusses perspectives for future research.

2. Two-Dimensional System

A general map in d-dimensions can be written as

$$\bar{x}_{n+1} = \bar{f}(\bar{x}_n) \tag{1}$$

where $\bar{x}_n \in \mathbf{R}^d$ is a finite-dimensional vector, being $\mathbf{R}^d$ the d-dimensional Euclidean space, and d is an integer number verifying $d > 1$.

In a two-dimensional vector space defined by the pair $(\bar{x}_{n+1}, \bar{x}_n)$, the equation $\bar{x}_{n+1} = \bar{x}_n$ represents a diagonal hyper-surface (DHS) [29]. In type I intermittency, the DHS surface, along with the local map, establishes a channel that allows the system to enter a laminar phase as the trajectory passes through it. The function of the DHS surface in two-dimensional maps is similar to that of the bisector line in one-dimensional maps.

In this paper, we analyze the two-dimensional map, $d = 2$, proposed by [29]:

$$\begin{aligned} x_{n+1} &= F(x_n, y_n) = 4\alpha x_n(1 - x_n) + \beta y_n(1 - x_n) \\ y_{n+1} &= G(x_n, y_n) = 4\alpha y_n(1 - y_n) + \beta x_n(1 - y_n) \end{aligned} \tag{2}$$

where α and β are control parameters, and the vector $\bar{x}_n = (x_n, y_n) \in \mathbf{R}^2$.

We perform a classical analysis of the dynamics of the system for a fixed value of β. In this analysis, the dynamics are determined by the parameter α. We calculate the fixed points and assess their stability, and we also generate bifurcation diagrams and basins of attraction for the system's attractors.

The fixed points of the system are all pairs (x^*, y^*) such that $x^* = F(x^*, y^*)$ and $y^* = G(x^*, y^*)$. The stability of these points is determined by the dynamic behavior in their vicinity. Some points can attract nearby trajectories, while others can repel them, and some may act as centers for periodic trajectories. The stability of fixed points can be analyzed by considering the eigenvalues of the Jacobian matrix.

$$J = \begin{vmatrix} \partial_x F(x^*, y^*) & \partial_y F(x^*, y^*) \\ \partial_x G(x^*, y^*) & \partial_y G(x^*, y^*) \end{vmatrix} \tag{3}$$

Evaluating the stability of a system's solutions requires a comprehensive understanding of the system dynamics. The eigenvalues of the Jacobian matrix are critical in determining the stability of the fixed points, as they provide important information about the system's response to perturbations. These eigenvalues exist within the complex plane, and a fixed point is classified as hyperbolic if no eigenvalue is located on the unit circle.

The stability condition indicates that if at least one eigenvalue lies outside the unit circle, the fixed point is unstable, whereas it is considered stable if all eigenvalues are within the unit circle. If at least one eigenvalue of the fixed point is on the unit circle, the fixed point is categorized as non-hyperbolic, for which the stability condition based on the eigenvalues of the Jacobian matrix is insufficient.

Bifurcation diagrams illustrate the behavior of dynamical systems, showing the solutions and their stability within the state-control space. In these diagrams, stable solutions are represented as stable branches, while unstable solutions are depicted as unstable branches. Generally, a branch of solutions will either commence, terminate, or change its stability at a bifurcation point [25].

Each attractor of the system, $\bar{X}$, possesses its basin or domain of attraction, which is the domain $D \in \mathbf{R}^d$ that includes all the initial conditions $\bar{x}_0$ such $\bar{f}^n(\bar{x}_0) \to \bar{X}$ as $n \to \infty$.

As a first step to determine the dynamics behavior, we start with the calculation of the fixed points of the map $\bar{f}(x,y)$, given by Equation (2). The fixed points have been calculated using analytic methods. For $\beta = 0.5$, they are:

$$x_1^* = 0 \qquad y_1^* = 0 \tag{4}$$

$$x_2^* = \frac{\alpha - 0.125}{\alpha + 0.125} \qquad y_2^* = \frac{\alpha - 0.125}{\alpha + 0.125} \tag{5}$$

$$x_3^* = \frac{0.09375 - 0.25\alpha}{0.046875 + (-0.5 + \alpha)\alpha + A} \qquad y_3^* = \frac{0.09375 - 0.25\alpha}{0.046875 + (-0.5 + \alpha)\alpha - A} \tag{6}$$

$$x_4^* = \frac{0.09375 - 0.25\alpha}{0.046875 + (-0.5 + \alpha)\alpha - A} \qquad y_4^* = \frac{0.09375 - 0.25\alpha}{0.046875 + (-0.5 + \alpha)\alpha + A} \tag{7}$$

where $A = \sqrt{(\alpha - 0.375)(\alpha - 0.125)(\alpha^2 + 0.046875)}$.

Once the control parameter β is established, the fixed points of the system depend only on the other control parameter, α. Figures 1 and 2 show the evolution of the fixed points with α. From the figures, we can observe that the fixed point (x_1^*, y_1^*) does not depend on α.

To generate a bifurcation diagram, we start by iterating the system from chosen initial values, denoted as (x_0, y_0). This iterative process continues until we arrive at a solution that characterizes the system's behavior. Once this is achieved, we repeat the iteration process using various values of the control parameter α.

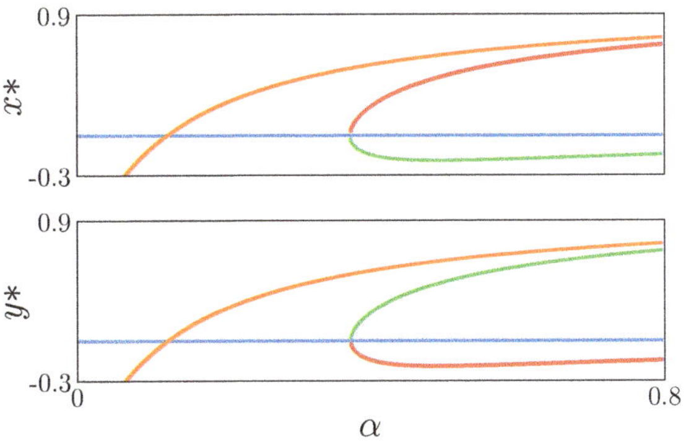

Figure 1. The evolution of fixed points as the control parameter α changes (see Equations (5)–(7)). Blue: (x_1^*, y_1^*). Orange: (x_2^*, y_2^*). Red: (x_3^*, y_3^*). Green: (x_4^*, y_4^*).

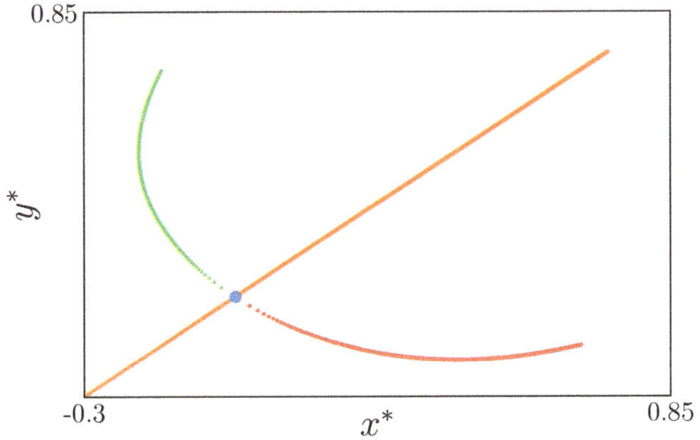

Figure 2. The evolution of the fixed points in the (x, y) plane. Blue: (x_1^*, y_1^*). Orange: (x_2^*, y_2^*). Red: (x_3^*, y_3^*). Green: (x_4^*, y_4^*).

Figure 3 presents a bifurcation diagram consisting of two superimposed plots: one in blue and the other in red. The blue plot illustrates the stationary solutions derived from initial conditions where $x_0 = y_0$, with each value of α held constant. This plot resembles a one-dimensional bifurcation diagram that follows the logistic equation, as the system described in Equation (2) is decoupled, functioning as two separate one-dimensional logistic maps.

In contrast, the red plot represents results from random initial conditions $(x_0 \neq y_0)$ in the interval $(0, 1)$ for each value of α. This curve exhibits its first bifurcation around $\alpha = 0.53$, indicating a period-doubling bifurcation. The blue curve's first bifurcation, however, occurs at $\alpha = 0.62$, as depicted in Figure 3. Each bifurcation corresponds to an eigenvalue departing from the unit circle through -1, resulting in a period-doubling bifurcation. Fixed points on the upper branches are unstable, while those on the lower branches remain stable until $\alpha \approx 0.85$ for the blue plot and $\alpha \approx 0.77$ for the red diagram. Fixed points on the lower branches become unstable or vanish beyond these values of α.

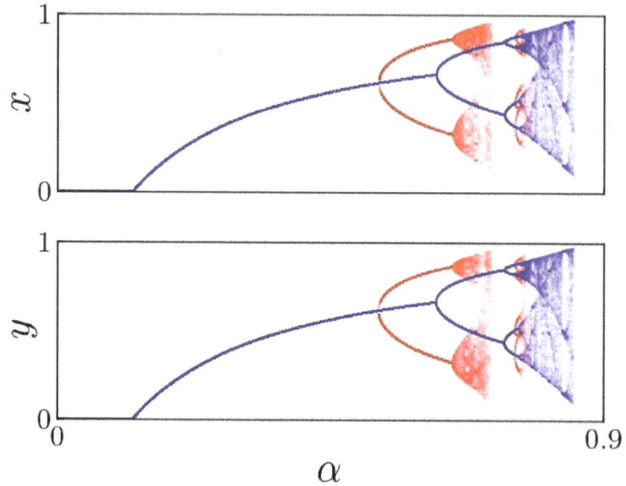

Figure 3. Numerical bifurcation diagram for $\beta = 0.5$.

The provided figures indicate a significant correlation between the initial conditions and the observed attractors. Consequently, each bifurcation diagram exhibits distinct basins of attraction. This information will be essential for developing a comprehensive understanding of the system's behavior and gaining insights into its dynamics.

As examples, we indicate some periodic points corresponding to different values of α that belong to solutions of periods 2, 4, 8, and 16, as shown in [32].

Fixing the β parameter at 0.3 and increasing α, with equal initial conditions $x_0 = y_0$ yields 2, 4, 8, and 16 period solutions for values of α 0.7, 0.79, 0.816, 0.8166.

With $\alpha = 0.7$ the fixed points are $(x_1 = 0.55, y_1 = 0.558)$, $(x_2 = 0.764, y_2 = 0.764)$, with $\alpha = 0.79$: $(x_1 = 0.467, y_1 = 0.467)$, $(x_2 = 0.861, y_2 = 0.861)$, $(x_3 = 0.413, y_3 = 0.413)$, $(x_4 = 0.838, y_4 = 0.838)$; for $\alpha = 0.816$: $(x_1 = 0.346, y_2 = 0.346)$, $(x_2 = 0.807, y_2 = 0.807)$, $(x_3 = 0.553, y_3 = 0.553)$, $(x_4 = 0.880, y_4 = 0.880)$, $(x_5 = 0.374, y_5 = 0.374)$, $(x_6 = 0.835, y_6 = 0.835)$, $(x_7 = 0.490, y_7 = 0.490)$, $(x_8 = 0.890, y_8 = 0.890$; and finally for $\alpha = 0.8166$: $(x_1 = 0.378, y_1 = 0.378)$, $(x_2 = 0.838, y_2 = 0.838)$, $(x_3 = 0.482, y_3 = 0.482)$, $(x_4 = 0.890, y_4 = 0.890)$, $(x_5 = 0.347, y_5 = 0.347)$, $(x_6 = 0.809, y_6 = 0.809)$, $(x_7 = 0.551, y_7 = 0.551)$, $(x_8 = 0.882, y_8 = 0.882)$, $(x_9 = 0.370, y_9 = 0.370)$, $(x_{10} = 0.831, y_{10} = 0.831)$, $(x_{11} = 0.499, y_{11} = 0.499)$, $(x_{12} = 0.891, y_{12} = 0.891)$, $(x_{13} = 0.344, y_{13} = 0.344)$, $(x_{14} = 0.805, y_{14} = 0.805)$, $(x_{15} = 0.558, y_{15} = 0.558)$, $(x_{16} = 0.879, y_{16} = 0.879)$.

If the initial conditions are now different $x_0 \neq y_0$, then we have two bifurcation regions, the first going into a 2-period solution before an explosive bifurcation takes place, then at $\alpha \sim 0.72$, a new period-doubling bifurcation starts, and it shows solutions of period 2, 4, 8, and 16 for α 0.73, 0.81, 0.815, and 0.817.

For $\alpha = 0.73$ the fixed points are: $(x_1 = 0.505, y_1 = 0.505)$ and $(x_2 = 0.804897, y_2 = 0.804897)$; for $\alpha = 0.81$: $(x_1 = 0.521, y_1 = 0.521)$, $(x_2 = 0.883, y_2 = 0.883)$, $(x_3 = 0.364, y_3 = 0.364)$, $(x_4 = 0.820, y_4 = 0.820)$; when $\alpha = 0.815$: $(x_1 = 0.808, y_1 = 0.808)$, $(x_2 = 0.550, y_2 = 0.550)$, $(x_3 = 0.880, y_3 = 0.880)$, $(x_4 = 0.373, y_4 = 0.373)$, $(x_5 = 0.833, y_5 = 0.833)$, $(x_6 = 0.494, y_6 = 0.494)$, $(x_7 = 0.889, y_7 = 0.889)$, $(x_8 = 0.348, y_8 = 0.348)$; and finally for $\alpha = 0.817$: $(x_1 = 0.379, y_1 = 0.379)$, $(x_2 = 0.840, y_2 = 0.840)$, $(x_3 = 0.479, y_3 = 0.479)$, $(x_4 = 0.890, y_4 = 0.890)$, $(x_5 = 0.347, y_5 = 0.347)$, $(x_6 = 0.809, y_6 = 0.809)$, $(x_7 = 0.550, y_7 = 0.550)$, $(x_8 = 0.883, y_8 = 0.883)$, $(x_9 = 0.368, y_9 = 0.368)$, $(x_{10} = 0.830, y_{10} =$

0.830), ($x_{11} = 0.502, y_{11} = 0.502$), ($x_{12} = 0.891, y_{12} = 0.891$), ($x_{13} = 0.343, y_{13} = 0.343$), ($x_{14} = 0.804, y_{14} = 0.804$), ($x_{15} = 0.560, y_{15} = 0.560$), ($x_{16} = 0.879, y_{16} = 0.879$);

The same analysis is performed for $\beta = 0.5$ but only for $x_0 \neq y_0$, showing period 2, 4, and 8 solutions for $\alpha = 0.72$ with fixed points ($x_1 = 0.838, y_1 = 0.838$) and ($x_2 = 0.457, y_2 = 0.457$); $\alpha = 0.75$ ($x_1 = 0.424, y_1 = 0.424$), ($x_2 = 0.826, y_2 = 0.826$), ($x_3 = 0.500, y_3 = 0.500$), ($x_4 = 0.874, y_4 = 0.874$); $\alpha = 0.756$ ($x_1 = 0.424, y_1 = 0.544$), ($x_2 = 0.833, y_2 = 0.809$), ($x_3 = 0.487, y_3 = 0.880$), ($x_4 = 0.895, y_4 = 0.860$), ($x_5 = 0.329, y_5 = 0.424$), ($x_6 = 0.809, y_6 = 0.833$), ($x_7 = 0.809, y_7 = 0.833$), ($x_8 = 0.860, y_8 = 0.895$); and $\alpha = 0.75$ ($x_1 = 0.912, y_1 = 0.837$), ($x_2 = 0.833, y_2 = 0.809$), ($x_3 = 0.487, y_3 = 0.880$), ($x_4 = 0.895, y_4 = 0.860$), ($x_5 = 0.329, y_5 = 0.424$), ($x_6 = 0.809, y_6 = 0.833$).

To explain the bifurcations displayed by bifurcation diagrams, we compute the stability of the fixed points for the maps $\bar{f}(x,y)$ and $\bar{f}^2(x,y) = \bar{f} \circ \bar{f}(x,y)$. In Figure 4, we observe the progression of the fixed points for $\bar{f}^2(x,y)$ as the control parameter α is modified.

The two eigenvalues of the Jacobian matrix for the fixed point (x_2^*, y_2^*), given by the yellow curve in Figure 1 and light blue one in Figure 4, exit the unit circle for different values of α: one for $\alpha = 0.53$ and another for $\alpha = 0.62$. The first eigenvalue has a strong influence on generating the red bifurcation diagram of Figure 3. However, the blue bifurcation diagram starts in the instability produced by the second eigenvalue. Also, in Figure 4, we can observe the instability and generation of new fixed points shown by red and blue curves.

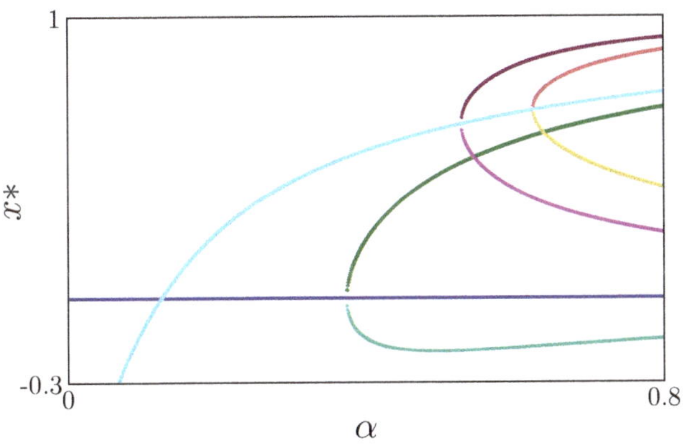

Figure 4. Fixed points for the map $f^2(x,y)$.

On the other hand, Figures 5–8 displays the vector field in the (x,y) plane together with the fixed points of map $\bar{f}^2(x,y)$ that appear as α grows.

Figure 5 shows the vector field for $\alpha = 0.3$. In this figure, we can see that there are only two fixed points which are shown in Figure 1 as blue and yellow lines. One fixed point is at $(0,0)$, and it is unstable, with the other one being stable at approximately $(0.42, 0.42)$. As we move to Figure 6, with an α value 0.5, we observe the bifurcation occurring at point $(0,0)$ and two more fixed points appearing. These two fixed points are saddle points, they attract alongside a direction and repel alongside the other. Figure 7 shows two new fixed points corresponding to the bifurcation shown in the violet solution of Figure 4. Finally, in Figure 8 ($\alpha = 0.65$), the directional field shows the appearance of a pair of fixed points that correspond to the ones shown in pink and yellow in Figure 4, which are saddle points with one eigenvalue inside the unit circle and the other outside of it.

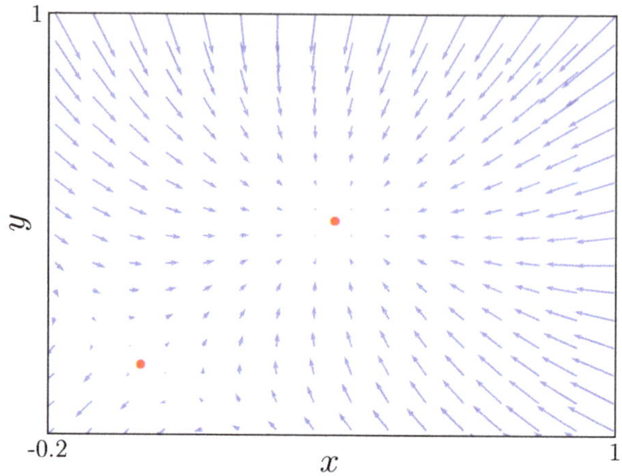

Figure 5. Vector field for $\bar{f}^2$ for $\alpha = 0.3$. Red points are the fixed points.

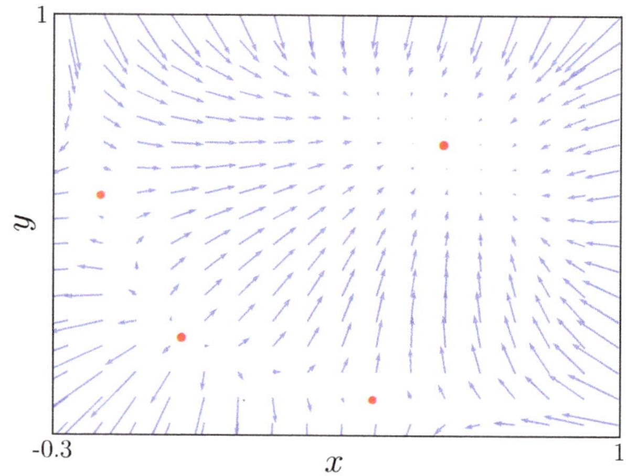

Figure 6. Vector field for $\bar{f}^2$ for $\alpha = 0.5$. Red points are the fixed points.

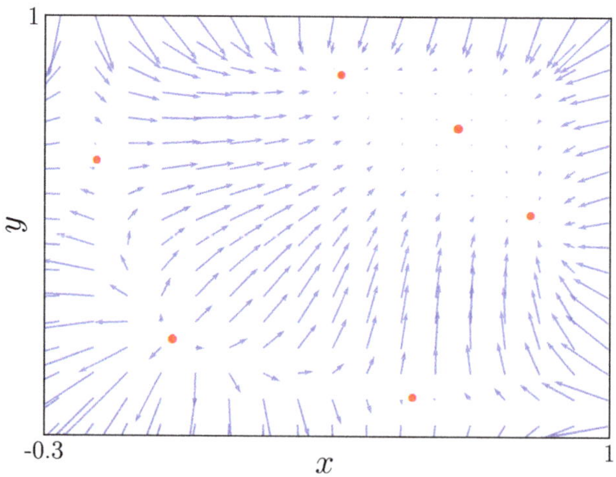

Figure 7. Vector field for $\bar{f}^2$ for $\alpha = 0.6$. Red points are the fixed points.

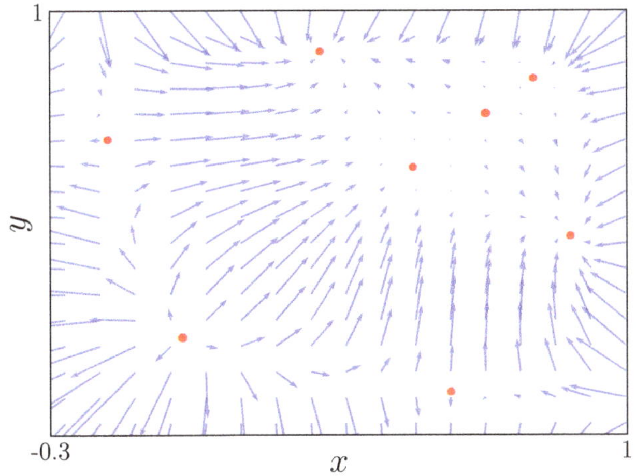

Figure 8. Vector field for $\vec{f}^2$ for $\alpha = 0.65$. Red points are the fixed points.

Figure 9 shows the bifurcation diagram used in [29]. From the figure, we see that for values of $\alpha \sim 0.7$ and ~ 0.8, the map presents a more complex behavior than those observed in the directional field (see Figures 5–8). There is a set of fixed points that meet the condition $x^* = y^*$, these fixed points correspond to the blue diagram shown in Figure 3, because solutions with $x = y$ decouple the system and transform it into two independent logistic maps (see blue diagram in Figure 3).

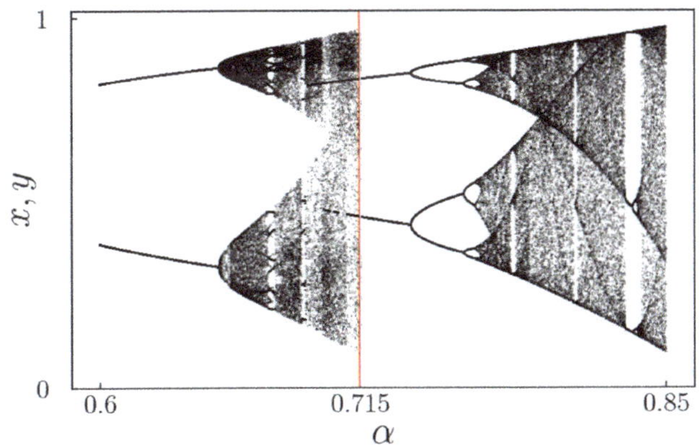

Figure 9. Bifurcation diagrams for x and y using deliberated initial conditions. The diagram is equal for x and y. $\beta = 0.5$.

Figure 9 is only feasible if the initial conditions of the iterative process for each α are deliberately selected. For an α lower to ~ 0.715, the initial conditions must verify $x_0 \neq y_0$. On the other hand, for an α greater than ~ 0.715, the initial conditions have to satisfy $x_0 = y_0$.

Figure 10 shows the bifurcation diagrams for x obtained for different initial conditions in the iterative process. The upper figure displays the diagram built with initial conditions $x_0 \neq y_0$ for every α, while the lower one was obtained only using $x_0 = y_0$ as initial condition for every α.

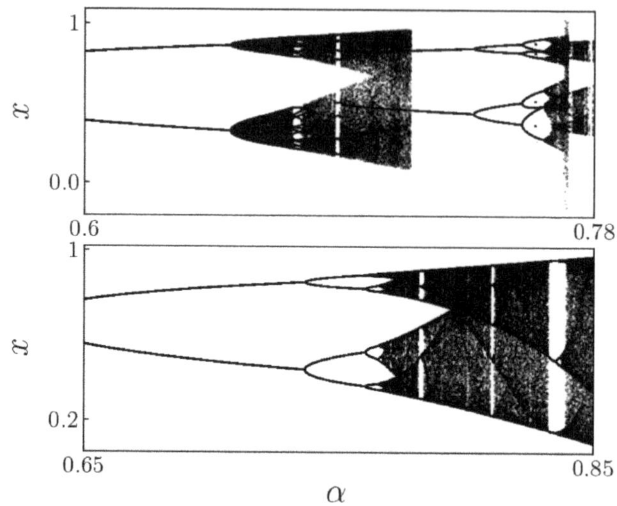

Figure 10. Bifurcation diagrams for x with $x_0 \neq y_0$ (**up**) and $x_0 = y_0$ (**down**). $\beta = 0.5$.

Figure 11 displays the relations between the variables x and y for the bifurcation diagrams of Figure 10. The left figure was calculated with initial conditions $x_0 \neq y_0$ for $0.6 \leq \alpha < 0.78$. The right figure was obtained using $x_0 = y_0$ as initial condition for $0.65 \leq \alpha \leq 0.85$.

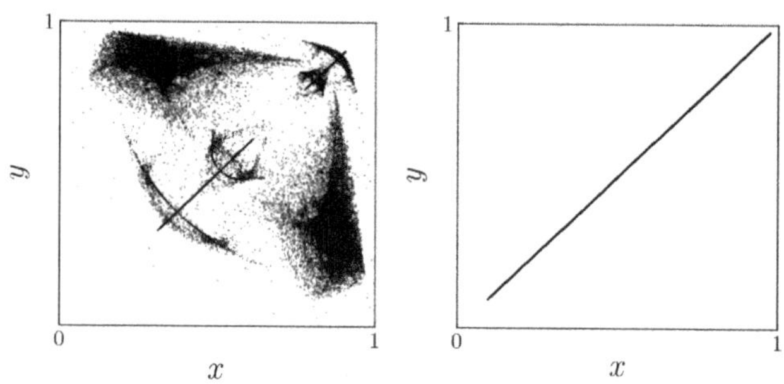

Figure 11. Bifurcation diagrams on x, y plane for $x_0 \neq y_0$ and $x_0 = y_0$. $\beta = 0.5$, $0.65 < \alpha < 0.85$.

For α greater than approximately 0.776, the basin of attraction for the attractor depicted in the upper Figure 10 becomes nearly non-existent. Additionally, once α exceeds approximately 0.77, the logistic attractor can be deemed a stable solution. This is achieved when the iterative processes are initiated on the bisector line in the (x, y) plane, specifically on points where $(x_0 = y_0)$.

3. Type I Intermittency

In this section, we examine three cases where type I intermittency occurs. We adhere to the criteria established by [29] to define type I intermittency for a two-dimensional map.

Figures 12 and 13 present the regions of interest in the bifurcation diagrams, showing the period-14 solution at $\alpha \sim 0.674$ and a period-10 solution at $\alpha \sim 0.689$, both with $\beta = 0.5$. With $\beta = 0.3$, a chaotic solution is shown for $\alpha \sim 0.778$ near a period-14 solution.

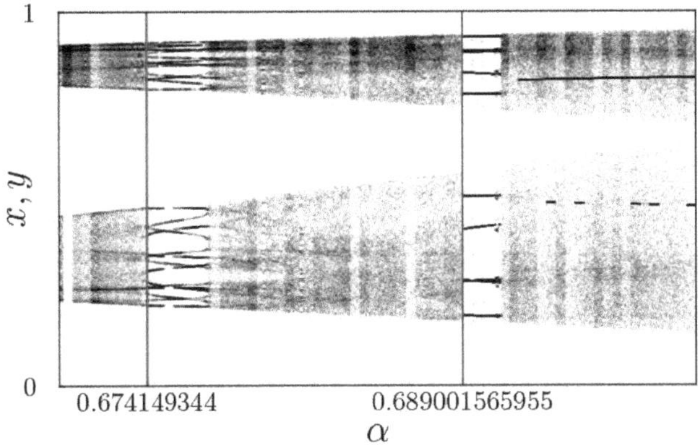

Figure 12. Bifurcation diagram of $f(x, y)$ map, with $\beta = 0.5$, period-14 (red) and period-10 (blue) solutions.

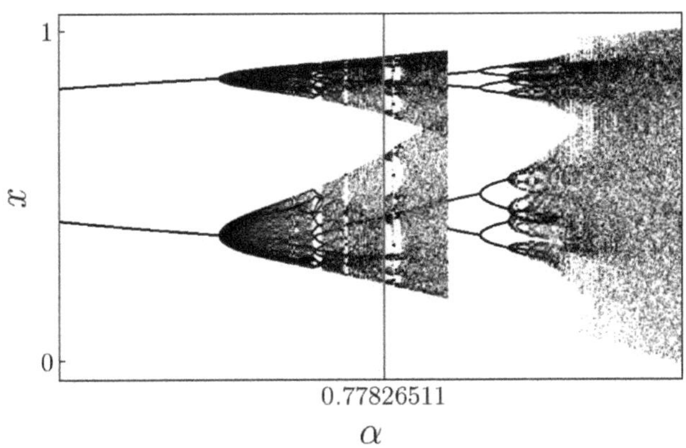

Figure 13. Bifurcation diagram of $f(x, y)$ map, with $\beta = 0.3$ and period-14 solution.

The bifurcation diagram presented in Figure 12 shows a period-14 solution that occurs at approximately $\alpha \sim 0.674$ with $\beta = 0.5$. The period-14 solution is placed between chaotic solutions for both lower and higher values of α, indicating the potential presence of intermittency. Therefore, examining the $n + 14$ map is particularly interesting in this context.

The solution for the map $\bar{f}^{14}(x, y)$, characterized by the parameter $\alpha = 0.67414$, is shown in Figure 14. As we analyze the dynamics of the system, we can observe that the trajectory initially follows one branch of the attractor for a certain duration. Subsequently, it transitions to the alternate branch, and this pattern continues in a cyclic fashion, occurring a total of fourteen times. This repetitive switching between branches culminates in the formation of a limit cycle solution.

When we examine the trajectory in the two-dimensional state space (x, y), it delineates a closed curve, as shown in Figure 15. This closed curve is indicative of the periodic nature of the oscillations within the system, demonstrating how the state variables evolve over time in a limit cycle.

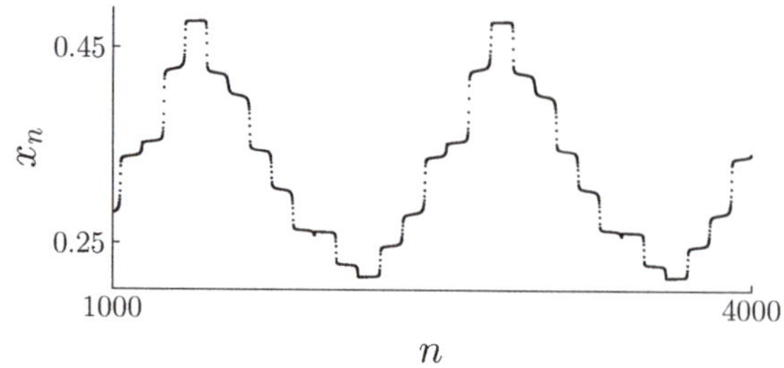

Figure 14. Temporal evolution of the $\bar{f}^{14}(x,y)$ map for $\alpha = 0.67414$. $\beta = 0.5$.

To gain a better understanding of the behavior of the solution, it is useful to analyze the map of x_{n+14} versus x_n for $\bar{f}^{14}(x,y)$. In Figure 16, we observe that the plateaus shown in Figure 14 are the result of the system solution approaching the bisector line $x_n = x_{n+14}$. This proximity of the map to the bisector line causes the trajectory to stay close for several iterations before being rapidly expelled and transported to a new region near the bisector line. Each time the trajectory approaches the line $x_n = x_{n+1}$, a narrow channel forms, resembling the behavior seen in type I intermittency in one-dimensional maps. In [29], this behavior is classified as type I intermittency, and a law for the mean or average laminar length is derived and compared with the results found for one-dimensional systems using the classic theory of chaotic intermittency.

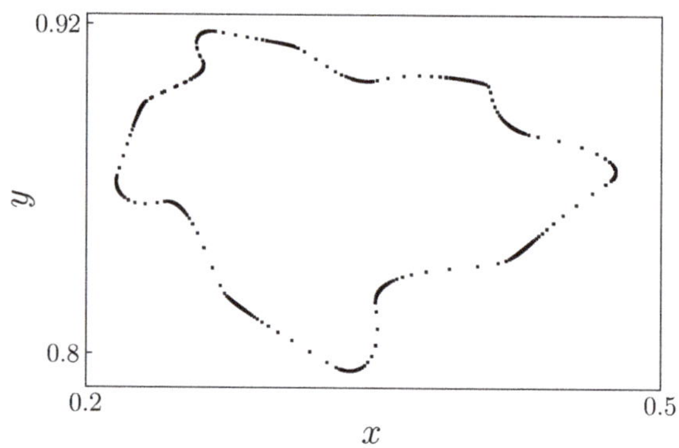

Figure 15. Attractor in (x,y) plane for $\alpha = 0.67414$. $\beta = 0.5$.

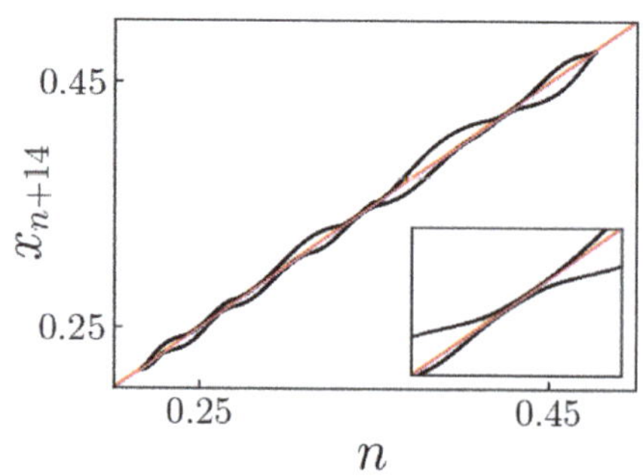

Figure 16. $\bar{f}^{14}(x,y)$ map for $\alpha = 0.67414$. $\beta = 0.5$.

The laminar length, in the context of intermittency, refers to the duration of the laminar phase. This duration is measured in iterations for discrete-time systems. For one-dimensional maps experiencing type I intermittency, the laminar length is a function of the distance between the map and the bisector line, known as the channel. The average laminar length depends on the control parameter ε in the following way [27]:

$$\langle l \rangle \sim \frac{1}{\sqrt{\varepsilon}} \tag{8}$$

where $\langle l \rangle$ is the average laminar length. In these systems, the value of ε is directly related to the distance between the map and the bisector line. This distance determines the width of the channel, which causes the trajectory to pass more slowly. In this region, the laminar flow characteristics of the intermittency phenomenon are defined.

The map $\bar{f}^{14}(x,y)$ showed a separation concerning the bisector line when the control parameter, defined as $\varepsilon = \alpha_c - \alpha$, was modified. The critical value of α at which intermittency is said to start and the limit cycle is found is known as α_c.

The laminar or regular interval is defined as the stages of evolution in which the trajectory did not significantly change position. These stages are understood as the *plateaus* in Figure 14. However, unlike in one-dimensional maps, the laminar region in two-dimensional maps is not connected. It consists of very confined domains through which the system rapidly jumps, generating a structure of multiple channels.

Figure 17 shows the influence of the control parameter ε on the distance between the map $\bar{f}^{14}(x,y)$ and the bisector. Note that as ε grows, the distance between $\bar{f}^{14}(x,y)$ and the bisector also increases.

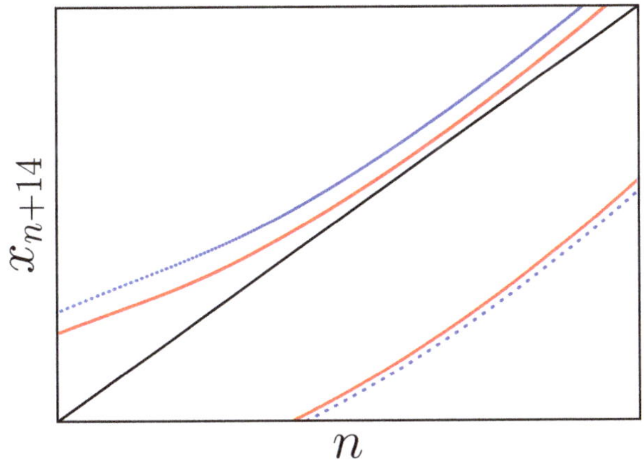

Figure 17. Displacement of region of the $\bar{f}^{14}(x,y)$ map with respect to bisector line for $\varepsilon = e^{-10}$ (red) and e^{-9} (blue).

To measure how many iterations the trajectory needs to pass through each channel, we define the relative error function of the variable x as follows:

$$x_{err} = \left| \frac{x_{n+14} - x_n}{x_n} \right| \tag{9}$$

When the changes in the variable are small, $x_{err} \ll 1$, it is detected that the trajectory is in a laminar region-iterating within one of the fourteen channels. Laminar intervals are defined by a relative error that is less than a certain fixed threshold. Figure 18 shows the temporal evolution of the solution x_{n+14} and the relative error function given by Equation (9).

The total number of iterations needed to complete the limit cycle was calculated by excluding the transition iterations between laminar regions, as they are insignificant when compared with others. The results obtained are presented in Figure 19. It shows the same slope as that achieved in [29].

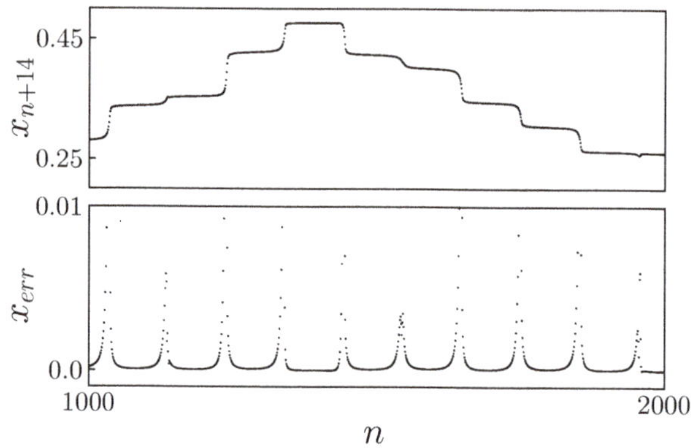

Figure 18. Temporal evolution of $\bar{f}^{14}(x,y)$ map and the x_{err} function. $\varepsilon = e^{-11}$.

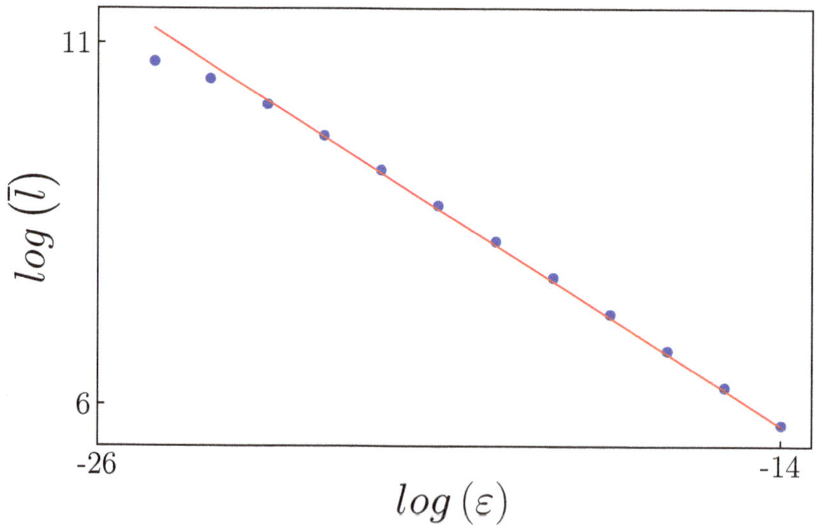

Figure 19. Mean laminar length and control parameter: in blue is the numerical result and in red is a line with slope -0.5. $\alpha \sim 0.674149$ with $\beta = 0.5$.

To verify the previous results, we study two other cases. The first one uses $\alpha \approx 0.689$ and $\beta = 0.5$. A period-10 solution in Figure 12 lies near a chaotic region which may indicate intermittency behavior as well as the period-14 solution in the same figure.

Figure 20 shows the change in laminar phase duration as the control parameter $\varepsilon = \alpha - \alpha_c$ is modified. As ε grows (α moves away α_c) the average laminar length decreases.

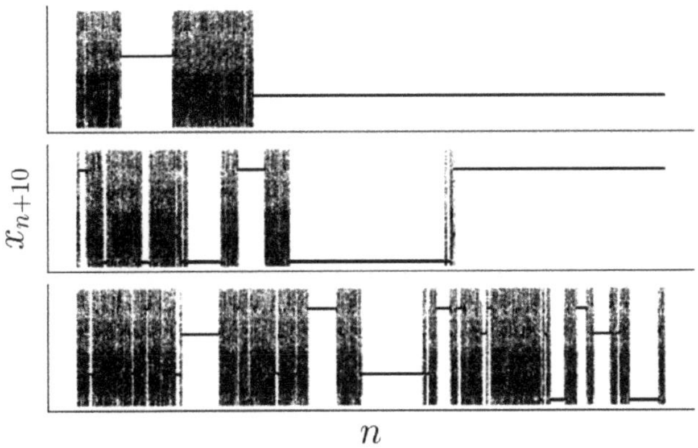

Figure 20. Change in duration in laminar phases as ε grows away from α_c: (**top**) $\varepsilon = e^{-20}$, (**middle**) $\varepsilon = e^{-18}$, (**bottom**) $\varepsilon = e^{-15}$. $\alpha_c \sim 0.6890011\ldots$, $\beta = 0.5$.

To determine the laminar or regular region, we use a second method. We define the distance between the map and the DHS surface. To determine this distance, we must find the minimum distance d from a 4th dimensional point $p_n = (x_n, y_n, x_{n+10}, y_{n+10})$ to a hyper-surface determined by DHS: $\{x_n, y_n, x_{n+10}, y_{n+10} \in \mathbf{R}^4 | \, x_n = x_{n+10} \wedge y_n = y_{n+10}\}$. So, we must find a point of the hyper-surface $p_s = (x_s, y_s, x_s, y_s)$ (because it satisfies the hyper-surface constraint) whose distance is the minimum to our point p_n. The 4th-dimensional Euclidean distance between the points will be

$$d = \sqrt{(x_n - x_s)^2 + (y_n - y_s)^2 + (x_{n+10} - x_s)^2 + (y_{n+10} - y_s)^2}, \tag{10}$$

minimizing the expression taking its derivatives with respect to x_s and y_s and equating them to zero, we obtain that

$$x_s = \frac{x_n + x_{n+10}}{2} \qquad y_s = \frac{y_n + y_{n+10}}{2} \tag{11}$$

Figure 21 shows the temporal evolution of the variables x_{n+10} and y_{n+10}, along with the distance to the DHS surface calculated using Equation (10).

The numerical results for the characteristic relations are presented in Figure 22. This figure illustrates the relationship between the average or mean laminar length and the control parameter. The blue points represent the numerical results, while the red line is derived from Equation (8). It is noteworthy that there is good agreement between the numerical findings and the theoretical predictions.

Finally, we analyze the following case: $\beta = 0.3$ and $\alpha \approx 0.778$ (see Figure 13). To determine the laminar interval, we employed the distance between the map and the DHS surface given by Equation (8). The results for the average laminar length are shown in Figure 23.

For the three analyzed cases, we numerically confirm the validity of Equation (8) for the two-dimensional map studied in this investigation. This equation indicates that the same scaling behavior of the laminar length as a function of the control parameter observed in one-dimensional maps is also applicable for the map given by Equation (2).

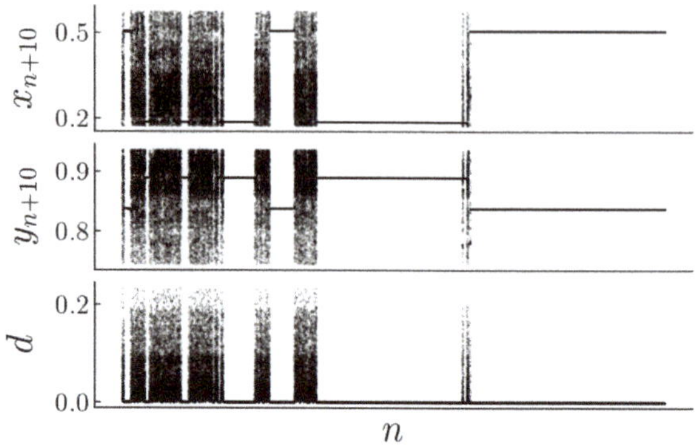

Figure 21. Temporal series for x_{n+10}, y_{n+10} and d (distance to DHS).

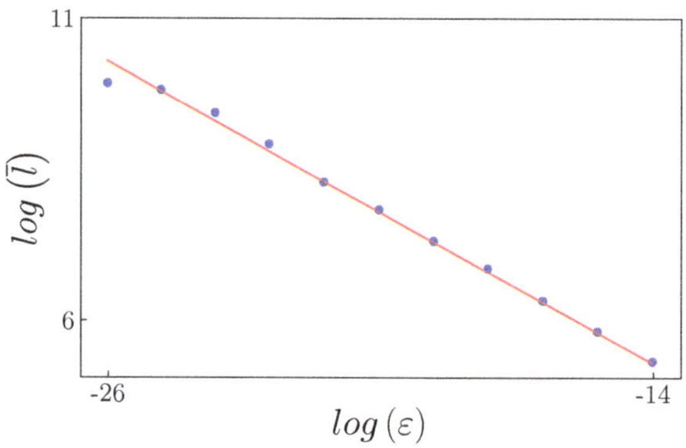

Figure 22. Mean laminar length and control parameter: in blue is the numerical result, and in red is a line with slope -0.5. $\alpha \sim 0.689011$ and $\beta = 0.5$.

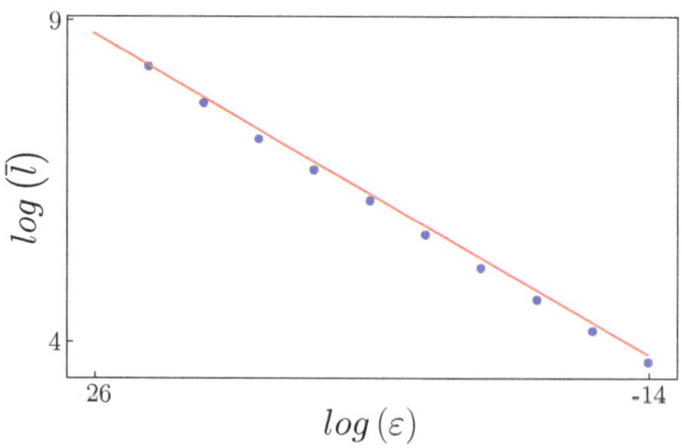

Figure 23. Mean laminar length and control parameter: in blue is the numerical result, and in red is a line with slope -0.5. $\alpha \sim 0.77826511\ldots$ and $\beta = 0.3$.

4. Conclusions

We explore the intricate dynamics of the two-dimensional map defined by Equation (2). Our analysis includes calculating the solutions and their stability, bifurcation diagrams, and the basins of attraction for the system's attractors. We observe that, for constant β, the solutions rapidly multiply when the control parameter α is altered, leading to significant changes in their stability. Additionally, we examine the intermittency phenomenon generated at distinct values of the control parameters α and β and numerically derive the characteristic relationship associated with two-dimensional intermittency.

The system's symmetry results in bifurcation diagrams that vary with the initial conditions. We discover that the symmetry of these initial conditions influences the solutions; different attractors emerge for cases where $x_0 = y_0$ compared with $x_0 \neq y_0$. Furthermore, we confirm that the bifurcations of fixed points and their stability changes depend on the chosen initial conditions.

We also investigate the relationship between the average laminar length and the control parameter $\varepsilon = \alpha_c - \alpha$. To identify the laminar or regular phases in high-dimensional maps, we propose two alternative approaches (see Equations (9) and (10)). One method utilizes the error function, while the other calculates the distance between the map and the DHS surface. The first method is simpler, but the second method takes both variables into account. Despite these differences, both approaches yield the same results. Our calculations confirm that, for all studied cases, the relationship we obtain for type I intermittency aligns with what has been established for one-dimensional maps using classical theory.

Author Contributions: Conceptualization, J.C. and S.E.; methodology, J.C. and S.E.; software, J.C.; validation, J.C. and S.E.; formal analysis, J.C. and S.E.; investigation, J.C. and S.E.; resources, J.C. and S.E.; writing—original draft preparation, J.C. and S.E.; writing—review and editing, J.C. and S.E.; visualization, J.C.; supervision, S.E.; project administration, S.E.; funding acquisition, S.E. All authors have read and agreed to the published version of the manuscript.

Funding: This research was funded by Proyecto Consolidar, SECyT-Universidad Nacional de Córdoba: "Desarrollo y aplicación de estudios teóricos, numéricos y códigos computacionales en mecánica de fluidos e intermitencia caótica". Also, the first author is a doctoral fellowship of CONICET.

Data Availability Statement: The data presented in this study are available on request from the corresponding author.

Acknowledgments: We acknowledge the Departamento de Ingeniería Aeroespacial, FCEFyN and Instituto de Estudios Avanzados en Ingeniería y Tecnología, UNC-CONICET.

Conflicts of Interest: The authors declare no conflicts of interest.

Abbreviations

The following abbreviations are used in this manuscript:

RPD	Reinjection probability density function
LBR	Lower boundary of reinjection
DHS	Diagonal hyper-surface

References

1. Petrzela, J. Chaotic Steady States of the Reinartz Oscillator: Mathematical Evidence and Experimental Confirmation. *Axioms* **2023**, *12*, 1101. [CrossRef]
2. Schmiegel, J.; Pons, F. Stochastic Intermittency Fields in a von Kármán Experiment. *Symmetry* **2021**, *13*, 1752. [CrossRef]
3. Irimiciuc, S.; Saviuc, A.; Tudose-Sandu-Ville, F.; Toma, S.; Nedeff, F.; Marcela Rusu, C.; Agop, M. Non-Linear Behaviors of Transient Periodic Plasma Dynamics in a Multifractal Paradigm. *Symmetry* **2020**, *12*, 1356. [CrossRef]
4. Stavrinides, S.; Miliou, A.; Laopoulos, T.; Anagnostopoulos, A. The intermittency route to chaos of an electronic digital oscillator. *Int. J. Bifurc. Chaos* **2008**, *18*, 1561–1566. [CrossRef]

5. Malasoma, J.; Werny, P.; Boiron, M. Multichannel type-I intermittency in two models of Rayleigh-Benard convection. *Phys. Rev Lett.* **2004**, *51*, 487–500. [CrossRef]
6. Elaskar, S.; del Rio, E.; Elaskar, S. Intermittency Reinjection in the Logistic Map. *Symmetry* **2022**, *14*, 481. [CrossRef]
7. Pizza, G.; Frouzakis, C.; Mantzaras, J. Chaotic dynamics in premixed Hydrogen/air channel flow combustion. *Combust. Theor Model* **2012**, *16*, 275–299. [CrossRef]
8. Sánchez-Arriaga, G.; Sanmartín, J.; Elaskar, S. Damping models in the truncated derivative nonlinear Schrödinger equation. *Phys Plasmas* **2007**, *14*, 082108. [CrossRef]
9. Manneville, P. Intermittency, self-similarity & 1/f spectrum in dissipative dynamical systems. *J. Phys.* **1980**, *41*, 1235–1243.
10. Saha, A.; Feudel, U. Characteristics of in-out intermittency in delay-coupled FitzHugh–Nagumo oscillators. *Eur. Phys. J. Spec. Top* **2018**, *227*, 1205–1219. [CrossRef]
11. Li, H.-H.; Xiao, J.-H.; Hu, G.; Hu, B. Intermittencies in complex Ginzburg–Landau equation by varying system size. *Chin. Phys. B* **2010**, *19*, 050516. [CrossRef]
12. Elaskar, S.; del Rio, E. Theoretical Evaluation of the Reinjection Probability Density Function in Chaotic Intermittency. *Symmetry* **2023**, *15*, 1591. [CrossRef]
13. Elnashaie, S.; Abashar, M.; Teymour, F. Bifurcation, instability and chaos in fluidized bed catalytic reactors with consecutive exothermic chemical reactions. *Chaos Solitons Fractals* **1993**, *3*, 1–33. [CrossRef]
14. Serre, T.; Nesme-Ribes, E. Nonlinear analysis of solar cycles. *Astron. Astrophys.* **2000**, *360*, 319–330.
15. Coulibaly, S.; Clerc, M.; Selmi, F.; Barbay, S. Extreme events following bifurcation to spatiotemporal chaos in a spatially extended microcavity laser. *Phys. Rev. A* **2017**, *95*, 023816. [CrossRef]
16. Sujith, R.; Unni, V. Complex system approach to investigate and mitigate thermoacoustic instability in turbulent combustors *Phys. Fluids* **2020**, *32*, 061401. [CrossRef]
17. Zambrano, S.; Mariño, I.P.; Sanjuán, M. Controlling crisis-induced intermittency using its relation with a boundary crisis. *New J. Phys.* **2009**, *11*, 023025. [CrossRef]
18. Zebrowski, J.; Baranowski, R. Type-I intermittency in nonstationary systems: Models and human heart-rate variability. *Phys. A* **2004**, *336*, 74–86. [CrossRef]
19. Velazquez, J.; Khosravani, H.; Lozano, A.; Bardakjian, B.; Carlen, P.; Wennberg, R. Type III intermittency in human partial epilepsy *Eur. J. Neurosci.* **1999**, *11*, 2571–2576. [CrossRef] [PubMed]
20. Chian, A. *Complex System Approach to Economic Dynamics. Lecture Notes in Economics and Mathematical Systems*; Springer: Berlin/Heidelberg, Germany, 2007.
21. Bhansali, R.; Holland, M.; Kokoszka, P. Intermittency, long-memory and financial returns. In *Long Memory in Economics*; Springer: Berlin/Heidelberg, Germany, 2007; pp. 39–68.
22. Bashkirtseva, I.; Nasyrova, V.; Ryashko, L. Scaling and intermittency of brains events as a manifestation of consciousness. *Chaos Solitons Fractals* **2018**, *110*, 76–81. [CrossRef]
23. Gardiner, J.; Atema, J. The function of bilateral odor arrival time differences in olfactory orientation of sharks. *Curr. Biol.* **2010**, *20*, 1187–1191. [CrossRef]
24. Hirsch, J.; Huberman, B.; Scalapino, D. Theory of intermittency. *Phys. Rev. Lett.* **1982**, *25*, 519–532. [CrossRef]
25. Nayfeh, A.; Balachandran, B. *Applied Nonlinear Dynamics*; Wiley: New York, NY, USA, 1995.
26. Schuster, H.; Just, W. *Deterministic Chaos*; Wiley VCH: Mörlenbach, Germany, 2005.
27. Elaskar, S.; del Rio, E. *New Advances on Chaotic Intermittency and Applications*; Springer: New York, NY, USA, 2017; ISBN 978-3-319-47836-4.
28. Elaskar, S.; del Rio, E. Review of Chaotic Intermittency. *Symmetry* **2023**, *15*, 1195. [CrossRef]
29. Kim, C.; Kye, W. Two-dimensional type-I intermittency. *Phy. Rev. E* **2001**, *63*, 037202. [CrossRef]
30. Kuznetsov, N.; Mokaev, T.; Ponomarenko, V.; Seleznev, E.; Stankevich, N.; Chua, L. Hidden attractors in Chua circuit: Mathematical theory meets physical experiments. *Nonlinear Dyn.* **2023**, *111*, 5859–5887. [CrossRef]
31. Colman, J.; Elaskar, S. Intermitencia en un mapa bidimensional. In Proceedings of the XXXIX Congreso Argentino de Mecánica Computacional, Concordia, Argentina, 6–11 November 2023; Mecánica Computacional; Volume 40, pp. 403–412.
32. Sajid, M. Chaotic Behaviour and Bifurcation in Real Dynamics of Two Parameter Family of Functions including Logarithmic Map. *Abstr. Appl. Anal.* **2020**, *2020*, 7917184. [CrossRef]

axioms

MDPI

Article

Strong Stability of the Thermoelastic Bresse System with Second Sound and Fractional Delay

Khaled Zennir and Loay Alkhalifa *

Department of Mathematics, College of Science, Qassim University, Buraydah 52571, Saudi Arabia; k.zennir@qu.edu.sa
* Correspondence: loay.alkhalifa@qu.edu.sa

Abstract: The thermoelastic Bresse system is a mathematical model that describes the dynamic behavior of elastic beams accounting for both mechanical deformations and thermal effects. Incorporating concepts such as second sound and fractional delay into this system enhances its ability to model complex physical phenomena. The paper studies a Bresse thermoelastic system with fractional delay and second sound. Firstly, we prove the existence and uniqueness of the solution for our system using semi-group theory. Additionally, we derive an exponential decay estimate for the associated semi-group utilizing suitable multiplier techniques.

Keywords: Bresse system; second-sound phenomenon; thermoelasticity; strong stability; fractional delay; multiplier techniques; fractional derivatives

MSC: 93D15; 74J30

1. Introduction and Problem Statement

Around 1867, Maxwell drew scientists' attention to a theoretical contradiction hidden in Fourier's law, which produces a contradiction in many scientific applications that have any kind of relationship to the subject: thermodynamics, machinists, thermal technicians, and so on. The core of the problem is very simple. The task of thermal diffusion described in Fourier's law leads to the equivalent differential equation, and as a result of the infinite velocity of diffusion. As a solution to this kind of contradiction, dozens of modified laws and methods of modification have been implemented, and the common feature of these efforts is that they all result in a hyperbolic differential equation and the propagation velocity becomes finite. This is the origin of the name "second sound", which has become the slogan of the entire phenomenon; see [1–3]. The extension of derivatives and integrals to fractional orders was discussed as soon as integral and differential calculus was introduced. However, even though the area has many applications, little attention has been paid to this area until recently. For instance, models of thermoelastic bodies, continuous media with memory, and temperature and humidity transformations in atmospheric layers and in diffusion equations make use of fractional calculus; see [4–6]. It is well known in the theory of thermoelasticity that the compound system that determines these phenomena includes differential equations and fractional equations. As the thermoelasticity theory is essentially a linear theory, these differential equations are also linear, so they can be solved using fairly simple methods. Similarly to integro-differential, systems of fractional-integral and fractional-differential equations usually do not have exact solutions. The presence of a fractional derivative with respect to time in the first equation of the Bresse system is interpreted as a reflection of a special property of the process being described, such as memory effects, or, in the case of a stochastic process, the influence of past states; see [7–9]. Fractional derivatives with respect to coordinates usually reflect the self-similar inhomogeneity of the structure or medium in which the process develops. Such structures are called fractals.

The new problem of interactions between the effects of the second-sound phenomenon and fractional delay on thermoelasticity has not been solved yet. The very complicated feature of the question has several signs; please see [10,11]. One of which is the impact of the delay and second sound on the stability. Another is related to thermoelasticity; see [12,13].

Let $x \in \Omega = (0,1)$ and $t \in (0,\infty)$. We consider a thermoelastic Bresse system

$$\begin{cases} \rho_1\varrho_{tt} - k(\varphi + \varrho_x + l\vartheta)_x - lk_0(\vartheta_x - l\varrho) + a_0\varrho_t + \mu\partial_t^{\alpha,\alpha_0}\varrho(x,t-\tau_0) = 0 \\ \rho_2\varphi_{tt} - b\varphi_{xx} + k(\varphi + \varrho_x + l\vartheta) + \gamma\theta_x = 0 \\ \rho_1\vartheta_{tt} - k_0(\vartheta_x - l\varrho)_x + lk(\varphi + \varrho_x + l\vartheta) = 0 \\ \rho_3\theta_t + q_x + \gamma\varphi_{tx} = 0 \\ \tau q_t + \beta q + \theta_x = 0 \\ \\ \varrho(x,0) = \varrho_0(x), \varrho_t(x,0) = \varrho_1(x), \theta(x,0) = \theta_0(x) \\ \varphi(x,0) = \varphi_0(x), \varphi_t(x,0) = \varphi_1(x), q(x,0) = q_0(x) \\ \vartheta(x,0) = \vartheta_0(x), \vartheta_t(x,0) = \vartheta_1(x), \varrho_t(x,-t) = f_0(x,t), t \in (0,\tau_0) \\ \varrho(0,t) = \varrho_x(1,t) = \varphi(1,t) = \varphi_x(0,t) = 0 \\ \vartheta(1,t) = \vartheta_x(0,t) = \theta(0,t) = q(1,t) = 0. \end{cases} \tag{1}$$

Here, the parameters $\rho_1, \rho_2, \rho_3, k, k_0, b, l, \alpha_0, a_0, \gamma, \tau, \beta$ are all positive, $\alpha \in (0,1)$, $\alpha_0 > 0$ and $\mu \in \mathbb{R}$, where the time delay is represented by $\tau_0 > 0$. Here, $\varrho = \varrho(x,t)$, $\varphi = \varphi(x,t)$, and $\vartheta = \vartheta(x,t)$ represent the vertical, longitudinal, and shear angle displacements, respectively, while the fourth and fifth coupled equations with variables θ and q represent the additional thermoelastic damping phenomenon. The system (1) is, of course, provided with specific boundary conditions (with respect to x) and initial conditions (with respect to t). The second sound physical properties come from the heat conduction, which is described by Fourier's law, which implies an infinite speed of heat propagation. However, in certain materials, especially at low temperatures, heat propagates at a finite speed, a phenomenon known as "second sound". This behavior is often modeled using Cattaneo's law, modifying the heat equation to account for finite thermal propagation speeds. In the context of the Bresse system, incorporating second sound leads to a more accurate representation of the thermoelastic interactions.

The operator $\partial_t^{\alpha,\alpha_0}$ is the generalized fractional derivative of order α, and it is expressed by:

$$\partial_t^{\alpha,\alpha_0}u(t) = \frac{1}{\Gamma(1-\alpha)}\int_0^t (t-s)^{-\alpha}e^{-\alpha_0(t-s)}\frac{du}{ds}(s)ds.$$

Fractional delay refers to the incorporation of memory effects into the system, acknowledging that the current state is influenced by its history. This is achieved by introducing terms that account for past states, often modeled using fractional calculus. In the Bresse system, the fractional delay can be represented through integral terms that capture the influence of past deformations and thermal states on the current behavior. In the following, we recall some works on the asymptotic behavior of solutions for thermoelastic Bresse systems. In [14], a Bresse system with thermal dissipation effective is considered

$$\begin{cases} \rho_1\varrho_{tt} - k(\varphi + \varrho_x + l\vartheta)_x - lk_0(\vartheta_x - l\varrho) = 0 \\ \rho_2\varphi_{tt} - b\varphi_{xx} + k(\varphi + \varrho_x + l\vartheta) + \gamma\theta_x = 0 \\ \rho_1\vartheta_{tt} - k_0(\vartheta_x - l\varrho)_x + lk(\varphi + \varrho_x + l\vartheta) = 0 \\ \theta_t - k_1\theta_{xx} + m\varphi_{tx} = 0. \end{cases}$$

The exponential stability is shown if and only if the speeds of wave propagation are equal. A similar model was studied later in [15], where the authors proposed a Timoshenko system of thermoelasticity of type III with a delay

$$\begin{cases} \rho_1\varrho_{tt} - k(\varrho_x + \varphi)_x + \mu_1\varrho_t + \mu_2\varrho_t(x, t-\tau) = 0 \\ \rho_2\varphi_{tt} - b\varphi_{xx} + k(\varphi + \varrho_x) + \beta\theta_{tx} = 0 \\ \rho_3\theta_{tt} - \delta\theta_{xx} + \gamma\varphi_{tx} - K\theta_{txx} = 0. \end{cases}$$

When certain conditions on the initial data were present, the authors proved the exponential decay of the solution when the wave prorogation speeds were equal, regardless of the presence of the delay term.

Motivated by the above articles, we study Problem (1). We structure our article as follows. In Section 2, some useful tools and results are listed, which will be used later. In the third section, we define a new system that is related to (1). Then, we give the existence and uniqueness result for the new system by using the semi-group theory. The strong stability for the new section is proved in Section 5 using the multiplier technique.

2. Preliminary

In this section, we state useful results for the model (1). We begin with the following theorem, and lemma are needed.

Theorem 1 ([16])**.** *Define the function ϑ as follows:*

$$\vartheta(\xi) = |\xi|^{(2\alpha-1)/2} \quad -\infty < \xi < +\infty, 0 < \alpha < 1.$$

Then, the 'input' U and the 'output' O of the system

$$\partial_t\varphi(\xi, t) + (\xi^2 + k)\varphi(\xi, t) - U(t)\vartheta(\xi) = 0,$$

$$\varphi(\xi, 0) = 0,$$

$$O(t) = (\pi)^{-1}\sin(\alpha\pi)\int_{-\infty}^{+\infty}\vartheta(\xi)\varphi(\xi, t)d\xi,$$

have a relationship that is given by

$$O = I^{1-\alpha,\alpha_0}U = D^{\alpha,\alpha_0}U,$$

where

$$[I^{\alpha,\alpha_0}f](t) = \frac{1}{\Gamma(\alpha)}\int_0^t (t-s)^{\alpha-1}e^{-\alpha_0(t-s)}f(s)ds.$$

The following lemma is given by [12], and it is important for our reformulation.

Lemma 1. *Let*

$$D_{\alpha_0} = \{\lambda \in \mathbb{C} : Re\lambda + \alpha_0 > 0\} \cup \{\lambda \in \mathbb{C} : Im\lambda \neq 0\}$$

If $\lambda \in D_{\alpha_0}$, *then*

$$\int_{-\infty}^{+\infty} \frac{\vartheta^2(\xi)}{\lambda + \alpha_0 + \xi^2} d\xi = \frac{\pi}{\sin(\alpha\pi)} (\lambda + \alpha_0)^{\alpha - 1}.$$

For positive real numbers a and b, and conjugate exponents p and q satisfying

$$\frac{1}{p} + \frac{1}{q} = 1,$$

Young's inequality states:

$$ab \leq \frac{a^p}{p} + \frac{b^q}{q}.$$

This can be extended beyond products to convolutions. For functions f and g in appropriate L^p spaces, the convolution $f * g$ satisfies:

$$\|f * g\|_r \leq \|f\|_p \|g\|_q,$$

where

$$\frac{1}{r} = \frac{1}{p} + \frac{1}{q}.$$

3. The Major Results

The system (1) can be reformulated to a suitable problem. To do this, the following variable will be introduced, as in [4]:

$$z(x, \rho, t) = \varrho_t(x, t - \rho\tau_0), \ \rho \in (0, 1).$$

With a simple differentiation, we can show that this variable satisfies

$$\tau_0 z_t(x, \rho, t) + z_\rho(x, \rho, t) = 0, \ \rho \in (0, 1).$$

Hypotheses on the weights of damping terms with/without delay are taken as

$$\mu\alpha_0^{\alpha-1} < a_0.$$

Consequently, Theorem 1 enables us to derive an equivalent system:

$$\begin{cases} \rho_1 \varrho_{tt} - k(\varphi + \varrho_x + l\vartheta)_x - lk_0(\vartheta_x - l\varrho) + a_0\varrho_t + \zeta \int_{-\infty}^{+\infty} \phi(v)\Psi(x, v, t) dv = 0 \\ \rho_2 \varphi_{tt} - b\varphi_{xx} + k(\varphi + \varrho_x + l\vartheta) + \gamma\theta_x = 0 \\ \rho_1 \vartheta_{tt} - k_0(\vartheta_x - l\varrho)_x + lk(\varphi + \varrho_x + l\vartheta) = 0 \\ \rho_3 \theta_t + q_x + \gamma\varphi_{tx} = 0 \\ \tau q_t + \beta q + \theta_x = 0 \\ \tau_0 z_t(x, \rho, t) + z_\rho(x, \rho, t) = 0, \\ \partial_t \Psi(x, v, t) + (v^2 + \alpha_0)\Psi(x, v, t) - z(x, 1, t)\phi(v) = 0, v \in \mathbb{R} \\ \varrho(x, 0) = \varrho_0(x), \varrho_t(x, -t) = f_0(x, t), \theta(x, 0) = \theta_0(x), t \in (0, \tau_0) \\ \varphi(x, 0) = \varphi_0(x), \varphi_t(x, 0) = \varphi_1(x), q(x, 0) = q_0(x) \\ \vartheta(x, 0) = \vartheta_0(x), \vartheta_t(x, 0) = \vartheta_1(x), z(w, 0, t) = \varrho_t(x, t), \\ \varrho(0, t) = \varrho_x(1, t) = \varphi(1, t) = \varphi_x(0, t) = 0 \\ \vartheta(1, t) = \vartheta_x(0, t) = \theta(0, t) = q(1, t) = 0, \\ \Psi(x, v, 0) = 0, v \in \mathbb{R}, \end{cases} \quad (2)$$

where

$$\zeta = \mu(\pi)^{-1}\sin(\alpha\pi),$$

and

$$I = \int_{-\infty}^{+\infty} \frac{\phi^2(v)}{v^2+\alpha_0} dv.$$

Now, the energy of solutions of (2) can be defined by

$$\begin{aligned}\mathcal{E}(t) &= \frac{1}{2}\int_0^1 \left[\rho_1\varrho_t^2 + \rho_2\varphi_t^2 + b\varphi_x^2 + \rho_1\vartheta_t^2 + \rho_3\theta^2 + \tau q^2\right]dx + \frac{\delta}{2}\int_0^1\int_0^1 z^2(x,\rho,t)d\rho dx \\ &+ \frac{\Lambda}{2}\int_0^1\int_{-\infty}^{+\infty} \Psi^2(x,v,t)dvdx + \frac{1}{2}\int_0^1 \left[k_0(\vartheta_x - l\varrho)^2 + k(\varrho_x + \varphi + l\vartheta)^2\right]dx,\end{aligned} \quad (3)$$

with

$$\Lambda I\tau_0 < \delta < \tau_0(2a_0 - \zeta I) \quad \text{and} \quad \zeta < \Lambda. \quad (4)$$

This energy equation satisfies the next estimate.

Lemma 2. *Let*

$$U = (\varrho, u, \varphi, v, \vartheta, \varpi, \theta, q, z, \Psi)^T,$$

be a solution to system (2)*, then the energy defined by* (3) *satisfies*

$$\mathcal{E}'(t) \le -C\left[\int_0^1 q^2 dx + \int_0^1 \varrho_t^2 dx + \int_0^1\int_{-\infty}^{+\infty}\left(v^2+\alpha_0\right)\Psi^2(x,v,t)dvdx + \int_0^1 z^2(x,1,t)dx\right]. \quad (5)$$

Proof. By multiplying $(2)_1, (2)_2, (2)_3, (2)_4, (2)_5, (2)_6$, and $(2)_7$ by $\varrho_t, \varphi_t, \vartheta_t, \theta, q, \delta z$, and $\Lambda\Psi$, respectively, and then integrating over Ω and summing up, we obtain

$$\begin{aligned}\mathcal{E}'(t) &= -\zeta\int_0^1\int_{-\infty}^{+\infty}\Psi(x,v,t)\varrho_t\phi(v)dvdx - \beta\int_0^1 q^2dx \\ &- \Lambda\int_0^1\int_{-\infty}^{+\infty}\Psi^2(x,v,t)(v^2+\alpha_0)dvdx \\ &- \Lambda\int_0^1\int_{-\infty}^{+\infty}\Psi(x,v,t)z(x,1,t)\phi(v)dvdx \\ &- a_0\int_0^1\varrho_t^2dx - \frac{\delta}{\tau_0}\int_0^1\int_0^1 z(x,\rho,t)z_\rho(x,\rho,t)d\rho dx.\end{aligned} \quad (6)$$

We have

$$\begin{aligned}-\frac{\delta}{\tau_0}\int_0^1\int_0^1 z(x,\rho,t)z_\rho(x,\rho,t)d\rho dx &= -\frac{\delta}{2\tau_0}\int_0^1\int_0^1\frac{\partial}{\partial\rho}z^2(x,\rho,t)d\rho dx \\ &= \frac{\delta}{2\tau_0}\int_0^1\left[\varrho_t^2 - z^2(x,1,t)\right]dx.\end{aligned}$$

Now, Young's inequality yields

$$\begin{aligned}
&-\zeta\int_0^1\int_{-\infty}^{+\infty}\Psi(x,v,t)z(x,1,t)\phi(v)dvdx\\
&\leq\frac{\zeta I}{2}\left(\int_0^1 z^2(x,1,t)dx\right)+\frac{\zeta}{2}\int_0^1\int_{-\infty}^{+\infty}(v^2+\alpha_0)\Psi^2dvdx,
\end{aligned}$$

and

$$-\Lambda\int_0^1\int_{-\infty}^{+\infty}\phi(v)\Psi(x,v,t)\varrho_t dvdx\leq\frac{\Lambda I}{2}\left(\int_0^1\varrho_t^2dx\right)+\frac{\Lambda}{2}\int_0^1\int_{-\infty}^{+\infty}(v^2+\alpha_0)\Psi^2dvdx.$$

Inserting the last two inequalities in (6) will lead to

$$\begin{aligned}
\mathcal{E}'(t)\leq&\left(-a_0+\frac{\zeta I}{2}+\frac{\delta}{2\tau_0}\right)\int_0^1\varrho_t^2dx+\left(\frac{\Lambda I}{2}-\frac{\delta}{2\tau_0}\right)\int_0^1 z^2(x,1,t)dx\\
&-\beta\int_0^1 q^2dx+\left(\frac{\zeta I}{2}-\frac{\Lambda}{2}\right)\int_0^1\int_{-\infty}^{+\infty}\left(v^2+\alpha_0\right)\Psi^2(x,v,t)dvdx,
\end{aligned}$$

from (4), the proof is completed. □

4. Existence and Uniqueness

The semi-group theory will be needed to prove that there exists a unique solution to the system (2). Define

$$U=(\varrho,u,\varphi,v,\vartheta,\varpi,\theta,q,z,\Psi)^T,$$

where $u=\varrho_t$, $v=\varphi_t$ and $\varpi=\vartheta_t$.

Now, we can rewrite (2) to be

$$\begin{cases}U'(t)=\mathbf{A}U(t)\\ U(t=0)=U_0=(\varrho_0,\varrho_1,\varphi_0,\varphi_0,\vartheta_0,\vartheta_1,\theta_0,q_0,z_0,0)^T,\end{cases}\tag{7}$$

where

$$\mathbf{A}:D(\mathbf{A})\subset\mathrm{H}\to\mathrm{H},$$

is the linear operator defined by

$$\mathbf{A}U=\begin{bmatrix}u\\ \frac{k}{\rho_1}(\varphi+\varrho_x+l\vartheta)_x+\frac{lk_0}{\rho_1}(\vartheta_x-l\varrho)-\frac{a_0}{\rho_1}u-\frac{\zeta}{\rho_1}\int_{-\infty}^{+\infty}\phi(v)\Psi(x,v,t)dv\\ v\\ \frac{b}{\rho_2}\varphi_{xx}-\frac{k}{\rho_2}(\varphi+\varrho_x+l\vartheta)-\frac{\gamma}{\rho_2}\theta_x\\ \varpi\\ \frac{k_0}{\rho_1}(\vartheta_x-l\varrho)_x-\frac{lk}{\rho_1}(\varphi+\varrho_x+l\vartheta)\\ -\frac{1}{\rho_3}q_x-\frac{\gamma}{\rho_3}v_x\\ -\frac{\beta}{\tau}q-\frac{1}{\tau}\theta_x\\ -\frac{1}{\tau_0}z_\rho\\ -(v^2+\alpha_0)\Psi+z(x,1,t)\phi(v),\end{bmatrix}\tag{8}$$

and H is the energy space given by

$$\begin{aligned} \mathrm{H} = & \mathrm{H}^1_*(\Omega) \times L^2(\Omega) \times \tilde{\mathrm{H}}^1_*(\Omega) \times L^2(\Omega) \times \tilde{\mathrm{H}}^1_*(\Omega) \times L^2(\Omega) \\ & \times L^2(\Omega) \times L^2(\Omega) \times L^2(\Omega \times \Omega) \times L^2(\Omega \times \mathbb{R}), \end{aligned}$$

with

$$\begin{aligned} \mathrm{H}^1_*(\Omega) &= \{f \in \mathrm{H}^1(\Omega) : f(0) = 0\} \\ \tilde{\mathrm{H}}^1_*(\Omega) &= \{f \in \mathrm{H}^1(\Omega) : f(1) = 0\} \\ \mathrm{H}^2_*(\Omega) &= \mathrm{H}^2(\Omega) \cap \mathrm{H}^1_*(\Omega) \\ \tilde{\mathrm{H}}^2_*(\Omega) &= \mathrm{H}^2(\Omega) \cap \tilde{\mathrm{H}}^1_*(\Omega). \end{aligned}$$

The inner product in H is defined by

$$\begin{aligned} (U, \tilde{U})_{\mathrm{H}} = & k \int_0^1 (\varrho_x + \varphi + l\vartheta)(\tilde{\varrho}_x + \tilde{\varphi} + l\tilde{\vartheta})dx + k_0 \int_0^1 (\vartheta_x - l\varrho)(\tilde{\vartheta}_x - l\tilde{\varrho})dx \\ & + \rho_1 \int_0^1 u\tilde{u}dx + b \int_0^1 \varphi_x \tilde{\varphi}_x dx + \rho_2 \int_0^1 v\tilde{v}dx + \rho_1 \int_0^1 \varpi\tilde{\varpi}dx + \rho_3 \int_0^1 \theta\tilde{\theta}dx + \tau \int_0^1 q\tilde{q}dx \\ & + \delta \int_0^1 \int_0^1 z\tilde{z}d\rho dx + \Lambda \int_0^1 \int_{-\infty}^{+\infty} \Psi(x, v, t)\tilde{\Psi}(x, v, t)dvdx. \end{aligned}$$

The domain of the linear operator $\mathbf{A}$ is

$$D(\mathbf{A}) = \left\{ \begin{array}{l} U \in \mathrm{H}/\varrho \in \mathrm{H}^2_*(\Omega); \varphi, \vartheta \in \tilde{\mathrm{H}}^2_*(\Omega); u, \theta \in \mathrm{H}^1_*(\Omega); v, \varpi, q \in \tilde{\mathrm{H}}^1_*(\Omega), \\ \varrho_x(1) = \varphi_x(0) = \vartheta_x(0) = 0; z, z_\rho \in L^2((0,1) \times L^2(\Omega)), z(x,0) = \varrho(x), \\ (v^2 + \alpha_0)\Psi - z(x,1,t)\phi(v) \in L^2(\Omega \times \mathbb{R}), \\ |v|\Psi \in L^2(\Omega \times \mathbb{R}) \end{array} \right\}. \quad (9)$$

We are going to show that the operator $\mathbf{A}$ generates a C_0 semi-group of contractions in H. To this end, we start by proving that $\mathbf{A}$ is monotone.

Lemma 3. *The linear operator $\mathbf{A}$ is monotone and for any $U \in D(\mathbf{A})$, the following inequality is satisfied:*

$$(\mathbf{A}U, U) < -C \left[\int_0^1 q^2 dx + \int_0^1 u^2 dx + \int_0^1 \int_{-\infty}^{+\infty} \left(v^2 + \alpha_0\right)\Psi^2(x, v, t)dvdx + \int_0^1 z^2(x, 1, t)dx \right]. \quad (10)$$

Proof. We can easily show that $D(\mathbf{A})$ is dense in H. Besides, for any

$$U = (\varrho, u, \varphi, v, \vartheta, \varpi, \theta, q, z, \Psi)^T \in D(\mathbf{A}),$$

we have

$$\mathcal{E}(t) = \frac{1}{2}\|U\|^2.$$

Then, from (7), we have

$$\begin{aligned} \mathcal{E}'(t) &= (U', U) \\ &= (\mathbf{A}U, U). \end{aligned}$$

Using (10), we conclude that the operator $\mathbf{A}$ is monotone. □

Next, we prove the following lemma with respect to the operator $(I - \mathbf{A})$.

Lemma 4. *The operator $(I - \mathbf{A})$ is surjective.*

Proof. For any

$$G = (g_1, g_2, g_3, g_4, g_5, g_6, g_7, g_8, g_9, g_{10}) \in \mathrm{H},$$

there exists $U \in D(\mathbf{A})$, which satisfies

$$(I - \mathbf{A})U = G. \tag{11}$$

It can be observed that Equation (11) is equivalent to

$$\begin{cases} -u + \varrho = g_1 \in \mathrm{H}_*^1(\Omega) \\ -k(\varphi + \varrho_x + l\vartheta)_x - lk_0(\vartheta_x - l\varrho) + (a_0 + \rho_1)u + \zeta \displaystyle\int_{-\infty}^{+\infty} \phi(\nu)\Psi(x,\nu,t)d\nu = \rho_1 g_2 \in L^2(\Omega) \\ -v + \varphi = g_3 \in \tilde{\mathrm{H}}_*^1(\Omega) \\ -b\varphi_{xx} + k(\varphi + \varrho_x + l\vartheta) + \gamma\theta_x + \rho_2 v = \rho_2 g_4 \in L^2(\Omega) \\ -\varpi + \vartheta = g_5 \in \tilde{\mathrm{H}}_*^1(\Omega) \\ -k_0(\vartheta_x - l\varrho)_x + lk(\varphi + \varrho_x + l\vartheta) + \rho_1\varpi = \rho_1 g_6 \in L^2(\Omega) \\ q_x + \gamma v_x + \rho_3\theta = \rho_3 g_7 \in L^2(\Omega) \\ (\tau + \beta)q + \theta_x = \tau g_8 \in L^2(\Omega) \\ z_\rho + \tau_0 z = \tau_0 g_9 \in L^2(\Omega \times (0,1)) \\ (\nu^2 + \alpha_0)\Psi - z(x,1,t)\phi(\nu) + \Psi = g_{10}(x,\nu) \in L^2(\Omega \times \mathbb{R}). \end{cases} \tag{12}$$

By $(12)_8$, we have

$$\tau \int_0^x g_8(y)dy - (\tau + \beta)\int_0^x q(y)dy = \theta,$$

which means that $\theta(0,t) = 0$. Given that

$$z(x,0) = u(x),$$

$$u = \varrho - g_1,$$

$$v = \varphi - g_3,$$

and

$$\varpi = \vartheta - g_5.$$

Integrating the Equation $(12)_9$ yields

$$z(x,\rho) = \varrho(x)e^{-\tau_0\rho} - e^{-\tau_0\rho}g_1(x) + \tau_0 e^{-\tau_0\rho}\int_0^\rho e^{\tau_0 s}g_9(x,s)ds,$$

then

$$z(x,1) = \varrho(x)e^{-\tau_0} - e^{-\tau_0}g_1(x) + \tau_0 e^{-\tau_0}\int_0^1 e^{\tau_0 s}g_9(x,s)ds.$$

From $(12)_{10}$, one has

$$\Psi = \frac{g_{10}(x,\nu) + z(x,1,t)\phi(\nu)}{\nu^2 + \alpha_0 + 1}.$$

Now, it can be easily shown that $\varrho,\varphi,\vartheta$ and q satisfy the following system

$$\begin{cases} -k(\varphi+\varrho_x+l\vartheta)_x - lk_0(\vartheta_x - l\varrho) + (a_0+\rho_1+\zeta M e^{-\tau_0})\varrho = h_1 \in L^2(\Omega) \\ -b\varphi_{xx} + k(\varphi+\varrho_x+l\vartheta) + \rho_2\varphi - \gamma(\tau+\beta)q = h_2 \in L^2(\Omega) \\ -k_0(\vartheta_x - l\varrho)_x + lk(\varphi+\varrho_x+l\vartheta) + \rho_1\vartheta = h_3 \in L^2(\Omega) \\ -q_x + \rho_3(\tau+\beta)\int\limits_0^x q(y)dy - \gamma\varphi_x = h_4 \in L^2(\Omega), \end{cases} \tag{13}$$

with

$$M = \int_{-\infty}^{+\infty} \frac{\phi^2(\nu)}{\nu^2+\alpha_0+1} d\nu,$$

and

$$\begin{cases} h_1 = \rho_1 g_2 + (a_0+\rho_1+\zeta M e^{-\tau_0})g_1 - \zeta M\tau_0 e^{-\tau_0}\int_0^1 e^{\tau_0 s} g_9(x,s)ds - \zeta\int_{-\infty}^{+\infty} \frac{g_{10}(x,\nu)\phi(\nu)}{\nu^2+\alpha_0+1}d\nu \\ h_2 = (g_3+g_4)\rho_2 - \gamma\tau g_8 \\ h_3 = (g_5+g_6)\rho_1 \\ h_4 = -\gamma g_{3x} - \rho_3\left(g_7 - \tau\int_0^x g_8(y)dy\right). \end{cases} \tag{14}$$

Multiplying $(13)_1, (13)_2, (13)_3$ and $(13)_4$ by $\tilde{\varrho}, \tilde{\varphi}, \tilde{\vartheta}$ and

$$(\tau+\beta)\int_0^x \tilde{q}(y)dy,$$

respectively. Then, integrating over Ω and summing up, we obtsain the variational formulation of (13), as

$$\mathcal{B}((\varrho,\varphi,\vartheta,q),(\tilde{\varrho},\tilde{\varphi},\tilde{\vartheta},\tilde{q})) = L(\varrho,\varphi,\vartheta,q), \tag{15}$$

where

$$\mathcal{B} : \left[\mathrm{H}^1_*(\Omega)\times\tilde{\mathrm{H}}^1_*(\Omega)\times\tilde{\mathrm{H}}^1_*(\Omega)\times L^2(\Omega)\right]^2 \to \mathbb{R},$$

is the bilinear form defined by

$$\begin{aligned} \mathcal{B}((\varrho,\varphi,\vartheta,q),(\tilde{\varrho},\tilde{\varphi},\tilde{\vartheta},\tilde{q})) &= k\int_0^1 (\varrho_x+\varphi+l\vartheta)(\tilde{\varrho}_x+\tilde{\varphi}+l\tilde{\vartheta})dx + k_0\int_0^1 (\vartheta_x - l\varrho)(\tilde{\vartheta}_x - l\tilde{\varrho})dx \\ &+ \rho_3(\tau+\beta)^2\int\limits_0^1 \left(\int_0^x q(y)dy\right)\left(\int_0^x \tilde{q}(y)dy\right)dx + \gamma(\tau+\beta)\int_0^1 \tilde{q}\varphi dx \\ &+ (a_0+\rho_1+\zeta M e^{-\tau_0})\int_0^1 \varrho\tilde{\varrho}dx \\ &+ b\int_0^1 \varphi_x\tilde{\varphi}_x dx + \rho_2\int_0^1 \varphi\tilde{\varphi}dx - \gamma(\tau+\beta)\int_0^1 q\tilde{\varphi}dx + \rho_1\int_0^1 \vartheta\tilde{\vartheta}dx + \gamma(\tau+\beta)\int_0^1 q\tilde{q}dx, \end{aligned}$$

and

$$L : \left[\mathrm{H}^1_*(\Omega)\times\tilde{\mathrm{H}}^1_*(\Omega)\times\tilde{\mathrm{H}}^1_*(\Omega)\times L^2(\Omega)\right] \to \mathbb{R},$$

is the linear functional given by

$$L(\varrho,\varphi,\vartheta,q) = \int_0^1 h_1\tilde{\varrho}dx + \int_0^1 h_2\tilde{\varphi}dx + \int_0^1 h_3\tilde{\vartheta}dx + (\tau+\beta)^2\int_0^1 h_4\left(\int_0^x \tilde{q}(y)dy\right)dx.$$

Let us now define a new space V by

$$V = \mathrm{H}^1_*(\Omega)\times\tilde{\mathrm{H}}^1_*(\Omega)\times\tilde{\mathrm{H}}^1_*(\Omega)\times L^2(\Omega),$$

equipped with the norm

$$\|(\varrho,\varphi,\vartheta,q)\|_V = \|(\varrho_x+\varphi+l\vartheta)\|_2^2 + \|(\vartheta_x-l\varrho)\|_2^2 + \|\varphi\|_2^2 + \|q\|_2^2.$$

It is easy to see, if l is small enough, that

$$\int_0^1 \left(\varrho_x^2+\varphi_x^2+\vartheta_x^2\right)dx \le c\int_0^1 \left[(\varrho_x+\varphi+l\vartheta)^2+(\vartheta_x-l\varrho)^2+\varphi_x^2\right]dx,$$

which shows us that $\mathcal{B}$ and L are bounded in $V\times V$ and V, respectively.
Moreover, the definition of $\mathcal{B}$ will lead to

$$\mathcal{B}((\varrho,\varphi,\vartheta,q),(\varrho,\varphi,\vartheta,q)) \ge c\|(\varrho,\varphi,\vartheta,q)\|_V^2,$$

which means that $\mathcal{B}$ is coercive. As a result, from the Lax–Milgram theorem, we conclude that the system (13) has a unique solution

$$(\varrho,\varphi,\vartheta,q)\in \mathrm{H}_*^1(\Omega)\times\tilde{\mathrm{H}}_*^1(\Omega)\times\tilde{\mathrm{H}}_*^1(\Omega)\times L^2(\Omega).$$

Now, by substituting $\varrho,\varphi,\vartheta$ and q into $(12)_1,(12)_3,(12)_5$ and $(12)_8$, respectively, we find that

$$(u,v,\varpi,\theta)\in \mathrm{H}_*^1(\Omega)\times\tilde{\mathrm{H}}_*^1(\Omega)\times\tilde{\mathrm{H}}_*^1(\Omega)\times L^2(\Omega).$$

If

$$(\tilde{\varphi},\tilde{\vartheta},\tilde{q})=(0,0,0)\in\tilde{\mathrm{H}}_*^1(\Omega)\times\tilde{\mathrm{H}}_*^1(\Omega)\times L^2(\Omega),$$

then, (15) provides us

$$k\int_0^1(\varrho_x+\varphi+l\vartheta)(\tilde{\varrho}_x+\tilde{\varphi}+l\tilde{\vartheta})dx+k_0\int_0^1(\vartheta_x-l\varrho)(\tilde{\vartheta}_x-l\tilde{\varrho})dx=\int_0^1 h_1\tilde{\varrho}dx, \tag{16}$$

for all $\varrho\in\mathrm{H}_*^1(\Omega)$. The latter implies that

$$-k\varrho_{xx}=k\varrho_x+l(k_0+k)\vartheta_x-\left(k_0l^2+\rho_1+a_0+\zeta Me^{-\tau_0}\right)\varrho+h_1\in L^2(\Omega). \tag{17}$$

Then, from the regularity theory for the linear elliptic equations, we obtain $\varrho\in\mathrm{H}_*^2(\Omega)$. Moreover, (16) is also true for any ϕ satisfying $\phi\in C^1([0,1])$ and $\phi(0)=0$, which is in $\mathrm{H}_*^1(\Omega)$. Therefore, for any $\phi\in C^1([0,1])$, we obtain

$$k\int_0^1\varrho_x\phi_x dx-\int_0^1\left[k\varrho_x+l(k_0+k)\vartheta_x-\left(k_0l^2+\rho_1+a_0+\zeta Me^{-\tau_0}\right)\varrho+h_1\right]\phi dx=0.$$

When the last equation is integrated in parts, using (17) will lead to

$$\phi(1)\varrho_x(1)=0\quad\forall\phi\in C^1([0,1]),$$

and, thus, $\varrho_x(1)=0$. In the same way, we can verify that

$$\begin{cases}-b\varphi_{xx}=-k\varrho_x-(k+\rho_2)\varphi-kl\vartheta-\gamma(\tau+\beta)q+h_2\in L^2(\Omega)\\ -b\vartheta_{xx}=-l(k_0+k)\varrho_x-kl\varphi+(\rho_1+l^2k_0)\vartheta+h_3\in L^2(\Omega)\\ -q_x=\gamma\varphi_x-(\tau+\beta)\rho_3\int_0^x q(y)dy+h_4\in L^2(\Omega).\end{cases}$$

Then, we have

$$\varphi,\vartheta\in\tilde{H}_*^2(\Omega),q\in\tilde{H}_*^1(\Omega),$$

and

$$\vartheta_x(0) = \varphi_x(0) = 0,$$

which leads to the existence of a unique solution $U \in D(\mathbf{A})$ to (11). This completes the proof. □

The previous two lemmas imply that the operator **A** is a maximal monotone operator. Then, **A** is the infinitesimal generator of a linear contraction C_0-semi-group on H. In other words, this can be considered as the proof of the following theorem (see [17]).

Theorem 2. *(Existence and uniqueness)*

1. *If $U_0 \in D(A)$, then there exists a unique strong solution to system* (7)*, and it is given by*

$$U \in C(\mathbb{R}^+, D(A)) \cap C^1(\mathbb{R}^+, \mathrm{H}).$$

2. *If $U_0 \in \mathrm{H}$, then there exists a unique weak solution to system* (7)*, and it is given by*

$$U \in C(\mathbb{R}^+, \mathrm{H}).$$

5. Exponential Stability

The exponential stability of the semi-group $S(t)$ in the Hilbert space H will be demonstrated in this section, then there exists a strong unique solution to the system (7). We will need to employ the necessary and sufficient conditions for C_0-semi-groups to be exponentially stable in a Hilbert space, which was achieved by Gearhart [18].

Theorem 3. *Let*

$$S(t) = e^{\mathrm{A}t},$$

be a C_0-semi-group of contractions on Hilbert space H. Then, $S(t)$ is exponentially stable if and only if

$$\rho(\mathrm{A}) \supseteq \{i\chi : \chi \in \mathbb{R}\} \equiv i\mathbb{R}, \tag{18}$$

$$\overline{\lim_{|\chi| \to \infty}} \left\| (i\chi I - \mathrm{A})^{-1} \right\| < \infty, \tag{19}$$

hold, where $\rho(\mathrm{A})$ denotes the resolvent set of A.

Theorem 4. *The C_0-semi-group of contractions $e^{\mathrm{A}t}$, $t > 0$, generated by* A*, is exponentially stable.*

Proof. Proving the exponential stability of $e^{\mathrm{A}t}$ requires demonstrating the validity of Theorem 3. By verifying the properties (18) and (19). To begin with, we establish the following

$$\rho(\mathrm{A}) \supseteq \{i\lambda : \lambda \in \mathbb{R}\} \equiv i\mathbb{R}. \tag{20}$$

This can be proved in contradiction. Assume that $\tilde{\lambda} \in \mathbb{R}$ with $\tilde{\lambda} \neq 0$ and $U \neq 0$, such that

$$\mathrm{A}U = i\tilde{\lambda}U.$$

Then

$$\begin{cases} i\tilde{\lambda}\varrho - u = 0 \\ i\tilde{\lambda}\rho_1 u - k(\varphi + \varrho_x + l\vartheta)_x - lk_0(\vartheta_x - l\varrho) + a_0 u + \zeta \int\limits_{-\infty}^{+\infty} \phi(v)\Psi(x,v,t)dv = 0 \\ i\tilde{\lambda}\varphi - v = 0 \\ i\tilde{\lambda}\rho_2 v - b\varphi_{xx} + k(\varphi + \varrho_x + l\vartheta) + \gamma\theta_x = 0 \\ i\tilde{\lambda}\vartheta - \varpi = 0 \\ i\tilde{\lambda}\rho_1\varpi - k_0(\vartheta_x - l\varrho)_x + lk(\varphi + \varrho_x + l\vartheta) = 0 \\ i\tilde{\lambda}\rho_3\theta + q_x + \gamma v_x = 0 \\ i\tilde{\lambda}\tau q + \beta q + \theta_x = 0 \\ i\tilde{\lambda}\tau_0 z + z_\rho = 0 \\ i\tilde{\lambda}\Psi + (v^2 + \alpha_0)\Psi - z(x,1,t)\phi(v) = 0. \end{cases} \tag{21}$$

From (10), we obtain

$$u = 0, \quad q = 0, \quad z(x,1) = 0.$$

From $(21)_{10}$ we obtain $\Psi = 0$, from $(21)_8$ we obtain $\theta = 0$, and $(21)_1$ gives us $\varrho = 0$. From $(21)_9$, we can write the solution

$$z(x,\rho) = Ce^{-i\tilde{\lambda}\tau_0\rho},$$

as the only one. With the fact $z(x,1) = 0$, we obtain $z(x,\rho) = 0$. We continue, using $(21)_7$ with the initial conditions to obtain $v = 0$, then $(21)_3$ gives us $\varphi = 0$. From $(21)_4$, we can conclude that $\vartheta = 0$. Finally, from $(21)_5$, we deal with $\varpi = 0$. In other words, $\|U\|_H = 0$, but this is a contradiction with $U \neq 0$; therefore, there are no imaginary eigenvalues.

Now, the proof of (19) will be given.

Assume (19) is false, that is

$$\lim_{|\lambda|\to\infty} \sup \left\| (i\lambda I - \mathrm{A})^{-1} \right\| = \infty.$$

Then, there exists a sequence $(V_n) \in H$ and $\lambda_n \in \mathbb{R}$, such that

$$\left\| (i\lambda_n I - \mathrm{A})^{-1} V_n \right\| > n\|V_n\|,$$

for all $n > 0$. Given

$$i\lambda_n \in \rho(\mathrm{A}),$$

it can be observed that there exists a unique sequence $(U_n) \in D(\mathrm{A})$, such that

$$i\lambda_n U_n - \mathrm{A}U_n = V_n, \quad \|U_n\| = 1,$$

i.e.,

$$U_n = (i\lambda I - \mathrm{A})^{-1} V_n,$$

and

$$\|U_n\| > n\|i\lambda_n U_n - \mathrm{A}U_n\|.$$

Now, define

$$F_n = i\lambda_n U_n - \mathrm{A}U_n,$$

which results in $\|F_n\| \leq \frac{1}{n}$, and then $F_n \to 0$ (strong) in H and $n \to \infty$.

Let

$$u = \varrho_t, v = \varphi_t, \omega = \vartheta_t,$$

and

$$U_n = (\varrho^n, u^n, \varphi^n, v^n, \vartheta^n, \omega^n, \theta^n, q^n, z^n, \Psi^n),$$

and

$$F_n = (f_1^n, f_2^n, f_3^n, f_4^n, f_5^n, f_6^n, f_7^n, f_8^n, f_9^n, f_{10}^n).$$

From

$$F_n = i\lambda_n U_n - \mathrm{A}U_n,$$

the following equations can be obtained

$$\begin{cases} i\lambda_n \varrho^n - u^n = f_1^n \\ i\lambda_n \rho_1 u^n - k(\varphi^n + \varrho_x^n + l\vartheta^n)_x - lk_0(\vartheta_x^n - l\varrho^n) + a_0 u^n + \zeta \int_{-\infty}^{+\infty} \phi(\nu)\Psi^n(x,\nu,t)d\nu = \rho_1 f_2^n \\ i\lambda_n \varphi^n - v^n = f_3^n \\ i\lambda_n \rho_2 v^n - b\varphi_{xx}^n + k(\varphi^n + \varrho_x^n + l\vartheta^n) + \gamma\theta_x^n = \rho_2 f_4^n \\ i\lambda_n \vartheta^n - \omega^n = f_5^n \\ i\lambda_n \rho_1 \omega^n - k_0(\vartheta_x^n - l\varrho^n)_x + lk(\varphi^n + \varrho_x^n + l\vartheta^n) = \rho_1 f_6^n \\ i\lambda_n \rho_3 \theta^n + q_x^n + \gamma v_x^n = \rho_3 f_7^n \\ i\lambda_n \tau q^n + \beta q^n + \theta_x^n = \tau f_8^n \\ i\lambda_n \tau_0 z^n + z_\rho^n = \tau_0 f_9^n \\ i\lambda_n \Psi^n + (\nu^2 + \alpha_0)\Psi^n - z^n(x,1,t)\phi(\nu) = f_{10}^n. \end{cases} \tag{22}$$

Taking the real part of the inner product of $(i\lambda_n I - \mathrm{A})U_n$ and U_n in H, noting that U_n is bounded and $F_n \to 0$ and using (10) will lead to

$$a_0 \int_0^1 (u^n)^2 dx + \beta \int_0^1 (q^n)^2 dx + \int_0^1 (z^n(x,1))^2 dx \to 0, \tag{23}$$

where

$$u^n \to 0, \quad q^n \to 0, \quad z^n(x,1) \to 0, \tag{24}$$

then, from $(22)_{10}$ we obtain $\Psi^n \to 0$.

Now, with the fact that

$$\frac{k}{\rho_1} = \frac{b}{\rho_2},$$

and $k = k_0$, after some calculations, we obtain

$$\begin{aligned} \int_0^1 \Big[& \rho_2(v^n)^2 + b(v_x^n)^2 + \rho_1(\omega^n)^2 + \rho_3(\theta^n)^2 + (z^n(x,1))^2 \\ & + k(\varphi^n + \varrho_x^n + l\vartheta^n)^2 + k(\vartheta_x^n - l\varrho^n)^2 \Big] dx \to 0, \end{aligned} \tag{25}$$

so that

$$i\lambda_n \|U_n\|^2 - (\mathrm{A}U_n, U_n) \to 0.$$

Then, $\lambda_n \|U_n\| \to 0$, which is true only if $\|U_n\| \to 0$. This contradicts $\|U_n\| = 1$; therefore, the proof of the theorem is now completed. □

6. Conclusions

The integration of second sound and fractional delay into the thermoelastic Bresse system provides a more comprehensive framework to model the dynamic behavior of thermoelastic beams, particularly in scenarios where the speed of propagation of the heat and historical effects are significant, and this is the case in the present work. An analysis of the exponential stability is conducted. The study establishes both the existence and uniqueness of solutions for the system through semi-group theory, deriving an exponential decay estimate for the associated semi-group via appropriate multiplier techniques.

Our system models the interplay between mechanical and thermal waves in materials, incorporating advanced concepts from fractional calculus and non-local effects.

Author Contributions: Writing—original draft preparation, K.Z. and, L.A.; writing—review and editing, K.Z. and L.A. All authors have read and agreed to the published version of the manuscript.

Funding: This research is funded by the Deanship of Graduate Studies and Scientific Research at Qassim University.

Data Availability Statement: The original contributions presented in the study are included in the article; further inquiries can be directed to the corresponding author.

Acknowledgments: The Researchers would like to thank the Deanship of Graduate Studies and Scientific Research at Qassim University for financial support (QU-APC-2025).

Conflicts of Interest: The authors declare no conflicts of interest.

References

1. Choucha, A.; Ouchenane, D.; Zennir, K. Stability for thermo-elastic Bresse system of second sound with past history and delay term. *Inter. J. Model. Ident. Control* **2021**, *6*, 315–328.
2. Lagnese, J.E.; Leugering, G.; Schmidt, E. J. P. Modelling of dynamic networks of thin thermo-elastic beams. *Math. Meth. Appl. Sci.* **1993**, *16*, 327–358. [CrossRef]
3. Lagnese, J.E.; Leugering, G.; Schmidt, E.J.P.G. *Modeling, Analysis and Control of Dynamic Elastic Multi-Link Structures, Systems and Control: Foundations and Applications*; Springer: Boston, MA, USA, 1994.
4. Nicaise, S.; Pignotti, C. Stability and instability results of the wave equation with a delay term in the boundary or internal feedbacks. *SIAM J. Control Optim.* **2006**, *45*, 1561–1585. [CrossRef]
5. Suh, I.H.; Bien, Z. Use of time delay action in the controller design. *IEEE Trans. Autom. Contr.* **1980**, *25*, 600–603. [CrossRef]
6. Beniani, A.; Bahri, N.; Alharbi, R.; Bouhali, K.; Zennir, K. Stability for Weakly Coupled Wave Equations with a General Internal Control of Diffusive Type. *Axioms* **2023**, *12*, 48. [CrossRef]
7. Choucha, A.; Ouchenane, D.; Mirgani, S.M.; Hassan, E.I.; Alfedeel, A.H.A.; Zennir, K. Exploring thermo-elastic Effects in Damped Bresse Systems with Distributed Delay. *Mathematics* **2024**, *12*, 857. [CrossRef]
8. Elhindi, M.; Zennir, K.; Ouchenane, D.; Choucha, A.; El Arwadi, T. Bresse-Timoshenko type systems with thermodiffusion effects: Well-possedness, stability and numerical results. *Rend. Circ. Mat. Palermo Ser.* **2023**, *72*, 169–194. [CrossRef]
9. Zennir, K.; Feng, B. One spatial variable thermo-elastic transmission problem in viscoelasticity located in the second part. *Math. Meth. Appl. Sci.* **2018**, *41*, 6895–6906. [CrossRef]
10. Djeradi, F.S.; Yazid, F., Georgiev, S.G.; Hajjej, Z.; Zennir, K. On the time decay for a thermo-elastic laminated beam with microtemperature effects, nonlinear weight, and nonlinear time-varying delay. *AIMS Math.* **2023**, *8*, 26096–26114. [CrossRef]
11. Dridi, H.; Zennir, K. Well-posedness and energy decay for some thermo-elastic systems of Timoshenko type with Kelvin-Voigt damping. *SeMA J.* **2021**, *78*, 385–400. [CrossRef]
12. Benaissa, A.; Gaouar, S. Stability result of the Lame′ system with a delay term in the internal fractional feedback. *Acta Univ. Sapientiae Math.* **2021**, *13*, 336–355. [CrossRef]
13. Li, G.; Luan, Y.; Liu, W. Well-posedness and exponential stability of a thermo-elastic-Bresse system with second sound and delay. *Hacet. J. Math. Stat.* **2020**, *49*, 523–538. [CrossRef]
14. Fatori, L.H.; Rivera, J.E.M. Rates of decay to weak thermo-elastic Bresse system. *IMA J. Appl. Math.* **2020**, *75*, 881–904. [CrossRef]
15. Kafini, M.; Messaoudi, S.A.; Mustafa, M.I.; Apalara, T. Well-posedness and stability results in a Timoshenko-type system of thermo-elasticity of type III with delay. *Z. Angew. Math. Phys.* **2015**, *66*, 1499–1517. [CrossRef]

6. Mbodje, B. Wave energy decay under fractional derivative controls. *IMA J. Math. Contr. Inf.* **2006**, *23*, 237–257. [CrossRef]
7. Pazy, A. *Semi-Groups of Linear Operators and Applications to Partial Differential Equations*; Springer Science & Business Media: Berlin/Heidelberg, Germany, 2012.
8. Liu, K. Characteristic conditions for exponential stability of linear dynamical systems in Hilbert spaces. *Chin. Sci. Bull.* **1985**, *44*, 1343.

axioms

MDPI

Article

Interaction of a Four-Level Atom with a Deformed Quantum Field: Mathematical Model and Quantum Resources

Mariam Algarni [1], Sayed Abdel-Khalek [2] and Kamal Berrada [3,*]

[1] Department of Mathematical Sciences, College of Science, Princess Nourah bint Abdulrahman University, P.O. Box 84428, Riyadh 11671, Saudi Arabia; mmalgarni@pnu.edu.sa
[2] Department of Mathematics and Statistics, College of Science, Taif University, P.O. Box 11099, Taif 21944, Saudi Arabia; sayedquantum@yahoo.co.uk
[3] Department of Physics, College of Science, Imam Mohammad Ibn Saud Islamic University (IMSIU), P.O. Box 90950, Riyadh 11432, Saudi Arabia
* Correspondence: berradakamal@ymail.com

Abstract: We introduce a framework presenting the interaction between a four-level atom (F-LA) and a field mode that begins in a coherent state within the para-Bose field (P-BF). The F-LA is considered in a cascade configuration and initially prepared in the upper level. We display the system dynamics by solving the motion equation. We discuss various dynamical behaviors of fundamental quantum resources used in quantum optics and information tasks, including atomic population inversion, quantum entanglement (QE), and the statistical properties of the P-BF based on the parameters of the quantum model. In this context, we demonstrate the impact of various system parameters on these quantum resources. Finally, we illustrate the dynamic relationships among the quantum resources within the model.

Keywords: para-Bose field; four-level atom; quantum entanglement; statistical properties

MSC: 20-xx; 81-xx

1. Introduction

In recent decades, numerous studies have explored extensions and modifications of the bosonic Fock–Heisenberg algebra to enhance various aspects of quantum field theory. Researchers have introduced different q-deformations of the simple harmonic oscillator using Jackson's q-calculus [1–4], leading to novel states associated with q-deformed Lie algebras, including q-coherent states, q-cat states, and q-squeezed states [4–12]. Another significant adaptation is the Wigner algebra, which integrates the reflection operator and the Wigner parameter into its structure. This formulation emerges within bosonic relationships and dynamics, yielding infinite-dimensional para-boson representations as well as finite-dimensional representations linked to parafermions [13]. These generalizations naturally lead to concepts involving para fields and para statistics [14,15].

The Jaynes–Cummings model (JCM) is widely utilized in quantum optics to depict the coupling between a two-level quantum system, such as an atom, and a single quantized mode of an electromagnetic field, adhering to the conditions of the rotating wave approximation [16]. This model has been expanded to encompass multi-photon transitions and various forms of fields, alongside an intensity-dependent coupling between the atom and the quantum field [17,18]. Extensions of the standard JCM have also explored additional levels, including three-level atomic systems [19–23]. In this context, many studies have examined the effects of the Kerr medium [24] and intensity-dependent coupling on the dynamics of three-level atomic systems. Furthermore, the interaction of two three-level atomic systems with a single-mode field, incorporating multi-photon transitions, has been examined in the presence of a Kerr nonlinear medium and detuning effects [25]. Recently, there has been growing interest in the quantum interaction between four-level atoms and cavity fields, with various configurations being explored [26,27].

Quantum entanglement is a fundamental feature of quantum theory, representing nonlocal correlations among composite quantum systems, where classical descriptions of correlations between subsystems are inadequate. It has been extensively studied in quantum information science [28–32] and is crucial for various applications, including quantum communication, teleportation, quantum entanglement swapping, cryptography, quantum computing, and dense coding [33–39]. The amount of entanglement can be quantified using measures such as von Neumann entropy, concurrence, linear entropy, and entanglement of formation [40,41]. Several methods have been proposed to quantify and identify quantum coherence within quantum systems [42]. Numerous studies have been undertaken to characterize and analyze quantum coherence, gaining significant attention through development and application of coherence quantification measures [43–45].

Beyond the specific domain of quantum optics, the mathematical methodologies and physical principles examined in this study have broader implications across multiple fields of physics. The deformed quantum algebras explored here, particularly para-Bose structures, have been extensively utilized in quantum gravity, where they play a crucial role in models of noncommutative space-time and extensions of the Heisenberg algebra [46–49]. Likewise, in condensed matter physics, these algebraic deformations have been instrumental in characterizing unconventional quantum phases, including topological insulators, superconductors, and quantum Hall systems, wherein fractional statistics arise as a consequence of strong electron correlations [50–53]. Specifically, para-statistics and deformed oscillator algebras provide a robust theoretical framework for investigating anionic excitations, which are fundamental to the description of fractional quantum Hall states and spin-liquid phases [54–56]. Furthermore, these mathematical structures contribute significantly to the theoretical modeling of correlated electron systems and quantum materials exhibiting nontrivial topological properties, where symmetry-protected quantum orders emerge [57–59]. In addition, the quantum resources analyzed in this work, such as entanglement and coherence, hold central importance in quantum information science, quantum computing, and quantum metrology. These properties are essential for advancing quantum cryptographic protocols, enhancing precision measurement techniques, and enabling the development of scalable quantum architectures [38,60–63]. By highlighting these interrelations, this study establishes a framework that extends beyond quantum optics and contributes to the broader landscape of modern physics. Moreover, our approach is closely aligned with recent experimental advances in superconducting qubit systems, engineered quantum states, and cavity quantum electrodynamics, further demonstrating the practical relevance of our findings beyond purely theoretical considerations [64–66].

Our manuscript focuses on examining the degree of entanglement, atomic coherence, and atomic inversion in a bipartite system where a four-level atom is coupled with a para-Bose field. We investigate how field deformation and photon transitions impact the dynamic behavior of quantifiers, particularly when the quantum field originates from a coherent state of the P-BF. The time evolution of entanglement between the four-level atom and para-Bose field is analyzed using quantum entropy, while atomic coherence is evaluated through the l_1 norm.

The manuscript is organized as follows: Section 2 describes the quantum model and dynamics, Section 3 presents the quantum quantifiers and discusses the numerical results, and Section 4 provides our conclusions.

2. Mathematical Model and Dynamics

This section describing the Hamiltonian of the interaction between one-mode P-BF with an F-LA has a state $|k\rangle$ ordered from upper to lower as $|1\rangle - |4\rangle$

$$\widehat{H}_{\text{int}} = \sum_{k=1}^{4} \varpi\left(\hat{a}^{J}|k\rangle\left\langle \mathrm{k}+1\right| + \hat{\mathrm{a}}^{\dagger J}\left|\mathrm{k}+1\right\rangle\langle \mathrm{k}|\right), \tag{1}$$

where ϖ represents the coupling constant between the F-LA and PB-field, J denotes the number of photons exchanged in transitions between (F-LA) and (P-BF), and $\widehat{a}^{\dagger}(\hat{a})$ is the creation (annihilation) operator of the quantized field, respectively, acting on the Fock states as

$$\hat{a}^{\dagger}|n\rangle = \sqrt{G(n+1)}|n+1\rangle, \;\; \hat{a}|n\rangle = \sqrt{G(n)}|n-1\rangle. \tag{2}$$

Here, the G is a positive function and is equal to $G(n) = n - \left(\left[\frac{n}{2}\right] - \left[\frac{n+1}{2}\right]\right)q$, and q is the P-BF deformed parameter.

The para-Bose field (P-BF) holds significance as it extends traditional bosonic field theory by introducing parastatistics, modifying the conventional commutation relations of annihilation and creation operators. These operators adhere to a parity-deformed oscillator algebra, where $\{R, \hat{a}\} = \{R, \hat{a}^{\dagger}\} = 0$ and $[\hat{a}, \hat{a}^{\dagger}] = G(N+1) - G(N)$, with $N = \hat{a}^{\dagger}\hat{a} + q(I - R)$, resulting in a more generalized Fock space representation. The operator R, known as the parity operator, is a Hermitian operator satisfying $R^2 = 1$, meaning it has eigenvalues ± 1, which classify states into even and odd parity components. This extension enables the study of systems where particles exhibit characteristics that differ from purely bosonic or fermionic behavior, making it a fundamental concept in quantum optics and quantum field theory [67]. The coherent states in the P-BF are characterized as the eigenstates associated with the field's annihilation operator. These states form an overcomplete and nonorthogonal basis, fulfilling the resolution of identity, akin to Glauber coherent states but with alterations due to parastatistical effects [67]. They exhibit notable quantum properties, such as photon antibunching, where the second-order intensity correlation function demonstrates a decreased probability of detecting two photons simultaneously. Additionally, they follow sub-Poissonian statistics, indicated by a negative Mandel parameter, signifying reduced photon number fluctuations compared to classical light sources [67]. Furthermore, these states show quadrature squeezing, where field quadratures x and p experience noise redistribution, confirming the presence of nonclassical effects [8]. Within the framework of JCM, extended to a single-mode P-BF, these states influence atomic inversion, modify Rabi oscillations, and enhance entanglement.

The final state of the (F-LA)–(P-BF) system at any time $\tau > 0$, where $\tau = \varpi t$ represents the scaled time, can be expressed as:

$$|\psi(\tau)\rangle = \sum_{n=0}^{\infty}\sum_{k=1}^{4} R_j(n,\tau)|n+k-1,k\rangle. \tag{3}$$

The amplitude $R_j(n,\tau), j = 1,2,3,4$ can be obtained by solving the equation of motion of this system:

$$-i\,\hbar\frac{\partial}{\partial t}|\psi(\tau)\rangle = \widehat{H}_{int}|\psi(\tau)\rangle. \tag{4}$$

At $\tau = 0$, the F-LA in the upper state and the field in the coherent state of the P-BF $|Z,q\rangle$. So, the initial state is assumed to be

$$|\psi(0)\rangle = |\psi_{\text{F-LA}}(0)\rangle \otimes |\psi_{\text{B-PF}}(0)\rangle = |1\rangle \otimes |Z,q\rangle, \tag{5}$$

where $|Z,q\rangle$ are provided as [41]

$$|Z,q\rangle = \frac{\exp\left(-\frac{|Z|^2}{2}\right)4^q\sqrt{(q!)^3}}{\sqrt{(2q)!}}\sum_{n=0}^{\infty} Z^n\sqrt{\frac{(q+[\frac{n}{2}])!}{[\frac{n}{2}]!(2q+n)!}}L_q^{[\frac{n-1}{2}]+\frac{1}{2}}\left(\frac{|Z|^2}{2}\right)|n\rangle. \quad (6)$$

Here, Z is the amplitude of the coherent state of the P-BF and $L_q^m(\ldots)$ are the associated Laguerre polynomials.

The coefficients R_j, representing the probability amplitudes, are determined by solving the time-dependent Schrödinger Equation (4) with the initial condition $|\psi(0)\rangle = |Z,q,1\rangle$. Consequently, these coefficients fulfill the following set of coupled differential equations:

$$\begin{pmatrix} R_1 \\ R_2 \\ R_3 \\ R_4 \end{pmatrix} = \begin{pmatrix} 0 & -i\varpi\sqrt{\frac{(n+J)!}{n!}} & 0 & 0 \\ -i\varpi\sqrt{\frac{(n+J)!}{n!}} & 0 & -i\varpi\sqrt{\frac{(n+2J)!}{(n+J)!}} & 0 \\ 0 & -i\varpi\sqrt{\frac{(n+2J)!}{(n+J)!}} & 0 & -i\varpi\sqrt{\frac{(n+3J)!}{(n+2J)!}} \\ 0 & 0 & -i\varpi\sqrt{\frac{(n+3J)!}{(n+2J)!}} & 0 \end{pmatrix}\begin{pmatrix} R_1 \\ R_2 \\ R_3 \\ R_4 \end{pmatrix}. \quad (7)$$

In this paper, we focus on the effects of single- and double-photon transitions, corresponding to $J = 1$ and 2, respectively. We analyze the time-dependent features of various quantum quantifiers related to the quantum system under investigation using the wave function $|\psi(\tau)\rangle$ (see Appendix A).

The atomic population inversion, quantum entropy, and coherence are all linked to the components of the atomic density matrix $\rho^{\text{F-LA}}(\tau)$, which is given by

$$\rho^{F\text{-}LA}(\tau) = Tr_{P\text{-}BF}|\psi(\tau)\rangle\langle\psi(\tau)| = \sum_{r=1}^{4}\sum_{l=1}^{4}\rho_{rl}(\tau)|r\rangle\langle l|. \quad (8)$$

The P-BF density matrix can be obtained as $\rho_{P\text{-BF}}(\tau) = Tr_{\text{F-LA}}|\psi(\tau)\rangle\langle\psi(\tau)| = \sum_m^{\infty}\rho_m|m\rangle\langle m|$.

3. Quantum Quantifiers

To investigate the effect of the P-BF deformed parameter q and single- and double-photon transition on the dynamics of quantum quantifiers, in Figures 1–4 illustrate the time-dependent behavior of the atomic inversion, second-order correlation function (S-OCF), atomic entropy, and atomic coherence.

3.1. Population Inversion Corresponding to the F-LA

Population inversion is one of the most significant quantities when considering quantum information. It can be applied to determine the collapse and revival times, which are crucial for characterizing the maximally entangled and separable state periods. We define the atomic population inversion through the diagonal elements of the atomic density matrix $\rho^{\text{F-LA}}(\tau)$ as

$$\rho_Z(\tau) = \rho_{11}(\tau) - \rho_{44}(\tau). \quad (9)$$

3.2. Nonclassical Effects

The S-OCF is widely employed to investigate the statistical characteristics of the field, as well as to assess photon bunching or antibunching phenomena. It is defined as:

$$g^{(2)}(\tau) = \frac{\left\langle \hat{L}^{\dagger 2}\hat{L}^2 \right\rangle}{\left\langle \hat{L}^{\dagger}\hat{L} \right\rangle^2}. \quad (10)$$

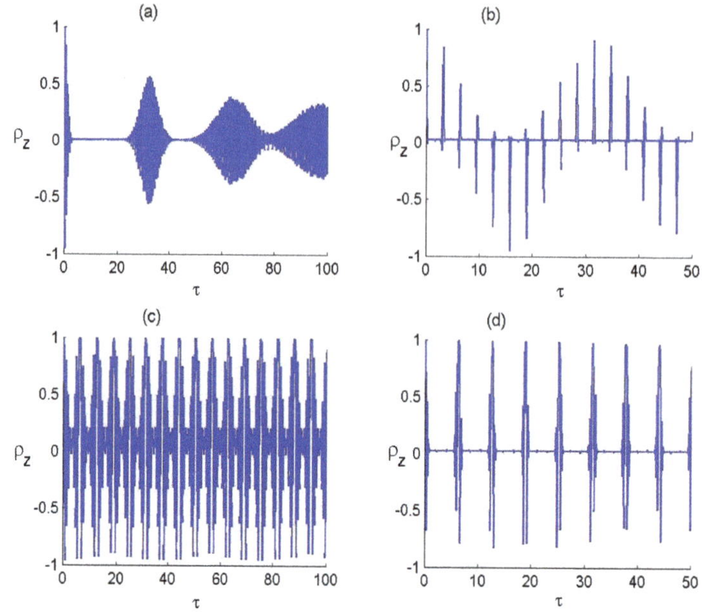

Figure 1. Dynamics of the atomic inversion ρ_Z of F-LA with $z = 4$ and for the parameter values of P-BF deformed parameter q and number of photons transitioned J as (**a**) $(q, J) = (\mathbf{0}, \mathbf{1})$, (**b**) $(q, J) = (\mathbf{0}, \mathbf{2})$, (**c**) $(q, J) = (\mathbf{20}, \mathbf{1})$, and (**d**) $(q, J) = (\mathbf{20}, \mathbf{2})$.

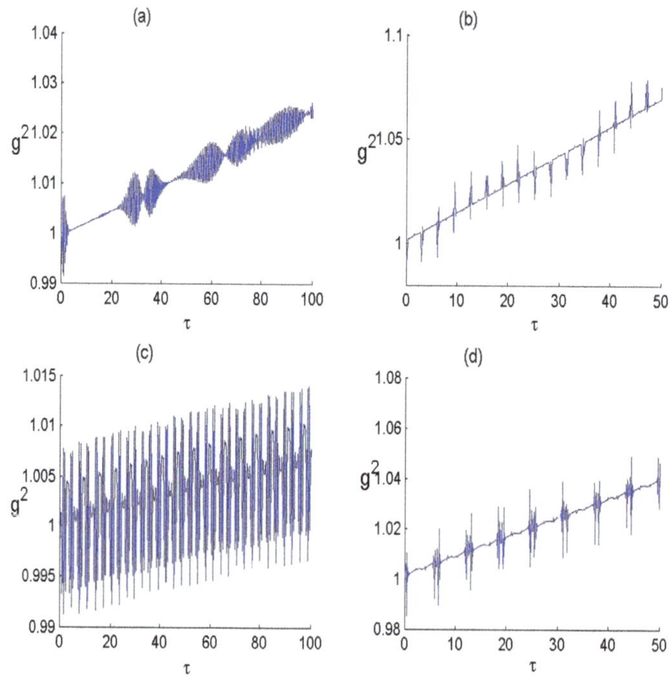

Figure 2. Dynamics of the S-OCF g^2, with $z = \mathbf{4}$ and for the parameter values of P-BF deformed parameter q and number of photons transitioned J as (**a**) $(q, J) = (\mathbf{0}, \mathbf{1})$, (**b**) $(q, J) = (\mathbf{0}, \mathbf{2})$, (**c**) $(q, J) = (\mathbf{20}, \mathbf{1})$, and (**d**) $(q, J) = (\mathbf{20}, \mathbf{2})$.

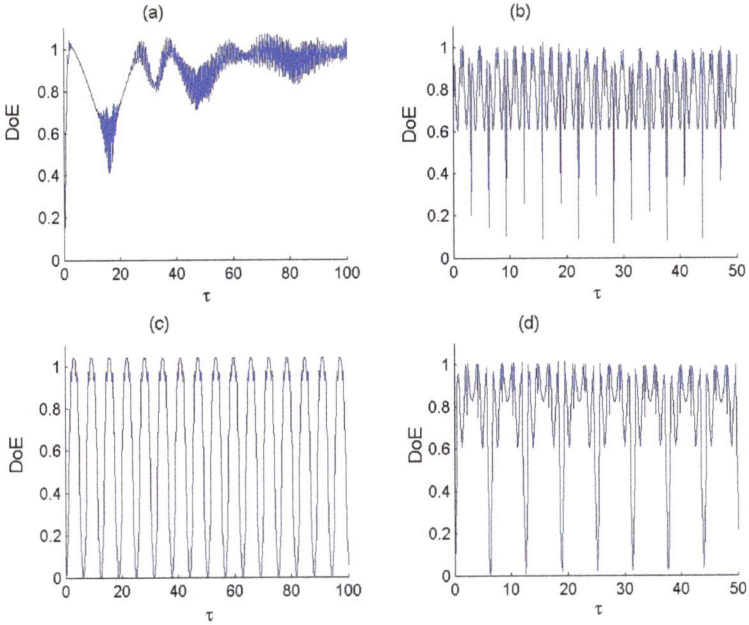

Figure 3. Dynamics of the $S_{F\text{-}LA}$ as a measure of QE between F-LA and P-BF with $z = \mathbf{4}$ and for the parameter values of P-BF deformed parameter q and number of photons transitioned J as **(a)** $(q, J) = (\mathbf{0}, \mathbf{1})$, **(b)** $(q, J) = (\mathbf{0}, \mathbf{2})$, **(c)** $(q, J) = (\mathbf{20}, \mathbf{1})$, and **(d)** $(q, J) = (\mathbf{20}, \mathbf{2})$.

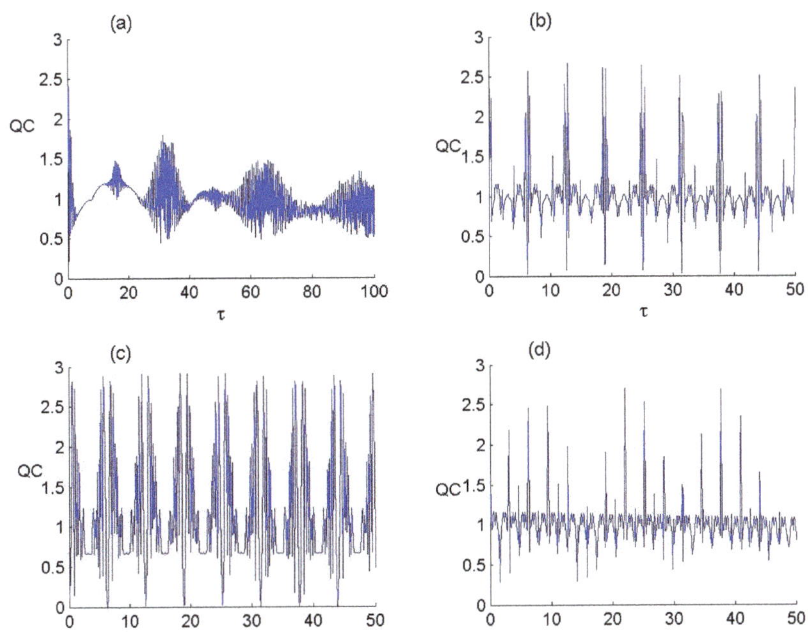

Figure 4. Dynamics of the quantum coherence Q_C, of F-LA with $z = \mathbf{4}$ and for the parameter values of P-BF deformed parameter q and number of photons transitioned J as **(a)** $(q, J) = (\mathbf{0}, \mathbf{1})$, **(b)** $(q, J) = (\mathbf{0}, \mathbf{2})$, **(c)** $(q, J) = (\mathbf{20}, \mathbf{1})$, and **(d)** $(q, J) = (\mathbf{20}, \mathbf{2})$.

We say that the quantized field is governed by super-Poissonian statistics if $g^{(2)} > 1$, Poissonian statistics if $g^{(2)} = 1$, and sub-Poissonian statistics if $g^{(2)} < 1$. The sub-Poissonian distribution of photons illustrates the quantum nature of the field.

3.3. *Quantum Entanglement*

The subsystem entropy, defined by the von Neumann entropy, can be used to determine the degree of entanglement (DoE) evolution of the (F-LA)–(P-BF) state. It is given by

$$DoE = -\mathrm{Tr}\left\{\rho^{\text{F-LA}}(\tau)\ln\left[\rho^{\text{F-LA}}(\tau)\right]\right\}, \tag{11}$$

where $\rho^{\text{F-LA}}(\tau)$ represents the F-LA density operator, as given by Equation (8). Based on refs. [40,41], the function $DoE_{(\text{F-LA})-(\text{P-BF})}$ takes the following form:

$$DoE_{(F\text{-}LA)-(P\text{-}BF)} = -\sum\nolimits_{j=1}^{4} r_j ln r_j, \tag{12}$$

where r_j is the jth eigenvalue of the state $\rho^{\text{F-LA}}$.

3.4. *Quantum Coherence*

The diagonal components of the system's density operator delineate the essential properties of coherence. The quantum coherence is determined by considering the absolute value of the non-diagonal elements and applying the l_1 norm. The coherence measure is the distance between the state in question and the nearest incoherent state from the point of view of the concept of entropy. To detect the amount of coherence, we consider the l_1 norm of coherence. This measure depends on off-diagonal elements for the density operator and it is defined by the formula [42]:

$$Q_c = \sum_{\substack{kl \\ k\neq l}} |\rho_{kl}|, \tag{13}$$

4. Numerical Results and Discussion

Figure 1 illustrates the dynamics of atomic population inversion in the F-LA system interacting with the P-BF under conditions of zero and non-zero deformation parameters, considering both single- and double-photon transitions. For a zero-deformation parameter, panels (a) and (b) depict the time evolution of atomic population for single- and double-photon excitations, respectively. In the single-photon excitation case, we observe distinct features of collapses and revivals in atomic population inversion. Initially, the collapses are well defined within the scaled time, but they become less distinct over time, with the revival amplitude gradually diminishing. In the double-photon excitation scenario, the atomic population exhibits brief revivals interspersed with adjacent collapses. These revivals are asymmetric around the zero-population inversion line, with fluctuations between positive and negative values of +1 and -1. The revival duration is notably shorter compared to the single-photon case. Panels (c) and (d) present the dynamics for a non-zero deformation parameter, set at 20 scaled units, for single and double photon transitions. In the single-photon case, we observe revivals in atomic population with very brief collapses, and the revival amplitude spans the entire range of population values. For the double-photon transition with a non-zero deformation parameter, the dynamics show collapses and revivals similar to the single-photon case, but with an increased collapse duration and a slightly reduced oscillation amplitude. Comparing the effects of varying photon transition numbers and deformation parameters, it is evident that these factors significantly influence the population inversion dynamics. For $q = 20$, increasing J from 1 to 2 leads to more frequent revivals and a reduction in their width. Conversely, for $q = 20$, increasing J does not increase the number of revivals but shortens the revival span. The collapse and revival phenomena observed in atom-field interactions indicate coherent quantum evolution, where revivals stem from constructive interference among atomic state amplitudes, while collapse periods reflect decoherence effects caused by transitions between energy levels. These results are consistent with previous research on Jaynes–Cummings models and intensity-dependent atom-field interactions, where nonlinearity and deformation significantly influence atomic transition dynamics. In particular, studies on q-deformed oscillators and para-Bose models reveal that deformation alters energy spectra and transition rates, leading to extended coherence times and modified revival patterns. The alignment of these findings with theoretical predictions in nonlinear optics and quantum field theories suggests that para-Bose field deformation serves as a controllable parameter for regulating atomic inversion dynamics.

Figure 2 shows the evolution of S-OCF g^2 for the F-LA system under conditions of zero and non-zero deformation parameters q, considering both single- and double-photon transitions $J = 1,2$, respectively. For $q = 0$, we can observe that $g^{(2)} < 1$ at the beginning of interaction for $J = 1,2$, indicating sub-Poissonian statistics. As the time increases, the function $g^{(2)}$ becomes larger than 1, indicating super-Poissonian statistics. For $q = 20$, we can observe that the function $g^{(2)}$ exhibits an oscillatory behavior with values greater and smaller than one, indicating super- and sub-Poissonian statistics. In the case of $J = 2$, we have $g^{(2)} < 1$ at the beginning of interaction and $g^{(2)} > 1$ as the time increases. The shift from sub- to super-Poissonian statistics suggests that interaction time significantly influences photon distribution. Studies on q-deformed oscillators and para-Bose fields demonstrate that deformation alters photon statistics by introducing nonlinear effects, leading to oscillatory behavior in $g^{(2)}$ for $q = 20$. Similar patterns have been observed in nonlinear quantum optics, such as Kerr media, where nonlinearity modulates photon distribution, indicating that para-Bose deformation introduces an additional degree of complexity to photon dynamics. The tunability of photon statistics enables the design of nonclassical light sources. Para-Bose deformation provides a useful method for controlling photon statistics, contributing to advancements in quantum optics applications.

Figure 3 displays the quantum entanglement (QE), as measured by the von Neumann entropy, for the F-LA–P-BF state under varying field deformation and photon transition numbers. For q = 0, panels (a) and (b) depict the $S_{F\text{-}LA}$ dynamics for single-photon (J = 1) and double-photon (J = 2) transitions, respectively. In the single-photon case, rapid oscillations are observed in the entanglement measure, with the amplitude fluctuating around a steady-state value before eventually stabilizing. In contrast, for the double-photon transition (J = 2), the entanglement exhibits quasi-periodic behavior. Unlike the single-photon case, the entanglement measure does not settle into a steady state. Panels (c) and (d) show the time-dependent behavior of entanglement for a non-zero field deformation parameter q for both single- and double-photon transitions, respectively. For J = 1, the function $S_{F\text{-}LA}$ exhibits consistent periodic behavior with a constant amplitude of oscillations throughout the dynamics. In the double-photon transition case (J = 2), the QE dynamics also display periodicity, but the amplitude of oscillations varies over time, introducing an additional layer of complexity to the system's behavior. Thus, the consideration of field deformation and double-photon transitions enhances the periodic nature of the entanglement measure during the evolution. These observations align with established studies in quantum optics, particularly the JCM, where single-photon transitions typically lead to periodic entanglement oscillations, while multi-photon transitions introduce interactions that increase quantum correlations. The quasi-periodic behavior in the J = 2 case suggests an enhanced interaction mechanism, as multi-photon absorption–emission processes can induce more complex quantum correlations. Studies on q-deformed oscillators and para-Bose fields have shown that deformation modifies energy levels and transition dynamics, which explains the stable periodic behavior in the J = 1 case and the varying oscillation amplitude in the J = 2 case. Additionally, entanglement dynamics in nonlinear quantum optics, such as Kerr-type media, exhibit similar periodic structures, indicating that para-Bose deformation effectively introduces an adjustable nonlinearity that influences quantum correlations. The ability to control entanglement oscillations through deformation and photon transition tuning presents promising applications in different tasks in quantum information and optics.

Figure 4 displays the dynamics of QC for the F-LA system for both zero and non-zero deformation parameters q of the P-BF, considering single- and double-photon transitions. For the zero-deformation parameter case, the dynamics of QC for single- and double-photon transitions are shown in panels (a) and (b), respectively. In the single-photon case, the QC dynamics exhibit collapses and revivals, with the collapse line fluctuating around a value of 1. In contrast, for the double-photon transition (J = 2), periodic behavior is observed in the QC dynamics, characterized by increased amplitude fluctuations and a shorter revival width compared to the single-photon case. Notably, no collapses are present in this scenario. For the non-zero deformation parameter case, the QC dynamics for single-photon transitions show periodic behavior with an increased amplitude of oscillations compared to the zero-deformation case. In the double-photon transition case (J = 2), oscillations are observed in the QC dynamics, but the amplitude of these oscillations varies over time, indicating more complex dynamic behavior. In summary, the introduction of non-zero deformation parameters enhances the periodic nature of quantum coherence, with single-photon transitions leading to more pronounced oscillations, while double-photon transitions result in oscillations with varying amplitude.

5. Conclusions

In this study, we have explored the dynamics of atomic population inversion, S-OCF, degree of entanglement, and quantum coherence in the F-LA system interacting with the P-BF under both zero and non-zero deformation parameters. For zero deformation parameter values, the system exhibits characteristic collapses and revivals in atomic population inversion during single-photon transitions, while double-photon transitions lead to brief, asymmetric revivals. The S-OCF similarly shows collapses and revivals, with an increasing slope of the collapse line that remains constant across both single- and double-photon transitions. The entanglement dynamics under single-photon transitions oscillate rapidly, stabilizing around a steady state, whereas double-photon transitions induce periodicity without reaching a steady state. Quantum coherence dynamics for single-photon excitations display collapses and revivals, with a collapse line that fluctuates around a steady value. The introduction of non-zero deformation parameters adds additional complexity to the system. For atomic population inversion, the period of oscillation remains the same as in the single-photon transition case, but with an extended collapse duration. The S-OCF and quantum coherence exhibit periodic behaviors, with increased amplitude and variable oscillations, particularly in double-photon transitions. The entanglement dynamics also show enhanced periodicity under non-zero deformation, highlighting the effects of deformation parameter and photon transition numbers on the overall system behavior. Overall, this work highlights the significant impact of field deformation and photon transition numbers on the quantum dynamics of the F-LA system. It provides valuable insights into how these parameters can be effectively controlled to extract and optimize quantum resources from the system. Regarding the experimental feasibility of our findings, we highlight that our model, which considers the interaction between a four-level atom and a deformed para-Bose field, can be realized using trapped atoms or ions in cavity quantum electrodynamics setups, where four-level atomic structures naturally arise in alkali or alkaline-earth atoms through well-defined energy level configurations. Another promising platform is cold atoms in optical lattices, where multi-level atomic transitions can be engineered via laser coupling.

Author Contributions: M.A.: investigation (equal); methodology (equal); software (equal); writing—original draft (equal). S.A.-K.: investigation (equal); methodology (equal); writing—review and editing (equal). K.B.: investigation (equal); resources (equal); writing—original draft (equal). All authors have read and agreed to the published version of the manuscript.

Funding: Princess Nourah bint Abdulrahman University Researchers Supporting Project number (PNURSP2025R225), Princess Nourah bint Abdulrahman University, Riyadh, Saudi Arabia.

Data Availability Statement: Not applicable.

Acknowledgments: The authors acknowledge to Princess Nourah bint Abdulrahman University Researchers Supporting Project number (PNURSP2025R225), Princess Nourah bint Abdulrahman University, Riyadh, Saudi Arabia.

Conflicts of Interest: The authors declare no conflict of interest.

Appendix A. Detailed Calculation

The evolution of the quantum state of the system is governed by the time-dependent Schrödinger equation:

$$i\hbar\frac{\partial}{\partial t}|\psi(t)\rangle = \widehat{H}_{\text{int}}|\psi(t)\rangle, \tag{A1}$$

where $\widehat{H}_{\text{int}}$ represents the interaction Hamiltonian describing the coupling between the four-level atom and the para-Bose field. The objective is to express this equation in terms of a set of differential equations governing the probability amplitudes associated with the atomic and field states.

Given that the system comprises an atom possessing four distinct energy levels coupled to a quantized field mode, the wavefunction is articulated as a superposition of the atomic states and the field's Fock states:

$$|\psi(t)\rangle = \sum_{k=1}^{4}\sum_{n=0}^{\infty} R_k(n,t)|n+k-1,k\rangle, \tag{A2}$$

where $R_k(n,t)$ represents the probability amplitude for the atom being in state $|k\rangle$ with $n+k-1$ photons in the field. Substituting this expansion into the Schrödinger equation and differentiating,

$$i\hbar\sum_{k=1}^{4}\sum_{n=0}^{\infty}\frac{dR_k(n,t)}{dt}|n+k-1,k\rangle = \widehat{H}_{\text{int}}\sum_{k=1}^{4}\sum_{n=0}^{\infty} R_k(n,t)|n+k-1,k\rangle. \tag{A3}$$

Multiplying both sides by $\langle n+k-1,k|$ and utilizing the orthonormality of the basis states, we obtain

$$i\hbar\frac{dR_k(n,t)}{dt} = \sum_{j=1}^{4}\langle n+k-1,k|\widehat{H}_{\text{int}}|n+j-1,j\rangle R_j(n,t). \tag{A4}$$

This equation provides a framework for obtaining the system of differential equations once we determine the Hamiltonian matrix elements. The interaction Hamiltonian for the quantum system is expressed as:

$$\widehat{H}_{\text{int}} = \sum_{k=1}^{4}\varpi\left(\hat{L}^{J}|k\rangle\left\langle k+1\right| + \hat{L}^{\dagger J}\left|k+1\right\rangle\langle k|\right), \tag{A5}$$

The operators and $\hat{L}^{\dagger}$ and $\hat{L}$ govern the transitions between atomic levels, leading to the coupling terms in the equations of motion. Using the matrix elements obtained from the

Hamiltonian action on the basis states, we obtain at the final system of coupled differential equations. The probability amplitudes evolve according to:

$$\frac{d}{dt}\begin{bmatrix} R_1 \\ R_2 \\ R_3 \\ R_4 \end{bmatrix} = \begin{bmatrix} 0 & -i\omega\sqrt{\frac{(n+J)!}{n!}} & 0 & 0 \\ -i\omega\sqrt{\frac{(n+J)!}{n!}} & 0 & -i\omega\sqrt{\frac{(n+2J)!}{(n+J)!}} & 0 \\ 0 & -i\omega\sqrt{\frac{(n+2J)!}{(n+J)!}} & 0 & -i\omega\sqrt{\frac{(n+3J)!}{(n+2J)!}} \\ 0 & 0 & -i\omega\sqrt{\frac{(n+3J)!}{(n+2J)!}} & 0 \end{bmatrix}\begin{bmatrix} R_1 \\ R_2 \\ R_3 \\ R_4 \end{bmatrix}. \quad \text{(A6)}$$

This system provides a full description of the time evolution of the probability amplitudes, incorporating the effects of multi-photon transitions and field deformation.

To determine the probability amplitudes $R_k(n,t)$, we solve the system of coupled differential equations. This system can be expressed in matrix form as

$$\frac{d}{dt}\mathrm{R}(t) = \mathrm{M}\mathrm{R}(t), \quad \text{(A7)}$$

where $\mathrm{R}(t)$ is the column vector of probability amplitudes and M is the coupling matrix. Since the matrix M is time-independent, the formal solution can be obtained using matrix exponentiation:

$$\mathrm{R}(t) = e^{\mathrm{M}t}\mathrm{R}(0). \quad \text{(A8)}$$

If M is diagonalizable, we write it as $\mathrm{M} = \mathrm{V}\mathrm{D}\mathrm{V}^{-1}$, leading to the solution:

$$\mathrm{R}(t) = \mathrm{V}e^{\mathrm{D}t}\mathrm{V}^{-1}\mathrm{R}(0), \quad \text{(A9)}$$

where V is the matrix whose columns are the eigenvectors of M, and $e^{\mathrm{D}t}$ is a diagonal matrix with elements $e^{\lambda_i t}$, where λ_i are the eigenvalues of M. Alternatively, numerical-method techniques can be used. Once the amplitudes $R_k(n,t)$ are determined, they allow analysis of quantum properties such as atomic population inversion, quantum coherence, and entanglement.

References

1. Arik, M.; Coon, D.D. Hilbert spaces of analytic functions and generalized coherent states. *J. Math. Phys.* **1976**, *17*, 524. [CrossRef]
2. Biedenharn, L.C. The quantum group SU_q (2) and a q-analogue of the boson operators. *J. Phys. A Math. Gen.* **1989**, *22*, L873. [CrossRef]
3. Macfarlane, A.J. On q-analogues of the quantum Harmonic oscillator and the quantum group *SU* (2). *J. Phys. A Math. Gen.* **1989**, *22*, 4581. [CrossRef]
4. Fakhri, H.; Nouraddini, M. Right SU_q (2)- and left $SU_{q^{-1}}$ (2)-invariances of the q-Hilbert–Schmidt scalar products for an adjoint representation of the quantum algebra $\check{U}_q$ (su_2). *J. Geom. Phys.* **2016**, *110*, 90. [CrossRef]
5. Fakhri, H.; Hashemi, A. Nonclassical properties of the q-coherent and q-cat states of the Biedenharn–Macfarlane q oscillator with q > 1. *Phys. Rev. A* **2016**, *93*, 013802. [CrossRef]
6. Fakhri, H.; Sayyah-Fard, M. Arik-Coon q-oscillator cat states on the noncommutative complex plane and their nonclassical properties. *Int. J. Geom. Meth. Mod. Phys.* **2017**, *14*, 1750060. [CrossRef]
7. Fakhri, H.; Sayyah-Fard, M. Nonclassical properties of the Arik-Coon q−1-oscillator coherent states on the noncommutative complex plane Cq. *Int. J. Geom. Meth. Mod. Phys.* **2017**, *14*, 1750165. [CrossRef]
8. Fakhri, H.; Sayyah-Fard, M. q-coherent states associated with the noncommutative complex plane C q^2 for the Biedenharn–Macfarlane q-oscillator. *Ann. Phys.* **2017**, *387*, 14. [CrossRef]
9. Fakhri, H.; Sayyah-Fard, M. Triplet q-cat states of the Biedenharn–Macfarlane q-oscillator with q > 1. *Quantum Inf. Process.* **2020**, *19*, 19. [CrossRef]
10. Fakhri, H.; Mousavi-Gharalari, S.E. Nonclassical properties of two families of q-coherent states in the Fock representation space of q-oscillator algebra. *Eur. Phys. J. Plus* **2020**, *135*, 253. [CrossRef]
11. Fakhri, H.; Sayyah-Fard, M. Noncommutative photon-added squeezed vacuum states. *Mod. Phys. Let. A* **2020**, *35*, 2050167. [CrossRef]

12. Sayyah-Fard, M. Nonclassicality of photon-added q-squeezed first excited states. *Phys. A* **2021**, *567*, 125636. [CrossRef]
13. Plyushchay, M.S. Deformed Heisenberg algebra with reflection. *Nucl. Phys. B* **1997**, *491*, 619. [CrossRef]
14. Wigner, E.P. Do the equations of motion determine the quantum mechanical commutation relations? *Phys. Rev.* **1950**, *77*, 711. [CrossRef]
15. Green, H.S. A generalized method of field quantization. *Phys. Rev.* **1953**, *90*, 270. [CrossRef]
16. Jaynes, E.T.; Cummings, F.W. Comparison of quantum and semiclassical radiation theories with application to the beam maser. *Proc. IEEE* **1963**, *51*, 89–109. [CrossRef]
17. Abdel-Aty, M. General formalism of interaction of a two-level atom with cavity field in arbitrary forms of nonlinearities. *Phys. A* **2002**, *313*, 471. [CrossRef]
18. Baghshahi, H.R.; Tavassoly, M.K. Entanglement, quantum statistics and squeezing of two Ξ-type three-level atoms interacting nonlinearly with a single-mode field. *Phys. Scr.* **2014**, *89*, 075101. [CrossRef]
19. Feneuile, S. Interaction of laser radiation with free atoms. *Rep. Prog. Phys.* **1977**, *40*, 1257. [CrossRef]
20. Li, X.-S.; Lin, D.L.; Gong, C.D. Nonresonant interaction of a three-level atom with cavity fields. I. General formalism and level occupation probabilities. *Phys. Rev. A* **1987**, *36*, 5209. [CrossRef]
21. Liu, Z.-D.; Li, X.-S.; Lin, D.L. Nonresonant interaction of a three-level atom with cavity fields. II. Coherent properties of the stimulated fields. *Phys. Rev. A* **1987**, *36*, 5220. [CrossRef]
22. Abdel-Wahab, N.H. The general formalism for a three-level atom interacting with a two-mode cavity field. *Phys. Scr.* **2007**, *76*, 233. [CrossRef]
23. Abdel-Wahab, N.H. A three-level atom interacting with a single mode cavity field: Different configurations. *Phys. Scr.* **2007**, *76*, 244. [CrossRef]
24. Yurke, B.; Stoler, D. One-step synthesis of multiatom Greenberger-Horne-Zeilinger states. *Phys. Rev. Lett.* **1993**, *57*, 13. [CrossRef] [PubMed]
25. Wang, H.; Goorskey, D.; Xiao, M. Dependence of enhanced Kerr nonlinearity on coupling power in a three-level atomic system. *Opt. Lett.* **2002**, *27*, 258–260. [CrossRef]
26. Baghshahi, H.R.; Tavassoly, M.K. Dynamics of different entanglement measures of two three-level atoms interacting nonlinearly with a single-mode field. *Eur. Phys. J. Plus* **2015**, *130*, 37. [CrossRef]
27. Liu, Z.D.; Zhu, S.-Y.; Li, X.-S. The properties of a light field interacting with a four-level atom. *J. Mod. Opt.* **1988**, *45*, 833. [CrossRef]
28. Vaglica, A.; Vetri, G. Irreversible decay of nonlocal entanglement via a reservoir of a single degree of freedom. *Phys. Rev. A* **2007**, *75*, 062120. [CrossRef]
29. Ficek, Z.; Tanas, R. Dark periods and revivals of entanglement in a two-qubit system. *Phys. Rev. A* **2006**, *74*, 024304. [CrossRef]
30. Vitali, D.; Gigan, S.; Ferreira, A.; Böhm, H.R.; Tombesi, P.; Guerreiro, A.; Vedral, V.; Zeilinger, A.; Aspelmeyer, M. Optomechanical entanglement between a movable mirror and a cavity field. *Phys. Rev. Lett.* **2007**, *98*, 030405. [CrossRef]
31. Zhang, Q.; Zhang, E.Y. Optimum parameters for biased two-state quantum key distribution protocol. *Acta Phys. Sin.* **2002**, *51*, 1684.
32. Moller, C. Dissipative Rabi model in the dispersive regime. *Phys. Rev. Res.* **2020**, *2*, 033046. [CrossRef]
33. Bennett, C.H.; Brassard, G.; Crépeau, C.; Jozsa, R.; Peres, A.; Wootters, W.K. Teleporting an unknown quantum state via dual classical and Einstein-Podolsky-Rosen channels. *Phys. Rev. Lett.* **1993**, *70*, 1895. [CrossRef] [PubMed]
34. Metwally, N.; Abdelaty, M.; Obada, A.-S.F. Quantum teleportation via entangled states generated by the Jaynes–Cummings model. *Chaos Solitons Fractals* **2004**, *22*, 529. [CrossRef]
35. Ekert, A.K. Quantum cryptography based on Bell's theorem. *Phys. Rev. Lett.* **1991**, *67*, 661. [CrossRef]
36. Bennett, C.H.; Wiesner, S.J. Communication via one-and two-particle operators on Einstein-Podolsky-Rosen states. *Phys. Rev. Lett.* **1992**, *69*, 2881. [CrossRef]
37. Yang, M.; Song, W.; Cao, Z.L. Entanglement swapping without joint measurement. *Phys. Rev. A* **2005**, *71*, 034312. [CrossRef]
38. Nielsen, M.A.; Chuang, I.L. *Quantum Computation and Quantum Information*; Cambridge University Press: Cambridge, UK, 2000.
39. Bennett, C.H.; Shor, P.W.; Smolin, J.A.; Thapliyal, A.V. Entanglement-assisted classical capacity of noisy quantum channels. *Phys. Rev. Lett.* **1999**, *83*, 3081. [CrossRef]
40. Phoenix, S.J.D.; Knight, P.L. Establishment of an entangled atom-field state in the Jaynes-Cummings model. *Phys. Rev. A* **1991**, *44*, 6023. [CrossRef]
41. Phoenix, S.J.D.; Knight, P. Comment on "Collapse and revival of the state vector in the Jaynes-Cummings model: An example of state preparation by a quantum apparatus". *Phys. Rev. Lett.* **1991**, *66*, 2833. [CrossRef]
42. Baumgratz, T.; Cramer, M.; Plenio, M.B. Quantifying coherence. *Phys. Rev. Lett.* **2014**, *113*, 140401. [CrossRef]
43. Berrada, K.; Algarni, M.; Marin, M.; Abdel-Khalek, S. Effects of Dipole-Dipole Interaction and Time-Dependent Coupling on the Evolution of Entanglement and Quantum Coherence for Superconducting Qubits in a Nonlinear Field System. *Symmetry* **2023**, *15*, 732. [CrossRef]

44. Algarni, M.; Berrada, K.; Abdel-Khalek, S. Quantum coherence and parameter estimation for mixed entangled coherent states. *Mod. Phys. Lett. A* **2022**, *37*, 2250159. [CrossRef]
45. Abdel-Khalek, S.; Algarni, M.; Marin, M.; Berrada, K. Entanglement, quantum coherence and quantum Fisher information of two qubit-field systems in the framework of photon-excited coherent states. *Opt. Quant. Elect.* **2023**, *55*, 1288. [CrossRef]
46. Majid, S. *Foundations of Quantum Group Theory*; Cambridge University Press: Cambridge, UK, 1995.
47. Madore, J. Noncommutative Geometry for Pedestrians. *Phys. Rep.* **1997**, *282*, 1.
48. Snyder, H.S. Quantized Space-Time. *Phys. Rev.* **1947**, *71*, 38. [CrossRef]
49. Freidel, L.; Livine, E.R. Ponzano-Regge model revisited III: Feynman diagrams and effective field theory. *Class. Quantum Grav.* **2006**, *23*, 2021. [CrossRef]
50. Wen, X.-G. *Quantum Field Theory of Many-Body Systems*; Oxford University Press: Oxford, UK, 2004.
51. Nayak, C.; Simon, S.H.; Stern, A.; Freedman, M.; Das Sarma, S. Non-Abelian anyons and topological quantum computation. *Rev. Mod. Phys.* **2008**, *80*, 1083. [CrossRef]
52. Das Sarma, S.; Freedman, M.; Nayak, C. Topologically protected qubits from a possible non-Abelian fractional quantum Hall state. *Phys. Rev. Lett.* **2005**, *94*, 166802. [CrossRef]
53. Read, N.; Rezayi, E. Beyond paired quantum Hall states: Parafermions and incompressible states in the first excited Landau level. *Phys. Rev. B* **1999**, *59*, 8084. [CrossRef]
54. Moore, G.; Read, N. Nonabelions in the fractional quantum Hall effect. *Nucl. Phys. B* **1991**, *360*, 362. [CrossRef]
55. Kitaev, A. Fault-tolerant quantum computation by anyons. *Ann. Phys.* **2003**, *303*, 2. [CrossRef]
56. Wen, X.-G. Topological orders and edge excitations in fractional quantum Hall states. *Adv. Phys.* **1995**, *44*, 405. [CrossRef]
57. Bernevig, B.A.; Hughes, T.L.; Zhang, S.C. Quantum spin Hall effect and topological phase transition in HgTe quantum wells. *Science* **2006**, *314*, 1757. [CrossRef]
58. Hasan, M.Z.; Kane, C.L. Topological insulators. *Rev. Mod. Phys.* **2010**, *82*, 3045. [CrossRef]
59. Kitaev, A. Periodic table for topological insulators and superconductors. *AIP Conf. Proc.* **2009**, *1134*, 22.
60. Bennett, C.H.; Brassard, G. Quantum cryptography: Public key distribution and coin tossing. *Theor. Comput. Sci.* **2014**, *560 Pt 1*, 7–11. [CrossRef]
61. Braunstein, S.L.; Caves, C.M. Statistical distance and the geometry of quantum states. *Phys. Rev. Lett.* **1994**, *72*, 3439. [CrossRef]
62. Dowling, J.P.; Milburn, G.J. Quantum technology: The second quantum revolution. *Phil. Trans. R. Soc. A* **2003**, *361*, 1655. [CrossRef]
63. Kimble, H.J. The quantum internet. *Nature* **2008**, *453*, 1023. [CrossRef]
64. Clarke, J.; Wilhelm, F.K. Superconducting quantum bits. *Nature* **2008**, *453*, 1031. [CrossRef] [PubMed]
65. Barends, R.; Kelly, J.; Megrant, A.; Veitia, A.; Sank, D.; Jeffrey, E.; White, T.C.; Mutus, J.; Fowler, A.G.; Campbell, B.; et al. Superconducting quantum circuits at the surface code threshold for fault tolerance. *Nature* **2014**, *508*, 500. [CrossRef] [PubMed]
66. Haroche, S.; Raimond, J.-M. *Exploring the Quantum: Atoms, Cavities, and Photons*; Oxford University Press: Oxford, UK, 2006.
67. Fakhri, H.; Sayyah-Fard, M. The Jaynes–Cummings model of a two-level atom in a single-mode para-Bose cavity field. *Sci. Rep.* **2021**, *11*, 22861. [CrossRef] [PubMed]

axioms

MDPI

Article

Relativistic Scalar Particle Systems in a Spacetime with a Spiral-like Dislocation

Ricardo L. L. Vitória

Faculdade de Física, Universidade Federal do Pará, Av. Augusto Corrêa, Guamá, Belém 66075-110, PA, Brazil; ricardovitoria@professor.uema.br or ricardo-luis91@hotmail.com

Abstract: We have analyzed solutions of bound states of a scalar particle in spacetime with torsion. In the first analysis, we investigate the confinement of a scalar particle in a cylindrical shell. In the second step, we investigate the Klein–Gordon oscillator. Then, we finish our analysis by searching for solutions of bound states of the Klein–Gordon oscillator by interacting with a hard-wall potential. In all these systems, we determine the relativistic energy profile in the background characterized by the presence of torsion in spacetime represented by a spiral-like dislocation.

Keywords: torsion; spiral-like dislocation; Klein–Gordon oscillator; solution of bound states

MSC: 81-10; 81Q05; 81T20; 81T45

1. Introduction

In analogy to phase transitions in condensed matter systems, it is believed that the decoupling of the fundamental interactions in the early Universe gave rise to cosmological objects known as topological defects (TDs) [1]. The best known TDs in the literature are the domain wall [2], global monopole [3,4] and the cosmic string [5–7]. In particular, the cosmic string is an example of a linear TD associated with the curvature of spacetime [8]. In crystallography, this type of defect is known as disclination [9]. In addition to the association between disclination and curvature, there are also linear defects associated with the torsion in a continuous solid [9]. These types of defects are known as dislocations, which, in cylindrical symmetry, can be typified as screw-like dislocation and spiral-like dislocation [10]. Recently, these two dislocations have been studied in quantum mechanics systems. For example, the screw-like dislocation has been investigated on the Landau quantization [11,12], on the harmonic oscillator [13], on a harmonic oscillator subjected to a linear potential [14], on the doubly anharmonic oscillator [15] and in non-inertial effects on a non-relativistic Dirac particle [16]. The spiral-like dislocation has been studied on an electron subjected to an electric field and an uniform magnetic field [17] and on the harmonic oscillator [18]. Other topological structures have been investigated in the gravitational context. For example, studies have evaluated the Hawking effect for a massive Dirac spinor under the effects of $\mathbb{RP}^3$ geon [19], quantum-gravitational effects produced in Minkowski spacetime with a periodic boundary condition [20] and the structure of the density matrix for two Unruh–DeWitt detectors coupled with a massless scalar field in two locally flat topologically nontrivial spacetimes constructed from identifications of Minkowski spacetime.

The screw-like and spiral-like dislocations have been reformulated in $(1+3)$-dimensions in Einstein–Cartan geometry through the generalized concept of the Volterra process [21], also known as the "cut and paste" process, in distorted spacetimes [22]. Another process capable of producing these types of structures is through the periodic identification of one of the spatial coordinates, imposing a periodic boundary condition on the fields in the background [20]. In particular, in the relativistic quantum mechanic context, recently, the screw-like dislocation has been investigated in several quantum systems [23–31]. The spiral-like dislocation has been studied on a scalar field subjected to a hard-wall confining potential [32] and in rotating effects on a Dirac field [33]. The metric that describes a spacetime with a spiral-like dislocation is given by [32] ($c = \hbar = 1$)

$$ds^2 = -dt^2 + (d\rho + \beta d\varphi)^2 + \rho^2 d\varphi^2 + dz^2, \tag{1}$$

where $\rho = (x^2 + y^2)^{1/2}$ and $\beta > 0$ are the parameters associated with the TD of the spacetime.

In this manuscript, we analyzed the effects of torsion on the relativistic quantum dynamics of a scalar particle immersed in spacetime with a spiral-like dislocation described by the line element given in Equation (1). Our first step is to investigate a relativistic scalar particle confined into a cylindrical shell. In addition, we analyze the dynamics of the Klein–Gordon oscillator [34] in the spacetime described by Equation (1), and thus, extend this discussion to the confinement of a hard-wall confining potential by searching for analytical solutions to the Klein–Gordon equation.

The structure of this paper is as follows: in Section 2, we investigate the topological effects of a spiral-like dislocation on the relativistic energy spectrum of a scalar particle into a cylindrical shell; in Section 3, we study the interaction between a scalar particle and the Klein–Gordon oscillator in spacetime with a spiral-like dislocation; in Section 4, we analytically determine the relativistic energy profile of the Klein–Gordon oscillator subjected to a hard-wall potential in this background with torsion; in Section 5, we present our conclusions.

2. On a Scalar Particle Confined to an Elastic Cylindrical Shell

A scalar particle associated with a field ϕ in a curved spacetime is described by the Klein–Gordon equation in the form [23]

$$\frac{1}{\sqrt{-g}}\partial_\mu(\sqrt{-g}g^{\mu\nu}\partial_\nu)\phi - m^2\phi = 0, \tag{2}$$

where $g = \det(g_{\mu\nu}) = -\rho^2$, by using Equation (1), $g^{\mu\nu} = (g_{\mu\nu})^{-1}$ and m is the parameter associated with the remaining mass of the field. From Equations (1) and (2), we obtain

$$-\frac{\partial^2\phi}{\partial t^2} + \left(1 + \frac{\beta^2}{\rho^2}\right)\frac{\partial^2\phi}{\partial\rho^2} + \left(\frac{1}{\rho} - \frac{\beta^2}{\rho^3}\right)\frac{\partial\phi}{\partial\rho} - \frac{2\beta}{\rho^2}\frac{\partial^2\phi}{\partial\rho\partial\varphi} + \frac{\beta}{\rho^3}\frac{\partial\phi}{\partial\varphi} + \frac{1}{\rho^2}\frac{\partial^2\phi}{\partial\varphi^2} + \frac{\partial^2\phi}{\partial z^2} - m^2\phi = 0. \tag{3}$$

Equation (3) describes the relativistic quantum motion of a spin-0 particle in spacetime with a spiral-like dislocation. The general solution to Equation (3) is

$$\phi(\rho,\varphi,z,t) = u(\rho)e^{il\varphi}e^{ikz}e^{-i\mathcal{E}t}, \tag{4}$$

where $l = 0, \pm1, \pm2\ldots$ are the quantum numbers associated with the angular momentum operator $\hat{L}_z = -i\partial_\varphi$, $-\infty < k < \infty$ are the quantum numbers associated with the linear momentum operator $\hat{p}_z = -i\partial_z$, where $[\hat{L}_z, \hat{H}] = [\hat{H}, \hat{L}_z]$ and $[\hat{p}_z, \hat{H}] = [\hat{H}, \hat{p}_z]$, with $\hat{H}$ as the Hamiltonian operator, and $u(\rho)$ is a radial function. Then, by substituting Equation (4) into Equation (3), we obtain the axial wave equation

$$\left(1+\frac{\beta^2}{\rho^2}\right)\frac{d^2u}{d\rho^2}+\left(\frac{1}{\rho}-\frac{\beta^2}{\rho^3}-\frac{2il\beta}{\rho^2}\right)\frac{du}{d\rho}+\frac{il\beta}{\rho^3}u-\frac{l^2}{\rho^2}u+\alpha^2u=0, \tag{5}$$

where

$$\alpha^2=\mathcal{E}^2-m^2-k^2. \tag{6}$$

Now, in order to analytically solve Equation (5), let us consider the axial wave function [32]

$$u(\rho)=R(\rho)e^{il\arctan\left(\frac{\rho}{\beta}\right)}, \tag{7}$$

that is, by substituting Equation (7) into (5), we obtain

$$\left(1+\frac{\beta^2}{\rho^2}\right)\frac{d^2R}{d\rho^2}+\left(\frac{1}{\rho}-\frac{\beta^2}{\rho^3}\right)\frac{dR}{d\rho}-\frac{l^2}{(\rho^2+\beta^2)}R+\alpha^2R=0. \tag{8}$$

Let us define $s=\alpha(\rho^2+\beta^2)^{1/2}$; then, Equation (8) becomes

$$\frac{d^2R}{ds^2}+\frac{1}{s}\frac{dR}{ds}-\frac{l^2}{s^2}R+R=0. \tag{9}$$

Equation (9) is the Bessel equation [35] and its general solution is

$$R(s)=C_1J_{|l|}(s)+C_2N_{|l|}(s), \tag{10}$$

where C_1 and C_2 are constants, $J_l(s)$ is the first type of Bessel function and $N_l(s)$ is the Neumann function [35]. In the interval $0\leq\rho<\infty$, we impose that $C_2=0$, since $N_{|l|}(s)\rightarrow\infty$ when $s\rightarrow 0$ ($\rho\rightarrow 0$). In this case, we obtain a simpler solution, $R(s)=C_1J_{|l|}(s)$; that is, the solution for a free scalar particle in spacetime with a spiral-like dislocation, as already discussed in Ref. [32].

From now on, let us consider a scalar particle confined to a cylindrical shell; that is, the relativistic quantum particle is restricted to move in interval $s_a\leq s\leq s_b$, where $s_a=\alpha\sqrt{\rho_a^2+\beta^2}$ and $s_b=\alpha\sqrt{\rho_b^2+\beta^2}$, with $\rho_a=a$ and $\rho_b=b$ fixed and $b>a$. In addition, let us consider the boundaries of this region as impenetrable walls, such that the axial wave function satisfies

$$R(s_a)=R(s_b)=0. \tag{11}$$

This type of confinement has been studied in spacetime with curvature and torsion [23], in Safka–Witten spacetime [36], in curved spacetime [37], on a non-relativistic particle in an environment with a magnetic dislocation [38], and on a neutral particle interacting with a dipole moment [39]. Equation (11) yields the following relation:

$$J_{|l|}(s_a)N_{|l|}(s_b)-J_{|l|}(s_b)N_{|l|}(s_a)=0. \tag{12}$$

Let us consider the case where $s_a\gg 1$, $s_b\gg 1$ and l are fixed numbers. In this specific case, $J_l(s)$ and $N_l(s)$ functions are rewritten, respectively, in the form [40]

$$J_{|l|}(s_i) \sim \sqrt{\frac{2}{\pi s_i}}\left[\cos\left(s_i - \frac{l\pi}{2} - \frac{\pi}{4}\right) - \frac{(4l^2-1)}{8s_i}\sin\left(s_i - \frac{l\pi}{2} - \frac{\pi}{4}\right)\right], \tag{13}$$

and

$$N_{|l|}(s_i) \sim \sqrt{\frac{2}{\pi s_i}}\left[\sin\left(s_i - \frac{l\pi}{2} - \frac{\pi}{4}\right) + \frac{(4l^2-1)}{8s_i}\cos\left(s_i - \frac{l\pi}{2} - \frac{\pi}{4}\right)\right], \tag{14}$$

where $i = a, b$. By substituting Equations (13) and (14) into Equation (12), we obtain

$$\alpha^2 \sim \frac{\pi^2 n^2}{(\sqrt{b^2+\beta^2} - \sqrt{a^2+\beta^2})^2} + \frac{4l^2-1}{4\sqrt{(a^2+\beta^2)(b^2+\beta^2)}}, \tag{15}$$

with $n = 0, 1, 2, \ldots$. By substituting Equation (6) into Equation (15), we obtain

$$\mathcal{E}_{k,l,n} \approx \sqrt{m^2 + k^2 + \frac{\pi^2 n^2}{(\sqrt{b^2+\beta^2} - \sqrt{a^2+\beta^2})^2} + \frac{4l^2-1}{4\sqrt{(a^2+\beta^2)(b^2+\beta^2)}}}. \tag{16}$$

Equation (16) gives us the relativistic energy spectrum of a scalar particle into a cylindrical shell in an environment with a spiral-like dislocation. We can see that the relativistic energy profile of this system is influenced by the spacetime topology. This influence is the correction made on the fixed axial radius $\rho_{\text{eff}} = \sqrt{\rho_i^2 + \beta^2}$, with $i = a, b$. In contrast to ref. [23], there is no gravitational effect analogous to the Aharonov–Bohm effect for bound states on the allowed energy values of the relativistic quantum system [26–28,30]. By making $\beta = 0$ into Equation (16) we recover the result discussed in refs. [23,36]; that is, the relativistic energy spectrum of a scalar particle into a cylindrical shell in Minkowski spacetime.

Figure 1 provides the relativistic energy levels for the first five radial modes of the system, which shows us how the permitted energy values of the system vary for each radial mode, both for the positive part and for the negative part (antiparticle). Figures 2 and 3 show the variation in the relativistic energy levels of the system through the variation in the TD. Figure 2 gives us the ground state ($n = 0$) of the system as a function of the torsion in spacetime, while Figure 3 gives us the first four excited states of the system as a function of the dislocation, both for $l = 1$. By observing Figures 2 and 3, we can note that the higher the value of n, the more abrupt the increase in energy (analyzing the positive side), while, in the fundamental state, the variation is minimal and occurs very tenuously when $m\beta \to 0$.

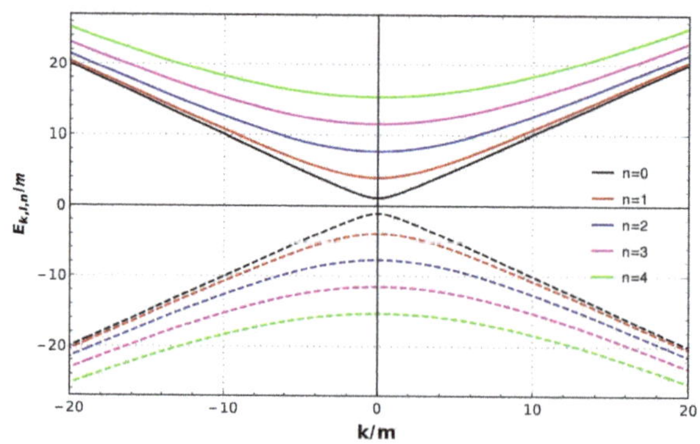

Figure 1. The positive and negative relativistic energy levels given in Equation (16) for $n = 0, 1, 2, 3$ and 4, with $a = 1$, $b = 2$, $l = 1$ and $\beta m = 1$.

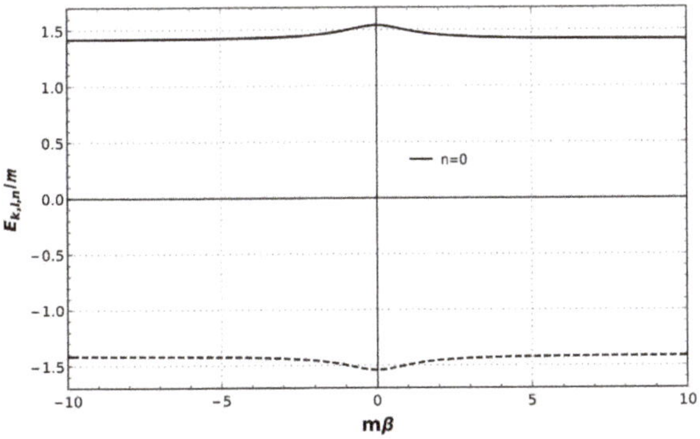

Figure 2. Relativistic energy level given in Equation (16) for the radial mode $n = 0$, with $a = 1$, $b = 2$, $l = 1$ and $k/m = 1$.

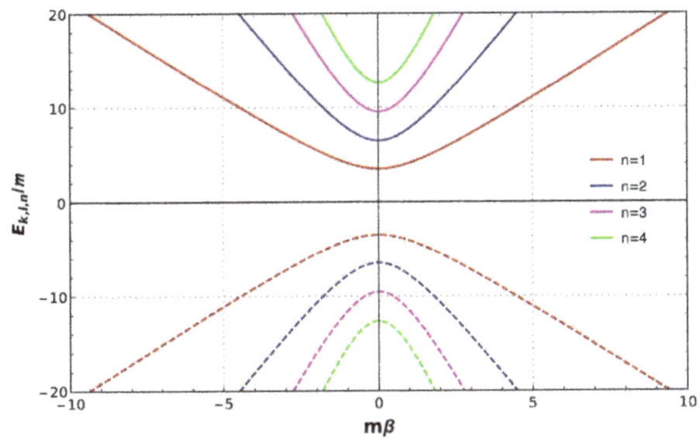

Figure 3. Positive and negative relativistic energy levels given in Equation (16) for $n = 1, 2, 3$ and 4, with $a = 1$, $b = 2$, $l = 1$ and $k/m = 1$.

By taking $b \to a$, we have a relativistic quantum particle restricted to move in a circle of radius of a. In Ref. [23], this confinement configuration has been investigated on a scalar field immersed in a spacetime with curvature and (time-like and space-like) torsion, while in Ref. [36], this confinement configuration is analyzed in a background characterized by a tubular matter source with axial interior magnetic field and a vanishing exterior magnetic field. However, for $b \to a$ into Equation (16), we have $\mathcal{E} \to \infty$, which is not a physically acceptable result. Next, let us introduce a potential of attractive nature in the interval $a < \rho < b$ to compete with the growth of the allowed energy values for the radial modes of the quantum system. In this case, Equation (16) is rewritten as follows

$$\mathcal{E}_{k,l} \approx \sqrt{m^2 + k^2 + \frac{l^2}{a^2 + \beta^2} - \frac{1}{4(a^2 + \beta^2)}}, \tag{17}$$

which represents the relativistic energy spectrum of a scalar particle confined into a quantum ring in the spacetime with spiral-like dislocation. We can note that the permitted values of relativistic energy of this system are influenced by the torsion present in the spacetime. This influence is the contribution that gives rise to an effective radius $\rho_{\text{eff}} = \sqrt{a^2 + \beta^2}$. By making $\beta = 0$ into Equation (17), we obtain a relativistic energy profile of a scalar particle confined into a quantum ring in Minkowski spacetime.

3. Klein–Gordon Oscillator Under Effect of a Spiral-like Dislocation

Inspired by the Dirac oscillator [41,42], Bruce and Minning [34] proposed a relativistic quantum oscillator model for scalar particles which became known as the Klein–Gordon oscillator (KGO) in the literature. This relativistic quantum oscillator model, in addition to providing an analytical solution at the non-relativistic limit, falls on the quantum harmonic oscillator described by the Schröndiger equation [43]. KGO has been investigated in a noncommutative space [44], on anti-de Sitter space [45], on a generalized uncertainty principle framework [46], on a topologically nontrivial spacetime [47], in position-dependent mass systems [48–50], in a curved spacetime [51], in the Som–Raychaudhuri spacetime [52], in possible Lorentz symmetry violation scenarios [53,54], and in the global monopole spacetime [55]. However, KGO has not yet been analyzed in a spacetime with a spiral-like dislocation. Here, we investigate the topological effects of a spiral-type dislocation on KGO. In this case, Equation (2) in the spacetime considered in this study can be rewritten as [29]

$$\frac{1}{\sqrt{-g}}(\partial_\mu + m\omega X_\mu)(\sqrt{-g}g^{\mu\nu})(\partial_\nu + m\omega X_\nu)\phi - m^2\phi = 0, \tag{18}$$

where ω is the angular frequency of KGO and $X_\mu = (0, \rho, 0, 0)$. Then, by following the steps from Equation (3) to Equation (5), we obtain the axial wave equation

$$\left(1+\frac{\beta^2}{\rho^2}\right)\frac{d^2u}{d\rho^2} + \left(\frac{1}{\rho} - \frac{\beta^2}{\rho^3} - \frac{2il\beta}{\rho^2}\right)\frac{du}{d\rho} + \frac{il\beta}{\rho^3}u - \frac{l^2}{\rho^2}u - m^2\omega^2\rho^2 u + \gamma u = 0, \tag{19}$$

with

$$\gamma = \mathcal{E}^2 - m^2 - k^2 - m^2\omega^2\beta^2 - 2m\omega. \tag{20}$$

By substituting Equation (7) into Equation (19), we obtain the differential equation

$$\left(1+\frac{\beta^2}{\rho^2}\right)\frac{d^2R}{d\rho^2} + \left(\frac{1}{\rho} - \frac{\beta^2}{\rho^3}\right)\frac{dR}{d\rho} - \frac{l^2}{(\rho^2+\beta^2)}R - m^2\omega^2\rho^2 R + \gamma R = 0. \tag{21}$$

Let us define the new variable $r = m\omega(\rho^2 + \beta^2)$, such that we obtain

$$\frac{d^2R}{dr^2} + \frac{1}{r}\frac{dR}{dr} - \frac{l^2}{4r^2}R + \frac{\delta}{r}R - \frac{1}{4}R = 0, \tag{22}$$

with

$$\delta = \frac{\gamma + m^2\omega^2\beta^2}{4m\omega} = \frac{\mathcal{E}^2 - m^2 - k^2 - 2m\omega}{4m\omega}. \tag{23}$$

We are interested in a well-behaved solution to Equation (22) in the limits $r \to 0$ and $r \to \infty$, and we have the following general solution:

$$R(r) = r^{\frac{|l|}{2}} e^{-\frac{r}{2}} f(r), \tag{24}$$

where $f(r)$ is a function to be determined. By substituting Equation (24) into Equation (22), we obtain

$$r\frac{d^2f}{dr^2} + (|l| + 1 - r)\frac{df}{dr} + \left(\gamma - \frac{|l|}{2} - \frac{1}{2}\right)f = 0, \tag{25}$$

which is the confluent hypergeometric differential equation [35] and $f(r)$ is the confluent hypergeometric series: $f(r) = {}_1F_1(A, B; r)$, with

$$A = \frac{1}{2} + \frac{|l|}{2} - \gamma; \quad B = |l| + 1. \tag{26}$$

The confluent hypergeometric series becomes a polynomial of degree n by imposing that $A = -n = 0, 1, 2, \ldots$, of which we obtain

$$\mathcal{E}_{k,l,n} = \pm\sqrt{m^2 + k^2 + 4m\omega\left(n + \frac{|l|}{2} + 1\right)}. \tag{27}$$

By observing Equation (27), we can see that the relativistic energy profile of KGO in the spiral-like dislocation spacetime is equal to the relativistic energy profile of KGO in the Minkowski spacetime [27,29,56]; that is, the relativistic energy levels of KGO are not influenced by the spacetime topology. This is due to Equation (23); note that the parameter δ is defined in terms of the parameter γ, where the latter is added by the term $m^2\omega^2\beta^2$, which cancels out with the term $-m^2\omega^2\beta^2$ that exists in the definition of the parameter γ. However, the eigenfunctions of KGO depend on the TD, since they are defined in terms of the confluent hypergeometric polynomials, which in turn depend on the parameter $A = A[\gamma(\beta^2)]$ given in Equation (26). In addition, there is no gravitational effect analogous to the Aharonov–Bohm effect for bound states on relativistic energy levels of the quantum system [26–28,30].

4. On the Klein–Gordon Oscillator Subjected to a Hard-Wall Potential in Spacetime with a Spiral-like Dislocation

In this section, we investigate the effects of the spacetime topology on KGO subjected to a hard-wall. This confinement type has been investigated in several quantum systems, for example, on a Dirac oscillator [57,58], in quantum systems under non-inertial effects [59,60], in a Landau-type quantization plus a Dirac field [61], in quantum system of geometric phase [62], in an environment with a pointlike defect [63] and on a massive scalar field under effects of the aether-like Lorentz symmetry violation [64]. This confining potential is important due its similarity to a box of certain dimensions, which is a very good approximation to consider when discussing the quantum properties of a gas molecule system and other particles, which are necessarily confined in a box.

Then, let us restrict a scalar particle in the following form:

$$u(\rho_0) = 0, \tag{28}$$

where $\rho_0 =$ const.. The boundary condition given in Equation (28) indicates that the radial wave function vanishes at a fixed radius ρ_0; that is, the quantum particle is under the effects of the hard-wall potential. To obtain the relativistic energy levels of this quantum system, let us consider the specific case $\gamma \gg 1$ and with l fixed. This means that parameters A and B is larger and fixed, respectively. Under these mathematical constraints, the confluent hypergeometric series is rewritten as follows

$${}_1F_1(A, B; r_0) \propto \cos\left(\frac{\pi}{4} - \frac{B\pi}{2} + \sqrt{2Br_0 - 4Ar_0}\right). \tag{29}$$

By substituting Equations (7) and (24) into Equation (28), we have

$$\mathcal{E}_{k,l,n} \approx \pm\sqrt{m^2 + k^2 + \frac{\pi^2}{(\rho_0^2 + \beta^2)}\left(n + \frac{|l|}{2} + \frac{3}{4}\right)^2 + 2m\omega}. \tag{30}$$

Equation (30) gives us the relativistic energy spectrum of KGO plus a hard-wall potential in the spacetime with a spiral-like dislocation, influenced by the TD present in spacetime. We can note this influence by the contribution that gives rise to an effective radius $\rho_{\text{eff}} = \sqrt{\rho_0^2 + \beta^2}$. We can also that there is no gravitational effect analogous to the Aharonov–Bohm effect for bound states on the relativistic energy profile of the quantum system [26–28,30]. In addition, by taking $\omega \to 0$ and $\beta \neq 0$ into Equation (30) we recover the result obtained in Ref. [32]. By making $\omega \neq 0$ and $\beta = 0$ into Equation (30) we obtain the relativistic energy spectrum of KGO interacting with a hard-wall potential in the Minkowski spacetime discussed in Ref. [65].

5. Conclusions

We have investigated some possible scenarios of a scalar particle interacting with confining potentials in spacetime with a spiral-like dislocation. We started our analysis with a scalar particle restricted in a cylindrical shell where we obtained the relativistic energy levels, which are influenced by the TD present in the spacetime. This influence is described explicitly through an effective radius defined by the parameter associated with the torsion. Next, we analyzed KGO in this background and analytically defined its relativistic energy levels, which are not influenced by the spiral-like dislocation; that is, the energy profile of KGO remains the same, despite being immersed in a background with torsion. In addition, we obtain the relativistic energy levels of KGO plus a hard-wall confining potential, which, again, are influenced by the spiral-like dislocation through an effective radius defined by the parameter associated with the TD. Finally, unlike the effects of the cosmic string and screw dislocation on confined quantum systems, we have observed that in all cases analyzed, there is no gravitational effect analogous to the Aharonov–Bohm effect for bound states on relativistic energy levels of the quantum system [26–28,30].

It is worth mentioning that the above results open up paths for extensions or generalizations. For example, the scalar particle subjected to relativistic Landau quantization [66] has already been studied in several distorted backgrounds [27,29], for different types of confinements [27,31,67]; however, this system has not been studied under the effects of spiral-like dislocation. Furthermore, confined quantum systems have recently been the object of study in the thermodynamic context [68–79], in which the effects of curvature and torsion on thermodynamic quantities, such as internal energy, entropy, specific heat, etc., are analyzed. In this sense, as a future perspective, the results obtained here can be used for this type of investigation.

Funding: Ricardo L. L. Vitória was supported by the CAPES (Coordenação de Aperfeiçoamento de Pessoal de Nível Superior—Brazil) project PNPD/CAPES.

Data Availability Statement: No new data were created or analyzed in this study. Data sharing is not applicable to this article.

Acknowledgments: The author would like to thank CAPES (Coordenação de Aperfeiçoamento de Pessoal de Nível Superior—Brazil).

Conflicts of Interest: The author declares that he has no known competing financial interests or personal relationships that could have appeared to influence the work reported in this paper.

References

1. Vilenkin, A.; Shellard, E.P.S. *Strings and Other Topological Defects*; Cambrigde University Press: Cambridge, UK, 1994.
2. Vilenkin, A. Cosmic strings and domain walls. *Phys. Rep.* **1985**, *121*, 263. [CrossRef]
3. Barriola, M.; Vilenkin, A. Gravitational field of a global monopole. *Phys. Rev. Lett.* **1989**, *63*, 341. [CrossRef]
4. de Mello, E.R.B. Physics in the Global Monopole Spacetime. *Braz. J. Phys.* **2001**, *31*, 2.
5. Vilenkin, A. Gravitational field of vacuum domain walls. *Phys. Lett. B* **1983**, *133*, 177. [CrossRef]
6. Hiscock, W.A. Exact gravitational field of a string. *Phys. Rev. D* **1985**, *31*, 3288. [CrossRef] [PubMed]
7. Linet, B. The static metrics with cylindrical symmetry describing a model of cosmic strings. *Gen. Relativ. Gravit. 1985*, *17*, 1109. [CrossRef]
8. Kibble, T.W.B. Topology of cosmic domains and strings. *J. Phys. A Math. Gen.* **1976**, *9*, 1387. [CrossRef]
9. Katanaev, M.O.; Volovich, I.V. Theory of defects in solids and three-dimensional gravity. *Ann. Phys.* **1992**, *216*, 1–28. [CrossRef]
10. Valanis, K.C.; Panoskaltsis, V.P. Material metric, connectivity and dislocations in continua. *Acta Mech.* **2005**, *175*, 77. [CrossRef]
11. Furtado, C.; Moraes, F. Landau levels in the presence of a screw dislocation. *Europhys. Lett.* **1999**, *45*, 279. [CrossRef]
12. Marques, G.A.; Furtado, C.; Bezerra, V.B.; Moraes, F. Landau levels in the presence of topological defects. *J. Phys. A Math. Gen.* **2001**, *34*, 5945. [CrossRef]
13. Furtado, C.; Moraes, F. Harmonic oscillator interacting with conical singularities. *J. Phys. A Math. Gen.* **2000**, *33*, 5513. [CrossRef]
14. Bueno, M.J.; Furtado, C.; Bakke, K. On the effects of a screw dislocation and a linear potential on the harmonic oscillator. *Phys. B* **2016**, *496*, 45. [CrossRef]
15. Bakke, K. Doubly anharmonic oscillator under the topological effects of a screw dislocation. *Phys. B* **2018**, *537*, 346. [CrossRef]
16. Bakke, K. Torsion and noninertial effects on a nonrelativistic Dirac particle. *Ann. Phys.* **2014**, *346*, 51. [CrossRef]
17. Maia, A.V.D.M.; Bakke, K. On an electron in an elastic medium with a spiral dislocation. *Int. J. Mod. Phys. A* **2019**, *34*, 1950153. [CrossRef]
18. Maia, A.V.D.M.; Bakke, K. Harmonic oscillator in an elastic medium with a spiral dislocation. *Phys. B* **2018**, *531*, 213. [CrossRef]
19. Langlois, P. Hawking radiation for Dirac spinors on the geon. *Phys. Rev. D* **2004**, *70*, 104008; Erratum in *Phys. Rev. D* **2005**, *72*, 129902. [CrossRef]
20. Foo, J.; Arabaci, C.S.; Zych, M.; Mann, R.B. Quantum superpositions of Minkowski spacetime. *Phys. Rev. D* **2023**, *107*, 045014. [CrossRef]
21. Volterra, V. Sur l'équilibre des corps élastiques multiplement connexes. *Ann. Sci. Éc. Norm. Supér.* **1907**, *24*, 401. [CrossRef]
22. Puntigam, R.A.; Soleng, H.H. Volterra distortions, spinning strings, and cosmic defects. *Class. Quantum Grav.* **1997**, *14*, 1129. [CrossRef]
23. Bezerra, V.B. Global effects due to a chiral cone. *J. Math. Phys.* **1997**, *38*, 5. [CrossRef]
24. Cravalho, J.; Furtado, C.; Moraes, F. Dirac oscillator interacting with a topological defect. *Phys. Rev. A* **2011**, *84*, 032109. [CrossRef]
25. Bakke, K.; Furtado, C. On the interaction of the Dirac oscillator with the Aharonov-Casher system in topological defect backgrounds. *Ann. Phys.* **2013**, *336*, 489. [CrossRef]
26. Vitória, R.L.L.; Bakke, K. Torsion effects on a relativistic position-dependent mass system. *Gen. Relativ. Gravit.* **2016**, *48*, 161. [CrossRef]
27. Vitória, R.L.L.; Bakke, K. Aharonov-Bohm effect for bound states in relativistic scalar particle systems in a spacetime with a spacelike dislocation. *Int. J. Mod. Phys. D* **2018**, *27*, 1850005. [CrossRef]
28. Vitória, R.L.L.; Bakke, K. On the interaction of the scalar field with a Coulomb-type potential in a spacetime with a screw dislocation and the Aharonov-Bohm effect for bound states. *Eur. Phys. J. Plus* **2018**, *133*, 490. [CrossRef]
29. Carvalho, J.; Carvalho, A.M.M.; Cavalcante, E.; Furtado, C. Klein-Gordon oscillator in Kaluza-Klein theory. *Eur. Phys. J. C* **2016**, *76*, 365. [CrossRef]
30. Vitória, R.L.L. Noninertial effects on a scalar field in a spacetime with a magnetic screw dislocation. *Eur. Phys. J. C* **2019**, *79*, 844. [CrossRef]
31. Ahmed, F. Klein-Gordon Oscillator in the Presence of External Fields in a Cosmic Space-Time with a Space-Like Dislocation and Aharonov-Bohm Effect. *Adv. High Energy Phys.* **2020**, *2020*, 691025. [CrossRef]
32. Vitória, R.L.L.; Bakke, K. Rotating effects on the scalar field in the cosmic string spacetime, in the spacetime with space-like dislocation and in the spacetime with a spiral dislocation. *Eur. Phys. J. C* **2018**, *78*, 175. [CrossRef]
33. Maia, A.V.D.M.; Bakke, K. Topological and rotating effects on the Dirac field in the spiral dislocation spacetime. *Eur. Phys. J. C* **2019**, *79*, 551. [CrossRef]
34. Bruce, S.; Minning, P. The Klein-Gordon oscillator. *Nuovo Cimento A* **1993**, *106*, 711. [CrossRef]
35. Arfken, G.B.; Weber, H.J. *Mathematical Methods for Physicists*, 6th ed.; Elsevier Academic Press: New York, NY, USA, 2005.
36. Bezerra, V.B. Gravitational Aharonov-Bohm effect in a locally flat spacetime. *Class. Quantum Grav.* **1991**, *8*, 1939. [CrossRef]

37. Bezerra, V.B.; dos Santos, I.B. Topological effects due to a cosmic string. *Eur. J. Phys.* **1992**, *13*, 122. [CrossRef]
38. Furtado, C.; Bezerra, V.B.; Moraes, F. Quantum scattering by a magnetic flux screw dislocation. *Phys. Lett. A* **2001**, *289*, 160 [CrossRef]
39. Bakke, K.; Furtado, C. Persistent currents for a moving neutral particle with no permanent electric dipole moment. *Eur. Phys. J. B* **2014**, *87*, 222. [CrossRef]
40. Abramowitz, M.; Stegum, I.A. *Handbook of Mathematical Functions*; Dover Publications Inc.: New York, NY, USA, 1965.
41. Moshinsky, M.; Szczepaniak, A. The Dirac oscillator. *J. Phys. A Math. Gen.* **1989**, *22*, L817. [CrossRef]
42. Vitória, R.L.L.; Belich, H. On the Dirac oscillator subject to a Coulomb-type central potential induced by the Lorentz symmetry violation. *Eur. Phys. J. Plus* **2020**, *135*, 247. [CrossRef]
43. Rao, N.A.; Kagali, B.A. Energy profile of the one-dimensional Klein-Gordon oscillator. *Phys. Scr.* **2008**, *77*, 015003. [CrossRef]
44. Mirza, B.; Narimani, R.; Zare, S. Relativistic oscillators in a noncommutative space and in a magnetic field. Commun. *Theor. Phys.* **2011**, *55*, 405.
45. Hamil, B.; Merad, M. Dirac and Klein-Gordon oscillators on anti-de Sitter space. *Eur. Phys. J. Plus* **2018**, *133*, 174. [CrossRef]
46. Khosropour, B. Statistical aspects of the Klein-Gordon oscillator in the frame work of GUP. *Indian J. Phys.* **2018**, *92*, 43. [CrossRef]
47. Santos, L.C.N.; Mota, C.E.; Barros, C.C., Jr. Klein-Gordon Oscillator in a Topologically Nontrivial Space-Time. *Adv. High Energy Phys.* **2019**, *2019*, 2729352. [CrossRef]
48. Bakke, K.; Furtado, C. On the Klein-Gordon oscillator subject to a Coulomb-type potential. *Ann. Phys.* **2015**, *355*, 48. [CrossRef]
49. Vitória, R.L.L.; Bakke, K. Relativistic quantum effects of confining potentials on the Klein-Gordon oscillator. *Eur. Phys. J. Plus* **2016**, *131*, 36. [CrossRef]
50. Vitória, R.L.L.; Furtado, C.; Bakke, K. On a relativistic particle and a relativistic position-dependent mass particle subject to the Klein–Gordon oscillator and the Coulomb potential. *Ann. Phys.* **2016**, *370*, 128. [CrossRef]
51. Deng, L.-F.; Long, C.-Y.; Long, Z.-W.; Xu, T. Generalized Dirac Oscillator in Cosmic String Space-Time. *Adv. High Energy Phys.* **2018**, *2018*, 2741694. [CrossRef]
52. Wang, Z.; Longa, Z.; Long, C.; Wu, M. Relativistic quantum dynamics of a spinless particle in the Som-Raychaudhuri spacetime. *Eur. Phys. J. Plus* **2015**, *130*, 36. [CrossRef]
53. Vitória, R.L.L.; Belich, H.; Bakke, K. A relativistic quantum oscillator subject to a Coulomb-type potential induced by effects of the violation of the Lorentz symmetry. *Eur. Phys. J. Plus* **2017**, *132*, 25. [CrossRef]
54. Vitória, R.L.L.; Belich, H. Effects of a linear central potential induced by the Lorentz symmetry violation on the Klein-Gordon oscillator. *Eur. Phys. J. C* **2018**, *78*, 999. [CrossRef]
55. Bragança, E.A.F.; Vitória, R.L.L.; Belich, H.; Bezerra de Mello, E.R. Relativistic quantum oscillators in the global monopole spacetime. *Eur. Phys. J. C* **2020**, *80*, 206. [CrossRef]
56. Boumali, A.; Messai, N. Klein-Gordon oscillator under a uniform magnetic field in cosmic string space-time. *Can. J. Phys.* **2014**, *92*, 1. [CrossRef]
57. Bakke, K. Noninertial effects on the Dirac oscillator in a topological defect spacetime. *Eur. Phys. J. Plus* **2012**, *127*, 82. [CrossRef]
58. Bakke, K. Rotating effects on the Dirac oscillator in the cosmic string spacetime. *Gen. Relat. Gravit.* **2013**, *45*, 1847. [CrossRef]
59. Castro, L.B. Noninertial effects on the quantum dynamics of scalar bosons. *Eur. Phys. J. C* **2016**, *76*, 61. [CrossRef]
60. Santos, L.C.N.; Barros, C.C., Jr. Relativistic quantum motion of spin-0 particles under the influence of noninertial effects in the cosmic string spacetime. *Eur. Phys. J. C* **2018**, *78*, 13. [CrossRef]
61. Vitória, R.L.L.; Belich, H. Effects of a Landau-Type Quantization Induced by the Lorentz Symmetry Violation on a Dirac Field. *Adv. High Energy Phys.* **2020**, *2020*, 4208161. [CrossRef]
62. Bakke, K. On the rotating effects and the Landau-Aharonov-Casher system subject to a hard-wall confining potential in the cosmic string spacetime. *Int. J. Theor. Phys.* **2015**, *54*, 2119. [CrossRef]
63. Vitória, R.L.L.; Belich, H. Harmonic oscillator in an environment with a pointlike defect. *Phys. Scr.* **2019**, *94*, 125301. [CrossRef]
64. Vitória, R.L.L.; Belich, H. On a massive scalar field subject to the relativistic Landau quantization in an environment of aether-like Lorentz symmetry violation. *Eur. Phys. J. Plus* **2020**, *135*, 123. [CrossRef]
65. Vitória, R.L.L.; Belich, H. A Central Potential with a Massive Scalar Field in a Lorentz Symmetry Violation Environment. *Adv. High Energy Phys.* **2019**, *2019*, 1248393. [CrossRef]
66. Medeiros, E.R.F.; Bezerra de Mello, E.R. Relativistic quantum dynamics of a charged particle in cosmic string spacetime in the presence of magnetic field and scalar potential. *Eur. Phys. J. C* **2012**, *72*, 2051.
67. Mustafa, O. KG-particles in a cosmic string rainbow gravity spacetime in mixed magnetic fields. *Eur. Phys. J. C* **2024**, *84*, 362. [CrossRef]
68. Song, X.-Q.; Wang, C.-W.; Jia, C.-S. Thermodynamic properties for the sodium dimer. *Chem. Phys. Lett.* **2017**, *673*, 50. [CrossRef]

Two typical classifications are the semi-classical Rabi model and the quantum Rabi model [14–24].

Definition 1. *A semi-classical Rabi model [1,2] is usually defined as* $H = \frac{\beta}{2}\sigma_z + \frac{g}{2}\cos(\omega t)\sigma_x$*, where* $\sigma_x, \sigma_y, \sigma_z$ *are Pauli matrices and* β *is the transition frequency of the two-level system. The parameters* ω *and* g *are the frequency and amplitude of harmonic driving. A quantum Rabi model [8,14] has the Hamiltonian as* $H = \omega a^\dagger a + \mu\sigma_z + \lambda\sigma_x(a^\dagger + a)$*, where* a $(a^\dagger)$ *is the destruction (creation) operator,* 2μ *is the qubit frequency,* ω *is the mode frequency, and* λ *is the coupling strength of the light–matter interaction.*

The semi-classical Rabi model can be regarded as the classical version of the effective Hamiltonian of the quantum Rabi model in the interaction picture. Recent theoretical developments, including analytical solutions for the quantum Rabi model, have further increased interest in the Rabi model. Braak's analytic solution [15] provided a basis for determining the full energy spectrum of the model, sparking ongoing research on various extensions, such as multi-photon, two-mode, and multi-atom Rabi models. The quantum Rabi model is focused on its eigenvalues, while the semi-classical Rabi model is focused on its evolution since its eigenvalue is trivial [21–24]. Both kinds of model can be transformed into an infinite matrix, to solve the above problem, although by different methods. Those matrices are unbound operators, and are often difficult to solve in mathematics.

In this paper, we present a new theoretical approach to obtain the eigenvalues and eigenvectors of certain types of infinite matrices, by establishing a link with the corresponding physical Rabi models. By solving this specific physical model problem, we actually also address the related mathematical problem of determining the eigenvalues of infinite unbounded matrices. The interesting thing is that confluent Heun functions appear in both the semi-classical and quantum Rabi models. We find that the eigenvalue of the matrix with the semi-classical Rabi model is determined by the confluent Heun functions, while the eigenvalue spectra of the quantum Rabi model are the roots of the equation defined by the confluent Heun functions. The analytical solution for the regular energy spectrum of the quantum Rabi model was first presented by Braak [15]. The results of Zhong [17] and Maciejewski [18] combine the regular energy spectrum with the other two special cases. The advantage of our approach lies in its ability to unify the regular case with the other two special cases. Additionally, we examine the energy spectrum of the quantum Rabi model, revealing intriguing phenomena and patterns. Our results enhance the understanding of Rabi models, broaden their potential applications in quantum optics and quantum information [3–7], and offer a framework for further exploration of confluent Heun functions in related fields.

We introduce the solvable infinite matrix generated by the semi-classical Rabi model in Section 2, while the infinite matrix for the quantum Rabi model is discussed in Section 3. Our discussions and conclusions are presented in Section 4 and Section 5, respectively.

2. Solvable Infinite Matrix Generated by Semi-Classical Rabi Models

2.1. The Infinite Matrix

We consider an infinite-dimensional Hermitian matrix $H_{\mathcal{F}}$, related to the semi-classical Rabi model under Fourier transform. Floquet theory can solve this so-called Floquet Hamiltonian $H_{\mathcal{F}}$, and here, we can continue to obtain the analytical expression of the eigenvalues q_i of $H_{\mathcal{F}}$ by solving the semi-classical Rabi model. Let us observe the expression of the infinite matrix $H_{\mathcal{F}}$, which can be divided into 2×2 block matrices as $H_{\mathcal{F}}^{m,n} = H_{\mathcal{F}}^{n,m} = \boldsymbol{h}_{m-n} \cdot \hat{\boldsymbol{\sigma}} + \delta_{mn} n\omega\mathcal{I}$, where $\mathcal{I}$ is the identity matrix, $\boldsymbol{h}_i = (x_i, y_i, z_i)^{\mathsf{T}}$, $\hat{\boldsymbol{\sigma}} = (\sigma_x, \sigma_y, \sigma_z)$, and $\sigma_x, \sigma_y, \sigma_z$ are Pauli matrices. Then, through the inverse Fourier transform, we can obtain the expression of the corresponding Hamiltonian as $H_f = \sum_{n=-\infty}^{\infty} \cos(n\omega t)\boldsymbol{h}_n \cdot \hat{\boldsymbol{\sigma}}$. Since $H_{\mathcal{F}}$ is Hermitian, the coefficient $\boldsymbol{h}_i$ must be symmetric as $\boldsymbol{h}_i = \boldsymbol{h}_{-i}$. We rewrite the Hamiltonian as $H_f = \boldsymbol{h} \cdot \hat{\boldsymbol{\sigma}}$, where $\boldsymbol{h} = \boldsymbol{h}_0 + 2\sum_{n=1}^{\infty} \boldsymbol{h}_n \cos(n\omega t)$.

For simplicity, we choose the semi-classical Rabi model as $H = \frac{\beta}{2}\sigma_z + \frac{g}{2}\cos(\omega t)\sigma_x$. The corresponding coefficients are $\boldsymbol{h}_0 = (0, 0, \beta/2)^{\mathsf{T}}$, $\boldsymbol{h}_1 = (g/4, 0, 0)^{\mathsf{T}}$, and $\boldsymbol{h}_{i\geq 2} = 0$. Then, the Floquet Hamiltonian $H_{\mathcal{F}}$ has the following infinite matrix representation in Floquet states

$$\begin{pmatrix} \ddots & & & & & & & & & \\ \cdot & s_{-2}^- & g/4 & 0 & 0 & 0 & 0 & 0 & 0 & \\ & g/4 & s_{-1}^+ & 0 & 0 & g/4 & 0 & 0 & 0 & \\ & 0 & 0 & s_{-1}^- & g/4 & 0 & 0 & 0 & 0 & \\ & 0 & 0 & g/4 & s_0^+ & 0 & 0 & g/4 & 0 & \\ & 0 & g/4 & 0 & 0 & s_0^- & g/4 & 0 & 0 & \\ & 0 & 0 & 0 & 0 & g/4 & s_1^+ & 0 & 0 & \\ & 0 & 0 & 0 & g/4 & 0 & 0 & s_1^- & g/4 & \\ & 0 & 0 & 0 & 0 & 0 & 0 & g/4 & s_2^+ & \cdot \\ & & & & & & & & & \ddots \end{pmatrix}, \tag{1}$$

where $s_n^{\pm} = n\omega \pm \beta/2$. To solve the eigenvalue of the infinite matrix $H_{\mathcal{F}}$ is in principle to solve $\det(H_{\mathcal{F}} - \lambda\mathcal{I}) = 0$. It is easy to check that, if λ is the eigenvalue of $H_{\mathcal{F}}$, $\lambda + n\omega$ is also an eigenvalue for any integer n. According to Floquet theory, the time evolution operator of the Hamiltonian H_f can be expressed as $U(t;t_0) = F(t)F^{-1}(t_0)$, and $F(t)$ has the form [25–28]

$$F(t) = M(t)\mathrm{e}^{-\mathrm{i}Qt}, \tag{2}$$

where $M(t)$ is a periodic matrix of t and the constant Q is the characteristic diagonal matrix as $Q = \mathrm{diag}(q_\alpha, q_\beta)$. Since we consider a two-level system here, the number of the characteristic eigenvalue is two, and the relation $q_\alpha + q_\beta = \mathrm{Tr}H_f = 0$ makes only one characteristic exponent independent. Thus, the characteristic matrix Q can be written as $Q = q_\alpha\sigma_z$.

2.2. Solution to the Characteristic Exponent

The solution to the characteristic exponent q_α is related to the time evolution operator $U(t;t_0)$ of a two-level system $H = \frac{\beta}{2}\sigma_z + \frac{g}{2}\cos(\omega t)\sigma_x$, which has been previously discussed [21–23]. Here, we recall the time evolution operator $U(t;t_0)$ in a more concise way. After a rotation $R = \mathrm{e}^{-\mathrm{i}\frac{\pi}{2}\sigma_x}\mathrm{e}^{-\mathrm{i}\frac{\pi}{4}\sigma_y}$, the efficient Hamiltonian takes a new form as $H_1 = RHR^{\dagger} = \frac{\beta}{2}\sigma_x + \frac{g}{2}\cos(\omega t)\sigma_z$, leaving the structure of the energy spectrum unchanged. The parameter ω can be regarded as a scaling parameter [23,29]. We choose a transform as $\tau = \omega t - \frac{\pi}{2}$; then, the Hamiltonian can be obtained as $H' = \frac{\beta'}{2}\sigma_x + \frac{g'}{2}\sin(\tau)\sigma_z$, where $\beta' = \beta/\omega$ and $g' = g/\omega$. For simplicity, we assume $\omega = 1$ and denote the Hamiltonian as $H = \frac{\beta}{2}\sigma_x + \frac{g}{2}\sin(t)\sigma_z$. The time period remains $T = 2\pi/\omega = 2\pi$. The Schrödinger equation is

$$\mathrm{i}\partial_t|\psi\rangle = H(t)|\psi\rangle = \left(\frac{\beta}{2}\sigma_x + \frac{g}{2}\sin(t)\sigma_z\right)|\psi\rangle, \tag{3}$$

where $|\psi\rangle = (c_1, c_2)^{\mathrm{T}}$ is the normalized wave function of the two-level system and $\hbar$ is set to 1. Then, after removing c_2 (or c_1), we obtain a second-order differential equation for c_1 (or c_2), as

$$\partial_t^2 c_1 + (\mathrm{i}\frac{g}{2}\cos t + \frac{g^2}{4}\sin^2 t + \frac{\beta^2}{4})c_1 = 0. \tag{4}$$

Next, applying the change in the variable from t to $z = \frac{1}{2}(1 - \cos t)$ and another transform $c_1 = e^{igz} f$, we can obtain the differential equation as

$$z(z-1)\frac{\partial^2 f}{\partial z^2} + \left[\frac{1}{2}(z-1) + \frac{1}{2}z - 2igz(z-1)\right]\frac{\partial f}{\partial z} + (-\frac{\beta^2}{4})f = 0. \tag{5}$$

Compared to the standard confluent Heun equation

$$z(z-1)y'' + [\gamma(z-1) + \delta z + z(z-1)\epsilon)]y' + (\alpha z - q)y = 0, \tag{6}$$

we can obtain the coefficients $q = \frac{\beta^2}{4}$, $\alpha = 0$, $\gamma = \frac{1}{2}$, $\delta = \frac{1}{2}$, $\epsilon = -2ig$. The solution that satisfies the confluent Heun equation is the confluent Heun function $\mathrm{HC}(q, \alpha; \gamma, \delta, \epsilon; z)$, with the initial condition $\mathrm{HC}(q, \alpha; \gamma, \delta, \epsilon; 0) = 1$ [30–32]. The confluent Heun function can be expressed as a standard power-series expansion around $z = 0$ as $\mathrm{HC}(q, \alpha; \gamma, \delta, \epsilon; z) = \sum_{n=0}^{\infty} b_n z^n$. The coefficients b_n are determined by the three-term recurrence relation $R_n b_n + Q_{n-1} b_{n-1} + P_{n-2} b_{n-2} = 0$ with the initial conditions $b_{-2} = b_{-1} = 0$ and $b_0 = 1$. Here, $R_n = n(n-1+\gamma)$, $Q_n = q - n(n-1+\gamma+\delta-\epsilon)$, and $P_n = -\alpha - \epsilon n$. Therefore, the solution to Equation (4) is

$$c_1(t) = e^{-igz}\mathrm{HC}\left(\frac{\beta^2}{4}, 0; \frac{1}{2}, \frac{1}{2}, -2ig; z\right) := e^{-igz}\mathrm{HC}(a_1; z), \tag{7}$$

where parameters $a_1 := \left(\frac{\beta^2}{4}, 0; \frac{1}{2}, \frac{1}{2}, -2ig\right)$, and $z = \sin^2 \frac{t}{2}$. Here, we choose the initial condition $c_1(t=0) = 1, c_2(t=0) = 0$.

From the symmetry of the two functions c_1 and c_2, we can observe that, apart from g changing sign to $-g$, c_1 and c_2 satisfy differential equations of the same form. Then, according to the initial condition $c_2(t=0) = 0$, we know that c_2 is the other linearly independent solution $z^{1-\gamma}\mathrm{HC}(q + (1-\gamma)(\epsilon - \delta), \alpha + (1-\gamma)\epsilon, 2 - \gamma, \delta, \epsilon, z)$, which is

$$c_2(t) = i^{\eta}\beta \sin\frac{t}{2} e^{igz}\mathrm{HC}\left(\frac{\beta^2 - 1}{4} + ig, ig; \frac{3}{2}, \frac{1}{2}, 2ig; z\right) := i^{\eta}\beta \sin\frac{t}{2} e^{igz}\mathrm{HC}(a_2; z), \tag{8}$$

where parameters $a_2 := \left(\frac{\beta^2-1}{4} + ig, ig; \frac{3}{2}, \frac{1}{2}, 2ig\right)$, $z = \sin^2 \frac{t}{2}$, and $\eta = 1 + 2\lfloor \frac{t-\pi}{T} \rfloor$ with the floor function $\lfloor x \rfloor$. The parameter η can be treated as a constant within each continuous period $t \in [(2n-1)\pi, (2n+1)\pi)$. Then, we can construct the time evolution operator as

$$U_1(t) = \begin{pmatrix} c_1(t) & -c_2(t)^* \\ c_2(t) & c_1(t)^* \end{pmatrix}. \tag{9}$$

According to the symmetry $H(t) = \sigma_x H(t - \frac{T}{2})\sigma_x$, we derive $U_2(t) = \sigma_x U_1(t - \frac{T}{2})\sigma_x$. Consequently, the total time evolution operator can be expressed (see Appendix B) as

$$U(t, 0) = U_2(t - NT)U_2^{\dagger}(0)e^{i2N\Theta\sigma_n/2}, \tag{10}$$

where $N = \lfloor \frac{t}{T} \rfloor$, $\Theta = 2\arcsin|c_2(\frac{T}{2}^-)|$, and $\sigma_n = \sin\Phi\sigma_x + \cos\Phi\sigma_y$ with $\Phi = \arg[c_1^*(\frac{T}{2}^-)c_2(\frac{T}{2}^-)]$. For simplicity, some notations (e.g., $f(t^-)$) are defined in Appendix A.

The continuity of the functions $c_1(t)$ and $c_2(t)$ in Equations (7) and (8) is worth mentioning. If the reader has no concerns about continuity, this section can be skipped. It should be noted that the two functions $c_1(t)$ and $c_2(t)$ are discontinuous at the periodic points $t = (2n+1)\pi$, $n \in \mathrm{Z}$. As a result, they only satisfy the differential Equation (3) within a single period. The parameter η indicates that the solution $c_2(t)$ differs by a negative sign between adjacent periodic intervals. Thus, we use $U_1(t)$ and $U_2(t)$ to construct the total time evolution operator $U(t,0)$, ensuring that $U(t,0)$ remains continuous at all times. This approach guarantees that $U(t,0)$ depends solely on the complete evolution during the first period. For example, we can obtain the continuity at $t = T$, as $N = 0$ and $U(T^-,0) = U_2(T^-)U_2^\dagger(0) = e^{i2\Theta\sigma_n/2} = U_2(0)U_2^\dagger(0)e^{i2\Theta\sigma_n/2} = U(T,0) = U(T^+,0)$.

Lemma 1. *Compared to the Floquet theory [25–28], an additional rotation is required, which is* $R_s = e^{-i\frac{\pi}{4}\sigma_x}e^{-i\frac{\Phi}{2}\sigma_z}$. *Then, we can obtain the Floquet operator* $F(t)$ *as*

$$F(t) = R_sUR_s^\dagger = R_sU_2(t-NT)U_2^\dagger(0)R_s^\dagger e^{iN\Theta\sigma_z}. \tag{11}$$

Proof of Lemma 1. Following Equations (3)–(10), the total time evolution operator $U(t,0)$ is given by (for a more detailed derivation, see Appendix B)

$$U = U(t,0) = U_2(t-NT)U_2^\dagger(0)e^{i2N\Theta\sigma_n/2}. \tag{12}$$

Since the direction of the spin in Equation (2) is σ_z, we need a rotation R_s to modify the direction σ_n, which is $\sigma_{n'} = R_s\sigma_nR_s^\dagger = e^{-i\frac{\pi}{4}\sigma_x}e^{-i\frac{\Phi}{2}\sigma_z}(\sin\Phi\sigma_x + \cos\Phi\sigma_y)e^{i\frac{\Phi}{2}\sigma_z}e^{i\frac{\pi}{4}\sigma_x} = e^{-i\frac{\pi}{4}\sigma_x}\sigma_y e^{i\frac{\pi}{4}\sigma_x} = \sigma_z$. Then, we can obtain the Floquet Operator as $F(t) = R_sUR_s^\dagger = R_sU_2(t-NT)U_2^\dagger(0)R_s^\dagger R_s e^{i2N\Theta\sigma_n/2}R_s^\dagger = R_sU_2(t-NT)U_2^\dagger(0)R_s^\dagger e^{iN\Theta\sigma_z}$. □

Theorem 1. *The characteristic value* q_α *is*

$$q_\alpha = \frac{\Theta}{T} = \frac{2\arcsin|c_2(\frac{T}{2}^-)|}{2\pi} \tag{13}$$

$$= \frac{1}{\pi}\arcsin\left(\sqrt{2}\beta\mathrm{Re}[e^{ig}\mathrm{HC}(a_1^*;\frac{1}{2})\mathrm{HC}(a_2;\frac{1}{2})]\right) \tag{14}$$

Proof of Theorem 1. Equation (11) is a little different from the standard Floquet operator (2). Thus, we modify Equation (11) as

$$\begin{aligned} F(t) &= R_sU_2(t-NT)U_2^\dagger(0)R_s^\dagger e^{iN\Theta\sigma_z} && (15)\\ &= R_sU_2(t-NT)U_2^\dagger(0)R_s^\dagger e^{-i(t-NT)\frac{\Theta}{T}\sigma_z}e^{i(t-NT)\frac{\Theta}{T}\sigma_z}e^{iNT\frac{\Theta}{T}\sigma_z} && (16)\\ &= R_sU_2(t-NT)U_2^\dagger(0)R_s^\dagger e^{-i(t-NT)\frac{\Theta}{T}\sigma_z}e^{it\frac{\Theta}{T}\sigma_z} && (17)\\ &\equiv M(t)e^{-iQt}, && (18)\end{aligned}$$

where $M(t) = R_sU_2(t-NT)U_2^\dagger(0)R_s^\dagger e^{-i(t-NT)\frac{\Theta}{T}\sigma_z}$ and $Q = \frac{\Theta}{T}\sigma_z$. Then, compared with $Q = q_\alpha\sigma_z$, we can obtain $q_\alpha = \frac{\Theta}{T} = \frac{\Theta}{\pi} = \arcsin|c_2(\frac{T}{2}^-)|/\pi$. □

2.3. Comparison with Previous Results

The approximate result for $\beta \ll 1$ was well studied in Refs. [5,27–29,33–39], and the one proposed earliest among them is [29]. The approximate result for β is $q_\alpha^{\mathrm{app}} \approx \frac{\sqrt{2}\beta}{\pi}\mathrm{Re}[e^{ig}\mathrm{HC}(a_1^*|_{\beta=0};\frac{1}{2})\mathrm{HC}(a_2|_{\beta=0};\frac{1}{2})] \equiv \frac{\beta}{2}J_0(g)$. These transformations, $\tau = \omega t - \pi/2$ and $\cos(\omega t) - \sin\tau$, introduce a bias of 1/2 to the characteristic value q_α, which should be noted when comparing with the previous work [29].

When $g \ll 1$, the approximate result [29] is

$$q_\alpha^{\mathrm{app}} \approx \frac{\beta}{2} - \frac{\beta}{8(1-\beta^2)}g^2 + \frac{\beta(3\beta^2+1)}{128(1-\beta^2)^3}g^4 + \ldots, \tag{19}$$

which can also be obtained by a perturbation expansion. Figure 1 shows the micro difference between the approximate and exact results when $g \ll 1$. If we compare the Taylor expansions of the two results, we will find some identities about the confluent Heun function, which are

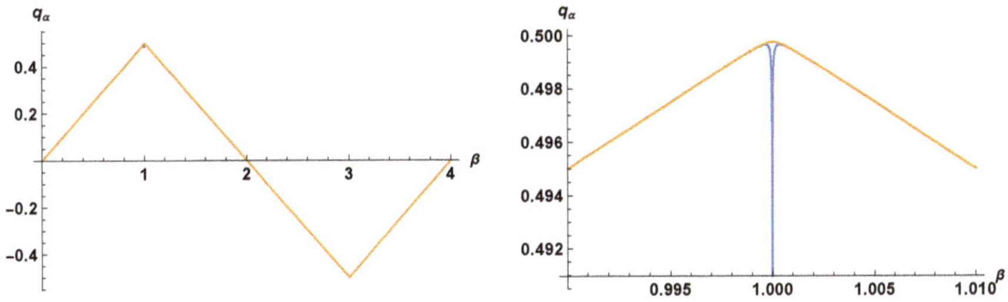

Figure 1. The difference between the exact and approximate characteristic value q_α with $g = 0.01$. The yellow line is the exact value q_α, while the blue line is the approximate value q_α^{app} . The right panel is an enlarged view near $\beta = 1$.

$$\left.\frac{\partial q_\alpha}{\partial g}\right|_{g=0} = 0, \left.\frac{\partial^2 q_\alpha}{\partial g^2}\right|_{g=0} = (-1)^{\lfloor \frac{\beta-1}{2} \rfloor} \frac{\beta}{4(1-\beta^2)}. \tag{20}$$

When β is large ($\beta \gg 1$), the approximate result [29] is

$$q_\alpha^{\text{app}} \approx \frac{1}{2} + \frac{g}{\pi x} \mathrm{E}(x), \tag{21}$$

where $x^2 = \frac{g^2}{g^2+(1-\beta)^2}$ and $\mathrm{E}(x)$ is the complete elliptic integral. As shown in Figure 2, the difference becomes very small when β is large.

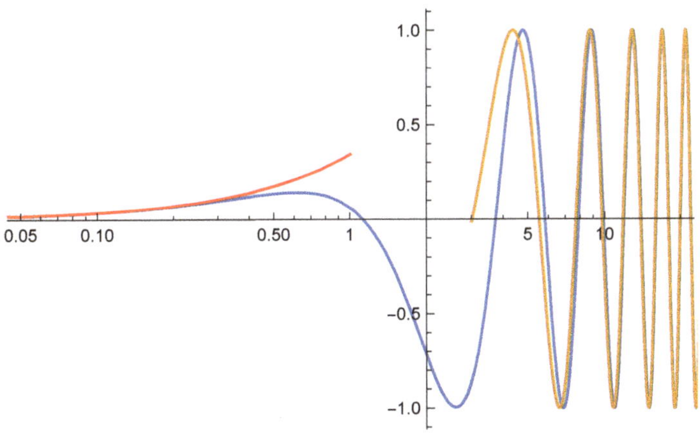

Figure 2. Comparison of the exact and approximate values of the characteristic value q_α when β is small or large. The continuous blue line is $\sin[q_\alpha \pi]$. The yellow line is $\sin\left[\frac{g}{x}\mathrm{E}(x)\right]$, $\mathrm{E}(x)$ is the average of the first and second kinds of the complete elliptic integral. The red line is $\sin\left[\frac{\beta}{2} J_0(g)\pi\right]$, where $J_0(g)$ is the first kind of the Bessel function of 0-order.

3. Solvable Infinite Matrix Generated by Quantum Rabi Models

3.1. The Quantum Rabi Model

The Hamiltonian of the quantum Rabi model [15–20] is described by

$$H = \omega a^\dagger a + \mu \sigma_z + \lambda \sigma_x \left(a^\dagger + a\right), \tag{22}$$

where a ($a^\dagger$) is the destruction (creation) operator, and $\sigma_{x,z}$ are Pauli matrices. The energy difference between the two levels is 2μ, and λ denotes the coupling strength between the two-level system and the bosonic mode. We set the frequency $\omega = 1$ for simplicity, without loss of generality. The eigenvalue equation $H|\psi\rangle = E|\psi\rangle$ can be regarded as a matrix equation $H_M|\psi\rangle = E|\psi\rangle$, where H_M is an infinite matrix and $|\psi\rangle$ is the eigenvector corresponding to eigenvalue E. The eigenstates $|\psi\rangle$ for the model can be written

$$|\psi\rangle = \sum_{n=0}^{\infty} c_n|n\rangle|\uparrow\rangle + d_n|n\rangle|\downarrow\rangle, \tag{23}$$

where $|n\rangle$ is the Fock state for the bosonic mode, and $|\uparrow\rangle$ and $|\downarrow\rangle$ are the eigenstates of σ_z with eigenvalues 1 and -1, respectively.

The infinite matrix H_M can be divided into 2×2 block matrices as $H_M^{m,n} = \boldsymbol{h}_{m,n} \cdot \hat{\boldsymbol{\sigma}} + \delta_{mn} n \mathcal{I}$, for $m, n \geq 0$. Here, $\boldsymbol{h}_{n,n} = (0, 0, \mu)^\mathsf{T}$, $\boldsymbol{h}_{m,n} = \sqrt{(m+n+1)/2}(\lambda, 0, 0)^\mathsf{T}$ for $|m-n| = 1$ and $\boldsymbol{h}_{m,n} = 0$ for $|m-n| \geq 2$. These terms for $|m-n| \geq 2$ arise when considering multi-photon interactions, which are not addressed in this paper. Then, the Hamiltonian $H_{\mathcal{M}}$ has the following infinite matrix representation

$$\begin{pmatrix} \mu & 0 & 0 & \lambda & 0 & 0 & 0 \\ 0 & -\mu & \lambda & 0 & 0 & 0 & 0 \\ 0 & \lambda & 1+\mu & 0 & 0 & \lambda\sqrt{2} & 0 \\ \lambda & 0 & 0 & 1-\mu+ & \lambda\sqrt{2} & 0 & \\ 0 & 0 & 0 & \lambda\sqrt{2} & 2+\mu & 0 & 0 \\ 0 & 0 & \lambda\sqrt{2} & 0 & 0 & 2-\mu & \lambda\sqrt{3} \\ 0 & 0 & 0 & 0 & 0 & \lambda\sqrt{3} & 3+\mu \\ & & & & & & \cdots & . \end{pmatrix}. \tag{24}$$

From the structure of the matrix, we can see that the solution space is naturally divided into two subspaces (odd and even), which can also be derived from the conditions (Equation (45)) formed by the confluent Heun functions later. Actually, it is very difficult to directly obtain the eigenvalue spectrum for this infinite matrix, as it is an unbounded operator. From an analytical perspective, the spectrum of unbounded operators may contain various components (e.g., point spectrum, continuous spectrum, and residual spectrum), whereas truncation methods struggle to handle the continuous and residual spectra. Numerically, the matrix elements of unbounded operators may grow rapidly as the row or column indices increase. When truncated to finite-dimensional matrices, issues such as truncation errors and convergence problems may arise, sometimes even introducing spurious eigenvalues unrelated to the original operator. However, its eigenvalue spectrum can be determined by connecting it to the physically relevant quantum Rabi model, which can be solved using creation and annihilation operators. This functional method yields Heun functions as exact solutions in a power series form. Even when considering finite truncations of these power series, the numerical precision can be controlled to any desired level of accuracy.

3.2. Conditions for Eigenvalues

There are several approaches to derive the conditions that the eigenvalues should satisfy. The earliest was the G-function form of the recurrence coefficient type given by Braak [15]. Next, Chen proposed a more physical way using Bogoliubov transformations [16]. Then, Zhong introduced a concise form by using the confluent Heun functions [17]. Here, we will follow some of Zhong's steps to solve the eigenvalues, then provide a more direct and concise expression for the conditions. We use analytical functions $\psi_{1,2}$ of the creation operator $a^\dagger$ to rewrite the eigenstates $|\psi\rangle$ in Equation (23) as

$$|\psi\rangle = \psi_1\left(a^\dagger\right)|0\rangle|\uparrow\rangle + \psi_2\left(a^\dagger\right)|0\rangle|\downarrow\rangle, \tag{25}$$

where $|0\rangle$ is the vacuum state for the bosonic mode.

From the eigenvalue equation $H|\psi\rangle = E|\psi\rangle$, the operator functions $\psi_{1,2}$ are found to satisfy the differential equations [17,40–42] as

$$z\frac{d\psi_1}{dz} + \lambda\left(\frac{d\psi_2}{dz} + z\psi_2\right) + \mu\psi_1 = E\psi_1, \tag{26}$$

$$z\frac{d\psi_2}{dz} + \lambda\left(\frac{d\psi_1}{dz} + z\psi_1\right) - \mu\psi_2 = E\psi_2, \tag{27}$$

where $z = a^\dagger$ can be formally regarded as a complex number. Using the linear combinations $f = \psi_1 + \psi_2$ and $g = \psi_1 - \psi_2$, the above equations can be transformed into a second-order differential equation for $f(z)$ or $g(z)$, which is

$$\frac{d^2 f}{dz^2} + p(z)\frac{df}{dz} + q(z)f = 0 \tag{28}$$

with $p(z) = [(1-2E-2\lambda^2)z - \lambda]/[z^2-\lambda^2], q(z) = [\lambda z - \lambda^2(z^2+1) + E^2 - \mu^2]/[z^2-\lambda^2]$.

We can transform the above equation into the standard confluent Heun equation by the two transformations as $f_1(z) = e^{-\lambda z}\phi_1(x_1)$ and $f_2(z) = e^{\lambda z}\phi_2(x_2)$, where $x_1 = \frac{\lambda - z}{2\lambda}$ and $x_2 = \frac{\lambda + z}{2\lambda}$. Firstly, we use the transformation $x_1 = \frac{\lambda - z}{2\lambda}$, and Equation (28) becomes

$$x_1(x_1-1)\phi_1'' + [\gamma(x_1-1) + \delta x_1 + x_1(x_1-1)\epsilon]\phi_1' + (\alpha x_1 - q)\phi_1 = 0, \tag{29}$$

where $q = \mu^2 - (E+\lambda^2)^2$, $\alpha = -4\lambda^2(E+\lambda^2)$, $\gamma = -(E+\lambda^2)$, $\delta = -(E+\lambda^2)+1$, $\epsilon = 4\lambda^2$. From the form of Equation (29), we can naturally express the eigenvalue E in terms of a new variable as $k = E + \lambda^2$. Here, k can be regarded as a quasi-energy value of a modified Hamiltonian $H' = H + \lambda^2$, which makes this formulation convenient for subsequent discussions. The parameters in the confluent Heun Equation (29) can be re-expressed as $q = \mu^2 - k^2, \alpha = -4k\lambda^2, \gamma = -k, \delta = 1-k, \epsilon = 4\lambda^2$. Therefore, the solution to Equation (28) is

$$f_1(z) = e^{-\lambda z}\mathrm{HC}\left(\mu^2 - k^2, -4k\lambda^2; -k, 1-k, 4\lambda^2; x_1\right) := e^{-\lambda z}\mathrm{HC}(a_3; x_1), \tag{30}$$

with the parameter $a_3 := \left(\mu^2 - k^2, -4k\lambda^2; -k, 1-k, 4\lambda^2\right)$. The other linearly independent solution of the Heun confluent function is $x_1^{1-\gamma}\mathrm{HC}(q + (1-\gamma)(\epsilon - \delta), \alpha + (1-\gamma)\epsilon; 2-\gamma, \delta, \epsilon; x_1)$, which requires separate discussion only when $1-\gamma \in \mathbb{N}$, due to the physical meaning of $z = a^\dagger$. Since $a^{\dagger n}|0\rangle = \sqrt{n!}|n\rangle$ in the Bargmann space, the analytical functions $\psi_{1,2}$ do not always correspond to valid states as they may not be normalized. Under certain conditions, the coefficients b_n in Heun confluent function $\mathrm{HC}(q, \alpha; \gamma, \delta, \epsilon; x)$ may satisfy $b_n/b_{n-1} \simeq -\epsilon/n$ for large n, where the analytical functions $\psi_{1,2}$ can be normalized and are thus valid. However, these conditions are not explicitly provided in the confluent Heun functions and are often related to the convergence at the singular point $x = 1$. Therefore, we use an alternative approach to determine the conditions for the eigenvalues, employing the next transformation and an additional solution.

We apply the second transformation $x_2 = \frac{\lambda + z}{2\lambda}$, and through a similar sequence of steps, we obtain another solution to Equation (28) as

$$f_2(z) = e^{\lambda z}\mathrm{HC}(a_4; x_2) := e^{\lambda z}\mathrm{HC}\left(\mu^2 - k^2 + 4\lambda^2, 4(1-k)\lambda^2; 1-k, -k, 4\lambda^2; x_2\right), \tag{31}$$

with the parameter $a_4 := (\mu^2 - k^2 + 4\lambda^2, 4(1-k)\lambda^2; 1-k, -k; 4\lambda^2)$. When E is an eigenvalue of the quantum Rabi model, the two forms of the solution $f(z)$ must coincide within the common domain of definition (up to a multiplicative constant), which implies that the Wronskian determinant vanishes. Noticing $x_1 + x_2 = 1$, we can obtain the Wronskian determinant [18,20] as

$$W(k,\lambda,\mu;y) = f_1\partial_z f_2 - f_2\partial_z f_1 \tag{32}$$

$$= \frac{1}{2\lambda}[4\lambda^2 \mathrm{H}_3(y)\mathrm{H}_4(1-y) + \mathrm{H}_3'(y)\mathrm{H}_4(1-y) + \mathrm{H}_3(y)\mathrm{H}_4'(1-y)], \tag{33}$$

where $y = x_1$, $\mathrm{H}_i(y) := \mathrm{HC}(a_i;y)$, and $\mathrm{H}_i'(y_0) := \partial_y \mathrm{HC}(a_i;y)|_{y=y_0}$.

Lemma 2. *The Wronskian can be expressed without explicitly involving derivatives, which is*

$$W(k,\lambda,\mu;y) = k^2\mathrm{H}_3(y)\mathrm{H}_3(1-y) - \mu^2\mathrm{H}_4(y)\mathrm{H}_4(1-y), \tag{34}$$

where a parameter $2k\lambda(y-1)$ *is multiplied.*

Theorem 2. *The Wronskian Equation* (34) *must vanish in the intersection of domains of solutions. By choosing* $y = 1/2$, *we can obtain a more concise form as*

$$w(k,\lambda,\mu) := W(k,\lambda,\mu;y=1/2) = k^2\mathrm{H}_3^2(1/2) - \mu^2\mathrm{H}_4^2(1/2) \tag{35}$$

$$= [k\mathrm{H}_3(1/2) - \mu\mathrm{H}_4(1/2)][k\mathrm{H}_3(1/2) + \mu\mathrm{H}_4(1/2)], \tag{36}$$

where $\mathrm{H}_i(1/2) := \mathrm{HC}(a_i;1/2)$. *From the above equation, we can see that the condition can be divided into two parts* $k\mathrm{H}_3(1/2) - \mu\mathrm{H}_4(1/2) = 0$ *and* $k\mathrm{H}_3(1/2) + \mu\mathrm{H}_4(1/2) = 0$, *and those conditions are more concise than previous results [15–19].*

Proof of Lemma 2 and Theorem 2. After applying the identity Equations (52) and (53), we can simplify Equation (33) as

$$\begin{aligned} W(k,\lambda,\mu;y) &= \frac{1}{2\lambda}[4\lambda^2\mathrm{H}_3(y)\mathrm{H}_4(1-y) + \frac{\mu^2\mathrm{H}_4(y) - k^2\mathrm{H}_3(y)}{k(1-y)}\mathrm{H}_4(1-y) \\ &\quad + \mathrm{H}_3(y)\frac{(k-4\lambda^2(1-y))\mathrm{H}_4(1-y) - k\mathrm{H}_3(1-y)}{1-y}] \qquad (37) \\ &= \frac{1}{2k\lambda(1-y)}[4k\lambda^2(1-y)\mathrm{H}_3(y)\mathrm{H}_4(1-y) + (\mu^2\mathrm{H}_4(y) - k^2\mathrm{H}_3(y))\mathrm{H}_4(1-y) \\ &\quad + k\mathrm{H}_3(y)\Big((k-4\lambda^2(1-y))\mathrm{H}_4(1-y) - k\mathrm{H}_3(1-y)\Big)] \qquad (38) \end{aligned}$$

$$\begin{aligned} &= \frac{1}{2k\lambda(1-y)}[\mathrm{H}_3(y)\mathrm{H}_4(1-y)(4k\lambda^2(1-y) - k^2 + k(k-4\lambda^2(1-y))) \\ &\quad - k^2\mathrm{H}_3(y)\mathrm{H}_3(1-y) + \mu^2\mathrm{H}_4(y)\mathrm{H}_4(1-y)] \qquad (39) \\ &= \frac{1}{2k\lambda(y-1)}\left[k^2\mathrm{H}_3(y)\mathrm{H}_3(1-y) - \mu^2\mathrm{H}_4(y)\mathrm{H}_4(1-y)\right]. \qquad (10) \end{aligned}$$

When $y = 1/2$, we can obtain

$$\begin{aligned} w(k,\lambda,\mu) &= 2k\lambda(y-1) * W(k,\lambda,\mu;y) \qquad (41) \\ &= k^2\mathrm{H}_3(1/2)\mathrm{H}_3(1-1/2) - \mu^2\mathrm{H}_4(1/2)\mathrm{H}_4(1-1/2) \qquad (42) \\ &= k^2\mathrm{H}_3^2(1/2) - \mu^2\mathrm{H}_4^2(1/2) \qquad (43) \end{aligned}$$

□

3.3. The Energy Spectrum of Quantum Rabi Model

We have now derived the conditions that the energy $E = k - \lambda^2$ needs to satisfy. These conditions are explicitly restated as

$$k\mathrm{HC}(a_3; 1/2) \pm \mu\mathrm{HC}(a_4; 1/2) = 0, \tag{44}$$

where $a_3 := (\mu^2 - k^2, -4k\lambda^2; -k, 1-k, 4\lambda^2)$ and $a_4 := (\mu^2 - k^2 + 4\lambda^2, 4(1-k)\lambda^2; 1-k, -k; 4\lambda^2)$. When the energy $E = k - \lambda^2$ satisfies Expression (44) above, we can reconstruct a physical eigenstate with the corresponding eigenvalue of E that can be normalized. If we look at the above equation from the perspective of parameter k, we will find that it has poles at $k \in \mathbb{Z}^+$. A new method is to multiply the condition expressions by a constant, the Gamma function $\Gamma(1-k)$, so that they no longer diverge at these poles. The use of Gamma functions to eliminate poles in the equivalent of G-functions for the asymmetric quantum Rabi model was also proposed theoretically in Refs. [43–45].

Remark 1. *The Wronskian condition* (44) *becomes* $l_\mp(k) = 0$, *where*

$$l_\mp(k) := \mathrm{HC}(a_3; 1/2)/\Gamma(-k) \mp \mu\mathrm{HC}(a_4; 1/2)/\Gamma(1-k). \tag{45}$$

Figure 3 shows the above functions $l_\mp$ and their zeros, which are consistent with the previous results [15–19]. Since these functions $l_\mp$ have no poles, we can observe their zero distributions more clearly.

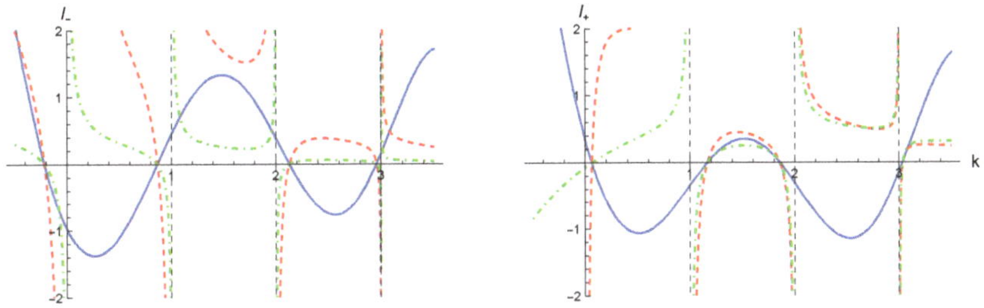

Figure 3. Comparison with previous results for $\mu = 0.4, \lambda = 0.7, \omega = 1$. The zeros of $G_\mp$ in Ref. [15], $G^+_{1(4)}|_{z=0}$ in Ref. [17], and $l_\mp$ in this paper are consistent. (**Left panel**): G_- (red dash lines), G^+_1 (green dot-dash lines), and l_- (blue solid lines). (**Right panel**): G_+ (red dash lines), G^+_4 (green dot-dash lines), and l_+ (blue solid lines). To enhance clarity, the values of the $l_\mp$ functions have been rescaled by a constant factor of 5.

The structure of the energy spectrum $E = k - \lambda^2$ is shown in Figure 4. The energies of the blue solid (red dashed) lines belong to the odd (even) subspace and satisfy the energy condition $l_- = 0$ ($l_+ = 0$). We can see that the non-trivial crossings occur only at $k \in \mathbb{Z}^+$ and there are trivial crossings when μ and k are half-integers, and $\lambda = 0$. The non-trivial crossings of the spectral lines occur only between lines of different colors or shapes, indicating that non-trivial energy degeneracy does not occur within the same subspace. We can then use the ordering of energies within the corresponding subspace to label the energy levels ($-$ for odd subspace and $+$ for even subspace), as illustrated in Figure 4. As λ approaches infinity, the quasi-energy value k converges to the corresponding marked level n. This type of marking indicates that non-trivial crossings occur only when the energies are at the same marked level, while trivial crossings occur between adjacent marked levels. This result has been verified using numerical methods; however, a theoretical proof would require a deeper understanding of confluent Heun functions and the quantum Rabi model, and is therefore not provided here. Numerical calculations show that when k is a half-integer, approximate crossing points appear. The lower right corner of the right panel in Figure 4 provides a magnified view of this situation.

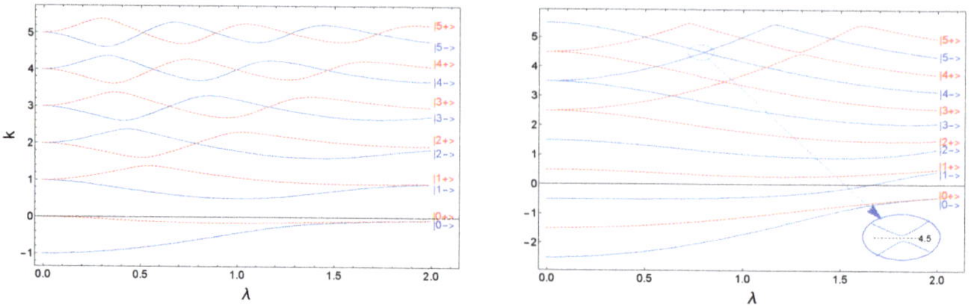

Figure 4. Quasi-energy spectrum ($k = E + \lambda^2$) of quantum Rabi models for $\mu = 1$ (**left panel**) and $\mu = 2.5$ (**right panel**). The energies of the blue solid lines belong to the odd subspace and satisfy the energy condition $l_- = 0$. The energies of the red dashed lines belong to the even subspace and satisfy the energy condition $l_+ = 0$.

When a non-trivial crossing occurs at $k_z \in Z^+$, the two condition functions $l_\mp$ also intersect at k_z, where the eigenstates degenerate into the Jude states [46–48] (polynomial states). We find that the number m of non-trivial crossings at $k_z \in Z^+$ is given by $m(\mu, k_z) = \lfloor \max(0, k_z + 1 - |\mu|) \rfloor$, where $\lfloor x \rfloor$ represents the floor function and $|x|$ represents the absolute value function; this result has also been verified by numerical methods. The result m represents the number of Juddian isolated exact solutions [45–47] and is consistent with the findings in Ref. [48] for the case $|\mu| < 1$. Another situation is that only one of the condition functions, l_- or l_+, equals zero at k_z. This situation implies that the limiting values of the two functions $H_3(1/2)/\Gamma(-k)$ and $\mu H_4(1/2)/\Gamma(1-k)$ at the pole k_z are either identical or opposite, corresponding to the odd or even subspace, respectively. Figure 5 shows these two situations, and we can regard these two special cases $k \in Z^+$ as the limiting situations at the poles, from the perspective of the criterion $l_\mp(k) = 0$. Our method unifies the conditions into a single consistent formula, whether k is a pole or not, indicating that we do not need to treat the poles as special cases. For both the regular and exceptional spectra, this consistent formula provides a clear understanding of the roots of conditional Equation (45).

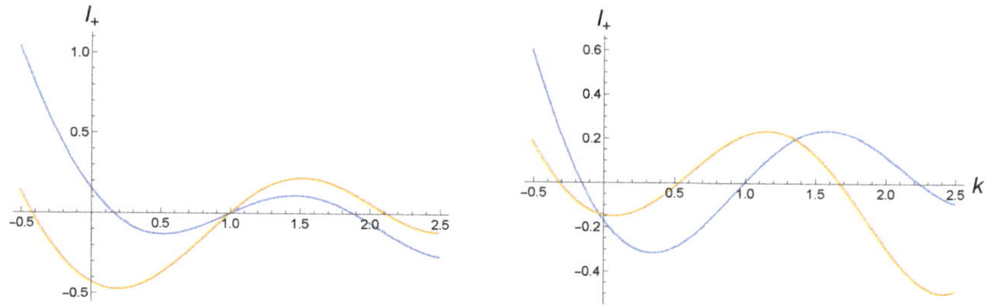

Figure 5. Exceptional quasi-energy $k = 1$ with the $l_\mp$ functions (yellow line for l_- and blue line for l_+). The **left** panel represents the degenerate case with $\mu = 1/2, \lambda = \sqrt{3}/4$, and the **right** panel represents the non-degenerate case with $\mu = 1, \lambda = 1.1647879$.

Although we have obtained the exact conditions for the eigenvalues of the quantum Rabi model, the explicit expressions for a specific energy level remain unclear, as the exact forms of the roots involving the confluent Heun functions are difficult to obtain. Here, we obtain the upper and lower bounds for the energy E_0, which is the ground state energy of the quantum Rabi model.

Remark 2. *The ground state energy is the lowest root of the odd parity condition $l_- = 0$, for which we obtain a lower bound, denoted as*

$$E_0 + \lambda^2 \geq e_g = -\mu + \frac{\mu}{1 + \lambda^{-2}(\mu + 1/2)}, \tag{46}$$

where we consider $\mu > 0$. When λ is small or large, we can obtain two more concise upper bounds $E_0 + \lambda^2 \leq \min(e_{\text{up}}^s, e_{\text{up}}^l)$ as

$$e_{\text{up}}^s = -\mu + \frac{\mu}{\frac{1/4}{\mu+1/2} + \lambda^{-2}(\mu + 1/2)}, \quad e_{\text{up}}^l = -\mu + \frac{\mu}{1 + \lambda^{-2}(\mu/4)}. \tag{47}$$

Figure 6 illustrates the differences between the three bounds and the exact ground quasi-energy k, which are negligible when λ is either small or large. This expression for small λ can be derived using perturbation theory (see Appendix C), while numerical checks are employed for other regions.

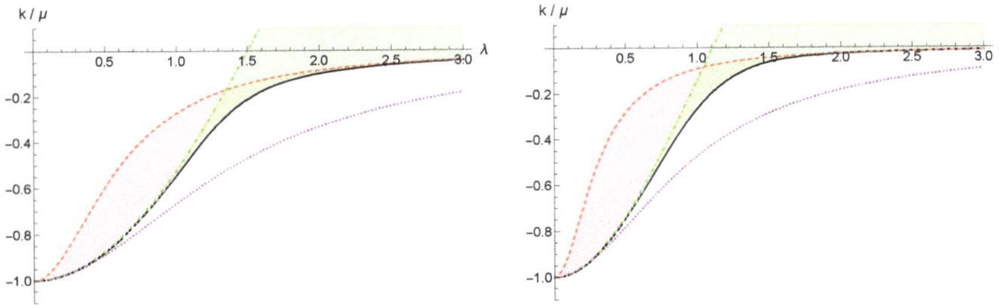

Figure 6. The upper and lower bound for the ground states with $\mu = 1.5$ (**left panel**) and $\mu = 0.4$ (**right panel**). The black solid lines are the exact quasi-energy of the ground states. The two upper bounds are e_{up}^l (red dashed line) and e_{up}^s (green dot-dash line), while the lower bound is e_g (purple dotted line) at the bottom right corner.

4. Discussion

The confluent Heun functions are used in both the semi-classical and quantum Rabi models, which is an interesting and noteworthy phenomenon. However, in these two cases, the relationship between the confluent Heun functions and the eigenvalue spectrum differs. In the semi-classical Rabi model, the eigenvalues q_α are expressed directly in terms of the confluent Heun functions as

$$q_\alpha = \frac{1}{\pi}\arcsin\left(\sqrt{2}\beta \text{Re}[e^{ig}\text{HC}(a_1^*; \frac{1}{2})\text{HC}(a_2; \frac{1}{2})]\right), \tag{48}$$

whereas in the quantum Rabi model, the eigenvalues $E = k - \lambda^2$ are determined as the zeros of a condition defined by the confluent Heun functions as

$$0 = \text{HC}(a_3; 1/2)/\Gamma(-k) \mp \mu\text{HC}(a_4; 1/2)/\Gamma(1-k). \tag{49}$$

In both cases, the special point $x = 1/2$ in confluent Heun functions $\text{HC}(a_i; x)$ is utilized, suggesting that this specific value $x = 1/2$ warrants further investigation. And we find that they are both related to the convergence at the singularity $x = 1$. In the semi-classical Rabi model, we ensure that the confluent Heun functions converge at $x = 1$ and take the value as

$$\text{HC}(a_1; x = 1) = \text{HC}^2(a_1; 1/2) - \frac{\beta^2}{2}e^{2ig}\text{HC}^2(a_2; 1/2). \tag{50}$$

In the quantum Rabi model, we find that the convergence of the confluent Heun function at $x = 1$ is a necessary condition for the energy E to be an eigenvalue. It should be clarified that the confluent Heun functions can also converge at $x = 1$ when E is not an eigenvalue. There are two modes of convergence. One mode in the semi-classical case is that $\mathrm{Re}(\delta) < 1$ ensures the convergence of the Heun confluent function. The other mode, relevant to the eigenvalue spectrum of the quantum Rabi model, requires the convergence to occur more rapidly, as the coefficients satisfy $b_n/b_{n-1} \sim -\epsilon/n$.

Within the convergence range of the function, we derive several useful identities. Among them, some have been obtained previously, while others are new and useful. In the semi-classical case, we obtain the following identity equation

$$e^{\epsilon x}\mathrm{HC}(q,\alpha;\gamma,\delta,\epsilon;x) = \mathrm{HC}(q-\gamma\epsilon,\alpha-\epsilon(\gamma+\delta);\gamma,\delta,-\epsilon;x), \tag{51}$$

which has also been presented in previous work [49]. In the quantum case, we obtain two identities as

$$k(1-x)\mathrm{HC}'(a_3;x) = \mu^2\mathrm{HC}(a_4;x) - k^2\mathrm{HC}(a_3;x), \tag{52}$$

$$x\mathrm{HC}'(a_4;x) = (k-4\lambda^2 x)\mathrm{HC}(a_4;x) - k\mathrm{HC}(a_3;x), \tag{53}$$

where $\mathrm{HC}'(a_i;x)$ represents the x-derivative of $\mathrm{HC}(a_i;x)$. Equations (52) and (53) above are identities involving the derivatives of the confluent Heun functions and have been used to simplify the Wronskian (33).

Our method can be generalized to handle more general cases. In the classical model, it can be extended to incorporate higher-order trigonometric functions, such as $\sin n\omega t$ and $\cos n\omega t$. From a theoretical perspective, based on the Fourier transform, such a series approximation can be applied to approximate any given function. Although this introduces additional complexity, it remains a feasible approach. In the quantum model, we can introduce multi-photon interactions, thereby enabling the expansion of our formalized matrix (24). Naturally, after such a modification, the resulting solution is no longer a Heun function; instead, it may correspond to the solution to a more complex equation. With a deeper understanding of the confluent Heun function, we hope to obtain explicit forms of eigenvalues in the future, which will require further research.

5. Conclusions

In conclusion, we establish the relationship between infinite-dimensional matrices and the Rabi model, and applying the confluent Heun functions, we present a unified approach to derive the eigenvalue spectrum of these unbounded matrices. For the first kind of matrix related to the semi-classical Rabi model, we obtain the explicit form of the eigenvalues, which is consistent with the previous approximate results. For the second kind of matrix related to the quantum Rabi model, we derive an explicit condition that the eigenvalue must satisfy. This condition is more concise than the previous results, and is valid to all situations. We have discussed the degeneracy of the energy spectrum, which aligns with the findings of previous studies. We obtain numerical upper and lower bounds in explicit forms for the eigenvalue, which fit well in the regimes where the interaction strength is either small or large.

The relationship between mathematics and physics is complementary since our approach actually solves the eigenvalue problem of infinite-dimensional unbounded matrices. We derive some identities involving the confluent Heun functions, which can not only be applied in the situation of this paper but also in many other related fields of mathematics and physics. The eigenvalues in the Rabi models are related to the special values of the confluent Heun functions and their convergence at the singular point $x = 1$. Our results enhance the understanding and potential applications of the Rabi model in quantum optics, quantum information, and condensed matter physics.

Author Contributions: Methodology, J.C.; Formal analysis, S.X., Y.S. and J.C.; Data curation, Y.C.; writing—original draft, H.L.; Writing—review and editing, H.L.; Funding acquisition, Y.C. and Y.S. All authors have read and agreed to the published version of the manuscript.

Funding: This work was supported by the National Natural Science Foundation of China (Grants No. 11975197 and No. 12247158) and the Talent introduction Project of Zhejiang Shuren University (Grant No. 2023R031).

Data Availability Statement: The original contributions presented in this study are included in the article. Further inquiries can be directed to the author.

Acknowledgments: The author would like to thank the National Natural Science Foundation of China and the Talent introduction Project of Zhejiang Shuren University.

Conflicts of Interest: The authors declare no conflicts of interest.

Appendix A. Notations in This Paper

x^* represents the complex conjugate of x. $\mathrm{Re}[x]$ represents the real part of x, while $\mathrm{Im}[x]$ represents the imaginary part of x. The function $\arg(x)$ represents the argument of the complex number x. $\lfloor x \rfloor$ represents the floor function as $\lfloor x \rfloor = \max\{m \in \mathbb{Z} | m \leq x\}$. $J_0(x)$ is the first kind of the Bessel function of 0-order and $j_0(n)$ represents the n-th zero point of the Bessel function $J_0(x)$. $f(x_0^{\pm})$ represents $f(x_0^{\pm}) \equiv \lim_{x \to x_0 + 0^{\pm}} f(x)$.

Appendix B. Key Derivations in the Semi-Classical Rabi Model

The Schrödinger equation is

$$\mathrm{i}\partial_t|\psi\rangle = H(t)|\psi\rangle = \left(\frac{\beta}{2}\sigma_x + \frac{g}{2}\sin(t)\sigma_z\right)|\psi\rangle, \quad \text{(A1)}$$

where $|\psi\rangle = (c_1, c_2)^{\mathrm{T}}$ is the normalized wave function. The Schrödinger equation can be written into two equations as

$$\mathrm{i}\frac{\partial c_1}{\partial t} - \frac{g}{2}c_1 \sin t = \frac{\beta}{2}c_2 \quad \text{(A2)}$$

$$\mathrm{i}\frac{\partial c_2}{\partial t} + \frac{g}{2}c_2 \sin t = \frac{\beta}{2}c_1 \quad \text{(A3)}$$

Then, after removing c_2 (or c_1), we obtain a second-order differential equation for c_1 (or c_2), as

$$\frac{\partial^2 c_1}{\partial t^2} + (\mathrm{i}\frac{g}{2}\cos t + \frac{g^2}{4}\sin^2 t + \frac{\beta^2}{4})c_1 = 0. \quad \text{(A4)}$$

Applying the change in the variable from t to $z = \frac{1}{2}(1 - \cos t) = \sin^2 \frac{t}{2}$, we can obtain (for $0 \leq t \leq \pi/2$)

$$\begin{aligned} \cos t &= 1 - 2z && \text{(A5)} \\ |\sin t| &= \sin t = 2\sqrt{z(1-z)} && \text{(A6)} \\ \frac{\partial z}{\partial t} &= \frac{1}{2}\sin t = \sqrt{z(1-z)} && \text{(A7)} \\ 0 &= z(1-z)\frac{\partial^2 c_1}{\partial z^2} + (\frac{1}{2} - z)\frac{\partial c_1}{\partial z} + (\mathrm{i}g(\frac{1}{2} - z) + g^2 z(1-z) + \frac{\beta^2}{4})c_1. && \text{(A8)} \end{aligned}$$

By applying another transform $c_1 = \mathrm{e}^{-\mathrm{i}gz} f$, we can obtain

$$\frac{\partial c_1}{\partial z} = \frac{\partial}{\partial z}(\mathrm{e}^{-\mathrm{i}gz} f) = \mathrm{e}^{-\mathrm{i}gz}(\frac{\partial f}{\partial z} - \mathrm{i}gf) \tag{A9}$$

$$\frac{\partial^2 c_1}{\partial z^2} = \frac{\partial}{\partial z}\left(\mathrm{e}^{-\mathrm{i}gz}(\frac{\partial f}{\partial z} - \mathrm{i}gf)\right) = \mathrm{e}^{-\mathrm{i}gz}\left(-g^2 f - 2\mathrm{i}g\frac{\partial f}{\partial z} + \frac{\partial^2 f}{\partial z^2}\right) \tag{A10}$$

$$z(1-z)\left(-g^2 f - 2\mathrm{i}g\frac{\partial f}{\partial z} + \frac{\partial^2 f}{\partial z^2}\right) + (\frac{1}{2} - z)(\frac{\partial f}{\partial z} - \mathrm{i}gf) + +(\mathrm{i}g(\frac{1}{2} - z) + g^2 z(1-z) + \frac{\beta^2}{4})f = 0 \tag{A11}$$

$$z(1-z)\frac{\partial^2 f}{\partial z^2} + \left[(\frac{1}{2} - z) - 2\mathrm{i}gz(1-z)\right]\frac{\partial f}{\partial z} + (\mathrm{i}g(\frac{1}{2} - z) + \frac{\beta^2}{4} - (\frac{1}{2} - z)\mathrm{i}g)f = 0 \tag{A12}$$

$$z(z-1)\frac{\partial^2 f}{\partial z^2} + \left[-2\mathrm{i}gz(z-1) + (z - \frac{1}{2})\right]\frac{\partial f}{\partial z} + (-\frac{\beta^2}{4})f = 0. \tag{A13}$$

Then, we can obtain the differential equation as

$$z(z-1)\frac{\partial^2 f}{\partial z^2} + \left[\frac{1}{2}(z-1) + \frac{1}{2}z - 2\mathrm{i}gz(z-1)\right]\frac{\partial f}{\partial z} + (-\frac{\beta^2}{4})f = 0. \tag{A14}$$

Compared to the standard confluent Heun equation

$$z(z-1)y'' + [\gamma(z-1) + \delta z + z(z-1)\epsilon)]y' + (\alpha z - q)y = 0, \tag{A15}$$

we obtain the coefficients $q = \frac{\beta^2}{4}$, $\alpha = 0$, $\gamma = \frac{1}{2}$, $\delta = \frac{1}{2}$, $\epsilon = -2\mathrm{i}g$. The solution that satisfies the confluent Heun equation is the confluent Heun function $H_C(q,\alpha;\gamma,\delta,\epsilon;z)$, with the initial condition $H_C(q,\alpha;\gamma,\delta,\epsilon;0) = 1$ [30–32]. The confluent Heun function can be expressed as a standard power-series expansion around $z = 0$ as $\mathrm{HC}(q,\alpha;\gamma,\delta,\epsilon;z) = \sum_{n=0}^{\infty} b_n z^n$. The coefficients b_n are determined by the three-term recurrence relation $R_n b_n + Q_{n-1}b_{n-1} + P_{n-2}b_{n-2} = 0$ with the initial conditions $b_{-2} = b_{-1} = 0$ and $b_0 = 1$. Here, $R_n = n(n-1+\gamma)$, $Q_n = q - n(n-1+\gamma+\delta-\epsilon)$, and $P_n = -\alpha - \epsilon n$. Thus, the solution to Equation (A4) is

$$c_1(t) = \mathrm{e}^{-\mathrm{i}gz}\mathrm{HC}\left(\frac{\beta^2}{4}, 0; \frac{1}{2}, \frac{1}{2}, -2\mathrm{i}g; z\right) := \mathrm{e}^{-\mathrm{i}gz}\mathrm{HC}(a_1; z), \tag{A16}$$

where parameters $a_1 := \left(\frac{\beta^2}{4}, 0; \frac{1}{2}, \frac{1}{2}, -2\mathrm{i}g\right)$, and $z = \sin^2\frac{t}{2}$. Here, we choose the initial condition $c_1(t=0) = 1, c_2(t=0) = 0$.

From the symmetry of the Equations (A2) and (A3), we can see that except for g becoming $-g$, c_1 and c_2 have differential equations of the same form. Then, according to the initial condition $c_2(t=0) = 0$, we know that c_2 is the other linearly independent solution $z^{1-\gamma}\mathrm{HC}(q + (1-\gamma)(\epsilon - \delta), \alpha + (1-\gamma)\epsilon, 2-\gamma, \delta, \epsilon, z)$, which is

$$c_2(t) = \mathrm{i}^{\eta}\beta z^{1/2}\mathrm{e}^{\mathrm{i}gz}\mathrm{HC}\left(\frac{\beta^2 - 1}{4} + \mathrm{i}g, \mathrm{i}g; \frac{3}{2}, \frac{1}{2}, 2\mathrm{i}g; z\right) := \mathrm{i}^{\eta}\beta \sin\frac{t}{2}\mathrm{e}^{\mathrm{i}gz}\mathrm{HC}(a_2; z), \tag{A17}$$

where parameters $a_2 := \left(\frac{\beta^2-1}{4} + \mathrm{i}g, \mathrm{i}g; \frac{3}{2}, \frac{1}{2}, 2\mathrm{i}g\right)$, $z = \sin^2\frac{t}{2}$, and $\eta = 1 + 2\lfloor\frac{t-\pi}{T}\rfloor$ with the floor function $\lfloor x \rfloor$. Then, we can construct the time evolution operator as

$$U_1(t) = \begin{pmatrix} c_1(t) & -c_2(t)^* \\ c_2(t) & c_1(t)^* \end{pmatrix}. \tag{A18}$$

The question is whether U_1 or c_2 is discontinuous at the points $t = (2k+1)\frac{T}{2}, k \in \mathbb{Z}$. Hence, an alternative form of the evolution operator U_2 is required to ensure continuity at these junctures. According to the symmetry $H(t) = \sigma_x H(t - \frac{T}{2})\sigma_x$, we derive $U_2(t) = \sigma_x U_1(t - \frac{T}{2})\sigma_x$. By combining U_1 and U_2, the evolution of half a period is attainable as $U_{\frac{T}{2}} \equiv U(\frac{T}{2}, 0) = U_2^\dagger(\frac{T}{4})U_1(\frac{T}{4})$. We need three parameter functions as follows: $\phi_1 = \arg(c_1^* c_2)$, $\theta_1 = 2\arcsin|c_2|$, and $\gamma_1 = -\arg(c_1 c_2)$. Now, we can obtain the evolution over a complete period as $U_T = U_2(T^-)U_2^\dagger(0) = e^{i2\Theta\sigma_n/2}$, where $\sigma_n = \sin\Phi\sigma_x + \cos\Phi\sigma_y$, $\Phi = \phi_1(\frac{T}{2}^-)$, and $\Theta = \theta_1(\frac{T}{2}^-)$. This U_T represents a clockwise rotation by an angle 2Θ in the $\boldsymbol{n}$-direction. Consequently, the total time evolution operator can be expressed as

$$U(t,0) = U_2(t - NT)U_2^\dagger(0)e^{i2N\Theta\sigma_n/2}, \tag{A19}$$

where $N = \lfloor \frac{t}{T} \rfloor$ and $U_2^\dagger(0) = U_{\frac{T}{2}}$. Here, $U_{\frac{T}{2}}$ as $U_{\frac{T}{2}} = e^{-\frac{1}{2}i\Phi\sigma_z}e^{-\frac{1}{2}i\Theta\sigma_y}e^{-\frac{1}{2}i\Gamma\sigma_z}$, where $\Phi = \phi_1(\frac{T}{2}^-)$, $\Theta = \theta_1(\frac{T}{2}^-)$ and $\Gamma = \gamma_1(\frac{T}{2}^-)$ with the notation $f(x_0^\pm) \equiv \lim_{x\to x_0+0^\pm} f(x)$.

As compared to Floquet theory [25–28], there is one more rotation needed, which is $R_s = e^{-i\frac{\pi}{4}\sigma_x}e^{-i\frac{\Phi}{2}\sigma_z}$. Then, we can obtain the operator $F(t)$ as

$$F(t) = R_s U R_s^\dagger = R_s U_2(t - NT)U_2^\dagger(0)R_s^\dagger e^{iN\Theta\sigma_z}. \tag{A20}$$

As we all can see, the characteristic value q_α should be

$$q_\alpha = \frac{\Theta}{T} = \frac{2\arcsin|c_2(\frac{T}{2}^-)|}{2\pi} \tag{A21}$$

$$= \frac{2}{\pi}\arcsin\left(\sqrt{2}\beta \mathrm{Re}[e^{ig}\mathrm{HC}^*(a_1;\frac{1}{2})\mathrm{HC}(a_2;\frac{1}{2})]\right) \tag{A22}$$

Appendix C. Perturbation Theory for the Ground State Energy

We use the perturbation theory to derive the explicit form for a small interaction strength λ. The Hamiltonian H of the system can be written as the sum of a solvable part H_0 (the unperturbed Hamiltonian) and a small perturbation V (the perturbing Hamiltonian):

$$H = H_0 + \lambda V, \tag{A23}$$

where λ is a small parameter controlling the strength of the interaction, $H_0 = a^\dagger a + \mu\sigma_z$, $V = \sigma_x(a^\dagger + a)$. The spectrum of the unperturbed Hamiltonian H_0 is $E_{n,\pm1}^{(0)} = n \pm \mu$. Consider the odd subspace. The spectrum becomes $e_n^{(0)} = E_{n,(-1)^{n+1}} = n + (-1)^{n+1}\mu$, while the corresponding eigenstates are denoted as $|n\rangle$. In the representation of $|n\rangle$, the perturbation Hamiltonian V and the transformation matrix U can be expressed as

$$V_{i,j} = \langle i|V|j\rangle,\ U_{i,j} = \langle i|U|j\rangle. \tag{A24}$$

The transformation matrix U can also be expressed in the power series of λ as $U = \sum_{i=0}^{\infty} \lambda^i U^i$. The first-order perturbation term for the energy is shown as

$$e_n^{(1)} = \langle n|V|n\rangle = 0. \tag{A25}$$

and the second-order perturbation term for the energy is shown as

$$e_n^{(2)} = \sum_{l\neq n} \frac{V_{n,l}V_{l,n}}{e_n^{(0)} - e_l^{(0)}} = \frac{2\mu(-1)^n(2n-1)+1}{4\mu^2 - 1}. \tag{A26}$$

We observe that the odd-order perturbation of the energy is always zero. Here, we are concerned with the ground state, so we obtain the perturbation term of the ground energy with the sixth-order as

$$e_0^{(0)} = -\mu,\ e_0^{(2)} = -\frac{1}{1+2\mu},\ e_0^{(4)} = -\frac{2\mu}{(2\mu+1)^3},\ e_0^{(6)} = -\frac{4\mu(4\mu^2+4\mu-1)}{(2\mu+1)^5(2\mu+3)}. \quad \text{(A27)}$$

Then, we expand the equations in (46) and (47) when λ is small, which are

$$e_g = -\mu + \lambda^2 - \frac{\lambda^2}{1+2\mu} - \frac{4\mu\lambda^4}{(2\mu+1)^2} + \frac{8\mu\lambda^6}{(2\mu+1)^3} + O\left(\lambda^7\right), \quad \text{(A28)}$$

$$e_{\text{up}}^s = -\mu + \lambda^2 - \frac{\lambda^2}{1+2\mu} - \frac{2\mu\lambda^4}{(2\mu+1)^3} + \frac{2\mu\lambda^6}{(2\mu+1)^5} + O\left(\lambda^7\right). \quad \text{(A29)}$$

Since $-\frac{4\mu(4\mu^2+4\mu-1)}{(2\mu+1)^5(2\mu+3)} < \frac{2\mu}{(2\mu+1)^5}$ when $\mu > 0$, we deduce that $e_g < E_0 + \lambda^2 < e_{\text{up}}^s$ for small λ.

References

1. Rabi, I.I. On the Process of Space Quantization. *Phys. Rev.* **1936**, *49*, 324–328. [CrossRef]
2. Rabi, I.I. Space Quantization in a Gyrating Magnetic Field. *Phys. Rev.* **1937**, *51*, 652–654. [CrossRef]
3. Nielsen, M.A.; Chuang, I.L. *Quantum Computation and Quantum Information;* Cambridge University: Cambridge, UK, 2000.
4. Bouwmeester, D.; Ekert, A.K.; Zeilinger, A. *The Physics of Quantum Information: Quantum Cryptography, Quantum Teleportation, Quantum Computation;* Springer: Berlin, Germany, 2000.
5. Ashhab, S.; Johansson, J.R.; Zagoskin, A.M.; Nori, F. Two-level systems driven by large-amplitude fields. *Phys. Rev. A* **2007**, *75*, 063414. [CrossRef]
6. Gerardot, B.D.; Öhberg, P. A Strongly Driven Spin. *Science* **2009**, *326*, 1489–1490. [CrossRef] [PubMed]
7. Fuchs, G.D.; Dobrovitski, V.V.; Toyli, D.M.; Heremans, F.J.; Awschalom, D.D. Gigahertz Dynamics of a Strongly Driven Single Quantum Spin. *Science* **2009**, *326*, 1520–1522. [CrossRef]
8. Jaynes, E.; Cummings, F. Comparison of quantum and semiclassical radiation theories with application to the beam maser. *Proc. IEEE* **1963**, *51*, 89–109. [CrossRef]
9. Milonni, P.W.; Ackerhalt, J.R.; Galbraith, H.W. Chaos in the SemiclassicalN-Atom Jaynes-Cummings Model: Failure of the Rotating-Wave Approximation. *Phys. Rev. Lett.* **1983**, *50*, 966–969. [CrossRef]
10. Bonci, L.; Roncaglia, R.; West, B.J.; Grigolini, P. Quantum irreversibility and chaos. *Phys. Rev. Lett.* **1991**, *67*, 2593–2596. [CrossRef]
11. Fukuo, T.; Ogawa, T.; Nakamura, K. Jaynes-Cummings model under continuous measurement: Weak chaos in a quantum system induced by unitarity collapse. *Phys. Rev. A* **1998**, *58*, 3293–3302. [CrossRef]
12. Su, Y.; Wang, X. Parametrized protocol achieving the Heisenberg limit in the optical domain via dispersive atom–light interactions. *Results Phys.* **2021**, *24*, 104159. [CrossRef]
13. Su, Y.; Lu, W.; Shi, H.L. Quantum metrology enhanced by the XY spin interaction in a generalized Tavis-Cummings model. *Phys. Rev. A* **2024**, *109*, 042614. [CrossRef]
14. Braak, D.; Chen, Q.H.; Batchelor, M.T.; Solano, E. Semi-classical and quantum Rabi models: In celebration of 80 years. *J. Phys. A* **2016**, *49*, 300301. [CrossRef]
15. Braak, D. Integrability of the Rabi Model. *Phys. Rev. Lett.* **2011**, *107*, 100401. [CrossRef] [PubMed]
16. Chen, Q.H.; Wang, C.; He, S.; Liu, T.; Wang, K.L. Exact solvability of the quantum Rabi model using Bogoliubov operators. *Phys. Rev. A* **2012**, *86*, 023822. [CrossRef]
17. Zhong, H.; Xie, Q.; Batchelor, M.T.; Lee, C. Analytical eigenstates for the quantum Rabi model. *J. Phys. A Math. Theor.* **2013**, *46*, 415302. [CrossRef]
18. Maciejewski, A.J.; Przybylska, M.; Stachowiak, T. Full spectrum of the Rabi model. *Phys. Lett. A* **2014**, *378*, 16–20. [CrossRef]
19. Xie, Q.; Zhong, H.; Batchelor, M.T.; Lee, C. The quantum Rabi model: Solution and dynamics. *J. Phys. A Math. Theor.* **2017**, *50*, 113001. [CrossRef]
20. Kam, C.F.; Chen, Y. Analytical approximations for generalized quantum Rabi models. *arXiv* **2024**, arXiv:2401.05615.
21. Ma, T.; Li, S.M. Floquet system, Bloch oscillation, and Stark ladder. *arXiv* **2007**, arXiv:0711.1458.
22. Xie, Q.; Hai, W. Analytical results for a monochromatically driven two-level system. *Phys. Rev. A* **2010**, *82*, 032117. [CrossRef]
23. Liang, H. Generating arbitrary analytically solvable two-level systems. *J. Phys. A Math. Theor.* **2024**, *57*, 095301 [CrossRef]

The FVM framework includes several essential computational steps. Initially, a mesh is generated to partition the computational domain into small, discrete control volumes that can be analyzed independently. Next, the evaluation of flux across the boundaries of these control volumes is performed, which involves calculating conserved quantities such as fluid velocity and pressure. Finally, appropriate boundary conditions are applied to define the behavior of the fluid at the edges of the computational domain. By carefully following these steps, the finite volume method provides an effective and reliable framework for simulating complex phenomena in fluid dynamics [1–3].

There have been several studies using numerical methods presented in the literature for solving nonlinear partial differential equations (PDEs). Recent studies have been proposed based on physics-informed neural networks (PINNs) and finite difference methods (FDMs), and they have shown promising performances for modeling complex waves and nonlinear dynamics, such as Burgers' and sine-Gordon equations [5,6]. Although these techniques provide valuable insights, this work chooses the finite volume method (FVM) framework due to its conservative implementation and robustness concerning sharp gradients and discontinuities, which are important when dealing with high-resolution schemes like TENO5.

The finite volume method (FVM) has been applied by researchers to address a variety of problems in computational fluid dynamics. The FVM is effective in solving the Poisson equation, heat equation, and diffusion equation, which govern numerous physical processes [7,8]. Additionally, its application with unstructured moving meshes for simulations highlights its capability to manage free surface flows [9].

In the finite volume method (FVM), various numerical schemes have unique characteristics, such as conservativeness, boundedness, and transportiveness. This research utilizes a high-order method, specifically the fifth-order targeted essentially non-oscillatory (TENO5) scheme, which aims to improve both numerical stability and accuracy.

The primary aim of this paper is to explore the fifth-order targeted essentially non-oscillatory (TENO5) scheme within the finite volume method for addressing a one-dimensional linear advection equation and a two-dimensional nonlinear Burgers' equation that includes diffusion. The finite volume method will be developed and utilized to tackle these equations, and numerical experiments will be conducted to evaluate the approximate solutions against the exact solutions.

This paper is organized as follows: Section 2 provides a brief overview of the targeted essentially non-oscillatory (TENO) scheme. Section 3 presents numerical experiments to evaluate the performance of the TENO scheme. Section 4 includes a discussion of the results. Finally, Section 5 concludes the paper and proposes future research directions, particularly focusing on extending the higher-order capabilities of the TENO scheme and exploring its application in 3D numerical experiments.

2. Targeted Essentially Non-Oscillatory (TENO) Scheme

The targeted essentially non-oscillatory (TENO) approach is crafted to minimize oscillations that may arise in the numerical solutions of problems featuring sharp gradients or discontinuities, commonly seen in computational fluid dynamics (CFD) and other areas that require the simulation of wave propagation or transport processes. TENO effectively addresses turbulence while maintaining controllable, low numerical dissipation. In the TENO approach, a scale separation technique adeptly distinguishes between discontinuities and minor fluctuations, leading to reduced dissipation when compared to conventional methods, which can produce oscillations and instabilities in the presence of strong shocks [10–12].

This paper will discuss the fifth-order version of the method, known as the fifth-order targeted essentially non-oscillatory (TENO5) scheme.

2.1. TENO Methodology in FVM Framework

The scalar hyperbolic conservation law in one dimension is given by

$$\frac{\partial u}{\partial t} + \frac{\partial f(u)}{\partial x} = 0. \tag{1}$$

An equivalent formulation is as follows:

$$u_t + f(u)_x = 0. \tag{2}$$

The initial condition is defined as

$$u(x,0) = u_0(x). \tag{3}$$

Discretizing Equation (1) on uniform cell elements, e.g., $I_i = \left[x_{i-\frac{1}{2}}, x_{i+\frac{1}{2}}\right]$ with $\Delta x = x_{i+\frac{1}{2}} - x_{i-\frac{1}{2}}$ for $i = 0, 1, \cdots, N$, the system reduces to a set of ordinary differential equations (ODEs) of the form

$$\frac{d\bar{u}_i}{dt} = -\frac{1}{\Delta x}\int_{x_i-\Delta x/2}^{x_i+\Delta x/2} \frac{\partial f}{\partial x}dx, \quad i = 0, 1, \cdots, N. \tag{4}$$

where

$$\bar{u}_i(t) = \frac{1}{\Delta x}\int_{x_i-\Delta x/2}^{x_i+\Delta x/2} u(x,t)dx, \tag{5}$$

expresses the cell-averaged conservative variable in I_i.

Moreover, Equation (4) could be approximated as

$$\frac{d\bar{u}_i}{dt} \approx -\frac{1}{\Delta x}\left(\hat{f}_{i+\frac{1}{2}} - \hat{f}_{i-\frac{1}{2}}\right), \tag{6}$$

The numerical fluxes at the cell interface $\hat{f}_{i+\frac{1}{2}}$ and $\hat{f}_{i-\frac{1}{2}}$ in the semi-discrete finite volume scheme, which is given in Equation (6), can be computed using a Riemann solver. For example, the flux $\hat{f}_{i+\frac{1}{2}}$ is given by

$$\hat{f}_{i+\frac{1}{2}} = f^{\text{Riemann}}_{i+\frac{1}{2}}\left(u^L_{i+\frac{1}{2}}, u^R_{i+\frac{1}{2}}\right). \tag{7}$$

Here, $u^L_{i+\frac{1}{2}}$ and $u^R_{i+\frac{1}{2}}$ represent left-biased reconstruction and right-biased reconstruction, respectively, within cell I_i.

Even though the exact Riemann problem can be solved at the cell interface, approximate Riemann solvers are commonly used for their high efficiency. There are many different variants of approximate Riemann solvers, such as the Rusanov flux, the Roe flux, and the HLLC flux, as detailed in [12,13]. They can be represented in a general form as follows:

$$f^{\text{Riemann}}_{i+\frac{1}{2}}\left(u^L_{i+\frac{1}{2}}, u^R_{i+\frac{1}{2}}\right) = \underbrace{\frac{1}{2}\left[f\left(u^L_{i+\frac{1}{2}}\right) + f\left(u^R_{i+\frac{1}{2}}\right)\right]}_{\text{Non-dissipative central flux term}} - \underbrace{\frac{1}{2}\left|\tilde{\eth}_{i+\frac{1}{2}}\right|\left(u^R_{i+\frac{1}{2}} - u^L_{i+\frac{1}{2}}\right)}_{\text{Numerical Dissipation term}}. \tag{8}$$

where $\tilde{\eth}_{i+\frac{1}{2}}$ denotes the characteristic signal velocity evaluated at the cell interface.

The reconstruction candidate stencils: To achieve high-order reconstruction, a polynomial can be found for each candidate stencil by solving a linear system through Equation (5) with an approximation that is represented by

$$u_r(x) \approx \hat{u}_r(x) = \sum_{l=0}^{k-1} a_{l,r} x^l. \tag{9}$$

where k indicates the stencil's width. The coefficient a_l is determined by solving the system of linear algebraic equations formed by substituting $u_r(x)$ into Equation (5) and evaluating the integral functions at the stencil nodes. In terms of the five-point scheme, the reconstructed conservative variable at the cell interface can be obtained as demonstrated in [10,11].

Scale separation: To separate smooth scales from discontinuities effectively, the smoothness indicators are defined as follows:

$$\gamma_r = \left(C + \frac{\tau_K}{\beta_{r,k} + \varepsilon} \right)^q. \quad r = 0, \ldots, 3. \tag{10}$$

where the parameters are $C = 1, q = 6$, and $\varepsilon = 10^{-40}$ to avoid a zero denominator, and K is the number of points.

$\beta_{r,k}$ can be determined using

$$\beta_{r,k} = \sum_{l=1}^{k-1} \Delta x^{2l-1} \int_{x_{i-\frac{1}{2}}}^{x_{i+\frac{1}{2}}} \left(\frac{d^l}{dx^l} \hat{u}_r(x) \right)^2 dx. \tag{11}$$

To obtain a high-order accurate scheme at the critical points, the global reference smoothness indicator τ is introduced for the five-point scheme, as presented in [11].

The TENO scheme is based on the principle of either abandoning the non-smooth stencil or applying the stencil with the optimal linear weights for the final reconstruction. To achieve this, the smoothness indicators are normalized as follows:

$$\chi_r = \frac{\gamma_r}{\sum_{r=0}^{3} \gamma_r}. \tag{12}$$

Here, the sharp cut-off function is defined by

$$\delta_r = \begin{cases} 0, & \text{if } \chi_r < C_T, \\ 1, & \text{otherwise.} \end{cases} \tag{13}$$

The cut-off parameter C_T determines the dissipation properties of the resulting scheme, and it is typically set to $C_T = 10^{-5}$.

If the large candidate stencil is judged to be smooth, i.e., $\delta_3 = 1$, the final reconstruction $u^L_{i+\frac{1}{2}}$ can be directly expressed as $u^L_{3,i+\frac{1}{2}}$. Otherwise, the final reconstruction is obtained through a nonlinear combination of the remaining small stencils, expressed as

$$u^L_{i+\frac{1}{2}} = \sum_{r=0}^{2} w_r u^L_{r,i+\frac{1}{2}}. \tag{14}$$

where the weight w_r is expressed as

$$w_r = \frac{\alpha_r}{\sum_{r=0}^{2} \alpha_r}, \quad \alpha_r = d_r \delta_r, \quad r = 0, 1, 2. \tag{15}$$

Here, d_r is the optimal weight to achieve the maximum accuracy order with the full stencil [10,11,14].

2.2. Time Discretization for TENO Scheme

After employing the finite volume method (FVM) and discretizing the spatial derivatives using the TENO scheme, the semi-discrete form of the governing equation can be expressed as

$$\frac{du}{dt} = L(u). \tag{16}$$

where $L(u)$ denotes the operator used for spatial discretization.

For time integration, a third-order strong-stability-preserving (SSP) Runge–Kutta method is utilized:

$$\begin{aligned} u^{(1)} &= u^{(n)} + \Delta t L\left(u^{(n)}\right), \\ u^{(2)} &= \frac{3}{4}u^{(n)} + \frac{1}{4}u^{(1)} + \frac{1}{4}\Delta t L\left(u^{(1)}\right), \\ u^{(n+1)} &= \frac{1}{3}u^{(n)} + \frac{2}{3}u^{(2)} + \frac{2}{3}\Delta t L\left(u^{(2)}\right). \end{aligned} \tag{17}$$

This explicit Runge–Kutta method provides strong stability characteristics while achieving third-order temporal accuracy [10–12].

3. Numerical Experiments

In this section, two numerical experiments will be carried out to solve the linear advection of multiple waves and two-dimensional Burgers' equation with diffusion for comparison purposes and to verify the results.

3.1. Linear Advection of Multiple Waves

Consider the one-dimensional linear advection equation

$$\frac{\partial u}{\partial t} + \frac{\partial u}{\partial x} = 0. \tag{18}$$

with the initial condition

$$u(x,0) = \begin{cases} \frac{1}{6}[G(x-1,\beta,z-\theta) + G(x-1,\beta,z+\theta) + 4G(x-1,\beta,z)], & \text{if } 0.2 \le x < 0.4, \\ 1, & \text{if } 0.6 \le x \le 0.8, \\ 1 - |10(x-1.1)|, & \text{if } 1.0 \le x \le 1.2, \\ \frac{1}{6}[F(x-1,\alpha,a-\theta) + F(x-1,\alpha,a+\theta) + 4F(x-1,\alpha,a)], & \text{if } 1.4 \le x < 1.6, \\ 0, & \text{otherwise.} \end{cases} \tag{19}$$

where

$$G(x,\beta,z) = e^{-\beta(x-z)^2}, \quad F(x,\alpha,a) = \sqrt{\max(1-\alpha^2(x-a)^2, 0)}. \tag{20}$$

The parameters are given as

$$a = 0.5, \quad z = -0.7, \quad \theta = 0.005, \quad \alpha = 10, \quad \beta = \frac{\log(2)}{36\theta^2}. \tag{21}$$

The initial condition consists of a Gaussian pulse, a square wave, a sharp triangle wave, and a half ellipse arranged from the left to the right in the computational domain $x \in [0,2]$.

The exact solution, representing the theoretical solution for the linear advection equation with a constant propagation speed c, is

$$u(x,t) = u_0(x - ct). \tag{22}$$

where $u_0(x) = u(x,0)$ represents the initial profile of the solution at time $t = 0$.

The final time for the experiment is $t_{end} = 0.5$. Spatial discretization is performed at various uniform grid points N_x of $25, 50, 100,$ and 200, with a Courant number of CFL $= 0.5$ (Table 1).

Table 1. Error analysis for TENO5 in the FVM framework at CFL = 0.5.

N_x	Error Type	TENO5
25	L_1 error	0.28068
	L_2 error	0.29093
	L_∞ error	0.72617
50	L_1 error	0.14012
	L_2 error	0.17126
	L_∞ error	0.41374
100	L_1 error	0.065585
	L_2 error	0.12042
	L_∞ error	0.5023
200	L_1 error	0.027077
	L_2 error	0.070048
	L_∞ error	0.3272

3.2. Burgers' Equation with Diffusion

Consider the two-dimensional Burgers' equation with diffusion

$$u_t + a\left[\left(\frac{u^2}{2}\right)_x + \left(\frac{u^2}{2}\right)_y\right] - D(u_{xx} + u_{yy}) = 0. \tag{23}$$

on the domain $[0,2]^2$.

When $a = 1$, the exact solution is given as

$$u(x,y,t) = -2D\pi\frac{\cos(\pi(x+y))\exp(-2D\pi^2 t)}{2+\sin(\pi(x+y))\exp(-2D\pi^2 t)}. \tag{24}$$

with CFL $= 0.5$, and at the final time, $t_{end} = 0.5$.

In this context, the diffusion coefficient, denoted as D, is given by the equation $D = \frac{1}{Re}$, where Re indicates the Reynolds number. In addition, different grid sizes are considered in this experiment, as represented in Table 2. The plots in this paper are specifically for a 40×40 uniform grid (Table 3).

This work also incorporates an additional study that investigates the performance of the TENO5 scheme at different Reynolds numbers (Re) to examine its suitability within the FVM framework.

The Reynolds number (Re) is an important dimensionless number in fluid dynamics that determines the relative importance of the inertial to viscous force in the system.

At low Re, viscous effects outweigh inertial effects, and the flow is smooth, while at high Re, inertial forces are larger, and the flow becomes turbulent or has sharp gradients.

Numerical simulations, which were aimed at investigating the performance of TENO5 in handling a flow regime and simulating both the sharp and smooth features at different

Re, were made to study its potential. The purpose of these tests was to determine the general operation of the scheme in a wide range of flows and to check the stability and accuracy of the solution in a smooth and complex flow.

The numerical results of these experiments are given below.

Table 2. Error analysis of the TENO5 scheme in the FVM framework for a diffusion coefficient of $D = 0.0002$ with CFL $= 0.5$.

$N_x \times N_y$	Error Type	TENO5
20 × 20	L_1 error	4.1892×10^{-8}
	L_2 error	6.7318×10^{-8}
	L_∞ error	1.8217×10^{-7}
40 × 40	L_1 error	1.2546×10^{-8}
	L_2 error	2.0612×10^{-8}
	L_∞ error	5.8097×10^{-8}
80 × 80	L_1 error	5.8603×10^{-9}
	L_2 error	9.967×10^{-9}
	L_∞ error	5.9789×10^{-8}
160 × 160	L_1 error	7.9686×10^{-9}
	L_2 error	1.1022×10^{-8}
	L_∞ error	3.2989×10^{-8}

Table 3. Error analysis for TENO5 in the FVM framework at various Reynolds numbers, performed on a 40×40 uniform grid with CFL $= 0.5$.

Error Type	Re = 50	Re = 100	Re = 500	Re = 1000
L_1 error	0.0028585	0.00034326	2.7898×10^{-6}	4.006×10^{-7}
L_2 error	0.0051578	0.00046317	4.1123×10^{-6}	6.1714×10^{-7}
L_∞ error	0.019154	0.00094257	1.2755×10^{-5}	2.2067×10^{-6}

4. Discussion

The numerical experiments presented in Section 3 illustrate the efficacy of the TENO5 scheme in addressing both linear and nonlinear issues within a finite volume context. The examination focuses on the advection of multiple waveforms and the two-dimensional Burgers' equation incorporating diffusion. The subsequent subsections discuss the accuracy, convergence behavior, and performance of the numerical method.

4.1. Effect of Final Time Integration, CFL Number, Reynolds Number, and Grid Resolution

In the present study, we use a final simulation time of $t_{\text{end}} = 0.5$ and a CFL number of 0.5, and we consider Reynolds numbers of Re $= 50, 100, 500, 1000,$ and 5000. So, $D = \frac{1}{\text{Re}}$, e.g., $D = 0.0002$ at Re $= 5000$. In addition to their direct effect, these attributes need to be accounted for in coordination with spatial resolution. Before moving on, we highlight its relationship to the number of grid points and grid optimization.

1. **Final simulation time (t_{end}):** A larger Δt means that it takes more steps to reach its location (as Δt is controlled by CFL), and it also amplifies the effect of spatial discretization errors. For coarser meshes, error propagation and numerical diffusion are more dominant over the long run; so when t_{end} is increased, one should ensure that the mesh (increasing N_x) is refined such that the target accuracy is maintained. The error analysis of the TENO5 scheme for the two experiments at different t_{end} is shown in Tables 4 and 5. The results indicate that the L_1, L_2, and L_∞ errors significantly increase as the t_{end} rises. Therefore, there is an accumulation of errors.

Hence, the determination of t_{end} is influenced by the selected experiment and other factors, such as parameters and diffusion.

Table 4. Error analysis for the one-dimensional linear advection of multiple waves using TENO5 in the FVM framework at different t_{end}, performed on a a uniform grid consisting of 200 points, with CFL = 0.5.

Error Type	$t_{end} = 0.5$	$t_{end} = 1.0$	$t_{end} = 1.5$	$t_{end} = 2.0$	$t_{end} = 2.5$
L_1error	0.027077	0.10487	0.18209	0.28088	0.32118
L_2 error	0.070048	0.26756	0.3707	0.45204	0.49381
L_∞ error	0.327	1.0053	1.0111	1.0122	1.0129

Table 5. Error analysis for two-dimensional Burgers' equation using TENO5 in the FVM framework at different t_{end}, performed on a 40 × 40 uniform grid with CFL = 0.5 and Re = 5000.

Error Type	$t_{end} = 0.5$	$t_{end} = 1.0$	$t_{end} = 1.5$	$t_{end} = 2.0$	$t_{end} = 2.5$
L_1error	1.2546×10^{-8}	2.5416×10^{-8}	4.0946×10^{-8}	5.9112×10^{-8}	8.012×10^{-8}
L_2 error	2.0612×10^{-8}	4.1019×10^{-8}	6.4118×10^{-8}	9.0932×10^{-8}	1.2343×10^{-7}
L_∞ error	5.8097×10^{-8}	1.2983×10^{-7}	2.1927×10^{-7}	3.2275×10^{-7}	4.4134×10^{-7}

2. **Courant–Friedrichs–Lewy number (CFL):** To simplify the method, the CFL condition in one dimension can be stated as follows: $\Delta t = \frac{\text{CFL}\,\Delta x}{c}$. For a specific CFL = 0.5, the decrease in the cell size Δx (increasing the number of cells N_x) splits Δt in half, which means that terms proceed through twice as many time steps, and consequently, the temporal and the spatial truncations are reduced. Conversely, when using extremely fine meshes, one can wisely raise the CFL to a maximum of 0.5 to lower overall expenses, though this comes at the cost of stability.
The error analysis of the TENO5 scheme for the linear advection of multiple waves, with various CFL, is presented in Table 6. The results indicate that the L_1, L_2, and L_∞ errors significantly increase as the CFL rises, and the determination of the CFL is also influenced by the selected experiment and other factors such as parameters.

Table 6. Error analysis for the one-dimensional linear advection of multiple waves using TENO5 in the FVM framework with different CFL, performed on a a uniform grid consisting of 200 points, at $t_{end} = 0.5$.

Error Type	CFL = 0.5	CFL = 1.0	CFL = 1.5	CFL = 2.0	CFL = 2.5
L_1error	0.027077	0.027251	0.027077	0.035564	0.04933
L_2 error	0.070048	0.072087	0.071968	0.08464	0.10223
L_∞ error	0.327	0.34092	0.34508	0.40645	0.4416

In the linear advection of multiple waves, errors and plot profiles are sharply and strongly influenced by the CFL number as the scheme must accurately follow wave propagation over many periods. A better temporal resolution and minimum phase error can be achieved for a lower CFL number.
Moreover, for the two-dimensional Burgers' equation with diffusion, diffusion has a smoothing effect since it removes small-scale oscillations and the dependence on the time step's size. Because the solution is smooth and decaying, temporal errors are much smaller than spatial errors.
In addition, with a short final time (e.g., $t_{end} = 0.5$), the time error dictated by the CFL is negligible.

3. **Reynolds number (Re) and diffusion coefficient (D):** The diffusion coefficient spans, in fact, from $D = \frac{1}{\text{Re}}$. With the Re value increasing, the physical diffusion becomes smaller, and as a result, the gradients of density become sharper such that a finer spatial resolution is needed. For a higher Re, a refined mesh is still needed to capture these steep features and fully exploit the low-dissipation nature of the TENO5 scheme for $D = 0.0002$ at 5000 (as well as higher Re).
4. **Grid optimization strategy:**
   To keep an acceptable balance between accuracy and efficiency, the choices of (t_{end}, CFL, Re, and N_x) should be implemented concurrently.
   In practice, it is common to use CFL to ensure stability. A grid convergence test is conducted by increasing N_x, based on which the error norms tend to stabilize. For a larger Re or longer t_{end}, additional finer meshes are necessary to resolve sharper gradients. This formulation guarantees accurate results and enables TENO5 to demonstrate its formal fifth-order convergence.

4.2. Linear Advection of Multiple Waves

The linear advection scenario involves a variety of waveforms, such as a Gaussian pulse, a square wave, a sharp triangle wave, and a half ellipse, that propogate without distortion according to governing Equation (18). Figures 1–4 depict the numerical solution achieved with the TENO5 scheme in comparison to the exact solution at $t_{\text{end}} = 0.5$. The numerical findings show a strong correlation with the exact solution, especially in accurately capturing smooth areas of the waves. Nonetheless, minor numerical dissipation and dispersion effects are noted around discontinuities and sharp gradients, which is typical for high-order schemes dealing with discontinuous issues.

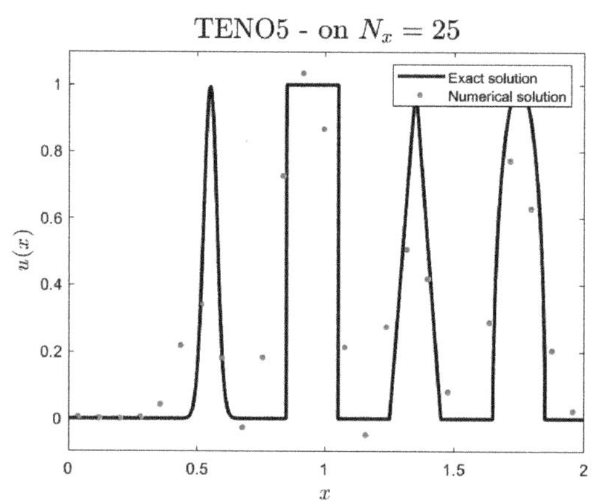

Figure 1. One-dimensional linear advection of multiple waves, comparing the exact solution and the numerical solution using the TENO5 scheme at simulation time $t_{\text{end}} = 0.5$. Spatial discretization is on $N_x = 25$ uniform grid points with CFL = 0.5.

The error analysis illustrated in Table 1 verifies that the numerical error diminishes as the grid becomes finer. The L_1 and L_2 errors consistently decrease with enhanced resolutions, indicating that the scheme attains high-order accuracy in smooth regions. However, the L_∞ error does not decrease as smoothly as the other norms, implying that the maximum error remains localized around discontinuities where numerical oscillations might arise. These results suggest that TENO5 achieves commendable accuracy while effectively managing spurious oscillations.

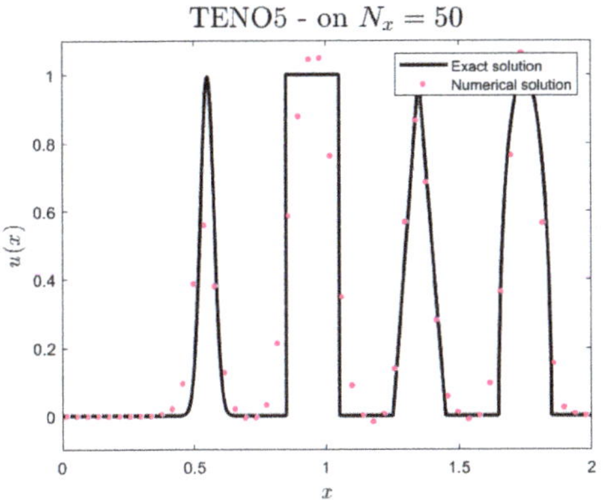

Figure 2. One-dimensional linear advection of multiple waves, comparing the exact solution and the numerical solution using the TENO5 scheme at simulation time $t_{\text{end}} = 0.5$. Spatial discretization is on $N_x = 50$ uniform grid points with CFL $= 0.5$.

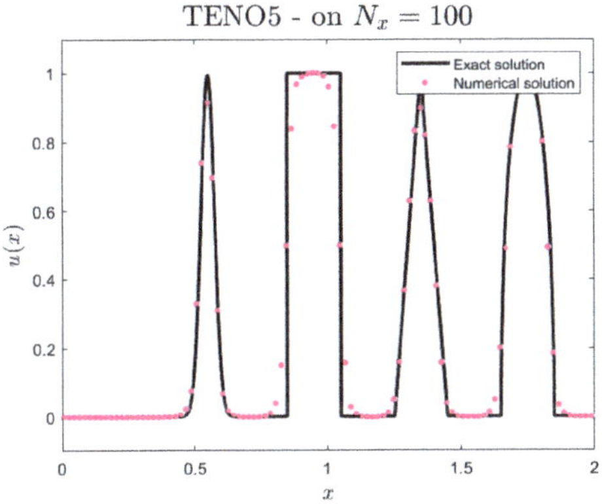

Figure 3. One-dimensional linear advection of multiple waves, comparing the exact solution and the numerical solution using the TENO5 scheme at simulation time $t_{\text{end}} = 0.5$. Spatial discretization is on $N_x = 100$ uniform grid points with CFL $= 0.5$.

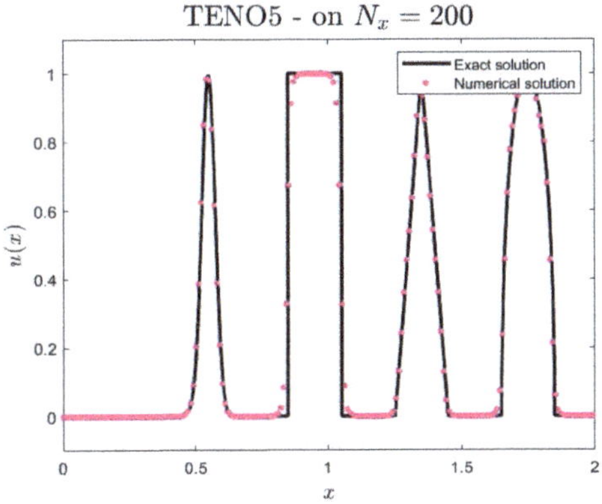

Figure 4. One-dimensional linear advection of multiple waves, comparing the exact solution and the numerical solution using the TENO5 scheme at simulation time $t_{\text{end}} = 0.5$. Spatial discretization is on $N_x = 200$ uniform grid points with CFL $= 0.5$.

4.3. Two-Dimensional Burgers' Equation with Diffusion

Regarding the two-dimensional Burgers' equation with diffusion, the findings expose the scheme's capacity to accurately capture the complexities of nonlinear advection–diffusion behavior. Figures 5 and 6 contrast the exact solution and the numerical solution for a diffusion coefficient of $D = 0.0002$ and Reynolds number of $\mathrm{Re} = 5000$. The TENO5 scheme successfully reflects the solution structure with minimal numerical artifacts, even when using a relatively coarse 40×40 grid.

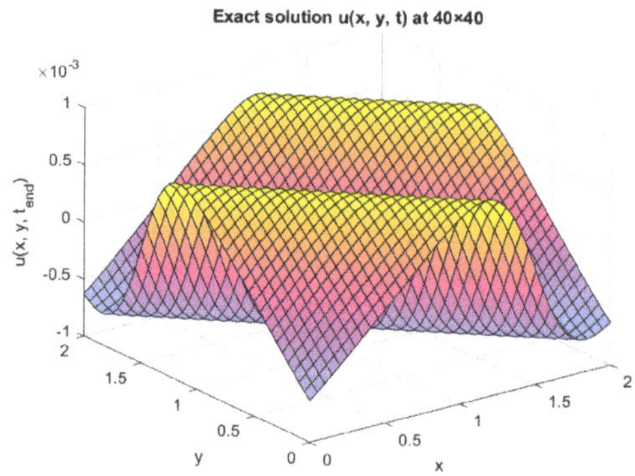

Figure 5. Exact solution of the two-dimensional Burgers' equation with diffusion. The value of the diffusion coefficient is $D = 0.0002$ and associated with $\mathrm{Re} = 5000$, with a CFL $= 0.5$. The domain is discretized using a 40×40 uniform grid.

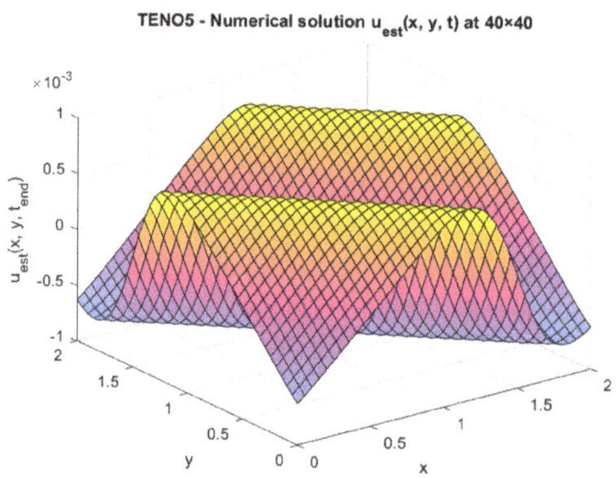

Figure 6. Numerical solution of the two-dimensional Burgers' equation with diffusion. The value of the diffusion coefficient is $D = 0.0002$ and is associated with $\mathrm{Re} = 5000$, with a CFL $= 0.5$. The domain is discretized using a 40×40 uniform grid.

The error analysis in Table 2 shows that enhancements in the grid's resolution lead to a significant drop in numerical errors. The L_1, L_2, and L_∞ errors decrease with grid refinement, corroborating the convergence of the scheme. Furthermore, the results presented in Figures 7–10 reveal how varying Reynolds numbers affect the numerical solution. As the Reynolds number escalates, sharper gradients and more defined features appear in the solution. The TENO5 scheme adeptly resolves these characteristics, affirming its robustness in managing advection-dominated flows.

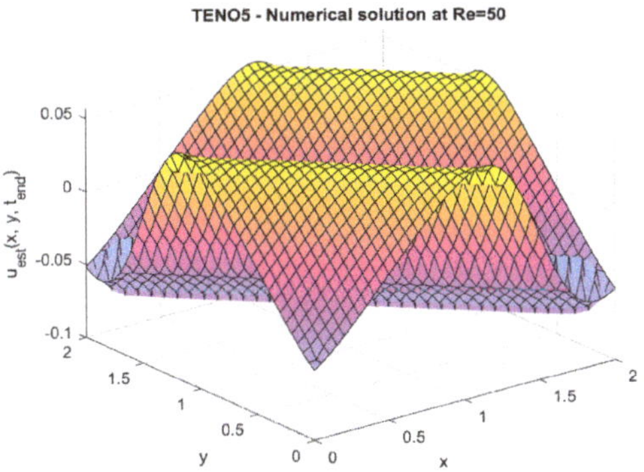

Figure 7. Numerical solution of the two-dimensional Burgers' equation with diffusion. The value of the diffusion coefficient is $D = 0.02$ and is associated with $\text{Re} = 50$, with a $\text{CFL} = 0.5$. The domain is discretized using a 40×40 uniform grid.

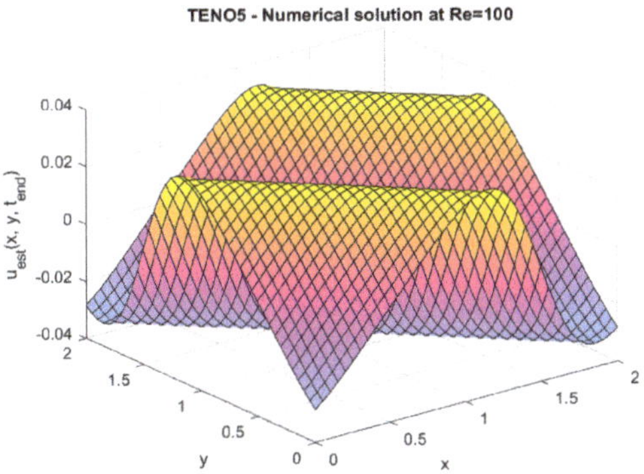

Figure 8. Numerical solution of the two-dimensional Burgers' equation with diffusion. The value of the diffusion coefficient is $D = 0.01$ and is associated with $\text{Re} = 100$, with a $\text{CFL} = 0.5$. The domain is discretized using a 40×40 uniform grid.

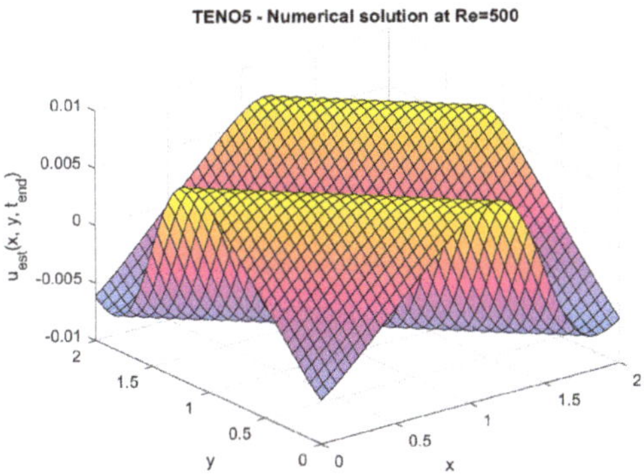

Figure 9. Numerical solution of the two-dimensional Burgers' equation with diffusion. The value of the diffusion coefficient is $D = 0.002$ and is associated with $\text{Re} = 500$, with a $\text{CFL} = 0.5$. The domain is discretized using a 40×40 uniform grid.

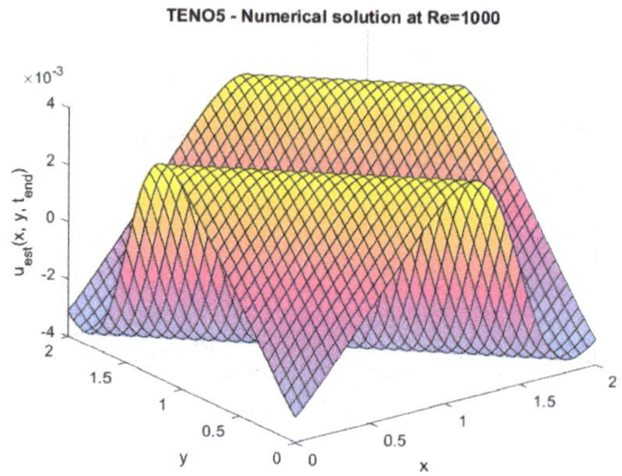

Figure 10. Numerical solution of the two-dimensional Burgers' equation with diffusion. The value of the diffusion coefficient is $D = 0.001$ and is associated with Re $= 1000$, with a CFL $= 0.5$. The domain is discretized using a 40×40 uniform grid.

The error analysis across different Reynolds numbers, as outlined in Table 3, reinforces these findings. The scheme retains its accuracy across various flow regimes, with slight differences in numerical errors resulting from increased sharpness in the solution at higher Reynolds numbers. This indicates that the scheme effectively balances numerical dissipation while resolving steep gradients.

5. Conclusions

This research evaluates the TENO5 scheme within a finite volume context for problems dominated by advection. Numerical tests on both linear and nonlinear cases reveal its precision, reliability, and convergence. The TENO5 scheme successfully captures smooth wave patterns in linear advection scenarios while maintaining low dissipation and dispersion errors, even though there are slight oscillations near discontinuities. In the case of the two-dimensional Burgers' equation with diffusion, it effectively addresses nonlinear dynamics at elevated Reynolds numbers and exhibits consistent convergence with grid refinement.

In summary, the TENO5 scheme demonstrates itself to be a very efficient method for problems driven by advection, striking a balance between numerical dissipation and resolution. Future research could broaden this study to encompass more intricate test cases, such as turbulent flows and multi-dimensional nonlinear systems. Moreover, examining higher-order extensions of the TENO framework could further improve accuracy, especially for issues involving fine-scale structures and turbulence. The extension to three-dimensional settings may provide some valuable insight into the performance and robustness properties of the scheme under increased complexity. However, there are difficulties in increased computational cost and the construction of the stencil in three dimensions.

Author Contributions: Conceptualization, A.M.S. and T.A.F.A.; methodology, A.M.S.; software, T.A.F.A.; validation, A.M.S. and T.A.F.A.; formal analysis, T.A.F.A.; investigation, A.M.S.; resources, T.A.F.A.; data curation, T.A.F.A.; writing—original draft preparation, T.A.F.A.; writing—review and editing, A.M.S.; visualization, T.A.F.A.; supervision, A.M.S. All authors have read and agreed to the published version of the manuscript.

Funding: This research received no external funding.

Data Availability Statement: The author declares that the data supporting the findings of this study are available within the paper or from the corresponding author upon reasonable request.

Acknowledgments: The authors gratefully acknowledge Qassim University, represented by the Deanship of Graduate Studies and Scientific Research, for the financial support for this research study under number QU-J-PG-2-2025-53063 during the academic year 1446 AH/2024 AD.

Conflicts of Interest: The author declares that there are no conflicts of interest or competing interests relevant to the content of this article.

Abbreviations

The following abbreviations are used in this manuscript:

ODEs	Ordinary differential equations;
CFD	Computational fluid dynamics;
TENO	Targeted essentially non-oscillatory;
FVM	Finite volume method;
PDEs	Partial differential equations;
SSP	Strong stability preserving;
CFL	Courant–Friedrichs–Lewy.

References

1. Moukalled, F.; Mangani, L.; Darwish, M.; Moukalled, F.; Mangani, L.; Darwish, M. *The Finite Volume Method*; Springer: Berlin/Heidelberg, Germany, 2016.
2. Petrova, R. *Finite Volume Method: Powerful Means of Engineering Design*; BoD—Books on Demand: Norderstedt, Germany, 2012.
3. Liang, S. Numerical Simulation of the Navier-Stokes Equations Using Finite Volume Method. Master's Thesis, Universitat Politècnica de Catalunya, Barcelona, Spain, 2017.
4. van Gestel, R.A.M. The Finite Volume Method for Systems of Conservation Laws. Master's Thesis, Eindhoven University of Technology, Eindhoven, The Netherlands, 2019.
5. Savović, S.; Ivanović, M.; Drljača, B.; Simović, A. Numerical Solution of the Sine—Gordon Equation by Novel Physics-Informed Neural Networks and Two Different Finite Difference Methods. *Axioms* **2024**, *13*, 872. [CrossRef]
6. Savović, S.; Ivanović, M.; Min, R. A Comparative Study of the Explicit Finite Difference Method and Physics-Informed Neural Networks for Solving the Burgers' Equation. *Axioms* **2023**, *12*, 982. [CrossRef]
7. Hadzic, H. Development and Application of Finite Volume Method for the Computation of Flows Around Moving Bodies on Unstructured, Overlapping Grids. Ph.D. Thesis, Hamburg University of Technology, Hamburg, Germany, 2006.
8. Zhang, Q.; Johansen, H.; Colella, P. A fourth-order accurate finite-volume method with structured adaptive mesh refinement for solving the advection-diffusion equation. *SIAM J. Sci. Comput.* **2012**, *34*, B179–B201. [CrossRef]
9. Jasak, H.; Tukovic, Z. Automatic mesh motion for the unstructured finite volume method. *Trans. FAMENA* **2006**, *30*, 1–20.
10. Fu, L. A low-dissipation finite-volume method based on a new TENO shock-capturing scheme. *Comput. Phys. Commun.* **2019**, *235*, 25–39. [CrossRef]
11. Huang, H.; Fu, L. A new troubled cell indicator and a new limiter based on TENO schemes for RKDG methods. *Comput. Methods Appl. Mech. Eng.* **2024**, *421*, 116795. [CrossRef]
12. Ji, Z.; Liang, T.; Fu, L. A class of new high-order finite-volume TENO schemes for hyperbolic conservation laws with unstructured meshes. *J. Sci. Comput.* **2022**, *92*, 61. [CrossRef]
13. Chandrashekar, P. *Numerical Methods for Hyperbolic System of Conservation Laws*; Tata Institute of Fundamental Research: Bangalore, India, 2019.
14. Tann, S.; Deng, X.; Shimizu, Y.; Loubère, R.; Xiao, F. Solution property preserving reconstruction for finite volume scheme: A bvd+ mood framework. *Int. J. Numer. Methods Fluids* **2019**.

axioms

MDPI

Article

On $(\bar{m}, m)$-Conformal Mappings

Branislav M. Randjelović [1,2,*], Dušan J. Simjanović [3], Nenad O. Vesić [4], Ivana Djurišić [5] and Branislav D. Vlahović [6]

1 Faculty of Electronic Engineering, University of Niš, 18000 Niš, Serbia
2 Faculty of Teachers Education, University of K. Mitrovica, 38218 Leposavić, Serbia
3 Faculty of Information Technology, Belgrade Metropolitan University, 11000 Belgrade, Serbia; dusan.simjanovic@metropolitan.ac.rs
4 Mathematical Institute of Serbian Academy of Sciences and Arts, 11000 Belgrade, Serbia
5 Institute for Multidisciplinary Research, University of Belgrade, 11000 Belgrade, Serbia
6 Department of Physics, North Carolina Central University, Durham, NC 27707, USA
* Correspondence: bane@elfak.ni.ac.rs; Tel.: +381-18-529-365

Abstract: Conformal mappings between Riemannian spaces $\bar{\mathbb{R}}_N$ and $\mathbb{R}_N$ are defined by the explicit transformation of the metric tensor of the space $\bar{\mathbb{R}}_N$ to the metric tensor of the space $\mathbb{R}_N$. Geodesic mapping between these two Riemannian spaces is a transformation that transforms any geodesic line of the space $\bar{\mathbb{R}}_N$ to a geodesic line of the space $\mathbb{R}_N$. In this research, we defined an m-conformal line of a Riemannian space, which is geodesic if $m = 0$. Based on this definition, we involved the concept of $(\bar{m}, m)$-conformal mapping as a transformation $\bar{\mathbb{R}}_N \to \mathbb{R}_N$ in which any $\bar{m}$-conformal line of the space $\bar{\mathbb{R}}_N$ transforms to an m-conformal line of the space $\mathbb{R}_N$. The result of this research is the establishment of three invariants for these mappings. At the end of this research, we gave an example of a scalar geometrical object which may be used in physics.

Keywords: mapping; Riemannian space; invariant; variation

MSC: 53B20; 53B50

1. Introduction

The theory of Riemannian spaces was given by L. P. Eisenhart [1]. Based on his research, this theory was developed to such a degree that it can be studied as a theoretical concept or a tool for applications in physics.

Many authors have developed the theory of mappings between Riemannian spaces. Some of them include J. Mikeš, with his research group [2–6], N. S. Sinyukov [7–9], U. C. De [10,11], among many others.

Motivated by Eisenhart's definition of a generalized Riemannian space, the theory of mappings of generalized Riemannian spaces has been developed. The most significant researchers in of subject are M. S. Stanković [12–16], M. Lj. Zlatanović [17–19], Lj. S. Velimirović [16,20], among many others.

An article [21] by N. Vesić developed the well known methodology for obtaining invariants of geometric mappings. In many later papers, like in this research paper, the article [15] and the methodology presented in [21] are applied, and the result is at least one new invariant for the analyzed mapping. In this research, we will review the results of Vesić's article and apply them to obtain invariants for a special mapping of a Riemannian space, which will be defined.

Conformal transformations are important for different applications in physics [22]. The Weyl tensor is composed by itself for generating the integrand for Einstein–Hilbert action. But this integrand leads the study of R^2-cosmology. We are interested in finding invariants for mappings which stay within the valid research topic of R^1-cosmology.

The integrand in Einstein–Hilbert action in [23] is very similar to invariants which Vesić obtained in [21]. In this research, we will study the Einstein–Hilbert action generated by Vesić's invariants.

In this manuscript, we aim to generalize the concept of conformal mappings by transforming the basic equation of conformal mapping between two Riemannian spaces. These results will provide different opportunities for theoretical research into this new class of mappings, and for its applications in cosmology as well.

1.1. Tensors as Indexed Geometrical Objects

An indexed magnitude $X^{\alpha_1\ldots\alpha_p}_{\beta_1\ldots\beta_q}$, $\alpha_i, \beta_j = 0, \ldots, N-1$, presented in the Cartesian coordinate system $(O, x^0, \ldots, x^{N-1})$, is a tensor of the type (p,q) if under a change of coordinate system to $(0', x'^0, \ldots, x'^{N-1})$, where the value $X^{\alpha_1\ldots\alpha_p}_{\beta_1\ldots\beta_q}$ transforms as [2,9]

$$X^{\alpha'_1\ldots\alpha'_p}_{\beta'_1\ldots\beta'_q} = x^{\alpha'_1}_{\alpha_1}\ldots x^{\alpha'_p}_{\alpha_p} x^{\beta_1}_{\beta'_1}\ldots x^{\beta_q}_{\beta'_q} X^{\alpha_1\ldots\alpha_p}_{\beta_1\ldots\beta_q},$$

where $x^{\alpha'_i}_{\alpha_i} = \dfrac{\partial x'^{\alpha_i}}{\partial x^{\alpha_i}}$, $x^{\beta_j}_{\beta'_j} = \dfrac{\partial x^{\beta_j}}{\partial x'^{\beta_j}}$, and Einstein's Summation Convention is used for repeated indices. Scalar functions are tensors of the type $(0,0)$.

From the last definition, we conclude that a partial derivative of a tensor of the type $(0,0)$ forms a tensor of the type $(0,1)$. Partial derivatives of a tensor of any another type do not form tensors.

1.2. Riemannian Spaces

An N-dimensional manifold $\mathcal{M} = \mathcal{M}(u^0, \ldots, u^{N-1})$ equipped with a symmetric metric tensor $g_{\mu\nu}$, $g_{\mu\nu} = g_{\nu\mu}$ is the Riemannian space $\mathbb{R}_N$ (see [2,9]). The Greek indices μ, ν, ... take values of $0, \ldots, N-1$.

Remark 1. *For studies in physics, especially in cosmology, it is important to make a distinction between indices which denote time and indices which denote space. It is standardized in physics that the Greek indices present both time and space, but Latin indices correspond to space. In our study, we will not make such a distinction, but for possibly easier applications, we will use the Greek indices.*

We assume that the matrix $[g_{\mu\nu}]$ is non-singular, i.e., $\det[g_{\mu\nu}] \neq 0$. Hence, the contravariant metric tensor is defined as $[g^{\mu\nu}] = [g_{\mu\nu}]^{-1}$. This means that $g^{\mu\alpha}g_{\nu\alpha} = \delta^\mu_\nu$.

Christoffel symbols of the second kind,

$$\Gamma^\pi_{\mu\nu} = \frac{1}{2}g^{\pi\alpha}(g_{\mu\alpha,\nu} - g_{\mu\nu,\alpha} + g_{\nu\alpha,\mu}),$$

where a comma denotes partial differentiation, are the affine connection coefficients of the space $\mathbb{R}_N$.

The Christoffel symbols are not tensors because they change as

$$\Gamma^{\pi'}_{\mu'\nu'} = x^{\pi'}_\pi x^\mu_{\mu'} x^\nu_{\nu'} \Gamma^\pi_{\mu\nu} + x^{\pi'}_\pi x^\pi_{\mu'\nu'},$$

where $x^{\pi}_{\mu'\nu'} = \dfrac{\partial^2 x^{\pi}}{\partial x'^{\mu} \partial x'^{\nu}}$.

The Christoffel symbols $\Gamma^{\pi}_{\mu\nu}$ and their traces $\Gamma_{\mu} = \Gamma^{\alpha}_{\mu\alpha}$ are not tensors.

1.3. Geodesic Lines of Riemannian Spaces

A curve $\ell = (\ell^{\mu}) = \ell(t)$ in Riemannian space $\mathbb{R}_N$ is geodesic if its tangential vector $\lambda^{\mu} = \dfrac{d\ell^{\mu}}{dt}$ satisfies the forthcoming system of differential equations

$$\frac{d\lambda^{\mu}}{dt} + \Gamma^{\mu}_{\alpha\beta}\lambda^{\alpha}\lambda^{\beta} = \rho\lambda^{\mu}, \tag{1}$$

where ρ is a scalar function. In one paper (Mikeš et al. [2], pp. 88–89), the definition of geodesics is discussed.

In spaces with a positive definite metric, the geodesic line is the shortest line between two points on manifolds by the path in it. The FLRW metric is not a positive definite one; light (the fastest unit in cosmology) moves along geodesic lines.

We are interested in obtaining some new invariants for a special geometric mapping and to present the corresponding action in four-dimensional cosmology.

1.4. Motivation

In cosmology, a geodesic line is defined in the case of homogeneous Equation (1), i.e., in the case of $\rho = 0$ (see [24], page 30, Equation (2.18)). For geodesics defined in such a way, we will prove that a geometrical object which determines a transformation of Christoffel symbols under geodesic mapping vanishes, (for the concrete methodology, see the sections on geodesic mappings in [2,9]).

After connecting the invariance of the Ricci tensor under geodesic mappings, we find that the standard Einstein–Hilbert action [24] $S = \dfrac{1}{2\kappa}\int d^4x\sqrt{-g}R$ is nothing more than action for the Lagrangian which is equal to the invariant $R_{\alpha\beta}$ composed by $g^{\alpha\beta}$, and for topological invariance multiplied by $\sqrt{-g}$.

Perturbations in cosmology are nothing more than summing the Friedmann–Lemaitre–Robertson–Walker metric $\bar{g}_{\mu\nu}$ with a tensor $\delta g_{\mu\nu}$ (named perturbation). In this way, any geodesic line of the initial space equipped with the FLRW metric transforms to a curve of perturbed space (equipped with metric $g_{\mu\nu} = \bar{g}_{\mu\nu} + \delta g_{\mu\nu}$).

Geodesics are defined by the non-homogeneous Equation (1) [1,2,9]. All special curves (F-planar, almost geodesic, … [2,9]) are generalizations of geodesics.

Until 2020, all invariants for mappings (Weyl projective tensor, Weyl conformal tensor, Weyl F-plannar tensor,…) were created in such a way that their traces by contravariant and covariant indices vanish. In (Vesić, 2020 [21]), the methodology for obtaining another invariant (whose traces do not vanish) was presented.

This other invariant, which does not lose the Ricci tensor after contraction, motivated us to pursue this research. The other motivation for our research is the significance of the conformal mappings of Riemannian spaces presented in [22]. The Lagrangian of Einstein–Hilbert action studied in [23] is very similar to the invariants for mappings obtained in [21], which is another motivation for our research, presented below.

This manuscript is organized as follows:

1. We will review the preferred methodology for obtaining invariants of geometric mappings from [15,21]. In this review, we will present the corresponding invariants for geodesic and conformal mappings of an N-dimensional Riemannian space.

2. In the next section, we will generalize the concept of conformal mapping by defining a special curve of a Riemannian space. A mapping from which any geodesic line from an initial space transforms to a curve of this special class of the deformed space will be the subject of our research.
3. We will obtain the basic equations for mappings mentioned in previous studies. After that, we will obtain the invariants for this mapping.
4. At the end of this paper, we will present the cosmology which corresponds to one of the invariants obtained herein and present the corresponding Einstein equations.

2. Review of Invariants for Geometric Mappings

In this section, we will review the process for obtaining invariants of mappings defined on N-dimensional Riemannian spaces [15,21]

Let $f : \bar{\mathbb{R}}_N \to \mathbb{R}_N$ be a mapping whose basic equation is

$$\Gamma^{\pi}_{\mu\nu} = \bar{\Gamma}^{\pi}_{\mu\nu} + \psi_\nu \delta^{\pi}_{\mu} + \psi_\mu \delta^{\pi}_{\nu} + \omega^{\pi}_{\mu\nu} - \bar{\omega}^{\pi}_{\mu\nu}. \tag{2}$$

After contracting this equation by π and ν, we obtain $\Gamma_\mu = \bar{\Gamma}_\mu + (N+1)\psi_\mu + \omega_\mu - \bar{\omega}_\mu$, i.e.,

$$\psi_\mu = \frac{1}{N+1}(\Gamma_\mu - \omega_\mu) - \frac{1}{N+1}(\bar{\Gamma}_\mu - \bar{\omega}_\mu). \tag{3}$$

With respect to (3), the basic Equation (2) is transformed to

$$\begin{aligned} \Gamma^{\pi}_{\mu\nu} = \bar{\Gamma}^{\pi}_{\mu\nu} + \omega^{\pi}_{\mu\nu} + \frac{1}{N+1}(\delta^{\pi}_{\mu}\Gamma_\nu + \delta^{\pi}_{\nu}\Gamma_\mu) - \frac{1}{N+1}(\delta^{\pi}_{\mu}\omega_\nu + \delta^{\pi}_{\nu}\omega_\mu) \\ - \bar{\omega}^{\pi}_{\mu\nu} - \frac{1}{N+1}(\delta^{\pi}_{\mu}\bar{\Gamma}_\nu + \delta^{\pi}_{\nu}\bar{\Gamma}_\mu) + \frac{1}{N+1}(\delta^{\pi}_{\mu}\bar{\omega}_\nu + \delta^{\pi}_{\nu}\bar{\omega}_\mu). \end{aligned} \tag{4}$$

The basic Equation (4) is expressed in the form $\Gamma^{\pi}_{\mu\nu} = \bar{\Gamma}^{\pi}_{\mu\nu} + d^{\pi}_{\mu\nu} - \bar{d}^{\pi}_{\mu\nu}$, where

$$\begin{aligned} d^{\pi}_{\mu\nu} &= \omega^{\pi}_{\mu\nu} + \frac{1}{N+1}(\delta^{\pi}_{\mu}\Gamma_\nu + \delta^{\pi}_{\nu}\Gamma_\mu) - \frac{1}{N+1}(\delta^{\pi}_{\mu}\omega_\nu + \delta^{\pi}_{\nu}\omega_\mu), \\ \bar{d}^{\pi}_{\mu\nu} &= \bar{\omega}^{\pi}_{\mu\nu} + \frac{1}{N+1}(\delta^{\pi}_{\mu}\bar{\Gamma}_\nu + \delta^{\pi}_{\nu}\bar{\Gamma}_\mu) - \frac{1}{N+1}(\delta^{\pi}_{\mu}\bar{\omega}_\nu + \delta^{\pi}_{\nu}\bar{\omega}_\mu). \end{aligned}$$

The basic invariants for the mapping f of the Thomas and Weyl type are $\mathcal{T}^{\pi}_{\mu\nu} = \Gamma^{\pi}_{\mu\nu} - d^{\pi}_{\mu\nu}$ and $\mathcal{W}^{\pi}_{\mu\nu\sigma} = R^{\pi}_{\mu\nu\sigma} - d^{\pi}_{\mu\nu|\sigma} + d^{\pi}_{\mu\sigma|\nu} + d^{\alpha}_{\mu\nu}d^{\pi}_{\alpha\sigma} - d^{\alpha}_{\mu\sigma}d^{\pi}_{\alpha\nu}$, and the corresponding $\bar{\mathcal{T}}^{\pi}_{\mu\nu}$ and $\overline{\mathcal{W}}^{\pi}_{\mu\nu\sigma}$. The invariants $\mathcal{T}^{\pi}_{\mu\nu}$ and $\mathcal{W}^{\pi}_{\mu\nu\sigma}$ are directly expressed as

$$\mathcal{T}^{\pi}_{\mu\nu} = \Gamma^{\pi}_{\mu\nu} - \omega^{\pi}_{\mu\nu} - \frac{1}{N+1}(\delta^{\pi}_{\mu}\Gamma_\nu + \delta^{\pi}_{\nu}\Gamma_\mu) + \frac{1}{N+1}(\delta^{\pi}_{\mu}\omega_\nu + \delta^{\pi}_{\nu}\omega_\mu), \tag{5}$$

$$\begin{aligned} \mathcal{W}^{\pi}_{\mu\nu\sigma} = {} & R^{\pi}_{\mu\nu\sigma} - \omega^{\pi}_{\mu\nu|\sigma} + \omega^{\pi}_{\mu\sigma|\nu} + \omega^{\alpha}_{\mu\nu}\omega^{\pi}_{\alpha\sigma} - \omega^{\alpha}_{\mu\sigma}\omega^{\pi}_{\alpha\nu} \\ & - \frac{1}{(N+1)^2}\delta^{\pi}_{\nu}\Big((N+1)\big(\Gamma_{\mu|\sigma} - \omega_{\mu|\sigma} + \omega^{\alpha}_{\mu\sigma}(\Gamma_\alpha - \omega_\alpha)\big) + (\Gamma_\mu - \omega_\mu)(\Gamma_\sigma - \omega_\sigma)\Big) \\ & + \frac{1}{(N+1)^2}\delta^{\pi}_{\sigma}\Big((N+1)\big(\Gamma_{\mu|\nu} - \omega_{\mu|\nu} + \omega^{\alpha}_{\mu\nu}(\Gamma_\alpha - \omega_\alpha)\big) + (\Gamma_\mu - \omega_\mu)(\Gamma_\nu - \omega_\nu)\Big), \end{aligned} \tag{6}$$

and the corresponding $\bar{\mathcal{T}}^{\pi}_{\mu\nu}$ and $\overline{\mathcal{W}}^{\pi}_{\mu\nu\sigma}$.

The equality $0 = \mathcal{W}^{\alpha}_{\alpha\nu\sigma} - \overline{\mathcal{W}}^{\alpha}_{\alpha\nu\sigma}$ is equivalent to the equality

$$\omega_{\nu|\sigma} - \omega_{\sigma|\nu} = \bar{\omega}_{\nu\|\sigma} - \bar{\omega}_{\sigma\|\nu},$$

which proves that the anti-symmetric part of $\omega_{\mu|\nu}$ by μ and ν is an invariant for the mapping f.

The equivalent forms of invariants, $\mathcal{W}^{\pi}_{\mu\nu\sigma}$ and $\overline{\mathcal{W}}^{\pi}_{\mu\nu\sigma}$ are

$$\begin{cases} \mathcal{W}^{\pi}_{\mu\nu\sigma} = R^{\pi}_{\mu\nu\sigma} - \omega^{\pi}_{\mu\nu|\sigma} + \omega^{\pi}_{\mu\sigma|\nu} + \omega^{\alpha}_{\mu\nu}\omega^{\pi}_{\alpha\sigma} - \omega^{\alpha}_{\mu\sigma}\omega^{\pi}_{\alpha\nu} + \delta^{\pi}_{\nu}X_{\mu\sigma} - \delta^{\pi}_{\sigma}X_{\mu\nu}, \\ \overline{\mathcal{W}}^{\pi}_{\mu\nu\sigma} = \bar{R}^{\pi}_{\mu\nu\sigma} - \bar{\omega}^{\pi}_{\mu\nu\|\sigma} + \bar{\omega}^{\pi}_{\mu\sigma\|\nu} + \bar{\omega}^{\alpha}_{\mu\nu}\bar{\omega}^{\pi}_{\alpha\sigma} - \bar{\omega}^{\alpha}_{\mu\sigma}\bar{\omega}^{\pi}_{\alpha\nu} + \delta^{\pi}_{\nu}\bar{X}_{\mu\sigma} - \delta^{\pi}_{\sigma}\bar{X}_{\mu\nu}, \end{cases}$$

where

$$\begin{cases} X_{\mu\nu} = -\frac{1}{N+1}\Big(\Gamma_{\mu|\nu} - \omega_{\mu|\nu} + \omega^{\alpha}_{\mu\nu}(\Gamma_{\alpha} - \omega_{\alpha})\Big) - \frac{1}{(N+1)^2}(\Gamma_{\mu} - \omega_{\mu})(\Gamma_{\nu} - \omega_{\nu}), \\ \bar{X}_{\mu\nu} = -\frac{1}{N+1}\Big(\bar{\Gamma}_{\mu\|\nu} - \bar{\omega}_{\mu\|\nu} + \bar{\omega}^{\alpha}_{\mu\nu}(\bar{\Gamma}_{\alpha} - \bar{\omega}_{\alpha})\Big) - \frac{1}{(N+1)^2}(\bar{\Gamma}_{\mu} - \bar{\omega}_{\mu})(\bar{\Gamma}_{\nu} - \bar{\omega}_{\nu}). \end{cases}$$

The invariance $\mathcal{W}^{\pi}_{\mu\nu\sigma} = \overline{\mathcal{W}}^{\pi}_{\mu\nu\sigma}$ is equivalent to the equality $0 = \mathcal{W}^{\pi}_{\mu\nu\sigma} - \overline{\mathcal{W}}^{\pi}_{\mu\nu\sigma}$, i.e.,

$$\begin{aligned} 0 = {} & (R^{\pi}_{\mu\nu\sigma} - \bar{R}^{\pi}_{\mu\nu\sigma}) - (\omega^{\pi}_{\mu\nu|\sigma} - \bar{\omega}^{\pi}_{\mu\nu\|\sigma}) + (\omega^{\pi}_{\mu\sigma|\nu} - \bar{\omega}^{\pi}_{\mu\sigma\|\nu}) + (\omega^{\alpha}_{\mu\nu}\omega^{\pi}_{\alpha\sigma} - \bar{\omega}^{\alpha}_{\mu\nu}\bar{\omega}^{\pi}_{\alpha\sigma}) \\ & - (\omega^{\alpha}_{\mu\sigma}\omega_{\alpha} - \bar{\omega}^{\alpha}_{\mu\sigma}\bar{\omega}_{\alpha}) + \delta^{\pi}_{\nu}(X_{\mu\sigma} - \bar{X}_{\mu\sigma}) - \delta^{\pi}_{\sigma}(X_{\mu\nu} - \bar{X}_{\mu\nu}). \end{aligned} \tag{7}$$

After contracting (7) by π and ν, one obtains

$$\begin{aligned} X_{\mu\sigma} - \bar{X}_{\mu\sigma} = {} & -\frac{1}{N-1}R_{\mu\sigma} + \frac{1}{N-1}(\omega_{\mu|\sigma} - \omega^{\alpha}_{\mu\sigma|\alpha} - \omega^{\alpha}_{\mu\beta}\omega^{\beta}_{\sigma\alpha} + \omega^{\alpha}_{\mu\sigma}\omega_{\alpha}) \\ & + \frac{1}{N-1}\bar{R}_{\mu\sigma} - \frac{1}{N-1}(\bar{\omega}_{\mu\|\sigma} - \bar{\omega}^{\alpha}_{\mu\sigma\|\alpha} - \bar{\omega}^{\alpha}_{\mu\beta}\bar{\omega}^{\beta}_{\sigma\alpha} + \bar{\omega}^{\alpha}_{\mu\sigma}\bar{\omega}_{\alpha}). \end{aligned} \tag{8}$$

If we substitute (8) into (7), we will obtain the relation $0 = W^{\pi}_{\mu\nu\sigma} - \bar{W}^{\pi}_{\mu\nu\sigma}$, for

$$\begin{aligned} W^{\pi}_{\mu\nu\sigma} = {} & R^{\pi}_{\mu\nu\sigma} - \frac{1}{N-1}(\delta^{\pi}_{\nu}R_{\mu\sigma} - \delta^{\pi}_{\sigma}R_{\mu\nu}) - \omega^{\pi}_{\mu\nu|\sigma} + \omega^{\pi}_{\mu\sigma|\nu} + \omega^{\alpha}_{\mu\nu}\omega^{\pi}_{\alpha\sigma} - \omega^{\alpha}_{\mu\sigma}\omega^{\pi}_{\alpha\nu} \\ & + \frac{1}{N-1}\delta^{\pi}_{\nu}(\omega_{\mu|\sigma} - \omega^{\alpha}_{\mu\sigma|\alpha} - \omega^{\alpha}_{\mu\beta}\omega^{\beta}_{\sigma\alpha} + \omega^{\alpha}_{\mu\sigma}\omega_{\alpha}) \\ & + \frac{1}{N-1}\delta^{\pi}_{\sigma}(\omega_{\mu|\nu} - \omega^{\alpha}_{\mu\nu|\alpha} - \omega^{\alpha}_{\mu\beta}\omega^{\beta}_{\nu\alpha} + \omega^{\alpha}_{\mu\nu}\omega_{\alpha}), \\ \bar{W}^{\pi}_{\mu\nu\sigma} = {} & \bar{R}^{\pi}_{\mu\nu\sigma} - \frac{1}{N-1}(\delta^{\pi}_{\nu}\bar{R}_{\mu\sigma} - \delta^{\pi}_{\sigma}\bar{R}_{\mu\nu}) - \bar{\omega}^{\pi}_{\mu\nu\|\sigma} + \bar{\omega}^{\pi}_{\mu\sigma\|\nu} + \bar{\omega}^{\alpha}_{\mu\nu}\bar{\omega}^{\pi}_{\alpha\sigma} - \bar{\omega}^{\alpha}_{\mu\sigma}\bar{\omega}^{\pi}_{\alpha\nu} \\ & + \frac{1}{N-1}\delta^{\pi}_{\nu}(\bar{\omega}_{\mu\|\sigma} - \bar{\omega}^{\alpha}_{\mu\sigma\|\alpha} - \bar{\omega}^{\alpha}_{\mu\beta}\bar{\omega}^{\beta}_{\sigma\alpha} + \bar{\omega}^{\alpha}_{\mu\sigma}\bar{\omega}_{\alpha}) \\ & + \frac{1}{N-1}\delta^{\pi}_{\sigma}(\bar{\omega}_{\mu\|\nu} - \bar{\omega}^{\alpha}_{\mu\nu\|\alpha} - \bar{\omega}^{\alpha}_{\mu\beta}\bar{\omega}^{\beta}_{\nu\alpha} + \bar{\omega}^{\alpha}_{\mu\nu}\bar{\omega}_{\alpha}). \end{aligned} \tag{9}$$

The traces of invariant $W^{\pi}_{\mu\nu\sigma}$ are

$$W^{\alpha}_{\alpha\nu\sigma} = -\frac{N-2}{N-1}(\omega_{\nu|\sigma} - \omega_{\sigma|\nu}), \quad W^{\alpha}_{\mu\alpha\nu} = -W^{\alpha}_{\mu\sigma\alpha} - 0.$$

The next theorem was proven above.

Theorem 1. *Let $f : \bar{\mathbb{R}}_N \to \mathbb{R}_N$ be a mapping between Riemannian spaces $\bar{\mathbb{R}}_N$ and $\mathbb{R}_N$. The geometrical objects $\mathcal{T}^{\pi}_{\mu\nu}$ and $\mathcal{W}^{\pi}_{\mu\nu\sigma}$ given by (5) and (6) are the basic invariants of the Thomas and Weyl type for the mapping f. The geometrical object $W^{\pi}_{\mu\nu\sigma}$ given by (9) is the derived invariant of the Weyl type for the mapping f. The geometrical object $\omega_{\mu|\nu} - \omega_{\nu|\mu}$ is an invariant for the mapping f.*

2.1. Review of Geodesic and Conformal Mappings

In this section, we will review the necessary results presented in [2,9] about geodesic and conformal mappings and their preferment with respect to the methodology for obtaining invariants of geometric mappings presented in [21], and its form, presented in [15], necessary for this research.

A mapping $f : \bar{\mathbb{R}}_N \to \mathbb{R}_N$ in which any geodesic line of the space $\bar{\mathbb{R}}_N$ transforms to a geodesic line of the space $\mathbb{R}_N$ is geodesic. The basic equation of mapping f is

$$\Gamma^{\pi}_{\mu\nu} = \bar{\Gamma}^{\pi}_{\mu\nu} + \psi_{\nu}\delta^{\pi}_{\mu} + \psi_{\mu}\delta^{\pi}_{\nu},$$

In comparison with (4), we conclude that $\omega^{\pi}_{\mu\nu} = 0$ and $\bar{\omega}^{\pi}_{\mu\nu} = 0$. That means that for geodesic mappings, the equalities $\omega_{\mu} = 0$ and $\bar{\omega}_{\mu} = 0$ are satisfied. Hence, the invariants for geodesic mapping f are

$$\mathcal{T}^{\pi}_{\mu\nu} = \Gamma^{\pi}_{\mu\nu} - \frac{1}{N+1}(\delta^{\pi}_{\mu}\Gamma_{\nu} + \delta^{\pi}_{\nu}\Gamma_{\mu}), \tag{10}$$

$$\mathcal{W}^{\pi}_{\mu\nu\sigma} = R^{\pi}_{\mu\nu\sigma} - \frac{1}{(N+1)^2}\delta^{\pi}_{\nu}(\Gamma_{\mu|\sigma} + \Gamma_{\mu}\Gamma_{\sigma}) + \frac{1}{(N+1)^2}\delta^{\pi}_{\sigma}(\Gamma_{\mu|\nu} + \Gamma_{\mu}\Gamma_{\nu}), \tag{11}$$

$$W^{\pi}_{\mu\nu\sigma} = R^{\pi}_{\mu\nu\sigma} - \frac{1}{N-1}(\delta^{\pi}_{\nu}R_{\mu\sigma} - \delta^{\pi}_{\sigma}R_{\mu\nu}). \tag{12}$$

For the Weyl projective tensor $W^{\pi}_{\mu\nu\sigma}$, the next identities are satisfied $W^{\alpha}_{\alpha\nu\sigma} \equiv 0$, $W^{\alpha}_{\mu\alpha\sigma} \equiv 0$, $W^{\alpha}_{\mu\nu\alpha} \equiv 0$, but $\mathcal{W}^{\alpha}_{\alpha\nu\sigma} \equiv 0$, $\mathcal{W}^{\alpha}_{\mu\alpha\sigma} = -\mathcal{W}^{\alpha}_{\mu\sigma\alpha} = R_{\mu\sigma} - \dfrac{N-1}{(N+1)^2}(\Gamma_{\mu|\sigma} + \Gamma_{\mu}\Gamma_{\sigma}) \not\equiv 0$.

The basic equation of conformal mapping $f : \bar{\mathbb{R}}_N \to \mathbb{R}_N$ is

$$\Gamma^{\pi}_{\mu\nu} = \bar{\Gamma}^{\pi}_{\mu\nu} + \psi_{\nu}\delta^{\pi}_{\mu} + \psi_{\mu}\delta^{\pi}_{\nu} - g_{\mu\nu}g^{\pi\alpha}\psi_{\alpha}. \tag{13}$$

After contracting (13) by π and ν, we obtain

$$\psi_{\mu} = \frac{1}{N}\Gamma_{\mu} - \frac{1}{N}\bar{\Gamma}_{\mu}. \tag{14}$$

Substituting (14) into the basic Equation (13), one can transform it to the form

$$\Gamma^{\pi}_{\mu\nu} = \bar{\Gamma}^{\pi}_{\mu\nu} + \frac{1}{N}(\delta^{\pi}_{\mu}\Gamma_{\nu} + \delta^{\pi}_{\nu}\Gamma_{\mu} - g_{\mu\nu}g^{\pi\alpha}\Gamma_{\alpha}) - \frac{1}{N}(\delta^{\pi}_{\mu}\bar{\Gamma}_{\nu} + \delta^{\pi}_{\nu}\bar{\Gamma}_{\mu} - \bar{g}_{\mu\nu}\bar{g}^{\pi\alpha}\bar{\Gamma}_{\alpha}).$$

This relation is equivalent to

$$\Gamma^{\pi}_{\mu\nu} = \bar{\Gamma}^{\pi}_{\mu\nu} + \delta^{\pi}_{\mu}\psi_{\nu} + \delta^{\pi}_{\nu}\psi_{\mu} - \frac{1}{N}g_{\mu\nu}g^{\pi\alpha}\Gamma_{\alpha} + \frac{1}{N}\bar{g}_{\mu\nu}\bar{g}^{\pi\alpha}\bar{\Gamma}_{\alpha}. \tag{15}$$

It is well known that the mapping $f : \bar{\mathbb{R}}_N \to \mathbb{R}_N$ is conformal if and only if the Christoffel symbols $\bar{\Gamma}^{\pi}_{\mu\nu}$ and $\Gamma^{\pi}_{\mu\nu}$ satisfy (13). It is not hard to prove that the relation (13) is identically satisfied for $\psi_{\mu} = \dfrac{1}{N}\Gamma_{\mu} - \dfrac{1}{N}\bar{\Gamma}_{\mu}$. Moreover, (15) is equivalent to (2) for $\omega^{\pi}_{\mu\nu} = -\dfrac{1}{N}g_{\mu\nu}g^{\pi\alpha}\Gamma_{\alpha}$ and $\bar{\omega}^{\pi}_{\mu\nu} = -\dfrac{1}{N}\bar{g}_{\mu\nu}\bar{g}^{\pi\alpha}\bar{\Gamma}_{\alpha}$.

Hence, the corresponding basic invariants of the Thomas and Weyl type, and the derived invariant of the Weyl type for conformal mapping, f are

$$\mathcal{T}^{\pi}_{\mu\nu} = \Gamma^{\pi}_{\mu\nu} - \frac{1}{N}\delta^{\pi}_{\mu}\Gamma_{\nu} + \frac{1}{N}\delta^{\pi}_{\nu}\Gamma_{\mu} + \frac{1}{N}g_{\mu\nu}g^{\pi\alpha}\Gamma_{\alpha},$$

$$\begin{aligned}\mathcal{W}^{\pi}_{\mu\nu\sigma} &= R^{\pi}_{\mu\nu\sigma} + \frac{1}{N^2} g_{\mu\nu} g^{\pi\alpha} (N\Gamma_{\alpha|\sigma} + \Gamma_\alpha \Gamma_\sigma) - \frac{1}{N^2} g_{\mu\sigma} g^{\pi\alpha} (N\Gamma_{\alpha|\nu} + \Gamma_\alpha \Gamma_\nu) \\ &- \frac{1}{N^2} \delta^{\pi}_{\nu} (N\Gamma_{\mu|\sigma} + \Gamma_\mu \Gamma_\sigma - g_{\mu\sigma} g^{\alpha\gamma} \Gamma_\alpha \Gamma_\gamma) \\ &+ \frac{1}{N^2} \delta^{\pi}_{\sigma} (N\Gamma_{\mu|\nu} + \Gamma_\mu \Gamma_\nu - g_{\mu\nu} g^{\alpha\gamma} \Gamma_\alpha \Gamma_\gamma), \\ W^{\pi}_{\mu\nu\sigma} &= R^{\pi}_{\mu\nu\sigma} - \frac{1}{N-1} (\delta^{\pi}_{\nu} R_{\mu\sigma} - \delta^{\pi}_{\sigma} R_{\mu\nu}) \\ &+ \frac{1}{N^2} g_{\mu\nu} g^{\pi\alpha} (N\Gamma_{\alpha|\sigma} + \Gamma_\alpha \Gamma_\sigma) - \frac{1}{N^2} g_{\mu\sigma} g^{\pi\alpha} (N\Gamma_{\alpha|\nu} + \Gamma_\alpha \Gamma_\nu) \\ &+ \frac{1}{N^2(N-1)} \delta^{\pi}_{\nu} \Big(N\Gamma_{\mu|\sigma} - \Gamma_\mu \Gamma_\sigma - g_{\mu\sigma} g^{\alpha\gamma} (N\Gamma_{\alpha|\gamma} - \Gamma_\alpha \Gamma_\gamma) \Big) \\ &- \frac{1}{N^2(N-1)} \delta^{\pi}_{\sigma} \Big(N\Gamma_{\mu|\nu} - \Gamma_\mu \Gamma_\nu - g_{\mu\nu} g^{\alpha\gamma} (N\Gamma_{\alpha|\gamma} - \Gamma_\alpha \Gamma_\gamma) \Big).\end{aligned}$$

2.2. *What Is Given byVesić's Method* [21]

If $f : \bar{\mathbb{R}}_N \to \mathbb{R}_N$ is a mapping between Riemannian spaces $\bar{\mathbb{R}}_N$ and $\mathbb{R}_N$, whose deformation tensor is $P^{\pi}_{\mu\nu} = \Gamma^{\pi}_{\mu\nu} - \bar{\Gamma}^{\pi}_{\mu\nu}$, the transformation rule of the curvature tensor $\bar{R}^{\pi}_{\mu\nu\sigma}$ to $\mathbb{R}^{\pi}_{\mu\nu\sigma}$ of the spaces $\bar{\mathbb{R}}_N$ and $\mathbb{R}_N$ is

$$R^{\pi}_{\mu\nu\sigma} = \bar{R}^{\pi}_{\mu\nu\sigma} + P^{\pi}_{\mu\nu\|\sigma} - P^{\pi}_{\mu\sigma\|\nu} + P^{\alpha}_{\mu\nu} P^{\pi}_{\alpha\sigma} - P^{\alpha}_{\mu\sigma} P^{\pi}_{\alpha\nu}. \tag{16}$$

If the mapping f is geodesic, then it is $P^{\pi}_{\mu\nu} = \psi_\nu \delta^{\pi}_{\mu} + \psi_\mu \delta^{\pi}_{\nu}$. After substituting this relation into (16), we will obtain [2,9]

$$R^{\pi}_{\mu\nu\sigma} = \bar{R}^{\pi}_{\mu\nu\sigma} + \delta^{\pi}_{\mu} (\psi_{\nu\|\sigma} - \psi_{\sigma\|\nu}) + \delta^{\pi}_{\nu} (\psi_{\mu\|\sigma} - \psi_\mu \psi_\sigma) - \delta^{\pi}_{\sigma} (\psi_{\mu\|\nu} - \psi_\mu \psi_\nu). \tag{17}$$

When one contracts (17) by π and μ, and by π and ν, the next relations will be obtained

$$\begin{aligned}\psi_{\nu\|\sigma} - \psi_{\sigma\|\nu} &= -\frac{1}{N+1} (R^{\alpha}_{\alpha\nu\sigma} - \bar{R}^{\alpha}_{\alpha\nu\sigma}) = 0, \\ \psi_{\mu\|\sigma} - \psi_\mu \psi_\sigma &= \frac{1}{N-1} R_{\mu\sigma} - \frac{1}{N-1} \bar{R}_{\mu\sigma}.\end{aligned}$$

The last two equalities, together with (17), give

$$R^{\pi}_{\mu\nu\sigma} = \bar{R}^{\pi}_{\mu\nu\sigma} + \frac{1}{N-1} (\delta^{\pi}_{\nu} R_{\mu\sigma} - \delta^{\pi}_{\sigma} R_{\mu\nu}) - \frac{1}{N-1} (\delta^{\pi}_{\nu} \bar{R}_{\mu\sigma} - \delta^{\pi}_{\sigma} R_{\mu\nu}).$$

From the last equality, the invariance of Weyl projective tensor $W^{\pi}_{\mu\nu\sigma}$ given by (12) is confirmed. Because $W^{\alpha}_{\alpha\nu\sigma} = 0$, $W^{\alpha}_{\mu\alpha\sigma} = 0$, and $W^{\alpha}_{\mu\nu\alpha} = 0$, we are not able to obtain an another invariant for the mapping f which contains $R^{\pi}_{\mu\nu\sigma}$ as a variable of a monic polynomial.

Vesić's approach [21] gives the significance. Namely, if $\Gamma^{\pi}_{\mu\nu} = \bar{\Gamma}^{\pi}_{\mu\nu} + d^{\pi}_{\mu\nu} - \bar{d}^{\pi}_{\mu\nu}$, for tensors $d^{\pi}_{\mu\nu}$ and $\bar{d}^{\pi}_{\mu\nu}$ of the type $(1,2)$, and symmetric by μ and ν, it was directly concluded that $\mathcal{T}^{\pi}_{\mu\nu} = \bar{\mathcal{T}}^{\pi}_{\mu\nu}$ for $\mathcal{T}^{\pi}_{\mu\nu} = \Gamma^{\pi}_{\mu\nu} - d^{\pi}_{\mu\nu}$ and the corresponding $\bar{\mathcal{T}}^{\pi}_{\mu\nu}$.

In the next step, the following relation was analyzed:

$$\bar{\mathcal{W}}^{\pi}_{\mu\nu\sigma} := \bar{\mathcal{T}}^{\pi}_{\mu\nu,\sigma} - \bar{\mathcal{T}}^{\pi}_{\mu\sigma,\nu} + \bar{\mathcal{T}}^{\alpha}_{\mu\nu} \bar{\mathcal{T}}^{\pi}_{\alpha\sigma} - \bar{\mathcal{T}}^{\alpha}_{\mu\sigma} \bar{\mathcal{T}}^{\pi}_{\alpha\nu} = \mathcal{T}^{\pi}_{\mu\nu,\sigma} - \mathcal{T}^{\pi}_{\mu\sigma,\nu} + \mathcal{T}^{\alpha}_{\mu\nu} \mathcal{T}^{\pi}_{\alpha\sigma} - \mathcal{T}^{\alpha}_{\mu\sigma} \mathcal{T}^{\pi}_{\alpha\nu} =: \mathcal{W}^{\pi}_{\mu\nu\sigma}.$$

The last equality is equivalent to $\bar{\mathcal{W}}^{\pi}_{\mu\nu\sigma} = \mathcal{W}^{\pi}_{\mu\nu\sigma}$, where $\mathcal{W}^{\pi}_{\mu\nu\sigma} = R^{\pi}_{\mu\nu\sigma} - d^{\pi}_{\mu\nu|\sigma} + d^{\pi}_{\mu\sigma|\nu} + d^{\alpha}_{\mu\nu} d^{\pi}_{\alpha\sigma} - d^{\alpha}_{\mu\sigma} d^{\pi}_{\alpha\nu}$, and the corresponding $\bar{\mathcal{W}}^{\pi}_{\mu\nu\sigma}$.

In the case of geodesic mapping f, the tensor $d^{\pi}_{\mu\nu}$ is $d^{\pi}_{\mu\nu} = \dfrac{1}{N+1}(\delta^{\pi}_{\mu}\Gamma_{\nu} + \delta^{\pi}_{\nu}\Gamma_{\mu})$. In the case of a conformal mapping, the tensor $d^{\pi}_{\mu\nu}$ is $d^{\pi}_{\mu\nu} = \dfrac{1}{N}(\delta^{\pi}_{\mu}\Gamma_{\nu} + \delta^{\pi}_{\nu}\Gamma_{\mu})$.

The corresponding basic invariants $\mathcal{W}^{\pi}_{\mu\nu\sigma}$ are not trace-free, nor is the Ricci-tensor vanished in their trace. The same holds for any of the above obtained basic invariants. That will help us to create an R^1-cosmological model as an example in this manuscript.

Furthermore, the invariance $\bar{\mathcal{W}}^{\pi}_{\mu\nu\sigma} = \mathcal{W}^{\pi}_{\mu\nu\sigma}$ gives us the chance to obtain an another invariant for analyzed mapping as a monic polynomial of curvature tensor $R^{\pi}_{\mu\nu\sigma}$. The Weyl projective and Weyl conformal tensors are examples of these other invariants.

Hence, by the methodology presented by H. Weyl, we are able to obtain only trace-free invariants for mappings. By Vesić's methodology, we obtained a novel invariant which makes it possible for linear cosmological models to be created from these invariants. Both of these invariants will present some significant magnitudes in physics, but we will not talk about these details in this paper.

3. Generalized Concept of Conformal Mappings

In this section, we are ready to define a curve of new kind in space $\mathbb{R}_N$. An m-conformal line of space $\mathbb{R}_N$ is a curve $\ell = \ell(t)$ whose tangential vector (λ^{μ}) satisfies the system of differential equations

$$\frac{d\lambda^{\mu}}{dt} + \Gamma^{\mu}_{\alpha\beta}\lambda^{\alpha}\lambda^{\beta} = \rho\lambda^{\mu} + m g_{\alpha\beta} g^{\mu\gamma}\Gamma_{\gamma}\lambda^{\alpha}\lambda^{\beta},$$

where ρ and m are scalar functions. The function m is the *conformality coefficient*.

A 0-conformal line of space $\mathbb{R}_N$ is a geodesic line of this space.

A $(-\frac{1}{N}, -\frac{1}{N})$-conformal mapping $f : \bar{\mathbb{R}}_N \to \mathbb{R}_N$ is the conformal mapping of space $\bar{\mathbb{R}}_N$.

A $(0,0)$-conformal mapping $f : \bar{\mathbb{R}}_N \to \mathbb{R}_N$ is geodesic mapping.

3.1. Invariants for $(\bar{m}, m)$-Conformal Mappings

A mapping $f : \bar{\mathbb{R}}_N \to \mathbb{R}_N$ in which any $\bar{m}$-conformal line of space $\bar{\mathbb{R}}_N$ transforms to an m-conformal line of space $\mathbb{R}_N$ is the $(\bar{m}, m)$-conformal mapping.

The $(0, m)$-conformal mapping $f : \bar{\mathbb{R}}_N \to \mathbb{R}_N$ transmits any geodesic line of space $\bar{\mathbb{R}}_N$ to an m-conformal line of space $\mathbb{R}_N$. The $(\bar{m}, 0)$-conformal mapping $f : \bar{\mathbb{R}}_N \to \mathbb{R}_N$ transforms any $\bar{m}$-conformal line of space $\bar{\mathbb{R}}_N$ to a geodesic line of the space $\mathbb{R}_N$.

Let us consider an $\bar{m}$-conformal line of the space $\bar{\mathbb{R}}_N$ and an m-conformal mapping of the space $\mathbb{R}_N$,

$$\begin{cases} \dfrac{d\lambda^{\mu}}{dt} + \bar{\Gamma}^{\mu}_{\alpha\beta}\lambda^{\alpha}\lambda^{\beta} = \bar{\rho}\lambda^{\mu} + \bar{m}\bar{g}_{\alpha\beta}\bar{g}^{\mu\gamma}\bar{\Gamma}_{\gamma}\lambda^{\alpha}\lambda^{\beta}, \\ \dfrac{d\lambda^{\mu}}{dt} + \Gamma^{\mu}_{\alpha\beta}\lambda^{\alpha}\lambda^{\beta} = \rho\lambda^{\mu} + m g_{\alpha\beta} g^{\mu\gamma}\Gamma_{\gamma}\lambda^{\alpha}\lambda^{\beta}. \end{cases} \tag{18}$$

Based on the expressions $\rho = \rho_{\alpha}\lambda^{\alpha}$, $\bar{\rho} = \bar{\rho}_{\alpha}\lambda^{\alpha}$, $\lambda^{\mu} = \delta^{\mu}_{\alpha}\lambda^{\alpha}$, from system (18), one obtains

$$\Big((\Gamma^{\mu}_{\alpha\beta} - \bar{\Gamma}^{\mu}_{\alpha\beta}) - \frac{1}{2}(\rho_{\alpha}\delta^{\mu}_{\beta} + \rho_{\beta}\delta^{\mu}_{\alpha}) + \frac{1}{2}(\bar{\rho}_{\alpha}\delta^{\mu}_{\beta} + \bar{\rho}_{\beta}\delta^{\mu}_{\alpha}) - (m g_{\alpha\beta} g^{\mu\gamma}\Gamma_{\gamma} - \bar{m}\bar{g}_{\alpha\beta}\bar{g}^{\mu\gamma}\bar{\Gamma}_{\gamma})\Big)\lambda^{\alpha}\lambda^{\beta} = 0.$$

The next lemma was proven above.

Lemma 1. *A mapping $f : \bar{\mathbb{R}}_N \to \mathbb{R}_N$ is an $(\bar{m}, m)$-conformal one if and only if*

$$\Gamma^{\pi}_{\mu\nu} = \bar{\Gamma}^{\pi}_{\mu\nu} + \delta^{\pi}_{\mu}\psi_{\nu} + \delta^{\pi}_{\nu}\psi_{\mu} + m g_{\mu\nu} g^{\pi\alpha}\Gamma_{\alpha} - \bar{m}\bar{g}_{\mu\nu}\bar{g}^{\pi\alpha}\bar{\Gamma}_{\alpha}, \tag{19}$$

where m is a scalar function and ψ_{μ} is a 1-form.

3.2. Invariants for $(\bar{m}, m)$-Conformal Mappings

Let $f : \bar{\mathbb{R}}_N \to \mathbb{R}_N$ be an $(\bar{m}, m)$-conformal mapping. After contracting its basic Equation (19) by π and ν, we obtain

$$\psi_\mu = -\frac{m-1}{N+1}\Gamma_\mu - \frac{\bar{m}-1}{N+1}\bar{\Gamma}_\mu. \tag{20}$$

After substituting (20) into the basic Equation (19), we obtain

$$\begin{aligned}\Gamma^\pi_{\mu\nu} = \bar{\Gamma}^\pi_{\mu\nu} &- \frac{m-1}{N+1}(\delta^\pi_\mu\Gamma_\nu + \delta^\pi_\nu\Gamma_\mu) + m g_{\mu\nu} g^{\pi\alpha}\Gamma_\alpha \\ &+ \frac{\bar{m}-1}{N+1}(\delta^\pi_\mu\bar{\Gamma}_\nu + \delta^\pi_\nu\bar{\Gamma}_\mu) - \bar{m}\bar{g}_{\mu\nu}\bar{g}^{\pi\alpha}\bar{\Gamma}_\alpha.\end{aligned} \tag{21}$$

(21) is equivalent to the equality $\mathcal{T}^\pi_{\mu\nu} = \bar{\mathcal{T}}^\pi_{\mu\nu}$, for

$$\mathcal{T}^\pi_{\mu\nu} = \Gamma^\pi_{\mu\nu} - m g_{\mu\nu} g^{\pi\alpha}\Gamma_\alpha + \frac{m-1}{N+1}(\delta^\pi_\mu\Gamma_\nu + \delta^\pi_\nu\Gamma_\mu), \tag{22}$$

and the corresponding $\bar{\mathcal{T}}^\pi_{\mu\nu}$.

From the basic Equation (21) of $(\bar{m}, m)$-mapping $f : \bar{\mathbb{R}}_N \to \mathbb{R}_N$, one obtains

$$\begin{cases} d^\pi_{\mu\nu} = -\dfrac{m-1}{N+1}(\delta^\pi_\mu\Gamma_\nu + \delta^\pi_\nu\Gamma_\mu) + m g_{\mu\nu} g^{\pi\alpha}\Gamma_\alpha, \\ \bar{d}^\pi_{\mu\nu} = -\dfrac{\bar{m}-1}{N+1}(\delta^\pi_\mu\bar{\Gamma}_\nu + \delta^\pi_\nu\bar{\Gamma}_\mu) + \bar{m}\bar{g}_{\mu\nu}\bar{g}^{\pi\alpha}\bar{\Gamma}_\alpha. \end{cases} \tag{23}$$

Remark 2. *From* (23) *we have* $\omega^\pi_{\mu\nu} = g_{\mu\nu} g^{\pi\alpha}\Gamma_\alpha$ *and* $\bar{\omega}^\pi_{\mu\nu} = \bar{m}\bar{g}_{\mu\nu}\bar{g}^{\pi\alpha}\bar{\Gamma}_\alpha$, *but it will be more simple to use the equality* $\mathcal{W}^\pi_{\mu\nu\sigma} = R^\pi_{\mu\nu\sigma} - d^\pi_{\mu\nu|\sigma} + d^\pi_{\mu\sigma|\nu} + d^\alpha_{\mu\nu}d^\pi_{\alpha\sigma} - d^\alpha_{\mu\sigma}d^\pi_{\alpha\nu}$.

For $d^\pi_{\mu\nu}$ given by (23), and with respect to $\Gamma_{\mu|\nu} = \Gamma_{\nu|\mu}$, one obtains

$$\begin{aligned} -d^\pi_{\mu\nu|\sigma} + d^\pi_{\mu\sigma|\nu} &= \frac{1}{N+1}\delta^\pi_\mu(\Gamma_\nu m_\sigma - \Gamma_\sigma m_\nu) + \frac{1}{N+1}\delta^\pi_\nu(\Gamma_\mu m_\sigma + (m-1)\Gamma_{\mu|\sigma}) \\ &- \frac{1}{N+1}\delta^\pi_\sigma(\Gamma_\mu m_\nu + (m-1)\Gamma_{\mu|\nu}) - g^{\pi\alpha}\Gamma_\alpha(g_{\mu\nu}m_\sigma - g_{\mu\sigma}m_\nu) \\ &- m g^{\pi\alpha}(g_{\mu\nu}\Gamma_{\alpha|\sigma} - g_{\mu\sigma}\Gamma_{\alpha|\nu}), \\ d^\alpha_{\mu\nu}d^\pi_{\alpha\sigma} - d^\alpha_{\mu\sigma}d^\pi_{\alpha\nu} &= m^2 g^{\pi\alpha}\Gamma_\alpha(g_{\mu\nu}\Gamma_\sigma - g_{\mu\sigma}\Gamma_\nu) \\ &+ \frac{1}{(N+1)^2}\delta^\pi_\nu\Big((N+1)m(m-1)g_{\mu\sigma}g^{\alpha\gamma}\Gamma_\alpha\Gamma_\gamma - (m-1)^2\Gamma_\mu\Gamma_\sigma\Big) \\ &- \frac{1}{(N+1)^2}\delta^\pi_\sigma\Big((N+1)m(m-1)g_{\mu\nu}g^{\alpha\gamma}\Gamma_\alpha\Gamma_\gamma - (m-1)^2\Gamma_\mu\Gamma_\nu\Big), \end{aligned}$$

and the corresponding differences $-\bar{d}^\pi_{\mu\nu\|\sigma} + \bar{d}^\pi_{\mu\sigma\|\nu}$ and $\bar{d}^\alpha_{\mu\nu}\bar{d}^\pi_{\alpha\sigma} - \bar{d}^\alpha_{\mu\sigma}\bar{d}^\pi_{\alpha\nu}$.

Hence, we obtain the following geometrical objects

$$\begin{aligned} \mathcal{W}^\pi_{\mu\nu\sigma} = R^\pi_{\mu\nu\sigma} &- g^{\pi\alpha}\Gamma_\alpha\Big(g_{\mu\nu}m_\sigma - g_{\mu\sigma}m_\nu - m^2(g_{\mu\nu}\Gamma_\sigma - g_{\mu\sigma}\Gamma_\nu)\Big) \\ &- m g^{\pi\alpha}(g_{\mu\nu}\Gamma_{\alpha|\sigma} - g_{\mu\sigma}\Gamma_{\alpha|\nu}) + \frac{1}{N+1}\delta^\pi_\mu(\Gamma_\nu m_\sigma - \Gamma_\sigma m_\nu) \\ &+ \frac{1}{(N+1)^2}\delta^\pi_\nu\Big((N+1)(m-1)(\Gamma_{\mu|\sigma} + m g_{\mu\sigma}g^{\alpha\gamma}\Gamma_\alpha\Gamma_\gamma) + \Gamma_\mu m_\sigma - (m-1)^2\Gamma_\mu\Gamma_\sigma\Big) \\ &- \frac{1}{(N+1)^2}\delta^\pi_\sigma\Big((N+1)(m-1)(\Gamma_{\mu|\nu} + m g_{\mu\nu}g^{\alpha\gamma}\Gamma_\alpha\Gamma_\gamma) + \Gamma_\mu m_\nu - (m-1)^2\Gamma_\mu\Gamma_\nu\Big), \end{aligned} \tag{24}$$

$$
\begin{aligned}
\bar{\mathcal{W}}^{\pi}_{\mu\nu\sigma} &= \bar{R}^{\pi}_{\mu\nu\sigma} - \bar{g}^{\pi\alpha}\bar{\Gamma}_{\alpha}\Big(\bar{g}_{\mu\nu}\bar{m}_{\sigma} - \bar{g}_{\mu\sigma}\bar{m}_{\nu} - \bar{m}^{2}\big(\bar{g}_{\mu\nu}\bar{\Gamma}_{\sigma} - \bar{g}_{\mu\sigma}\bar{\Gamma}_{\nu}\big)\Big) \\
&\quad - \bar{m}\bar{g}^{\pi\alpha}\big(\bar{g}_{\mu\nu}\bar{\Gamma}_{\alpha\|\sigma} - \bar{g}_{\mu\sigma}\bar{\Gamma}_{\alpha\|\nu}\big) + \frac{1}{N+1}\delta^{\pi}_{\mu}\big(\bar{\Gamma}_{\nu}\bar{m}_{\sigma} - \bar{\Gamma}_{\sigma}\bar{m}_{\nu}\big) \\
&\quad + \frac{1}{(N+1)^{2}}\delta^{\pi}_{\nu}\Big((N+1)(\bar{m}-1)\big(\bar{\Gamma}_{\mu\|\sigma} + \bar{m}\bar{g}_{\mu\sigma}\bar{g}^{\alpha\gamma}\bar{\Gamma}_{\alpha}\bar{\Gamma}_{\gamma}\big) + \bar{\Gamma}_{\mu}\bar{m}_{\sigma} - (\bar{m}-1)^{2}\bar{\Gamma}_{\mu}\bar{\Gamma}_{\sigma}\Big) \\
&\quad - \frac{1}{(N+1)^{2}}\delta^{\pi}_{\sigma}\Big((N+1)(\bar{m}-1)\big(\bar{\Gamma}_{\mu\|\nu} + \bar{m}\bar{g}_{\mu\nu}\bar{g}^{\alpha\gamma}\bar{\Gamma}_{\alpha}\bar{\Gamma}_{\gamma}\big) + \bar{\Gamma}_{\mu}\bar{m}_{\nu} - (\bar{m}-1)^{2}\bar{\Gamma}_{\mu}\bar{\Gamma}_{\nu}\Big).
\end{aligned}
\tag{25}
$$

The traces of the geometrical objects $\mathcal{W}^{\pi}_{\mu\nu\sigma}$ and $\bar{\mathcal{W}}^{\pi}_{\mu\nu\sigma}$ from Equations (24) and (25) by π and μ are $\mathcal{W}^{\alpha}_{\alpha\nu\sigma} = -\dfrac{N}{(N+1)^{2}}(\Gamma_{\nu}m_{\sigma} - \Gamma_{\sigma}m_{\nu})$ and $\bar{\mathcal{W}}^{\alpha}_{\alpha\nu\sigma} = -\dfrac{N}{(N+1)^{2}}(\bar{\Gamma}_{\nu}\bar{m}_{\sigma} - \bar{\Gamma}_{\sigma}\bar{m}_{\nu})$. The traces of these geometrical objects by π and ν are

$$
\begin{aligned}
\mathcal{W}^{\alpha}_{\mu\alpha\sigma} &= R_{\mu\sigma} - \frac{2m+N-1}{N+1}\Gamma_{\mu|\sigma} + m g_{\mu\sigma}g^{\alpha\gamma}\Gamma_{\alpha|\gamma} - \left(\frac{2}{N+1}m + \frac{N-1}{N+1}\right)g_{\mu\sigma}g^{\alpha\gamma}\Gamma_{\alpha}\Gamma_{\gamma} \\
&\quad + \left(\frac{N^{2}+N+2}{(N+1)^{2}}m^{2} + \frac{2N-2}{(N+1)^{2}}m - \frac{N-1}{(N+1)^{2}}\right)\Gamma_{\mu}\Gamma_{\sigma} + g_{\mu\sigma}g^{\alpha\gamma}\Gamma_{\alpha}m_{\gamma} \\
&\quad - \frac{1}{N+1}\Gamma_{\sigma}m_{\gamma} - \frac{N^{2}+1}{(N+1)^{2}}\Gamma_{\mu}m_{\sigma}, \\
\bar{\mathcal{W}}^{\alpha}_{\mu\alpha\sigma} &= \bar{R}_{\mu\sigma} - \frac{2\bar{m}+N-1}{N+1}\bar{\Gamma}_{\mu\|\sigma} + \bar{m}\bar{g}_{\mu\sigma}\bar{g}^{\alpha\gamma}\bar{\Gamma}_{\alpha\|\gamma} - \left(\frac{2}{N+1}\bar{m} + \frac{N-1}{N+1}\right)\bar{g}_{\mu\sigma}\bar{g}^{\alpha\gamma}\bar{\Gamma}_{\alpha}\bar{\Gamma}_{\gamma} \\
&\quad + \left(\frac{N^{2}+N+2}{(N+1)^{2}}\bar{m}^{2} + \frac{2N-2}{(N+1)^{2}}\bar{m} - \frac{N-1}{(N+1)^{2}}\right)\bar{\Gamma}_{\mu}\bar{\Gamma}_{\sigma} + \bar{g}_{\mu\sigma}\bar{g}^{\alpha\gamma}\bar{\Gamma}_{\alpha}\bar{m}_{\gamma} \\
&\quad - \frac{1}{N+1}\bar{\Gamma}_{\sigma}\bar{m}_{\gamma} - \frac{N^{2}+1}{(N+1)^{2}}\bar{\Gamma}_{\mu}\bar{m}_{\sigma}.
\end{aligned}
$$

Because $\mathcal{W}^{\pi}_{\mu\nu\sigma} = -\mathcal{W}^{\pi}_{\mu\sigma\nu}$ and $\bar{\mathcal{W}}^{\pi}_{\mu\nu\sigma} = -\bar{\mathcal{W}}^{\pi}_{\mu\sigma\nu}$, the traces of $\mathcal{W}^{\pi}_{\mu\nu\sigma}$ and $\bar{\mathcal{W}}^{\pi}_{\mu\nu\sigma}$ by π and σ are $\mathcal{W}^{\alpha}_{\mu\nu\alpha} = -\mathcal{W}^{\alpha}_{\mu\alpha\nu}$ and $\bar{\mathcal{W}}^{\alpha}_{\mu\nu\alpha} = -\bar{\mathcal{W}}^{\alpha}_{\mu\alpha\nu}$.

After substituting the previously obtained geometrical objects necessary for the derived invariant $W^{\pi}_{\mu\nu\sigma}$, we get

$$
\begin{aligned}
W^{\pi}_{\mu\nu\sigma} &= R^{\pi}_{\mu\nu\sigma} - \frac{1}{N-1}\big(\delta^{\pi}_{\nu}R_{\mu\sigma} - \delta^{\pi}_{\sigma}R_{\mu\nu}\big) - g^{\pi\alpha}\Gamma_{\alpha}\big(g_{\mu\nu}m_{\sigma} - g_{\mu\sigma}m_{\nu}\big) \\
&\quad - m g^{\pi\alpha}\big(g_{\mu\nu}\Gamma_{\alpha|\sigma} - g_{\mu\sigma}\Gamma_{\alpha|\nu}\big) + m^{2}g^{\pi\alpha}\Gamma_{\alpha}\big(g_{\mu\nu}\Gamma_{\sigma} - g_{\mu\sigma}\Gamma_{\nu}\big) \\
&\quad + \frac{1}{N-1}\delta^{\pi}_{\nu}\Big(m\Gamma_{\mu|\sigma} + \Gamma_{\mu}m_{\sigma} - m^{2}\Gamma_{\mu}\Gamma_{\sigma} - g_{\mu\sigma}g^{\alpha\gamma}\big(m\Gamma_{\alpha|\gamma} + \Gamma_{\alpha}m_{\gamma} - m^{2}\Gamma_{\alpha}\Gamma_{\gamma}\big)\Big) \\
&\quad - \frac{1}{N-1}\delta^{\pi}_{\sigma}\Big(m\Gamma_{\mu|\nu} + \Gamma_{\mu}m_{\nu} - m^{2}\Gamma_{\mu}\Gamma_{\nu} - g_{\mu\nu}g^{\alpha\gamma}\big(m\Gamma_{\alpha|\gamma} + \Gamma_{\alpha}m_{\gamma} - m^{2}\Gamma_{\alpha}\Gamma_{\gamma}\big)\Big),
\end{aligned}
\tag{26}
$$

and the corresponding $\bar{W}^{\pi}_{\mu\nu\sigma}$.

The traces $W_{\nu\sigma} = W^{\alpha}_{\alpha\nu\sigma}$ and $W_{\mu\sigma} = W^{\alpha}_{\mu\alpha\sigma}$ of the invariant $W^{\pi}_{\mu\nu\sigma}$ given by (26) are $W_{\nu\sigma} = -\dfrac{N-2}{N-1}(\Gamma_{\nu}m_{\sigma} - \Gamma_{\sigma}m_{\nu})$ and $W_{\mu\sigma} = 0$.

The next theorem was proven above.

Theorem 2. *Let $f : \mathbb{R}_N \to \mathbb{R}_N$ be an $(\bar{m}, m)$-mapping. The geometrical object $\mathcal{T}^{\pi}_{\mu\nu}$ given by* (22) *is the basic invariant for mapping f of the Thomas type. The geometrical object $\mathcal{W}^{\pi}_{\mu\nu\sigma}$ given by* (24) *is the basic invariant for mapping f of the Weyl type. The geometrical object $W^{\pi}_{\mu\nu\sigma}$ given by* (26) *is the derived invariant for mapping f of the Weyl type.*

3.3. Lagrangian Caused by $(\bar{m}, m)$-Conformal Mappings

In [23], the Lagrangian is taken to be

$$\mathcal{L}_N = \sqrt{-g}g^{\mu\nu}\left(G^{\alpha}_{\mu\nu,\alpha} + \frac{1}{N-1}G^{\alpha}_{\alpha\mu}G^{\beta}_{\beta\nu} - G^{\alpha}_{\beta\mu}G^{\beta}_{\alpha\nu}\right),$$

for $G^{\pi}_{\mu\nu} = \Gamma^{\pi}_{\mu\nu} - \frac{1}{2}(\delta^{\pi}_{\mu}\Gamma_{\nu} + \delta^{\pi}_{\nu}\Gamma_{\mu})$.

The value $G^{\pi}_{\mu\nu}$ is similar to the Thomas projective parameter (10). As we mentioned above, the basic invariant $\mathcal{W}_{\mu\sigma} = \mathcal{W}^{\alpha}_{\mu\alpha\sigma}$ for the geodesic mapping given by (11) reduces to the Ricci tensor $R_{\mu\sigma}$.

We obtained the basic invariant $\mathcal{W}^{\pi}_{\mu\nu\sigma}$ for an $(\bar{m}, m)$-conformal mapping. In this example, we will study the transformation of $\bar{\Gamma}^{\pi}_{\mu\nu}$ to $\Gamma^{\pi}_{\mu\nu}$ such that any $\bar{m}$-conformal line of an N-dimensional Riemannian space $\bar{\mathbb{R}}_N$ equipped with an FLRW-metric whose square form is $ds^2 = -dt^2 + a^2(dx^{1^2} + \ldots + dx^{N-1^2})$, where $a = a(t)$ is the scale factor, transforms to an m-conformal line of the perturbed space.

To simplify our computing, we will start from the basic equation of the form $\Gamma^{\pi}_{\mu\nu} = \bar{\Gamma}^{\pi}_{\mu\nu} + d^{\pi}_{\mu\nu} - \bar{d}^{\pi}_{\mu\nu}$, where

$$\begin{cases} d^{\pi}_{\mu\nu} = -\dfrac{m-1}{N+1}(\delta^{\pi}_{\mu}\Gamma_{\nu} + \delta^{\pi}_{\nu}\Gamma_{\mu}) + m g_{\mu\nu}g^{\pi\alpha}\Gamma_{\alpha}, \\ \bar{d}^{\pi}_{\mu\nu} = -\dfrac{\bar{m}-1}{N+1}(\delta^{\pi}_{\mu}\bar{\Gamma}_{\nu} + \delta^{\pi}_{\nu}\bar{\Gamma}_{\mu}) + \bar{m}\bar{g}_{\mu\nu}\bar{g}^{\pi\alpha}\bar{\Gamma}_{\alpha}. \end{cases}$$

is given by (23).

The corresponding basic invariant of the Weyl type in the perturbed space is

$$\mathcal{W}_{\mu\sigma} = \mathcal{W}^{\alpha}_{\mu\alpha\sigma} = R_{\mu\sigma} - d_{\mu|\sigma} + d^{\alpha}_{\mu\sigma|\alpha} + d^{\alpha}_{\mu\beta}d^{\beta}_{\sigma\alpha} - d^{\alpha}_{\mu\sigma}d_{\alpha}.$$

The corresponding Einstein–Hilbert action is

$$2\kappa S^{+}_{0} = \int d^N x\sqrt{-g}g^{\alpha\beta}\mathcal{W}_{\alpha\beta},$$

i.e.,

$$\begin{aligned} 2\kappa S^{+}_{0} = &\int d^N x\sqrt{-g}R - \int d^N x\sqrt{-g}g^{\alpha\beta}d_{\alpha|\beta} + \int d^N x\sqrt{-g}g^{\alpha\beta}d^{\gamma}_{\alpha\beta|\gamma} \\ &+ \int d^N x\sqrt{-g}g^{\alpha\beta}d^{\gamma}_{\alpha\delta}d^{\delta}_{\beta\gamma} - \int d^N x\sqrt{-g}g^{\alpha\beta}d^{\gamma}_{\alpha\beta}d_{\gamma}. \end{aligned} \tag{27}$$

Because $\Gamma_{\mu} = \left(\ln\sqrt{-g}\right)_{,\mu} = \dfrac{\sqrt{-g}_{,\mu}}{\sqrt{-g}}$, we get $\sqrt{-g}_{,\mu} = \sqrt{-g}\Gamma_{\mu}$.

For this reason, if τ^{α} is a tensor of the type $(1,0)$, we obtain

$$\sqrt{-g}\tau^{\alpha}_{|\alpha} = \sqrt{-g}\tau^{\alpha}_{,\alpha} + \sqrt{-g}\Gamma^{\alpha}_{\beta\alpha}\tau^{\beta} = \sqrt{-g}\tau^{\alpha}_{,\alpha} + \sqrt{-g}_{,\beta}\tau^{\beta} = \left(\sqrt{-g}\tau^{\alpha}\right)_{,\alpha}.$$

Because $\delta g^{\mu\nu} = 0$ at the border of integration, and based on the Stokes Theorem, we conclude that the variation $\delta\left(\int d^N x\sqrt{-g}d^{\alpha}_{|\alpha}\right)$ vanishes. For this reason, and because $g^{\alpha\beta}d_{\alpha|\beta} = \left(g^{\alpha\beta}d_{\alpha}\right)_{|\beta}$ and $g^{\alpha\beta}d^{\gamma}_{\alpha\beta|\gamma} = \left(g^{\alpha\beta}d^{\gamma}_{\alpha\beta}\right)_{|\gamma}$, the variations of the second and third integral of (27) are equal to zero.

The variation of the scalar curvature R is

$$\begin{aligned} \delta R &= \delta g^{\mu\nu}R_{\mu\nu} + g^{\mu\nu}\left((\delta\Gamma^{\alpha}_{\mu\alpha})_{,\nu} - (\delta\Gamma^{\alpha}_{\mu\nu})_{,\alpha} + \delta\Gamma^{\beta}_{\mu\alpha}\Gamma^{\alpha}_{\nu\beta} + \Gamma^{\beta}_{\mu\alpha}\delta\Gamma^{\alpha}_{\nu\beta} - \delta\Gamma^{\alpha}_{\mu\sigma}\Gamma_{\alpha} - \Gamma^{\alpha}_{\mu\sigma}\delta\Gamma_{\alpha}\right) \\ &= (\delta\Gamma_{\mu}|)_{|\sigma} - \left(\delta\Gamma^{\alpha}_{\mu\sigma}\right)_{|\alpha}. \end{aligned}$$

For this reason, because $\delta\sqrt{-g} = -\frac{1}{2}\sqrt{-g}\delta g^{\mu\nu} g_{\mu\nu}$, and with respect to the Stokes Theorem, we obtain

$$\delta\Big(\int d^N x\sqrt{-g}R\Big) = \int d^N x\sqrt{-g}\delta g^{\mu\nu}\big(R_{\mu\nu} - \frac{1}{2}Rg_{\mu\nu}\big).$$

Because $\bar{m}$ and m are scalars, the variation $\delta m = m - \bar{m}$ is a scalar too. With respect to the tensor $\delta g^{\mu\nu}$ of the type $(0,2)$, and the quotient rule, there exists a tensor $M_{\mu\nu}$ of the type $(0,2)$ such that $\delta m = M_{\mu\nu}\delta g^{\mu\nu}$.

Because $0 = \delta(\delta^\alpha_\beta) = \delta(g^{\alpha\gamma} g_{\beta\gamma}) = \delta g^{\alpha\gamma} g_{\beta\gamma} + g^{\alpha\gamma}\delta g_{\beta\gamma}$, we conclude that

$$\delta g_{\beta\delta} = -\delta g^{\alpha\gamma} g_{\alpha\beta} g_{\gamma\delta}.$$

The variation of the vector $\Gamma_\alpha = \Gamma^\beta_{\alpha\beta}$ is

$$\begin{aligned}
\delta\Gamma_\alpha &= \frac{1}{2}\delta\big(g^{\beta\delta}(g_{\alpha\beta,\delta} - g_{\alpha\delta,\beta} + g_{\beta\delta,\alpha})\big) = \frac{1}{2}\delta g^{\beta\delta} g_{\beta\delta,\alpha} + \frac{1}{2}g^{\beta\delta}(\delta g_{\beta\delta})_{,\alpha} \\
&= \frac{1}{2}\delta g^{\beta\delta} g_{\beta\delta,\alpha} - \frac{1}{2}g^{\epsilon\zeta}(\delta g^{\beta\delta} g_{\beta\epsilon} g_{\delta\zeta})_{,\alpha} \\
&= \frac{1}{2}\delta g^{\beta\delta} g_{\beta\delta,\alpha} - \frac{1}{2}(\delta g^{\beta\delta})_{,\alpha} g_{\beta\delta} - \frac{1}{2}\delta g^{\beta\delta} g_{\beta\delta,\alpha} - \frac{1}{2}\delta g^{\beta\delta} g_{\beta\delta,\alpha} = -\frac{1}{2}(\delta g^{\beta\delta} g_{\beta\delta})_{,\alpha}.
\end{aligned}$$

For $d^\pi_{\mu\nu}$ given by (23), the following equalities hold:

$$\begin{aligned}
g^{\alpha\beta} d^\gamma_{\alpha\delta} d^\delta_{\beta\gamma} &= -\Big(\frac{N^2+N-2}{(N+1)^2}m^2 + \frac{2(N^2+N-2)}{(N+1)^2}m + \frac{N+3}{(N+1)^2}\Big)g^{\alpha\gamma}\Gamma_\alpha\Gamma_\gamma, \\
g^{\alpha\beta} d^\gamma_{\alpha\beta} d_\gamma &= \Big(\frac{N^2+N-2}{(N+1)^2}m + \frac{2}{N+1}\Big)g^{\alpha\gamma}\Gamma_\alpha\Gamma_\gamma.
\end{aligned}$$

Hence, the difference $I = g^{\alpha\beta} d^\gamma_{\alpha\delta} d^\delta_{\beta\gamma} - g^{\alpha\beta} d^\gamma_{\alpha\beta} d_\gamma$ between the last two integrands in (27) is

$$I = -\Big(\frac{N^2+N-2}{(N+1)^2}m^2 - \frac{3(N^2+N-2)}{(N+1)^2}m + \frac{N+5}{(N+1)^2}\Big)g^{\alpha\gamma}\Gamma_\alpha\Gamma_\gamma.$$

The variation of term $\sqrt{-g}I$ is

$$\begin{aligned}
\delta(\sqrt{-g}I) &= \frac{1}{2}\sqrt{-g}\delta g^{\mu\nu} g_{\mu\nu}\Big(\frac{N^2+N-2}{(N+1)^2}m^2 - \frac{3(N^2+N-2)}{(N+1)^2}m + \frac{N+5}{(N+1)^2}\Big)g^{\alpha\gamma}\Gamma_\alpha\Gamma_\gamma \\
&\quad - \sqrt{-g}\delta g^{\mu\nu}\Big(\frac{N^2+N-2}{(N+1)^2}m^2 - \frac{3(N^2+N-2)}{(N+1)^2}m + \frac{N+5}{(N+1)^2}\Big)\Gamma_\mu\Gamma_\nu \\
&\quad - \frac{N^2+N-2}{(N+1)^2}\sqrt{-g}\delta g^{\mu\nu} M_{\mu\nu}(2m-3)g^{\alpha\gamma}\Gamma_\alpha\Gamma_\gamma \\
&\quad + \sqrt{-g}\Big(\frac{N^2+N-2}{(N+1)^2}m^2 - \frac{3(N^2+N-2)}{(N+1)^2}m + \frac{N+5}{(N+1)^2}\Big)g^{\alpha\gamma}\Gamma_\alpha(\delta g^{\mu\nu} g_{\mu\nu})_{,\gamma}
\end{aligned}$$

The following equality is satisfied

$$\sqrt{-g}\Big(\frac{N^2+N-2}{(N+1)^2}m^2-\frac{3(N^2+N-2)}{(N+1)^2}m+\frac{N+5}{(N+1)^2}\Big)g^{\alpha\gamma}\Gamma_\alpha(\delta g^{\mu\nu}g_{\mu\nu})_{,\gamma}$$
$$=\Big(\sqrt{-g}\Big(\frac{N^2+N-2}{(N+1)^2}m^2-\frac{3(N^2+N-2)}{(N+1)^2}m+\frac{N+5}{(N+1)^2}\Big)g^{\alpha\gamma}\Gamma_\alpha\delta g^{\mu\nu}g_{\mu\nu}\Big)_{,\gamma}$$
$$-\sqrt{-g}\Big(\frac{N^2+N-2}{(N+1)^2}m^2-\frac{3(N^2+N-2)}{(N+1)^2}m+\frac{N+5}{(N+1)^2}\Big)\delta g^{\mu\nu}g_{\mu\nu}g^{\alpha\gamma}\Gamma_\alpha\Gamma_\gamma$$
$$-\sqrt{-g}\frac{N^2+N-2}{(N+1)^2}\delta g^{\mu\nu}g_{\mu\nu}(2m-3)g^{\alpha\gamma}\Gamma_\alpha m_\gamma$$
$$-\sqrt{-g}\Big(\frac{N^2+N-2}{(N+1)^2}m^2-\frac{3(N^2+N-2)}{(N+1)^2}m+\frac{N+5}{(N+1)^2}\Big)\delta g^{\mu\nu}g_{\mu\nu}g^{\alpha\gamma}(\Gamma_{\alpha|\gamma}-\Gamma_\alpha\Gamma_\gamma).$$

Finally, the variation of Einstein–Hilbert action (27) vanishes if and only if

$$0=R_{\mu\nu}-\frac{1}{2}Rg_{\nu\nu}-\Big(\frac{N^2+N-2}{(N+1)^2}m^2-\frac{3(N^2+N-2)}{(N+1)^2}m+\frac{N+5}{(N+1)^2}\Big)\Gamma_\mu\Gamma_\nu$$
$$-\frac{1}{2}\Big(\frac{N^2+N-2}{(N+1)^2}m^2-\frac{3(N^2+N-2)}{(N+1)^2}m+\frac{N+5}{(N+1)^2}\Big)g_{\mu\nu}g^{\alpha\gamma}\Gamma_\alpha\Gamma_\gamma$$
$$-\frac{N^2+N-2}{(N+1)^2}(2m-3)g^{\alpha\gamma}\Gamma_\alpha(M_{\mu\nu}\Gamma_\gamma+g_{\mu\nu}m_\gamma)$$
$$-\Big(\frac{N^2+N-2}{(N+1)^2}m^2-\frac{3(N^2+N-2)}{(N+1)^2}m+\frac{N+5}{(N+1)^2}\Big)g_{\mu\nu}g^{\alpha\gamma}(\Gamma_{\alpha|\gamma}-\Gamma_\alpha\Gamma_\gamma).$$

The corresponding energy–momentum tensor is

$$\begin{aligned}T_{\mu\nu}=&R_{\mu\nu}-\frac{1}{2}Rg_{\nu\nu}-\Big(\frac{N^2+N-2}{(N+1)^2}m^2-\frac{3(N^2+N-2)}{(N+1)^2}m+\frac{N+5}{(N+1)^2}\Big)\Gamma_\mu\Gamma_\nu\\&-\frac{1}{2}\Big(\frac{N^2+N-2}{(N+1)^2}m^2-\frac{3(N^2+N-2)}{(N+1)^2}m+\frac{N+5}{(N+1)^2}\Big)g_{\mu\nu}g^{\alpha\gamma}\Gamma_\alpha\Gamma_\gamma\\&-\frac{N^2+N-2}{(N+1)^2}(2m-3)g^{\alpha\gamma}\Gamma_\alpha(M_{\mu\nu}\Gamma_\gamma+g_{\mu\nu}m_\gamma)\\&-\Big(\frac{N^2+N-2}{(N+1)^2}m^2-\frac{3(N^2+N-2)}{(N+1)^2}m+\frac{N+5}{(N+1)^2}\Big)g_{\mu\nu}g^{\alpha\gamma}(\Gamma_{\alpha|\gamma}-\Gamma_\alpha\Gamma_\gamma).\end{aligned}\tag{28}$$

If the scalar functions m and $\bar{m}$ are equal, which means that is $\delta m=0$, the energy–momentum tensor $T_{\mu\nu}$ given by (28) reduces to

$$T_{\mu\nu}=R_{\mu\nu}-\frac{1}{2}Rg_{\nu\nu}-\Big(\frac{N^2+N-2}{(N+1)^2}m^2-\frac{3(N^2+N-2)}{(N+1)^2}m+\frac{N+5}{(N+1)^2}\Big)\Gamma_\mu\Gamma_\nu$$
$$-\frac{1}{2}\Big(\frac{N^2+N-2}{(N+1)^2}m^2-\frac{3(N^2+N-2)}{(N+1)^2}m+\frac{N+5}{(N+1)^2}\Big)g_{\mu\nu}g^{\alpha\gamma}\Gamma_\alpha\Gamma_\gamma$$
$$-\frac{N^2+N-2}{(N+1)^2}(2m-3)g^{\alpha\gamma}\Gamma_\alpha g_{\mu\nu}m_\gamma$$
$$-\Big(\frac{N^2+N-2}{(N+1)^2}m^2-\frac{3(N^2+N-2)}{(N+1)^2}m+\frac{N+5}{(N+1)^2}\Big)g_{\mu\nu}g^{\alpha\gamma}(\Gamma_{\alpha|\gamma}-\Gamma_\alpha\Gamma_\gamma).$$

If m and $\bar{m}$ are equal numbers, which means $M_{\mu\nu} = 0$ and $m_\mu = \bar{m}_\mu = 0$, the energy–momentum tensor $T_{\mu\nu}$ given by (28) reduces to

$$
\begin{aligned}
T_{\mu\nu} = R_{\mu\nu} - \frac{1}{2}Rg_{\nu\nu} &- \left(\frac{N^2+N-2}{(N+1)^2}m^2 - \frac{3(N^2+N-2)}{(N+1)^2}m + \frac{N+5}{(N+1)^2}\right)\Gamma_\mu\Gamma_\nu \\
&- \frac{1}{2}\left(\frac{N^2+N-2}{(N+1)^2}m^2 - \frac{3(N^2+N-2)}{(N+1)^2}m + \frac{N+5}{(N+1)^2}\right)g_{\mu\nu}g^{\alpha\gamma}\Gamma_\alpha\Gamma_\gamma \\
&- \left(\frac{N^2+N-2}{(N+1)^2}m^2 - \frac{3(N^2+N-2)}{(N+1)^2}m + \frac{N+5}{(N+1)^2}\right)g_{\mu\nu}g^{\alpha\gamma}\left(\Gamma_{\alpha|\gamma} - \Gamma_\alpha\Gamma_\gamma\right).
\end{aligned}
$$

The free parameters $M_{\mu\nu}$, m_μ and m make possible some cosmological measuring to be presented exactly by the model. In this way, the problems with Einstein's model of cosmology that makes relatively high numerical errors in some experiments may be attempted to be solved.

4. Conclusions

In this paper we reviewed the methodology for obtaining invariants of geometric mappings, already published by Vesić [21] and developed by Vesić, Stanković, and Mihajlović [15]. We also defined the m-conformal line of a Riemannian space. The conformal mappings of Riemannian spaces are generalized to $(\bar{m}, m)$-conformal mappings. This represents a completely new approach in the field of conformal mappings that is very important, especially from an application perspective.

At the end of this research, we introduced one example from cosmology that illustrates how the results can be applied in further physical research.

In future research, we will determine the general equations of motion for various cosmological models defined in Riemannian spaces of different dimensions. In the simplest case, these general equations of motion will reduce to those obtained in classical mechanics. Furthermore, since the geometric mappings transform all curves of a given class in the initial Riemannian space into curves of a corresponding class in the deformed space, and since the transformation laws for the Christoffel symbols and the associated invariants are determined based on this, we will use these transformed curves to identify the corresponding mechanical properties of a particle moving along such a curve. A special case will be the Navier–Stokes equations, when the moving particle is considered to be a fluid particle.

Author Contributions: Conceptualization, I.D. and N.O.V.; methodology, N.O.V.; software, D.J.S.; validation, I.D.; formal analysis, N.O.V.; investigation, B.M.R.; resources, B.D.V.; data curation, D.J.S.; writing—original draft preparation D.J.S.; writing—review and editing, B.M.R.; visualization, D.J.S.; supervision, B.D.V.; project administration, B.M.R.; funding acquisition, B.D.V. All authors have read and agreed to the published version of the manuscript.

Funding: This research was funded by the Ministry of Science, Innovations and Technological Development of Serbia, through the grants 451-03-137/2025-03/200251 and 451-03-137/2025-03/200102, and funded by the Faculty of Teacher Education, Leposavić, through grant IMP-003.

Data Availability Statement: Data is contained within the article.

Acknowledgments: The authors wish to thank the anonymous referees for their significant recommendations for the editing of this manuscript. Nenad Vesić wishes to thank the Serbian Ministry of Science, Technological Developments and Patents, which financially supported this research through the Mathematical Institute of Serbian Academy of Sciences and Arts.

Conflicts of Interest: The authors declare no conflicts of interest.

References

1. Eisenhart, L.P. *Riemannian Geometry*; Princeton University Press: Princeton, NJ, USA, 1947.
2. Mikeš, J. *Differential Geometry of Special Mappings*, 1st ed.; Olomouc University Press: Olomouc, Czech Republic, 2015; pp. 257–280.
3. Shandra, I.G.; Mikeš, J. Geodesic Mappings of $V_n(K)$-Spaces and Concircular Vector Fields. *Mathematics* **2019**, *7*, 692. [CrossRef]
4. Berezovsky, V.; Mikeš, J. On special almost geodesic mappings of type π_1 of spaces with affine connection. *Acta Univ. Palacki. Olomuc. Fac. Rerum Natur. Math.* **2004**, *43*, 21–26.
5. Chuda, H.; Mikeš, J. Conformally geodesic mappings satisfying a certain initial condition. *Arch. Math.* **2011**, *47*, 389–394.
6. Mikeš, J. Geodesic mappings of affine-connected and Riemannian spaces. *J. Math. Sci.* **1996**, *78*, 311–333. [CrossRef]
7. Sinyukov, N.S.; Sinyukova, E.N.; Movchan, Y.A. Some actual aspects of development of the theory of geodesic mappings of Riemannian spaces and its generalization. *Rus. Math.* **1994**, *38*, 74–78.
8. Sinyukov, N.S.; Sinyukova, E.N. Holomorphically projective mappings of special Kähler spaces. *Math. Notes* **1984**, *36*, 417–423. [CrossRef]
9. Sinyukov, N.S. *Geodesic Mappings of Riemannian Spaces*, 1st ed.; Nauka: Moscow, Russia, 1979.
10. De, U.C.; Ghosh, G.; De, K. Characterization of a paraSasakian manifold admitting Bach tensor. *Commun. Fac. Sci. Univ. Ank. Ser. A1 Math. Stat.* **2023**, *72*, 826–838. [CrossRef]
11. De, U.C.; Chaubey, S.K.; Shenawy, S. Perfect fluid spacetimes and Yamabe solitons. *J. Math. Phys.* **2021**, *62*, 032501. [CrossRef]
12. Milenković, V.M.; Stanković, M.S.; Vesić, N.O. Invariant Geometric Objects of the Equitorsion Canonical Biholomorphically Projective Mappings of Generalized Riemannian Space in the Eisenhart Sense. *Mathematics* **2025**, *13*, 1334. [CrossRef]
13. Stanković, M.S.; Minčić, S.M.; Velimirović, L.S. On holomorphically projective mappings of generalized Kahlerian spaces. *Mat. Vesn.* **2002**, *54*, 195–202. [CrossRef]
14. Stanković, M.S.; Minčić, S.M.; Velimirović, L.S.; Zlatanović, M.L. On equitorsion geodesic mappings of general affine connection spaces. *Rend. Sem. Mat. Univ. Padova* **2010**, *124*, 77–90. [CrossRef]
15. Vesić, N.O.; Milenković, V.M.; Stanković, M.S. Two Invariants for Geometric Mappings. *Axioms* **2022**, *11*, 239. [CrossRef]
16. Vesić, N.; Velimirović, L.; Stanković, M. Some Invariants of Equitorsion Third Type Almost Geodesic Mappings. *Mediterr. J. Math.* **2016**, *13*, 4581–4590. [CrossRef]
17. Zlatanović, M.; Hinterleitner, I.; Najdanović, M. On equitorsion concircular tensors of generalized Riemannian spaces. *Filomat* **2014**, *28*, 463–471. [CrossRef]
18. Maksimović, M.D.; Zlatanović, M.L. Einstein Type Curvature Tensors and Einstein Type Tensors of Generalized Riemannian Space in the Eisenhart Sense. *Mediterr. J. Math.* **2022**, *19*, 217. [CrossRef]
19. Zlatanović, M.L.; Maksimović, M.D. Quarter-symmetric generalized metric connections on a generalized Riemannian manifold. *Filomat* **2023**, *37*, 3927–3937. [CrossRef]
20. Najdanović, M.; Velimirović, L.; Vesić, N. Geodesic infinitesimal deformations of generalized Riemannian spaces. *Mediterr. J. Math.* **2022**, *19*, 149. [CrossRef]
21. Vesić, N.O. Basic invariants of geometric mappings. *Miskolc Math. Notes* **2020**, *21*, 473–487. [CrossRef]
22. Danehkar, A. On the significance of the Weyl curvature in a relativistic cosmological model. *Mod. Phys. Let. A* **2009**, *24*, 3113–3127. [CrossRef]
23. McKeon, D.G.C. The Canonical Structure of the First-Order Einstein-Hilbert Action. *Phys. Rev. A.* **2010**, *25*, 3453–3480. [CrossRef]
24. Dodelson, S. *Modern Cosmology*, 1st ed.; Elsevier: Oxford, UK, 2003.

MDPI AG
Grosspeteranlage 5
4052 Basel
Switzerland
Tel.: +41 61 683 77 34

Axioms Editorial Office
E-mail: axioms@mdpi.com
www.mdpi.com/journal/axioms

www.ingramcontent.com/pod-product-compliance
Lightning Source LLC
Chambersburg PA
CBHW061820210926
51850CB00006B/764
9783725851997